The Psychology of
Sex and Gender

For my parents, Edward and Jo-Ellen.
Mom, you always said I'd write a book one day.
J. K. B.

For Nick.
J. A. V.

For Chrismarie Baxter, Janet Spence,
and my beloved family.
C. E. B.

The Psychology of Sex and Gender

Jennifer K. Bosson
University of South Florida

Joseph A. Vandello
University of South Florida

Camille E. Buckner
Marymount University

Los Angeles | London | New Delhi
Singapore | Washington DC | Melbourne

FOR INFORMATION:

SAGE Publications, Inc.
2455 Teller Road
Thousand Oaks, California 91320
E-mail: order@sagepub.com

SAGE Publications Ltd.
1 Oliver's Yard
55 City Road
London EC1Y 1SP
United Kingdom

SAGE Publications India Pvt. Ltd.
B 1/I 1 Mohan Cooperative Industrial Area
Mathura Road, New Delhi 110 044
India

SAGE Publications Asia-Pacific Pte. Ltd.
3 Church Street
#10-04 Samsung Hub
Singapore 049483

Acquisitions Editor: Lara Parra
Associate Editor: Zachary Valladon
Development Editor: Lucy Berbeo
Editorial Assistant: Morgan Shannon
Marketing Manager: Katherine Hepburn
Production Editor: Kelle Schillaci Clarke
Copy Editor: Jared Leighton
Typesetter: C&M Digitals (P) Ltd.
Proofreader: Sarah J. Duffy
Indexer: Beth Nauman-Montana
Cover Designer: Anupama Krishnan

Library of Congress Cataloging-in-Publication Data

Names: Bosson, Jennifer K., author. | Vendello, Joseph A., author. | Buckner, Camille E., author.

Title: The psychology of sex and gender / Jennifer K. Bosson, University of South Florida, Joseph A. Vendello, University of South Florida, Camille E. Buckner, Marymount University.

Description: First Edition. | Thousand Oaks : SAGE Publications, [2018] | Includes bibliographical references and index.

Identifiers: LCCN 2017042023 | ISBN 9781506331324 (pbk. : alk. paper)

Subjects: LCSH: Sex (Psychology) | Sex. | Gender identity. | Interpersonal relations.

Classification: LCC BF692 .B67 2018 | DDC 155.3—dc23
LC record available at https://lccn.loc.gov/2017042023

Printed in the United States of America

ISBN: 9781506331324

This book is printed on acid-free paper.

Certified Chain of Custody
Promoting Sustainable Forestry
www.sfiprogram.org
SFI-01268

SFI label applies to text stock

19 20 21 22 10 9 8 7 6 5 4 3 2

Brief Contents

Preface   xix

Acknowledgments   xxv

About the Authors   xxix

UNIT I   FOUNDATIONS   1

Chapter 1   Introducing Sex and Gender   3

Chapter 2   Studying Sex and Gender   37

UNIT II   BECOMING GENDERED: BIOLOGICAL AND SOCIAL FACTORS   73

Chapter 3   The Nature and Nurture of Sex and Gender   75

Chapter 4   Gender Development   111

UNIT III   STEREOTYPES, DISCRIMINATION, AND POWER   145

Chapter 5   The Contents and Origins of Gender Stereotypes   147

Chapter 6   Power, Sexism, and Discrimination   183

UNIT IV   COGNITION, EMOTION, AND COMMUNICATION   219

Chapter 7   Cognitive Abilities and Aptitudes   221

Chapter 8   Language, Communication, and Emotion   255

UNIT V   SEXUALITY, RELATIONSHIPS, AND WORK   289

Chapter 9   Sexual Orientation and Sexuality   291

Chapter 10   Interpersonal Relationships   331

Chapter 11   Work and Home   369

UNIT VI   HEALTH AND WELL-BEING   405

Chapter 12   Gender and Physical Health   407

Chapter 13   Gender and Psychological Health   443

Chapter 14   Aggression and Violence   477

Glossary   G-1

References   R-1

Index   I-1

Detailed Contents

Preface   xix

Acknowledgments   xxv

About the Authors   xxix

UNIT I FOUNDATIONS   1

Chapter 1   Introducing Sex and Gender   3

How Do We Explain Central Concepts in the
Psychology of Sex and Gender?   5
   Sex and Gender   6
   The Sex and Gender Binaries   7
   Gender Identity   9
   Sexual Orientation   10
   Intersectionality   10
   Masculinity and Femininity   11

What Makes Sex and Gender So Complicated?   11
   Complexity and Change   12
   Ubiquity and Invisibility   13

How Have Gender Movements Shaped History?   16
   Structures of Power and Inequality   16
   Women's Movements and the Rise of Feminisms   17
     Women's Movements   17
     Feminisms   21
     ▶ **Debate:** Are Men Overlooked in Feminist Movements?   24
   Men's Movements   26
   Gay Rights Movements   27
   The Transgender Movement   27
   Where Are We Now? Inclusivity and Intersectionality   30

About This Book   30
   Our (Interdisciplinary) Psychological Approach   30
   Our Challenge to You: Critical Thinking   31

Chapter 2   Studying Sex and Gender   37

What Is the Meaning of Difference?   40
   ▶ **Debate:** Should Psychologists Study Sex Differences?   42

What Is Science?   43
   The Scientific Method   44

▶ **Journey of Research:** Conceptualizing and
Measuring Masculinity and Femininity   46

What Are the Primary Methods Used in
Sex and Gender Research?   47
  Quantitative Research Methods   47
    Experimental Designs   47
    Ex Post Facto Designs   50
    Quasi-Experiments   50
    Correlational Designs   52
  Qualitative Research Methods   54
    Case Studies   55
    Interviews   55
    Focus Groups   55
  Mixed Methods   56

What Do Meta-Analyses and Effect Sizes
Tell Us About Sex Differences?   57
    Effect Sizes   58
    Overlap and Variance   60
    Beyond Overall Effect Sizes   62

What Are Some Biases Common in
Sex and Gender Research?   63
  Identifying the Research Question   63
  Designing the Study and Collecting Data   64
  Interpreting and Communicating the Results   65

How Do We Address the Challenges in
Sex and Gender Research?   66
  Guidelines for Gender-Fair Research Design   67
  Diversity Issues in the Study of Sex and Gender   68

UNIT II BECOMING GENDERED: BIOLOGICAL AND SOCIAL FACTORS   73

Chapter 3 The Nature and Nurture of Sex and Gender   75

Nature *Versus* Nurture or Nature *and* Nurture?   78
  Gene-by-Environment Interactions   78
  Epigenetics   79
How Do Nature and Nurture Shape Sex Differentiation?   80
  Typical Sex Differentiation   80
    Chromosomes and Genes   81
    Hormones and Anatomy   82
    ▶ **Journey of Research:** Unlocking Genetic and
    Hormonal Contributions to Sex   84

Intersex Conditions   86

     Chromosomes and Genes   87

     Hormones and Anatomy   88

     ▶ **Debate:** Should Intersex Individuals Be Allowed to
Compete in Athletic Competitions?   91

How Do Nature and Nurture Shape Sex Assignment and Gender Identity?   92

Optimal Sex   92

Gender Identity   93

Gender Confirmation Procedures   96

What Do Sex Differences in Brain Structure Reveal?   98

Sex Differences in the Brain   98

Equating the Brain With "Nature"   99

Neuroscience or Neurosexism?   100

How Do Theories of Sex Differences Account for Nature and Nurture?   100

Evolutionary Psychology   100

Biosocial Constructionist Theory   103

Chapter 4   Gender Development   111

How Central Are Sex and Gender in Early Development?   112

What Are the Major Theoretical Approaches to Gender Development?   113

Social Learning Theories and Sources of Socialization   115

     Parents   116

     Siblings   119

     Teachers and Peers   119

     Media   119

     ▶ **Debate:** Should Toys Be Marketed as Gender Neutral?   122

Cognitive Theories   123

     Cognitive-Developmental Theory   123

     Gender Schema Theory   124

     Developmental Intergroup Theory   125

     Gender Self-Socialization Model   127

Evaluating Social Learning and Cognitive Theories   127

What Are the Experiences of Gender-Nonconforming Children?   127

Biological and Social Contributions to Gender Nonconformity   128

Nonconforming Identities and Milestones   129

How Do Sex and Gender Shape Development in Adolescence and Emerging Adulthood?   131

Puberty and the Transition to Young Adulthood   131

Relationships With Parents   133

Friendship, Dating, and Social Networking 134
Gendered Self-Views Across Time and Cultures 136

How Do Sex and Gender Shape Development in Middle and Late Adulthood? 137

Cultural Ideals of Womanhood and Manhood 137
Gendered Self-Views 140
Women's Gender Advantage? 140
The Double Standard of Aging 141

UNIT III STEREOTYPES, DISCRIMINATION, AND POWER 145

Chapter 5 The Contents and Origins of Gender Stereotypes 147

What Are the Contents and Structure of Gender Stereotypes? 149

Communion and Agency 152
The Stereotype Content Model 152
The Women-Are-Wonderful Effect 155
▶ **Journey of Research:** Think Manager–Think Male 156
Subgroups and Intersectionality 158
Transgender Stereotypes 163
Sexual Orientation Stereotypes 163

What Are Some Consequences of Gender Stereotyping? 165

Penalizing Gender Role Violators 165
Confirming Negative Stereotypes 166

Where Do Gender Stereotypes Come From? 168

Evolutionary Psychology 168
Social Role Theory 169
Biosocial Constructionist Theory 170

Are Gender Stereotypes Accurate? 172

Challenges: Defining "Reality" and Accuracy 172
Cognitive Stereotypes 173
Personality Stereotypes 173
Nonverbal and Verbal Communication Stereotypes 174
Stereotypes Across Multiple Domains 174
▶ **Debate:** Are Gender Stereotypes Accurate? 176

So How Universal Are Gender Stereotypes, Really? 177

Chapter 6 Power, Sexism, and Discrimination 183

How Do Power and Privilege Relate to Sex and Gender? 184

Patriarchal and Matriarchal Social Structures 184
Structural Versus Dyadic Power 186

Ways of Exerting Power 188

   Force 188

   Resource Control 190

   Cultural Ideologies 190

Privilege 192

Intersectionality, Double Jeopardy, and Invisibility 192

What Is Sexism, and Why Does It Persist? 195

Ambivalent Sexism Toward Women 195

Ambivalent Attitudes Toward Men 199

  ▶ **Journey of Research:** Measuring Gender Role and Sexist Attitudes 201

Social Dominance and System Justification Theories 202

Why Do Sexist Attitudes Matter? 203

  ▶ **Debate:** Do Men Experience Sexism? 204

What Is Gender Discrimination? 205

Overt Discrimination and Microaggressions 206

Global Gender Discrimination in Education and Politics 207

How Can We Resist and Reduce Gender Discrimination? 209

Affirmative Action: It's the Law 209

Confronting Gender Discrimination: Individual Efforts 210

Resisting Gender Discrimination: Collective Action 212

Being an Ally 214

UNIT IV COGNITION, EMOTION, AND COMMUNICATION 219

Chapter 7 Cognitive Abilities and Aptitudes 221

What Is Cognitive Ability? 223

  ▶ **Journey of Research:** Measuring the Brain From Phrenology to fMRI 224

Sex Differences in General Mental Ability 227

What Are the Sex Differences and Similarities in Cognitive Abilities? 228

Verbal Performance 228

   Vocabulary and Verbal Fluency 230

   Reading and Writing 230

   Verbal Reasoning 231

Quantitative Performance 231

Visual-Spatial Performance 232

   Mental Rotation 234

   Spatial Perception and Visualization 234

   Spatial Location Memory 234

Sex Differences in the Variability of Cognitive Abilities 235

How Do Individual Differences and Context Influence Cognitive Performance? 237

Culture   239
Stereotype Threat   239
Willingness to Guess on Tests   241
Achievement Motivation and Sensitivity to Feedback   242

How Do Sex and Gender Matter in Educational Systems and STEM Fields?   242

Education and School Performance   242
Cultural Influences   242
Home and Classroom Dynamics   243
▶ **Debate:** Do Children Fare Better in Single-Sex Classrooms?   244
Sex, Gender, and STEM Fields   246
Discrimination   246
Interests, Values, and Expectations   247
Gendered Family Responsibilities   248

Chapter 8   Language, Communication, and Emotion   255

How Does Gender-Related Language Influence Social Perception?   257

Gendered Features of Language   257
The Generic Masculine   257
Grammatical Gender   260
Diminutives and Gender Labels   260
The Influence of Gendered Language on Perceptions   261

What Roles Do Sex and Gender Play in Verbal Communication?   262

Sex Differences in *How* People Communicate   263
Who Talks More?   263
Who Interrupts More?   264
Sex Differences in *What* People Communicate   265
Gossip   265
Social Media   265
Beyond Sex Differences: Intersectionality in Communication   268
Verbal Communication: What's the Big Picture?   270

What Roles Do Sex and Gender Play in Nonverbal Communication?   270

Smiling and Eye Contact   271
Personal Space and Touch   272
Body Posture and Gait   273
Nonverbal Communication: What's the Big Picture?   275

How Do Sex and Gender Shape the Experience, Expression, and Identification of Emotions?   277

Emotional Experience and Expression   277
▶ **Debate:** Are Women More Emotional Than Men?   278
Display Rules   281

Encoding and Decoding Accuracy   282

Empathy and Emotional Intelligence   283

▶ **Journey of Research:** Understanding Empathy,
From Darwin to Mirror Neurons   283

UNIT V SEXUALITY, RELATIONSHIPS, AND WORK   289

Chapter 9 Sexual Orientation and Sexuality   291

How Do Understandings of Sexuality and
Sexual Orientation Differ Across Time and Culture?   293

▶ **Journey of Research:** Sexual Orientation Change Efforts   295

What Is Sexual Orientation?   297

Sexual Identity   297

Motivation: Desire and Love   299

Sexual Behavior   302

Complexity of Sexual Orientation   303

How Does Sexual Orientation Develop?   304

Phase Models of Sexual Identity Development   304

Milestone and Narrative Models of Sexual Minority
Identity Development   307

Why Do People Differ in Sexual Orientation?   309

Biological Theories   310

Evolutionary Theories   312

The Integrative Approach   314

Evaluation of Theories   315

How Do Sex and Gender Contribute to the
Experience of Sexuality?   315

Sexual Behavior and Attitudes   316

▶ **Debate:** Do Men Have a Stronger Sex Drive Than Women?   318

Orgasm Frequency and Sexual Satisfaction   319

Sexual Fluidity   322

How Does Sexuality Change Over the Life Course?   323

Sexual Trajectories   323

The Medicalization of Sexual Changes   325

Chapter 10 Interpersonal Relationships   331

What Roles Do Sex and Gender Play in Social Networks and
Friendships?   333

Social Networks   333

Friendships   334

Sex Differences in Friendship Intimacy   335

Cross-Sex Friendships   336

Friends With Benefits   337

LGBT Friendships   338

What Roles Do Sex and Gender Play in Interpersonal Attraction?   339

Mate Preferences: Similarities and Differences   339

Mate Selection: Whom Do We Choose?   342

Dating Relationships   344

Dating Scripts and Paternalistic Chivalry   344

Experiencing Love and Romance   345

What Is the Nature of Marriage—Past and Present?   346

A Brief Social History of Marriage   346

Contemporary Marriage-Like Relationships   347

The Changing American Family   347

Arranged Versus Autonomous Marriages   349

Polygyny and Polyandry   350

Consensual Nonmonogamy and Polyamory   351

What Roles Do Sex and Gender Play in Committed Relationships?   352

Happy Relationships: Equity and Love   352

Making Decisions   352

Dividing Labor and Childcare   353

Showing Love   354

Relationship Struggles: Jealousy and Conflict   355

Jealousy   355

Dealing With Conflict   355

▶ **Debate:** Did Women and Men Evolve Different Jealousy Reactions?   356

Separation and Divorce   358

What Roles Do Sex and Gender Play in Parenting and Family Relationships?   359

Parent to Parent: Gender and Parental Relationships   360

Parent to Child: Gender and Caring for Children   361

Chapter 11 Work and Home   369

How Have Work and Home Labor Divisions Changed?   371

How Do People Divide Housework and Childcare at Home?   372

Trends and Inequities   372

Who Does What?   374

Childcare   375

Predictors of the Division of Domestic Labor   376

Time Availability   376

Relative Income   377

Gender Role Ideology   377

Maternal Gatekeeping   378

How Does Gender Operate in the Workplace?   379
Gender and Leadership   379
Glass Ceilings, Glass Cliffs, and Sticky Floors   381
Bias Against Women   382
Sexual Orientation, Gender Identity, and Race   383
Bias Against Men   385

How Can We Explain the Gender Wage Gap?   386
What Is the Gender Wage Gap?   387
▶ Debate: Is the Gender Wage Gap a Myth?   389
Possible Explanations for the Gender Wage Gap   391
Education and Occupational Segregation   391
Occupational Feminization   393
Salary Negotiation   394
Relocations and Career Interruptions   395
Overwork   397
Conclusions About the Gender Wage Gap   397

How Do Work and Family Roles Interact?   398
▶ **Journey of Research:** From Work–Family Conflict to
Work–Life Enrichment   398
Conflict and Enrichment   399
Flexible Work and Family Leave Policies   400

UNIT VI   HEALTH AND WELL-BEING   405

Chapter 12   Gender and Physical Health   407

How Have Understandings of Health and
Longevity Changed Over Time?   408
Changes in Life Expectancy   409
Mortality (Death) and Morbidity (Sickness)   410
▶ **Debate:** Do Women or Men Experience Better Physical Health?   412

How Do Biological Factors Shape Sex
Differences in Health?   413
Genetic Factors   413
Hormonal Influences   415
An Evolutionary Theory of Health and Longevity   415

How Do Social Factors Contribute to Sex
Disparities in Health?   416
Health-Relevant Behavior: Things That People *Do*   417
Accidents and Risky Sex   417
Smoking, Alcohol Use, and Diet   419
Physical Activity and Exercise   422
Health-Relevant Traits: Ways That People *Are*   423
Accessing Health Care   425

Seeking Health Care 425

Receiving Health Care 426

Gender-Egalitarian Communities and Health 427

How Do Multiple Systems of Discrimination
Shape Health and Health Care? 429

Race, Ethnicity, and Sex 429

Socioeconomic Status, Sex, and Race/Ethnicity 430

Sexual Orientation and Gender Identity 431

How Has Reproductive Health Been Medicalized? 434

▶ **Journey of Research:** Pregnancy and Childbirth
Advice Through the Centuries 438

Chapter 13 Gender and Psychological Health **443**

How Are Mental Illnesses Defined, Classified,
and Conceptualized? 445

The *Diagnostic and Statistical Manual* and the
International Classification of Diseases 446

The Transdiagnostic Approach: Internalizing and
Externalizing Disorders 446

▶ **Journey of Research:** Treatment of Transgender
Identity in the *DSM* 447

What Factors Contribute to Sex Differences
in Internalizing Disorders? 449

Gender Role Factors 450

Abuse and Violence Factors 452

Personality Factors 452

Biological Factors 452

What Factors Contribute to Sex Differences
in Externalizing Disorders? 453

Gender Role Factors 454

Personality Factors 454

Biological Factors 455

▶ **Debate:** Do Women Suffer From Depression More Than Men? 456

What Roles Do Sex and Gender Play in Eating
and Body Image Disorders? 458

Objectification Theory, Body Image, and Eating Disorders 460

Links to Women's Mental Health 460

Roles of Media and Culture 461

Intersectionality and Eating Disorders Among Women 463

Gender Identity, Body Dissatisfaction, and
Eating Disorders 464

The Desire for Muscularity 464

How Do Sexual and Gender Minority
Statuses Relate to Mental Health?   465
    Victimization, Discrimination, and Rejection   466
    Homelessness   466
    Institutional Discrimination: A Hostile Environment   467
    Internalized Stigma: Homophobia and Transphobia From Within   467

What Roles Do Sex and Gender Play in
Mental Health Help-Seeking?   468
    Sex Differences in Rates of Help-Seeking   468
    Intersectionality and Help-Seeking   469

What Roles Do Sex and Gender Play in
Happiness and Well-Being?   470
    Subjective Well-Being   470
    Communion, Agency, and Well-Being   472

Chapter 14   Aggression and Violence   **477**

Are There Sex Differences in Aggression?   479
    Sex Differences in Perpetrating Aggression   479
      Physical Aggression   479
      Verbal Aggression   482
      Relational Aggression   483
      Cyberbullying   483
    Sex Differences in Experiencing Aggression   484
    What's the Big Picture?   484

What Are the Major Forms of Gender-Based
Aggression and Violence?   485
    Intimate Partner Violence   485
      Situational Couple Violence Versus Intimate Terrorism   486
      ▶ **Debate:** Do Men Perpetrate Intimate Partner
      Violence More Often Than Women?   487
    Sexual Violence: Rape and Sexual Assault   488
      How Common Is Sexual Violence?   489
      Who Commits Sexual Violence?   492
      The Aftermath of Sexual Violence   493
    Sex-Based Harassment   495

What Explains Gender-Based Aggression and Violence?   499
    Biological Factors   500
      Testosterone   500
      Evolved Jealousy   500
    Sociocultural Factors   501
      Honor Cultures   501
      Precarious Manhood   502

Power and Structural Gender Inequality   502

I³ Theory   504

What Is the Relationship Between Pornography and Sexual Aggression?   505

Definitions and Prevalence   505

▶ **Journey of Research:** Science, Politics, and Pornography   505

Pornography and Sexual Aggression   506

Glossary   G-1

References   R-1

Index   I-1

Preface

· ·

This book reflects a new approach to the psychology of sex and gender. As instructors of undergraduate psychology of gender courses, we regularly face three challenges when selecting a textbook. First, some textbooks can read as light on science. Second, existing gender textbooks often emphasize the psychology of women rather than giving equal weight to the experiences of people of all sexes and gender identities. Third, the field of gender research changes at a remarkable pace, making textbooks feel dated quickly. In writing this book, we specifically tackled each of these challenges to yield an exciting new offering to the field.

To tackle the first challenge—that gender textbooks can seem light on science—our book puts cutting-edge science at the center. This approach reflects our belief that students must critically evaluate the empirical evidence and draw their own conclusions about controversial issues and findings. Given the centrality of sex and gender to most of our lives, people tend to approach these topics with preconceived views, but such views often stem from cultural stereotypes, folk beliefs, and outdated assumptions rather than from systematic, empirical observations. Our book emphasizes science as a useful, albeit imperfect, method for reducing biases. At the same time, we cover politically charged topics and tackle challenging discussions when relevant. Research on sex and gender has inevitable social and political implications, and when such implications arise, we invite students to consider multiple perspectives and question their assumptions.

To tackle the second challenge—that existing textbooks often prioritize the psychology of women—our book takes a broad approach to the psychology of sex and gender. When we first set out to write this book, we noticed that many of the top-selling psychology of gender textbooks were primarily about women. These books fill an important social and historical need, as women and women's experiences were largely neglected by mainstream psychology for many decades. That said, we think that the time is ripe for a different kind of textbook, one that closely reflects current sociocultural contexts and understandings of sex and gender. Our book includes not only the rich literature on men and masculinity but also the expanding literatures on transgender, nonbinary, and gender-nonconforming identities and experiences. It also highlights sexual orientation diversity and intersectionality and pushes students to think about ever more inclusive ways of conceptualizing sex and gender.

To tackle the third challenge—that the field of gender research proceeds at a breakneck pace—we cover the most up-to-date findings and interweave these with classic, time-honored theories, approaches, and studies. In the past decade, scientific understandings of sex and gender saw rapid transitions. We know more than ever before about topics like gender identity and sexual orientation, genes and hormones, the effects of gender stereotypes on their targets, and the nature of sexism. Old theories and assumptions that long held sway are regularly upended by new findings. At the same time, underlying these rapid changes are some enduring psychological truths. Psychology of gender instructors need a book that both keeps up with the changes and uncovers the enduring truths. As scholars in this field who follow the most updated findings, we are well positioned to report on the vanguard and situate it within the fundamentals of psychology.

Not only does this book fill needs specific to the psychology of sex and gender, it also fills a more general need shared by all high-quality textbook users: to enhance students' learning by promoting deep processing of information. Specifically, this text utilizes current best practices from the scholarship of teaching and learning to facilitate students' understanding of material by prompting them to develop habits of critical and integrative thinking.

Finally, a word about our title. We realize that many books on the same topic will opt for the simpler *Psychology of Gender*. Many gender researchers avoid the term *sex* because of the convention in the field that *sex* means biological differences between women and men while *gender* refers to sociocultural assumptions and roles that accompany maleness and femaleness. Breaking from this convention, we embrace the term *sex* and use it simply to refer to the categories of being male, female, or otherwise. We therefore include *sex* in our title to illustrate that categories of sex are conceptually distinct from *gender*, rather than to imply any distinction between biological and social causes. In fact, throughout the book, we regularly insist that nature and nurture are intertwined in ways that make them impossible to separate. This reflects a growing awareness within psychology of the inseparability of nature and nurture: Biological factors shape how people and cultures conceptualize gender, and social factors shape our interpretations of the anatomy and physiology of sex. We highlight this theme explicitly in Chapter 3 ("The Nature and Nurture of Sex and Gender") but return to it repeatedly throughout other chapters as well.

Intended Courses and Readers

We intend this book to be used as a core text for undergraduate courses in the psychology of gender, the psychology of women, and the psychology of men. As such, it covers requisite content including sex versus gender, the sex and gender binaries, gender stereotypes, gender role socialization, sexism, and sex similarities and differences in cognitive, emotional, relational, workplace, and health outcomes. Many universities—both public and private, research oriented and teaching focused—offer these or similar courses as part of the regular curriculum in the Psychology Department, but other departments offering courses in the psychology of gender include Sociology Departments, Women's and Gender Studies Departments, and Men's Studies Departments. A course in the psychology of gender has wide appeal for students, regardless of academic major. While many are majors in psychology, sociology, or women's and gender studies who plan to pursue graduate study in this topic area, others take the course out of interest in the topic or because understanding gender will prepare them for a career in an applied area. Thus, this textbook should appeal to a broad range of students, and our writing reflects this by incorporating cross-disciplinary material regularly.

Organization, Features, and Pedagogy

The book is organized into six units, although instructors can easily shift the order of chapters without disrupting the flow too much. Unit I lays the foundation for the rest of the book by introducing the concepts of sex and gender, defining essential terminology, and placing the study of sex and gender within sociohistorical contexts in Chapter 1. This unit also discusses some of the unique methodological approaches and challenges in the study of sex and gender and prepares students to evaluate critically the validity of research designs and researchers' conclusions (Chapter 2). Unit II covers material on how people become gendered beings, from their prenatal origins and sex assignment at birth (Chapter 3) to childhood gender role socialization and adult development (Chapter 4). In Unit III, we focus on gendered social perception and systems of gender-based status and power by examining gender stereotypes (Chapter 5) and sex-related differences in structural power and patterns of discrimination (Chapter 6).

In Unit IV, we examine cognitive and emotional aspects of sex and gender, including similarities and differences in cognitive ability (Chapter 7) and gendered aspects of communication and emotion (Chapter 8). Unit V focuses on domains of personal and social life, including sexuality, relationships, and the work–home interface. While Chapter 9 offers in-depth analyses of sexual orientation and sexuality, Chapter 10 covers friendships, romantic relationships, and parenting. Chapter 11 then examines the interconnection between work and home life in the context of changing family arrangements and societal norms. Unit VI, which covers health and well-being, considers the roles of sex and gender in both physical health (Chapter 12) and psychological health (Chapter 13). This unit also considers the gendered aspects of aggression and violence that have bearing on health (Chapter 14).

The themes that guided our writing, which are evident throughout each chapter, include the following:

Updated science. We cover up-to-date findings in the psychology of sex and gender. This keeps students abreast of the latest scholarship in the field, prepares them to evaluate unfounded assumptions about sex and gender critically, and offers them a solid foundation of knowledge upon which to build.

Diversity emphasis. We wrote this book to meet the needs of an increasingly globally aware and sophisticated student population. To this end, we focus on a diversity of gender identities, sexual orientations, races and ethnicities, cultural and subcultural backgrounds, and intersections among these dimensions. Moreover, we routinely intersperse diversity and intersectionality into the central chapter text rather than boxing them separately and treating them as afterthoughts. This emphasis on diversity benefits students in several ways. First, exposure to inclusive content increases feelings of belonging among underrepresented students, who see their own experiences reflected in the text. This can foster interest in and engagement with the material, as students realize that the psychology of sex and gender is about everyone, not just those who occupy mainstream or privileged social groups. Second, exposure to diverse content can increase students' awareness of the unique backgrounds of others who differ from them, foster an appreciation for issues of social justice, and help students build interpersonal skills that will assist them in their chosen careers and life paths. Finally, exposure to diverse perspectives and experiences can increase students' creativity, cognitive flexibility, and problem-solving abilities, and these skills can generalize beyond the learning environment into other aspects of life.

Scholarship of teaching and learning. This book utilizes current best practices in the scholarship of teaching and learning (SOTL), which is relevant application of the principles of cognitive psychology to educational contexts. SOTL uses empirically sound strategies to enhance student learning. This means that, throughout the book, we present information in such a manner so as to increase the chances of attaining the gold standard in any educational setting: the transfer of new student knowledge beyond the end of the learning experience. Some of the SOTL best practices that we employ are as follows:

- We illustrate text concepts with current popular culture and relevant real-world examples to capture and hold student interest and prompt students to connect new material to what they already know.

- We prompt students to engage in metacognition about their knowledge, perspectives, and assumptions. This increases the likelihood that readers will use information and evidence to calibrate their understanding of concepts and that they will gain insight into what they do and do not fully understand, allowing them to ask more targeted questions.

- We weave thematic content (e.g., diversity and critical thinking) throughout the text and revisit it after presenting new material to reinforce student learning and help students organize the new material in deeper and more meaningful associative networks that span different chapters. We take a similar approach with our coverage of gender-related theories. Rather than including a stand-alone theories chapter, we integrate theories directly in the text where relevant. This encourages students to use and apply theories as organizing frameworks and not simply consider theories in isolation from the phenomena they explain.

- We encourage students to apply the knowledge that they acquire from reading this book to other course material, current events, and their own personal experiences. This allows them to evaluate how the new knowledge relates and does not relate to material they already know, thus deepening the level of processing and increasing the likelihood of retention.

To ensure that readers get the most out of this book, we also employ several specific pedagogical tools in each chapter that we hope will enhance their experience. These include the following:

Learning objectives. We begin each chapter with learning objectives, which contain the main takeaway ideas and cognitive skills that we hope students will learn through a careful reading of the chapter. In keeping with SOTL best practices, we state these as concrete actions (e.g., describe, analyze, and apply) that demonstrate mastery of the material.

Knowledge pre- and post-tests. Each chapter begins with a short "Test Your Knowledge" quiz that gives the reader a sense of the coverage to come and challenges intuitions about sex and gender. These quizzes prompt metacognition and allow readers to track changes in their understanding of the material by comparing their pretest answers with the correct answers, which appear at the end of each chapter.

Journey of research. Many topics in the study of gender have long and colorful histories. The "Journey of Research" feature traces these histories by examining changes in scholars' thinking about specific questions over time. This situates students' understanding of topics within context and illustrates concretely how the endeavor of science evolves continually.

Stop-and-think questions. Each chapter contains four to six "Stop and Think" questions that activate and fine-tune students' critical thinking skills. These questions engage all levels of Bloom's taxonomy—from the lowest-level domain (*remembering*) to the highest-level domain (*creating*)—and many of them engage multiple domains (e.g., both *applying* and *evaluating*). For instance, stop-and-think questions may ask readers to consider a topic more deeply, draw connections between different topics, interpret a finding from multiple theoretical perspectives, or evaluate the pros and cons of a given outcome.

Debates. The study of gender is punctuated by many lively intellectual disagreements, and we detail many of these within the chapter "Debate" feature. While some debates are theoretical, others pertain to the robustness, interpretation, or implications of empirical evidence. Debate features present both sides of an issue in an unbiased way and invite readers to weigh the evidence and draw their own informed conclusions. These debates activate readers' critical thinking skills while offering a sense of the reflexive and iterative nature of science.

Sidebars. To capture attention and offer additional detail about topics of particular interest or new and exciting research findings, each chapter includes several short (one- or two-paragraph) sidebars, such as "100 Million Missing Girls," "Is Androgyny Good for Your Health?" and "Practicing the Principles of Polyamory."

Chapter summaries. Each chapter ends with a summary that reiterates the learning objectives from the beginning of the chapter and then briefly recaps the chapter material that is central to student reflection in the process of meeting these objectives.

Resources for Instructors and Students

SAGE edge is a robust online environment featuring an impressive array of free tools and resources. At **edge.sagepub.com/bosson**, instructors using this book can access customizable PowerPoint slides, along with an extensive test bank built on Bloom's taxonomy that features multiple-choice, true/false, essay and short answer questions for each chapter. The site also features lecture notes, discussion questions, and class activities. Also at **edge.sagepub.com/bosson**, students can access multimedia resources and Gender in the News exercises to enhance their understanding of key topics and explore concepts further.

Acknowledgments

We are indebted to many people for their assistance and guidance during the writing of this book. First, we offer our warmest thanks to our friends at SAGE, without whom there would be no book. Reid Hester originally approached us about writing this textbook and convinced us that the timing was right for such a project. Lucy Berbeo read each chapter of the original manuscript and made many wise suggestions for improvement. Zachary Valladon lent a conscientious eye to the visuals and permissions. Jared Leighton carefully copyedited the book. And Lara Parra, our enthusiastic advocate and friend, offered us copious amounts of support, reassurance, insight, and delightful company. We could not have asked for a better team.

Many anonymous reviewers provided invaluable feedback on early drafts of our chapters, often going above and beyond to offer input, suggestions, and support. Reviewer feedback shed light on our own blind spots and guided us toward research that might otherwise have escaped our notice. We can say with confidence that this book would not be what it is without them.

Carolyn E. Adams-Price, Mississippi State University

Nicole M. Capezza, Stonehill College

Adrienne R. Carter-Sowell, Texas A&M University

Joan C. Chrisler, Connecticut College

Lisa Kratz Denton, State University of New York at Fredonia

Jeannie D. DiClementi, Purdue University–Fort Wayne

Lisa Marie Dillon, Wayne State University

Betty Carter Dorr, Fort Lewis College

LeAnne Epling, University of Pikeville

Jamie Loran Franco-Zamudio, Spring Hill College

Ashleigh Gallagher, University of North Carolina at Greensboro

Justin D. Hackett, California University of Pennsylvania

Linda Hoke-Sinex, Indiana University

Mary-Theresa Howard, University of Ottawa

Jill Kaplan, The University of Miami

Jennifer Katz, State University of New York at Geneseo

Iva Katzarska-Miller, Transylvania University

Elizabeth Kudadjie-Gyamfi, Long Island University Brooklyn Campus

Lisa Mask, Bishop's University

Madhavi Menon, Nova Southeastern University

Courtney Mozo, Old Dominion University

Joan M. Ostrove, Macalester College

Dongxiao Qin, Western New England University

Cheryl A. Rickabaugh, University of Redlands

Heidi Rose Riggio, California State University, Los Angeles

Sharon Scales Rostosky, University of Kentucky

Lisa Sinclair, University of Winnipeg

Leslie Templeton, Hendrix College

Janice D. Yoder, University of Akron

We also offer special thanks to Desdamona Rios of the University of Houston–Clear Lake and J. Michael Bailey of Northwestern University for providing valuable in-depth feedback on several chapters.

We thank our graduate students, especially Sophie Kuchynka and Liz Kiebel, who read and gave feedback on some early drafts, and Curtis Puryear, who assisted with supplementary materials.

And thank you, as well, to the countless students we have had the pleasure of teaching and learning from over the years. Their insights have sharpened our thinking in more ways than they can imagine.

In addition, each author would like to thank specific individuals who helped along the way.

Jennifer: I love writing about social psychology, and for that, I have to thank my graduate school mentor, Bill Swann. Writing articles and chapters with Bill taught me more about the process of writing than I could ever have hoped. I am also indebted to two teachers who, respectively, sparked and then fueled my love of social psychology: Hubert O'Gorman (my undergraduate social psychology instructor) and Constantine Sedikides (my undergraduate research advisor). For my lifetime loves of gender and social justice, I thank my parents, Jo-Ellen and Ed: You taught me through example about the importance of feminism and gender equality. I think it is safe to say that all three of us coauthors owe a debt of gratitude to David Davisson—my spouse and reference librarian extraordinaire—for the research assistance that he patiently and expertly provided when we needed to track down esoteric and hard-to-find data, scholarship, and anecdotes. But far and above these professional thanks, I also give Dave my personal thanks for his patience, love, support, and inspiration—not only during these past 2 years but also during the 15 years that came before. I hit the jackpot when it comes to life partners.

Joe: My teaching has been most inspired by my own teachers, whose passion and enthusiasm for their subjects were infectious. Three teachers, in particular, remain with me today: Gary Steeples (my seventh-grade math teacher), Bob Baron (my undergraduate psychology instructor, who solidified my career path), and Dov Cohen (my graduate school advisor, whose many lessons resonate with me daily).

Camille: Much of what I know about teaching, I learned from my colleague and friend Chrismarie Baxter at Frostburg State. An exceptional teacher, she channeled her expertise and kindness into teaching me how to teach. Similarly, I learned much of how I think about gender from Janet Spence, and her spunky character and insights about gender will remain with me always. I am also particularly grateful to three teachers who shaped my academic path: Betty Esslinger, my high school English teacher, for loving writing and reading as much as I did; Carol Quillen, for sparking my interest in gender in a women's history course at Rice University; and Lucia Gilbert, for reinforcing this interest in a graduate gender seminar at UT-Austin. I kept all of the books from these two classes and still use them to this day. Finally, I am grateful for my dear friends, my loving and eccentric kin (especially Jeff, Maxine, Vincent, Levi, and Evy), and my Marymount family, whose steady support and kindheartedness helped see me through the intense and exacting process of writing this book.

Jennifer K. Bosson
Joseph A. Vandello
Camille E. Buckner

About the Authors

Jennifer K. Bosson is a professor of psychology at the University of South Florida in Tampa, Florida. The middle of three daughters raised in Yorktown Heights, New York, she attended Wesleyan University as an undergraduate and earned her PhD in social psychology from the University of Texas at Austin in 2000. Jennifer became interested in gender and feminism at a young age. As a fifth grader in 1981, she vowed to one day "join a women's liberation club." Although this particular life goal never panned out, she did end up writing this book, which reflects her 20-plus years' worth of interest in social psychology. Her primary research interests include gender roles, stereotypes, sexism, and sexual prejudice. She lives in Tampa, Florida, with her husband and their two dogs. The opportunity to write this book with two of her favorite people feels like a rare gift indeed.

Joseph A. Vandello grew up as the second of three children in a small town in Iowa. He received his BS from the University of Iowa in 1994 and received his PhD from the University of Illinois at Urbana-Champaign in 2000. In 2002, he joined the Psychology Department at the University of South Florida. His culturally homogenous (i.e., White, middle-class) upbringing fed a curiosity about understanding the diversity of the human experience outside of his small corner of the world and led him to study social psychology as a career. He has broad research interests in understanding manhood and masculinity, aggression, honor, underdogs, interracial interactions, and moral judgments. In his spare time, he enjoys playing the guitar, painting, and watching superhero shows with his son. Although not empirically verified, he is confident that he has substantially higher concentrations of testosterone than his coauthors. Whether this is a good thing is debatable.

Camille E. Buckner loves to think and learn new things, especially about gender. She has a good sense of humor but prefers not to show it in author bios. After graduating from Rice University with a BA in psychology and French in 1991, she got her PhD in social-personality psychology from the University of Texas at Austin in 1997. At UT, she had the good fortune to meet her coauthor Jennifer Bosson and to study gender under the mentorship of Janet Spence. After teaching at Wesleyan College and Frostburg State University, Camille joined the faculty at Marymount University in Arlington, Virginia, in 2006. She is a professor of psychology at MU and recently wrapped up a term as department chair. She loves teaching, learning from her students, and following their paths after graduation. She most enjoys teaching courses on research design, cultural psychology, and gender psychology, and her research interests include gender stereotyping and discrimination, attitudes toward parents and parenting, and best practices in teaching and learning. With one daughter and three sons, she and her partner appreciate raising their family in the multicultural DC metro area, where they regularly get their fill of politics, museums, and good music.

Foundations

Chapter 1   Introducing Sex and Gender

Chapter 2   Studying Sex and Gender

Transgender actress and activist Laverne Cox.

Source: Frederick M. Brown/Stringer/Getty Images Entertainment/Getty Images

Test Your Knowledge: True or False?

1.1 Life experiences can cause biological differences between women and men.

1.2 There are only two biological sexes: male and female.

1.3 Throughout human history, there is evidence that some societies were true matriarchies in which women ruled the society, controlled how it operated, and held more power than men.

1.4 Many people who believe in feminist principles do not identify as feminists.

1.5 The American Psychiatric Association considers transgender identity to be a clinically diagnosable psychological disorder.

CHAPTER

1

Introducing Sex and Gender

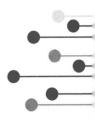

Key Concepts

How Do We Explain Central Concepts in the Psychology of Sex and Gender?

Sex and Gender

The Sex and Gender Binaries

Gender Identity

Sexual Orientation

Intersectionality

Masculinity and Femininity

What Makes Sex and Gender So Complicated?

Complexity and Change

Ubiquity and Invisibility

How Have Gender Movements Shaped History?

Structures of Power and Inequality

Women's Movements and the Rise of Feminisms

Women's Movements

Feminisms

Debate: Are Men Overlooked in Feminist Movements?

Men's Movements

Gay Rights Movements

The Transgender Movement

Where Are We Now? Inclusivity and Intersectionality

About This Book

Our (Interdisciplinary) Psychological Approach

Our Challenge to You: Critical Thinking

Learning Objectives

Students who read this chapter should be able to do the following:

1.1 Explain central terminology in the study of sex and gender.

1.2 Evaluate how culture, gender identity, and sexual orientation shape the experience and expression of sex and gender.

1.3 Evaluate the meaning and relevance of feminisms, gender movements, and systems of power, privilege, and inequality.

1.4 Demonstrate how to approach the textbook material in "critical thinking mode."

Introducing Sex and Gender

Why study sex and gender? One answer to this question lies in how these topics are, at the same time, both central to our daily lives and near-constant sources of controversy and change. Think about how dramatically different our views of sex and gender are today from those held 20, 10, or even 5 years ago. A few recent examples from around the world illustrate these changes. In 2016, for the first time in U.S. history, a woman ran for president as the candidate of a major party. Hillary Rodham Clinton won the popular vote against Donald J. Trump but lost the election, and following Trump's inauguration in early 2017, women and men around the world staged the largest collective protest in human history (the "Women's Marches") to bring attention to gender issues raised during the campaign. In 2014, 17-year-old Malala Yousafzai, a Pakistani girl who survived a murder attempt by the Taliban, became the youngest ever Nobel Peace Prize winner for her education rights advocacy for young girls around the world. Also in 2014, Laverne Cox became the first openly transgender person to be nominated for a Primetime Emmy Award for acting, and in 2017, the Boy Scouts of America opened its doors to transgender children for the first time. In 2016, the *New York Times* profiled a college football coach at the University of Houston, Tom Herman, who defies gender stereotypes by motivating his players with hugs and kisses on the cheek. In 2017, following a brutal attack on a gay couple holding hands in the Netherlands, men all over the country walked hand in hand in public to show their solidarity. In 2015, the United Nations endorsed an initiative called "Planet 50-50 by 2030: Step It Up for Gender Equality," with over 90 countries vowing to take concrete steps to decrease gender inequality. And the list goes on and on.

Sex and gender play substantial roles in shaping our identities, interpersonal interactions, opportunities, and societal institutions. It would be difficult to escape their influence, even if we tried. In this book, we examine the roles that sex and gender play on individual, interpersonal, social, and cultural levels. Along the way, we address questions such as these: How have ideas about sex and gender changed over the time, and how do they vary from culture to culture? How do gendered environments shape brain development? How do various sexes and gender identities differ? How do sex, gender, race, class, and sexual orientation interact to shape our identities, life experiences, and opportunities? We hope that you share our interest in these—and many other—questions about the psychology of sex and gender.

While the field of psychology got its official start in the late 1800s, researchers in mainstream psychology did not consider gender a legitimate topic of study for much of the field's history (Crawford & Marecek, 1989). This began to change in the 1970s, largely due to an upsurge in the scholarship of feminist psychologists at the time (for more on this, see the "Women's Movements and the Rise of Feminisms" section of this chapter). Since then, the scientific study of sex and gender has grown exponentially, with methods becoming more sophisticated and theories more advanced. In this book, you will learn about the most central theories and recent research findings on sex and gender.

This chapter sets the stage for the rest of the book by introducing you to some important terms and concepts and situating the study of sex and gender within a historical context. Chapter 1 covers a lot of territory in order to set the stage for future chapters that will go into greater depth and detail.

How Do We Explain Central Concepts in the Psychology of Sex and Gender?

To communicate about sex and gender effectively, it is important to understand some basic terminology. In this section, we clarify the terminology used throughout this book, but keep in mind that not all scholars agree on the definitions of terms such as *sex* and *gender*. When relevant, we acknowledge disagreements and clarify our preferred conceptualizations. See Table 1.1 for an overview of terms.

Table 1.1 Central Terminology in the Psychology of Sex and Gender.

Term	Central Question	Examples
Sex	To which category do I belong?	Male, female, intersex
Gender	What attributes, tendencies, and experiences (traits, interests, roles, attitudes, stereotypes, socialization practices, etc.) are associated with my sex?	Masculine (or male-typed), feminine (or female-typed), androgynous, agendered
Gender identity	How do I identify myself and experience my gender internally?	Boy, girl, man, woman, transgender man (transman), transgender woman (transwoman), agender, genderqueer, nonbinary
Sex–gender correspondence	Does my gender identity match my assigned sex?	Cisgender, transgender
Gender expression	How do I express myself outwardly (via dress, social behavior, etc.)?	Masculine (or male-typed), feminine (or female-typed), androgynous
Gender roles	What socially expected gender-related behavior patterns do I enact?	Provider/caretaker, leader/follower, protector/protected
Gender traits	What are my personality characteristics?	Masculine (or male-typed), feminine (or female-typed), androgynous
Gender role attitudes	What do I believe are the proper roles for women and men in society?	Traditional, transitional, egalitarian
Gender stereotypes	What attributes do I believe men share? What attributes do I believe women share?	Women are emotional and kind (communal). Men are decisive and independent (agentic).
Sexual orientation	What is my sexual orientation? To whom am I attracted?	Straight, gay, bisexual, pansexual, polysexual, asexual

Sex and Gender

In a classic article, Rhoda Unger (1979) argued that the meaning of the word *sex* was conceptually unclear in psychological research because it was overextended. For example, *sex* was used to refer to *sex* chromosomes and *sexual* anatomy—both of which are biological factors—as well as to *sex* roles and *sex* differences in personality, which arguably reflect sociocultural influences. And yet, despite being used to refer to different types of factors, the term *sex* was often interpreted in a primarily biological sense. Thus, differences between men and women, labeled sex differences, were assumed to reflect biological causes. However, differences between women and men do not always—or even mostly—stem from biological factors.

To reduce ambiguity about the causes and interpretations of sex differences, Rhoda Unger (1979) suggested using the term *gender* to refer to the nonbiological, culturally constructed aspects of being female or male and the term *sex* when discussing the biological aspects. Unfortunately, this is not as easy as it might seem, for at least two reasons. First, for any given difference between women and men, we do not know precisely how much of that difference stems from biology and how much stems from socialization, cultural norms, and life experience. Take differences in physical aggression rates, for example. On average, boys and men are more physically aggressive in comparison with girls and women (Archer, 2004). But this difference reflects a complex combination of biological and social factors. For instance, the hormone testosterone predicts aggression, and men have higher levels of testosterone than women do (Severson & Barclay, 2015). But boys and men are also socialized to perform physically active, risky behavior and to deal with negative emotion by directing it outward. Both of these factors likely contribute to sex differences in aggression, which makes it very difficult to disentangle the root cause of any observed sex difference.

Second, even the very meanings of *biological* and *social* factors can be somewhat fuzzy. For instance, people generally understand hormones as biological factors and socialization as a set of social factors. However, performing male-typed behaviors can increase testosterone in women, and performing female-typed behaviors can decrease testosterone in men. Since women and men learn from experience to perform male-typed and female-typed behaviors at different rates, some researchers question whether seemingly *biological* testosterone differences between women and men might actually reflect the result of gender socialization experiences (van Anders, Steiger, & Goldey, 2015; van Anders, Tolman, & Jainagaraj, 2014). In other words, differentiating biological from social causes of difference is not a straightforward process, a topic we will explore more fully in Chapter 3 ("The Nature and Nurture of Sex and Gender").

To resolve the issue in this book, we follow a convention adopted by Alice Eagly (2013) and use the word **sex** when we refer to male, female, and intersex as categories or groups of people. For example, we will refer to *sex differences* when discussing average differences between women, men, and those identifying as nonbinary (where available) on some variable of interest. By using the word sex in this context, however, we do not imply anything about the causes (biological or social) of the observed difference. In contrast, we use the term **gender** to refer to the meanings that people give to the different sex categories. Thus, gender refers to broad sets of identities, traits, interests, roles, tendencies, attitudes, stereotypes, and socialization practices commonly associated with maleness and femaleness. For instance, gender roles are social roles (e.g., provider or

Sex:
A term used to categorize people according to whether they are male, female, or intersex.

Gender:
The meanings that people give to the different sex categories. Gender consists of broad sets of attributes and tendencies (e.g., identities, traits, interests, roles, attitudes, stereotypes, and socialization practices) commonly associated with maleness and femaleness.

caretaker) that are typically associated with people as a function of their sex. Importantly, aspects of gender often differ by age, race and ethnicity, sexual orientation, culture, social class, and historical era, a point that we will emphasize throughout this book. As with sex, however, our use of the term gender does not imply anything about the causes of the phenomenon in question. That is, the gender roles that men and women tend to occupy likely result from a combination of biological and social factors (W. Wood & Eagly, 2012). Finally, we suggest that you do not get overly preoccupied with wording. While language is important, people often use terms differently, and consensus eventually emerges over time.

Soothing a crying infant can cause temporary decreases in men's testosterone levels, which raises this question: Do hormones cause changes in gender-typed behavior, or does gender-typed behavior cause changes in hormones?

Source: © iStockPhoto .com/bukharova

The Sex and Gender Binaries

Do sex and gender exist solely in binary (either/or) form? Are all people either male or female, boy or girl, man or woman, masculine or feminine? The **sex and gender binaries** refer to overarching social systems that conceptualize sex (male or female) and gender (masculine or feminine) as consisting of two opposite, nonoverlapping categories. Most—though not all—human societies and cultures operate under the framework of the sex binary, in large part because this binary tends to simplify social interactions, organize labor divisions, and maintain order in social institutions. However, the binary also oversimplifies the complexity of the natural world. According to biologist Anne Fausto-Sterling (2000), nature offers us a lot of variety when it comes to the biological components of sex. In a review of medical studies published between 1955 and 2000, Fausto-Sterling and her colleagues estimated that approximately 1.7% of human infants are born with some form of intersexuality (Blackless et al., 2000). **Intersexuality** is a condition in which the biological components of sex (chromosomes, hormones, genitals, and internal and external sex organs) do not consistently fit the typical male pattern or the typical female pattern. For example, an individual may be genetically male (XY) with undescended testicles and external genitalia that look female. This happens when people are born with Complete Androgen Insensitivity Syndrome (CAIS). Because they appear female, infants with CAIS often are assigned female at birth and raised as girls, leading them to develop a female gender identity despite having male sex chromosomes.

The complexity of biological factors underlying sex illustrates that sex does not operate cleanly in a binary fashion with only two categories. Taking this idea further, some scholars propose that the very idea of "biological sex" (the categories of male, female, and intersex) is a social construction (Marecek, Crawford, & Popp, 2004). This means that the categories of sex are not fixed, universal facts in nature but instead are shaped and constructed by different belief systems within specific cultures. Of course,

Gender binary:
Conceptualization of gender as consisting of two opposite and nonoverlapping categories, such as masculine or feminine.

Sex binary:
Conceptualization of sex as consisting of two opposite and nonoverlapping categories, such as male or female.

by extension, the sex binary is also not a fixed, natural reality. To illustrate this, consider the following quote:

Intersexuality: A condition in which biological components of sex (chromosomes, hormones, genitals, and internal and external sex organs) do not consistently fit the typical male pattern or the typical female pattern.

> The genitals of [intersexual individuals] are only ambiguous if they must be labeled as female or male (i.e., seen in terms of two nonoverlapping categories). If sex is not dimorphic, then the intersexed do not have ambiguous genitals but *variations* of the two more commonly known forms. In other words, what looks like ambiguity from the perspective of a two-sex categorization scheme is natural variation viewed from outside that scheme. (Golden, 2008, p. 139)

Similar to the sex binary, the gender binary—the assumption that individuals embody either masculine or feminine traits and tendencies—is also socially constructed. The concept of **androgyny** is relevant here. Androgyny refers to possessing high levels of both stereotypically masculine (e.g., assertive and confident) and feminine (e.g., warm and generous) traits (Bem, 1974). As we will discuss, masculinity and femininity are complex, multidimensional constructs, and some dimensions (e.g., gender-related occupational preferences) show more evidence of being binary than others (e.g., gender-related personality traits; Lippa, 2005b).

Androgyny: High levels of both stereotypically male-typed and female-typed traits.

In sum, the sex and gender binaries are oversimplified categorical structures that people often impose on the world. However, some cultures recognize more than two sexes and genders, with a great deal of cross-cultural variety emerging in the meanings, norms, and beliefs that people attach to these groups. For example, *two-spirit people* live outside the sex/gender binary in traditional Native American societies and adopt elements of both the female and male gender roles. In different Native American societies, two-spirit people may be lesbian or gay, live as the other sex, hold sacred or spiritual roles, or perform work typically associated with another sex. In India, *hijras* are a separate caste of people who live as neither men nor women. Considered sacred within Hinduism, hijras often play important roles in religious rites such as births and weddings, but they also tend to occupy a low social status and face negative stereotypes. In the western Balkans, *sworn virgins*, though biologically female, either are raised as boys from childhood or become men later in life. These individuals dress and live as men but must pledge to remain virgins and never marry. In contrast, *mustergil* are girls and women in Iraq who live like men but can return to the female gender role to marry (Lang & Kuhnle, 2008). These examples demonstrate some of the many ways that cultures attach meaning to *nonbinary* individuals who are neither male nor female. While many Western cultures have been slow to recognize and accept people who fall outside the sex and gender binaries, this is starting to change. We will return to this idea later in this chapter (see the section "Complexity and Change").

Stop and Think

Why do you think certain people and certain cultures enforce sex and gender binaries? What do cultures gain from this? Why are some people and some cultures more accepting *than others of going beyond sex and gender binaries? What other features of a culture might correlate with the tendency to acknowledge more than two sexes and genders?*

Gender Identity

Gender identity refers to individuals' psychological experience of their gender and how they identify their gender as that of a man, woman, girl, boy, or something else. Gender identity often (though not always) involves feeling a basic sense of belongingness to a sex category. Many people—referred to as **cisgender**—experience a match between their assigned sex at birth and the gender with which they feel a sense of belonging. On the other hand, **transgender** individuals experience a mismatch between their assigned sex at birth and their psychological sense of their gender. Moreover, some people are **agender**, meaning that they do not feel a sense of belonging to any category of sex.

Sidebar 1.1: Gender-Neutral Pronouns?

Some transgender, agender, and gender-neutral individuals prefer that others use gender-neutral pronouns (e.g., *ze* instead of *she* or *he* and *zir* instead of *her* or *him*) when referring to them (Bennett, 2016). Others prefer a plural pronoun (e.g., *them*). Because it can be difficult to know which pronouns people prefer, it is generally considered polite simply to ask.

In her multifactorial theory of gender identity, Janet Spence notes that a wide variety of attributes (e.g., roles, traits, interests, and attitudes) shapes gender identity and that these attributes are uncorrelated factors that vary greatly from person to person (Spence, 1993; Spence & Buckner, 1995). For example, knowing that someone identifies as a man (a male gender identity) would not necessarily allow us to predict accurately whether he also likes sports (a male-typed interest), makes decisions easily (a male-typed trait), occupies a leadership position (a male-typed role), or believes that men make better leaders than women (a traditional gender role attitude). For some individuals, these attributes do align in a male-typed manner; for others, they do not. Moreover, there are many different constellations of these gender attributes that can contribute to a person's gender identity. Despite this variability, most people develop a sense of belongingness to their assigned biological sex early in life and maintain this identity throughout life. They do so by staking their gender identity on the sex-typical attributes they possess and by discounting the importance of the sex-typical attributes they do not possess.

While Spence's (1993) theory acknowledges the multidimensionality of gender, it fails to account for the full spectrum of gender identities that people feel and express. For instance, her theory does not consider people who are agender or **genderqueer** (neither, both, or a combination of man and woman). More current conceptualizations not only recognize a wider range of gender identities, they also allow for dynamic identities such as **gender fluid**, which describes people whose gender identities shift over time and depend on the situation. Examples of gender-fluid identities include **bigender** (shifting between woman and man) and **trigender** (shifting among female, male, and third gender identities). Recognizing this complexity, Kay Deaux and Abigail Stewart (2001) conceptualize gender identity formation as a dynamic process and caution against viewing gender identity as a single, inflexible identity that emerges early in life and remains stable throughout life. They instead view gender identity as a set of overlapping identities

Gender identity: Individuals' psychological experience of their gender and how they identify internally as a man, woman, or something else.

Cisgender: Describes people who experience a match between their sex assigned at birth and their psychological gender identity.

Transgender: Describes people whose psychological gender identity does not align with their assigned sex at birth.

Agender: Describes people who feel internally ungendered.

Genderqueer: Describes people who identify as neither, both, or a combination of man and woman.

Gender fluid:
Describes people
whose gender
identity shifts or
changes flexibly
rather remaining
constant.

Bigender:
Describes people
who shift between
gender identities as
woman and man.

Trigender:
Describes people
who shift among
woman, man,
and third gender
identities.

Gay: Refers to
a man who is
attracted only (or
primarily) to men.

Lesbian: Refers
to a woman who
is attracted only
(or primarily) to
women.

Bisexual:
Signifies being
attracted to women
and men.

that are negotiated dynamically and shaped by norms and other people in social contexts (Deaux & Stewart, 2001).

Sexual Orientation

Unlike gender identity, sexual orientation refers to people's tendency to develop romantic and sexual attractions to others based on their sex. Note that both cisgender and transgender individuals can have any sexual orientation. For example, a biologically female person who identifies as a woman and is attracted only to women would be considered a cisgender lesbian, whereas a biologically male person who identifies as a woman and is attracted only to men would be a transgender heterosexual woman (or heterosexual transwoman). Sexual orientation category labels include **gay**, **lesbian**, **bisexual**, **heterosexual**, **polysexual**, **pansexual**, and **asexual**. Of course, just as imposing category labels oversimplifies sex and gender, some argue that labeling sexual orientation categories is also an oversimplification. Proponents of this view point to the fact that sexual orientation is a complex, multidimensional construct that consists—at the very least—of cognitive, motivational, and behavioral factors (Herek, 2000), as you will read more about in Chapter 9 ("Sexual Orientation and Sexuality").

Intersectionality

Traditional psychological perspectives on sex and gender tend to view "women" and "men" as uniform groups rather than focusing on the differences among them. This approach ignores the fact that people do not belong solely to a sex or gender identity category but simultaneously occupy categories of race, class, age, nationality, physical ability, and sexual orientation. Moreover, because different social categories correlate with different levels of privilege and discrimination, people who occupy more than one disadvantaged group may face unique experiences not shared by other members of their sex or gender identity group. The notion of **intersectionality** refers to the ways in which different forms of discrimination and oppression (e.g., sexism, racism, classism, heterosexism, and transphobia) interact to shape people's experiences (Crenshaw, 1993; Hurtado, 1996; McCall, 2005). For instance, rather than just focusing on how "women" as a group are affected by sexism, an intersectional perspective might focus on how sexism interacts with racism and classism to shape the experiences of poor Latinas.

Sociologist Patricia Collins (2000) proposes the idea of a matrix to represent the intersecting identities that exist within cultural and historical contexts. All individuals and social groups occupy a specific social location within a matrix that is defined by cross-cutting social categories (e.g., sex, race and ethnicity, and sexual orientation). Each social location within the matrix is associated with different levels of privilege or oppression and, accordingly, with different life experiences. Proponents of intersectionality argue that a nuanced understanding of sex and gender will require psychologists to examine more fully the intersecting identities and oppressions that shape people's lives. We return to this idea in the upcoming section "Women's Movements and the Rise of Feminisms."

Masculinity and Femininity

What makes someone masculine, feminine, androgynous, or other? It has been surprisingly difficult for gender researchers to answer these questions (Spence & Buckner, 1995). In a groundbreaking article, Ann Constantinople (1973) declared masculinity and femininity to be two of the muddiest concepts in the psychological literature. Despite this, researchers generally agree that **masculinity** refers to the possession of physical and psychological attributes typically associated with men, and **femininity** refers to the possession of physical and psychological attributes typically associated with women. As noted, psychological androgyny refers to the possession of high levels of both masculine and feminine attributes.

Heterosexual: Signifies being attracted only (or primarily) to persons of the other sex.

Stop and Think

Do you consider yourself masculine, feminine, androgynous, or none of the above? What do the terms masculine and feminine mean to you? How do you interpret it when, for example, someone describes a man as being "in touch with his 'feminine' side"? When you think of people who are androgynous, how do you picture their personality? What about their physical appearance?

Sidebar 1.2: Is Androgyny Good for Your Health?

Having an androgynous personality means being high in both male-typed traits (e.g., "analytical" and "independent") and female-typed traits (e.g., "affectionate" and "understanding"). Since both of these types of traits predict positive outcomes in important life domains (e.g., personal achievement and interpersonal relationships), some researchers propose androgyny to be "good for your health." In fact, one large study of over 4,800 White, Black, and Latino youth examined the correlations between androgyny scores and quality of life across physical, emotional, social, and school domains (S. M. Scott et al., 2015). Androgyny correlated positively with quality of life but only among White and Latino girls. Among boys, high levels of male-typed traits and low levels of female-typed traits best predicted quality of life. Why do you think these different patterns of associations might emerge for girls and boys?

Polysexual: Signifies being attracted to people of many different sexes and gender identities.

Pansexual: Signifies being attracted to people of all sexes and gender identities.

Asexual: Signifies having a lack of desire for sex or sexual partners.

Intersectionality: The ways in which different forms of discrimination and oppression (e.g., sexism, racism, classism, heterosexism, and transphobia) interact to shape people's experiences.

What Makes Sex and Gender So Complicated?

"There is nothing simple about sex and gender."

—Rhoda Unger (2001, p. vi)

In this statement, Unger conveys the complexity of sex and gender well. Even something as seemingly simple as identifying and naming the different sexes is more complicated than it first appears. In this section, we discuss some complexities in how people and cultures think about sex and gender, as well as the tendency for sex and gender to fall out of consciousness and become invisible.

Complexity and Change

While several non-Western cultures have long recognized third and fourth categories of sex and gender, most Western cultures recognize only two sexes. However, this is beginning to change, as understandings of sex and gender become more complex. Consider the cases of Alex MacFarlane and Norrie May-Welby in Australia. In 2003, Alex Mac-Farlane became the first Australian (and likely the first person in the world) to indicate a third sex ("X") identity on a passport ("Ten Years of 'X' Passports," 2013). MacFarlane has Klinefelter syndrome, a genetic condition and type of intersexuality in which the individual's sex chromosomes are XXY, rather than the more common XX (female) or XY (male). In Western cultures, people with Klinefelter syndrome are typically assigned male at birth and accordingly develop a male gender identity, but MacFarlane identifies as neither male nor female.

Between 2003 and 2011, the Australian government offered the third sex option on passports only for diagnosed intersex individuals like MacFarlane. Then, from 2011 to 2014, Australia gradually broadened its policies to allow all nonbinary transgender individuals to specify a third sex/gender option on official documents as long as they provided a letter signed by a medical doctor. This change came about largely due to the efforts of Norrie May-Welby. Assigned male at birth, May-Welby had **genital reconstructive surgery** in 1989 but subsequently came to identify as both male and female simultaneously (or "spansexual," in May-Welby's words). In 2014, the High Court of Australia ruled that May-Welby had the legal right to register as gender nonspecific, which paved the way for other gender-neutral Australians to do the same (Rawstron, 2014). Now, this third gender is recognized by the Australian census, as well as by at least one health insurance provider in Australia (Pash, 2016).

Between 2007 and 2015, several other countries followed suit and acknowledged a third sex/gender option. For instance, Nepal, India, Bangladesh, Thailand, Pakistan, New Zealand, Germany, Denmark, and Malta added a third sex/gender option on various official documents (Byrne, 2014; Macarow, 2015). Though Argentina, Columbia, and Ireland do not allow this third option on official documents, they do allow individuals to change their sex category (from female to male or vice versa) without requiring any medical or psychological documentation. In the United States, no third sex/gender option was offered on official documents until recently, when New York City issued the first intersex birth certificate in late 2016 to Sara Kelly Keenan (Scutti, 2017). In 2017, Oregon became the first state to allow a third gender option on identity cards such as driver's licenses (A. Ferguson, 2017). Overall, policies regarding changing one's sex designation on birth certificates and other official documents vary from state to state in the United States, with most states requiring proof of genital reconstructive surgery before allowing the change (Byrne, 2014; "Changing Birth Certificate," 2015).

Why is this important? Cases like those of Alex MacFarlane and Norrie May-Welby illustrate not only the complexity of sex and gender but also the powerful roles of social and cultural factors in shaping our understandings of sex and gender. Some social understandings of sex and gender have remained remarkably similar across time and cultures while others change quite rapidly. For example, the tendency to view women as more warm, moral, and appearance oriented than men seems to transcend time and culture (Glick et al., 2000). In contrast, beliefs about the existence and acceptability of third sex/gender options show a great deal of cross-cultural variability and, in some cultures, have changed substantially over the past 10 years.

Sidebar 1.3: Toddler Fashion Flashback

Sex-typed styles of dress have changed a lot over time. For example, take a look at the famous American depicted in the image below. Who do you think this is? In fact, this is a 2-year-old Franklin D. Roosevelt (the 32nd president of the United States) in 1884. In the late 19th century, Americans considered this outfit gender neutral rather than feminine. At the time, people dressed girls and boys similarly—in dresses—until the age of 6 or 7 (Paoletti, 2012).

Regardless of this change, sex and gender are powerful *schemas*—or mental frameworks—through which most people process their social worlds. At the same time, we do not always notice their influence. Let's examine this paradox further.

Ubiquity and Invisibility

Sex and gender play pervasive roles in many aspects of life, from our occupations and our physical health to our educational and political outcomes, our appearance and dress, and even our understandings and interpretations of basic constructs like colors, numbers, and food. For example, across cultures, people typically associate red meat (especially steak and hamburgers), potatoes, and beer with men and salad, pasta, yogurt, fruit, and chocolate with women (Sobal, 2005). In the United States, people tend to associate pink with girls and blue with boys (Paoletti, 2012). Around the world, about 55% of all languages are gendered, with nouns designated as masculine, feminine, or gender neutral

Who is this famous American?

Source: https://www
.smithsonianmag.com/
arts-culture/when-did-
girls-start-wearing-
pink-1370097/

(Prewitt-Freilino, Caswell, & Laakso, 2012). Even numeric digits are gendered. Consider this: Which number, 1 or 2, do you view as more masculine? When James Wilkie and Galen Bodenhausen (2012) asked people this question, they found a tendency for the number 1 to be perceived as more masculine than the number 2. Wilkie and Bodenhausen reasoned that the number 1 represents a solitary, autonomous entity, which makes it seem masculine relative to the more relational, "feminine" number 2.

Sex and gender clearly permeate our lives. A quick Internet search for "gender in the news" reveals hundreds of recent stories about topics such as gender role norms ("Jameis Winston Apologizes After Saying Girls Should Be 'Silent and Polite,'" 2017), gender in politics ("What's Next for the Women's Movement?" 2017), and gender in the workplace ("When a Company Is Failing, Female CEOs Get Blamed More Frequently Than Men"; Peck, 2016). At the same time, because the influence of gender on our everyday interactions and behaviors is so routine and normalized, we sometimes fail to notice it. Sociologist Judith Lorber (1994) argues that we should attempt to reverse this trend and make gender even more visible in order to challenge dominant gender norms, beliefs, and institutions because these often reinforce gender inequality. But how can we make sex and gender more visible?

One way is by flipping gender norms for men and women to expose how they operate. For example, in a 2015 video created by the Cover the Athlete campaign, reporters asked world-class male athletes questions routinely asked of female athletes. Examples included the following: "If you could date anyone in the world, who would you date?" "How has your weight gain affected your mobility?" and "Could you give us a twirl and tell us about your outfit?" Male athletes responded with disbelief and open irritation to these questions, illustrating the absurdity of gender norms that make topics such as appearance and sexuality acceptable fodder for interviews with female athletes.

People can also make the influence of sex and gender more visible by discussing it directly. To this end, we will regularly ask you in this book to reflect on and evaluate how sex and gender shape people at individual, interpersonal, and societal levels. Perhaps not surprising, the extent to which people recognize the influence of sex and gender depends on the groups to which they belong. For example, the more dominant and privileged the group (as with male or cisgender individuals), the less group members tend to recognize the influence of sex and gender in their daily lives (Case, Hensley, & Anderson, 2014; McIntosh, 2012). Conversely, less privileged groups (female and transgender individuals, for example) tend to more readily recognize the influence of gender in their lives.

Privilege is an automatic, unearned advantage that accompanies membership in certain social groups. In many Western cultures, privilege is associated with being male, White, cisgender, heterosexual, able-bodied, and wealthy. Because privilege often comes with an absence of certain experiences (e.g., an absence of discrimination or an absence of stressful identity-based encounters), it can be difficult to recognize when one has it. Inspired by an essay about White privilege by Peggy McIntosh (1989), some educators use "privilege lists" to encourage members of dominant groups to recognize how their group status shapes their experiences (Killermann, 2013). See Table 1.2 for examples of cisgender, male, and heterosexual privilege lists. Interestingly, exposure to videotaped discussions of male and heterosexual privilege can reduce people's sexist attitudes and increase their motivation to avoid prejudice (Case et al., 2014).

Stop and Think

Do you fall into any of the categories of privilege listed in Table 1.2? McIntosh (1989) asserts that members of privileged groups should reflect on the automatic advantages that their group membership affords them. What are the pros and cons of this sort of reflection? What other ways might there be to encourage people to think about their privileged statuses?

Table 1.2 Lists of Cisgender Privilege, Male Privilege, and Heterosexual Privilege. Privilege can be difficult to detect when one has it because it is often characterized by an *absence* of stressful and unpleasant experiences, rather than by the *presence* of pleasant experiences. As a class exercise, instructors sometimes ask their students to consider which of these experiences are familiar to them.

Cisgender Privilege

1. You can use public restrooms without fear of verbal abuse, physical intimidation, or arrest.

2. Strangers don't assume they can ask you what your genitals look like and how you have sex.

3. You can walk through the world and generally blend in, not being constantly stared or gawked at, whispered about, pointed at, or laughed at because of your gender expression.

4. You can reasonably assume that you will not be denied services at a hospital, bank, or other institution because the staff does not believe the gender marker on your ID card to match your gender identity.

5. You don't have to fear interactions with police officers due to your gender identity.

Male Privilege

1. A decision to hire you won't be based on whether the employer assumes you will be having children in the near future.

2. You can generally work comfortably (or walk down a public street) without the fear of sexual harassment.

3. You can decide not to have children and not have your masculinity questioned.

4. You can have promiscuous sex and be viewed positively for it.

5. You are less likely to be interrupted in conversation.

Heterosexual Privilege

1. You can count on immediate access to your loved one in case of accident or emergency.

2. You can easily find a neighborhood in which residents will accept the make-up of your household.

3. You can expect to share joint child custody.

4. You can go wherever you wish knowing that you will not be harassed, beaten, or killed because of your sexuality.

5. You do not have to worry that people won't let their children play with your children because of your sexuality.

Source: Excerpted from Killermann (2013).

Finally, sex and gender sometimes become more salient when we encounter patterns that do not match our expectations. For example, consider this scenario:

> A man and his son get into a car accident. The man dies instantly, but the boy is rushed to the hospital for surgery. The surgeon enters the room and says, "I cannot operate on this boy. He is my son." How is this possible?

When Margo Monteith, then president of the Midwestern Psychological Association, mentioned this riddle during her presidential address at a conference, she listed a variety of answers that her students had generated over the years. Some solved the riddle by assuming that the boy's parents were a gay male couple; others thought that the surgeon must be the boy's stepfather; one even suggested that the surgeon was a Catholic priest who called all male people "my son" (Monteith, 2014). In contrast, people less frequently guess the actual solution to the riddle, that the surgeon is the boy's mother. Revealing this answer to those who are stumped by the riddle can bring visibility to otherwise invisible gendered assumptions. Note, however, that not everyone finds this riddle perplexing. Children tend to have an easier time identifying the surgeon as the boy's mother. What might this say about the role of learning in our gendered associations?

How Have Gender Movements Shaped History?

Structures of Power and Inequality

Patriarchal: Describes a societal structure in which men/fathers occupy the leadership positions in the society and control how it operates.

Matriarchal: Describes a societal structure in which women/mothers occupy the leadership positions in the society and control how it operates.

Not all individuals within any given society share the same rights and enjoy equal access to resources and power. Some form of hierarchical social structure exists in all human societies, though the specific forms that hierarchies take vary from culture to culture (Pratto, Sidanius, & Levin, 2006). Within hierarchies, *dominant groups* have more access to education, leadership positions, and resources, and *subordinate groups* have less access to these opportunities and resources. In turn, access to power and resources allows dominant group members to shape the norms and laws that govern society and thus to shape the outcomes of subordinate groups.

Though not the only factors, sex and gender shape status hierarchies within societies. In **patriarchal** societies, men as a group rule the society and control how it operates. In contrast, **matriarchal** societies are defined as ones in which women rule the society and control how it operates. While we lack evidence of any true matriarchal societies throughout human history, there are many known matrilineal societies in which family relationships and ancestry are traced through the mother's line. For example, among the Garo people in India and Bangladesh, daughters inherit property from their mothers, and sons move in with their wives' families upon marriage (Burling, 1963). Similarly, several Native American societies, including the Navajo, Hopi, Iroquois, and Tinglit, are traditionally matrilineal. Note, however, that being matrilineal does not make a society matriarchal because men still tend to hold more political and decision-making power than women do in these societies.

Social scientists offer many theories to explain how social hierarchies operate. For example, according to social dominance theory, group-based social hierarchies and dominant group advantages result from a system of discrimination that operates on individual, interpersonal, and institutional levels (Sidanius & Pratto, 1999). In this theory, *legitimizing myths* (consensually shared values and beliefs that primarily reflect the interests of dominant group members) emerge to justify unequal social hierarchies. An example of a legitimizing myth is the belief that women have qualities that men lack, such as gentleness and moral purity, that make them both well suited for mothering roles and needful of protection from men. Another legitimizing myth is the model of **hegemonic masculinity**, which refers to a culturally idealized yet difficult-to-attain version of manhood characterized by aggression, competition, success, emotional restraint, toughness, courage, and antifemininity. Framing manhood in this way can serve to reinforce and justify male dominance (Connell & Messerschmidt, 2005).

The Navajo of North America are traditionally matrilineal, passing property from mothers to daughters. Here, a Navajo woman and her mother (seated) pose in front of their hogan (traditional dwelling).

Source: © iStockPhoto .com/tobkatrina

Throughout history, group-based power imbalances have sometimes prompted disempowered groups to organize and advocate for equal and fair treatment. Relevant here is the distinction between **equality** (treating everyone the same, regardless of background or differences) and **equity** (treating everyone fairly by taking background and difference into account). Whereas equality can still disadvantage some people relative to others if they possess different capabilities or attributes, equity typically leads to more just outcomes. As an example, consider using an equality versus an equity principle to guide the treatment of vision problems. Because people differ in how well their eyes focus on distant objects, treating all vision problems with the same eyeglass prescription would be truly "equal," but it would not be equitable: Some people's vision would be improved by the prescription while others would still have difficulty seeing. Many gender movements—including the women's movements, gay rights movements, and transgender movement—tackle these issues of equality and equity head on, and men's movements often address how gender shapes men's experiences. Although the goals of men's movement groups vary, some focus on how the male gender role can be oppressive and harmful to men. We will now examine the progress made by women, sexual minorities, transgender individuals, and men as a result of political movements.

Hegemonic masculinity: A culturally idealized version of manhood that reinforces men's control over women.

Women's Movements and the Rise of Feminisms

Women's movements. As discussed in the opening of this chapter, the Women's Marches of January 2017 were possibly the largest collective protest in history. With an estimated 4.2 million people participating in the United States and hundreds of thousands of people marching in over 200 other nations (Frostenson, 2017), it is difficult to discount the power and organization of this social effort. Moreover, despite the name, the Women's Marches were attended by people of all sexes, and they represented a range

EQUALITY   VS.   EQUITY

Treating everyone identically (equality) does not always lead to the fairest outcomes. In contrast, equity sometimes requires giving some people more of a boost than others.

Source: http://groundswellcenter .org/october-from-the-director

Equality: A principle in which each individual is treated the same, regardless of background.

Equity: A principle in which each individual is treated fairly, by taking background into account.

of gender identities, sexual orientations, ages, races, ethnicities, nationalities, religions, and socioeconomic classes. These marches did not emerge in a vacuum but instead drew on decades of political action and effort by feminists and gender activists.

So what efforts preceded the Women's Marches? Some argue that the women's movement in the United States occurred in three waves, each punctuated by a series of major social and political events (see Figure 1.1). However, not everyone agrees that the wave metaphor is the best way to describe the progress of the women's movements. For instance, Linda Nicholson (2010) contends that labeling "waves" in the women's movement ignores the work and progress made outside of the waves (e.g., in the 1920s–1960s) and fails to acknowledge the diversity of feminists with differing perspectives who contributed to each wave. To this end, some propose that a river metaphor better captures the development of women's movements over time, since a river—though at times expanding and narrowing—is always flowing (Laughlin et al., 2010). Although we sometimes use the wave terminology in this book, keep in mind that these waves do not represent the unitary voice of all feminists and that much gender activism takes place outside of the "waves."

Scholars generally agree that the first wave of the women's movement in the United States began in Seneca Falls, New York, in 1848 at the first women's rights convention. The 68 women and 32 men present at this convention endorsed the goal of attaining

On January 21, 2017, the day after Donald J. Trump was inaugurated, millions of protestors marched in Washington, D.C., and hundreds of other cities throughout the world.

Source: Mario Tama/Getty Images News/Getty Images

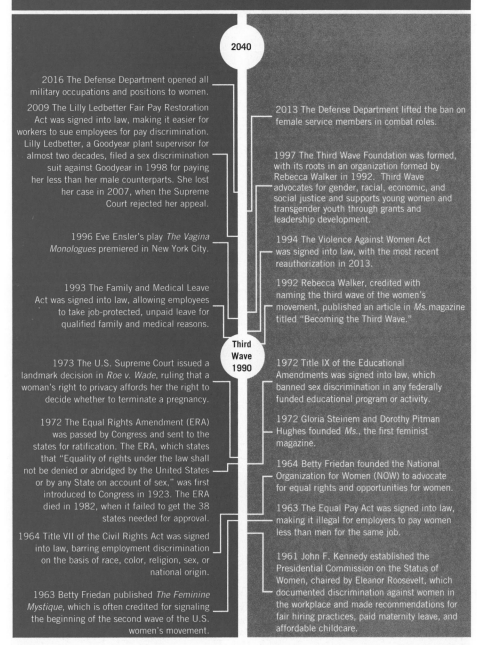

Figure 1.1 Timeline of Important Events Across the First, Second, and Third "Waves" of the Women's Movement in the United States

2040

2016 The Defense Department opened all military occupations and positions to women.

2009 The Lilly Ledbetter Fair Pay Restoration Act was signed into law, making it easier for workers to sue employees for pay discrimination. Lilly Ledbetter, a Goodyear plant supervisor for almost two decades, filed a sex discrimination suit against Goodyear in 1998 for paying her less than her male counterparts. She lost her case in 2007, when the Supreme Court rejected her appeal.

1996 Eve Ensler's play The Vagina Monologues premiered in New York City.

1993 The Family and Medical Leave Act was signed into law, allowing employees to take job-protected, unpaid leave for qualified family and medical reasons.

1973 The U.S. Supreme Court issued a landmark decision in Roe v. Wade, ruling that a woman's right to privacy affords her the right to decide whether to terminate a pregnancy.

1972 The Equal Rights Amendment (ERA) was passed by Congress and sent to the states for ratification. The ERA, which states that "Equality of rights under the law shall not be denied or abridged by the United States or by any State on account of sex," was first introduced to Congress in 1923. The ERA died in 1982, when it failed to get the 38 states needed for approval.

1964 Title VII of the Civil Rights Act was signed into law, barring employment discrimination on the basis of race, color, religion, sex, or national origin.

1963 Betty Friedan published The Feminine Mystique, which is often credited for signaling the beginning of the second wave of the U.S. women's movement.

Third Wave 1990

2013 The Defense Department lifted the ban on female service members in combat roles.

1997 The Third Wave Foundation was formed, with its roots in an organization formed by Rebecca Walker in 1992. Third Wave advocates for gender, racial, economic, and social justice and supports young women and transgender youth through grants and leadership development.

1994 The Violence Against Women Act was signed into law, with the most recent reauthorization in 2013.

1992 Rebecca Walker, credited with naming the third wave of the women's movement, published an article in Ms. magazine titled "Becoming the Third Wave."

1972 Title IX of the Educational Amendments was signed into law, which banned sex discrimination in any federally funded educational program or activity.

1972 Gloria Steinem and Dorothy Pitman Hughes founded Ms., the first feminist magazine.

1964 Betty Friedan founded the National Organization for Women (NOW) to advocate for equal rights and opportunities for women.

1963 The Equal Pay Act was signed into law, making it illegal for employers to pay women less than men for the same job.

1961 John F. Kennedy established the Presidential Commission on the Status of Women, chaired by Eleanor Roosevelt, which documented discrimination against women in the workplace and made recommendations for fair hiring practices, paid maternity leave, and affordable childcare.

(Continued)

Figure 1.1 (Continued)

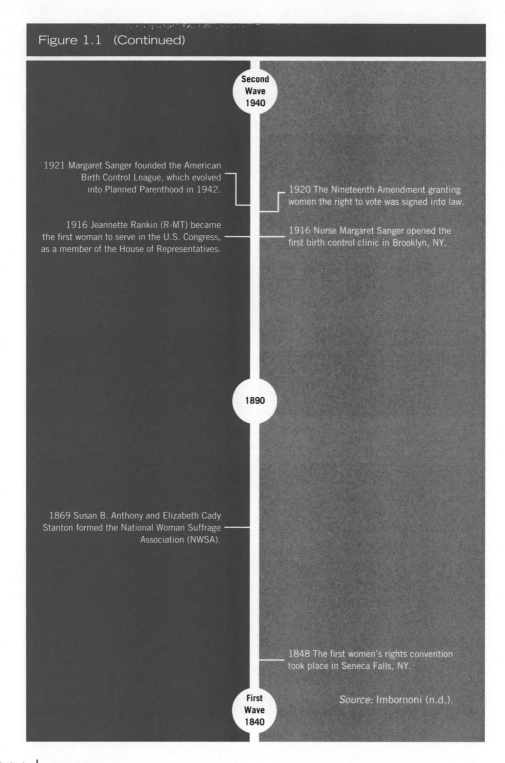

Second
Wave
1940

1921 Margaret Sanger founded the American
Birth Control League, which evolved
into Planned Parenthood in 1942.

1920 The Nineteenth Amendment granting
women the right to vote was signed into law.

1916 Jeannette Rankin (R-MT) became
the first woman to serve in the U.S. Congress,
as a member of the House of Representatives.

1916 Nurse Margaret Sanger opened the
first birth control clinic in Brooklyn, NY.

1890

1869 Susan B. Anthony and Elizabeth Cady
Stanton formed the National Woman Suffrage
Association (NWSA).

1848 The first women's rights convention
took place in Seneca Falls, NY.

Source: Imbornoni (n.d.).

First
Wave
1840

equal treatment of women and men under the law, with a particular emphasis on economic and voting rights for women. At the time, no country in the world granted women the right to vote in elections, and women who pursued higher education routinely faced discrimination. For example, in the late 19th century, Mary Whiton Calkins, who would later become the first female president of the American Psychological Association (APA), was denied a PhD from Harvard, despite having fulfilled the requirements to earn the degree (Rutherford & Granek, 2010). As a result of international suffrage movements, women began gaining the right to vote in many countries around the world, starting in 1893. By the end of the 1970s, only a small number of nations in Africa and the Middle East still denied women voting rights, and in 2015, Saudi Arabia—the last holdout—gave women the right to vote.

Scholars frequently trace the beginning of the second wave of the U.S. women's movement to Betty Friedan's publication of *The Feminine Mystique*. In this book, Friedan discussed "the problem that has no name," by which she meant the dissatisfaction that middle-class (primarily White) women felt in the 1950s and 1960s when their lives were restricted to roles as housewives and mothers. As in the first wave, second-wave activists sought equal rights and opportunities for women, but they expanded their focus to issues such as domestic violence, sexual harassment, pay equality, and reproductive rights. Gender activism in this era had bearing on the field of psychology in that researchers began including women as research participants and studying topics of relevance to women (e.g., domestic violence and androgyny) that previously went unexamined (Rutherford & Granek, 2010). Furthermore, the field saw the emergence of new journals devoted to sex and gender, such as *Sex Roles* in 1975; new organizations, such as the Society for the Psychology of Women (Division 35 of the APA) in 1973; and new university courses, such as "The Psychology of Women." To get a sense of some of the rights and freedoms that resulted from the second wave of the women's movement, see Table 1.3.

In 1992, Rebecca Walker, daughter of writer Alice Walker, published an article in *Ms.* magazine that is credited with galvanizing what some identify as the third wave of the women's movement. This article, titled "Becoming the Third Wave," emphasized intersectionality by simultaneously confronting issues of sex and race. Third-wave feminists reject the idea that all women experience a common oppression, and they are critical of the primarily White, middle-class, second-wave feminists for failing to include diverse women and identities. Specifically, third-wave feminists more often view race, class, sexual orientation, and gender identity as central issues, and they take more global perspectives on sex and gender. In psychology, proponents of the third wave emphasize how diverse experiences (e.g., poverty, racism, and educational barriers) interact to influence women's health and outcomes (Baumgardner & Richards, 2010). Note, however, that these ideas were not new in the early 1990s, as they appeared in the earlier works of Cherríe Moraga, bell hooks, and Audre Lorde, among others (hooks, 1980; Lorde, 1984; Moraga & Anzaldúa, 1981). Nonetheless, it was not until the early 1990s that these ideas garnered more widespread attention among feminists.

Feminisms. Do you consider yourself a feminist? Why or why not? Though many different types of **feminisms** exist (see Table 1.4)—and we emphasize this by using the plural *feminisms* here, rather than the singular *feminism*—some core issues hold all of them

Feminisms: Movements for the social, political, and economic equality of women and men or, according to bell hooks, movements "to end sexism, sexist exploitation, and oppression."

Table 1.3 Things That American Women Could Not Do Before the 1970s.
Consider how much has changed in the past several decades. If you value any of these rights, you can thank a gender activist!

Keep a job if pregnant	Women could be fired from their job for being pregnant, until the passage in 1978 of the Pregnancy Discrimination Act.
Report workplace sexual harassment	Workplace sexual harassment was not legally recognized until 1977, and it was not until 1980 that it was legally defined by the Equal Employment Opportunity Commission.
Run in the Boston Marathon	Women were not allowed to run in this race until 1972.
Get a credit card	Women could not apply for credit cards until 1974, under the Equal Credit Opportunity Act.
Refuse to have sex with her husband	Marital rape was not recognized as rape in most states until the mid 1970s. In 1993, it became criminalized in all 50 states.
Get an easy divorce	Prior to the No Fault Divorce law of 1969, it was very difficult to divorce unless a spouse could prove that the other spouse did something wrong (e.g., adultery).
Have a legal abortion	Women could not legally seek an abortion in all states until the 1973 Supreme Court decision *Roe v. Wade*, which stated that a woman's decision to terminate a pregnancy was protected under the guaranteed right to privacy.

Source: Excerpted from N. Turner (2013).

together. For instance, feminists share a common goal of social, political, and economic equality of women and men (Baumgardner & Richards, 2010). However, as discussed, writer bell hooks (2000) criticizes this narrow emphasis on equality between the sexes because it ignores important factors like race and class. That is, not all men have the same status and opportunities, nor do all women experience similar levels of disadvantage. To address this, hooks (2014) defines feminisms as movements "to end sexism, sexist exploitation, and oppression" because this addresses systems of power and oppression rather than individual women and men (p. 1).

Feminisms and feminist identities have evolved over time in the women's movements, with liberal feminism predominating in the first and second waves and radical feminism emerging during the second wave. Transnational feminism, though present in some form since the first wave, coalesced in the mid-1980s to focus on worldwide issues such as poverty, gender violence, and access to education and health care (Moghadam, 2010).

Where are the various feminisms now? Have their missions been accomplished? While advances have been made, particularly in the United States from the gender activism of the women's movements, much remains to be done throughout the world for

Table 1.4	**Different Types of Feminisms.** Feminisms tend to share the common goal of gender equality, but they also assume various forms that reflect their different emphases and values.
Liberal feminism	Asserts that men and women should be treated equally because they are equal in characteristics and ability. Supports legislation that removes barriers for women and leads to greater opportunity.
Radical feminism	Believes that patriarchy (male control in society and over women) must be dismantled. Seeks to rid society of rigid gender roles and oppression of women.
Socialist feminism	Views the gendered division of labor, capitalism, and the value put on men's work in the public sphere as disadvantaging women. Seeks economic independence for women.
Womanism	Calls out the exclusion of women of color from mainstream feminism and recognizes that race, gender, and class intersect to shape experiences.
Cultural/difference feminism	Asserts that there are fundamental differences between men and women. Advocates that the qualities of women be as valued and respected as the qualities of men.
Transnational feminism	Seeks to alleviate the discrimination and suffering of girls and women across national boundaries. Focuses on issues such as poverty, health, gender violence, and educational access.

people of all sexes to experience social, political, and economic equality. In addition, some question whether feminisms are healthy in their current forms, and their concerns center around three main issues. First, for feminisms to be viable, they need supporters, but fewer and fewer young people identify as feminists. While young people espouse many of the beliefs of feminists (that women and men should have equal rights), they often do not take the next step to identify as feminists (Liss, Crawford, & Popp, 2004; Zucker, 2004). Negative stereotypes about feminists likely contribute to this. For example, in comparison with their nonfeminist counterparts, feminist women are seen as more radical, unattractive, cold, intolerant, and uncooperative, and feminist men are seen as more weak, fragile, emotional, feminine, and likely to be gay (V. N. Anderson, 2009; Rudman, Mescher, & Moss-Racusin, 2012).

Stop and Think

Comedian and actress Amy Poehler had this to say about people who support gender equity but do not identify as feminists: "That's like someone being like 'I don't really believe in cars, but I drive one every day and I love that it gets me places and makes life so much easier and faster and I don't know what I would do without it'" ("Amy Poehler," 2014). What do you think of Amy's point? Is it fair?

Second, to remain relevant, feminisms must be more inclusive of nonbinary and transgender individuals. For instance, the focus on attaining equality "between women and men" reinforces the sex binary and fails to acknowledge the issues confronting those who fall outside this binary. In addition, as noted, many first- and second-wave feminists generally ignored how factors like gender, race, class, and sexual orientation interacted to shape experiences. Similarly, many feminists fail to acknowledge the ways in which rigid and restrictive gender roles negatively impact men. For more on this issue, see "Debate: Are Men Overlooked in Feminist Movements?"

Finally, to remain viable, feminist movements must flexibly adapt to the updated needs and experiences of younger generations. Given their focus on diversity, intersectionality, and globalism, third-wave feminists tend to prioritize issues such as environmental justice, prison reform, the living wage, marginalized people (e.g., women of color and trans people), and **reproductive justice** (the human right to personal bodily autonomy, parenthood choices, and safe communities in which to raise children). But these issues do not always overlap with the goals of earlier feminists, and tensions sometimes arise between second-wave feminists and younger generations (Baumgardner & Richards, 2010).

Sidebar 1.4: Reproductive *Rights* or Reproductive *Justice*?

In 2003, the SisterSong Women of Color Reproductive Justice Collective offered the term *reproductive justice* to add to and build on conversations about *reproductive rights* (L. Ross, 2011). While *reproductive rights* often boil down to the issue of women's access to birth control and safe abortion, SisterSong noted that conditions in marginalized communities, such as environmental dangers and lack of health care access, often restrict women's reproductive rights and choices on a broader level. In other words, women who live in marginalized communities face restrictions to their reproductive outcomes that go beyond issues of individual choice and birth control. Therefore, advocates of *reproductive justice* work to make marginalized communities safer and healthier, with increased social support structures so that women will have more autonomy to make healthy reproductive choices and to parent their children in safe environments.

Debate

Although gender equality seems like a noble ideal, many respond to feminist movements with ambivalence or derision, and stereotypes of feminists tend to be negative (V. N. Anderson, 2009). Why do people often feel uncomfortable labeling themselves feminists? Why do feminist movements often inspire resentment? Some argue that any movement that challenges the status quo will face resistance, but others argue that feminisms elicit resentment because they ignore a significant component of the human population (i.e., men). Do men's concerns get left behind in feminist movements? Can men, who generally have more structural power than women do, be disempowered? Throughout this book, we engage readers in intellectual debates to expand on some of the issues that we cover. Here, we consider whether feminist movements overlook men and, if so, whether this is a problem. Let's examine both sides.

Yes, Feminist Movements Overlook Men

For a social justice movement to be effective, it needs to be inclusive. Equality means respecting everyone's outcomes, not just those of a particular group. While many feminists intend to promote the rights of women and not to degrade the rights of men, they sometimes cast men as oppressors who stand in opposition to women's advancement. This can alienate men who might otherwise serve as useful allies.

Feminisms also tend to overlook the ways that men experience mistreatment and exploitation. For instance, by seeking to attain equality between men and women, feminisms ignore inequalities within the sexes (i.e., not all men are similarly privileged). As social psychologist Roy Baumeister (2010) notes, despite being at the top of the social hierarchy, men are also at the bottom. Many men are disempowered: They swell the prisons; they perform much of the riskiest, low-paid work; they experience more violent crime than women; and they pay enormous prices in terms of stress and health. This view of men as expendable gets lost in the feminist emphasis on structural power differences between the sexes.

In short, feminist movements have failed to gain more traction and widespread support because they alienate too much of the population, both by treating men as the problem and by ignoring the ways in which cultures exploit men. To be more viable going forward, feminist movements need to become more inclusive of men and recognize that gendered systems can harm men as well as women.

No, Feminist Movements Do Not Overlook Men

Social justice movements arise when groups that lack power fight against this inequality. Feminisms must necessarily focus on addressing structural inequalities, which traditionally empower men and disempower women. Despite the negative stereotypes, feminists are not against individual men, but they *are* against the patriarchal power structures that perpetuate inequality. As long as wage gaps exist, as long as so few women hold positions of political and economic power, and as long as women make up the vast majority of victims of sexual assault, feminist movements must remain focused on women's disempowerment. Men can be allies in this fight, but women must be at the center. That said, feminist movements *do* help men because both women and men benefit from a more equal, just world.

It is true that traditional gender role norms can negatively impact men. However, men who wish to challenge these gender role norms must organize social change efforts, just as women have led feminist movements. Men's movements need not be in opposition to women's movements. In fact, the two can complement each other, as they have largely the same goals of equality. However, because each group faces unique issues, each needs its own voice to address these issues.

What do you think? Do feminist movements overlook men and ignore how rigid gender expectations and structures harm men? Or is the focus on women by women a necessary approach to empower women and gain equality? Which evidence do you find most and least convincing? Why?

Men's Movements

Just like women's movements, men's movements come in many different forms. Here, we consider examples of two very different men's movements, the National Organization for Men Against Sexism (NOMAS) and the Promise Keepers. NOMAS took its current form in 1990 but has roots going back to the first annual Men and Masculinity Conference in Tennessee in 1975 (Cochran, 2010). It is a pro-feminist organization of men and women who seek to enhance the lives of men by combating sexism, racism, and heterosexism and by changing the institutions that create inequality. As NOMAS took shape, a new subfield for the study of men and masculinity emerged in psychology. Scholars who study men and masculinity develop new theories and conduct research about the male gender role, often focusing on destructive aspects of the traditional male gender role for men's physical and psychological health.

Sidebar 1.5: Men Under the Microscope

In the 1970s and 1980s, academic courses and conferences on men's studies began to blossom at U.S. universities. Journals on the topic began emerging in the 1990s, including the *Journal of Men's Studies, Men and Masculinities,* and the *Psychology of Men & Masculinity.* In 1997, the Society for the Psychological Study of Men and Masculinity was officially included as Division 51 of the APA (Bosson, Vandello, & Caswell, 2013).

Operating from a different perspective, the Promise Keepers, founded in 1990, is an evangelical Christian men's movement (Bartkowski, 2003). This organization focuses on men's spiritual health and social responsibilities by encouraging men to worship Jesus Christ, fulfill their role as head of the family, and maintain fidelity within the context of heterosexual marriage. The Promise Keepers have enjoyed extraordinary popularity over the years, reaching millions of men through their use of large ministry rallies, books, radio programs, and merchandise, such as caps and bumper stickers. While they included women at their events from 2009 to 2011, they reverted back to an all-male organization in 2012 due to the belief that all-male environments allow men greater freedom to express themselves. Given their emphasis on living a godly life through traditional gender and family arrangements, the Promise Keepers are vocal about promoting men's authority and denouncing same-sex sexuality.

While NOMAS and the Promise Keepers differ in their values and visions of progress, both share the goal of enhancing the lives of men through social change. Note that men's movements, just like feminist movements, conceptualize progress and change in very different ways. Some men's movements seek to reclaim men's power while emphasizing the benefits of traditional gender role ideologies. Others promote feminisms and LGBT inclusiveness, push for fathers' rights, encourage spirituality or religiosity, or promote various forms of masculinity. The main theme that ties together the men's movements is that they explicitly address and create a space for men to examine the role of gender in men's lives. This may be very important, especially in light of the invisibility of

LGBT: An acronym for "lesbian, gay, bisexual, and transgender."

sex and gender discussed earlier. As noted, members of more privileged groups often do not notice how sex and gender influence their lives (Case et al., 2014). This can create a conundrum for some men: The privilege of not having to think about gender means, simultaneously, that gender goes largely unacknowledged even when it creates problems in men's lives (Kimmel & Messner, 1989). Some men therefore appreciate men's movements for reducing the invisibility of gender in their lives.

Gay Rights Movements

The gay rights movements in the United States started to take shape in the 1920s, when Henry Gerber founded the first gay rights organization (see Figure 1.2 for a timeline of milestones). Gay people at the time faced extreme stigmatization and criminal penalties, and Gerber's organization soon crumbled under legal and social antigay pressure. About 30 years later, psychologist Evelyn Hooker (1957) published a groundbreaking study that showed no differences in psychological adjustment between heterosexual and gay male participants. This finding, which contradicted popular beliefs at the time, ultimately led the American Psychiatric Association to remove homosexuality from its classification as a psychological disorder in the *Diagnostic and Statistical Manual of Mental Disorders* (DSM-II) in 1973. From this point forward, the gay rights movements gained momentum and have remained active ever since. We see evidence of this progress in the area of marriage equality, for example, which culminated in the 2015 Supreme Court ruling that granted same-sex couples the right to marry in all 50 U.S. states.

Over the past several decades, the study of **sexual minority** issues developed as a productive area of psychological research. For example, the *Journal of Homosexuality* emerged in 1974 and the Society for the Psychological Study of Lesbian, Gay, Bisexual, and Transgender Issues (Division 44 of the APA) began in 1985. As sexual minority researchers expanded their focus to include topics such as relationships, parenting, discrimination, and well-being, the APA updated the *Guidelines for Psychological Practice with Lesbian, Gay, and Bisexual Clients* (APA, 2012). Among other things, these guidelines encourage psychotherapists and counselors to remain sensitive to the effects of stigma on the lives of lesbian, gay, and bisexual individuals and to understand that *sexual orientation change efforts* (therapies that seek to assist individuals in changing their sexual orientation) are neither effective nor safe.

Sexual minority: Referring to lesbian, gay, bisexual, and other nonheterosexual sexual orientations.

The Transgender Movement

In 1993, a 21-year-old transman named Brandon Teena was beaten, raped, and murdered by two male acquaintances in Nebraska. (His life is the subject of the 1999 film *Boys Don't Cry* starring Hilary Swank.) In 1995, Tyra Hunter, a 24-year-old transwoman, was critically injured in a car accident in Washington, D.C., but was left untreated by paramedics when they discovered that she had male genitals. Tyra later died in the emergency room of D.C. General Hospital (Taylor, 2007). More recently, Joshua Vallum became the first person to be prosecuted and sentenced under a federal hate crime statute for the murder of a transgender individual. In 2015, Vallum murdered Mercedes Williamson, his ex-girlfriend, when his fellow gang members found out she was transgender. Sadly, cases such as these occur frequently, and they illustrate the harsh and brutal treatment

Figure 1.2 Timeline of Important Events of the Gay Rights Movements in the United States

2020

2015 In *Obergefell v. Hodges*, the Supreme Court issued a landmark 5-4 decision that the Fourteenth Amendment guarantees same-sex couples the right to marry.

2010 The U.S. Senate voted to repeal Don't Ask, Don't Tell, making it legal for gay, lesbian, and bisexual people to serve openly in the military.

2004 Massachusetts became the first state to legalize same-sex marriage.

1996 President Clinton signed the Defense of Marriage Act (DOMA), which defined marriage as a legal union between one man and one woman.

1990

1988 The Centers for Disease Control and Prevention (CDC) mailed an *Understanding AIDS* brochure to 107 million households in the United States

1982 Wisconsin became the first state to ban discrimination on the basis of sexual orientation.

1978 Dan White assassinated Harvey Milk, the first openly gay politician elected in California.

1969 Police raided a gay bar in Greenwich Village called the Stonewall Inn, which led to riots and several days of demonstrations. These riots served as a catalyst for the modern gay rights movement in the United States

1962 Illinois became the first U.S. state to decriminalize homosexuality.

1957 Psychologist Evelyn Hooker published her study, "The Adjustment of the Overt Male Homosexual," showing no significant differences in psychological adjustment between heterosexual and gay male participants.

1960

1953 President Eisenhower signed Executive Order 10450, which considered gay people to be security risks and banned them from employment with the federal government or its private contractors.

1950 Harry Hay founded the Mattachine Society, the first national gay rights organization.

1930

Source: http://www.pbs.org/wgbh/american experience/features/timeline/stonewall

2011 President Obama instructed the Justice Department to stop supporting the Defense of Marriage Act (DOMA).

2010 A federal judge in California ruled that Proposition 8 was unconstitutional. Prop 8 was a ballot measure approved by voters in 2008 that made same-sex marriage illegal in California.

2000 Vermont became the first state to legalize civil unions for same-sex couples.

1993 The Department of Defense issued the "Don't Ask, Don't Tell" policy, which prevented the military from barring service on the basis of sexual orientation as long as service members did not openly disclose their sexual orientation.

1987 The AIDS advocacy group ACT UP (AIDS Coalition to Unleash Power) was formed in New York City, with the motto "Silence = Death."

1979 Over 75,000 people participated in the National March on Washington for Lesbian and Gay Rights.

1973 The American Psychiatric Association voted to remove homosexuality as a disorder from its *Diagnostic and Statistical Manual of Mental Disorders* (DSM-II).

1958 In One, *Inc. v. Oleson*, the Supreme Court ruled in favor of the First Amendment rights of *One: The Homosexual Magazine*, an LGBT magazine considered obscene by the U.S. Postal Service and the FBI.

1955 Del Martin and Phyllis Lyon founded the Daughters of Bilitis, the first lesbian rights organization.

1952 The American Psychiatric Association listed homosexuality as a "sociopathic personality disturbance" in the (*Diagnostic and Statistical Manual of Mental Disorders DSM-I*).

1924 Henry Gerber founded the Society for Human Rights, the first gay rights organization, in Chicago.

that people sometimes receive when they do not fit cleanly into the sex and gender binaries. In the face of this treatment, the transgender movement emerged to advance the rights, protections, and visibility of transgender individuals. The movement gained momentum in the past two decades in part due to the Internet, which allows transgender individuals to connect and create supportive communities such as TQ Nation and the Facebook Transgender Alliance. In addition, the spotlight on transgender celebrities, such as Chaz Bono, Caitlyn Jenner, and Laverne Cox, and the popularity of TV shows that include major transgender characters, such as *Transparent* and *Orange is the New Black*, increase the visibility of the transgender rights movement.

Another arm of the transgender movement consists of organizations like the Intersex Campaign for Equality (ICE), which advocates for the rights of intersex individuals to physical integrity, self-determination, and legal recognition. ICE criticizes the medical community for defining intersexuality as a disorder and argues that societies should not pathologize those whose bodies do not conform to sex and gender norms (http://oii-usa.org/about).

The efforts of activists in the transgender movement have borne fruit. In 1993, Minnesota became the first state to pass a law banning discrimination against transgender people, and by 2016, 18 states plus the District of Columbia had similar laws ("Know Your Rights," 2016). In 2008, the APA approved a resolution on *Transgender, Gender Identity, and Gender Expression Non-Discrimination* (APA, 2008), and 4 years later, the Equal Employment Opportunity Commission (EEOC) ruled that Title VII of the 1964 Civil Rights Act, which prohibits employment discrimination on the basis of sex, race, and religion, also protects transgender employees. Finally, in 2013, the American Psychiatric Association updated its diagnostic manual to replace the diagnosis of *gender identity disorder* with the less stigmatizing *gender dysphoria*. Now, the condition of being transgender is no longer considered a diagnosable mental illness in itself. Instead, people may meet diagnostic criteria for gender dysphoria only if they experience clinical levels of distress arising from a mismatch between their gender identity and the sex that others assign them (APA, 2013).

Sidebar 1.6: What's in an Acronym?

Throughout this book, we will sometimes use acronyms to refer to sexual minority (e.g., lesbian, gay, and bisexual) and gender identity minority (e.g., transgender and genderqueer) groups and individuals. To avoid confusion, we'll start by explaining all of the terms that go into the acronym LGBTQIA+, which some use to signify a wide range of sexual and gender minority statuses. LGBTQIA+ means lesbian, gay, bisexual, transgender, queer (a broad term that refers to a variety of sexual and gender identities), intersex, and asexual. So what does the "+" signify? Despite the number of terms in the LGBTQIA+ acronym, the "+" indicates that even more identities exist, such as questioning (undecided about sexual orientation or gender identity but considering one's options), two-spirit, pansexual, bigender, and so on. In this book, when we refer specifically to sexual minority groups or individuals, we might use LGB only. If we refer to both sexual and gender identity minority groups, we may use LGBT. When using LGBTQIA+, we intentionally refer to the whole range of possibilities. As you read this book, you may wish to refer back to this chapter for a refresher on terminology when needed.

Where Are We Now?
Inclusivity and Intersectionality

Each movement discussed in this section has made impressive strides for its constituents. Stepping back and looking at the movements collectively, we see a common pattern in the push for greater inclusivity over time. For example, sexual minority rights movements now include bisexual and asexual people, whereas early organizations did not; third-wave feminists explicitly address the concerns of poor and minority women, whereas many of their predecessors did not. Another commonality involves greater recognition of the need to include and address intersectionality. What implications will these new understandings have as gender activism moves forward? Though difficult to say, it will be exciting to find out.

Stop and Think

Consider the Women's Marches in January 2017. Do you think the Women's Marches were sufficiently inclusive of different sexes, gender identities, and sexual orientations? Did they sufficiently address issues of intersectionality, diversity, class, and globalism? Did they represent the future of gender activism, or were they just more of the "same old same old"? Why or why not?

About This Book

Given that you have been immersed in a sex- and gender-focused culture since birth, you have likely developed many beliefs and expectations about sex and gender, and you may already feel (and, in fact, actually be) fairly knowledgeable on these topics. Still, we expect and hope that this book will, at times, lead you to question some of your beliefs and reflect on them more carefully. But how will you know whether to trust the information you read throughout this book? To help you consider this question, we provide some background on our approach to writing the book, and we offer a challenge for you to keep in mind while reading. You will also likely find the material in the next chapter ("Studying Sex and Gender") useful in helping you distinguish between trustworthy and untrustworthy claims.

Our (Interdisciplinary) Psychological Approach

Since we aim to help you evaluate sex and gender in all their complexity, this book draws on ideas and research findings from psychology, sociology, anthropology, biology, history, epidemiology, and gender studies. Though the primary approaches and methods used in these disciplines vary, there is some degree of commonality. In general, psychologists examine how sex and gender norms shape individual thoughts, feelings, and behavior;

sociologists examine how sex and gender are constructed within specific social and historical contexts; and anthropologists examine the roles of sex and gender in the development of human societies across cultures and time. Similarly, biologists might examine the genetic and physiological factors that contribute to sex-related outcomes at the level of cells and organisms, epidemiologists might study how the incidence of disease and health outcomes differs across sex or sexual orientation within a population, and historians might analyze how meanings of sex and gender have changed across eras. Other fields, such as gender studies, are interdisciplinary by design, drawing on content and methods from multiple disciplines to understand the complexity of gendered identities and social systems.

We are social psychologists, and most of our expertise thus reflects our own educational backgrounds. However, we intentionally draw from a multitude of academic disciplines because we believe that the complexity of sex and gender calls for a mixed-methods approach. In mixed-methods research, researchers incorporate multiple worldviews and methods to develop a better understanding of a topic than can be afforded by a single-worldview, single-method approach (Creswell & Clark, 2011). Because sex and gender do not operate solely on an individual level—the level at which psychologists generally conduct their work—the contents of this book do not cover only the individual level. Instead, we cover the full gamut, from the cellular level to the individual, interpersonal, societal, cross-cultural, and cross-historical levels. When pulling from different disciplines, however, we remain focused on selecting high-quality information. That is, we carefully vet the scholarship described in this book to ensure that it reflects rigorous theories, methods, and analysis by those who conducted it.

Our Challenge to You: Critical Thinking

That said, scholars and scientists are humans with their own biases and tendencies toward error. If and when you encounter material in this book that strikes you as imprecise or that challenges your pre-existing beliefs, we hope that you will inspect your own beliefs, as well as the quality of scholarship that produced the material. In other words, we challenge you to engage in critical thinking. What does this mean? According to Carole Wade (2008), critical thinking consists of several mental practices, including asking questions, examining the evidence, evaluating underlying assumptions, avoiding emotional reasoning, and considering other ways of interpreting findings. These are all skills that can be learned and perfected with practice. To get into the habit of thinking critically about the material in this book, you might ask yourself questions and then try to generate answers. For example, when you read our assertion that "biological sex is a social construction," you might ask yourself these questions:

- What does this mean?

- How does this relate to information that I already have? How is it inconsistent with what I already know (or think I know)?

- What evidence supports this point? What is the quality of this evidence?

- What is another way to view this point? What evidence counters this point? What is the quality of this evidence?

- Why is this point important? How might it apply to my own or someone else's everyday life?

To prompt such thinking, we regularly pose questions (labeled "Stop and Think") throughout this book that await your evaluation. Considering these questions—and developing the habit of asking and answering your own critical thinking questions—should not only lead to interesting thoughts and conversations, it should also enhance your learning of the material. Cognitive psychologists find that college students' memory and understanding of course material increases substantially when they think deeply about the meaning of material and connect it to information that is already stored in their long-term memory (Eysenck, 2011).

Subsequently, we list the learning objectives that helped guide us in writing this book. These are the concrete knowledge and skill sets that you should demonstrate upon reading the material in this book. Specifically, you should be able to do the following:

- Critically evaluate current concepts, theories, and research findings in the psychology of sex and gender.

- Examine sex and gender through the lens of psychological science, identify sources of bias, and distinguish between valid and invalid claims.

- Understand the complexity of sex, gender, gender identity, and sexual orientation, and recognize the diversity of gender and sexual orientation identities.

- Analyze how biological forces (nature) and social forces (nurture) interact in complex ways to shape sex assignment, gender development, and gendered outcomes.

- Evaluate how cultural norms, values, and social structures shape the construction, experience, and expression of sex and gender.

- Examine sex and gender through the lenses of status and power, and evaluate how different systems of inequality intersect to shape experiences.

- Apply gender concepts, theories, and research findings to real-world situations and events.

- Demonstrate mastery of the material by engaging in strategies and methods that facilitate deep learning.

Finally, given the pervasiveness of sex and gender, we hope that you will continue to use the concepts, theories, and research findings discussed throughout this textbook to analyze real-world situations and events long after you finish reading the book. The three of us have had a lifelong fascination with the topics of sex and gender, and we hope that you will discover (if you have not already done so) how captivating these topics can be.

CHAPTER SUMMARY

1.1 Explain central terminology in the study of sex and gender.

Understanding basic terminology in the psychology of sex and gender leads to more effective communication in the field. We use the term *sex* to refer to the categories of being male, female, and intersex and the term *gender* to refer to the meanings that people give to the different sex categories (e.g., the identities, traits, interests, roles, and attitudes commonly associated with maleness and femaleness). Counter to many gender scholars, we do not view sex as solely biologically determined and gender as solely socioculturally determined because biological *and* sociocultural factors play important roles in shaping both sex and gender. Although sex is an important category of identity, individuals simultaneously have identities based on other social categories, such as race, class, age, and sexual orientation. An individual's position across these social categories (e.g., young, gay, Asian, and male) conveys different levels of privilege and discrimination, and *intersectionality* refers to how different forms of discrimination (e.g., sexism, racism, and heterosexism) interact to shape people's experiences.

1.2 Evaluate how culture, gender identity, and sexual orientation shape the experience and expression of sex and gender.

Cultures with *sex and gender binaries* conceptualize sex (male and female) and gender (masculine and feminine) as having only two categories. But sex is not binary in nature, as shown when the biological components of sex (chromosomes, hormones, and anatomy) do not align consistently as male or female in *intersex* individuals. Some cultures more readily go beyond the binary, recognizing third sex/gender individuals, such as Indian hijras and Native American two-spirit people. In the past decade, more countries around the globe have officially recognized the status of transgender/nonbinary individuals on legal documents, such as birth certificates and passports. *Transgender*

individuals experience a mismatch between their assigned sex at birth and the sex with which they feel a sense of belonging, whereas *cisgender* individuals experience a match between their assigned sex and gender identity. Both cisgender and transgender individuals can have any *sexual orientation*, which refers to the tendency to develop romantic and sexual attractions to others based on their sex. Examples of different sexual orientation identities include gay, lesbian, bisexual, heterosexual, polysexual, and asexual.

1.3 Evaluate the meaning and relevance of feminisms, gender movements, and systems of power, privilege, and inequality.

All societies are arranged hierarchically, with dominant groups having more access to education, leadership positions, and resources than subordinate groups. Sex and gender shape status hierarchies within societies. In *patriarchal* societies, men as a group rule the society and control how it operates. While we lack evidence of any true *matriarchal* societies (in which women control how the society operates), many societies are *matrilineal*, meaning that family relationships and ancestry are traced through the mother's line. Across time, group-based imbalances in power and privilege have prompted disempowered groups, such as women and LGBT individuals, to organize and advocate for equal and fair (equitable) treatment. Though great diversity exists within each of these movements, their collective efforts have led to improved outcomes over time. Similarly, although there are many types of feminisms (liberal, radical, womanist, and transnational), they share a common goal of attaining the social, political, and economic equality of women and men. Men's movements often focus on how gender shapes men's experiences.

1.4 Demonstrate how to approach the textbook material in "critical thinking mode."

Although you have already formed many beliefs and expectations about sex and gender, we encourage you to examine them critically as you read this book. Critical thinking involves asking questions, examining evidence, evaluating underlying assumptions, avoiding emotional reasoning, and considering other ways of interpreting findings. Because these are skills that improve with practice, we prompt you to engage in critical thinking regularly throughout the book (e.g., in the debates and "Stop and Think" questions). We hope that you will not only become versed in analyzing the main concepts, theories, and research findings in the psychology of gender but that you will be able to use this information to become a more sophisticated thinker about gender-related events in the world around you.

Test Your Knowledge: True or False?

1.1. Life experiences can cause biological differences between women and men. (True: Performing male-typical behaviors can increase women's testosterone levels, and performing female-typical behaviors can reduce men's testosterone levels.) [p. 6]

1.2. There are only two biological sexes: male and female. (False: Biology also offers several different types of intersexuality, in which the biological components of sex do not consistently fit the typical male pattern or the typical female pattern.) [p. 7]

1.3. Throughout human history, there is evidence that some societies were true matriarchies in which women ruled the society, controlled how it operated, and held more power than men. (False: There are no known human matriarchies. There are, however, many examples of matrilineal societies.) [p. 16]

1.4. Many people who believe in feminist principles do not identify as feminists. (True: Many people support the principles of feminism but reject the label, perhaps due to negative stereotypes of feminists.) [p. 21]

1.5. The American Psychiatric Association considers transgender identity to be a clinically diagnosable psychological disorder. (False: The most recent edition of the *Diagnostic and Statistical Manual of Mental Disorders* no longer considers transgender identity a disorder. People may, however, receive a diagnosis of gender dysphoria if they experience distress about a mismatch between their gender identity and the sex that others assign them.) [p. 27]

Test Your Knowledge: True or False?

2.1 Gender researchers disagree about whether or not it is appropriate to study sex differences.

2.2 If a study finds that women and men differ on some variable of interest—for instance, the frequency of smiling behavior—the researcher can therefore conclude that sex (being female or male) causes differences in smiling behavior.

2.3 Qualitative methods (non-numerical methods that involve in-depth interpretations, such as case studies) are defined as nonscientific.

2.4 Across most psychological variables, sex differences are generally very small.

2.5 Gender researchers generally agree that psychological science, if done correctly, can be objective and unbiased.

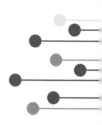

CHAPTER 2

Studying Sex and Gender

Key Concepts

What Is the Meaning of Difference?
Debate: Should Psychologists Study Sex Differences?

What Is Science?
The Scientific Method
Journey of Research: Conceptualizing and Measuring Masculinity and Femininity

What Are the Primary Methods Used in Sex and Gender Research?
Quantitative Research Methods
Experimental Designs
Ex Post Facto Designs
Quasi-Experiments
Correlational Designs
Qualitative Research Methods
Case Studies
Interviews
Focus Groups
Mixed Methods

What Do Meta-Analyses and Effect Sizes Tell Us About Sex Differences?
Effect Sizes
Overlap and Variance
Beyond Overall Effect Sizes

What Are Some Biases Common in Sex and Gender Research?
Identifying the Research Question
Designing the Study and Collecting Data
Interpreting and Communicating the Results

How Do We Address the Challenges in Sex and Gender Research?
Guidelines for Gender-Fair Research Design
Diversity Issues in the Study of Sex and Gender

Studying Sex and Gender

We have taught enough psychology courses over the years to anticipate how some readers might feel about a chapter on research methods. While research methods do captivate some students, more common reactions range from boredom to intimidation to annoyance. In this chapter, we hope to illustrate that research methods need not be painful. Exploring methods is important and can even be exciting and fun. Think of the study of gender as a mystery and the researcher as the detective trying to crack the case.

Rather than presenting a thorough, technical review of research methods, this chapter instead focuses on common methodological approaches and challenges in gender research. Why is it important to study questions of gender systematically? Without systematic research, people would likely rely too heavily on stereotypes and intuitions to understand questions of gender, making them prone to misconceptions. They might overlook many of the complex and counterintuitive findings that emerge through a careful study of gender phenomena. For example, consider the following beliefs that do not stand up to empirical scrutiny:

- **Many believe that men inherently possess greater math ability than women**. However, large-scale reviews show no overall sex differences in math performance (Lindberg, Hyde, Petersen, & Linn, 2010). In fact, math performance is predicted less by sex than it is by other factors, such as socioeconomic status, primary school effectiveness, home learning environment, and mother's education level (Melhuish et al., 2008). Nonetheless, girls do tend to have higher levels of math anxiety than boys (Else-Quest, Hyde, & Linn, 2010), and this anxiety can sometimes interfere with their performance on math tests. (For more on this topic, see Chapter 7, "Cognitive Abilities and Aptitudes.")

- **Many people regard women as more talkative than men**. But when Matthias Mehl and colleagues recorded women and men in their daily lives, they found no sex differences in numbers of words spoken per day (Mehl, Vazire, Ramírez-Esparza, Slatcher, & Pennebaker, 2007). Other studies do reveal sex differences, but they are small and depend on age. For example, Leaper and Smith (2004) found young girls (under the age of 3) to be slightly more talkative than young boys, whereas Leaper and Ayres (2007) found men to be slightly more talkative than women.

- **Common Western views dating back to the Victorian era hold that women—in comparison with men—are less interested in sex**. For example, when approached by an attractive stranger who offered casual sex, women declined the offer much more frequently than men did (R. D. Clark & Hatfield, 1989). Much more recently, however, Terri Conley (2011) found that there are two primary reasons for American college women's reluctance to accept casual sex offers: (1) They fear that they will be stigmatized as promiscuous, and (2) they do not expect the sex to be pleasurable. When Conley controls for these factors, American women show just as much interest in casual sex as men do.

Throughout this book, we describe the results from hundreds of studies. Some will confirm your prior beliefs about sex and gender, but others will fly in the face of conventional wisdom and debunk common gender myths. Developing an understanding of sound research methodology should help you learn how to distinguish between accurate and inaccurate claims about gender. Again, as you read this book, we challenge you to examine your existing beliefs about gender and think critically about the research findings that we present before drawing conclusions.

Women's reluctance to accept casual sex offers stems, at least in part, from their expectations that sex with a stranger is unlikely to be very pleasurable.

Source:
© iStockPhoto.com/hoozone

Of course, we do not suggest that there are perfect research methods or studies. Each methodology and study has flaws and can be legitimately criticized. However, the accumulation of multiple, well-designed studies on a given topic increases confidence in the conclusions. In this chapter, we will explain what makes a *well-designed study* and how even the best studies have limitations. Before launching into methods, however, we will begin by analyzing what researchers mean when they refer to *sex differences*.

Sidebar 2.1: A Brief History of Sex Difference Research

In the 19th century, medical researchers interested in sex differences focused mainly on identifying structural brain differences that could explain women's intellectual inferiority to men (Shields, 1975). Around the turn of the 20th century, Helen Thompson-Woolley (1903) criticized the biases in this earlier work and sought to improve the quality of sex difference research in her psychology dissertation. Her carefully designed experiment revealed only negligible sex differences in motor and intellectual abilities. Sex difference research in the 1920s and 1930s focused mostly on emotional and social tendencies and culminated in Terman and Miles's (1936) personality measure of masculinity and femininity. Still, research on sex differences was slow to take root in psychology, likely because most early psychologists were men who generally did not find the research interesting or valuable. This began to change in the United States in the 1970s, when the second wave of the women's movement brought greater attention to women's issues. In 1974, Eleanor Maccoby and Carol Nagy Jacklin published a landmark book titled *The Psychology of Sex Differences* in which they reviewed over 1,400 published studies of sex differences. Though Maccoby and Jacklin's (1974) results showed overall evidence of sex similarity, differences emerged in the areas of verbal ability (favoring girls) and math ability, visuospatial ability, and aggression (favoring boys).

What Is the Meaning of Difference?

Let's return to the finding that girls have higher levels of math anxiety than boys (Else-Quest et al., 2010). What does this mean? Does it suggest that girls and boys have very different levels of math anxiety or, alternatively, that they are merely slightly different in math anxiety? Researchers can use statistical methods to quantify the size of sex differences, and we will explain how to do this later in the chapter. For now, the point is that many people, including researchers, tend to give certain meanings to sex differences. Whereas those who take a **maximalist approach** emphasize differences between sex groups, those who take a **minimalist approach** emphasize similarity. As you can see in Figure 2.1, someone with a maximalist approach might envision that girls and boys have completely nonoverlapping distributions of math anxiety scores (such that even the most math-anxious boys would be lower in math anxiety than the least math-anxious girls). In contrast, someone with a minimalist approach might envision that the distributions of math anxiety scores of girls and boys are largely similar and overlapping, with girls scoring just slightly higher than boys on average.

As another example, consider a study by Basow and Rubenfeld (2003) that examined sex differences in support provision. In this study, male and female participants imagined that a friend confided a problem to them and then rated their likelihood of each of these possible responses to their friend: (a) giving advice, (b) offering sympathy, (c) changing the subject, (d) sharing a similar problem, (e) joking about it, and (f) telling the friend not to worry. Overall, women rated themselves as more likely than men to give sympathy, and men rated themselves as more likely than women to change the subject. However, on the other four types of support, there were no sex differences. Despite finding sex differences on only two of six total responses, Basow and Rubenfeld interpreted their findings to suggest that men and women communicate differently, with women prioritizing interpersonal connection and men prioritizing autonomy. Thus, the researchers

Maximalist approach: A tendency to emphasize differences between members of different sex groups and view them as qualitatively different.

Minimalist approach: A tendency to emphasize similarities between members of different sex groups.

Figure 2.1 Maximalist and Minimalist Approaches.

These theoretical distributions represent (a) the maximalist approach and (b) the minimalist approach. The maximalist approach assumes little or no overlap between the distributions of women's and men's scores. In contrast, the minimalist approach assumes that although women's and men's mean scores differ, there is a lot of overlap in their distributions.

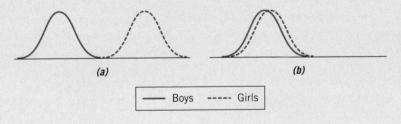

(a) *(b)*

—— Boys   ----- Girls

Source: R. Unger and Crawford (1996).

emphasized difference rather than similarity, which might lead readers to develop a view of women and men as fundamentally different in their communication styles. Later, however, Erina MacGeorge and her colleagues reanalyzed Basow and Rubenfeld's data and concluded that there was more evidence of similarity than difference in how women and men claimed to offer support (MacGeorge, Graves, Feng, Gillihan, & Burleson, 2004). As shown in Figure 2.2, when you visualize the data across all six types of support, the sex similarities in communication seem more pronounced than the differences.

The maximalist approach has a potential danger in that it encourages people to ignore the overlap that often characterizes people of different sexes. Given this, some minimalist theorists argue that the study of sex differences promotes gender stereotypes and is

Figure 2.2 MacGeorge et al.'s (2004) Reanalysis of Basow and Rubenfeld's (2003) Data.

When MacGeorge et al. (2004) graphed Basow and Rubenfeld's (2003) data, it made a powerful visual point: The two statistically significant sex differences (in offering sympathy and changing the subject) appear quite small in comparison with the overall pattern of sex similarity that characterizes the data.

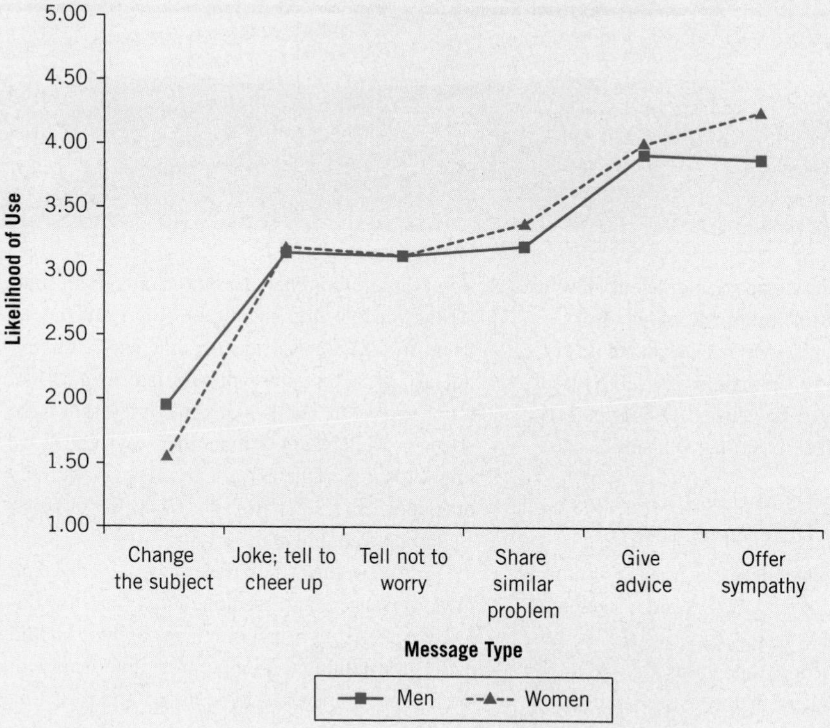

Source: MacGeorge, Graves, Feng, Gillihan, and Burleson (2004).

therefore irresponsible. (For more on this issue, see "Debate: Should Psychologists Study Sex Differences?") That is, by focusing on differences and ignoring similarities, researchers may perpetuate overgeneralized and exaggerated beliefs about the sexes. Of course, one could also argue that the minimalist approach ignores potentially important sex differences. In other words, to conclude that people of different sexes are "mostly alike" may be technically accurate in some cases, but it also fails to acknowledge the differences that do exist. Perhaps the more important point is that if researchers approach the study of sex differences with either a maximalist or a minimalist bias, this bias may influence how they and others interpret their findings. Try to keep these biases in mind as you read the results of sex difference research presented throughout this book. And when you encounter sex differences, we encourage you to ask yourself, *What does this difference mean?*

Stop and Think

Are you a maximalist, a minimalist, or neither? Which approach do you prefer, and why? Can you strike a compromise between these perspectives when *interpreting sex differences? What would such a compromise look like?*

Debate

Should psychologists study sex differences? What important and useful information can be gained by studying sex differences? A debate about these questions emerged in psychology several decades ago and continues to this day (Eagly, 2013; Kitzinger, 1994). Let's examine both sides.

No, Psychologists Should Not Study Sex Differences

Research on sex differences can have the unfortunate consequence of reinforcing gender stereotypes (Baumeister, 1988). This occurs, in part, because of *publication bias* (also known as the *file drawer problem*), which refers to the biased tendency in the field of psychology to publish studies that find

significant group differences more often than studies that do not find significant group differences. Since studies that fail to find differences less frequently get accepted for publication, we may not know as much about sex similarities as we do about sex differences. Put another way, if what we know about sex differences is based almost entirely on published studies, we likely have an exaggerated understanding of these differences.

Furthermore, since the popular media tend toward exaggerating sex differences (because difference is attention grabbing), researchers should avoid contributing to this by providing them with sex difference material. By studying and reporting sex differences, psychologists communicate that such differences merit attention. If we want people to focus less on sex and gender, then researchers should lead the way by discontinuing research that calls attention to sex differences (Baumeister, 1988).

Finally, some argue that comparisons of women and men stem from a faulty conceptualization of gender (Hare-Mustin & Maracek, 1994). Comparing men and women assumes that gender can be accurately viewed as a quality that resides within people. In contrast, some view gender as a dynamic and complex system of behaviors, shaped by societal institutions and practices, that emerges through social interaction. In this way, gender is not what someone *is*, but rather what someone *does* (West & Zimmerman, 1987). From this perspective, sex difference research reinforces an overly simplistic and inaccurate view of gender.

Yes, Psychologists Should Study Sex Differences

Science is the best tool we have to develop accurate understandings of sex differences (Halpern, 1994). While not perfect, science is a systematic method with built-in checks and balances that decrease error and increase valid findings over time. The knowledge gained from sex difference research, moreover, can help counter gender bias and misconceptions. For example, because "experts" in the 19th century believed women to be intellectually inferior to men, women were often denied access to higher education (Shields, 1975). Research on sex differences in cognitive abilities debunked the myth of women's intellectual inferiority (Halpern, 2012), paving the way for increases in women's access to education. Thus, many believe that the benefits of studying sex differences outweigh the costs, especially in the long run (Eagly, 1994).

Studying sex differences also allows psychologists to identify the contexts in which such differences do or do not emerge, which can assist theory development. For example, when examining the literature on sex differences in helping behavior, Eagly and Crowley (1986) found that men, relative to women, showed greater helpfulness toward strangers. They reasoned that this difference reflected social norms of male chivalry, which led them to predict—and find—a larger sex difference when an audience was present to observe the helping behavior. In communicating such findings, researchers demonstrate the complexity of sex differences.

Now that you have read the arguments on both sides, what do you think? Should psychologists study sex differences or focus their attention elsewhere? Which perspective makes the most sense? Which evidence do you find most and least convincing? Why?

What Is Science?

This textbook emphasizes the scientific study of sex and gender. But what exactly makes research on sex and gender scientific? When you think of the word *science*, what images come to mind? People in lab coats holding test tubes? People peering through microscopes at microbial life? When conceptualizing science, most people think of the "hard" or natural sciences (e.g., physics, chemistry, and biology) more readily than the "soft" or social sciences (e.g., psychology, sociology, and political science). In fact, some consider psychology and other social sciences to be less scientific than the hard sciences because human behavior does not follow precise mathematical laws the same way that planets or atoms do. Gravity is gravity—its rules do not change—but people are unique and can be difficult to predict.

Sidebar 2.2: The Unfalsifiable Freud

The perception of psychology as unscientific may have been bolstered by the work of Sigmund Freud, perhaps the most well-known psychologist in history. Though Freud's psychoanalytic theories of development and personality have been quite influential, many of his ideas are unfalsifiable. A *falsifiable theory* is one that can be disproved with evidence. This means that the researcher must specify a set of conditions that, if they occurred, would clearly invalidate the theory. In other words, the researcher must state, "If my theory is correct, then *x* will happen. If, instead, *y* happens, then my theory is not correct." If there is no set of conditions (*y*) that will be taken as invalidation of a theory, then a theory is not truly scientific. Unfortunately, Freud tended to focus on evidence that he viewed as consistent with his theories, rather than carefully specifying the patterns of data that could invalidate his theories. Nonetheless, his ideas did help to shape early understandings of gender.

So what is the definition of science? In *Broca's Brain: Reflections on the Romance of Science*, astrophysicist Carl Sagan (1980) writes,

> Science is a way of thinking much more than it is a body of knowledge. Its goal is to find out how the world works, to seek what regularities there may be, to penetrate to the connections of things—from subnuclear particles, which may be the constituents of all matter, to living organisms, the human social community, and thence to the cosmos as a whole. (p. 15)

As Sagan indicates, science is as an ongoing process of discovery, defined more by its methods than by its contents (the specific topics under investigation). Science is a systematic, empirical way of investigating the world in order to identify rules and patterns in the way it works.

The Scientific Method

Scientific method: A process by which researchers conduct systematic studies in order to test hypotheses derived from theory.

Hypothesis: A testable prediction about the outcome of a study, stated in terms of the variables tested.

Although the range of topics studied by scientists is vast, from astrophysics to psychology, the common thread through all science is the use of the scientific method. Thus, to determine which fields do and do not qualify as science, we must examine the type and rigor of the methods used. Let's examine what this means, more specifically.

When using the **scientific method**, a researcher conducts systematic studies to test theory-driven **hypotheses**, or testable predictions about the outcome of a study. The scientific method unfolds in a series of steps, including hypothesis generation, study design, data collection and analysis, results dissemination, and *replication* (repeating a study to determine whether the results will recur). Figure 2.3 provides a general model of the scientific method. A researcher begins by making an observation about the world (e.g., women and men seem to exhibit different body language in public) and then develops a hypothesis (e.g., in public, women generally sit in ways that take up less space compared with men). To test the hypothesis, the researcher designs a study, which may take any number of different forms (more on specific methods in a bit). After gathering

Figure 2.3   The Steps in the Scientific Method.

Rather than following a strict linear path, the steps in the scientific method occur in a loop, with no final endpoint.

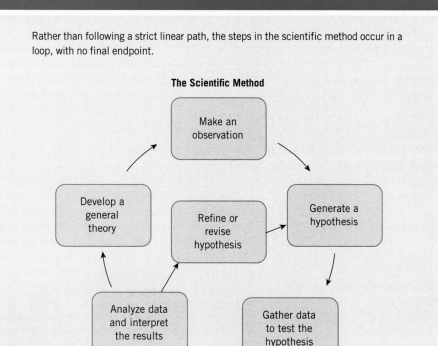

The Scientific Method

and analyzing data, the researcher decides whether the hypothesis has been supported or refuted and then may alter or refine the hypothesis for future testing. After interpreting the results, the researcher can also develop or refine general theories about the phenomenon. For instance, in finding that men sit in ways that take up more space than women, the researcher may develop a theory about how people use personal space as a signal of dominance. To the extent that men care more than women about issues of social dominance, they may use more personal space to demonstrate their dominance. This theory can then be used to generate new hypotheses. For example, perhaps individuals who are made to feel relatively powerless (whether male or female) will sit in ways that occupy less space than individuals who are made to feel powerful. Going forward, the researcher could do the following: (a) conduct an experiment in which she manipulates participants' feelings of power to be either high or low and then measures how this impacts sitting behavior, (b) analyze the results, (c) further refine the theory, and (d) generate new hypotheses to test. As this example and Figure 2.3 illustrate, the steps of the scientific method—rather than being linear—occur in a loop. There is no final endpoint in the scientific process, as each new discovery leads to the refinement of theories and hypotheses, which starts the process anew. For an example of how researchers continue to build and refine theories, turn to "Journey of Research: Conceptualizing and Measuring Masculinity and Femininity."

Conceptualizing and Measuring Masculinity and Femininity

Before devising methods to measure any construct of interest, researchers must first clarify its meaning. Consider masculinity and femininity. What is the best way to conceptualize and measure these constructs? As you may recall from Chapter 1, gender psychologists have struggled with this question for quite some time. Here, we summarize three significant shifts in psychological thinking about masculinity and femininity.

Unidimensional Conceptualization

In the 1920s, Lewis Terman and Catharine Cox Miles began to develop the first measure of psychological masculinity and femininity, the M–F Test. Published in 1936, the M–F Test had over 400 items that were included based on their ability to distinguish between men and women. In retrospect, the scale was odd in that many items did not seem centrally connected to psychological masculinity or femininity. For example, some items presented respondents with a target word like *TENDER* and asked them to select which of four words (*kind, loving, meat,* or *sore*) they most associated with the target word. Response options for each item were coded as masculine, feminine, or neutral, and an overall score was calculated for each respondent.

Decades later, Anne Constantinople (1973) published an influential article that identified problems with measures of masculinity and femininity, including the M–F Test. Among other things, she criticized these tests for conceptualizing masculinity–femininity as a single dimension with two endpoints. In other words, Constantinople challenged the assumption that the opposite of masculine is feminine (and vice versa) because this ignores the possibility that individuals can simultaneously possess elements of both masculinity and femininity.

Two-Dimensional Conceptualization

In the early 1970s, researchers developed the Personal Attributes Questionnaire (PAQ; Spence, Helmreich, &

Stapp, 1974) and the Bem Sex-Role Inventory (BSRI; Bem, 1974), both of which included separate subscales of male-typed (M) or agentic traits (e.g., independent and competitive) and female-typed (F) or communal traits (e.g., gentle and kind). These items were selected-based on how well they distinguished typical men and women or whether they were perceived as more desirable for one sex than the other. Importantly, the M and F trait scales were uncorrelated, meaning that individuals could be either high or low on each set of traits (Bem, 1974; Helmreich, Spence, & Wilhelm, 1981). This

The best indicators of people's masculinity and femininity include gender-related hobbies and everyday activities.

Source: © iStockPhoto.com/michal-rojek; © iStockPhoto.com/AleksandarNakic

led researchers to develop the construct of androgyny, defined as possessing high levels of both M and F traits.

Multidimensional Conceptualizations

Despite the progress made in the 1970s, researchers soon began questioning whether gendered traits alone could capture masculinity and femininity. For instance, Janet Spence (1993) proposed that a person's sense of gender reflects not only traits but also attitudes, roles, and interests that may or may not relate to one another. Inspired by Spence's approach, new theories better capture the multidimensionality of masculinity and femininity. For example, Richard Lippa (1991) uses individuals' preferences for gender-related occupations, hobbies, and everyday activities to capture their levels of masculinity and femininity in what he calls a **gender diagnosticity (GD) score**. Lippa (2005a) finds that GD scores do a better job—in comparison with M and F trait scales—in predicting gender-related outcomes, and he argues that the core of masculinity and femininity consists of occupational interests, hobbies, everyday activities, nonverbal behavior, and sexual orientation.

As you can see, overly simplistic conceptualizations of masculinity and femininity from earlier eras gave way to more sophisticated, multifaceted conceptualizations as researchers continually refined the definitions of these constructs.

What Are the Primary Methods Used in Sex and Gender Research?

Once a researcher identifies a topic of interest and a research question, the next steps involve designing a study to examine the research question, collecting and analyzing data, and communicating the results. When designing a study, the researcher may choose from many different methods, often categorized broadly as quantitative or qualitative. In this section, we examine some common quantitative and qualitative methods used in gender psychology, along with some methodological challenges and biases in the research process.

Quantitative Research Methods

Quantitative methods allow researchers to turn variables of interest into numbers that can be submitted to statistical analyses. All of the methods reviewed in this section share the property of relying on numerical data. These methods are summarized in Table 2.1.

Experimental designs. Well-conducted experiments allow researchers to establish cause-and-effect relationships between variables. Thus, to know whether smiling *causes* happiness or whether effective studying *reduces* test anxiety, you have to conduct an **experiment**. In experiments, the researcher manipulates variables of interest (called **independent variables**) to observe whether this causes changes in outcome variables (called **dependent variables**). For instance, to determine whether dominance causes people to use more physical space, a researcher might ask some people to think and write about a time when they were socially dominant while other people think and write about what they ate yesterday. The researcher might then guide people to a waiting room, ask them to take a seat, and unobtrusively observe how much space they take up. In this experiment, the independent variable is dominance and it is manipulated by having people think about either their own dominance or a neutral topic. The dependent variable is people's physical use of space while seated.

Gender diagnosticity (GD) score: The estimated probability that an individual is male or female given the individual's gender-related interests. A GD score of .85 means that the individual has an 85% chance of being male and a 15% chance of being female.

Quantitative methods: Methods in which researchers convert variables of interest into numbers and use statistical analyses to test hypotheses. Examples include experimental, ex post facto, quasi-experimental, and correlational designs.

Researchers also use **random assignment** in experiments, meaning that each participant has an equal chance of being assigned to each of the different experimental conditions in the study. Why is this important? Participants naturally vary in many ways (e.g., age, race, and socioeconomic status), and random assignment increases the likelihood that these pre-existing differences are spread out evenly across conditions at the outset of a study, before the manipulation of the independent variable. Thus, by manipulating an independent variable, using random assignment, and holding all other variables constant, researchers can establish whether an independent variable causes changes in a dependent variable. If a study has good *experimental control*—meaning that no variables other than the independent variable differ systematically across the conditions—then the researcher can confidently conclude that any observed differences in the dependent variable were caused by the manipulation of the independent variable. This ability to determine cause-and-effect relationships leads many to view experiments as the gold standard of the scientific method.

Gender research faces a special challenge when it comes to experimental methods because, strictly speaking, sex cannot be treated as an independent variable. If you cannot easily or ethically assign people into the different conditions or levels

Table 2.1   Quantitative (Numerical) Research Methods and Techniques.

Design	Main Concepts/Issues	Description
Experimental	Independent variables, dependent variables, random assignment, experimental control	A researcher manipulates an independent variable, randomly assigns participants to different conditions, and measures their standing on a dependent variable. If the study has good experimental control, cause-and-effect relationships can be determined.
Ex post facto	Participant variables	A researcher compares groups of people who differ on some participant variable (e.g., women versus men). Cause-and-effect relationships cannot be determined because of reverse causation and the third variable problem.
Quasi-experimental (person-by-treatment)	Independent variables, participant variables, dependent variables, interaction effects	A researcher selects groups of people who differ on some participant variable (e.g., women versus men) and randomly assigns them to different levels of an independent variable. Interaction effects may occur when the effect of the independent variable on the dependent variable differs as a function of the participant variable.
Correlational	Participant variables, reverse causation, the third variable problem, cross-sectional designs, longitudinal designs	A researcher measures people's standing on two continuous variables and examines the strength and direction of the association between them. Cause-and-effect relationships cannot be determined because of reverse causation and the third variable problem. In a cross-sectional design, all variables are measured at one time; in a longitudinal design, variables are measured at multiple points across time.

of a variable, then it is not a true independent variable. Despite this, many gender researchers conduct true experiments. How is this possible? Although researchers cannot manipulate *actual* sex, they can manipulate the *perceived* sex of a target and measure people's reaction to that target (Deaux, 1984).

Imagine, for instance, a psychologist interested in whether people treat female and male babies differently. Using a nonexperimental method, she could observe people as they interact with female and male babies, but if she found differences, it would be difficult to know whether those differences were due to the sex of the babies or to some other associated variable (e.g., differences in the babies' clothing or temperament). A better method would be to allow adults to interact with a baby who is dressed in gender-neutral clothing (e.g., a diaper and a white shirt) after telling half of them that the baby is a girl and half that the baby is a boy. In this way, the baby's perceived sex is a true independent variable. Here's another example. To determine whether employers have a sex bias in hiring, a researcher could conduct an experiment by randomly assigning real employers to receive nearly identical résumés that differ only in the name and sex of the applicant (e.g., Ana Garcia versus Antonio Garcia). The researcher could then ask employers to rate how competent, hirable, and likable the applicant is and then compare across the résumés. Both of these examples allow for tests of cause-and-effect because the researcher manipulates perceived sex in an experimental setting while holding all other variables constant.

Gender researchers could also conduct experiments by manipulating a variable that is related to sex and gender. For instance, suppose a researcher hypothesizes that men exhibit more dominance than women in the workplace because men more frequently hold positions of status in these settings. While the researcher cannot manipulate participants' sex, she can systematically manipulate status, for example, by randomly assigning both women and men to play either a supervisory role (higher status) or a subordinate role (lower status) in some work-related task. If status causes differences in dominance behavior, then both women and men should exhibit more dominance when playing a supervisor role as compared to a subordinate role. However, it is also possible that displaying dominance in the workplace causes men to attain positions of status and power in the workplace, instead of the other way around. If so, then the study just described will produce *null results*, or results that do not support the hypothesis. At this point, the researcher might design a second study to examine this alternative cause-and-effect relationship between dominance and workplace status. The point is that a well-designed experiment allows researchers to rule out some cause-and-effect relationships and identify others. Of course, experiments are not always a viable option. In many cases, gender researchers turn to nonexperimental designs, which we examine next.

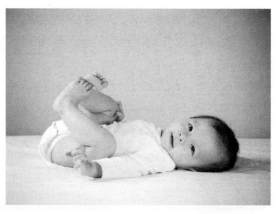

What sex is this baby? We have no idea, and neither would participants in an experiment. But consider this important question: Would people treat this baby differently depending on whether they believed it to be female or male?

Source: © iStockPhoto .com/DONOT6

Dependent variable: An outcome variable in an experiment, the dependent variable is the one hypothesized to change as a result of manipulation of an independent variable.

Random assignment: A process of assigning participants to experimental conditions randomly, so that each person has an equal chance of ending up in each condition.

What are some more examples of experiments that involve manipulating variables related to sex and gender? To generate more examples, first think of a sex difference that you have observed (e.g., men speak up in class more than women do). Then, think of a gender-relevant social factor that might explain this difference (e.g., men receive more approval than women do for speaking up in class). Finally, plan a way to manipulate *this social factor and examine its effects on the behavior of women and men (e.g., assign women and men to receive either social approval or no approval for speaking up in class, and observe whether they both speak up at similar rates when they receive social approval for doing so). Try to generate more examples on your own, and make predictions about what you might find.*

Participant variable: A naturally occurring feature of research participants (e.g., sex, personality, or nationality) that is measured in a study rather than manipulated.

Ex post facto design: A nonexperimental design in which participants are assigned to conditions on the basis of a preexisting participant variable (e.g., sex) and compared on some dependent variable.

Quasi-experiment (or person-by-treatment design): A design in which the researcher measures at least one participant variable and manipulates at least one independent variable.

Ex post facto designs. As mentioned, sex and gender identity cannot be treated as true independent variables. Instead, they are **participant variables**, or naturally occurring features of research participants that are measured instead of manipulated. If researchers want simply to compare the responses or behaviors of men or boys against those of women or girls, they can do so using an ex post facto design. In **ex post facto designs**, researchers compare groups of people (e.g., smokers and nonsmokers or women and men) to see whether they differ on some participant variable of interest. Ex post facto designs look similar to experiments on the surface, but they include neither the manipulation of an independent variable nor the random assignment of participants to conditions that allow for cause-and-effect conclusions (Cook & Campbell, 1979). Thus, researchers might use an ex post facto design to test the hypothesis that women tend to smile more than men, but even if they find sex differences in smiling rates, they cannot conclude that sex causes these differences. There may be other, unmeasured variables that cause women to smile more than men, such as norms that encourage women to be friendly. The true cause of the smiling sex difference cannot be determined on the basis of ex post facto studies alone.

Despite their inability to answer cause-and-effect questions, ex post facto studies can lay the foundation for future research that clarifies or explains the results. For instance, we know that sex differences in smiling do not emerge until approximately the age of 13 (Else-Quest, Hyde, Goldsmith, & Van Hulle, 2006). This suggests that sex differences in smiling may have less to do with people's sex and more to do with other factors that covary with sex, such as gender socialization processes that encourage people to adopt gender role norms.

Quasi-experiments. In **quasi-experiments** (sometimes called **person-by-treatment designs**), researchers incorporate both a participant variable and a manipulated or independent variable in the design (Pelham & Blanton, 2013). Let's return to the example of sex differences in smiling. If adherence to gender role norms plays a role in smiling, then sex differences in smiling should be larger when people think they are being observed by others. In a quasi-experiment, a researcher can compare the smiling behavior (dependent variable) of men and women (a participant variable) after randomly assigning them to contexts in which they are either observed or not observed (an independent variable).

Using this type of design, LaFrance, Hecht, and Paluck (2003) found that sex differences in smiling are greatest when people believe that they are being observed. Note that this type of design allows researchers to test for **interaction effects**, which occur when the strength or direction of the association between one independent or participant variable (e.g., sex) and a dependent variable (e.g., smiling behavior) differs as a function of another independent or participant variable (e.g., observation condition). See Figure 2.4 for an example of an interaction effect.

When they believe that they are being observed—as people posing for a picture clearly do—women tend to smile more than men.

Source: © iStockPhoto .com/guvendemir

Figure 2.4   An Interaction Effect.

In an interaction effect, the strength of the association between an independent or participant variable and a dependent variable differs as a function of another independent or participant variable. Here, the researchers randomly assigned women and men to receive feedback that either threatened or affirmed their gender status and then measured their aggressive cognitions. As you can see, the effects of the feedback manipulation (independent variable) on aggressive cognitions (dependent variable) were stronger for men than they were for women (participant variable).

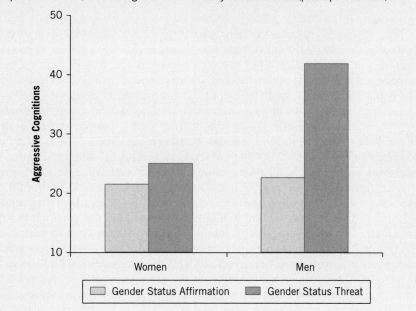

Source: Vandello, Bosson, Cohen, Burnaford, and Weaver (2008).

Interaction effect: A pattern in which the strength or direction of the association between an independent (or participant) variable and a dependent variable differs as a function of another independent (or participant) variable.

Correlational designs. In correlational designs, researchers test hypotheses about the strength and direction of relationships between pairs of variables. In contrast to ex post facto designs, which compare two or more groups on some variable of interest (e.g., whether women are higher than men in body image problems), the most prevalent correlational design examines the relationships between continuous variables (e.g., feminine personality traits and body image problems). While correlations do not allow conclusions regarding cause-and-effect relationships, they are useful because they allow researchers to make predictions. If two variables (*x* and *y*) are correlated, then given a person's score on variable *x*, you can predict that person's score on *y*. However, the accuracy of predictions based on correlations differs as a function of the strength of the correlation. The stronger the correlation between two variables, the more accurate the prediction.

Sidebar 2.3: A Correlation Refresher

Pearson correlation coefficients, or *r* values, range from −1.0 to +1.0, and the farther the *r* value is from 0 in either direction, the stronger the relationship. In terms of direction, *r* values can be positive or negative. *Positive correlations* indicate that the variables change in the same direction (i.e., as one increases, the other increases, and vice versa). For example, as agentic traits increase, self-esteem increases, and as agentic traits decrease, self-esteem decreases. *Negative correlations* indicate that the variables change in opposite directions (i.e., as one increases, the other decreases, and vice versa). For example, as stress increases, body esteem decreases, and as stress decreases, body esteem increases.

Reverse causation: In correlational research, the possibility that the true cause-and-effect relationship between two variables is the reverse of what is initially assumed (also known as the directionality problem). For instance, instead of X causing Y, it is always possible that Y causes X.

Third variable problem: In correlational research, the possibility that an unmeasured third variable (*z*) is responsible for the relationship between two correlated variables (*x* and *y*).

Let's consider an example of a correlational design. Kevin Swartout (2013) surveyed college men about their attitudes toward women and sexual aggression, as well as their perceptions of their peers' attitudes toward women and sexual aggression. He found that perceived peer rape-supportive attitudes were positively correlated with men's own hostility toward women. It might be tempting to assume a causal relationship here—for instance, that hanging out with peers who are believed to have hostile attitudes toward women causes men to develop hostile attitudes themselves. However, we cannot draw this conclusion from a correlational design. As shown in Figure 2.5, there are at least two alternative possibilities. First, the possibility of **reverse causation** means that the causal relationship might be the reverse of what is initially assumed. That is, rather than perceived peer attitudes (*x*) causing individual men's attitudes (*y*), men's hostile attitudes toward women (*y*) might lead them to associate with others whom they perceive as like-minded (*x*). Second, the **third variable problem** means that some unmeasured third variable (*z*) could be responsible for the association between two correlated variables (*x* and *y*). For instance, perhaps men's adherence to male gender role norms (*z*) shapes men's attitudes toward women (*x*) and leads them to associate with peers whom they perceive to hold similar attitudes (*y*). So it may appear that peer attitudes influence individuals' attitudes toward women, but really the unmeasured variable (*z*, adherence to male gender role norms) may be causing both individual attitudes (*x*) and peer attitudes (*y*).

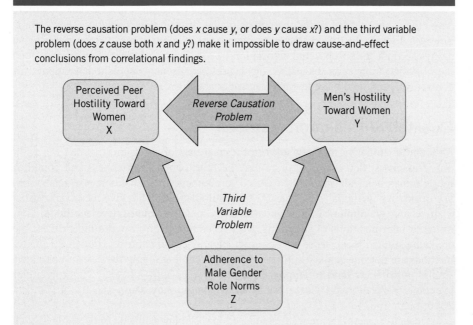

Figure 2.5 Problems With Determining Cause-and-Effect Relationships in Correlational Designs.

The reverse causation problem (does *x* cause *y*, or does *y* cause *x*?) and the third variable problem (does *z* cause both *x* and *y*?) make it impossible to draw cause-and-effect conclusions from correlational findings.

Perceived Peer Hostility Toward Women
X

Reverse Causation Problem

Men's Hostility Toward Women
Y

Third Variable Problem

Adherence to Male Gender Role Norms
Z

Source: Adapted from https://sccpsy101.files.wordpress.com/2011/06/correlation_problems.jpeg?
w=500

Although causal ambiguity is an inherent problem of correlational research, longitudinal designs can help address the problem of reverse causation. In *longitudinal designs*, researchers follow people over time and measure variables at multiple points, whereas in *cross-sectional designs*, researchers measure variables at one point in time. For example, suppose a researcher theorizes that the amount of contact between heterosexual and gay people correlates with heterosexual people's attitudes toward gay people. To test this, the researcher conducts a cross-sectional study and finds a positive correlation between amount of intergroup contact and heterosexual people's attitudes toward gay people (the greater the contact, the more positive the attitudes). Due to the possibility of reverse causation and the third variable problem, the researcher cannot conclude that the amount of contact itself causes the changes in heterosexual people's attitudes. However, a longitudinal design can help reduce this ambiguity. To this end, Gregory Herek and John Capitanio (1996) measured both contact with and attitudes toward gay people over a 2-year period in a sample of heterosexual U.S. adults. They found that more contact with gay people at Time 1 predicted increases in favorable attitudes toward gay people 2 years later at Time 2. We know that Time 2 attitudes could not have caused the Time 1 contact that occurred 2 years earlier, so the much more likely conclusion is that Time 1 contact caused the changes in Time 2 attitudes. However, Herek and Capitanio also found that more favorable Time 1 attitudes predicted increases in contact with gay people at Time 2.

Thus, the causal relationship between these variables likely goes both ways: More contact leads to more favorable attitudes, and more favorable attitudes also lead to more contact.

Although longitudinal designs do not fully safeguard against reverse causation problems, they can increase confidence in particular directions of causality. They cannot, however, address the third variable problem because some unmeasured variable could always account for an observed association in correlational designs. For instance, perhaps having a more agreeable personality causes heterosexual people to have more daily contact with and hold more favorable attitudes about gay people.

Qualitative Research Methods

Qualitative methods: Methods in which researchers collect in-depth, non-numerical information in order to understand participants' subjective experiences within a specific context. Examples include case studies, interviews, and focus groups.

Although quantitative methods allow for a great deal of precision, they are not without weaknesses. For example, there may be times when the richness and complexity of human behavior cannot be reduced to numbers. In such cases, researchers may use qualitative methods (see Table 2.2 for a summary of qualitative methods). Rather than relying on numerical data and statistical analyses, **qualitative methods** allow in-depth interpretations of situations, with an emphasis on how the individuals who are being studied make sense of their own experiences in context. Though qualitative methods are not one unitary approach, there are some unifying themes. In qualitative studies, researchers tend to emphasize depth over breadth, subjective interpretations over objective reality, and contextualized understandings over universal truths (Gergen, 2010; Kidd, 2002).

Qualitative methods are well established in disciplines outside of psychology, such as sociology and education, but what about within psychology? Although qualitative

Table 2.2 Qualitative (Non-Numerical) Research Methods and Techniques.

Design	Main Features	Description
Case study	In-depth investigation, generalizability	A researcher conducts an in-depth investigation of a single entity, such as a person, group, or event. Data provide rich detail but may lack generalizability, and interpretations may differ based on researcher's perspective.
Interview	Open-ended questions	A researcher asks participants a series of open-ended questions in an unstructured, semistructured, or structured format.
Focus group	Open-ended questions, group format, moderator	A moderator conducts an interview in a semistructured group format.
Narrative research	Written documents, texts	A researcher analyzes the stories that people tell (e.g., in journals, autobiographies, and letters).
Ethnography	Immersion within a culture or subculture	A researcher attempts to understand the meanings and practices of a particular culture or subculture by living with the group for an extended period of time.

methods have been used by many prominent psychologists (e.g., Sigmund Freud, William James, and Jean Piaget), and they are widely used in some areas of psychology (e.g., feminist psychology), quantitative methods remain the dominant research paradigm in mainstream psychology (Wertz, 2014). This has been shifting recently, however, with qualitative methods gaining some ground. In 2011, the Society for Qualitative Inquiry in Psychology (http://qualpsy.org) was established as a section of Division 5 of the American Psychological Association (APA). Then, in 2014, the APA began publishing *Qualitative Psychology*, its first journal dedicated solely to psychological research that uses qualitative methods, such as case studies, interviews, and focus groups.

Case studies. In a case study, the researcher conducts an in-depth investigation of a single entity, usually a person, although case studies are sometimes conducted on a group or event (such as a natural disaster). As an example, Roe-Sepowitz, Gallagher, Risinger, and Hickle (2014) did a case study of female pimps charged with child sex-trafficking crimes in the United States. By examining arrest and court records, personal histories, and media releases for each pimp, the researchers were able to describe different types of female pimps and develop a better understanding of their role in this male-dominated industry. Although case studies provide rich detail about the cases under study, their results tend to lack **generalizability**, which means that it is difficult to generalize the findings to the larger population. Moreover, the interpretation of the results can vary widely based on the perspective of the researchers. As you will see, these strengths and weaknesses are associated with the interview and focus group methods as well.

Generalizability: The extent to which the findings of a study would apply beyond the sample in the original study to the larger population.

Interviews. Interviews typically involve asking participants (either individuals or groups) to answer open-ended questions that vary in how structured versus unstructured they are. As one example, Chen, Granato, Shipherd, Simpson, and Lehavot (2017) interviewed 201 transgender military veterans about both the challenges and the strengths associated with their unique identity. The researchers asked each person three open-ended questions and then analyzed their responses to identify themes. While negative themes included the discrimination and stigma that the veterans faced from both the outside world and within the military, positive themes included personal resilience, authenticity, and pride in both their gender expression and their ability to serve their country.

Focus groups. Focus groups, or interviews conducted in a group format, are often guided by a moderator. On principle, qualitative researchers seek to represent marginalized groups in their research, and focus groups serve this purpose well by convening people with similar backgrounds to describe their experiences in their own voices (Gergen, 2010). For example, Parra-Cardona, Córdova, Holtrop, Villarruel, and Wieling (2008) used a focus group format to study the parenting experiences of foreign-born and U.S.-born Latino parents in the United States. By conducting group sessions in the preferred language of the participants at familiar community sites, the researchers aimed to make the participants feel comfortable describing their experiences. Their findings revealed that the two groups were similar in many ways, although the foreign-born parents felt greater language barriers and isolation.

In a focus group, a moderator guides a group interview with people who share similar experiences.

Source: © iStockPhoto .com/asiseeit

Mixed-methods approach: A research approach that combines both qualitative and quantitative methods within the same study or same program of research to develop a more complete understanding of a phenomenon.

Mixed Methods

You may wonder which method— qualitative or quantitative—is more effective or more "scientific." Taking a historical look, people's thinking on this question has evolved over time. As mentioned, quantitative methods have dominated the field of psychology, and researchers did not begin to advocate for the use of qualitative methods in psychology until the 1960s (Wertz, 2014). This push gained momentum in the 1970s as feminist psychologists criticized quantitative research approaches on several grounds (Eagly & Riger, 2014). For example, critics suggested that quantitative methods were *androcentric*, meaning that they treated men and men's experiences as universal while viewing women and women's experiences as deviations from the male norm. This was reflected in the fact that quantitative research was conducted primarily by men, used only male participants, and assumed a male standard for all humans. Moreover, the emphasis in quantitative methods on experimental control and numerical reductionism implies an objectivity and value neutrality that some view as misleading. In fact, no type of research can be completely objective and value neutral because all research is conducted by humans who inevitably bring their biases to their work. In pushing for the use of qualitative methods, feminist psychologists emphasized the idea of *reflexivity*, which means recognizing and acknowledging that the value orientations of the researcher play an active role in shaping the design, findings, and interpretations in any study (Gergen, 2010). The push toward qualitative methods also emphasized the need to include the voices and perspectives of marginalized groups, not just those of people in positions of privilege. Ultimately, this debate led many to recognize both qualitative and quantitative methods as equally effective and scientific. The primary difference between them is thus not *whether* they produce valid knowledge but *how* they produce this knowledge.

Today, many psychology researchers capitalize on the strengths of both approaches by using **mixed methods** (R. B. Johnson, Onwuegbuzie, & Turner, 2007). In mixed-methods approaches, researchers may use qualitative methods as a first step to develop ideas or hypotheses that they later test with quantitative methods, or they may integrate qualitative and quantitative methods within the same study. For example, Mary Crawford and Michelle Kaufman (2008) did a case study analysis of 20 girls rescued from the sex-trafficking industry in Nepal and then statistically summarized the main themes in the cases. By examining the girls' case files, the researchers developed a detailed picture of the typical trafficking experiences of Nepali girls, as well as the common behavioral and physical symptoms experienced by survivors. Then, by quantitatively analyzing data regarding survivors' experiences, the researchers provided empirical evidence that survivors of sex trafficking can be successfully reintegrated into their communities.

As social psychologists, we (the authors of this book) are trained in quantitative methods, and you may notice an emphasis on quantitative over qualitative methods in the research that we cite. Despite this, we are proponents of mixed-methods research because single-method approaches of any kind tend to yield an incomplete picture. When trying to understand a phenomenon as complex as gender, approaching it from multiple perspectives and methods can lead to a more complete understanding than would be afforded by a single-method approach.

Stop and Think

Some people view qualitative research as less scientific than quantitative research. What do you think about this view? Remember that we defined science as a systematic, empirical way of investigating the world in order to identify rules and patterns in the way it works. That said, do you think that qualitative and quantitative methods differ in how scientific they are? If so, how? If not, why not?

What Do Meta-Analyses and Effect Sizes Tell Us About Sex Differences?

So far, we have discussed the methods of individual studies, but researchers can also use methods that combine many individual studies to look at overall trends in the results. This can allow researchers to draw broad conclusions and to identify why inconsistencies sometimes emerge across individual studies. A **meta-analysis** is a quantitative technique for analyzing the results across a set of individual studies. In meta-analysis, the unit of analysis is typically an **effect size**, which quantifies the magnitude and direction of a difference between groups or the strength of a relationship between variables. Let's look more closely at effect sizes and how to interpret them.

Meta-analysis: A quantitative technique for analyzing a large collection of results from individual studies for the purpose of integrating the research findings.

Effect size: A quantitative measure of the magnitude and direction of a difference between groups or of the strength of a relationship between variables.

Sidebar 2.4: Getting Very Meta

Just as a meta-analysis summarizes the results of a set of individual studies, a *second-order meta-analysis* (or *meta-synthesis*) summarizes the results of a set of meta-analyses (Zell, Krizan, & Teeter, 2015). Of course, second-order meta-analysis is only possible when a given topic is studied enough that there exist multiple meta-analyses of the research. Why would a researcher want to conduct a second-order meta-analysis? Researchers who conduct individual meta-analyses may have different criteria for which individual studies to include, or they may focus on some subsets of studies while ignoring others (given their research questions and interests). These practices can introduce error. A second-order meta-analysis can reduce some sources of error and allow an even broader, more comprehensive view of an entire body of research findings.

Effect sizes. Many gender studies compare the responses of women or girls to those of men or boys. For example, a study might compare the reading comprehension scores of girls and boys on a standardized test. If the scores show a statistically significant difference (that is, a difference that is very unlikely to result from chance), the researcher will conclude that there is a sex difference in reading comprehension. But finding a statistically significant sex difference still leaves questions unanswered. Is the difference large or small, meaningful or trivial? To address these questions, researchers calculate effect sizes, which quantify the magnitude of research findings. Whereas statistical significance tells us how likely it is that an observed difference occurred by chance, the effect size tells us how large or small the effect is.

d **statistic:** An effect size statistic that expresses the magnitude and direction of a difference between group means, or of the strength of association between variables, in standardized units.

Standard deviation: A statistical measure of variability that indicates how far the scores in a distribution deviate, on average, from the mean value of the distribution.

The *d* **statistic**, one common measure of effect size, quantifies the difference between two group means (averages) in standardized units. This statistic can be calculated in a single study, or in a meta-analysis across a set of studies. For example, the *d* statistic in a single study of sex differences in reading comprehension would express the difference between the average male and female reading scores in standard deviation units. (More on this in a moment.) In a meta-analysis, the *d* statistic would express the average reading comprehension sex difference (in standard deviation units) across all studies included in the meta-analysis.

What does it mean to standardize a variable or express it in standard deviation units? Researchers standardize variables to allow for meaningful comparisons across studies. If one study measures reading comprehension on a 10-point scale and another uses a 100-point scale, it would be impossible to make meaningful comparisons across the two studies. By standardizing the variables, the researcher converts them statistically to the same measurement scale, which allows them to be compared. The **standard deviation**, a crucial part of the standardization process, is a measure of variability, meaning that it tells you how spread out the scores are in a sample or population. Consider a distribution of reading scores with a mean of 75 and a standard deviation of 5.0. The standard deviation tells you how much the scores in the set differ, on average, from the mean value. So the scores in the distribution are, on average, 5.0 points away from the mean. Then, by expressing each individual's score in terms of how many standard deviation units it is from the mean value, the researcher creates standard scores. For example, an individual with a reading comprehension score of 90 is 3.0 standard deviations above the mean, and an individual with a score of 65 is 2.0 standard deviations below the mean.

Let's revisit the example of comparing the reading comprehension scores of girls and boys. To compare scores across sex, we would separate the reading comprehension distributions by sex and calculate a mean and standard deviation (*SD*) separately for each distribution. Suppose that the mean reading score for girls is 76 (*SD* = 6.0), and the mean reading score for boys is 74 (*SD* = 4.0). Recall that the effect size statistic, *d*, is the standardized difference between two group means (see Figure 2.6 for the formula). To calculate *d* for the sex difference in reading comprehension scores, subtract the female mean from the male mean (74 − 76) and then divide this difference by the average standard deviation for the two groups (5.0). The resulting statistic, *d* = −0.40, is considered medium in size (see Table 2.3). It tells us that, on average, boys in this study are slightly less than one-half of a standard deviation lower than girls in reading comprehension. To estimate the effect size in a meta-analysis, we would locate all available studies of sex differences in reading comprehension and then calculate the average *d* statistic across all of

Figure 2.6   Cohen's d (1988).

This is the formula for computing Cohen's d statistic, formatted for sex difference research. The d value is an estimate of the size of the effect. See Table 2.3 for information about how to interpret the d value.

$$d = \frac{M_m - M_f}{SD_{pooled}}$$

Source: J. Cohen (1988).

Note: M_m = mean of male scores; M_f = mean of female scores; SD_{pooled} = pooled standard deviation (weighted average of each group's standard deviation).

these studies. When Hedges and Nowell (1995) did this, they found $d = -0.09$ for the sex difference in adolescents' reading comprehension. This means that, averaged across all of the studies, there was a negligible (close-to-zero) sex difference in adolescents' reading comprehension scores.

We will report d statistics many times throughout this book, so take a moment to familiarize yourself with Table 2.3, which summarizes the size designations conventionally associated with various d values. Note that effect size designations range from *close to zero* to *very large* (Hyde, 2005). However, the size of an effect does not always correspond with its importance: A small effect can have important consequences, and a large effect may be unimportant in the grand scheme of things. For example, a small effect size associated with sex differences in reading scores might have important real-world consequences if teachers use these scores to determine student placements into advanced or remedial classes.

Table 2.3 · **Interpreting Effect Sizes.** The column on the right provides descriptive labels to accompany various ranges of d values (column on the left). This helps researchers interpret the magnitude of effects. The d values in this table are expressed in absolute value terms. The sign (+ or −) of the d statistic is irrelevant in determining its size.

d value	Description of size
0.00–0.10	Close to zero
0.11–0.35	Small
0.36–0.65	Medium
0.66–1.00	Large
> 1.00	Very large

Source: Hyde (2005).

Within-group variance: A measure of how spread out the values are among people within the same group (or within the same condition of an experiment).

Between-group variance: The difference between the average values for each group in a study.

Overlap and variance. Another way of thinking about effect sizes is in terms of how much overlap exists in the two distributions being compared. More overlap (i.e., more similarity) between two distributions yields a smaller effect size, whereas less overlap (i.e., less similarity) yields a larger effect size. Understanding two types of variance helps clarify this (see Figure 2.7). **Within-group variance** reflects how spread out the values are among people within the same group. For instance, although the average height of U.S. women is 64 inches, not all women are the same height; if there is a lot of within-group variance in women's height, it would mean that women generally differ a lot from the average height. On the other hand, **between-group variance** reflects the difference between the average values for each group (e.g., men are about 6 inches taller than

Figure 2.7 Within-Group and Between-Group Variance.

Within-group variance refers to how spread out the values are within a given group. Between-group variance refers to the difference between the average values of each group.

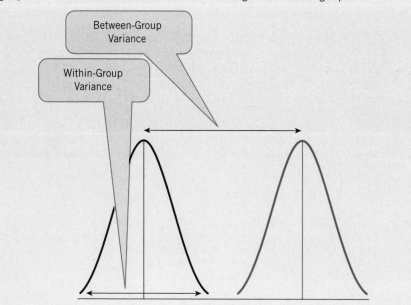

women, on average). With relatively large between-group variance and small within-group variance, there is little overlap between the distributions, and the effect size is large. Conversely, with small between-group variance and large within-group variance, there is a lot of overlap, and the effect size is small. As shown in Figure 2.8, a small effect size ($d = 0.20$) means that there is a lot of overlap (85%) between the two distributions, a medium effect size ($d = 0.50$) means that there is a moderate amount of overlap (67%), and a large effect size ($d = 0.80$) means that there is relatively less overlap (52%) between the distributions.

To provide some concrete examples of sex differences with different levels of overlap, academic cheating behavior has a small effect size ($d = 0.17$; Whitley, Nelson, &

Figure 2.8 Overlap for Distributions Given Different Effect Sizes.

The figures below show how much overlap occurs between two distributions when the effect size for the difference between the groups is small (top figure), medium (middle figure), and large (bottom figure).

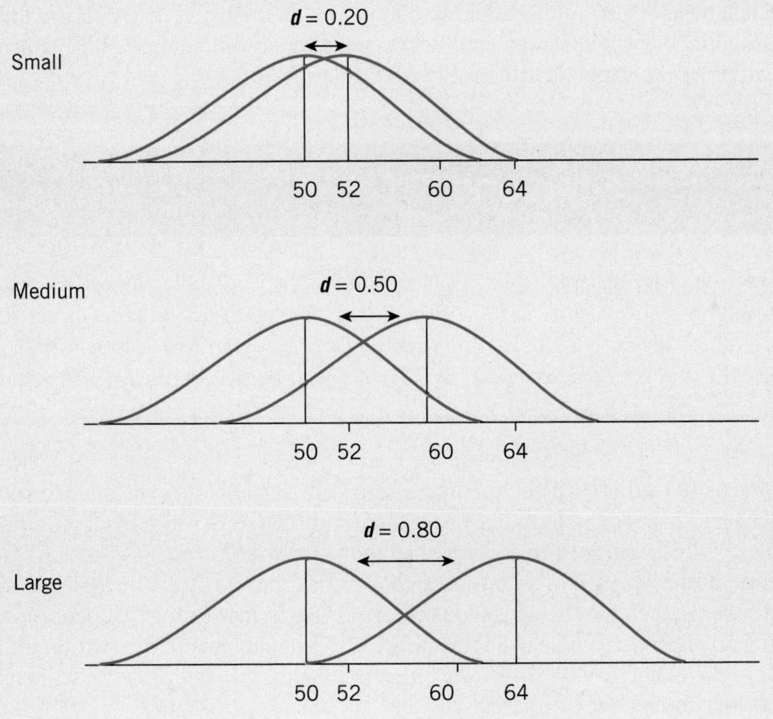

Source: J. Cohen (1988).

Note:

A. Small Effect Size ($d = 0.20$): 85% overlap in two distributions.

B. Medium Effect Size ($d = 0.50$): 67% overlap in two distributions.

C. Large Effect Size ($d = 0.80$): 52% overlap in two distributions.

Jones, 1999), physical activity level has a medium effect size ($d = 0.49$; W. O. Eaton & Enns, 1986), and mental rotation ability (a perceptual skill) has a large effect size ($d = 0.73$; Linn & Petersen, 1985). Let's consider what overlap in distributions means, taking the medium effect size in activity level as an example. The average man has a higher activity level than the average woman; however, with about 67% overlap between the male and female activity level distributions, it would not be unusual for a given woman (selected at random) to have a higher activity level than a given man. In fact, for medium effect sizes, sex accounts for only about 6% of the total variance in the behavior, which means that 94% of the population variation in activity level is accounted for by something other than people's sex.

Some sex differences fall in the very large range, but these typically occur for physical variables such as throwing velocity ($d = 2.18$; J. R. Thomas & French, 1985). The majority of psychological sex differences are in the small or close-to-zero ranges (Hyde, 2005), a point we will revisit shortly. For most psychological variables, then, female and male score distributions overlap substantially, even when statistically significant differences emerge between the average scores of women and men. Why does this matter? When talking about sex and gender, we often focus on the between-group variability by talking about how women and men differ on some variable of interest while ignoring the large within-group variability that the sexes display.

Stop and Think

Suppose you were a gender researcher and you conducted three different meta-analyses. Consider the following research outcomes: (a) a d statistic of −0.43 in spelling ability, (b) a d statistic of +0.01 in life satisfaction, *and (c) a d statistic of +0.28 in physical aggression. What do these three effects tell you about the size and direction of the difference between men and women for spelling ability, life satisfaction, and physical aggression?*

Beyond overall effect sizes. In comparison with single studies, meta-analyses allow researchers to uncover patterns across multiple studies in order to provide meaning and coherence, which can lead to theory generation and refinement. Researchers find this especially useful when individual research findings are inconsistent. For example, as noted earlier in this chapter, many consider gender to be something that people perform within particular social contexts, not simply a stable quality that resides within individuals (Deaux & Major, 1987). This means that the size of sex differences may increase or decrease depending on the context.

As an illustration, consider gender and leadership. For years, researchers have been interested in the qualities of effective leaders, a particularly important research topic given women's underrepresentation in high-level leadership positions in the United States and around the world (Noland, Moran, & Kotschwar, 2016). Alice Eagly and her collaborators conducted a meta-analysis of 76 leadership studies and found that, overall, men and women were equally effective as leaders, with an effect size near zero ($d = -0.02$; Eagly, Karau, & Makhijani, 1995). But when they examined contextual factors, an interesting pattern emerged. In leadership roles in highly male-dominated contexts, such as the military, men were more effective leaders ($d = 0.42$). In contrast, in leadership roles in less male-dominated contexts, such as education, women were more effective leaders ($d = -0.11$). In other words, Eagly and her collaborators identified an interaction effect, such that the association between participant sex and leadership effectiveness differed as a function of context. Had they focused only on the overall finding of no sex difference in leadership effectiveness, they would not have detected the more nuanced interaction pattern.

What Are Some Biases Common in Sex and Gender Research?

As you've likely gathered, no research is completely free of bias and error, and sex and gender research comes with some of its own unique challenges and biases. With *researcher bias*, researchers behave in subtle ways that influence the outcome of a study. For example, in a meta-analysis of sex differences in intrusive interruptions, K. J. Anderson and Leaper (1998) reported that studies with female first authors found larger sex differences (favoring men) in interruptions than did studies with male first authors. This raises the possibility that female and male researchers may have subtly—and perhaps without awareness—acted in ways that confirmed what they expected to find (for example, in choosing how to measure interruptions or in choosing how to analyze or interpret data). In another form of error known as *participant bias*, participants' behavior or responses are influenced by what they think the researcher expects. For example, in a classic study, women directly informed about the researchers' interest in menstrual symptoms reported significantly more of these types of symptoms than women not informed about the researchers' specific interest (Aubuchon & Calhoun, 1985). As you will see, bias can enter the research process at any step: in identifying the research question, designing the study, collecting the data, and interpreting and communicating the results.

Identifying the Research Question

Try as they might to be objective, researchers have values and beliefs that can introduce bias into the kinds of research questions that they ask. For example, some gender researchers frame their research questions from the perspective of a *female deficit model*, which is the tendency to view sex differences as arising from something that women lack (Hyde, 1994). The female deficit model is rooted in *androcentrism*, which, again, is the tendency to view men as the universal or default for the species and women as exceptions in need of explanation (Bem, 1993). The question of whether "girls lack math abilities compared with boys" is framed within the female deficit model. To move away from that model, researchers might ask, "Under what specific conditions do girls and boys perform differently on math exams?" As mentioned in the chapter opener, girls tend to have higher levels of math anxiety than boys (Else-Quest et al., 2010), which can impair their performance. Similarly, negative stereotypes about women's math abilities can lower their performance on math tests (Spencer, Steele, & Quinn, 1999) while

positive stereotypes about men's math competence can inflate their math performance (Danaher & Crandall, 2008). A researcher who operates within the female deficit model, however, may fail to ask questions about contextual or social factors that can drive sex differences in math performance.

At times, the questions that researchers ask reflect gendered differences in power, status, and social roles. For instance, researchers have long examined how working parents balance the demands of their work and home lives and the stressors that result from competing pressures and time constraints. But which type of parent—mothers or fathers—do you think receives the bulk of research attention on this topic? Far more of this research focuses on mothers, which reflects long-standing labor divisions in which women are expected to fill the role of primary caregivers at home, and men are expected to fill the role of paid workers. Women's entrance into the workforce in the United States and other industrialized nations over the past 50 years led researchers to ask questions about how mothers balance work and home roles while they paid relatively less attention to how fathers balance these roles. Researchers pay even less attention to how single parents, same-sex parents, and parents in nonindustrialized cultures balance work and home roles (Chang, McDonald, & Burton, 2010). Consider what these trends in research questions suggest about the values, expectations, and assumptions of researchers.

Until the 1960s, it was standard in psychology for researchers to use only men as participants and then generalize their findings to "all people." What do you think? Are these people the default for the human species?

Source: © iStockPhoto .com/asiseeit

Designing the Study and Collecting Data

After identifying a research question, the researcher determines specific methods to use for sampling participants, measuring variables, and collecting data. Poor sampling procedures can compromise the generalizability of research findings. As standard practice until the 1960s, psychologists used all-male samples to represent all people. During the second wave of the women's movement, this biased sampling method came under fire from feminist psychologists and subsequently began to decline steadily (Gannon, Luchetta, Rhodes, Pardie, & Segrist, 1992).

Beyond sampling, bias can enter a study through the measures and procedures used to collect data. For example, which sex do you think is more helpful? It turns out that the answer depends on the specific measures and methods used to test helpfulness. In a meta-analysis of sex differences in helping behavior, Eagly and Crowley (1986) found that men were significantly more likely than women to help. To clarify this finding, Eagly and Crowley distinguished between heroic or chivalrous helping (part of the male gender role) and nurturant or caring helping (part of the female gender role). They noted that the studies included in their meta-analysis disproportionately measured heroic helping. This suggests that researchers had a bias at the time toward conceptualizing and measuring helping behavior in a very specific, male-typical manner. In contrast, other studies of helping behavior show that women are more likely than men to donate to charities (Mesch, Brown, Moore, & Hayat, 2011) and to enter into people-oriented helping professions (Lippa, Preston, & Penner, 2014). Thus, the way that researchers measure their variables can influence both their findings and conclusions.

Interpreting and Communicating the Results

After data collection and analysis, researchers interpret and communicate their results, which creates yet another opportunity for bias. Here, androcentric thinking can shape how researchers interpret and frame their results. For example, the tendency to state conclusions in the form of the *masculine generic*—that is, using masculine pronouns and nouns (e.g., *he* and *men*) to refer to all people—used to be common but is becoming less so in psychology journals (Hegarty & Buechel, 2006). This decrease can be partly attributed to the APA publishing its "Guidelines for Nonsexist Language in APA Journals" in the 1970s (APA, 1977) and subsequently incorporating these guidelines into the third edition of its *Publication Manual* (APA, 1983). For more on the masculine generic and other gender-related language issues, see Chapter 8 ("Language, Communication, and Emotion").

As you read earlier in this chapter, taking a maximalist approach can sometimes lead people to ignore the great amount of overlap that often characterizes female and male distributions. In fact, Hyde (2005) found that 78% of the effect sizes associated with sex differences in cognitive, social, and motor variables were in the small or close-to-zero ranges, with only 8% of the effect sizes in the large or very large ranges. More recently, Zell and colleagues examined 386 effect sizes from 106 meta-analyses (including 12 million participants from over 20,000 studies) and found that 85% of the effect sizes were in the small or close-to-zero range, with a small average overall effect size of $d = 0.21$ (see Table 2.4; Zell et al., 2015).

Table 2.4 **How Big Are Psychological Sex Difference Effects?** Summarizing the data from 12 million participants in over 20,000 studies of sex differences, this table shows that the vast majority of sex differences on psychological variables falls into the close-to-zero and small ranges.

Effect sizes	Effect size range				
	0.00–0.10 Close to zero	0.11–0.35 Small	0.36–0.65 Medium	0.66–1.00 Large	> 1.00 Very large
Number	152	178	46	7	3
% of total	39.4%	46.1%	11.9%	1.8%	0.8%

Source: Zell, Krizan, and Teeter (2015).

What do you think about the finding that sex differences in most psychological (cognitive and social) and motor variables are close to zero or small? Think back to the chapter debate about whether or not researchers should

study sex differences. Now that you know that most sex differences are actually quite small, do you think that gender researchers should continue to study sex differences? Why or why not?

How Do We Address the Challenges in Sex and Gender Research?

Postpositivism:
An orientation that views empirical investigation as a useful method for acquiring knowledge but recognizes its inherent biases and values.

Scientific positivism: An orientation that emphasizes the scientific method and proposes that objective and value-free knowledge is attainable through empirical investigation.

We have summarized a host of methodological challenges that sex and gender researchers face, but how do we address these challenges? Researchers working within a **postpositivism** framework offer a set of guidelines for conducting gender-fair research. These researchers view empirical investigation as a useful, although inherently flawed, method for acquiring knowledge (Eagly & Riger, 2014). Their views arose in response to **scientific positivism**, which is the philosophical position that objective and value-free knowledge is attainable through empirical investigation. While postpositivists respect science as a process, they disagree with the positivistic view of science as objective and value free. Despite this, postpositivists choose to march forward—with specific scientific standards in place—toward the goal of arriving at better understandings. As Diane Halpern and her colleagues state,

> We recognize that all social-science research is conducted in a cultural context that influences the nature of the questions that may be asked and the evidence that is accepted as valid. Science can never be free of all biases, but it is the best method available for finding answers to politically charged questions. . . . We also recognize that science is a cumulative process, so that the conclusions that are drawn today may change as additional data are collected over time, as society and people change, and as our understanding of the phenomenon being studied evolves. (Halpern et al., 2007, p. 2)

Subsequently, we summarize a number of methodological guidelines that address some of the challenges outlined in this chapter. We offer these guidelines to raise awareness and stimulate discussion about gender bias in psychological research, with the ultimate goal of decreasing this bias.

Sidebar 2.6: A Battle of "-isms"

Social constructivism is an epistemology (theory of knowledge) that views knowledge as subjective, actively constructed representations of reality (Hare-Mustin &

Maracek, 1988). In psychology, social constructivists challenge the tradition of *positivism*, the philosophical position that knowledge develops from an objective, unbiased observation of facts about reality. Social constructivists also challenge the perspective of *essentialism*, the tendency to believe that human differences arise from stable and essential (usually biological) qualities within individuals. Currently, the dominant perspective in psychology is *postpositivism*, an epistemology that, while viewing empirical investigation as a useful method for acquiring facts about reality, recognizes that all scientific inquiry is subject to error and bias.

Guidelines for Gender-Fair Research Design

To promote gender-fair research designs, psychologists offer the following guidelines:

- **Researchers should work to eliminate sex bias from sampling and always report the demographic characteristics of their samples.** This means that researchers should not generalize findings from single-sex samples to all people and should not select samples based on biased assumptions (e.g., selecting female-only samples when studying contraception). In addition to reporting demographic characteristics of samples, researchers should regularly examine whether their findings differ by these characteristics (Denmark, Russo, Frieze, & Sechzer, 1988).

- **Researchers should use precise, non-gender-biased, nonevaluative terminology when describing their participants and research findings.** In particular, researchers should not use androcentric or negatively toned terms and should avoid interpreting findings from within a female deficit model (e.g., describing men as "rational" and women as "irrational").

- **Researchers should not exaggerate the prevalence and magnitude of sex differences.** Journal editors and researchers should place more emphasis on publishing studies that find sex similarities, rather than privileging studies that show sex differences. Researchers should clarify the distinction between statistical and practical significance because not every statistically significant difference has important practical implications. Finally, to communicate the magnitude of sex differences, researchers should report effect sizes (Hyde, 1994).

- **Researchers should not imply or state that sex differences are due to biological causes when biological factors have not been properly tested.** This guideline is relevant, for example, when evaluating some of the claims made by evolutionary psychologists (whose work you will encounter in Chapter 3, "The Nature and Nurture of Sex and Gender"). For instance, David Buss (1989) studied the mate preferences of women and men across 37 cultures and found consistent evidence that men more than women prioritized attractiveness in a mate while women more than men prioritized wealth and status in a mate. Although Buss did not measure any biological factors, he concluded nonetheless that sex differences in mate preferences reflect genetically inherited tendencies. This practice violates the postpositivistic guideline of only making biological claims if biological variables are measured.

- **Researchers should engage in more critical reflection about their research questions, methods, and findings.** They should actively examine their underlying assumptions, seek and examine both confirming and disconfirming evidence for their hypotheses, evaluate the convergence and divergence of findings across studies, and engage in professional debates about research values and methods (McHugh, Koeske, & Frieze, 1986). Researchers should also critically examine other variables (job status, age, race, and socioeconomic class) that might interact with sex or gender in interesting and important ways.

Stop and Think

What do you think of these gender-fair research guidelines? Do they seem reasonable or overly restrictive? What are some opposing views that researchers might raise in response to these guidelines? Do you think gender researchers should be required to follow these guidelines to get their work published? Why or why not?

Diversity Issues in the Study of Sex and Gender

How well do gender researchers in psychology examine issues of diversity, particularly in terms of race, ethnicity, culture, class, and sexual orientation? Turning a critical eye on this issue reveals that researchers could do well to pay more attention to diversity. Most psychological studies in the United States are conducted using largely White, middle-class samples. Furthermore, gender researchers tend to study sex and gender by comparing the attributes of men as a group against those of women as a group. This practice necessarily ignores individual differences that exist within the sexes. Women clearly differ from each other in many ways, and the same is true of men.

Our discussion of intersectionality from Chapter 1 is relevant here. Intersectionality refers to the idea that people's experiences are shaped by multiple, interconnected identities, as well as by the power and privilege associated with these identities. Some psychologists push researchers to engage in a more careful examination of individual differences within group categories, especially those shaped by power differences associated with sex, race, class, age, ability, religion, and sexual orientation (Cole, 2009; Sawyer, Salter, & Thoroughgood, 2013). Proponents of intersectionality argue that examining single identities in isolation (e.g., comparing women and men, without taking race, class, or sexual orientation into consideration) lacks meaning because it is the *intersection* of multiple identities that shapes a person (Parent, DeBlaere, & Moradi, 2013). However, others propose a "both/and" approach in which researchers examine *both* single identities (as a baseline for comparison) *and* the intersections of multiple identities in order to understand the unique properties that emerge when people simultaneously occupy multiple social categories (Shields, 2008).

Given the suggestion that mainstream gender psychology should pay greater attention to issues of diversity, where are the next steps? Academic psychology would benefit from more ethnic, racial, and class diversity among its professional ranks (Eagly, 2013), and academic psychologists should strive to diversify their research samples, not just within the United States but cross-culturally as well. Researchers should also avoid making global statements about sex differences without considering the conditions under which these differences emerge and disappear (Hyde, 2014). This gets to the issue of generalizability that we raised earlier—a sex difference found among primarily White, Western, middle-class, heterosexual young adults may not generalize to people of other races, ethnicities, ages, social classes, and so on. Given this, gender researchers should avoid language that implies generalizability to all people.

Researchers can also expand the number of demographic questions routinely asked of participants in their studies to capture a wider range of identities than is typically measured (Sawyer et al., 2013). This simple practice would help build databases for use in meta-analyses that examine issues of intersectionality. In fact, meta-analysis offers a good tool for exploring identities at the intersections of sex, race, and class (Else-Quest & Hyde, 2016). Moreover, cross-cultural meta-analyses can allow researchers to examine how sex differences in some variable of interest (e.g., math achievement) relate to gender equity measures (e.g., in educational and job opportunities for girls and women) across different nations (Else-Quest et al., 2010).

Of course, not everyone agrees about which methods will lead to the most complete understanding of sex and gender, but this tension is healthy. As social psychologists, we (the authors of this book) see great value in continuing to use the scientific method to answer our research questions while simultaneously remaining aware of and questioning its flaws and imperfections. We welcome a diversity of perspectives and methods in this process. When trying to understand a phenomenon as complex as gender, having a diverse group of individuals approaching it from multiple perspectives and methods makes good sense.

CHAPTER SUMMARY

2.1 Evaluate the meaning of sex differences.

When researchers find that people of different sexes differ significantly on some variable (e.g., optimism), it means that the average difference found in the optimism levels of women and men is unlikely to have occurred due to chance. It does not convey anything about the size or importance of the sex difference in optimism levels. Still, some gender researchers and consumers of research exhibit a bias in their interpretation of sex differences. Those who take a maximalist approach emphasize differences between sex groups, believing them to be qualitatively different from each other. Those who take a minimalist approach emphasize similarities between sex groups, believing them to be largely alike in their psychological characteristics. Each type of bias may have negative consequences: Maximalist interpretations tend to ignore the large amount of overlap that often characterizes people of different sexes while minimalist approaches ignore potentially important sex differences. These perspectives are reflected in a long-standing debate in the field about whether or not sex differences should be studied.

2.2 Explain the scientific method and specific quantitative and qualitative methods used in the study of sex and gender.

In adopting the scientific method, researchers test hypotheses derived from theory by conducting studies and interpreting results. The scientific method is defined by its approach rather than the content investigated. It is a systematic, empirical way of investigating the world in order to identify rules and patterns in the way it works. The researcher starts with an observation, generates a hypothesis, tests the hypothesis, analyzes the results, and interprets the results to generate or refine a theory. The process is then repeated to develop theories further and to gather more data about the way the world operates.

The methods that researchers use to test hypotheses generally fall into one of two categories: quantitative or qualitative. With quantitative methods, researchers turn variables of interest into quantities that are analyzed with statistics. Examples of quantitative methods include experiments, ex post facto designs, quasi-experiments, and correlational designs. Qualitative methods allow in-depth interpretations of situations, emphasizing how the participants make sense of their own experiences in context. Examples of qualitative methods include case studies, interviews, and focus groups. In a mixed-methods approach, researchers use both qualitative and quantitative methods within the same study or program of research to seek a more complete understanding of a research topic.

2.3 Describe meta-analyses and how to interpret effect sizes of different magnitudes.

Meta-analysis is a quantitative technique for analyzing a large collection of results from individual studies on a given topic. It allows researchers to integrate the findings, identify contextual factors that shape the outcomes, and build theories. The most common effect size measure used in sex and gender meta-analyses is the d statistic, which communicates the magnitude and the direction of the difference between women and men on some variable of interest (in standardized units). A small effect size signifies a relatively large amount of overlap between female and male distributions on some variable, a medium effect size signifies

a moderate amount of overlap, and a large effect size signifies relatively less overlap.

For most psychological variables, effect sizes are small, meaning that female and male score distributions overlap substantially. Gender researchers and consumers of their research have a tendency to emphasize the average differences between women and men (between-sex variability) while ignoring the larger variability that exists within women as a group and within men as a group (within-sex variability).

2.4 Analyze methodological challenges and biases in sex and gender research.

No research study is free of bias or error, and gender research has its own unique set of challenges. Bias can enter at any step in the research process, from identifying the research question to interpreting and communicating the results. Androcentric thinking, a form of bias in gender research, refers to male-centered thinking that assumes men to be the norm and representative of all humans. For example, in the past, researchers tested male-only samples and generalized the results to all people. Other common sources of bias include researcher bias and participant bias, whereby researchers and participants introduce error into the research process.

2.5 Discuss the principles of gender-fair research design and the issues of diversity in sex and gender research.

Postpositivistic gender psychologists view the scientific method as a useful but flawed method for acquiring knowledge. In that spirit, they offer guidelines, such as eliminating sex bias in sampling and using non-gender-biased terminology in describing findings, for conducting gender-fair research. Properly implemented, these guidelines help to decrease bias and improve the quality of research findings. Gender researchers should also be attentive to issues of diversity in their research and should work to include participants of all backgrounds in their studies. Finally, researchers should recognize that people's experiences are shaped by multiple interconnected identities and by the degree of power and privilege associated with these identities, a concept at the heart of intersectional research.

Test Your Knowledge: True or False?

2.1. Gender researchers disagree about whether or not it is appropriate to study sex differences. (True: There is a long-standing debate among gender researchers about whether or not it is appropriate and ethical to study sex differences.) [p. 42]

2.2. If a study finds that women and men differ on some variable of interest— for instance, the frequency of smiling behavior—the researcher can therefore conclude that sex (being male or female) causes differences in smiling behavior. (False: Because sex and gender identity are not true independent variables—that is, they cannot be manipulated, nor can people be randomly assigned to occupy different levels of them— researchers cannot draw cause-and-effect conclusions from studies that compare women and men.) [p. 50]

2.3. Qualitative methods (non-numerical methods that involve in-depth interpretations, such as case studies) are defined as nonscientific. (False: Qualitative methods are scientific. Science is a systematic, empirical way of investigating the world, and it consists of both quantitative and qualitative methods.) [p. 54]

2.4. Across most psychological variables, sex differences are generally very small. (True: Sex differences on most psychological variables are in the close-to-zero and small ranges.) [p. 65]

2.5. Gender researchers generally agree that psychological science, if done correctly, can be truly objective and unbiased. (False: Researchers generally acknowledge that psychological science is not truly objective because researchers always bring biases to their studies.) [p. 63]

Becoming Gendered: Biological and Social Factors

Chapter 3   The Nature and Nurture of Sex and Gender

Chapter 4   Gender Development

Caster Semenya is a world-class track athlete who won Olympic gold for South Africa in the 800 m in 2016.

Source: Courtesy of Erik van Leeuwen

Test Your Knowledge

3.1 Sex (whether a person is male, female, or other) is shaped entirely by biological factors.

3.2 Genetic female individuals who get exposed to high levels of androgens in utero can appear masculine at birth and are sometimes raised as boys.

3.3 All female individuals have an XX pair of chromosomes, and all male individuals have an XY pair.

3.4 From twin studies, we know that gender identity is determined primarily by socialization (nurture).

3.5 Within the past decade, neuroscientists identified structural sex differences in the brain and linked them directly to specific psychological sex differences.

The Nature and Nurture of Sex and Gender

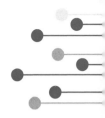

Key Concepts

Nature *Versus* Nurture or Nature *and* Nurture?
   Gene-by-Environment Interactions
   Epigenetics

How Do Nature and Nurture Shape Sex Differentiation?
   Typical Sex Differentiation
      Chromosomes and Genes
      Hormones and Anatomy
   Journey of Research: Unlocking Genetic and Hormonal
      Contributions to Sex
   Intersex Conditions
      Chromosomes and Genes
      Hormones and Anatomy
   Debate: Should Intersex Individuals Be Allowed to
      Compete in Athletic Competitions?

**How Do Nature and Nurture Shape Sex Assignment
and Gender Identity?**
   Optimal Sex
   Gender Identity
   Gender Confirmation Procedures

What Do Sex Differences in Brain Structure Reveal?
   Sex Differences in the Brain
   Equating the Brain With "Nature"
   Neuroscience or Neurosexism?

**How Do Theories of Sex Differences Account
for Nature and Nurture?**
   Evolutionary Psychology
   Biosocial Constructionist Theory

Learning Objectives

Students who read this chapter should be able to do the following:

3.1   Explain how nature and nurture interactively contribute to the development of sex and gender.

3.2   Explain how chromosomes, genes, and hormones shape sex differentiation in both typical and atypical (intersex) cases.

3.3   Analyze the biological and sociocultural factors that shape sex assignment and gender identity.

3.4   Evaluate evidence for sex differences in the brain and the prevalence of neurosexism.

3.5   Examine the roles of nature and nurture in theories of the origins of sex differences.

The Nature and Nurture of Sex and Gender

In 2009, a teenage South African runner, Caster Semenya, burst onto the world track scene when she won gold at the World Championships in the 800 meter race. Caster quickly gained notice not only for her dominance in track but for her appearance as well: Because she has a masculine, muscular appearance, rumors spread that she might not be a woman. Pierre Weiss, the general secretary of the International Association of Athletics Federations (IAAF), was quoted expressing doubts about Caster's sex: "She is a woman, but maybe not 100%" (Longman, 2016). A day after Caster won the gold, the IAAF ordered her to undergo a sex verification test, and she was forced to withdraw from competition for almost a year based on the results of her test. Although Caster's results were never officially published, leaked reports suggested that she had internal testes, no uterus or ovaries, and unusually high levels of testosterone and other male hormones. In short—if the leaked reports are to be trusted—Caster Semenya is intersex in a world that largely recognizes only two sexes. By intersex , we mean that, for Caster, the biological components of sex do not consistently fit either the typical male or the typical female pattern.

Intersex: Individuals for whom the biological components of sex (chromosomes, hormones, genitals, and internal and external sex organs) do not consistently fit either the typical male pattern or the typical female pattern.

What is sex verification testing? Just like it sounds, sex verification tests seek to determine a person's sex through various indicators. The earliest method of athletic sex verification, spurred by suspicions that some Soviet and Eastern European female athletes were actually men, simply involved physical examinations to assess whether the athletes looked male anatomically. By the late 1960s, testing was more advanced and involved examining an individual's pattern of sex chromosomes (XX, XY, etc.). More recently, testing shifted to include an examination of testosterone levels (K. Thomas, 2008). Each of these testing methods has shortcomings, however, because atypical cases exist. As discussed in Chapter 1, sex is complexly determined and consists of many components, including genes, hormones, and internal and external anatomy. While these components typically line up as consistently male or female, this is not the case for intersex individuals like Caster Semenya. Despite the predominant cultural tendency to view sex as a binary, sex actually falls along a continuum from consistently female to consistently male. In fact, biologist Anne Fausto-Sterling (1993) long ago argued for the recognition of five or more biological sexes. For instance, a person can be male at the chromosomal (XY) level but have female-typical genitalia and developed breasts and identify as a woman. And non-intersex individuals, whose internal and external attributes generally align as male or female, also show great within-sex variability in characteristics such as facial and body hair, breast size, and muscle tone.

In Caster Semenya's case, based on her sex verification test results, the IAAF required her to take medication to lower her testosterone levels to the female-typical range before returning to competition (Engber, 2016). Several years later, however, a female Indian sprinter named Dutee Chand brought a successful lawsuit against the IAAF after she was banned from competition in women's events due to her unusually high androgen levels. The court found insufficient evidence of a relationship between testosterone and performance in female athletes to justify requiring drug treatment, and the IAAF reversed its policy on female athletes with atypically high levels of androgens (Branch, 2015).

In the end, although Caster experienced some distress from the public scrutiny surrounding her case (B. Smith, 2015), she went on to win an Olympic gold medal for South Africa in 2016 in the women's 800 meter race.

The question of how to determine a person's sex resonates beyond the world of sports. Recent changes to athletic sex verification policies reflect our evolving understanding of the biology of sex and gender (see the chapter debate titled "Should Intersex Individuals Be Allowed to Compete in Athletic Competitions?"). We are presently witnessing a rapid redefinition of what it means to be female or male and a growing recognition that these labels alone do not adequately capture nature's range of outcomes. Ultimately, these issues are both biological and sociocultural in nature.

Cultures vary in the extent to which they accept more than two categories of sex and gender, with some granting intersex and transgender individuals a special social status (Lang & Kuhnle, 2008). As discussed in Chapter 1, *hijras*—who may be intersex or transgender—are considered sacred within Hinduism and constitute a legally recognized third sex category in India. *Kathoeys* (translated loosely as *ladyboys*) are transgender women or effeminate gay men in Thailand. Thai boxing champion Nong Toom, arguably the most famous kathoey, had her life story portrayed in the film *Beautiful Boxer*. The *fa'afafine* in Samoa are men who identify as women and tend to have sexual relationships with men. Note that some of these identities blur the boundaries between gender identity (as man, woman, or other) and sexual orientation (as heterosexual, gay, lesbian, bisexual, or other). In some cultures, boys who exhibit gender nonconformity in childhood, such as female-typical interests or play preferences, are socialized to occupy female, rather than male, gender roles (VanderLaan, Ren, & Vasey, 2013). In adulthood, these individuals may occupy a category that blends assumptions about gender and sexuality.

In this chapter, we will examine the biological and sociocultural pieces that shape sex and gender identity, with a particular focus on how *nature*—or biological factors, such as genes, chromosomes, and hormones—interacts with *nurture*—or social and cultural factors, such as environments, life experiences, and socialization. We end the chapter by discussing how major theories about the origins of sex differences account for the roles of nature and nurture.

Hijras are transgender women in India who are assigned male at birth but live as women. They are considered sacred in Hinduism but tend to occupy a low social status.

Source: © iStockPhoto.com/ ClaudineVM

Stop and Think

When a 1997 NBC poll asked people to choose the main reason for the difference between men and women, 53% chose nurture, 31% chose nature, 13% chose both, and 3% were unsure (Applegate, 1997). How would *you respond to such a poll? Which factor—nature or nurture—do you think has a stronger influence on sex differences and similarities? On gender identity? On masculinity and femininity? Why?*

Nature *Versus* Nurture
or Nature *and* Nurture?
···

The "nature versus nurture" question has a long history. As early as 350 BCE, Greek philosophers such as Plato and Aristotle tackled questions about whether people's traits reflected nature (biological factors) or nurture (sociocultural factors). While many great thinkers came down solidly on one side versus the other, scholars today generally find it overly simplistic to ask questions about nature *or* nurture. In reality, both nature *and* nurture shape sex and gender in powerful ways, and we see an increasing consensus that nature and nurture jointly shape sex and gender (W. Wood & Eagly, 2013).

Gene-by-Environment Interactions

Biology and the environment interact in ways that make them impossible to separate. Genes are the basic units of heredity—passed down from parents to offspring—that carry the instructions for shaping the offspring's characteristics. Environmental factors influence whether and how genes get expressed as actual physical and psychological traits. A gene-by-environment interaction occurs when a genetic tendency emerges only under certain environmental circumstances or when an environment shapes traits or behavior only for individuals with a particular genetic makeup. Gene-by-environment interactions can be passive, evocative, or active as children develop (Scarr & McCartney, 1983). In *passive gene-by-environment interactions*, parents create certain rearing environments that cannot be separated from their own (and thus their child's) genetic makeup. For instance, consider parents who are genetically skilled at reading and who both pass along reading skills to their children genetically and create reading-rich environments for them. With *evocative interactions*, an individual's genetic tendency evokes specific treatment from others, such as a boy with an active temperament who elicits rough-and-tumble play from his parents and peers. Finally, with *active interactions*, an individual's genetic tendency guides her to choose certain environments, such as a genetically shy person who deliberately chooses quieter environments than her more extroverted sibling chooses. In each of these cases, a biological difference (nature) influences an environmental factor (nurture). Conversely, nurture can influence nature. For example, when a child experiences more active and vigorous play at a young age, it can alter the wiring of the brain, strengthening neural connections that would otherwise not be strengthened. As another example, when girls experience environments of higher family stress, they tend to have an earlier age of menstruation (Moffitt, Caspi, Belsky, & Silva, 1992). Here, the environment (nurture) alters the individual's neural circuitry or hormones (nature).

Avshalom Caspi and his colleagues found an interesting gene-by-environment interaction when investigating the environmental and genetic roots of depression (Caspi et al., 2003). In a large longitudinal study, they measured both stressful life experiences and a genetic marker of depression, a variation of the serotonin transporter gene (referred to as 5-HTT). Caspi and his colleagues did not find direct links between the 5-HTT gene and later depression or between stressful life experiences (e.g., childhood maltreatment) and later depression. Instead, it was individuals who displayed the risky 5-HTT gene

Genes: Basic units of heredity passed down from parents to offspring, consisting of specific sequences of DNA (deoxyribonucleic acid) that carry instructions for the offspring's characteristics.

Gene-by-environment interaction: When a genetic effect on a trait or behavior emerges only under certain environmental circumstances or when the environmental effect on a trait or behavior depends on a person's genetic makeup.

variant and also experienced a lot of stress who had a higher prevalence of depression. These findings support the *diathesis-stress model* in which a genetic predisposition for a disorder emerges only under certain stressful environmental circumstances.

But how do gene-by-environment interactions relate to sex differences? We will address this topic more specifically in other chapters of this book. For instance, in Chapter 13 ("Gender and Psychological Health"), you will read about how girls experience higher rates of depression than boys, a difference that emerges around the onset of puberty. One explanation for sex differences in depression is that girls' pubertal hormones (e.g., estrogen and progesterone) interact uniquely with interpersonal and social stressors during adolescence to produce depression (Nolen-Hoeksema, 2001). In Chapter 7 ("Cognitive Abilities and Aptitudes"), you will read about how Diane Halpern's biopsychosocial model rejects the nature/nurture dichotomy and argues that biology (genes and hormones) and environment (culture and learning experiences) mutually influence each other in shaping sex differences and similarities in various cognitive abilities (Halpern, 2012).

Epigenetics

Further evidence of the interconnectedness of nature and nurture is found in *epigenetics*. Whereas **genetics** is the study of genes (the basic units of heredity) and how traits are inherited, **epigenetics** is the study of the biological mechanisms that guide whether or not certain genes get expressed or activated (Nugent & McCarthy, 2011). *Epigenetic marks* are molecular structures that sit on genes and instruct them to activate or deactivate. Although every somatic cell (e.g., cells that make up organs, blood, bones, and connective tissue) in the human body contains identical gene sequences, only certain genes are activated in particular cells, leading them to become very different types of cells (e.g., hair, muscle, or eye cells).

The functioning of epigenetic marks can be influenced by the environment, either in the uterus or after birth. This phenomenon can help to explain why identical twins, who are exact genetic copies of each other, nonetheless differ in subtle ways and become increasingly different over time as their environments diverge: Epigenetic marks may activate different genes in the cells of identical twins. Some research shows that epigenetic marks can be transmitted from mother to offspring (M. M. McCarthy et al., 2009). For example, a mother's diet, sleep patterns, or stress levels during pregnancy may affect not only her own epigenetic environment (the biochemical changes around the genes that can cause the genes to turn on or off over time) but also the epigenetic environments of her offspring. In other words, a mother's environmental experiences may alter which genes will be expressed in her offspring, thus illustrating the complex interaction between nature and nurture. Although some claims regarding epigenetics require further research, the evidence to date suggests that life experiences can influence epigenetic environments and thus genetic expression (Heard & Martienssen, 2014).

Thus, although biological and sociocultural factors are conceptually independent, they interact in ways that make them difficult to disentangle. In the sections that follow, we will explore how these biological and sociocultural factors operate to shape sex and gender.

Genetics: The study of genes (the basic units of heredity) and how physical traits are inherited.

Epigenetics: The study of the biological mechanisms that guide whether or not certain genes get expressed.

How Do Nature and Nurture Shape Sex Differentiation?

The processes that ultimately create our sex—our maleness, femaleness, or something else—begin at the moment a sperm fertilizes an egg. Sex differentiation refers to the complex series of processes that unfolds as the sex-undifferentiated embryo transitions into an individual with male, female, or intersex gonads and genitalia (see Figure 3.1; C. A. Wilson & Davies, 2007). Although much of sex differentiation occurs prenatally, further differentiation occurs during puberty. In this section, after outlining the stages of typical sex differentiation, we will address several intersex conditions in which the components of biological sex (genes, hormones, and anatomy) do not align as consistently female or male.

Sex differentiation: The complex processes that unfold as sex-undifferentiated embryos transition into individuals with male, female, or intersex internal and external genitalia.

Typical Sex Differentiation

What determines a person's sex? This turns out to be a complicated question. Sex cannot be determined simply by looking at a person's external genitalia, as the earliest method of sex verification testing in sports would suggest. Nor can it be determined simply by

Figure 3.1 The Biological Components of Sex Differentiation.

Typical sex differentiation in utero follows a complex process starting with the sex chromosomes, which guide the development of gonads, the production of hormones, and the development of a vulva or penis and scrotum.

Chromosomes	XX	XY
	No SRY gene	SRY gene
	Gonadal Differentiation	
Gonads	Ovaries	Testes
Hormones	Estrogen, progesterone	Testosterone
External Genitalia	Vulva	Penis, scrotum
	Male phenotype	Female phenotype

looking at the sex chromosomes. Sex chromosomes initiate the biological process of sex differentiation, but when viewed alone, they provide an incomplete picture. Biological sex is a product of chromosomes, genes, hormones, internal sex organs, and external genitalia. In most cases, these various factors align in a consistent manner to produce a biologically female or male person. Let's examine what happens at each stage in typical cases.

Chromosomes and genes. The human body has two major categories of cells: *somatic cells* (e.g., organ, blood, bone, and connective tissue cells) and *reproductive cells* (egg and sperm). In turn, all cells contain **chromosomes** , which are organized units of genes. Every somatic cell in the human body has 23 pairs of chromosomes, with the mother and father each contributing one set of 23 chromosomes. In contrast, reproductive cells contain 23 *unpaired* chromosomes. In each type of cell, all but one chromosome or chromosome pair are *autosomes* (non-sex chromosomes), which contain genes that code for all attributes other than sex (e.g., eye color, hair color, and height). The remaining chromosome or chromosome pair is an *allosome* (sex chromosome), which contains genes that code for sex (see Figure 3.2). Each sperm cell contains either an X or Y chromosome, whereas egg cells always contain an X chromosome. Thus, at the point of

Chromosomes:
The organized units of genes inside the cells of all living organisms. Every somatic cell in the human body has 23 pairs of chromosomes, with the mother and father each contributing one set of chromosomes.

Figure 3.2 Chromosomes of the Somatic Cells.

Somatic cells (e.g., organ, blood, and bone cells) typically have 23 pairs of chromosomes. These consist of 22 autosome pairs (that code for attributes such as eye color and height) and one allosome pair (that codes for sex).

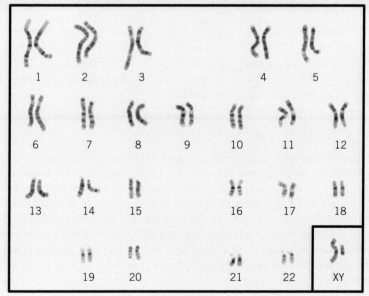

Autosomes   Sex chromosomes

fertilization, the sperm provides either an X or Y chromosome to pair with the X chromosome provided by the egg (Griffiths, Wessler, Carroll, & Doebley, 2015). In typical development, a pairing of XY chromosomes produces a male individual, and a pairing of XX chromosomes produces a female individual. At the genetic level, female and male are thus defined by the presence or absence of a Y chromosome. More precisely, a single gene on the Y chromosome called SRY regulates genital and testicular development causing a fetus to develop as male, although we will note some exceptions in a moment.

Sidebar 3.1: The Tiny but Indispensable Y Chromosome

Unlike all the other chromosomes in the human genome, the Y ("male") chromosome does not have a duplicate partner. This makes it the most vulnerable chromosome, as its genes have to fend for themselves in the event of harmful mutations. In fact, over millions of years of evolution, the Y chromosome has lost almost all of its genes. Whereas most chromosomes contain thousands of genes, the stubby little Y contains fewer than 100 genes, including the SRY gene, which guides male sex development (C. A. Wilson & Davies, 2007).

Stop and Think

Suppose that technology allowed parents to choose the sex of their children easily and reliably. Would this practice be morally justifiable? What if parents have a family history of a sex-linked hereditary disease, and choosing a child's sex could protect the child? What if they already had several children of one sex and wanted a child of another sex? What if they lived in a culture that highly valued boys over girls? Would some of these reasons be more acceptable than others? Why or why not?

Gonads: The sex organs (ovaries and testes) that produce sex cells (egg and sperm) and sex hormones (estrogen and testosterone).

Genital ridge: The precursor to female or male gonads (ovaries or testes). It appears identical in genetic female and male embryos.

Hormones and anatomy. **Gonads** are sex organs that produce sex cells (egg and sperm) and sex hormones (estrogen and testosterone). Until about the sixth week of development, the gonads of female and male human embryos do not differ by sex. Instead, all embryos contain an undifferentiated internal reproductive structure called the **genital ridge**. At about the sixth week after conception, the SRY gene initiates the development of the male gonads or testes. In the absence of the SRY gene, the female gonads or ovaries develop. By about the eighth week of gestation, the gonads begin producing **hormones**, which are chemical substances that regulate bodily functions, such as digestion, growth, and reproduction. In particular, the testes produce androgens, such as testosterone, which initiate the biological masculinization process in the male internal **genitalia** or reproductive structures (testes, seminal vesicles, and vas deferens). In genetic females, the ovaries do not produce many hormones prenatally, and the genital ridge develops into female internal genitalia (ovaries, uterus, and fallopian tubes) in the absence of androgens (Hines, 2004).

Just as all internal genitalia originate from the same undifferentiated structure, so too do the external genitalia (see Figure 3.3). Until about the 12th week of gestation, the external genitalia of human embryos consists of a **genital tubercle** (a small bump

Hormones:
Chemical substances in the body that regulate bodily functions such as digestion, growth, and reproduction.

Genitalia:
Internal and external reproductive organs. For females, these include the cervix, uterus, fallopian tubes, and ovaries (internal) and the labia and clitoris (external). For males, these include the seminal vesicles, vas deferens, and testes (internal) and penis and scrotum (external).

Genital tubercle: The undifferentiated embryonic structure that becomes the clitoris or the penis.

Figure 3.3   Prenatal Development of Genitalia.

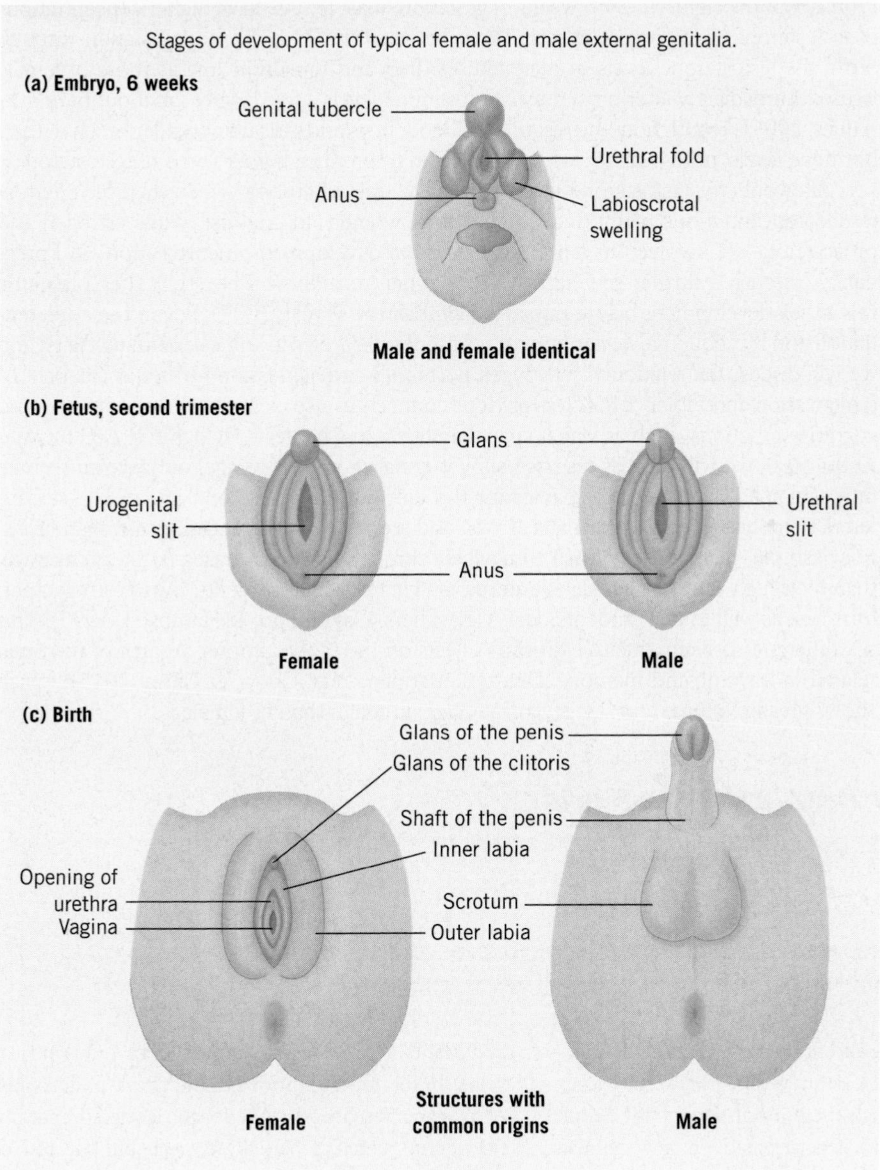

Stages of development of typical female and male external genitalia.

(a) Embryo, 6 weeks

Genital tubercle ——
Anus ——
—— Urethral fold
—— Labioscrotal swelling

Male and female identical

(b) Fetus, second trimester

—— Glans ——
Urogenital slit ——
—— Urethral slit
—— Anus ——

Female   **Male**

(c) Birth

Glans of the penis —
Glans of the clitoris
Shaft of the penis —
— Inner labia
Opening of urethra —
Vagina —
Scrotum —
— Outer labia

Female   **Structures with common origins**   **Male**

Chapter 3 | The Nature and Nurture of Sex and Gender   83

between the legs) with a small opening, surrounded by a swelling of skin on either side. After 12 weeks, in most cases, the genital tubercle and swellings develop into either a penis and scrotum or a clitoris and labia (M.-H. Wang & Baskin, 2008). Thus, the presence of androgens typically leads to the development of male-pattern genitalia, and their absence typically leads to the development of female-pattern genitalia.

We should clarify a common misperception about hormones. People often view testosterone as a male hormone and estrogen and progesterone as female hormones. In fact, almost everyone produces all of these hormones, but the amounts produced differ by sex. From about the eighth to 24th weeks of gestation, male fetuses have higher concentrations of testosterone than female fetuses. Then, between the 24th week of gestation through birth, the testosterone levels of male fetuses drop and remain as low as those of female fetuses. Immediately after birth, boys' testosterone levels surge briefly for about 6 months (Hines, 2004). Throughout the rest of childhood, boys and girls do not differ much in their hormone levels, until puberty, when boys begin to produce higher levels of testosterone.

After puberty, testosterone levels peak in young adulthood, when men have testosterone concentrations many times higher than women. In contrast, while estrogen and progesterone are involved in reproductive system development, menstruation, and pregnancy (discussed further in Chapter 12, "Gender and Physical Health"), they play little role in sex development before puberty (Hampson & Moffat, 2004). Beyond sex differentiation and reproductive development, hormones play roles in some sex-linked traits, and we will discuss the relationship between hormones and aggression further in Chapter 14 ("Aggression and Violence"). A less obvious connection also exists between hormones and cognitive functions, such as visual-spatial abilities. In Chapter 7 ("Cognitive Abilities and Aptitudes"), we will discuss research showing that men, on average, outperform women on visual-spatial tasks, such as navigating through a three-dimensional space. This sex difference emerges in other mammals as well and seems to be influenced by estrogen levels. For example, male rodents learn to navigate through complex mazes faster, on average, than their high-estrogen female counterparts, whereas female rodents low in estrogen perform just as well as male rodents (Galea, Kavaliers, Ossenkopp, & Hampson, 1995). This sex difference is likely due to estrogen's effects on the hippocampus, an area of the brain related to learning and memory (Duarte-Guterman, Yagi, Chow, & Galea, 2015), which shows greater volume and density, on average, in males than in females.

Journey of Research

Unlocking Genetic and Hormonal Contributions to Sex

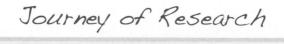

We know that genes and hormones guide the development of biological sex, but how do we know the precise mechanisms by which these processes unfold? People have speculated and experimented on how animals and plants become female and male for thousands of years. In the fifth century BCE, the Greek philosopher Anaxagoras reasoned that sex must be determined by the sperm, which is partially correct, but the rest of his logic fell short of reality: Anaxagoras thought that sperm produced in the right testicle would create male children, and those produced in the left testicle would create female children (Mukherjee, 2016). It was not until the discoveries of genes (dating back to Gregor Mendel's work in the mid-19th century) and hormones (a term first used in 1905 by physiologist Ernest Starling) that scientists began speculating about their roles in guiding biological sex development in sexually reproducing species.

In 1905, biologist Nettie Stevens conducted groundbreaking research on mealworm beetles that led to the discovery of the role of genes in sex determination. While analyzing male beetle sperm, she discovered that chromosomes in the sperm came in two different sizes, large (later called X chromosomes) and small (later called Y chromosomes). Stevens then observed that fertilizing an egg with the large chromosome (X) sperm created female offspring, whereas fertilizing an egg with the small chromosome (Y) sperm created male offspring. She concluded that sperm must contain the genes that code for biological sex, meaning that male members of the species determined biological sex (Brush, 1978). This pattern was later confirmed in other animals, including humans.

If genes carried by sperm provide the initial blueprint for biological sex, hormones get the ball rolling. Some of the earliest work on hormonal regulation of sex began in the late 1940s with the work of Alfred Jost, who removed the testes of fetal male rabbits and found that the rabbits appeared female at birth. In other experiments, Jost reversed this procedure by transplanting testes into female rabbit fetuses and found that these rabbits appeared male at birth. Jost's research showed that the Y chromosome carried by some sperm instructs undifferentiated gonads to develop into testes and produce hormones, such as testosterone, that are critical to the development of male sex characteristics (including internal and external sex organs). In the absence (or inactivity) of these hormones, fetuses will typically develop as biologically female (Jost, Vigier, Prepin, & Perchellet, 1973).

More recent advances in molecular biology highlighted the complexity of chromosomes and genes in the development of biological sex. For instance, in the early 1950s, scientists predicted that certain genes on the Y chromosome must be responsible for initiating the masculinization of fetal gonads; they called these genes the *testis-determining factor*. By the 1990s, geneticists confirmed that the SRY gene on the Y chromosome did, in fact, produce fetal gonad masculinization, at least in most cases. Very rarely, the SRY gene can show up on an X chromosome in the father, which causes an XX fetus to appear male. At other times, the SRY gene does not work properly on the Y chromosome, and an XY fetus develops largely as female.

To complicate matters, hormonal anomalies can sometimes occur with otherwise typical female (XX) or male (XY) babies. Although scientists studied intersex individuals prior to the 20th century under the labels *true* and *pseudohermaphrodites* (Holmes, 2016), a more complete understanding of genetic and hormonal causes of intersexuality emerged much later. For example, in androgen insensitivity syndrome, first identified in 1953, cells fail to "hear" masculinizing androgens, leading a genetic (XY) male to appear female at birth (Hines, Ahmed, & Hughes, 2003). Conversely, a genetic female (XX) can be exposed to atypically high levels of masculinizing hormones prenatally, due to a malfunctioning adrenal gland (a condition called congenital adrenal hyperplasia). Genetic females with this condition may have male-appearing genitals, and they are sometimes raised as boys (Woelfle et al., 2002).

Determining what makes someone female or male at the biological level can be quite complicated. As we learn more about biological sex differentiation, a more nuanced picture emerges, with sex appearing less categorical than previously believed. With further advances in genetics, molecular biology, and endocrinology, the future holds the promise of an increased understanding of biological sex and intersexuality in all their varieties.

Intersex Conditions

Even though all individuals vary in sex-related physical attributes (e.g., hormone levels and genital size), some individuals show greater degrees of variation than others. In most cases, the various biological components of sex (chromosomes, genes, hormones, and internal and external reproductive organs) line up to produce typical female or male babies, but in approximately 1%–2% of cases, babies are born intersex (Arboleda, Sandberg, & Vilain, 2014; Fausto-Sterling, 2000). An intersex individual has inconsistency across the biological components of sex, showing some combination of male and female components (e.g., an XY individual with female external genitalia). The medical community refers to intersex conditions as **differences/or disorders/of sex development (DSDs)**.

Differences (or disorders) of sex development (DSDs): Conditions present at birth in which sex development is atypical in terms of chromosomes, gonads, or anatomy.

Examining DSDs not only gives visibility to the variety of forms that sex can take, but it also sheds light on how biological and social factors contribute to sex and gender. For example, how does gender identity develop in someone with an unpaired X chromosome? What about in someone with an XXY chromosome pattern? And what about in a genetic male (XY) whose body cannot respond to androgens? Or a genetic female (XX) who produces unusually high concentrations of androgens? By examining the different patterns that emerge across a variety of intersex conditions (see Table 3.1), we can draw inferences about the relative influences of biological and sociocultural factors in shaping gender identity.

Table 3.1 **Intersex Conditions.** Intersex conditions can result from irregularities occurring at either the chromosomal or hormonal levels. Note that the links between the specific type of atypicality (chromosomal vs. hormonal) and the individual's most likely gender identification are complex and depend on several factors.

Chromosomal Condition	Typical Gender Identity?	Typical Traits
XO (Turner's syndrome)	Female	Infertile; shorter than average; female-typical external genitalia; undeveloped sex organs at puberty; increased risk for heart defects, diabetes, and hearing problems.
XXX (triple X syndrome)	Female	Fertile; taller than average; female-typical internal and external anatomy; increased risk for language delays and learning disabilities.
XXY (Klinefelter syndrome)	Male	Infertile; appear male at birth; tend to have small testicles and enlarged breasts; increased risk for language delays and learning disabilities.
XYY (Jacob's syndrome)	Male	Fertile; tall and thin; tend to have severe acne in adolescence and high testosterone levels; increased risk for speech and reading delays.

Hormonal Condition	Typical Gender Identity?	Typical Traits
Congenital adrenal hyperplasia (CAH)	Affects genetic males and females; genetic females with CAH may identify as either male or female.	Reduced fertility rates. Genetic females: female internal reproductive organs; male-appearing external genitalia.
Complete androgen insensitivity syndrome (CAIS)	Clinically relevant in genetic males; genetic males with CAIS typically identify as female.	Infertile; cannot menstruate; female-appearing external genitalia; internal male gonads (testes).
Partial androgen insensitivity syndrome (PAIS)	Clinically relevant in genetic males; gender identity may be either male or female.	Variations in fertility; minimal body hair; enlarged breasts; atypical external genitalia (enlarged clitoris or small penis).

Sidebar 3.2: An Intersex God?

Greek God Hermaphroditus, the son of Aphrodite and Hermes, had both female and male features. For this reason, Edwin Klebs (1876) referred to intersex individuals as *hermaphrodites*, a term that is now considered outdated and imprecise when referring to humans. This term technically refers to nonhuman species, such as earthworms and some types of snails and fish, that have both female and male functioning reproductive organs.

Chromosomes and genes. Four deviations from the typical XX or XY chromosome pattern have been widely studied (see Table 3.1). Typically identifying as female, individuals with *Turner's syndrome* have only a single X chromosome in each cell (Powell & Schulte, 2011), whereas those with *triple X syndrome* have an XXX chromosomal pattern (Otter, Schrander-Stumpel, & Curfs, 2010). Typically identifying as male, individuals with *Klinefelter syndrome*, the most common male sex chromosome atypicality, have an XXY chromosomal pattern in each cell, whereas this pattern is XYY in individuals with *Jacob's syndrome* (J. L. Ross et al., 2012).

What do these atypical conditions tell us about the role of chromosomes in sex? It appears that the presence of a Y chromosome strongly predicts having a male appearance and gender identity while the absence of a Y chromosome strongly predicts having a female appearance and gender identity. However, developing a female gender identity does not require two X chromosomes. As we will see in the next section, other factors, such as hormones, can override these genetic influences in contributing to gender identity development.

Hormones and anatomy. Occasionally, due to genetically transmitted disorders, fetuses experience atypical levels of sex hormones in the womb, by having either unusually high concentrations of androgens or an inability to process androgens (see Table 3.1). In *congenital adrenal hyperplasia* (CAH), the body overmanufactures androgens. Genetic females (XX) with CAH have internal female reproductive anatomy but tend to have more masculine-appearing genitalia. Typically assigned female at birth, XX individuals with CAH often undergo feminization surgery of their genitalia in infancy, although such surgery raises ethical questions. While most CAH individuals who are assigned female at birth ultimately identify as female, they tend to show less satisfaction with their sex assignment and more male-typical gender identity than do non-CAH girls (Berenbaum & Bailey, 2003; Hines et al., 2004).

Let's revisit the case of Caster Semenya from the chapter opener. The diagnosis that presumably applies to Semenya is *hyperandrogenism*, a medical condition characterized by an excess of androgens in the female body. Note that hyperandrogenism can result from CAH, but it may also reflect other causes. Therefore, we cannot know for sure whether Caster was born with CAH, but her androgen levels in adulthood are consistent with this disorder. And consistent with what we know about CAH, Semenya exhibited male-typical play preferences in childhood: She spent her time playing only with boys, and she loved soccer (B. Smith, 2015). Similarly, when compared with their siblings without CAH, girls with CAH play with male-typical toys more than their sisters do but less than their brothers do. This pattern emerges even though parents often encourage more female-typical toy play in daughters with CAH than in daughters without CAH (Pasterski et al., 2005).

In the rare condition of *complete androgen insensitivity syndrome* (CAIS), the cells of the body do not respond to the influence of androgens. For genetic females (XX), the insensitivity to androgens in utero does not disrupt sex development, but for genetic males (XY), it does. Because testosterone (an androgen) directs the masculinization of genitals in fetuses, genetic males with CAIS appear female at birth and typically develop a female gender identity. By developing a gender identity inconsistent with their genetic sex in a relatively straightforward manner, CAIS XY individuals illustrate the importance of external appearance and assigned sex in the identity formation process. Likewise, *partial androgen insensitivity syndrome* (PAIS), characterized by a partial inability of cells to respond to androgens, only disrupts sex development for genetic males (XY), who are typically born with genitals that look like an enlarged clitoris or a small penis, depending on the degree of androgen insensitivity (Deeb, Mason, Lee, & Hughes, 2005).

These anomalies suggest that hormones sometimes override the influence of chromosomes in guiding both sex assignment at birth and the development of gender identity. That is, due to atypically high or low testosterone exposure, people can develop a gender identity at odds with their chromosomal sex. But hormones cannot tell the whole story. Consider the fact that genetic females with CAH and genetic males with PAIS can develop an identity as either girls *or* boys. In other words, among infants with CAH, their parents' decision about how to raise them can lead them to internalize a gender identity that is inconsistent with either their chromosomal sex (CAH XX individuals raised as male) or their hormone levels (CAH XX individuals raised as female). If this sounds complicated, it is, and we will explore the implications for gender identity in more detail shortly.

Individuals who do not fit cleanly into the sex binary live in all cultures, and cultural responses to intersexuality vary widely. For example, consider the *guevedoces* of the Dominican Republic (Knapton, 2015). Because of a rare genetic disorder that is unusually prevalent in an isolated Dominican village, about 1 in 90 genetic boys lacks an enzyme that produces testosterone. As a result, these individuals do not undergo male sex differentiation in utero, and their testes remain hidden inside their bodies. Because they appear to have a vagina at birth, parents raise them as girls. But when they enter puberty at around age 12 and experience a surge of male hormones, their testicles descend, and they grow a penis (*guevedoces* translates to "penis at 12"). The villagers usually welcome and celebrate this transformation, perhaps due to the higher social status of men in Dominican society. Rather than stigmatizing the guevedoces, Dominicans' cultural narrative recognizes their unique experiences and identities. See Table 3.2 for examples of other cultures that have unique third sex or gender categories to accommodate and give meaning to the lives of intersex, transgender, and sexual minority individuals.

Unlike in the cultures described in Table 3.2, predominant narratives in the United States and many other Western cultures tends to exclude the experiences of intersex individuals and others who do fit within the sex and gender binaries. This can have implications for violence. Though intersex and transgender individuals are at an increased risk for violence in any culture (see Chapter 14, "Aggression and Violence"), the stigma and violence that they face is generally higher in countries where they experience more social and legal exclusion (Badgett, Nezhad, Waaldijk, & van der Meulen Rodgers, 2014).

Maria Patiño, a Spanish hurdler with androgen insensitivity syndrome (AIS), was dismissed from the Spanish Olympic team in 1986 for failing a sex verification test.

Source: Courtesy of 20 Minutos

Stop and Think

Recall from Chapter 1 that transgender individuals have a gender identity that does not align with their assigned sex at birth while cisgender individuals experience a match between their gender identity and their birth sex. Research has thus far not identified any hormonal or genetic anomalies that differentiate transgender and cisgender individuals (Hines, 2004). In other words, most transgender individuals are not intersex. How does this inform the debate about what factors shape gender identity, especially in terms of nature and nurture?

Table 3.2 Third Sex and Gender Statuses in Non-Western Cultures. Many non-Western cultures around the world recognize third sex or gender categories that accommodate the lives and experiences of intersex, transgender, and sexual minority individuals. The social status of these third sex and gender categories can vary widely, from "accepted but may face stigma" to "respected and valued."

Name	Nation/Culture/ Region	Sex/Gender Category	Description/Role	Status
Guevedoce	Dominican Republic	Intersex	Initially raised female but some change to male or a third gender status at puberty	Celebrated
Kwolu-Aatmwol	Papua New Guinea	Intersex	Initially raised female but change to a third gender status at puberty	Seen as sad and mysterious but accepted
Nadleehe (or Bedarche[1])	North America, Navajo culture	Most are biologically male	Live in the gender role of the other sex but considered a third gender category	Respected; viewed as sacred, spiritual, and possessing unique skills
Hijra	India	Most are biologically male	Live as a third gender category that is neither male nor female; some have their penis and testicles removed	Have low social status but considered sacred in Hinduism
Sworn virgins	Western Balkans	Biologically female	Raised as boys from childhood; live in the male gender role but cannot marry	Accepted; act as heirs to family property when family lacks sons
Mustergil	Southern Iraq	Biologically female	Live in the male gender role but can return to female role	Accepted
Kawe-kawe	Indonesia	Biologically male	Live partially or not at all in the male gender role	Accepted
Calabi	Indonesia	Biologically female	Refuse to adopt the female gender role	Accepted
Fa'afafine	Samoa, Papua New Guinea	Biologically male	Raised as girls from childhood but considered a third gender category	Respected and valued
Kathoey	Thailand	Biologically male	Live as either transgender women or effeminate gay men	Generally accepted but may face stigma

Source: Adapted from Lang and Kuhnle (2008).

1. The term Bedarche is generally considered offensive today but has historical significance.

The case of Caster Semenya, highlighted in the chapter opener, raises questions about fairness in sports. Many would agree that it is unfair for men to compete against women in athletic competitions for which speed and strength generally give men a significant advantage. But what about when a person's sex does not fit neatly into the categories of female and male? Should intersex athletes be allowed to compete along with members of the sex with which they identify, or does their atypical physiology give them an unfair advantage? Note that this debate only affects female-identified athletes with intersex conditions. Officials do not conduct sex verification on male athletes because male-identified intersex athletes competing as men would not be seen as having an unfair competitive advantage. Let's examine both sides of the debate.

No, They Should Not Be Allowed to Compete

Almost all sports are divided by sex, and these sex-based divisions make sense. If women competed against men, men would have an advantage. Men tend to be larger and stronger than women, on average, and they typically run faster, jump farther, and throw harder and farther. These sex differences are substantial: Recall from Chapter 2 that sex differences in physical traits are among the largest known sex effects (J. R. Thomas & French, 1985). It follows that if women have biological anomalies that push them into the male range, it creates a disadvantage to the great majority of women who lack these features.

Performance-enhancing drugs such as artificial testosterone are banned in sports—and for good reason. Bicyclist Lance Armstrong, winner of seven consecutive Tour de France titles, was banned for life from competitive cycling in 2012 after testing positive for several steroids. The home run records of baseball stars Mark McGwire and Barry Bonds are similarly tainted by their use of steroids and human growth hormones, actions that keep them locked out of the Baseball Hall of Fame.

Just as the public would find it unacceptable for an athlete to elevate his or her testosterone levels artificially, atypical conditions that naturally elevate testosterone levels create the same unfair competitive advantage. If an intersex woman has testosterone levels much higher than her opponents, as Caster Semenya apparently did, then the same logic should apply.

Yes, They Should Be Allowed to Compete

By definition, elite athletes have atypical physiologies. They are bigger, stronger, faster, and more agile than average humans. Legendary NBA basketball player Shaquille O'Neal's unusual physique (7 ft. 1 in., 325 lbs.) gave him an obvious competitive advantage. No one would deny that O'Neal's towering frame helped him dominate his opponents. Similarly, the almost superhuman body of Olympic swimmer Michael Phelps—abnormally long torso and tremendous arm span—is acknowledged as a primary reason for his astonishing swimming abilities. Tennis star Serena Williams has a famously muscular physique and one of the fastest serves in the game. These athletes' unique bodies clearly play a substantial role in their athletic victories. And yet, some people question whether an intersex

(Continued)

(Continued)

athlete's atypical physiology (say, a testosterone concentration several times higher than her competitors) renders her performance problematic. If intersex athletes have a unique advantage because of their physiology, how does this differ from the unique physical gifts of O'Neal, Phelps, and Williams?

Moreover, research to date does not clearly show how much competitive advantage, if any, elevated testosterone levels provide (Longman, 2016). Even if testosterone did confer a competitive physical advantage in women, the exclusive focus on androgen (testosterone) testing in *female* athletes presents a bias. Both women and men have testosterone, and men also vary from each other in their testosterone levels. Given this, why have officials only felt compelled to regulate the testosterone levels of female athletes? Should we not also regulate those of male athletes to ensure that men with very high levels of testosterone do not have an unfair competitive advantage?

In fact, the larger issue may stem from gender role norms about how much masculinity people accept in women: The concerns may have less to do with supposed competitive advantages and more to do with challenges to conventional notions of femininity that some intersex female athletes represent. In reality, people come in all shapes and sizes, and the physiology of men and women exists on a spectrum. Naturally occurring, elevated levels of testosterone should thus not preclude women from competing in athletic events.

Which side of the debate seems more compelling to you? Which points do you find most and least convincing? Why?

How Do Nature and Nurture Shape Sex Assignment and Gender Identity?

How do we identify the sex of a fetus or infant? The most common method is very simple—we look at the genitals. This can be done at birth or prenatally with sonograms that allow for a visual inspection of a penis or labia between the third and seventh months of pregnancy (G. F. Cunningham et al., 2014). Another method, known as noninvasive prenatal testing, can determine a fetus's genetic sex (and test for chromosomal abnormalities) by drawing blood from the mother about 9 weeks after conception (Chandrasekharan, Minear, Hung, & Allyse, 2014). The typical method of assigning sex based on a visual inspection of the genitals highlights a potential clash between nature and nurture. As discussed, while nature offers us a continuum of sex configurations (Fausto-Sterling, 2000), most—though not all—cultures choose to dichotomize sex as either male or female based on a simple glance at the genitals. But what happens when a visual inspection of the genitals does not offer a clear male/female answer?

Optimal sex:
The binary (male or female) sex perceived to be most advantageous to assign to a newborn whose genitalia appear atypical at birth.

Optimal Sex

Optimal sex refers to the binary sex that doctors and parents perceive as the best option for a newborn whose genitalia appear atypical at birth. (Although most scholars refer to this concept as *optimal gender*, we use the term *optimal sex* instead because it reflects how we define sex in this book, as referring to the categories of male, female, or intersex.) Prior to the 1950s, the scientific community lacked consensus on how to treat the small percentage of newborns whose genitals could not easily be categorized into the male/female binary. Then, psychologist John Money and his colleagues at Johns Hopkins University developed the *optimal sex policy*, which proposed that intersex infants should be socialized as either boys or girls beginning in the first 18 months of life (Money, Hampson, & Hampson, 1955). Money believed that gender identity was largely a product of socialization and that social factors could override any role that biology played in gender identity. He also generally advocated for early corrective surgery when the genitals were not clearly female or male, followed by hormone treatments to ensure typical hormone levels for the assigned sex. The optimal sex policy thus prioritized the goal of creating a physical appearance consistent with assigned sex. In this way, the scientific community viewed intersex children as a problem that needed solving, and the favored solution constrained them to fit into a binary system of sex.

Social and medical opinions have changed slowly over time. Professionals today increasingly reject the optimal sex policy on ethical grounds and instead recommend to parents of intersex infants that they postpone surgeries and hormone treatments until children are old enough to understand their situation, contribute to decisions about their sex assignment and gender identity, and consent to treatment (Wiesemann, Ude-Koeller, Sinnecker, & Thyen, 2010). This rethinking of the optimal sex policy reflects, in part, the difficulties of deciding what constitutes "typical" versus "atypical" genitalia at birth. As one example, physicians disagree on how to diagnose *clitoromegaly* (an atypically large clitoris) in infants because accurately measuring clitoral length poses challenges, and clitoral size can vary based on nationality, ethnicity, and race (Kutlu & Akbiyik, 2011). With typical infant clitoral lengths averaging about 3–4 mm, some define clitoromegaly in infants as a clitoral length over 10 mm (not quite 0.5 inches). But this standard has been criticized for representing such a small difference—about 6.5 mm, or 0.25 inches—between a "normal" clitoris and an "atypical" one.

The evolving response that society has to intersex individuals reveals an important point about sex and gender: Even though biological factors do play a role, sex is also socially and culturally constructed. The moment the sex of a fetus or infant becomes known, social values and beliefs enter the process. When doctors recommend surgery to alter an infant's genitalia, they reflect and reinforce a cultural worldview that recognizes two and only two categories of sex (Marecek, Crawford, & Popp, 2004). The movement away from such procedures and the increasing cultural visibility of intersex and transgender individuals in the United States and around the world suggest that cultural constructions of sex as binary may be changing.

Gender Identity

Let's return to John Money's assumption that nurture is stronger than nature in determining individuals' gender identity. Money assumed that a child born with visually atypical genitals could be raised as either female or male, contingent upon strong and consistent socialization pressures from parents and the surrounding environment. How accurate is this belief? To what extent do intersex individuals who get assigned either female or

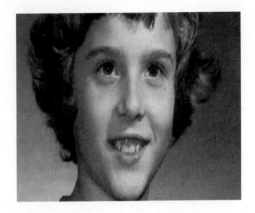

Brenda Reimer as a child and David Reimer after assuming a male gender identity.

Source: REUTERS/ Str Old

male at birth come to embrace versus reject their assigned sex? The evidence is mixed. One the one hand, the majority of genetically female individuals with CAH who are assigned female at birth do tend to develop a female gender identity (Berenbaum & Bailey, 2003; Hines et al., 2004). On the other hand, the famous case story of David (born Bruce) Reimer, a genetic boy raised as a girl, offers some vivid evidence that socialization cannot always override biological factors in shaping gender identity. In 1965, when circumcising Bruce and his identical twin brother, a surgeon accidentally removed most of Bruce's penis. Since surgical reconstruction of the penis was impossible, Bruce's parents followed John Money's advice and had Bruce reassigned as female. This meant surgically constructing a vagina for him and giving him hormonal and psychological treatments (Mukherjee, 2016).

For years, Money claimed that Bruce (raised as Brenda) developed a typical female gender identity and adjusted well, but this was far from true, as chronicled in John Colapinto's (2000) book, *As Nature Made Him: The Boy Who Was Raised as a Girl*. In reality, Brenda never felt like a girl. She cut up dresses she felt forced to wear, preferred her brother's toys over her dolls, and chose to stand while urinating. At age 14, upon learning the truth about his botched circumcision in infancy, Reimer adopted a male gender identity, took the name David, and sought testosterone treatments. Although David Reimer married as an adult, he suffered from depression and anger issues and ultimately committed suicide at age 38, almost 2 years after his twin brother died of an overdose (Mukherjee, 2016).

David Reimer's story suggests that he and his twin brother had struggles in life that perhaps went beyond David's traumatic gender upbringing, which underscores the difficulties of generalizing from a single case. That said, Reimer's story does indicate that gender identity cannot necessarily be shaped entirely by rearing and socialization in a person who undergoes typical sex differentiation in utero. In fact, a larger study of intersex individuals like Reimer corroborates this conclusion. These individuals were genetic males (XY) who were androgenized normally in utero but were raised female due to the absence of male-typical genitalia at birth (Meyer-Bahlburg, 2005). Although the majority (78%) of them developed a female gender identity, 13% experienced symptoms of *gender dysphoria*, which is defined as clinically significant levels of distress arising from a mismatch between people's felt sense of gender identity and the sex they were assigned at birth. Moreover, 22% of the sample ultimately transitioned to a male gender identity, a rate that is almost 37 times larger than the estimated rate (0.6%) of transgender people in the United States (Flores, Herman, Gates, & Brown, 2016). Thus, on the one hand, these findings offer partial support for Money's beliefs because the majority of the sample developed the female gender identity that they were socialized to adopt, despite their genetic maleness. On the other hand, that 22% of the sample chose to transition to a male identity seems to suggest the reverse—that chromosomes and hormones can override rearing and socialization. Also noteworthy is the fact that in a comparison sample of intersex XY babies raised as boys, none changed gender identity, and only one experienced possible gender dysphoria (Meyer-Bahlburg, 2005).

Another way to assess the relative roles of biology versus socialization in gender identity is to estimate its genetic heritability. Using twin studies, researchers can compute heritability estimates that quantify the extent to which genes versus nongenetic factors shape a given trait or tendency. A **heritability estimate** is a statistic that specifies the proportion of total population variance in a given trait, such as gender identity, that is due to genetic differences among the people in the population. Heritability estimates (signified by h^2) can range from 0% to 100% (or 0.0–1.0). An h^2 of 0 would indicate that genetic differences among people account for none of the population variance in a trait, and an h^2 of 100% (or 1.0) would indicate that genetic differences among people account for all of the population variance in a trait. For example, if h^2 for extraversion is .42, this means that genes explain 42% of the population variance in extraversion. However, it does not mean that 42% of your extraversion (or of any individual's extraversion) is caused by genes. Instead, it means that 42% of the extent to which people differ from one another in extraversion is due to genetic differences among them.

Heritability estimates are calculated by comparing the similarity of *monozygotic (identical) twins* to the similarity of *dizygotic (fraternal) twins*. Monozygotic twins have 100% of their genes in common while dizygotic twins share, on average, 50% of their genes. Thus, to the extent that monozygotic twins are more similar to one another than dizygotic twins are on a given trait, we can estimate the extent to which genes shape the trait. Using this logic, Heylens et al. (2012) selected 23 monozygotic twin pairs and 34 dizygotic twin pairs in which one twin was transgender and then measured the gender identity (transgender or cisgender) of the other twin. The monozygotic twins had transgender identities in common in nine pairs (39%); in contrast, the dizygotic twins had no cases in which both twins shared a transgender identity. Another twin study of children reported a heritability estimate of 62% for gender identity based on parents' ratings of their children's gender identity (Coolidge, Thede, & Young, 2002). With heritability estimates closer to 50% than to 100%, these studies suggest that biological and social factors both contribute substantially to gender identity status. If genes predominantly determined gender identity, you would see greater similarity in the gender identities of identical twin pairs and thus higher heritability estimates. For the sake of comparison, a meta-analysis of heritability estimates of major personality traits yielded an overall estimate of 40% (Vukasović & Bratko, 2015). Therefore, what little data we have on the heritability of gender identity indicate that it is roughly as heritable as other aspects of personality.

Heritability estimate: A statistic that specifies the proportion of total population variance in a given trait, such as gender identity, that is due to genetic differences among the people in the population. Heritability estimates (signified by h^2) can range from 0% to 100%.

Monozygotic (identical) twins share 100% of their genes. Therefore, if they are more similar to one another on a given trait than dizygotic (fraternal) twins are, it suggests that genes exert an influence on the trait.

Source:
© iStockPhoto.com/
Image Source

As with research on gender identity, twin studies also illuminate the role of genes in masculine and feminine attributes. In a study of 38 monozygotic twin pairs and 32 dizygotic twin pairs, each member of the pair completed self-report measures of masculine and feminine traits (Mitchell, Baker, & Jacklin, 1989). The monozygotic twins had more similar scores to one another than did the dizygotic twins, resulting in heritability estimates of 20%–48%, findings that have been corroborated in more recent research (Verweij, Mosing, Ullén, & Madison, 2016). These estimates mean that genetic differences among people explain between 20% and 48% of the population variance in masculine and feminine traits, with social and environmental factors explaining the remainder (52%–80%) of the population variance. Studies with children document similar moderate genetic influences on sex-typed preferences for toys (dolls and toy guns) and activities (dressing up and playing soldier; Iervolino, Hines, Golombok, Rust, & Plomin, 2005).

Biological factors—genes and hormones—clearly contribute to both gender identity and sex-linked attributes, although they cannot explain the full picture. Just as we have discussed throughout this chapter, nature and nurture interact and influence each other in ways that make them difficult to disentangle. Particularly relevant in the interpretation of findings from twin studies, identical twin pairs tend to be treated more similarly than do fraternal twin pairs, which confounds nature and nurture. Note that we will address the specific factors that contribute to the development of male- and female-typed traits and preferences further in Chapter 4 ("Gender Development"). Similarly, we will address the nature and nurture of sexual orientation in detail in Chapter 9 ("Sexual Orientation and Sexuality").

Gender Confirmation Procedures

Gender confirmation procedures: Procedures (including hormone treatments, surgeries, and psychotherapies) that transgender individuals sometimes seek to bring their physical bodies into greater alignment with their psychological identities.

As discussed, controversy surrounds the hormone treatments and surgeries used by doctors and parents to bring the bodies of intersex infants and children in line with their assigned sex. In a different context, transgender individuals sometimes voluntarily seek surgeries and other procedures to bring their physical bodies into greater alignment with their gender identities. These **gender confirmation procedures** include surgery, hormone treatments, and psychological therapy. Transmen (female-to-male, or FtM, individuals) who undergo surgical procedures may opt for genital reconstruction of a penis through *phalloplasty* (the lengthening of the urethra and construction of a penis using grafted tissue) or *metoidioplasty* (the enlargement and separation of the clitoris to form a penis). FtM individuals may also elect to have a *mastectomy* (removal of breast tissue). Transwomen (male-to-female, or MtF, individuals) who undergo surgical procedures may seek *vaginoplasty* (the surgical construction of a vagina) and breast augmentation. Although transgender people have regularly altered their appearance to satisfy their gender identity, options for safe and medically sound surgical alterations to the body are relatively new. For instance, the first vaginoplasty was performed in 1931 (Munro, 2017), and the first phalloplasty was conducted in 1946 (Kennedy, 2007). Still, many transgender individuals, especially those of color or low income, continue to face difficulties in accessing medical care for these procedures (Strousma, 2014).

Sidebar 3.3: Changing Terminology

Individuals who transition from their assigned sex to their felt gender identity have often been (and sometimes still are) referred to as *transsexual*, but not all individuals who transition identify with this term. In this book, we use the terms *transwomen* or *MtF (male-to-female) individuals and transmen or FtM (female-to-male) individuals* to signify people who undergo a formal (physical or psychological) transition from their assigned sex to their felt gender. Furthermore, some dislike terms such as *sex change* or *sex reassignment surgery* because *change* is not an accurate way to describe an identity that many trans individuals have always felt. While some prefer the term *gender confirmation surgery*, others opt for *genital reconstructive surgery* since it simply describes the procedure with no added meanings about sex or gender being reassigned or confirmed. *Gender confirmation procedures*, in contrast, refer to a broad range of treatments that bring the body into greater alignment with gender identity, including surgeries, hormone treatments, and psychotherapies.

Of course, surgery can be cost prohibitive, painful, difficult, or inconsistent with people's values. Thus, some transgender individuals who want to alter their bodies physically opt instead for hormone treatments, and these treatments are also often used as a preliminary stage in the transition process, preceding any surgical procedures. Relatively less expensive feminizing or masculinizing hormones (e.g., estrogen and testosterone, respectively) can be administered in many forms (injections, pills, patches, and implants) and effectively stimulate the development of secondary sex characteristics such as increased breast tissue in MtF individuals and facial and body hair in FtM individuals. In terms of mental health, one review of longitudinal studies found that both MtF and FtM individuals showed significant decreases in anxiety and depression symptoms 3–12 months after initiating hormone treatments (White Hughto & Reisner, 2016). Still other transgender individuals opt out of both surgery and hormone treatments for a variety of reasons.

Stop and Think

If one goal of the transgender movement is to push society beyond a binary conceptualization of sex as either male or female, then how do MtF and FtM individuals fit into this picture? Do you think that fewer people would transition from male to female or from female to male if society moved beyond a binary system of sex? Why or why not?

What Do Sex Differences in Brain Structure Reveal?

Some of the physical sex differences that we have discussed so far, including chromosomes and hormones, are understood fairly well. In contrast, identifying sex differences in the brain is a less straightforward task. While there appear to be some (small) sex differences in the brain, little is known about what causes them and what they signify. Neuroscientists debate questions of how to understand and interpret sex differences in the brain, with some contending that sex differences in the brain matter greatly (Cahill, 2006) and others that the findings are overstated (deVries & Södersten, 2009).

Sex Differences in the Brain

If you placed a pile of human brains on a table, would an expert be able to sort them by sex based on visual inspection alone? Not likely. One analysis of the brains of over 1,400 people between the ages of 13 and 85 concluded that male and female brains overlap a great deal in terms of the structure of both *cortical gray matter* (neuron cell bodies and dendrites in the cerebral cortex) and *cortical white matter* (myelinated axons in the cerebral cortex) and connective tissue (Joel et al., 2015). When averaging across all brains scanned, the researchers did identify a number of regions that differed in size between female and male brains. However, approximately 92% of the individuals in the sample did not follow this sex-typical pattern in its entirety and showed what Joel and her colleagues (2015) called a "unique mosaic" of male-typical and female-typical patterns in their brains.

Magnetic resonance imaging (MRI): An imaging procedure that uses magnetic fields and radio waves to create high-resolution images of brain structures.

Since the late 1970s, brain imaging techniques have become much more sophisticated and include techniques such as **magnetic resonance imaging (MRI)** and **functional magnetic resonance imaging (fMRI)**. While MRI creates vivid, high-resolution images of brain *structures* (size, shape, and form), fMRI measures brain activity by detecting changes in blood flow in the brain, thereby allowing insight into brain *functions* (processes that underlie cognition, behavior, emotion, or perception). These and other sophisticated imaging techniques led to a proliferation of research on sex differences in the brain. Although structural differences between male and female brains are not obvious to the naked eye, male brains are, on average, about 11% larger in volume than female brains, as measured in total volume and not corrected for body size differences (Ruigrok et al., 2014). There are also sex differences in specific regions of the brain, with some areas larger or denser in male brains and some areas larger or denser in female brains. For example, women show greater volume and density than men in the frontal pole cortex (responsible for strategic planning and decision making). And men often show greater volume and density than women in the left hippocampus (part of the limbic system that regulates memory, learning, and emotion) and in the left amygdala (part of the limbic system involved in processing and expressing emotion, especially fear; Ruigrok et al., 2014).

Functional magnetic resonance imaging (fMRI): A brain imaging technique that uses magnetic fields and radio waves to map brain activity.

How do these structural brain differences arise? Some evidence suggests that they are set in motion prenatally by the production of gonadal hormones that shape fetal brains, and they continue to develop during the phase of brain plasticity in adolescence.

Plasticity (or neuroplasticity), which refers to the brain's ability to reorganize and adapt physically in response to environmental factors, is especially high during adolescence. During this time, the brain undergoes several major developmental changes that are regulated internally by pubertal increases in sex hormones (including testosterone, estrogen, progesterone, and estradiol) and that are also shaped by life experiences such as individuals' patterns of eating, sleeping, and caffeine and tobacco use (Arain et al., 2013). But the (perhaps) more interesting question concerns the precise manner in which structural sex differences in the brain relate, if at all, to psychological sex differences. And when it comes to this question, the fact is that psychologists do not yet have an answer. Neuroscientists do not fully understand the connections between brain structure and brain function, and hypotheses about human sex differences in brain functions tend to be speculative (deVries & Södersten, 2009). Therefore, an important question might be this: If the size or structure of various brain regions does not reliably predict meaningful behavioral or psychological differences between women and men, then what is the value of searching for sex differences in the brain? (We will further examine the links between sex differences in the brain and cognitive abilities in Chapter 7, "Cognitive Abilities and Aptitudes.")

Plasticity (or neuroplasticity): The ability of the brain to reorganize and adapt physically throughout life in response to environmental changes.

Equating the Brain With "Nature"

Several challenges confront researchers who study sex differences in the brain. Recall from Chapter 2 ("Studying Sex and Gender") that bias can enter a study at any point in the research process. In the case of brain research, some neuroscientists exhibit a bias toward equating the brain with nature. Upon documenting sex differences in the brain, they assume that these differences must result from innate biological differences between female and male individuals. Consider what might be problematic about this assumption. In particular, think back to our discussions of the malleability of the brain and the interconnectedness between nature and nurture. As neuroscientist Lise Eliot (2009) documents in her book *Pink Brain, Blue Brain*, adults' gender stereotypes can enlarge small sex differences that are present in infants' brain structures at birth or even create sex differences in brain structures that were not present at birth. This can occur because of the brain's plasticity, which renders it susceptible to modification via life experiences. The different experiences that girls and boys have from very young ages may enlarge or create structural sex differences in the brain, and these brain differences can then grow over time as the environments of boys and girls become increasingly different. Therefore, the observation of sex differences in brain structures does not necessarily imply a stronger role of nature than nurture in causing these differences.

The environment continues to shape neural structures and sex differentiation past infancy and childhood. Furthermore, just because hormones—a biological factor—contribute to sex differences in brain structures, it does not mean that biology is the sole driver of these effects. In fact, social factors can alter hormone levels. As we discussed in Chapter 1, performing male-typed and female-typed behaviors can change people's testosterone levels. For example, women who role-played having power over someone (i.e., firing a subordinate) subsequently showed increases in testosterone relative to a neutral condition (van Anders, Steiger, & Goldey, 2015), and men who soothed a simulated crying infant showed a decrease in testosterone relative to those who listened to but did not soothe the infant (van Anders, Tolman, & Jainagaraj, 2014). These findings led Sari van Anders and her colleagues to theorize that adult sex differences in testosterone levels may reflect sex differences in the types of behaviors that women and men are routinely socialized to perform.

Neuroscience or Neurosexism?

Neuroscience is the scientific study of the nervous system, including neurons and the brain. Although powerful neuroimaging technologies (such as fMRI) opened the door for neuroscientists to peer into the brain in new ways, these technologies, like any tool, can be misused, and the images they produce can be misinterpreted. In her book *Delusions of Gender*, Cordelia Fine (2010) introduced the concept of neurosexism, which occurs when people interpret the findings from neuroscience research in ways that reinforce gender stereotypes without valid supporting evidence. When researchers catalog structural sex differences in the brain without linking these to meaningful functional differences, they may run the risk of perpetuating gender stereotypes. Moreover, as we noted, a focus on structural sex differences in the brain can imply that these differences stem from biological factors, which is not necessarily true. Thus, neurosexist research practices can reinforce *essentialist beliefs* that men and women have inherent, unique, and natural attributes that make them two qualitatively different sexes, which then fuels the popularity of these beliefs within the media (Bluhm, 2013b; Fine, 2013). To encourage responsibility in neuroscience research, the subdiscipline of *neuroethics* recently emerged. Neuroethics prompts neuroscientists to reflect systematically on their perspectives and research practices and to consider the social, legal, and ethical implications of their findings (Clausen & Levy, 2015).

Neurosexism: Interpreting the findings from neuroscience research in ways that reinforce gender stereotypes without valid supporting evidence.

Evolutionary psychology: A theoretical approach that explains much of human thought and behavior in terms of genetically heritable adaptations that evolved because they helped ancestral humans survive and reproduce.

Biosocial constructionist theory: A theory that explains how biological differences between women and men lead to sex-based labor divisions in society, which then shape the development of role-relevant skills and gender stereotypes.

How Do Theories of Sex Differences Account for Nature and Nurture?

As noted earlier, scholars throughout history often favored either a biological or a social-environmental account of human development. Reflecting this either/or approach, some theories of sex differences focus more on biological influences (e.g., newborn temperaments or activity levels), and some focus more on environmental influences (e.g., parental socialization). Increasingly, however, gender researchers embrace interactionist models that acknowledge the roles of both types of factors. In this section, we will outline two important theories that attempt to explain the ultimate origins of sex differences and similarities: evolutionary psychology and biosocial constructionist theory. Each theory examines why people of different sexes exhibit certain traits, gender roles, and sex-related preferences. Because we will return to these theories repeatedly throughout this book, it is worth considering them in some detail. Note that although both theories consider nature and nurture, they differ in the emphasis placed on each factor.

Evolutionary Psychology

Using Charles Darwin's theory of evolution as a guiding framework, evolutionary psychologists assert that humans' physical, behavioral, and psychological attributes today are products of what our ancestors did to survive and reproduce hundreds of thousands of years ago. People vary genetically across many attributes, and sometimes these variations give some people advantages in terms of survival and reproduction. When this happens, advantageous variations more frequently get passed down genetically to future generations. But how does evolution shape sex and gender differences? According to the logic, sex differences should arise in domains in which women and men faced different *adaptive problems* in our evolutionary past (Buss & Schmitt, 2011). An adaptive problem is any environmental condition that challenges an organism's ability to survive or reproduce. Some adaptive problems affect people equally regardless of sex, and thus we would not expect sex differences to evolve in response to these challenges. However, women have faced unique challenges when it comes to pregnancy, birthing, and nursing offspring, and men have faced the unique challenge of *paternity uncertainty*, which is the problem of not knowing with certainty whether a given child is one's biological offspring. Therefore, according to evolutionary psychology, women and men should have evolved different psychological and behavioral tendencies in adaptation to these different challenges.

Natural selection is a process whereby heritable features increase or decrease an organism's survival, and **sexual selection** is a process in which heritable features make an organism more or less likely to reproduce and pass on its genes. According to evolutionary psychologists, sexual selection takes two main forms. First, in **intrasexual selection**, an individual may have a feature that gives it a competitive edge against other same-sex members in the contest for access to mates. For example, male bighorn sheep use their large curved horns to head-butt rivals in an attempt to gain status and access to mates. Second, in **intersexual selection**, an individual may have a feature that gives it an advantage by increasing its attractiveness to the other sex. For example, peacocks evolved elaborate colorful plumage presumably because peahens select the peacocks with the biggest, most elaborate feathers as mates. You can thus think of these two evolutionary processes in this way: Intersexual selection results in attractive ornamentation for enticing lovers while intrasexual selection produces weaponry for besting one's competitors.

Let's return now to the notion of sex differences in adaptive challenges. According to evolutionary psychology, one adaptive challenge faced by ancestral men was gaining access to mates. Whereas most ancestral women had a high likelihood of reproducing, ancestral men displayed much greater variance in reproductive success: High-status men at the top of social hierarchies often had multiple mates while those at the bottom of status hierarchies sometimes did not mate at all (M. Wilson & Daly, 1992). To adapt to this challenge, men should have evolved qualities that helped them during intrasexual competitions, including larger physical size, greater strength, and more competitive and aggressive tendencies. These qualities helped men to win competitions against other men, and men who won such competitions would have had more mating opportunities with women.

Next, an adaptive problem faced by women was the fact that women (and female members of many other species) must invest more in reproduction and parenting than males do. For women, successful child-rearing requires, at the very least, a 9-month commitment of energy, nutrients, and physical resources during pregnancy, plus an additional 1–3 years of lactation and nursing. Compare this to the brief investment required of men—potentially as brief as a single act of sexual intercourse—in order to produce a child. According to **parental investment theory**, the member of the species who invests

Natural selection: The evolutionary process by which heritable features that increase the likelihood of an organism's survival get passed down through genes.

Sexual selection: The evolutionary process by which heritable features that increase the likelihood of successful mating get passed down through genes.

Intrasexual selection: The process by which heritable features get passed down because they give an animal a competitive advantage in contests against other same-sex animals for access to mates.

Intersexual selection: The process by which heritable features get passed down because they give an animal an advantage by increasing its attractiveness to other-sex mates.

The horns of a bighorn sheep (left) are the product of intrasexual selection, allowing it to compete against other sheep in head-butting status competitions for access to mates. The peacock's elaborate plumage (right) is a product of intersexual selection, serving as an enticing ornament to attract peahens.

Source: © iStockPhoto.com/phototropic & iStockPhoto.com/galindr

Parental investment theory: Theory proposing that the sex that invests more in parenting (usually female) will be more selective in its choice of mates and will prefer mates who have social status and resources.

more in producing offspring and parenting will generally be more selective when choosing mates because they have more to lose from bad choices (Trivers, 1972). How does this relate to intersexual selection? Across cultures, women, on average, demonstrate a stronger preference than men do for high-status, resource-rich mates (Buss, 1989). Presumably, women evolved a preference for such mates because mates with higher social status have more access to resources and can therefore provide for offspring. Like the peacock's flashy tail, men's displays of resources and status are like ornaments that advertise their ability to provide a woman and child with resources.

At the same time, men across cultures demonstrate a stronger preference than women do for physically attractive and younger mates (Buss, 1989). Women's physical attractiveness and youth signals health, good genes, and fertility, and these qualities convey a greater likelihood of carrying healthy offspring to term. Moreover, because of paternity uncertainty, men should have evolved a heightened tendency toward sexual jealousy because men who jealously guard their mates against rivals have a lower risk of supporting offspring who do not carry their genes (for more on this topic, see Chapter 10, "Interpersonal Relationships"). So according to evolutionary psychologists, beauty, youth, and signs of sexual fidelity are ornaments that women can use to indicate their mating potential to men.

As noted, however, the evolutionary psychology perspective suggests that sex differences in mate preferences should only emerge for qualities that are relevant to sex differences in our ancestors' adaptive problems. And, in fact, the qualities that both sexes rank as most essential in a mate, including kindness, understanding, and sense of humor, show little evidence of sex differences (Hatfield & Sprecher, 1995). Moreover, evolutionary psychologists argue that environmental or cultural cues can evoke different adaptive cognitive modules that evolved in the ancestral environment (Gangstead, Haselton, & Buss, 2006). In other words, while genes (nature) are the driving force of evolution, the human mind is responsive to local environments (nurture) and varying contexts. For example, in cultures characterized by higher levels of gender equality, sex differences in preferences for a mate with earning potential are smaller (Eagly & Wood, 1999). This may reflect the fact that the reproductive success of women in more gender-egalitarian cultures is not as contingent on their ability to secure a resource-rich mate as it is in cultures where women have less access to education, jobs, and financial security.

Evolutionary psychology is both an incredibly influential and an incredibly controversial approach. One criticism of it centers on the scientific merit of the theory, in that its tenets tend to be speculative and difficult, if not impossible, to test empirically (Gannon, 2002). After all, we cannot go back 200,000 years, randomly assign some women to mate with high-status men and others to mate with low-status men, and observe how their offspring fare. Despite being speculative about the conditions of the distant past, however, the theory is still useful in generating testable predictions about present-day behavior, and we will consider many of these predictions throughout this text. Evolutionary psychology is also criticized as heteronormative in its emphasis on heterosexual mating preferences and reproductive sex. And yet, evolutionary psychologists have contributed several sophisticated hypotheses regarding the origins and maintenance of same-sex sexual activity and lesbian and gay sexual orientations, and we will consider these in depth in Chapter 9 ("Sexual Orientation and Sexuality").

Sidebar 3.4: Are Evolutionary Psychology and Feminism Incompatible?

Evolutionary psychologists and feminist psychologists often do not see eye to eye about sex differences, as each camp occupies a different location on the nature–nurture continuum. Evolutionary psychologists criticize feminist psychologists for overstating sex similarities and ignoring the role of biology in order to advance a feminist political agenda. Feminist psychologists criticize evolutionary psychologists for espousing an essentialist view of women and men, one that roots sex differences in biology and reinforces power differences and inequality between women and men (C. A. Smith & Konik, 2011). In 2011 and 2013, the debate between feminism and evolutionary psychology took center stage in special issues of the journal *Sex Roles*. A call for a more integrative approach emerged from this dialogue, with the recognition that positions that go too far in the direction of *either* nature *or* nurture do not accurately depict the complexity of sex and gender (Eagly & Wood, 2013). In their feminist evolutionary approach, Daniel Kruger and his colleagues called for greater critical thinking about sex and gender and for greater recognition of women as active agents in evolutionary processes, such as intrasexual and intersexual selection (Kruger, Fisher, & Wright, 2013).

Biosocial Constructionist Theory

Biosocial constructionist theory integrates the roles of distal (distant) biological factors and proximal (close) social and cultural influences in explaining sex differences and similarities in behavior and traits (W. Wood & Eagly, 2012). According to this theory, the key to understanding sex differences and similarities is the division of labor in societies (see Figure 3.4). All societies have to solve the problem of dividing labor, and most do this by assigning women and men different jobs. Why? Let's start with basic physical differences.

Men are, on average, larger and physically stronger than women, which tends to make them better suited for some types of physically demanding and dangerous occupations. In some ecologies, this might mean chopping down trees; in others, it might mean mining, deep-sea fishing, or big-game hunting. Women's reproductive activities (pregnancy and nursing) make it less efficient for them to do jobs that require them to be away from home for long periods of time and more efficient for them to perform domestic activities that keep them close to nursing infants and young children.

Figure 3.4 The Biosocial Constructionist Model of Sex Differences.

The biosocial constructionist model assumes that biological factors contribute to sex-based labor divisions, which then drive social factors, such as gender roles, socialization patterns, and gender stereotypes.

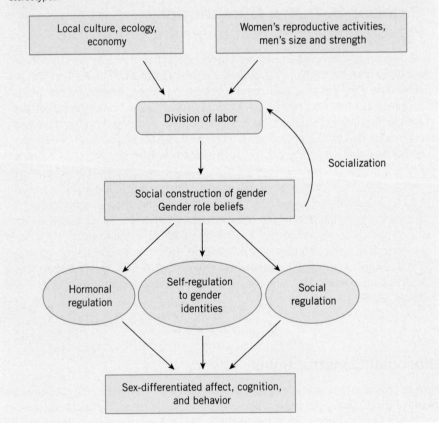

Source: W. Wood and Eagly (2012).

In other words, societies can function with greater efficiency when men do certain types of jobs and women do others. Two important implications follow from this gendered division of labor. First, men and women must acquire different skills, which children begin to learn early in life. Adults and peers socialize young girls to become caretakers and homemakers by providing rewards and encouragement for things like playing with dolls, taking care of younger siblings, or playing house. Adults and peers also teach young boys to become physically active risk-takers by rewarding them for bravery, rough-and-tumble play, and activities that foster physical skill development. Second, people form expectations about the qualities and abilities of men and women as a result of their socialized skills and gendered social roles. Because of their roles as primary caretakers of children, women are expected to be—and perceived as—more warm, emotional, and nurturing than men. Because of their roles as providers, men are expected to be—and perceived as—more independent, assertive, and risk-taking than women. According to biosocial constructionist theory, this is how gender stereotypes are formed, a topic we will examine in detail in Chapter 5 ("The Contents and Origins of Gender Stereotypes"). So gender role beliefs are learned, reinforced, and perpetuated through socialization and the practice of skills. These expectations tend to become internalized as well, meaning that people often regulate their own behaviors and interests to be consistent with gender role stereotypes.

Of course, as societies change, the types of occupations that women and men do change as well. In contemporary Western, industrialized societies, most people do not work in the fields or hunt big game all day. Advances in technology have led to decreases in some physically demanding jobs and to increases in more cognitively oriented jobs, with a trend toward women and men doing more similar jobs. In some societies, the introduction of birth control allows women to delay or forgo having children, just as breast pumps and baby formula now allow men to assume more active roles in child-rearing, compared with generations past. According to the biosocial constructionist theory, these changes should lead to different (and more similar) skills and expectations for women and men and, consequently, to changes in gender stereotypes. Thus, this theory emphasizes not only biological differences between women and men that lead to gendered labor divisions but also more immediate environmental influences that shape gender roles and stereotypes.

Girls are encouraged to learn caretaking skills early in life by, for example, taking care of dolls.

Note that this leads to a divergence between evolutionary theory and the biosocial constructionist perspective. Evolutionary theorists tend to view the human brain as a fossil that represents adaptations to conditions that occurred tens of thousands of years ago, which means that recent changes to occupational or social roles should not change our fundamental psychology much. Moreover, evolutionary psychologists propose that sex differences in tendencies such as mating preferences, competitiveness, sexual jealousy, and nurturance are genetically coded at the species level and therefore are unlikely to change over the short term. And yet, as noted earlier, evolutionary psychologists do view the brain as flexibly adaptive to local contexts and environments (Gangstead et al., 2006). In contrast, biosocial constructionist theory assumes that while some *biological* sex differences are coded in genes, sex differences in *psychological* factors, such as personality traits, mating preferences, and jealousy, are not genetically heritable. Therefore, this theory predicts that changes in social roles can create fairly rapid changes to the psychology of men and women, and these can lead rather rapidly to changes in cultural gender stereotypes. Thus, as noted earlier, the divergence between these theories boils down to one of emphasis: Evolutionary psychology primarily emphasizes biology while acknowledging the essential role of environments, and biosocial constructionists primarily emphasize the environment while acknowledging the essential role of biology. However, both approaches have a weakness in common in that they conceptualize sex and gender as binary categories, which, as we discussed earlier, oversimplifies reality.

Stop and Think

Consider the major changes to the workforce that occurred in the United States and similar nations as women entered the workforce in record numbers beginning in the second half of the 20th century. How might these changes shape the psychology of women and men according to the biosocial constructionist theory? What about according to evolutionary theory?

So what should a comprehensive theory of sex differences and similarities look like? First, it should be *interactionist*, recognizing the influences of both nature and nurture. Second, it should address how physical and biological differences (e.g., in size, strength, and reproductive capabilities) among the sexes may produce different behaviors and traits. In doing so, however, it should consider a range of physical and biological differences, including those that give rise to intersexuality. It should also consider the factors that motivate not just heterosexual, reproductive mating but also same-sex behaviors and sexuality, which are central in both human and nonhuman animal species. Finally, a comprehensive theory should also acknowledge that the environment can alter physiology and biology in ways that, although not necessarily noticeable to the naked eye, can have significant consequences (think back to the discussion of epigenetics). As we have tried to emphasize throughout this chapter, biological and social factors are inextricably intertwined and flexibly responsive to one another: Biology shapes our social and cultural experiences, and sociocultural factors shape our biology. We encourage you to keep these ideas in mind not only as you read this book but also as you observe sex and gender in your daily life. Remember—it's not "nature *or* nurture" but "nature *and* nurture."

CHAPTER SUMMARY

3.1 Explain how nature and nurture interactively contribute to the development of sex and gender.

Determining the relative contributions of nature (biological factors) and nurture (environmental factors) in shaping sex and gender is challenging. Scholars today generally recognize that both nature *and* nurture play complex, interconnected roles in creating and shaping sex and gender. In gene-by-environment interactions, a genetic effect on behavior only emerges under certain environmental circumstances. Epigenetics is the study of the biological mechanisms that guide whether or not certain genes get activated. Life experiences can influence epigenetic environments and thus genetic expression. Thus, although biological and sociocultural factors are conceptually independent, they interact in ways that make them difficult to disentangle.

3.2 Explain how chromosomes, genes, and hormones shape sex differentiation in both typical and atypical (intersex) cases.

Sexual differentiation begins at conception, when a sperm carrying either an X (female) or Y (male) chromosome fertilizes an egg. For the first 6 weeks of life, male and female embryos remain largely undifferentiated, having the same internal and external structures. Female sex is the biological default, but a gene called SRY on the Y chromosome instructs the body to produce androgenizing hormones that cause male gonads (testes) to develop. In the absence of the SRY gene, female gonads (ovaries) develop. The external genitalia remain undifferentiated until about the 12th week of gestation, when the penis and scrotum or the clitoris and labia typically develop.

Children are sometimes born with sex-atypical genes or hormones that can produce intersex conditions, in which the biological components of sex (chromosomes, hormones, genitals, and internal and external sex organs) do not align consistently as either male or female. Differences from the typical XX or XY chromosome pair include XO (Turner's syndrome), XXX (triple X syndrome), XXY (Klinefelter syndrome), and XYY (Jacob's syndrome). These intersex conditions suggest that the presence of a Y chromosome strongly predicts having a male appearance and gender identity while the absence of a Y chromosome strongly predicts having a female appearance and gender identity. But hormones can override chromosomes in shaping gender identity. Genetic females (XX) who overmanufacture androgens, a condition called congenital adrenal hyperplasia (CAH), sometimes have masculinized external genitalia (but female internal reproductive organs) and adopt male gender identities. Conversely, genetic males (XY) who are unable to respond to androgens, a condition called complete androgen insensitivity syndrome (CAIS), often have an outward female appearance and adopt female gender identities.

3.3 Analyze the biological and sociocultural factors that shape sex assignment and gender identity.

Although people often equate sex with nature and gender with nurture, even "biological" sex is a social construction. That is, cultures define and give meaning to the categories of sex. Many cultures acknowledge only two sexes, male and female, even though biological sex extends beyond this binary to include other variations. In these cultures, intersex or transgender individuals whose identities go beyond the sex binary may be shunned, stigmatized, or pressured to conform to conventional notions of sex. Parents often elect for their intersex newborns to undergo surgery to bring their physiology in line with their optimal sex, as defined by doctors. Transgender individuals sometimes experience gender dysphoria, which is clinically significant levels of distress arising from the discrepancy between their assigned sex at birth and their psychological gender identity. Some—though not all—transgender individuals choose to undergo gender confirming procedures, including hormone treatments or surgery, to bring congruence between their physiology and their psychological gender identity.

3.4 Evaluate evidence for sex differences in the brain and the prevalence of neurosexism.

There are small but reliable sex differences in the structure of the brain. Some brain regions, such as in the hippocampus and the amygdala, tend to be larger or denser in male brains, whereas other brain regions, such as the frontal pole cortex, tend to be larger or denser in female brains. Researchers debate the meaning and importance of these differences. It is important to understand that structural sex differences in brains are not necessarily innate. Adults may create different environments for newborn girls and boys, which—due to the malleability of the brain—can produce or enlarge structural sex differences in the brain. Neurosexism occurs when people interpret the findings of neuroscience research in ways that reinforce gender stereotypes without valid supporting evidence.

3.5 Examine the roles of nature and nurture in theories of the origins of sex differences.

Theories that explain the origins of sex differences and similarities increasingly incorporate both nature and nurture. Evolutionary theories assume that much of human thought and behavior reflects adaptive psychological mechanisms that helped our ancestors survive and reproduce. Biosocial constructionist theory argues that biological differences lead to a division of labor between the sexes. This division of labor between the sexes, in turn, leads to the socialization and acquisition of different skills and behaviors in boys/men and girls/women. Differing roles then create different expectations and self-perceptions of male and female behavior.

Test Your Knowledge: True or False?

3.1. Sex (whether a person is male, female, or other) is shaped entirely by biological factors. (False: Sex is shaped by complex interactions between nature and nurture.) [p. 78]

3.2. Genetic female individuals who get exposed to high levels of androgens in utero can appear masculine at birth and are sometimes raised as boys. (True) [p. 84]

3.3. All female individuals have an XX pair of chromosomes, and all male individuals have an XY pair. (False: While most girls have XX pairs and most boys have XY pairs, some female-identifying and male-identifying individuals have different combinations of chromosomes.) [p. 87]

3.4. From twin studies, we know that gender identity is determined primarily by socialization (nurture). (False: Twin studies indicate that gender identity is determined by a combination of genetic and environmental factors.) [p. 95]

3.5. Within the past decade, neuroscientists identified structural sex differences in the brain and linked them directly to specific psychological sex differences. (False: Neuroscientists do not fully understand the connections between brain structure and function, and hypotheses about human sex differences in brain functions remain speculative.) [p. 84]

David and Storm Stocker-Witterick.

Source: Bernard Weil/Toronto Star/Getty Images

Test Your Knowledge: True or False?

4.1 Parents are generally accurate in their perceptions of sex differences in infant boys' and girls' physical abilities.

4.2 By calling attention to sex in the classroom (e.g., referring to "girls and boys" rather than "children"), teachers can increase children's gender stereotyping and their preferences for members of their own sex.

4.3 Children who display cross-sex play preferences in childhood (e.g., girls who prefer rough-and-tumble play and boys who prefer dolls) are no more likely than other children to identify as gay or lesbian later in life.

4.4 Young women are more likely than young men to post about relationships on social network sites while young men are more likely than young women to post about abstract societal issues.

4.5 As people enter middle and late adulthood, gender becomes a less central part of the self.

Gender Development

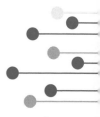

Key Concepts

How Central Are Sex and Gender in Early Development?

What Are the Major Theoretical Approaches to Gender Development?

Social Learning Theories and Sources of Socialization

Parents

Siblings

Teachers and Peers

Media

Debate: Should Toys Be Marketed as Gender Neutral?

Cognitive Theories

Cognitive-Developmental Theory

Gender Schema Theory

Developmental Intergroup Theory

Gender Self-Socialization Model

Evaluating Social Learning and Cognitive Theories

What Are the Experiences of Gender-Nonconforming Children?

Biological and Social Contributions to Gender

Nonconformity

Nonconforming Identities and Milestones

How Do Sex and Gender Shape Development in Adolescence and Emerging Adulthood?

Puberty and the Transition to Young Adulthood

Relationships With Parents

Friendship, Dating, and Social Networking

Gendered Self-Views Across Time and Cultures

How Do Sex and Gender Shape Development in Middle and Later Adulthood?

Cultural Ideals of Womanhood and Manhood

Gendered Self-Views

Women's Gender Advantage?

The Double Standard of Aging

Learning Objectives

Students who read this chapter should be able to do the following:

4.1 Explain how gender stereotypes influence expectant parents and early child development.

4.2 Differentiate social learning and cognitive theories of gender development.

4.3 Describe the experiences of gender-nonconforming children and the factors underlying gender nonconformity in childhood.

4.4 Explain how sex and gender influence biological, social, and identity changes in adolescence and emerging adulthood.

4.5 Evaluate how cultural ideals and gender shape the experiences of women and men in middle and late adulthood.

Gender Development

In 2011, the *Toronto Star* published a story about Canadian parents David Stocker and Kathy Witterick, who decided to raise their baby, Storm, in a gender-neutral way. Though they knew Storm's sex at birth, David and Kathy did not publicly disclose this information. Instead, just as they did with Storm's older siblings, Jazz and Kio, they allowed Storm to select the gender identity (if any) that felt right. To explain their choice to friends and family, David and Kathy sent an e-mail: "We've decided not to share Storm's sex for now—a tribute to freedom and choice in place of limitation, a stand up to what the world could become in Storm's lifetime (a more progressive place? . . .)." This decision elicited strong opinions from others. Friends criticized David and Kathy, worried that Storm would be bullied. Some strangers sent angry letters or accused them of child abuse; still others rallied around Storm's family, offering them support and encouragement. Several years after the story first made headlines, a follow-up story revealed that Storm identifies as a girl (Botelho-Urbanski, 2016). For their part, David and Kathy remain happy with their decision to allow their children to choose their gender. In reflection, Kathy notes, "Now that I have that exposure I realize what a great choice we made. At the time, I didn't know it was such a great choice" (Poisson, 2013).

Why do some people have such strong, negative reactions to gender-neutral parenting? What effects might this parenting approach have on children like Storm? It is difficult to pinpoint the psychological effects of raising a child without gender roles and norms because there are so few examples of it. One common concern is that children raised without gender will be confused about their gender identity later in life. However, given that most transgender, nonbinary, and agender people are initially socialized *with* a gender, such concerns are probably unwarranted: Just as being socialized to adopt a given gender identity cannot ensure that such adoption will occur, being socialized without a gender identity does not necessarily produce confusion. As you read in Chapter 3 ("The Nature and Nurture of Sex and Gender"), biological and social factors interact in complex ways to produce gender identity, and we lack evidence that parenting can successfully override a child's sense of their gender.

This chapter is about how people come to be gendered beings, from birth through adulthood. What role does gender play in shaping infants, children, adolescents, and adults? Socialization is a big part of the picture, but so is the child's maturing brain, which affords increasingly sophisticated attempts to understand the world through the lens of gender. Often, developmental psychology focuses on childhood, but gender development does not stop when childhood does. In this chapter, we will consider the role of gender in people's behaviors, relationships, and self-views throughout life. Note, however, that several of the themes of adulthood that we touch upon here briefly, such as relationships, work and home, and physical and psychological health, are covered more extensively in later chapters of this book.

How Central Are Sex and Gender in Early Development?

Let's face it: As cute as newborn babies are, they are pretty nondescript. In infancy, clad only in a diaper, most infants are similar in size and appearance, have few distinguishing traits, and spend most of their time sleeping, crying, or sucking on things. Despite this, parents attribute all sorts of unique qualities to their newborns, and sex is one of the main cues that they use. Proud parents project gender onto their infants with proclamations such as "What a strong grip he has!" and "She's got such delicate features!" In one study from the early 1970s, researchers asked 30 pairs of parents to rate their newborn infants on adjectives like "strong versus weak" and "small versus large." The researchers also measured the babies on various physical characteristics and found no sex differences. Although the male and female babies were physically indistinguishable, their parents rated them differently. Parents of boys rated their babies as stronger, larger, more alert, and more coordinated than parents of girls (J. Z. Rubin, Provenzano, & Luria, 1974). This study was replicated in the 1990s, with similar results (Karraker, Vogel, & Lake, 1995). Thus, parents engage in gender stereotyping shortly after the birth of their infants. In doing so, parents help to create gender, not only in a social sense but in a biological sense as well: As you may recall from Chapter 3, the gendered actions that parents encourage from children can shape children's brain development (Eliot, 2009).

Even before birth, a child's sex is often of central importance. Expectant parents may wish to know the sex of a child before birth so they can pick out gender-typical clothes, decorate the infant's room, and select names. Most cultures have folk wisdoms about determining the sex of a fetus, such as consulting the Chinese lunar calendar or dangling a ring on a chain over the pregnant woman's belly and observing how it swings. When a new child arrives, acquaintances most commonly ask about the baby's sex. Today, some parents throw a "gender reveal" party during which they disclose and then celebrate their child's sex with friends and family (Sirois, 2016). In contrast, parents of intersex children report feeling at a loss for how to describe their newborn without being able to use the language of the sex/gender binary (Gough, Weyman, Alderson, Butler, & Stoner, 2008).

Not only does assigned sex influence the way adults and others socialize children, but sex and gender are also important schemas that children use to organize and make sense of their worlds. Sex is the first social category that infants recognize, as early as 3 months of age (P. C. Quinn, Yahr, Kuhn, Slater, & Pascalis, 2002), and by age 2, some toddlers make associations between people's sex and the gender-typed activities that they perform (Poulin-Dubois & Serbin, 2006). From that point on, children grow increasingly sophisticated in their beliefs about sex and gender. In this chapter, we will consider gender development from a number of theoretical perspectives, some of which emphasize external forces that socialize children into gendered beings, and some of which emphasize children's changing cognitive understanding of the world and themselves. Although we will address biology in this chapter, our primary focus is on sociocultural influences.

What Are the Major Theoretical Approaches to Gender Development?

Major theories of gender development fall into two broad categories: social learning theories and cognitive theories. To a large degree, both types of theories address a set of common questions about how children acquire gendered beliefs and preferences. For instance, they both address the acquisition of gender identity (the sense of belonging to a sex category), gender stereotypes (beliefs about the qualities associated with people of

Social learning theories: Theories that propose that children learn gendered beliefs, behaviors, and preferences by observing and imitating models and by receiving reinforcement and punishment from others.

different sexes), gendered self-views (beliefs about the self along masculine and feminine trait dimensions), gender roles (sets of behaviors associated with gender), gendered preferences (such as toy and play activity preferences), and gender-based prejudices (positive or negative feelings about people of different sexes). These theories differ, however, in their assumptions about how gender development unfolds and which factors drive it. **Social learning theories** emphasize how external factors, such as socialization agents (e.g., parents, peers, and the media), shape children's gender development while **cognitive theories** emphasize how children's growing cognitive abilities lead them to develop gender. In this section, we cover the main points of several social learning and cognitive theories (see Table 4.1 for a summary).

Table 4.1 **Major Theories of Childhood Gender Development.** While social learning theory emphasizes the role of external socializing agents and experiences in children's gender development, cognitive theories emphasize the role of children's cognitive abilities and interpretations in guiding their gender development.

Theoretical Approach	Main Concepts	Primary Assumptions
Social learning theory	Sex typing, reinforcement, punishment, observation and imitation, models	Children learn gendered beliefs and preferences (sex typing) by observing and imitating models and by receiving reinforcement and punishment. Behaviors and the rewards they elicit cause children to develop gender beliefs (gender identity, stereotypes, and self-views).
Cognitive-developmental theory	Gender identity, gender stability, gender constancy	Children learn gendered beliefs and preferences as they mature cognitively through a series of stages (gender identity, gender stability, and gender constancy). A cognitive understanding of gender identity causes children to develop other aspects of gender (gender roles, self-views, and stereotypes).
Gender schema theory	Gender schemas, gender schematic and gender aschematic processing	Children develop gender schemas that filter and organize how they interpret, process, and remember gender-relevant information. There are individual differences in the extent to which children rely on their gender schemas to understand the world, with some people being gender schematic and others gender aschematic.
Developmental in-group theory	Groups, in-group bias	Once children identify with a given gender in-group, they evaluate it more positively than gender out-groups. Children learn early on that sex is a highly meaningful social group; adults can influence children's stereotyping and in-group biases by drawing more or less attention to sex as a category.

Theoretical Approach	Main Concepts	Primary Assumptions
Gender self-socialization model	Gender identity, gender stereotypes, gendered self-views, cognitive consistency	Gender identity, gender stereotypes, and gendered self-views are all cognitive associations that differ in strength. Because of people's need for cognitive consistency, the strength of each association is influenced by the strength of the other two associations. For instance, having a strong gender identity ("I am a girl") and endorsing gender stereotypes more strongly ("Girls are friendly") should lead one to develop gendered self-views ("I am friendly").

Sidebar 4.1: Penis or Womb Envy?

In one of the earliest influential theories of gender development, Sigmund Freud's *psychosexual stage theory*, Freud proposed that children identify with and model themselves after their same-sex parent as a means of resolving unconscious anxieties about sexual urges, resentment and jealousy, and punishment concerns. Karen Horney, a psychoanalytic theorist and contemporary of Freud's, challenged some of his ideas about gender. For instance, Freud proposed that young girls develop penis envy when they discover that they lack a penis, and this envy contributes to the unconscious anxiety that they must resolve through identification with the mother. In contrast, Horney proposed that girls do not desire a penis per se, but instead they desire what the penis symbolizes: men's greater social status than women's. Horney further proposed that boys experience womb envy, or jealousy of women's ability to bear children. To compensate for this lack, boys and men strive to achieve in other realms, which explains why achievement is so central to the male gender role. While some credit Horney as the founder of feminist psychology (Paris, 1994) and regard Freud as one of the most influential thinkers of the 20th century, many aspects of psychoanalytic theory do not hold up to empirical scrutiny.

Cognitive theories: Theories that propose that children learn gender by progressing through a series of increasingly sophisticated cognitive stages and that the emergence of sex-typed cognitions causes children to learn sex-typed behaviors and preferences.

Sex typing: In social learning theories, the processes by which individuals acquire gendered behavior patterns.

Social Learning Theories and Sources of Socialization

Social learning theories of gender development grew out of behaviorist learning theories that dominated psychology in the first half of the 20th century and emphasized direct learning though reward and punishment and indirect learning through observation and imitation of others. Walter Mischel (1966), the first theorist to apply social learning theory to gender development, defined **sex typing** as the processes by which individuals acquire gendered behavior patterns. According to social learning theory, certain behaviors elicit different patterns of reward and punishment for children of different sexes. For example, a boy might observe his father roughhousing with his brother, imitate this aggressive behavior, and receive praise from his parents. In contrast, a girl might be ignored or even reprimanded for the same aggressive behavior. Children learn which

Reinforcement:
Any response
following a behavior
that increases the
likelihood of the
behavior occurring
again.

Punishment: Any
response following
a behavior that
decreases the
likelihood of the
behavior occurring
again.

Model: In social
learning theories,
a person who
performs a behavior
that is observed
and later imitated
by a learner.

**Cross-sex
behavior:**
Behavior that is
strongly associated
with a sex group
other than one's
own.

behaviors are associated with their sex through these processes of observation, imitation, **reinforcement**, and **punishment**. Reinforcement is any response following a behavior that increases the likelihood of the behavior occurring again. Conversely, punishment is any response that decreases the likelihood of a given behavior recurring. Reinforcement and punishment can be obvious things, such as praise ("Good girl!") or a smack on the hand, but they can also be quite subtle: A simple smile can communicate that a certain behavior is desired while withdrawing attention can serve as an effective punishment. Importantly, social learning theories posit that behaviors and the rewards they elicit *cause* children to develop gender beliefs and preferences. That is, a child observes that he receives rewards for doing "boy things" and concludes that he must be a boy (C. L. Martin, Ruble, & Szkrybalo, 2002). Of course, children typically have many **models** to observe and imitate and many sources of rewards and punishments for their behavior. In the following sections, we outline several major socialization agents, including those within the family (parents and siblings) as well those outside the family (teachers, peers, and the media).

Parents. Parents, often as the first major source of socialization for children, teach gender to children in several ways. First, parents serve as models of expected gender roles and behaviors. For example, children of fathers who are actively involved in childcare tend to hold less traditional gender stereotypes, presumably because their fathers model nurturing as well as agentic behaviors (Deutsch, Servis, & Payne, 2001). Similarly, children raised by same-sex parents are less likely to endorse certain gender stereotypes than children raised by heterosexual parents (Fulcher, Sutfin, & Patterson, 2008), likely because of their exposure to nontraditional gender arrangements in the home. Second, parents hold gender stereotypes that may translate into different parenting practices. For instance, in one study, 11-month-old girls and boys displayed no sex differences in their crawling abilities; still, mothers estimated that their sons could crawl down steeper slopes than their daughters (Mondschein, Adolph, & Tamis-LeMonda, 2000). If parents hold the gender stereotype that boys are more physically agile and strong than girls, they may be more willing to let sons than daughters take physical risks.

Third, parents are an important source of reward and punishment for children's sex-typed activities. One meta-analysis of 172 studies conducted in Western cultures found that parents treated boys and girls very similarly, except when it comes to encouraging sex-typical preferences and activities (Lytton & Romney, 1991). Parents shape young children's gendered interests through the room décor, clothing, toys, and play activities that they encourage and reinforce. In older children, parents encourage sex-typical behavior by directing sons and daughters toward different types of activities and academic interests and through differential allocation of household chores (McHale, Crouter, & Whiteman, 2003). In fact, one trend observed around the world is that parents assign girls, compared with boys, more household chores, such as cleaning, cooking, and caring for younger siblings (Larson & Verma, 1999). In this sense, parents socialize daughters for homemaker and caregiver roles.

Interestingly, parents generally allow boys less flexibility than girls to pursue **cross-sex behavior**, or behavior associated with the other sex (Lytton & Romney, 1991). Moreover, fathers, as compared with mothers, tend to be less tolerant of female-typed activities in sons. In a classic illustration of this, Judith Langlois and Chris Downs (1980) had children engage in both sex-typical and cross-sex play activities while either their mother or their father watched. When boys did sex-typical play (e.g., playing with toy trucks and dressing in a fireman's uniform), fathers got on the floor and played with them, giving them lots of reinforcement. In contrast, when boys did cross-sex play (e.g., playing with a tea set and dressing in a princess costume), fathers largely ignored them. By withdrawing attention, parents can give powerful messages about the sorts of activities and interests that children ought (and ought not) to have.

Stop and Think

What do you think would happen if Langlois and Downs's (1980) study were replicated today? Would *fathers show similar levels of disinterest in their sons' sex-atypical play? Why or why not?*

Aside from these different practices of gender role socialization, cultural differences exist in the extent to which parents and the wider culture value girls and boys. Some cultures in North Africa, South and East Asia, and the Middle East tend to value boys more because they carry on the family name and bring the economic benefits of a wife and her dowry into the family. In contrast, girls in these cultures may be viewed as an economic burden because their dowries will go to another family. These cultures show a male bias by giving boys better nutrition and health care and more educational opportunities, by selectively aborting female fetuses or killing or abandoning infant girls, and by selling young girls into marriage (Rafferty, 2013). Even in more gender-egalitarian nations, such as the United States, boys tend to receive preferential treatment when families' economic resources are tight. For instance, among U.S. families with limited economic resources, sons are more likely than daughters to receive developmentally beneficial (but costly) activities, such as extra classes, lessons, and sports involvement (McHale et al., 2003).

Sidebar 4.2: 100 Million Missing Girls?

In cultures that value sons over daughters, the practices of sex-selective abortion and infanticide can lead to skewed **sex ratios** (the numbers of men per woman in a population). Consider China, which implemented a policy in 1980 limiting the number of children that couples could have to only one (the one-child policy). Because boys tend to be valued more than girls in China, the one-child policy resulted in disproportionate rates of abortion and infanticide of female infants. According to a 2014 report by UNICEF, the sex ratio at birth in China by 1982 was 109 male infants to 100 female infants (109:100), and this ratio rose to 118:100 by 2010. Economist Amartya Sen (1990) estimated that selective abortion and infanticide resulted in 100 million girls "missing" from the global population. However, a study conducted in 2016 indicated that up to 25 million of these girls may be alive: In rural villages in China, where it was harder for officials to enforce the one-child policy, families often did not report the births of daughters and allowed them to remain unregistered until they were of marriage age (Shi & Kennedy, 2016). In 2015, the Chinese government ended its one-child policy, allowing Chinese couples to have two children. How do you think this will influence China's sex ratio?

Sex ratio: The number of men per woman in a given population or locale.

What about same-sex parents? If parents are a source of children's gender role development, does it make a difference what sex they are? Some people express concerns that the children of same-sex parents will have trouble developing a gender identity or that the lack of parents of both sexes will deprive them of important gender role models. These fears appear unwarranted, however, as research consistently shows that gender identities, gender role behaviors, and sexual orientations develop in similar ways among children of gay and straight parents (Patterson, 2004). In fact, evidence from studies conducted in both the United States and Europe indicates that, in comparison with children of heterosexual parents, children of same-sex parents do not differ in psychological adjustment or well-being (Patterson, 2006). One exception, noted earlier, is that children of same-sex parents endorse fewer gender stereotypes than children raised by heterosexual parents (Fulcher et al., 2008).

A related question concerns the gender socialization of children raised in single-parent households. Although there is relatively little research on the topic, existing studies show no obvious differences in the gender development of children raised in single-parent versus two-parent households. For example, one meta-analysis that compared children in father-absent versus father-present families found small effects and inconsistent patterns for boys: Preschool boys from father-absent homes were less sex typed than those from father-present families, but this pattern was reversed among older boys (Stevenson & Black, 1988). Another study found that parents in single-parent families tend to socialize children in a more gender-egalitarian manner than parents in two-parent families (Leve & Fagot, 1997). This may occur because single parents themselves often must adopt both male-typed (financial provider) and female-typed (caregiver) roles. Perhaps adopting gender-egalitarian values can assist single parents in fulfilling these dual parenting roles, and their egalitarian values are then reflected in their gender socialization of children.

Note that parents not only influence children, but children influence parents as well (Pomerantz, Ng, & Wang, 2004). These patterns of mutual influence are called **parent–child interactions**, and they can take a couple of different forms. First, children's temperaments can influence how parents treat them. For example, girls tend to respond better than boys do to gentle discipline, which can help to explain why parents use harsher discipline with boys than girls. Second, even when parents treat male and female children similarly, children may respond differently to such treatment. For example, boys tend to be more reluctant than girls to accept socialization attempts from their parents. Although most research focuses on parents as socialization agents, gender socialization is a two-way street. Children may not have as much power as their parents do, but they can be active players in their own socialization.

Siblings. For many young children, siblings represent a daily source of gender messages. Consider a child with older brothers versus older sisters. Would you expect the child to be exposed to different gender messages, have access to different types of toys, and observe different gender modeling? In one study, researchers examined more than 5,000 preschoolers, some with older brothers, some with older sisters, and some without siblings (Rust, Golombok, Hines, & Johnston, 2000). Girls with older sisters and boys with older brothers displayed the most traditionally sex-typical behaviors. Boys and girls with cross-sex older siblings displayed the least traditionally sex-typical behaviors, and children without siblings were somewhere in the middle. These patterns suggest that older siblings influence children's gender role development. Of course, these data are correlational, and causation therefore cannot be determined.

Teachers and peers. In many cultures, children spend several hours each day at school, where teachers can have a substantial impact on gender development. Not only do teachers serve as models of gendered behavior, they can also influence children's adoption of gender stereotypes by drawing attention to sex as a category. If teachers regularly use gendered language (e.g., by saying, "Good morning, boys and girls," instead of "Good morning, children") or draw attention to sex (e.g., lining children up according to sex), this can encourage children to endorse gender stereotypes more strongly and favor their own sex group over others. You'll read more about this in the upcoming section on *developmental intergroup theory.*

With regard to peers, children's peer and friendship circles tend to be quite sex segregated. Beginning at about age 3, most children show an increasing preference for peers and friends of their own sex, and this lasts until about puberty (C. L. Martin & Ruble, 2004). By the age of about 5 or 6, children spend about 70%–75% of their unsupervised free time in the company of same-sex peers, with most of the rest of the time in mixed-sex groups. Similar patterns of sex segregation are observed among children of different races and ethnicities in the United States (Halim, Ruble, Tamis-LeMonda, & Shrout, 2013) and in cultures around the world (Whiting & Edwards, 1988). Interestingly, segregation by sex seems to be chosen and preferred by children. In school settings, even when teachers encourage mixed-sex play, children choose to spend most of their time with same-sex playmates (Fabes, Martin, & Hanish, 2003).

What role might sex segregation have in children's gender socialization? Some posit that increasing exposure to same-sex peers as models, combined with reinforcement from such peers, ultimately leads children to adopt more sex-typical behavior and reduce their cross-sex behavior. Over time, peer socialization can produce sex differences in behavior, relationship styles, and even emotional expressions. To illustrate, a study that tracked children over a 1-year period found that girls who spent more time interacting with same-sex peers showed increases in their expressions of sadness, and boys who spent more time interacting with same-sex peers increased their expressions of anger (Lindsey, 2016). This suggests that peers act as socialization agents who teach one another sex-typical ways of expressing emotion.

Media. Of course, children gain exposure to many models beyond their families, teachers, and peers. In fact, the average child in the United States watches 3 hours of television per day and uses other media (e.g., books, video games, and the Internet) for an additional

3 hours per day (APA, 2007). Across industrialized nations in North America, East Asia, and Europe, television viewing constitutes the largest category of media use among children, with boys consistently spending more time, on average, watching television than girls (Larson & Verma, 1999). Think about the many gender models that children see in cartoons, advertisements, books, fairy tales, movies, and games. What messages do children get from these media? One answer may be that what children *don't* see is just as important as what they *do* see, and girls and women are relatively less visible in much of children's media. Take books, for instance. In one analysis of over 5,600 children's books published between 1900 and 2000, 57% of main characters were male while only 31% were female. By the 1990s, there was greater parity in gender representation, but male characters were still more common (McCabe, Fairchild, Grauerholz, Pescosolido, & Tope, 2011). Children's television shows also underrepresent female characters. One study examined the contents of children's fictional television programs in 24 countries around the world and found that only 32% of all lead characters were female while 68% were male (Götz et al., 2008). As shown in Figure 4.1, gender bias in favor of male main characters is even more pronounced when the characters are nonhuman animals, monsters, objects, and robots. Video games and coloring books also portray more male than female lead characters (M. C. R. Burgess, Stermer, & Burgess, 2007; Fitzpatrick & McPherson, 2010).

Figure 4.1 Sex of Lead Characters in Children's Television.

As you can see, across 6,375 fictional children's television programs in 24 countries, the percentages of male lead characters far outweigh the percentages of female lead characters. The sex differences are even larger for nonhuman characters than for human characters.

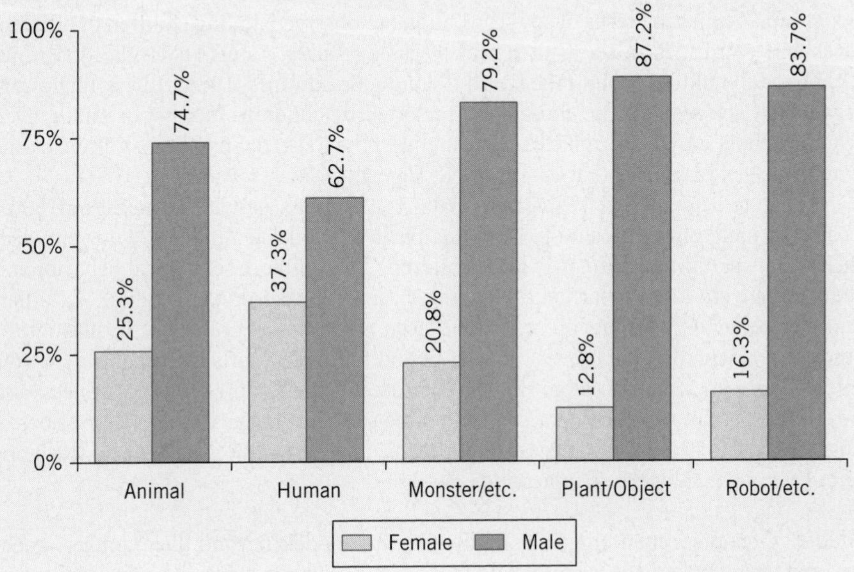

Source: Götz et al. (2008).

Beyond differences in the visibility of female and male characters, decades' worth of research documents how children's entertainment reinforces gender stereotypes. Television programs and advertisements portray male characters in more active and leadership roles than female characters (Götz et al., 2008; Kahlenberg & Hein, 2010). In contrast, they more often portray female characters in a sexualized manner and as having a thin body (APA, 2007; Götz et al., 2008). Researchers know relatively little about children's consumption of entertainment media in nonindustrialized and rural cultures, where there is less access to television, radio, and the Internet (Larson & Verma, 1999). How do you think cultural differences in access to media might influence the development of children's gender stereotypes in industrialized versus nonindustrialized cultures?

Stop and Think

Consider the ways in which children's media portray female and male lead characters. How can we know whether gender representations in the media directly influence children's gender development? What type of study would you have to conduct to test the hypothesis that gender images in children's entertainment influence children's gender development?

Another gender stereotype that is regularly modeled in the media regards toy preferences. As one of the strongest, most consistent sex differences in childhood, sex-typed toy preferences emerge across cultures. By age 2, girls tend to prefer playing with dolls and household objects, and boys prefer cars, trucks, and weapons (A. Campbell, Shirley, & Caygill, 2002). But how much of this reflects children's natural preferences versus their exposure to media images and toy ads?

Although a difficult question to answer, evidence suggests that preferences for sex-typical toys emerge early in life. Studies of infants often use a technique called **preferential looking** that consists of showing infants two different things and examining how much time they spend looking at each one. Researchers find that infants as young as 3–8 months of age prefer looking at sex-typical toys over sex-atypical ones (G. M Alexander, Wilcox, & Woods, 2009). Moreover, toy and play preferences have a moderate genetic component (Hines, 2013), and sex differences in toy preferences are not unique to humans: Rhesus monkeys, who lack any exposure to children's entertainment media, display toy preferences based on sex that are similar to children's preferences (Hassett, Siebert, & Wallen, 2008). Still, while children spend about 20% of their play time with sex-typical toys and only about 5% of play time with sex-atypical toys, most of their play time, by far (75%), is spent with gender-neutral toys such as crayons and puzzles (Fagot, Rodgers, & Leinbach, 2000). Given that children seem to prefer gender-neutral toys over all other toys, why bother marketing toys for children in ways that can potentially reinforce gender stereotypes? We address this question in "Debate: Should Toys Be Marketed as Gender Neutral?"

Preferential looking: A method for determining preferences among preverbal infants that involves showing them two different objects or stimuli and examining how much time they spend looking at each one.

Walk into the toy section of a department store, and you will likely find separate toy aisles for girls and boys. Now, step back, and look at the colors. In many toy sections, you will notice an explosion of pinks, lavenders, and pastels in some aisles and bright blues, blacks, and reds in other aisles. Some argue that gender-typed marketing of toys is unnecessary and even harmful because it perpetuates stereotypes that can ultimately lead to sex differences in competencies and occupational choices. Why limit children's options by suggesting that only girls can play with dolls and only boys can play with toy cars?

In 2012, Europe's largest toy company, Top-Toy, began advertising toys in a gender-neutral way (Molin, 2012). The ads show both boys and girls playing with beauty kits, girls holding toy guns and playing with cars, and boys pushing toy vacuums. In 2015, U.S. department store Target dropped gender-based labels and marketing in the toy aisles of their stores (Robinson, 2015). No longer are there "boys' building sets" and "girls' building sets" but simply "building sets." Are these moves helpful correctives to unnecessary gender-based marketing, or are they simply a case of political correctness gone too far?

Yes, Toy Marketing Should Be Gender Neutral

The consequences of gender-typed toy marketing can be great because playing with toys provides opportunities for children to develop important skills. For example, playing with construction and sports toys helps children develop spatial abilities and motor skills (Serbin, Zelkowitz, Doyle, Gold, &

Wheaton, 1990), and playing with dolls helps them develop language skills through conversations and playacting (O'Brien & Nagle, 1987). Given this, marketing toys as gender neutral might encourage children to play with both male-typed and female-typed toys, which could benefit them by increasing their range of skills and interests.

Furthermore, because of the plasticity of the brain, experiences with different types of toys can strengthen neural circuits while unused neural circuits tend to weaken (Eliot, 2009). In other words, a child who regularly plays with a building set will strengthen brain pathways that contribute to spatial skills and motor coordination, and one who plays with dolls may strengthen brain pathways that underlie verbal skills and relational competencies. Thus, marketing toys in a gender-typed manner can perpetuate sex differences that take root at the level of the brain's architecture. Conversely, gender-neutral marketing may encourage brain growth in ways that can increase children's life opportunities.

No, Toy Marketing Need Not Be Gender Neutral

Some people question whether any of this matters. Sex differences in toy preferences show up very early in life, are consistent across cultures, and are even evident in monkeys (Hassett et al., 2008). These trends suggest that socialization, including exposure to gender-typed toy marketing, plays little role in children's toy choices.

Consider Lego. The wildly successful toy company enjoyed enormous growth in the first decade of the 21st century, but 91% of the children who bought Lego sets in the United States were boys, despite Lego's history of gender-neutral advertising (Reddy, 2012). In an effort to expand the market to girls, Lego introduced "Lego Friends" in 2012, with sets marked by pastel colored cafés, beauty salons, and grocery stores and figures that are taller, curvier, and more doll-like than the traditional, boxy Lego figures (Orenstein, 2011). These efforts paid off. The number of girls who played with Legos tripled by the end of 2012, and "Lego Friends" became the company's fourth-best-selling toy line (C. Allen, 2014). In essence, by changing Lego from a "building set" toy to a toy that features dolls and interpersonal environments, Lego successfully attracted the little-girl market. If girls appreciate and use this product, is there anything inherently wrong with marketing it in a gendered way?

Is marketing a product as a "girl" or "boy" toy a rational response to children's already strong gendered toy preferences? Or does this type of marketing reinforce gender stereotypes? Which side of the debate seems more reasonable to you? Which evidence do you find most and least convincing? Why?

The "Lego Friends" toy characters (left) are marketed for girls. Compare them with the more traditional Lego figures (right), which are boxier and have less expressive faces.

Source: © iStockPhoto.com/fieldwork; © iStockPhoto.com/mattjeacock

Cognitive Theories

As you likely noticed, social learning theories focus on the external influences that contribute to children's gender development, but they tell us very little about children's internal worlds. What do children think about gender? How do they view themselves as gendered beings? These questions are the focus of cognitive theories, which address the mental changes that children undergo as they mature and develop increasingly sophisticated understandings of themselves and the world. As you will see, cognitive approaches treat children as active, curious perceivers of their social environments.

Cognitive-developmental theory. According to Lawrence Kohlberg's (1966) cognitive-developmental theory, children's understanding of gender progresses through three stages of increasing maturity. In the first stage, children develop gender identity, which is the ability to identify the self as a boy or a girl and to label others according to sex. Note that Kohlberg's use of *gender identity* largely matches our use of this term elsewhere in this book, though it emphasizes a binary view of sex and specifically focuses on the *cognitive* aspect of gender identity. Most children develop gender identity by about age 2 to 3, and once they do, they begin to perform behaviors consistent with that sex in order to receive rewards for doing so. Notice that this is the opposite causal sequence from that proposed by social learning theorists: In social learning theory, being rewarded for sex-typical behavior leads children to develop gender identity; in cognitive-developmental theory, the emergence of gender identity causes children to perform sex-typical behavior.

Gender stability:
The understanding that sex remains (largely) constant across time.

Gender constancy: The recognition that sex is (largely) fixed and does not change as a result of external, superficial features.

Gender schema:
A mental model about gender, based on prior learning and experience, that guides how people interpret, process, and remember new gender-relevant information.

Self-concept:
The entire set of an individual's beliefs, feelings, and knowledge about the self.

The second stage of gender development, **gender stability**, usually occurs around the age of 4 or 5 and is signified by an understanding that sex remains constant across time. To illustrate, a cisgender girl who has gender stability understands that she may be a "mommy" when she grows up but not a "daddy." Finally, the third stage is **gender constancy**, which is the recognition that sex is (largely) fixed and does not change as a result of external, superficial features. Before children master gender constancy, they may think that a girl can turn into a boy by getting a short haircut, or a man can become a woman by wearing a dress. Most children master gender constancy by the age of 6 or 7. In support of cognitive-developmental theory, longitudinal studies show that children who enter the gender identity stage earlier tend to show stronger sex-typical preferences and gender stereotypes later (Fagot & Leinbach, 1989). More generally, the idea that children's cognitions about sex and gender precede and guide their gender stereotypes, preferences, and behaviors remains a hallmark of cognitive gender theories.

Gender schema theory. Gender schema theory proposes that **gender schemas**—mental networks of information about gender—guide how people interpret, process, and remember new gender-relevant information (Bem, 1981). As soon as boys and girls can identify their own sex and that of others, they begin to build a schema for gender by seeking out additional information about gendered traits, behaviors, and roles. For instance, a child might see that her mother usually does the laundry and therefore assimilate into her gender schema the belief that "laundry is a female behavior." Moreover, as children learn the traits, behaviors, and roles associated with gender, they incorporate these into their **self-concepts** to varying degrees. This can help explain how people come to develop self-concepts that are high in gendered self-views, such as masculine or feminine traits.

As noted, gender schemas influence how people interpret and remember gender-relevant information. One meta-analysis found that girls were more likely than boys to remember items depicting feminine activities and objects ($d = -0.35$), whereas boys were more likely than girls to remember items depicting masculine activities and objects ($d = 0.34$; Signorella, Bigler, & Liben, 1997). Children rely on gender schemas to guide their personal preferences as well. In one study, researchers offered preschool children gender-neutral toys, like magnets and flip books, and initially noted no sex differences in the children's toy preferences. However, in a follow-up study, the researchers presented another group of children with the same toys but placed half of them in a box labeled "Girls" and half in a box labeled "Boys." Under these conditions, girls and boys preferred the toys in the "sex-appropriate" box over the toys in the "sex-inappropriate" box. Moreover, children generalized these preferences beyond themselves by assuming that other children of their sex would also prefer the same toys that they did (C. L. Martin, Eisenbud, & Rose, 1995). This illustrates how gender schemas allow children to go beyond the information that is given and make inferences about other people based on gender.

One interesting contribution of gender schema theory is the notion that people differ reliably in how much they use gender schemas to process information about the world. Sandra Bem (1983) proposed that people who rely on **gender schematic** processing are especially likely to notice gender and use it as a way of understanding and organizing the world. In contrast, those who do not use gender as a dimension for interpreting the world are referred to as **gender aschematic**. For instance, one study conducted with Chinese students found that exposure to male and female faces activated gender stereotypes and allowed faster processing of gender-relevant trait information for gender schematic individuals. In contrast, gender aschematic individuals did not differ in how quickly they processed gender-relevant trait information after exposure to male and female faces. This suggests that the sight of the faces did not activate gender stereotypes for gender aschematic individuals (Yan, Wang, & Zhang, 2012).

Gender schematic: Having a tendency to use gender as a salient schema for understanding the world.

Gender aschematic: Lacking the tendency to use gender as a salient schema for understanding the world.

Stop and Think

Consider how sex-typical toys might contribute to children's levels of gender schematicity. Do you think that children who are exposed primarily to sex-typical toys are likely to become more gender schematic than children exposed to a wide range of toys? Why or why not?

Developmental intergroup theory. Developmental intergroup theory is a variant of gender schema theory that emphasizes how groups shape the formation of gender stereotypes and prejudices in children (Bigler & Liben, 2007). The theory assumes that individuals tend to appraise groups positively as soon as they identify with the group (or, in gendered terms, as soon as they form a gender identity). Though true of any social group, this is particularly true for salient and meaningful groups, and sex is one such group. Appearance differences between boys and girls make sex a salient category, and authority figures regularly make sex groupings meaningful for children by forming separate lines for boys and girls, segregating teams or clubs by sex, building separate male and female bathrooms, and so on. As children observe adults' pervasive tendency to divide the world based on sex, they develop the belief that there must be inherent, natural differences between male and female people. This paves the way for children to develop gender stereotypes and gender-based prejudices, most notably **in-group bias** (a preference for their own sex group over other sex groups).

Thus, adults can influence children's gender stereotypes and in-group biases by making sex more (or less) salient as a grouping dimension. In an experimental demonstration of this, teachers of two preschool classes made sex either more or less salient over a period of 2 weeks (Hilliard & Liben, 2010). In one classroom, teachers made sex salient by organizing play and educational activities by sex, lining children up by sex, and using gender-specific language (e.g., "I need a girl to pass out the markers").

In-group bias: A preference for one's own social group over other groups.

In another classroom, teachers avoided sex-based organization of activities and gendered language. The researchers measured children's gender stereotypes and their in-group bias both before and after the 2-week period and observed striking differences between the classes. In the classroom where teachers made sex salient, children engaged in more gender stereotyping, displayed more in-group bias, and played less with other-sex peers (see Figure 4.2). Importantly, the effects remained several weeks later when the researchers returned for follow-up testing. This suggests that children's gender stereotypes and in-group bias can be increased or decreased by the amount of labeling that teachers use, even in a relatively short amount of time.

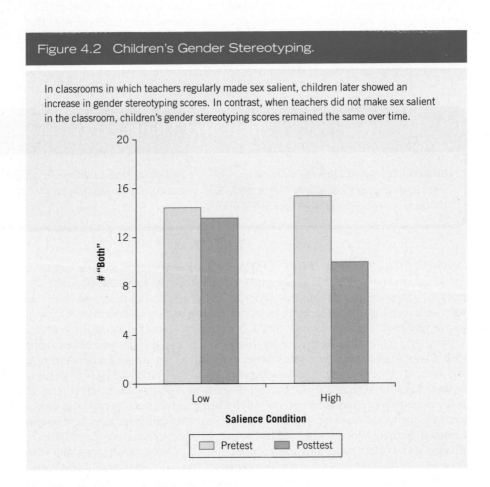

Figure 4.2   Children's Gender Stereotyping.

In classrooms in which teachers regularly made sex salient, children later showed an increase in gender stereotyping scores. In contrast, when teachers did not make sex salient in the classroom, children's gender stereotyping scores remained the same over time.

Source: Hilliard and Liben (2010).

Note: Children's gender stereotyping was assessed both before and after a 2-week period during which their teachers either did (high-salience condition) or did not (low-salience condition) make sex salient as a social category. The gender stereotype measure assesses children's tendency to say that "both women and men" should do various male-typed (e.g., be a firefighter) and female-typed (e.g., be a dancer) activities and occupations. Higher scores indicate lower endorsement of gender stereotypes.

Gender self-socialization model. The gender self-socialization model integrates assumptions from other cognitive approaches and focuses on the dynamic links among gender identity, gender stereotypes, and gendered self-views (Tobin et al., 2010). The model proposes that children form three sets of cognitive associations about gender: those that connect the self to a sex group (gender identity), those that connect sex groups to traits (gender stereotypes), and those that connect the self to traits (gendered self-views). These associations vary in strength from one person to another, depending on how strongly they are learned and reinforced. Moreover, each association is influenced by the other two associations because of people's need for cognitive consistency among their beliefs. Thus, for instance, children who identify more strongly with their sex (e.g., "I am a girl") and endorse gender stereotypes more strongly (e.g., "Girls are friendly") will be especially likely to develop gendered self-views (e.g., "I am friendly"). While provocative, this model is relatively new and has not undergone as much empirical testing as other cognitive development theories have.

Evaluating Social Learning and Cognitive Theories

Social learning theories make a compelling case for the influence of parents, siblings, teachers, peers, and the media in children's gender socialization. However, these approaches have been criticized for treating children as somewhat passive recipients of environmental influences and for ignoring how children think about gender. In contrast, the cognitive approaches emphasize how children strive actively to make sense of the world, selectively attending to (and ignoring) information depending on its relevance to them. Of course, the cognitive perspectives can be criticized for de-emphasizing the role of the external world—and particularly the role of culture—in gender development. So which is it? Do children develop gender because they imitate others and receive reinforcement? Or do children develop gender because their beliefs guide their actions and their interpretations of the world? The evidence suggests that both processes are at work. Children develop gender schemas based, in part, on observation and imitation of others in their environment, and they use their schemas as guides in their own gender-relevant behavior and responses. Thus, these sets of processes are dynamic in nature and each reinforces the other.

What Are the Experiences of Gender-Nonconforming Children?

Thus far, we have focused on typical gender development. However, not all children fit into the sex binary or display sex-typical interests and behaviors. Psychologists tend to study two forms of gender nonconformity in childhood. First, some children display cross-sex behavior, such as play preferences that deviate from traditional expectations. Examples of such children might be girls who prefer rough-and-tumble play or boys who prefer dress-up games. Second, some children display a gender identity that is at odds with the sex they are assigned at birth. These children might be transgender or nonbinary.

Biological and Social
Contributions to Gender Nonconformity

As discussed in the previous sections, powerful social and cognitive factors encourage children to adopt gender-typical roles, traits, and interests. If gender nonconformity goes against the normative messages that children receive, why does it occur? Genes and biology likely play some role. For instance, both cross-sex play preferences and gender identity (as cisgender versus transgender) are moderately heritable (M. J. Bailey & Zucker, 1995; M. Diamond, 2013). Moreover, adolescents who identify as lesbian or gay at age 15 are much more likely than their heterosexual peers to display cross-sex play preferences between the ages of 2 and 5, and the effect sizes are large for both girls ($d = 0.9$) and boys ($d = 1.2$; G. Li, Kung, & Hines, 2017). This suggests that genes that code for childhood play preferences may also code for sexual orientation. However, biological factors only account for some of the variance in gender nonconformity, indicating that social factors must play a role. What might these social factors be?

Parents are an obvious candidate since they do vary in how much gender nonconformity they tolerate in children. Think of the decision by David and Kathy Stocker-Witterick, described in the chapter opener, to allow their children to choose their own gender identities freely. While Storm identifies as a girl, her oldest sibling, Jazz, identifies as a transgender girl, and Kio identifies as nonbinary (Botelho-Urbanski, 2016). This raises the question: Had they been raised in a more traditional manner, would the Stocker-Witterick children display less gender nonconformity? Or alternatively, would the expression of their gender nonconformity merely have been delayed until a later stage of life? While it is not possible to answer these questions conclusively, we know that parenting by itself cannot prevent people from displaying gender nonconformity. Among a sample of transgender adults, 56% of MtF (male-to-female) adults and 20% of FtM (female-to-male) adults reported that their parents did not tolerate any cross-gender identity expression in childhood (M. Diamond, 2013), and yet, they developed a transgender identity nonetheless.

Rather than attempting to identify the precise social factors that predict childhood gender nonconformity, Milton Diamond's (2006) biased-interaction theory addresses the broad question of how people come to think of themselves as male, female, or something else. This theory begins with the assumption that biological factors, including chromosomes and prenatal hormones, predispose individuals to display temperaments and tendencies that are classified by societies as "masculine" or "feminine." However, natural variance exists in the degree to which biological factors translate into masculine versus feminine tendencies, and some children's preferences do not align with their biological sex. Once sex is assigned at birth, social contexts, such as family and society, offer the developing child a rich body of information about the typical traits, preferences, and attitudes of male and female individuals. Early in life, children begin to assess their similarity to others around them by comparing their internal sense of self—their own likes and dislikes, attitudes, and preferences—to those of "girls" and "boys." Gender identity emerges from this comparison of self with others: The majority of individuals initially view themselves as similar to others of their sex and accordingly develop a cisgender identity while some perceive themselves as "different" from their sex, gradually distance themselves cognitively and emotionally from that group, and align themselves instead with the group to which they feel most similar. Thus, this theory defines the *social factors* that shape gender identity as the entire body of gender-relevant information that children use as bases of self–other comparisons. Moreover, it captures the early childhood experiences of gender-nonconforming individuals, who often recall feeling "different" from others of their assigned sex early in life. Consider this memory by an MtF adult: "I found a pic in a catalogue. I felt it would be really good to be able to dress and look like that. I took the catalogue to my mum . . . and asked her if I could have it. She said I couldn't because I was a boy and this was for girls" (Riley, Clemson, Sitharthan, & Diamond, 2013, p. 249). According to biased-interaction theory, this brief exchange teaches the child both that "self is not like boys" and that "self is like girls."

Stop and Think

Consider this mother–child exchange from the perspectives of both social learning and cognitive theories. What gender identity outcome might a social learning theorist expect based on this parent–child interaction?

What gender identity outcome might a cognitive theorist expect? Do social learning and cognitive theories do a good job of explaining the emergence of transgender identity? Why or why not?

Nonconforming Identities and Milestones

Some people express skepticism of the idea that prepubertal children can have a stable transgender identity and believe instead that these children are likely confused or play-acting. To examine this issue, Kristina Olson and her colleagues studied the gender identities of 32 transgender children between the ages of 5 and 12 (Olson, Key, & Eaton, 2015). They also recruited an age-matched sample of cisgender children to use as a comparison group. To measure the children's gender identities, Olson and colleagues used self-report and implicit (indirect) measures. On self-report measures, transgender children and their cisgender peers looked identical: Transgender girls reported the same toy, food, and play preferences as cisgender girls, and transgender boys looked just like cisgender boys. Similarly, the indirect measures revealed identical responses between transgender and cisgender children. Indirect measures capture automatic responses over which people do not have full conscious control. For example, the Implicit Association Test—a reaction time test that measures how strongly different concepts are associated in memory—revealed that transgender children associate themselves just as strongly as cisgender children do with concepts that match their gender identity (i.e., pictures of girls or boys). Transgender and cisgender children also distance themselves equally strongly from concepts that match the other gender identity. In short, these findings suggest that transgender children are not confused or pretending to be another sex but, in fact, genuinely identify as members of a sex group that does not match their assigned sex.

However, a great deal of variety exists in how transgender and nonbinary individuals experience the development of their gender identity. The study conducted by Olson and her colleagues examined the responses of children who presented as transgender early in life (Olson et al., 2015). This suggests that by young childhood, some transgender children have a clear and consistent sense of themselves as belonging to a sex group that differs from their assigned sex. Other transgender people, however, take longer to realize that their initial gender identity and assigned sex do not match. These people might feel a sense of unhappiness whose source they cannot identify until they learn, in adolescence or adulthood, about the existence of other transgender people. Still others might temporarily adopt an identity as gay or lesbian as they strive to understand themselves but ultimately realize that this does not "fit." These differences in transgender people's development may reflect diverse factors, such as their family, religious, and cultural backgrounds; their race and ethnicity; and even the historical time in which they live. For instance, people who grow up with access to the Internet can learn about other transgender people at a much younger age relative to people from previous generations or to those who lack Internet access. To capture this variety, Beemyn and Rankin (2011) proposed a "milestone" model of transgender identity development based on interviews with almost 3,500 transgender adults in the United States (see Table 4.2). This model captures several of the major turning points reported by FtM and MtF people in their gender identity development. However, note that not all transgender people experience all of these milestones, and people may go through them in different orders.

Table 4.2 **Milestone Model of Transgender Identity Development.** Based on interviews with thousands of transgender and gender-nonconforming adults, this model describes important milestones that many transgender people experience as their gender identity develops. Note that not all transgender people experience all of these milestones, and they may experience them in different orders and at different ages.

FtM Individuals	MtF Individuals
Feeling and (sometimes) expressing a male gender identity from a young age	Feeling and (sometimes) expressing a female gender identity from a young age
Hiding or repressing one's male gender identity to avoid hostility and isolation	Hiding or repressing one's female gender identity to avoid hostility and isolation
Identifying as lesbian but realizing, over time, that this identity does not "fit"	Recognizing oneself as transgender instead of a "cross-dresser"
Learning about and meeting other FtM individuals	Learning about and meeting other MtF individuals
Overcoming denial and internal resistance; accepting oneself as male	Overcoming denial and internal resistance; accepting oneself as female
Taking hormones and perhaps having surgery to look more like one's self-image as male	Taking hormones and perhaps having surgery to look more like one's self-image as female
Deciding whether and when to tell others; undergoing changes to relationships after disclosure	Deciding whether and when to tell others; undergoing changes to relationships after disclosure
Having a sense of wholeness as a man	Having a sense of wholeness as a woman

Source: Adapted from Beemyn and Rankin (2011).

As shown in Table 4.2, both FtM and MtF individuals report a time in their childhood when they hid their feelings of difference in order to avoid hostility and rejection from others. Perhaps not surprisingly, treatment of gender-nonconforming children within families varies widely, depending on personal, cultural, and religious attitudes. When parents reject or abuse gender-nonconforming children, their risk for depression, attempted suicide, drug and substance use, and risky sex behavior increases substantially (Simons, Schrager, Clark, Belzer, & Olson, 2013). Among peers, gender-nonconforming children and youth experience increased risk for all sorts of harassment, including threats, rejection, and verbal and physical abuse (Kosciw, Diaz, & Greytak, 2008). Gender-nonconforming boys, in particular, experience especially high rates of rejection and bullying (Pauletti, Cooper, & Perry, 2014). We will return to these issues in Chapter 6 ("Power, Sexism, and Discrimination") and Chapter 13 ("Gender and Psychological Health").

Sidebar 4.3: It Gets Better!

In 2010, writer and media commentator Dan Savage started the It Gets Better Project to provide support and hope for bullied LGBT teens (see http://www.itgetsbetter.org). To contribute to the project, people can submit video confessionals that offer support, optimism, and personal stories about dealing with gender nonconformity. Celebrities who have submitted videos to the project include President Obama, E. J. Johnson (Magic and Cookie Johnson's son), and Canadian pop stars Tegan and Sara.

How Do Sex and Gender Shape Development in Adolescence and Emerging Adulthood?

As we have discussed, gender socialization in childhood typically results in children adopting a gender identity and gendered self-views, developing a gender schema, and learning gender stereotypes. Moreover, children often display sex-typed play activities, interests, and emotional expressions. Still, girls and boys are fairly similar to each other, both physically and cognitively, until adolescence. With the onset of puberty, young women and men diverge physically and, in some ways, psychologically. In addition, sources of gender socialization shift during this phase as adolescents become more autonomous. While parental gender socialization may decline in adolescence and young adulthood, the influence of peers and media grows.

Puberty and the Transition to Young Adulthood

Puberty consists of a series of biological changes typically including the development of secondary sex characteristics, such as an Adam's apple and facial hair in young men, enlarged breasts in young women, and pubic hair. It also involves the onset of menstruation in women and the production of sperm in men. On average, girls enter puberty about 2 years earlier than boys, but there are differences within sex in age of pubertal onset, and these age differences predict certain psychological and behavioral outcomes. One consistent finding is that, in Western cultures, early puberty relates to more negative outcomes among girls than among boys (Mendle, Turkheimer, & Emery, 2007). Girls who enter puberty earlier tend to have a more negative body image, perhaps, in part, because puberty involves an increase in and redistribution of body fat as breasts develop and hips widen. Moreover, early puberty among girls relates to depression, anxiety, and eating disorders, as well as to risky behavior, such as alcohol and drug use, smoking, vandalism, and sexual activity. This may occur because early maturation sets young women apart from their same-age peers and activates changes for which they may not be emotionally ready. Moreover, their physical (if not emotional) readiness for sexual activity may encourage early maturing girls to spend more time with older male peers, which can increase their access to alcohol, drugs, and sexual partners. It is not clear whether all of these early maturity effects generalize across adolescents of different races and ethnicities. While some studies find that early maturing Black and Latino girls experience the same depression and body image symptoms as early maturing White girls do, other studies find no evidence of negative psychological outcomes for early maturing Black and Latino girls (Mendle et al., 2007).

The relationship between early puberty and negative outcomes is less consistent for boys than for girls, although early maturing boys do experience a heightened risk for antisocial behaviors, mood disturbances, and early sexual activity (Mendle &

A young Ethiopian man from an Omo Valley tribe performs the bull jumping ceremony as a rite of passage into manhood.

Source: © iStockPhoto .com/itpow

Ferrero, 2012). Still, early maturing boys experience some benefits that early maturing girls do not. For instance, such young men often are more popular and have higher self-esteem than late maturing boys. Early maturing boys also tend to have a more positive body image than late maturing boys, partly because puberty brings about increases in height and muscle mass that promote athletic competence (Weichold, Silbereisen, & Schmitt-Rodermund, 2003).

Regardless of the specific age at which young people enter puberty, many cultures consider puberty an important life transition, celebrating it with formal rites of passage. For instance, among the Satere-Mawe of Amazonian Brazil, pubertal boys become men by sticking their hand into a glove full of painful, stinging ants (Hogue, 1987). In the Omo Valley of Ethiopia, young men prove their manhood and readiness for marriage by running naked across the backs of bulls (Forssman, 2015). Malawian girls take part in an initiation ceremony, often involving singing and dancing, at the onset of menstruation (Munthali & Zulu, 2007), and Mexican girls have a quinceañera celebration on their 15th birthday (Stavans, 2010). Formal rites of passage to adulthood tend to be less common in Western, industrialized countries, so how do people in these cultures know when they are adults? Given that there is no single milestone, people rely on different symbolic events to mark the transition. These include biological changes (e.g., menstruation and reaching the age of 18 or 21), role transitions (e.g., getting married and moving out of parents' house), and developing family capacities (e.g., being able to support and care for a family; L. J. Nelson et al., 2007).

Sidebar 4.4: Intensify Your Gender?

One early hypothesis, the **gender intensification hypothesis**, proposed that gender socialization pressures increase during adolescence as children prepare for the social roles that they are most likely to perform in adulthood (J. P. Hill & Lynch, 1983). According to this hypothesis, young women approaching puberty undergo increasing pressure to adopt caregiving traits of emotionality and self-sacrifice while young men face increasing pressure to adopt masculine qualities, such as confidence and self-esteem, that will prepare them for competitive workplace roles. This logic may sound reasonable, but the data do not cleanly support it. Contemporary adolescents, at least in the United States, do not appear to undergo a consistent increase in gendered self-views (Priess, Lindberg, & Hyde, 2009). Moreover, to the degree that gender socialization intensifies in adolescence, it seems to differ as a function of sex: Adolescent boys, relative to girls, face more intense pressure from peers to avoid sex-atypical behavior.

Gender intensification hypothesis: The hypothesis that gender role socialization pressures increase during adolescence, resulting in increases in adolescents' gendered self-views.

Emerging adulthood: In Western industrialized nations, the period of life between ages 18 and 25 when people transition to more adult roles and responsibilities.

Relationships With Parents

In adolescence, gender socialization sometimes reflects a double standard whereby parents, especially those who hold more traditional gender role ideologies, afford sons and daughters different levels of freedom. One study of Mexican American families illustrates this point nicely. Among more traditional families with both a daughter and a son, parents allowed adolescent daughters fewer privileges (e.g., attending parties and staying out late) than they gave to sons, even when daughters were the older sibling. At the same time, parents in these families assigned adolescent daughters more household chores than they assigned to sons (McHale, Updegraff, Shanahan, Crouter, & Killoren, 2005).

Regardless of parents' gender socialization practices, adolescence is a developmental phase during which relationships with parents often become destabilized as young people seek greater autonomy. For both young women and men, levels of conflict with parents tend to be highest in early and middle adolescence and then decline in frequency toward late adolescence and **emerging adulthood**, which is the period of life between ages 18 and 25 when people in Western, industrialized nations typically transition to more adult roles and responsibilities (Parra, Oliva, & del Carmen Reina, 2015). Conflict with parents during adolescence often arises from disagreements regarding the criteria for determining when adolescents become adults. As noted in the prior section, people raised in Western cultures define the transition to adulthood in a variety of ways, and parents and adolescents do not always see eye to eye on this issue. For instance, parents tend to place more importance on norm compliance (e.g., avoiding juvenile misbehavior, such as drunkenness, drug use, and sexual promiscuity) as a sign of adulthood than their sons and daughters do. In contrast, young adults often view their own biological changes and role transitions (e.g., getting married and finishing college) as evidence of their adulthood more than parents do. Some sex differences emerge as well, with young women viewing relational maturity (e.g., becoming less self-centered) as a more important criterion for adulthood than young men (L. J. Nelson et al., 2007).

Stop and Think

Do you consider yourself an adult? If so, what happened to turn you into an adult? If not, why not? What criteria do you use for determining whether or not you are an adult? Do you agree or disagree with your *parents, family, and friends about when people become adults? Do you think having a formal manhood or womanhood ritual might make the transition easier? Why or why not?*

When conflicts arise, parental tendencies to support or undermine adolescents' expressions of autonomy can have long-term consequences for the functioning of young adults. In Western contexts, when parents negotiate conflicts by supporting adolescents' autonomy (e.g., respecting their positions and accepting their input), adolescents display stronger relationship skills as they enter adulthood (Oudekerk, Allen, Hessel, & Molloy, 2015). Adolescents in Western and individualistic cultures often equate strict parental control with rejection and respond more favorably to permissive parenting. In contrast, in collectivistic cultures, such as Mexico, China, Korea, and Russia, adolescents expect and respect strict parental control, interpreting it as a sign of warmth and caring (Tamm, Kasearu, Tulviste, & Trommsdorff, 2016; Zimmer-Gembeck & Collins, 2006). For instance, let's return to the study mentioned earlier in which traditional Mexican American parents treated daughters and sons differently. When these parents imbued in their children values of **familism**—collectivistic values of loyalty, support, and interdependence among family members—adolescent daughters were less likely to view their parents' stricter control of them as unfair (McHale et al., 2005). This suggests that levels of parental control versus autonomy interact with cultural values to influence how adolescents react to this treatment.

Familism: A set of collectivistic social values that promote loyalty, support, and interdependence among family members.

Cross-sex friendships: Friendships with people who do not share one's sex.

Friendship, Dating, and Social Networking

As discussed earlier, children across cultures tend to segregate themselves by sex until the age of 12 or so. Then, during adolescence, rates of **cross-sex friendships** increase, particularly in Western cultures. In one longitudinal study of U.S. adolescents, the proportion of students' mixed-sex friendship groups increased from only 10% in Grade 6 to 22% in Grade 9 (Molloy, Gest, Feinberg, & Osgood, 2014). Around this time, adolescents' involvement in dating relationships also increases steadily. The percentages of U.S. adolescents who report experiencing a romantic relationship in the past 18 months increases from less than 30% at age 12 to about 70% by age 18. These dating rates are generally comparable across White, Black, Latino, and Native American adolescents while Asian teenagers are relatively less likely to report romantic relationships at each age (Carver, Joyner, & Udry, 2003). Same-sex romantic relationships are statistically rare in adolescence, with only about 2.2% of boys and 3.5% of girls reporting a same-sex relationship in the past 18 months. Interestingly, sexual minority youths report dating other-sex partners more frequently than same-sex partners in adolescence (S. T. Russell & Consolacion, 2003). These other-sex dating experiences may provide a context for sexual minority youths to explore their identity, gain self-awareness, and develop social competencies (Glover, Galliher, & Lamere, 2009).

In addition to face-to-face friendships and dating relationships, many adolescents today use online social networking sites to connect with larger networks of acquaintances. Sites like Instagram, Snapchat, and tumblr provide opportunities for young adults to experiment with different ways of presenting themselves and gain exposure to people with different backgrounds and worldviews. These platforms serve a unique purpose for young adults, with both women and men reporting that they use social networking sites for expressing ideas or beliefs that they would not feel comfortable expressing in face-to-face contexts (Norona, Preddy, & Welsh, 2016). So do young women and men use social networking sites differently? In some ways, yes. For instance, women tend to discuss friends, relationships, and significant others in their online posts more often than men do while men discuss society and abstract problems more often than women do (Magnuson & Dundes, 2008; Mazur & Kozarian, 2010; see Table 4.3). The images that people post also differ by sex—with women more likely to appear in photos of two

Table 4.3 **Social Network Topics by Sex.** While some of the topics that adolescent and emerging adult women and men discuss on social network sites differ by sex, others show similarity across the sexes.

Topic Discussed	Women	Men
Self[1]	81.0%	71.1%
Friends or peers[1]	11.4%	6.7%
Parents[1]	2.5%	0
Other family members[1]	3.8%	0
Society[1]	0	6.7%
Significant other[2]	84.0%	57.0%
Love[2]	19.0%	7.0%

1. Data are from Mazur and Kozarian (2010). Values are average percentages of blog entries that contained each topic within a 4-month period. Participants were adolescents, ages 15–19.
2. Data are from Magnuson and Dundes (2008). Values are overall percentages of women and men, ages 17–29, whose online profiles contained each topic.

On social network sites, men are more likely to appear in large, all-male groups while women are more likely to appear in pairs.

Source: © iStockPhoto .com/LeoPatrizi; © iStockPhoto.com/ franckreporter

women and men more likely to appear in photos of large, all-male groups—and this sex difference is evident around the world (David-Barrett et al., 2015). That said, there is also a lot of similarity in how young adults present themselves online. Women and men tend to use similar narrative and emotional tones, and they discuss similar content, such as daily activities, philosophical thoughts, and future goals (Norona et al., 2016).

Gendered Self-Views Across Time and Cultures

By the time they enter emerging adulthood, the self-concepts of women and men tend to differ. On average, women score higher than men do on measures of communal self-views (e.g., viewing the self as warm, kind, and understanding) while men score higher than women do on measures of agentic self-views (e.g., viewing the self as decisive, independent, and competitive). However, when examining changes in gendered self-views across the years of 1973 to 1994, Jean Twenge (1997) noticed a trend for sex differences in gendered self-views to decrease with time. This trend was driven primarily by women's increases in agentic self-views: While women displayed large increases in agentic self-views over the two decades, men's communal self-views increased by a smaller amount. Subsequent research showed that the increase in women's agentic self-views over time occurred on some traits (e.g., active, ambitious, and self-reliant) but not others (e.g., aggressive, competitive, and forceful; Spence & Buckner, 2000).

Why might this be the case? Think back to the material you read in Chapter 1 about the women's movements in the United States. From the mid-1960s to the early 1980s, a time of great social change in the United States, women increasingly entered the workforce and gained economic and political power. These changes in women's behaviors and roles likely led to changes in young women's gendered self-views. But what about men's communal self-views, which changed very little during the same time span? Perhaps men's communal self-views did not change as much because men at the time were slower to embrace more caregiving and domestic roles. However, men today assume more childcare and household responsibilities than ever before (Parker, 2015). How do you think these shifting roles might influence men's self-views over time?

Looking at gendered self-views across cultures, a counterintuitive pattern emerges: Sex differences in young adults' gendered self-views are larger in cultures that have more gender equality. For example, although women score higher than men on warmth, and men score higher than women on competitiveness, these sex differences are larger in European and North American cultures than they are in African and Asian cultures (Costa, Terracciano, & McCrae, 2001). Why do you think this occurs? To solve this puzzle, Serge Guimond and his colleagues propose that people learn about their standing on traits by comparing themselves with different groups of people (Guimond et al., 2007). In cultures characterized by greater gender equality, women and men are more likely to learn about their own traits by comparing themselves with peers of all sexes. Conversely, in cultures that are lower in gender equality, people tend to live more sex-segregated lives, and cross-sex social comparisons are relatively rare. Consider how this might influence people's gendered self-views: In gender-egalitarian cultures, women decide how "aggressive" they are, for example, by comparing themselves with both women and men (rather than only with women). Since men tend to be more aggressive than women, on average, a woman who determines her own aggressiveness by comparing herself with women *and* men may conclude that she is relatively low on aggression. In more traditional cultures, a woman who compares herself only with other women may end up concluding that she is average on aggression. The net result is that sex differences in gendered self-views appear exaggerated in more gender-egalitarian cultures. This hypothesis was confirmed across several studies in France, Belgium, the Netherlands, the United States, and Malaysia.

Stop and Think

How do you the think the use of online social networking sites might create different opportunities for people to compare themselves with members of other sex groups?

Do you think that the sexes of people against whom we compare ourselves might differ in online contexts, or would it remain the same as it is in face-to-face contexts?

How Do Sex and Gender Shape Development in Middle and Late Adulthood?

During adulthood, most people spend time engaging in paid or unpaid labor, building relationships and families, and bearing responsibility for major life decisions. What role does gender play in these life tasks? How do gendered self-views, expectations, stereotypes, and roles change as women and men mature? In what ways do gender roles prepare us—or fail to prepare us—for the later stages of life? We address these topics in this last section of the chapter.

Cultural Ideals of Womanhood and Manhood

As we discuss throughout this book, most human societies rely on sex-based divisions of labor in which men are primarily responsible for paid labor in the public sphere, and women are primarily responsible for unpaid domestic labor, including housework and childcare (Eagly & Wood, 1999). Even in the contemporary United States and other nations higher in gender equality, where gender norms increasingly allow women to pursue workplace and leadership roles, "ideal" women are still expected to be mothers and caretakers. For instance, perceivers in one study rated agentic women leaders less favorably than they rated agentic male leaders, but this difference disappeared if perceivers learned that the agentic female leader had children (Heilman & Okimoto, 2007; see Figure 4.3). In other words, it is okay for a woman to be a leader, as long as she is a mother as well. This suggests that the **motherhood mandate** (Russo, 1976)—the norm dictating that women should have children—is still operative in the contemporary United States. In fact, women who are *child-free by choice* tend to be stereotyped as lacking in warmth, and they elicit in others feelings of envy, contempt, and moral outrage (Ashburn-Nardo, 2017; Bays, 2016). Another expectation of "ideal" women is that they will exert effort, time, and money into beautifying their faces and bodies (Gimlin, 2007). This expectation puts great pressure on women, and those who perceive themselves as

Motherhood mandate: The societal expectation that women should have children and invest significant time and energy in raising them.

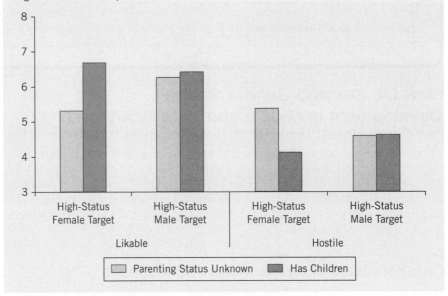

Figure 4.3   Ratings of High-Status Female and Male Targets.

For both likability and hostility, high-status male targets' parenting status has no bearing on how they are viewed. However, high-status female targets are viewed as more likable and less hostile if they are described as parents than if no information about their parenting status is offered. Also, high-status female targets are viewed as less likable and more hostile than high-status male targets when no information about parenting is offered, but this sex difference disappears when targets are described as parents.

Source: Heilman and Okimoto (2007).

not living up to ideal beauty standards report feelings of shame and low self-esteem (Clarke & Griffin, 2008). We will return to the topic of body image in Chapter 13 ("Gender and Psychological Health").

What about "ideal" manhood? As you encountered in Chapter 1, hegemonic masculinity refers to a culturally idealized and exaggerated version of manhood that consists of competition, aggression, success, toughness, and the avoidance of femininity (Connell & Messerschmidt, 2005). In terms of roles, a core element of hegemonic masculinity across cultures is the expectation that men will work and earn enough to provide for family. As sociologist Michael Kimmel (2006) describes it, hegemonic masculinity in the United States is an "impossible synthesis of sober, responsible breadwinner, imperviously stoic master of his fate, and swashbuckling hero" (p. 173). Because hegemonic masculinity sets an almost impossible-to-achieve cultural standard, men often experience a sense of insecurity about their masculine adequacy. For instance, in China, hegemonic masculinity centers on the notion of *chenggong*, which is an outstanding and highly important career accomplishment, such as becoming a billionaire entrepreneur or a scientist who makes world-changing discoveries (Liu, 2017). While many Chinese men realize that their likelihood of achieving such extreme work success is slim, they nonetheless feel driven by a sense of urgency combined with anxiety about the possibility of failure.

While women who fail to meet ideal standards of womanhood are evaluated negatively, people do not typically question their very status as "real women." In contrast, men across cultures experience chronic pressure to prove that they are "real men." According to the **precarious manhood hypothesis**, there is a cross-cultural tendency to define manhood as a precarious social status that is hard to earn and easy to lose and that requires continual validation in the form of public action and risk-taking (Vandello & Bosson, 2013). Womanhood, by comparison, is more commonly conceptualized as a stable social status that emerges inevitably from biological changes (Gilmore, 1990). This has some consequences for how cultures define "ideal" manhood. First, ideal manhood requires social achievements, such as success in paid labor, that ideal womanhood does not. Second, when men fail to achieve ideal manhood standards, they risk losing their gender status in other people's eyes. As a result, men often feel motivated to prove their masculinity by engaging in active and risky behavior and by avoiding anything that might be construed as feminine.

Men's felt pressure to prove manhood can potentially illuminate sex differences in a wide range of domains, including physical health, aggression, risk-taking, occupational preferences, and relationship tendencies (Vandello & Bosson, 2013). For instance, given the centrality of paid work to the male gender role, men who experience involuntary job loss—in comparison with women who lose their jobs—expect others to view them much more negatively (Michniewicz, Vandello, & Bosson, 2014). Moreover, among unemployed adults, men who believe that others viewed them as "less of a man" at the time of their job loss report experiencing more depression and anxiety. For unemployed women, there is no correlation between their beliefs about being seen as "less of a woman" and their psychological symptoms. While these correlational data cannot demonstrate that losing gender status *causes* men to feel depressed, they do indicate that gender status loss is linked closely to men's mental health, a pattern not seen in women.

Precarious manhood hypothesis: Hypothesis that manhood, relative to womanhood, is widely conceptualized as a social status that is hard to earn and easy to lose and that requires continual validation in the form of public action.

Gendered Self-Views

Degendering theory: The theory that gender becomes a less central aspect of the self as people age.

If the gendered self-views of men and women derive from their differential socialization into roles as paid laborers and caretakers, then might the strength of these self-views fade with time as children mature and leave home and as adults retire from the paid labor force? This should be true according to **degendering theory**, which proposes that gender becomes a less central aspect of the self as people grow older. However, one 20-year longitudinal study of women found just the opposite: As women aged from 39 to 59, they showed an average *increase* in both their communal and agentic self-views (Kasen, Chen, Sneed, Crawford, & Cohen, 2006). Another cross-sectional study that compared people's gendered self-views across groups of young adults (ages 25–39), middle adults (ages 40–59), and older adults (60 or older) also found no evidence of degendering. Across all age groups, women rated themselves higher in communal than in agentic traits, and men rated themselves higher in agentic than in communal traits. Further, the strength of people's gendered self-views did not differ across the age groups, indicating no overall trend for older people to become degendered (Lemaster, Delaney, & Strough, 2017). It is possible, however, that degendering occurs primarily among older adults than those examined in current studies. Alternatively, perhaps degendering primarily affects those who experience chronic illness or socioeconomic hardships that interfere with their ability to meet gendered expectations.

Stop and Think

Do you think that degendering theory makes intuitive sense? Why or why not? Do you think that the research described here does a convincing job of disproving degendering theory? Are there other ways of testing *this theory that might yield different findings? If you were going to test degendering theory, what approach would you use? Which aspects of gender would you measure?*

Women's Gender Advantage?

Research consistently shows that women tend to have richer social networks than men do, meaning that women generally have larger sets of people on whom they can rely for both emotional support and practical assistance as they age (Umberson, Chen, House, & Hopkins, 1996). This sex difference may result from socialization processes that cultivate and encourage women's relational tendencies more strongly than men's. Similarly, as we have discussed throughout this chapter, gender socialization practices around the world train women more consistently than men in practical homemaking skills, such as cooking, cleaning, and laundry. Later in life, these socialization practices may confer an advantage to women, who tend to care for themselves better and have more sources of assistance, in comparison with men. In fact, heterosexual men tend to rely more heavily on their spouses than women do, and men's well-being later in life depends more on their spouse than does women's (Cable, Bartley, Chandola, & Sacker, 2013). Men who lose a spouse due to divorce or widowhood have a higher likelihood than women of depression and even death (Lee, DeMaris, Bavin, & Sullivan, 2001; Shor, Roelfs, Bugyi, & Schwartz, 2012).

Poverty and traditional labor divisions can intensify sex differences in self-reliance later in life. One qualitative interview study of older adults living in poverty in Nairobi, Kenya, identified several themes of gender-based disadvantage in men's reports (Mudege & Ezeh, 2009). Older retired men in these communities, who spent their adulthood doing paid work in the male-dominated public sector, often lacked knowledge of how to perform domestic chores at home. Those who lived alone therefore felt unable to care for themselves, ill prepared to face old age, and useless. While some men had female relatives who helped them with housework on occasion, those who lacked such assistance reported elevated levels of stress and despondency. In general, both women and men in these communities viewed older men as idle, weak, and constantly worried while they viewed older women as resourceful, cooperative, and stronger than men. Thus, while the stresses of poverty and isolation negatively impact both women and men, there may be some ways in which women's gender role socialization better prepares them to live independently in old age.

The Double Standard of Aging

Decades ago, writer and social critic Susan Sontag (1978) wrote about the **double standard of aging**. This refers to the idea that women's social value tends to decline with age as their beauty and sexual appeal fade while men's value increases with age as their life experience and social status increase. Some findings are consistent with the idea of this double standard. For example, women are perceived to be "old" at a younger age than men are (Nolan & Scott, 2009), and evaluations of women's likability take a bigger hit as women age than do evaluations of men's likability (Kite, Stockdale, Whitley, & Johnson, 2005). Also, women tend to view aging as having a more negative impact on their appearance than men do: While women report feeling ever more invisible as their youth and physical beauty fade, men feel like their appearance becomes more distinguished with age (Clarke & Griffin, 2008; Halliwell & Dittmar, 2003). And yet, other research on the double standard of aging yields mixed findings. For instance, evaluations of men's competence decline more with age than do evaluations of women's competence (Kite et al., 2005). This suggests that double standards of aging may affect both women and men in domains that are especially relevant to their gender roles: likability and appearance for women and

Double standard of aging: The idea that women's social value declines with age as their beauty and sexual appeal fade while men's value increases with age as their life experience and social status increase.

As women age, they often report feeling invisible.

Source: © iStockPhoto .com/ysbrandcosijn

competence for men. Moreover, men are not free from concerns about their physicality as they age. Men express concerns about declining physical health, failing eyesight and hair loss, and reductions in athletic prowess (Nolan & Scott, 2009). And, as noted in the prior section, men who are unpartnered later in life often have concerns about their ability to care for themselves and receive support from others.

While many young people fear aging for these very reasons—declining health and fading of youthful beauty—we do not want to leave you with the message that gender development later in life is marked entirely by feelings of loss. When researchers surveyed over 8,000 British adults about the advantages and disadvantages of being their age, between 40% and 50% of older adults (ages 60–69) identified "freedom" as a unique advantage associated with their life stage (Nolan & Scott, 2009). Whereas women tended to appreciate freedom from caregiving and family responsibilities, men appreciated freedom from breadwinning responsibilities. Thus, just as gender roles give people a sense of identity and meaning throughout life, there may also be some relief when gendered expectations and responsibilities decrease in salience in the later years.

CHAPTER SUMMARY

4.1 Explain how gender stereotypes influence expectant parents and early child development.

Adults create binary, gendered worlds for infants before they are even born. Parents often desire to know the sex of fetuses so as to prepare gender-typical room décor, select names, and buy sex-typical clothes. The first question that others ask about newborn infants is their sex. Despite having few distinguishing characteristics, infant girls and boys are treated differently by adults. Parents attribute sex-based traits to infants and begin to apply gender stereotypes to them shortly after birth. Sex is also one of the first social categories that infants recognize, and it serves as a powerful schema that guides how children interpret the world.

4.2 Differentiate social learning and cognitive theories of gender development.

Social learning theories of gender development propose that children learn gendered beliefs (gender identity, stereotypes, and self-views) and preferences (play preferences and interests) by observing and imitating models and by receiving reinforcement and punishment from others. Parents, siblings, teachers,

peers, and the media all provide children with messages about gender, including rewards (such as praise, encouragement, or attention) and punishment (such as scolding, teasing, or withdrawal of attention) for certain sex-typed behaviors.

Cognitive theories of gender development propose that children learn gender via a predictable series of cognitive changes. By age 2 or 3, most children tend to recognize that they belong to a sex category and then use this to guide their performance of sex-related behavior and their understanding of gender stereotypes and roles. Gender schema theory proposes that people develop elaborate networks of knowledge about gender that guide how they interpret, process, and remember gender-relevant information. People vary in the extent to which they rely on gender schemas to make sense of the world, with gender schematic people noticing and using gender a lot and gender aschematic people paying less attention to it.

A main distinction between social learning and cognitive theories is the direction of causation they posit between sex-typed behaviors and cognitions. Whereas social learning theories propose that performing sex-typed behaviors causes children to develop gendered cognitions (identity, stereotypes, and self-views), cognitive theories propose that developing gendered cognitions causes children to learn sex-typed behaviors and preferences. The evidence suggests that children develop gender through *both* social learning processes (imitation, modeling, and reinforcement) *and* active cognitive processes (using schemas as flexible guides).

4.3 Describe the experiences of gender-nonconforming children and the factors underlying gender nonconformity in childhood.

Childhood gender nonconformity may involve displaying cross-gender toy and play preferences or developing a gender identity that does not match the sex assigned at birth. While both types of nonconformity show moderate heritability, little is known about the specific social factors that contribute to transgender identity. One theory proposes that such identity emerges from social comparisons that children make between themselves and the groups "boys" and "girls." When children display a strong transgender identity early in childhood, their gender identity is very similar to that of same-gender cisgender children. However, transgender individuals experience a great deal of variety in the development of their identity, with some realizing their gender identity early in life and others making a more gradual transition. Gender-nonconforming children tend to experience much higher rates of rejection, bullying, and abuse from parents and peers than gender-conforming children, and this treatment can have long-term consequences for mental health. Gender-nonconforming boys, in particular, receive more harsh treatment and rejection.

4.4 Explain how sex and gender influence biological, social, and identity changes in adolescence and emerging adulthood.

Many cultures celebrate puberty as an important transition into young adulthood. In the United States, girls who enter puberty at earlier ages are more likely to exhibit mental health problems. Boys who enter puberty early also experience some negative outcomes, but early maturing boys experience some social benefits as well. During adolescence and emerging adulthood, relationships with parents may become destabilized as young people seek more autonomy. In families with more traditional views of gender, parents allow adolescent daughters fewer privileges and assign them more chores than sons. How children respond to strict or permissive parenting differs by culture. In individualistic cultures, adolescents perceive permissive parenting more favorably, whereas in collectivistic cultures, adolescents expect and appreciate stricter parental control.

Adolescents spend increasing time with mixed-sex friend groups, and most U.S. adolescents enter dating relationships by the time they are 18. Young women and men rely heavily on social media as a platform for presenting themselves in different ways, gaining exposure to people from different backgrounds, and expressing things that they do not feel comfortable expressing in face-to-face contexts. While there is a lot of similarity in how women and men use social media, young women are more likely to discuss friends and relationships, and young men are more likely to discuss society and abstract problems online.

4.5 Evaluate how cultural ideals and gender shape the experiences of women and men in middle and late adulthood.

"Ideal" women are expected to be mothers and to put effort into beautifying themselves. "Ideal" men are expected to perform paid labor and provide for family. Both women and men who fall short of cultural ideals experience insecurity, but manhood is often conceptualized as a more precarious social status than womanhood. This means that men feel extra pressure to prove their masculinity and may experience negative psychological outcomes if they feel that they do not meet cultural expectations. Degendering theory proposes that as people age, gender becomes a less central aspect of the self, but research does not show declines in gendered self-views or traits with age. Among older adults who live alone, women's gender socialization may give them an advantage over men because women often have larger social networks and more homemaking skills. Sex differences in self-reliance are especially pronounced in cultures characterized by poverty and more traditional labor divisions. The aging double standard refers to the idea that women's social value declines with age while men's increases. There is some evidence that aging affects women more negatively than men in domains of appearance and likability, but aging affects men more negatively than women in the domain of competence. Older adults of both sexes identify failing health as a disadvantage, but they also identify freedom from responsibilities as a unique advantage of their age.

Test Your Knowledge: True or False?

4.1.   Parents are generally accurate in their perceptions of sex differences in infant boys' and girls' physical abilities. (False: Parents tend to overestimate the physical abilities of boys, when, in fact, there are no sex differences in infants' physical competencies.) [p. 116]

4.2.   By calling attention to sex in the classroom (e.g., referring to "girls and boys" rather than "children"), teachers can increase children's gender stereotyping and their preferences for members of their own sex. (True: Simply labeling children by their sex category can increase children's endorsement of sex stereotypes and their preference for their own sex over others.) [p. 125]

4.3.   Children who display cross-sex play preferences in childhood (e.g., girls who prefer rough-and-tumble play and boys who prefer dolls) are no more likely than other children to identify as gay or lesbian later in life. (False: Children who display cross-sex play preferences are substantially more likely to identify as gay or lesbian in adolescence and adulthood.) [p. 128]

4.4.   Young women are more likely than young men to post about relationships on social network sites while young men are more likely than young women to post about abstract societal issues. (True: Young women are more likely to post about relationships while young men are more likely to discuss society.) [p. 134]

4.5.   As people enter middle and late adulthood, gender becomes a less central part of the self. (False: Counter to the de-gendering hypothesis, there is no evidence that gender becomes less central to the self as people age.) [p. 140]

UNIT

III

Stereotypes, Discrimination, and Power

Chapter 5   **The Contents and Origins of Gender Stereotypes**

Chapter 6   **Power, Sexism, and Discrimination**

Test Your Knowledge: True or False?

5.1 The contents of gender stereotypes tend to vary a lot from one culture to another.

5.2 In the United States, the strength of people's gender stereotypes has not weakened over the past several decades.

5.3 Being reminded of a negative gender stereotype can cause people to behave consistently with the stereotype.

5.4 Gender stereotypes largely map onto the types of social roles and occupations that women and men perform.

5.5 Most of the evidence indicates that widely held gender stereotypes are inaccurate.

CHAPTER 5

The Contents and Origins of Gender Stereotypes

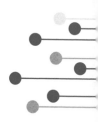

Key Concepts

What Are the Contents and Structure of Gender Stereotypes?
Communion and Agency
The Stereotype Content Model
The Women-Are-Wonderful Effect
Journey of Research: Think Manager–Think Male
Subgroups and Intersectionality
Transgender Stereotypes
Sexual Orientation Stereotypes

What Are Some Consequences of Gender Stereotyping?
Penalizing Gender Role Violators
Confirming Negative Stereotypes

Where Do Gender Stereotypes Come From?
Evolutionary Psychology
Social Role Theory
Biosocial Constructionist Theory

Are Gender Stereotypes Accurate?
Challenges: Defining "Reality" and Accuracy
Cognitive Stereotypes
Personality Stereotypes
Nonverbal and Verbal Communication Stereotypes
Stereotypes Across Multiple Domains
Debate: Are Gender Stereotypes Accurate?

So How Universal Are Gender Stereotypes, Really?

Learning Objectives

Students who read this chapter should be able to do the following:

5.1 Describe the contents and structure of gender stereotypes, especially in terms of the dimensions of agency and communion.

5.2 Discuss the social consequences of violating prescriptive and proscriptive gender stereotypes.

5.3 Evaluate the major theories of gender stereotypes.

5.4 Analyze research and perspectives on the accuracy of gender stereotypes.

The Contents and Origins
of Gender Stereotypes

Who are better college instructors, women or men? One seemingly obvious way to answer this question is to compare the teaching evaluations that female and male college instructors receive from their students. But this approach is problematic because students in face-to-face university classrooms observe much more than just their instructor's sex and the instruction that she or he offers. Many other factors—the instructor's appearance, speaking and lecturing style, nonverbal behaviors, and personality—can influence teaching evaluations. So even if you compared the course evaluations that female and male instructors of the same courses receive from their students, you could not be certain that the sex of the instructors alone caused any observed differences in teaching evaluations.

To control for the potential influence of extraneous factors, Lillian MacNell and her collaborators took this question to the online class environment (MacNell, Driscoll, & Hunt, 2015). MacNell and her team randomly assigned students in an online anthropology course to one of four discussion sections that were taught by two different instructors, one of whom was male and the other of whom was female. Both instructors taught two discussion sections but there was a catch: Each instructor taught one section under his or her real identity and the other section under the other instructor's identity. Thus, of the two sections that the female instructor taught, one section believed they had the male instructor. Similarly, of the two sections that the male instructor taught, one believed they had the female instructor. You may recall this methodology from Chapter 2 ("Studying Sex and Gender"), when we discussed how researchers sometimes manipulate the *perceived* sex of targets. At the conclusion of the course, students in all of the discussion sections rated their instructor on teaching effectiveness (e.g., professional, prompt, and fair) and interpersonal traits (e.g., respectful, warm, and caring).

The results were clear: Regardless of actual sex, the same instructor received better teaching evaluations from students who thought the instructor was a man. But keep in mind that each instructor treated the students in both of their sections in an identical manner, using the same grading rubrics, giving the same types of feedback, and following the same timeline for returning grades. This means that students viewed the same grading behavior as more "prompt" and "fair" and the same interpersonal style as more "respectful" and "enthusiastic" if they believed that their instructor was male relative to female.

Why do you think this happened? According to MacNell et al. (2015), student evaluations of college instructors are biased by **gender stereotypes**, or shared beliefs about the traits, qualities, and tendencies associated with members of different sex categories (Deaux & Lewis, 1984). Given that no actual differences in teaching effectiveness or interpersonal behavior existed between the two sections that each instructor taught, any perceived differences on the part of the students likely resulted from their gender stereotypes. Perhaps the same behavior appeared more professional and effective when enacted by a man because students believe that men are higher in authority and competence than women. Or maybe the female instructor's personality seemed less warm because of the stereotype that women are better suited for domestic, caregiving roles

Gender stereotypes: Shared beliefs about the traits, qualities, and tendencies associated with different sex categories.

than professional, leadership roles. If so, a female college instructor might be viewed as less warm because she violates gender stereotypes.

It is important to realize, moreover, that gender stereotypes can subtly shape people's reactions, even outside of their awareness. For instance, the students in MacNell et al.'s (2015) study likely did not realize that stereotypes influenced their evaluations. Nonetheless, these sorts of biases can contribute to systematic gender inequalities in academic settings that favor male over female faculty members (Monroe, Ozyurt, Wrigley, & Alexander, 2008). Given the weight that colleges and universities place on students' evaluations when deciding whether to hire and promote faculty, the gender stereotypes that students hold can have large and long-lasting, practical consequences.

In this chapter, we will take a broad look at gender stereotypes. We will consider their contents and structure, consequences, origins, and accuracy. We will also discuss cross-cultural variations in gender stereotypes that reflect long-standing sex differences in status and power. Then, in the next chapter, we will expand on the material presented here and focus more explicitly on gender discrimination and the systems of status and power that underlie many of our gender-based beliefs.

What Are the Contents and Structure of Gender Stereotypes?

What are women like, as a group? If you took a minute to jot down a few adjectives that you associate with the social category of "women," what words would make your list? These questions get at the root of stereotyping. A stereotype is a belief about the traits associated with a given social group, such as the belief that "athletes are physically fit" or that "grandmothers are sweet." Stereotyping, then, is the process of assigning a trait or quality to members of a social group. Note also that stereotypes are shared beliefs. You may think that women are bossy or men are lazy, but unless many others believe this to be true as well, psychologists do not consider it a stereotype. Whether you like it or not, we all engage in stereotyping, and we do so regularly. According to theories of social categorization, we automatically categorize people into social groups on the basis of appearance or other distinguishing features and then generalize from one category member to the group as a whole (Allport, 1954; Fiske, 1998). This can be a highly useful tendency because it allows us to make sense of a complex world by constructing and then using mental categories that filter, organize, and store information in meaningful ways. Think about how routinely you do this with inanimate objects: When you see a pen, even a new pen that you have never seen before, you quickly categorize it into the proper mental category labeled "pens." Next, you rapidly generalize from all of the past pens in your life and assume, with great confidence, that this new pen contains ink with which you can make markings on paper. This latter process, called **generalization**, is one of the defining features of stereotyping because a stereotype is basically a generalization about the members of a given social category. Of course, it's one thing to assume that "pens contain ink" and another thing to assume that "women are warm and friendly." The latter type of

Generalization:
Tendency to assume that a new member of a category has the same qualities as other category members.

generalization is less likely to hold true from one woman to the next because people are more variable and less predictable than pens.

Still, that doesn't stop us from stereotyping on the basis of people's sex. So what are the contents of our gender stereotypes? A great many gender stereotypes have been documented, and you can probably think of several of them without much effort. We have gender stereotypes about personality traits, cognitive abilities, social roles and occupations, hobbies and interests, religiosity and political orientation, sexual behavior, physical appearance, mental health, emotional tendencies, and nonverbal communication, to name a few. For example, men are stereotyped as messy, hardworking, and interested in sports (Ghavami & Peplau, 2012; Rudman, Moss-Racusin, Phelan, & Nauts, 2012). Women are stereotyped as smiley and expressive, concerned about their appearance, and well suited to occupations in teaching and nursing (Briton & Hall, 1995; Conley, 2013; Koenig & Eagly, 2014). To simplify the array of ways in which we stereotype women and men, Deaux and Lewis (1984) proposed four primary components of gender stereotypes: *trait dimensions* (such as "nurturing" or "assertive"), *role behaviors* (such as "financial provider" or "takes care of children"), *occupations* (such as "elementary school teacher" or "truck driver"), and *physical appearance* (such as "strong" or "graceful"). See Table 5.1 for a summary of these stereotypes. Throughout this chapter, we will address each of these components of stereotypes to varying degrees. To begin, we will consider two trait dimensions: communion (warmth) and agency (competence).

Table 5.1 **Common Gender Stereotypes.** Gender stereotypes fall into domains of traits, role behaviors, physical characteristics, and occupations.

Male Stereotypes	Female Stereotypes
Traits	
Active	Able to devote self to others
Competitive	Aware of feelings of others
Feels superior	Emotional
Independent	Gentle
Makes decisions easily	Helpful
Never gives up easily	Kind
Self-confident	Understanding
Stands up under pressure	Warm

Male Stereotypes	Female Stereotypes
Role Behaviors	
Always tries to win	Cooks the meals
Financial provider	Defers to judgments of others
Head of household	Does household chores
Is a leader	Does the laundry
Is athletic	Is family oriented
Is responsible for household repairs	Takes care of children
Makes major decisions	Tends the house
Takes initiative with other sex	Source of emotional support
Physical Characteristics	
Big hands	Dainty
Broad-shouldered	Delicate
Deep voice	Fashionable
Muscular	Graceful
Solid	Physically attractive
Strong	Short
Sturdy	Soft voice
Tall	Wears jewelry
Occupations	
Cable installer	Administrative assistant
Chemist	Bank teller
Construction worker	Elementary school teacher
Engineer	Hairdresser
Firefighter	Librarian
Insurance agent	Nurse
Politician	Occupational therapist
Truck driver	Speech pathologist

Source: Summarized from Haines, Deaux, and Lofaro (2016).

Communion and Agency

Women as a group are stereotyped as high (or at least higher than men) on **communion**. Communion refers to a broad set of traits that reflect concern for and connectedness with others, such as warmth, kindness, nurturance, agreeableness, cooperativeness, and emotional sensitivity. What about men? Men are generally stereotyped as higher than women on the dimension of **agency**, which embodies traits that facilitate individual success, status, and leadership. Such traits include competence, assertiveness, competitiveness, and effectiveness (Kite, Deaux, & Haines, 2008).

The stereotype content model. Importantly, communion and agency are not opposites of each other. According to the **stereotype content model**, because communion and agency constitute separate dimensions of evaluation, different social groups can be (and are) stereotyped as high on both dimensions, low on both dimensions, or high on one and low on the other. Figure 5.1 shows the combined communion and

Communion: A dimension, stereotypically associated with women, that reflects traits such as warmth, connectedness, generosity, and kindness.

Figure 5.1   Stereotypes of Social Groups on Communion (Warmth) and Agency (Competence).

As shown, social groups are stereotyped along dimensions of communion and agency. This means that stereotypes of many groups (e.g., "rich people") are not entirely flattering or entirely unflattering but are a mix of flattering (e.g., high agency) and unflattering (e.g., low communion).

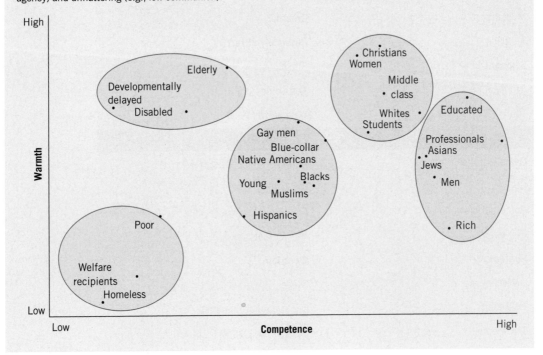

Source: Fiske, Cuddy, Glick, and Xu (2002).

agency stereotypes that characterize some of the social groups that Susan Fiske and her collaborators have examined (Fiske, Cuddy, Glick, & Xu, 2002). Note that women fall into a cluster of groups at the top right: They are rated very high on communion and moderately high on agency. Men, who fall into the cluster at the far right, are rated as average on communion and very high on agency.

You may have noticed by now that communion and agency are major themes in the psychology of sex and gender. While communion contains many traits that are considered feminine, agency contains traits that are considered masculine. Some theorists propose that these dimensions have broad relevance for predicting our reactions to other persons in general (not just on the basis of sex and gender) because communion and agency offer important, survival-relevant information (Abele & Wojciszke, 2013). In other words, they help us to determine other people's intentions toward us (e.g., do they *intend* to befriend or harm me?), as well as their ability to act on those intentions (e.g., are they *capable* of helping or hurting me?). Therefore, a tendency to make quick assessments of others along these two dimensions may facilitate our ability to navigate the social world effectively (Fiske, Cuddy, & Glick, 2007).

These dimensions, moreover, underlie many aspects of our gender stereotypes beyond just traits. The role behaviors (e.g., "providing emotional support") and occupations (e.g., "nursing") that are most strongly associated with women often reflect communion while the role behaviors (e.g., "being a leader") and occupations (e.g., "insurance agent") that are most strongly associated with men tend to reflect and require agency. Even some of our physical-appearance stereotypes reflect communion and agency: Women are stereotyped as "smiley" (communal), and men are stereotyped as "big and tall" (agentic).

Much of the original work identifying male and female stereotypes was done in the United States. Do people in other cultures share the same gender stereotypes? Data collected around the world indicate a great deal of cross-cultural consistency in stereotypes of women and men, suggesting that these stereotypes may be universally held. For example, John Williams and Deborah Best presented university students in 27 different cultures with a list of 300 adjectives and asked the students to indicate whether, in their culture, each adjective was associated more frequently with women or with men (Williams & Best, 1990). Some interesting cultural patterns emerged. For example, stereotypes of women and men overlapped the most in Scotland, Bolivia, and Venezuela while women and men were stereotyped as being least alike in Germany, the Netherlands, and Finland. Moreover, nations differed in how positive their stereotypes were, with some countries (Italy, Peru, and Australia) stereotyping women more favorably, and others (Japan, South Africa, and Nigeria) stereotyping men more favorably (Best & Williams, 2001). Despite these differences, high cross-cultural agreement regarding the contents of gender stereotypes emerged: People consistently associated women with traits such as nurturance, agreeableness, and affection and men with traits such as adventurousness, independence, and dominance. A recent update of this work replicated these findings in 10 different nations representing both Europe (e.g., Spain and the Netherlands) and East Asia (e.g., Japan and South Korea; Cuddy et al., 2009). However, this cross-cultural tendency does show some exceptions, which we will consider toward the end of this chapter.

Agency: A dimension, stereotypically associated with men, that reflects traits such as competence, intelligence, assertiveness, and competitiveness.

Stereotype content model: Theory proposing that stereotypes about social groups fall along communion and agency dimensions and that groups may be seen as high or low on both dimensions.

Sidebar 5.1: No Matter the Culture, Commercials Portray Gender Stereotypes

Do commercials reflect and reinforce gender stereotypes? Does this differ across cultures? A study of 1,755 commercials from 13 Asian, American, and European countries sought to answer these questions (Matthes, Prieler, & Adam, 2016). The authors found that despite the diversity of cultures, portrayals of women and men are similar and stereotypical. Across nearly all cultures, people associate female characters with beauty and personal care products, toiletries, and cleaning products, whereas they associate male characters with technical products and cars. Reflecting stereotypes of male agency, men (62%) more frequently do voiceovers in commercials—in comparison with women (32%)—and this difference emerges across cultures.

While the contents of gender stereotypes show consistency across cultures, what about the strength with which people endorse gender stereotypes? How about in the United States, a culture that saw large increases in women's participation in workplaces, higher education, and athletics over the past several decades? Did these changes in women's roles lead to a weakening of gender stereotypes? To answer this question, Elizabeth Haines and her colleagues presented raters with the same gender traits that Deaux and Lewis (1983) used several decades ago and asked them to rate the likelihood that either a typical man or a typical woman possessed each trait (Haines, Deaux, & Lofaro, 2016). They found evidence that participants endorsed gender stereotypes just as strongly in 2016 as they did in 1983, leading them to conclude that gender stereotypes in the United States have not weakened over time.

What do you think about the fact that the strength of people's gender stereotypes did not change substantially since the early 1980s? Do you think this finding is likely limited to stereotypes about traits, or would it also apply to stereotypes about occupations, hobbies, *interests, and appearance? If you measured a wide range of gender stereotypes, where would you expect the largest changes over time? Where would you expect the smallest changes?*

The women-are-wonderful effect. So which is more favorable, "communal" stereotypes or "agentic" stereotypes? On the one hand, agentic qualities, such as leadership and competitiveness, are important for achieving success and status. In Western, individualistic cultures, we value these traits highly and have great respect for people who embody them. We also tend to offer generous financial compensation to individuals who succeed in high-status occupations requiring effectiveness and skill, such as doctors, engineers, software programmers, and corporate leaders. On the other hand, qualities such as kindness and generosity are very attractive for different reasons—we tend to adore warm and kind people. When Eagly and Mladinic (1994) asked people how positively versus negatively they felt about the communal and agentic traits associated with women and men, they found strong evidence that stereotypes of women are more favorable than stereotypes about men. This phenomenon is dubbed the **women-are-wonderful effect**.

A wonderful woman? The women-are-wonderful effect is reserved primarily for White, middle-class women who fulfill domestic roles.

Source:
© iStockPhoto.com/ George Marks

There are a few things to keep in mind about the women-are-wonderful effect, however. First, Eagly and Mladinic (1994) argue that favorable stereotypes about women as warm, nurturing, and generous apply primarily to women who conform to traditional gender role expectations. Women who occupy high-status or leadership positions or who push to increase women's opportunities (i.e., activist or radical feminists) are neither stereotyped as warm nor evaluated especially favorably. In fact, while traditional women are stereotyped in a positive and seemingly flattering manner—as warm, morally pure, and virtuous—nontraditional women tend to be stereotyped in a hostile and insulting manner, as overly bossy, manipulative, and untrustworthy (Rudman et al., 2012).

Next, the women-are-wonderful effect differs as a function of women's race and socioeconomic status. In comparison with middle-class women, lower-class women are stereotyped as lower in both communion and agency. In comparison with White women, Black women are stereotyped as lower on communal traits (e.g., emotional and dependent) but higher on agentic traits (e.g., self-reliant and assertive; Landrine, 1985).

Women-are-wonderful effect: Tendency for people to view stereotypes about women more favorably than they view stereotypes about men.

Think manager–think male effect: Effect in which stereotypes of men and good leaders overlap more strongly than stereotypes of women and good managers.

Thus, the women-are-wonderful effect may apply mostly to White, middle-class women who fill traditional domestic roles. Finally, although people seem to like women more than men because of their stereotyped warmth, they respect men more than women because of their stereotyped agency (Vescio, Schlenker, & Lenes, 2010). In other words, being stereotyped positively does not necessarily offer women a route to social status and power, a point that we will elaborate in the "Journey of Research: Think Manager–Think Male" section.

If lower-class and Black women are stereotyped less favorably than middle-class and White women, could this reflect something about the people who are doing the stereotyping? After all, although demographic trends at U.S. universities have changed over time, most of the people who participated in studies of stereotyping in the past several decades have been middle-class, White college students. Perhaps the race and class of these participants helps to explain why White, middle-class, and traditional women are stereotyped so favorably. To address this question, Terri Conley measured the stereotypes of White women that were held by persons of color, including Black, Asian American, and Latina/o individuals. Among the most frequently listed traits that Black, Asian American, and Latina/o respondents used to describe White women were *dumb, conceited, sexually easy,* and *beautiful* (Conley, 2013). Rather than reflecting the women-are-wonderful effect, these traits seem to correspond to media images that portray White women as beautiful and sexually available "arm candy." Thus, the belief that women are wonderful is reserved for a specific type of (White, middle-class, traditional) woman, and this belief may not be shared by people of color.

Journey of Research

Think Manager–Think Male

What traits should a typical business manager display? Do stereotypes of managers align more with stereotypes of men or of women? As you might guess, manager stereotypes tend to be pretty masculine. This has important consequences because if gender stereotypes predispose people to assume that men are better suited than women for leadership positions, then qualified women may be disadvantaged in hiring decisions.

This topic has inspired decades of empirical research. Victoria Schein (1973) first demonstrated the links between stereotypes of men and managers in a sample of 300 male managers at insurance companies. Schein presented the managers with a list of 92 gender-typed traits and asked them to rate how characteristic

the traits were of either "women in general," "men in general," or "successful middle managers." She then correlated ratings of managers with ratings of women and men to determine how much overlap there was with each group. Overall, ratings of managers and men (MM ratings) correlated much more strongly ($r = .62$) than did ratings of managers and women (MW ratings; $r = .06$). Additional research replicated this pattern of findings, which is dubbed the **think manager–think male effect**, among a sample of female managers (Schein, 1975). Thus, both male and female managers espoused the stereotype linking men more strongly than women to leadership traits.

Over the next few decades, researchers replicated this effect in dozens of studies. By the mid-1990s, however, a change emerged in the stereotypes held by female respondents. Three separate studies in the 1980s and 1990s found that women's MM ratings and their MW ratings were similar in size (Brenner, Tomkiewicz, & Schein, 1989; Dodge, Gilroy, & Fenzel, 1995; Schein, Mueller, & Jacobson, 1989). Male managers' ratings, in contrast, replicated the original think manager–think male effect, showing strong positive MM correlations and nonsignificant MW correlations. Thus, a shift had occurred in how female managers thought of women's leadership traits, but this shift was not evident among male managers.

In 2011, Anne Koenig and her colleagues meta-analyzed data from 40 studies of the think manager–think male phenomenon and examined changes in the strength of the effect over time (Koenig, Eagly, Mitchell, & Ristikari, 2011). Between 1973 and 2010, the strength of the MW correlation increased while the strength of the MM correlation remained constant. Koenig and her colleagues also examined overall sex and culture (Eastern versus Western) differences in the strength of the think manager–think male effect. The MM correlation was $r = .63$ among men raters and $r = .58$ among women raters, and these correlations did not differ significantly from each other. However, the MW correlation among men raters ($r = .11$) was smaller than the MW correlation among women raters ($r = .37$). Similarly, the MM correlation was equally strong among Eastern and Western samples ($rs = .68$ and $.60$) while the MW correlation was smaller in Eastern ($r = .09$) than in Western ($r = .27$) samples. Thus, over the past 40 years, stereotypes about men's leadership traits have remained constant while stereotypes about women's leadership traits have increased, especially among women and Westerners.

Why did this shift occur? Recall that MW correlations require two sets of ratings, one of managers and another of women in general. Thus, changes in MW correlations could reflect changes in (a) beliefs about the traits of good managers, (b) beliefs about the traits associated with women, or (c) both. Koenig et al. (2011) found that between 1979 and 2007, stereotypes of "good managers" have

In 2009, Ursula Burns was named CEO of Xerox Corporation, becoming the first Black woman to head a Fortune 500 company.

Source: http://www.gettyimages.com/license/454285738

remained high in agentic traits, but these stereotypes have also increased in communal traits. Idealized views of leadership in the United States increasingly favor managers who are collaborative, supportive, and emotionally intelligent (Eagly, 2007), and these qualities align more with stereotypes about women than men. As Koenig et al. (2011) concluded, "Leadership now, more than in the past, appears to incorporate more feminine relational qualities such as sensitivity, warmth, and understanding . . . [in addition to] masculine dominance and strength" (p. 634). And yet, in practice, women still constitute only 26% of chief executive officers (CEOs) in the United States and only 4.5% of CEOs worldwide (Noland, Moran, & Kotschwar, 2016). Black and Latina women also remain disadvantaged relative to White and Asian American women in upper-level management positions (U.S. Bureau of Labor Statistics, 2015c). It will be interesting to see if— and for how long—these trends continue.

Subgroups and Intersectionality

We started this chapter by asking you to consider your stereotypes about the broad category of "women." But when we encounter individuals in our daily lives, we rarely see them merely as women or men—instead, we view them as belonging to more differentiated subgroups within larger categories (Richards & Hewstone, 2001). For example, you might think of individual women you know as homemakers, feminists, or athletes; similarly, men might be blue-collar workers, fathers, or outdoorsy types. To examine stereotypes about gender subgroups, Thomas Eckes (2002) asked participants to rate 17 female and 24 male subgroups on communal and agentic dimensions (see Table 5.2

Table 5.2 Common Subgroups of Women and Men. Gender stereotypes can pertain not only to broad categories of people, such as "women" and "men," but also to more specific subgroups. These are some of the most common gender subgroups about which there are specific stereotypes.

Woman Subgroups	Man Subgroups
Arrogant type	Arrogant type
Artistic woman	Athlete
Athlete	Blue-collar worker
Bitch	Business man
Career woman	Family man
Common/vulgar woman	Gay man
Feminist	Hippie
Housewife	Homemaker/housefather
Mother	Intellectual
Secretary/nurse	Mama's boy/sissy
Slut/whore	Ordinary man
Snob	Sexist/macho man
Student	Student
Submissive woman	Womanizer/eternal bachelor
Working woman	Yuppie

Source: Vonk and Ashmore (2003).

for a list of some of the most common gender subgroups). Eckes's findings show that people make clear-cut distinctions between different gender subgroups. For instance, "hippie" men are stereotyped as lower in competence but higher in warmth than "manager" men, and "career" women are stereotyped as higher in competence but lower in warmth than "housewife" women. This indicates that we do not stereotype all men or all women similarly. In fact, some researchers argue that thinking about subgroups is a good way of combatting our gender stereotypes because it forces us to confront the reality that broad-based stereotypes are overgeneralizations (Richards & Hewstone, 2001). Of course, stereotypes about subgroups are also overgeneralizations but perhaps less egregious ones than stereotypes about "women" and "men" in general. Moreover, considering the multiple subgroups that individuals belong to, such as "woman, young, student," can increase our tendencies to view group members as unique individuals, to see them as similar to us, and to like them (Crisp, Hewstone, & Rubin, 2001). Thus, thinking about people at the level of their subgroups may help us to better acknowledge their differences.

This may remind you of the concept of intersectionality, which is the study of the ways in which different forms of discrimination and oppression interact to shape people's experiences (Crenshaw, 1993; McCall, 2005). As you read in Chapter 1, all individuals occupy cross-cutting social categories, such as sex, age, race or ethnicity, social class, sexual orientation, and physical ability. Thus, people who study stereotypes from an intersectional perspective might focus on widespread beliefs about "gay Black women" or "low-income, elderly Latinos."

Sidebar 5.2: The Manifesto That Began It All

An early expression of intersectionality appeared in a manifesto written in the late 1970s by a Boston-based Black feminist group called the Combahee River Collective. In its manifesto, the collective articulated the difficulties of disentangling the various types of oppression that affected them: "We . . . find it difficult to separate race from class from sex oppression because in our lives they are most often experienced simultaneously" (Combahee River Collective, 1977/1995, p. 234).

When researchers examine stereotypes from an intersectional perspective, an interesting finding emerges: Stereotypes about people who occupy multiple subordinate status categories (e.g., gay Black men) sometimes contain unique elements that are not found in stereotypes of any of the individual groups (e.g., gay people, Black people, and men) that intersect to form the identity. A study by Nevin Ghavami and Letitia Peplau (2012) illustrates this point. These researchers asked participants to list 10 characteristics that were part of common cultural stereotypes about various social groups, including sex groups (women and men), racial and ethnic groups (Black, Asian American, Latino/a, Middle Easterner, and White people), and groups that reflected combinations of the two sex groups and the five racial/ethnic groups (Black women, Middle Eastern men, and so on). Table 5.3 lists the most frequently mentioned

characteristics associated with several different groups. Note that stereotypes about people in the cross-cutting categories contain unique traits. For example, participants associated the traits *quiet* and *oppressed* with Middle Eastern women, but these traits did not appear among the stereotypes associated with either "Middle Easterners" or "women." Thus, stereotypes about people who occupy multiple subordinate groups do not merely reflect a sum of the stereotypes about their constitutive social categories.

Two other interesting findings emerged from this study. First, stereotypes about male cross-cutting identities

Members of the Combahee River Collective, which was active from 1974 until 1980 in Boston, MA. The manifesto written by this collective contained an early reference to intersectionality.

Source: Photo @Ellen Shub

Table 5.3 **Intersectional Gender and Racial/Ethnic Stereotypes in the United States.** In a study conducted on U.S. college students, these were the 15 most frequently listed traits associated with each category of gender and race/ethnicity. Unique attributes (attributes that only appear in one gender/ethnicity category) are designated with an asterisk. Note that the category "Middle Eastern Women" has the most unique attributes; it is also the only category listed here that combines two subordinate group statuses (woman and ethnic minority).

Men	Women
Tall	Emotional
Physically strong	Caring
Respected	Soft
Intelligent	Care about appearance
Have high status	Talkative
Leaders	Small build/petite
Sexist	Submissive
Like sports	Dependent

Men		Women	
Providers		Motherly	
Aggressive		Feminine	
Unfaithful		Manipulative	
Ambitious		Attractive	
Arrogant		Sexual objects	
Messy		Materialistic	
Fixer-uppers		Jealous	

Middle Easterners	Middle Eastern Men	Middle Eastern Women
Terrorists	Bearded	Quiet*
Dark-skinned	Dark-skinned	Religious
Oppress women	Terrorist	Covered*
Muslim	Sexist	Oppressed*
Hairy	Speak English with accent	Conservative
Wear turban	Dirty	Submissive
Rich	Muslim	Attractive
Dangerous	Wear turban	Dependent
Dirty	Religious	Muslim
Intelligent	Intelligent	Family oriented*
Speak English with accent	Anti-West*	Have many children*
Violent	Suspicious*	Small build/petite
Bearded	Dangerous	Sexually conservative*
Conservative	Good at bargaining*	Housewives*
Religious	Rich	Submissive

Whites	White Men	White Women
High status	Rich	Arrogant
Rich	Tall	Blond
Intelligent	Intelligent	Rich

(Continued)

Table 5.3 (Continued)

Whites	White Men	White Women
Arrogant	Assertive*	Attractive
Privileged	Arrogant	Small build/petite
Blond	Successful*	Ditsy*
Racist	High status	Tall
All-American	Blond	Materialistic
Ignorant	Racist	Racist
Redneck	All-American	Intelligent
Tall	Educated*	Feminine
Attractive	Leaders	Sexually liberal*
Patronizing	Privileged	Emotional
Blue eyes	Attractive	Submissive
Overweight	Sexist	High status

Source: Ghavami and Peplau (2012).

(e.g., Middle Eastern men) have more traits in common with stereotypes about the over-arching racial/ethnic group (e.g., Middle Easterners) than do stereotypes about female cross-cutting identities (e.g., Middle Eastern women). As you can see in Table 5.3, stereotypes about Middle Eastern men have fewer unique traits than stereotypes about Middle Eastern women. Next, stereotypes about White women and men share more overlapping traits with stereotypes of "women" and "men" in general than do the stereotypes of women and men of color. What do these findings suggest to you about gender and racial/ethnic stereotypes? According to intersectional theory, this reflects the fact that cultural stereotypes about gender and ethnicity are rooted in systems of power in which the most powerful members of social groups serve as the prototypes of those groups. A **prototype** is the most typical cognitive representation of a given category, or the cultural default. Therefore, stereotypes about "Blacks" and "Middle Easterners" evoke images of Black *men* and Middle Eastern *men* while stereotypes about "women" and "men" evoke images of *White* women and men. In other words, the default representative of racial/ethnic stereotypes is a man while the default representative of gender stereotypes is a White person. This tendency can result in feelings of invisibility among people who occupy cross-cutting non-male and non-White identities because they are not viewed as the most representative members of either their sex or race groups (Purdie-Vaughns & Eibach, 2008). Keep these ideas in mind because we will return to them in the next chapter.

Prototype:
The most typical cognitive representation of a category; with social groups, the prototype is the cultural default for representing the group.

You may have noticed that researchers study the contents of gender stereotypes in several different ways. Some measure stereotypes by asking respondents to rate members of gender groups along trait dimensions (e.g., "low warmth" to "high warmth") while others ask respondents to estimate the likelihood that women *and men possess certain traits or to list the common stereotypes that come to mind when they think about women and men. What are the strengths and weaknesses of each of these different approaches? What types of unique information does each approach yield? Which is the best way to examine gender stereotypes? Why?*

Transgender Stereotypes

To date, there is not a lot of systematic psychology research on stereotypes about transgender individuals. Moreover, the studies that exist measure stereotypes about male-to-female (MtF) and female-to-male (FtM) transgender people and do not consider stereotypes about other variations of transgender people (e.g., genderqueer or non-binary people). One finding is that stereotypes about MtF women largely align with stereotypes about cisgender women, in that they include feminine traits, interests, and appearances (Gazzola & Morrison, 2014). In contrast, stereotypes about FtM men are more androgynous than are stereotypes of cisgender men, in that they contain both feminine and masculine traits and hobbies. Next, unlike cisgender women and men, transgender women and men are stereotyped as being *confused* and *gay*. Why might this be the case? Perhaps these stereotypes indicate a tendency for perceivers to conflate gender identity with sexual orientation and assume that they are the same thing. In fact, transgender people generally experience their gender identity and sexual orientation as distinct components of the self, much like cisgender people do (Mizock & Hopwood, 2016). It will be interesting to see if and how these stereotypes change as transgender awareness expands.

Sexual Orientation Stereotypes

A large body of research examines the contents of stereotypes about sexual minority individuals. One well-documented stereotype about gay men and lesbians is that their gender attributes are similar to members of the other sex. This belief has roots in late-19th-century theorizing about sexual orientation, particularly in *sexual inversion theory*, which posited that lesbians and gay men have an external appearance of one sex but an internal experience of the other sex. Although outdated and inconsistent with the evidence, the assumptions behind sexual inversion theory continue to influence stereotypes of lesbian women and gay men. For example, cultural stereotypes paint lesbians as having agentic and dominant personalities, as likely to pursue male-typed hobbies and occupations, and as masculine in appearance and clothing style (Blashill & Powlishta, 2009; Kite & Deaux, 1987). Gay men are stereotyped as having feminine personality traits, as well suited for female-typed occupations, as having feminine mannerisms, and as likely to suffer from female-typed mental health concerns, such as eating, anxiety, and mood disorders (Boysen, Vogel, Madon, & Wester, 2006; Kite & Deaux, 1987; Madon, 1997). One notable exception to this pattern, however, is in stereotypes about sexual promiscuity. Gay men are stereotyped as similar to heterosexual men when it comes to their presumed high levels of sexual promiscuity, and lesbians are stereotyped as similar to heterosexual women in this tendency (Burke & LaFrance, 2016).

Just as with the gender stereotypes considered earlier, stereotypes about gay men and lesbians fall into more differentiated subgroups as well. For example, Geiger and her colleagues identified eight distinct lesbian stereotypes, including "lipstick lesbians," "angry butch" types, and "free spirits," that differed in both their contents and their overall favorability (Geiger, Harwood, & Hummert, 2006). Similarly, Clausell and Fiske (2005) found evidence of 10 distinct gay man stereotypes that vary in their perceived communion and agency. For instance, "flamboyant" and "feminine" gay men are stereotyped as high in communion and somewhat low in agency while "hypermasculine" and "activist" gay men are stereotyped as low in communion and high in agency.

What about bisexual men and women? Interestingly, stereotypes about bisexual people tend to be more negative overall than stereotypes of heterosexual, gay, or lesbian people. This may be because of the stereotyped belief that bisexual people are highly sexual, indecisive, and confused (Burke & LaFrance, 2016; Zivony & Lobel, 2014). Further, bisexual people are stereotyped—by gay men and lesbians, as well as by heterosexual people—as having an unstable sexual orientation that is likely to change. Burke and LaFrance (2016) suggest that this stereotype might stem from a preference for simple, binary thinking and a discomfort with people who appear to straddle the boundaries between social categories.

Finally, little research examines stereotypes of heterosexual women and men, most likely because of **heteronormative** assumptions about sexuality. In other words, because of the dominant cultural assumption of heterosexuality as "normal" sexuality, most people are assumed heterosexual unless proven otherwise. Therefore, stereotypes of heterosexual women and men largely mimic the gender stereotypes that we have discussed throughout this chapter (Burke & LaFrance, 2016). But just as with the women-are-wonderful effect described earlier, the contents of stereotypes about heterosexual people differ as a function of who is doing the stereotyping. When Jes Matsick and Terri Conley (2016) asked lesbian, gay, bisexual, queer, and transgender (LGBQT) adults about their stereotypes of heterosexual men and women, they found some interesting themes. While some of the stereotype contents overlapped with widespread gender stereotypes, others were distinct and unflattering. For example, heterosexual men were stereotyped as *aggressive* and *macho* but also as *homophobic*, *intolerant*, and *ignorant*; heterosexual women were stereotyped as *emotional*, *hyperfeminine*, *appearance obsessed*, and *close-minded*. These stereotypes reveal the intergroup dynamics and tensions that exist between heterosexual people and members of sexual and gender minorities. Stereotypes of heterosexual people held by LGBQT individuals may thus reflect negative past experiences with heterosexual people or awareness of widespread, stigmatizing attitudes that are directed toward the LGBQT community.

Heteronormative: The assumption that "normal" sexuality is heterosexual.

Stop and Think

We have considered several cases in which the contents of social group stereotypes differ depending on who holds the stereotypes. What does this imply about the function that stereotypes serve for perceivers?

If social dynamics and relationships between social groups were to change, would you expect the contents of stereotypes to change as well? In what ways?

What Are Some Consequences of Gender Stereotyping?

Gender stereotypes double as gender rules. That is, they do not merely describe what we think women and men are like—they also convey cultural expectations about the traits that women and men ought (and ought not) to have. Whereas **gender prescriptions** indicate traits that women and men should exhibit, **gender proscriptions** indicate traits that women and men should not exhibit (Rudman et al., 2012). For women, prescriptions include the traits *warm*, *interested in children*, and *attentive to appearance* while proscriptions include *rebellious*, *arrogant*, and *promiscuous*. For men, prescriptions include *athletic*, *self-reliant*, and *rational*, and proscriptions include *emotional*, *childlike*, and *gullible*.

The fact that gender stereotypes serve as rules for behavior has two important consequences. First, if a culture values a stereotype (for example, the stereotype that men should be assertive and that women should be child oriented), people will feel pressure to conform to it, and those who do not conform can face punishment. Second, when a gender stereotype is negative (for example, the stereotype that girls do not excel at math or science), this can lead to personal anxieties or interpersonal behaviors that reinforce the stereotype. We will consider each of these processes in turn.

Penalizing Gender Role Violators

What happens when people violate gender rules? Recall that in Chapter 4 ("Gender Development"), we considered some of the consequences of gender nonconformity among children and adolescents. Just as children and teenagers who violate gender rules receive social sanctions, adult gender role violators similarly receive negative evaluations from others. We already alluded to a few of these negative evaluations when we discussed both the women-are-wonderful effect and subgrouping: Women who belong to nontraditional subgroups (e.g., "feminists") are stereotyped less favorably than traditional women, especially if these subgroups are associated with gender proscriptions (e.g., rebellious and stubborn; Eagly & Mladinic, 1994).

But why are gender role–violating women viewed so negatively? According to the **status incongruity hypothesis**, people stigmatize such women because they seem "too high" in dominance (Rudman et al., 2012). This hypothesis argues that gender rules serve to justify and reinforce the unequal gender hierarchy in which men, across cultures

Gender prescriptions: Traits that people believe women and men should have.

Gender proscriptions: Traits that people believe women and men should not have.

Status incongruity hypothesis: Assumption that gender role–violating women are viewed negatively because they are seen as too dominant while gender role–violating men are viewed negatively because they are seen as too low in status. These perceptions violate the gender status hierarchy and make people uncomfortable.

and times, routinely have higher social status than women. Because the behavior of agentic women appears incongruous with their expected low social status, it raises questions about the very legitimacy of the gender hierarchy. After all, if women can demonstrate agentic traits associated with high status, then why do we routinely allow men more access to power and status than women? To avoid this uncomfortable question, we penalize women who display high-status, agentic traits by viewing them as less likable and less hireable than similarly agentic men. Likewise, when men exhibit proscriptive traits associated with low status, such as modesty, they are liked less than comparably modest women (Moss-Racusin, Phelan, & Rudman, 2010). Again, Rudman and her colleagues explain this by suggesting that men who violate gender rules challenge the gender status quo, which makes people uncomfortable.

Confirming Negative Stereotypes

As noted, many gender stereotypes are negative. For example, people in many cultures view girls as less interested in and less capable at science and math than boys. How do you think this stereotype might affect girls? According to research on **stereotype threat**, members of negatively stereotyped groups often feel anxiety about the possibility of confirming negative group stereotypes. This anxiety, in turn, can undermine performance in high-stakes testing situations. To illustrate, when women or girls are reminded about negative math stereotypes prior to completing a series of difficult math problems, they perform more poorly than when *not* first reminded about the negative stereotype (Schmader & Johns, 2003). This performance decrement seems to occur because reminders of negative stereotypes increase test-taking anxiety and reduce working memory capacity (Rydell, McConnell, & Beilock, 2009). As you will read about further in Chapter 7 ("Cognitive Abilities and Aptitudes"), several meta-analyses indicate that stereotype threat can affect the performance of girls and women on math tests, but

Stereotype threat: Anxiety individuals feel when concerned that their behavior or performance might confirm a negative group stereotype.

Sidebar 5.3: Stereotype Threat Can Cost You College Credit

Even subtle reminders of gender, such as having students indicate their sex on a test booklet shortly before they take an exam, can activate negative stereotypes about women's math competencies and undermine women's math performance. For instance, Stricker and Ward (2004) manipulated when (either before or after the exam) approximately 2,000 high school students indicated their sex during a national Advanced Placement (AP) calculus exam. Women performed better when they indicated their sex after, as compared with before, the exam. This difference can have real consequences because students receive college credit if they achieve certain scores on the AP calculus exam. Danaher and Crandall (2009) estimated that a simple change to testing strategies, like routinely asking students to indicate their sex only *after* they complete this standardized exam, could result in an additional 4,700 women receiving college calculus credit each year.

the effects are modest and depend on several factors (Flore & Wicherts, 2015; Picho, Rodriguez, & Finnie, 2013). For instance, negative effects of stereotype threat on girls' math performance are larger in world regions characterized by greater gender inequality (e.g., southern Europe and East Africa) than they are in more gender-egalitarian regions (e.g., western and northern Europe). Within the United States, stereotype threat effects are larger in southern and Midwestern states than in the Northeast and West. This may suggest that stereotypes linking gender to math performance may be weaker in regions with more relaxed gender rules.

Negative stereotypes can also have interpersonal consequences, affecting people's expectations and therefore their behaviors toward members of stereotyped groups. For example, if a teacher holds the stereotype that girls lack proficiency at math, she may interact in subtly different ways with girls and boys in her classroom. She may give more attention to boys than girls during math class, or she may provide hints to boys (but not girls) who struggle with math problems. Over time, these repeated interactions can undermine girls' confidence in math, leading them to exert less effort or to disengage from math. Psychologists refer to this interpersonal process—in which a stereotype shapes how group members are treated, which then yields outcomes that "prove" the stereotype true—as a **self-fulfilling prophecy** (see Figure 5.2). The existence of self-fulfilling prophecies means that gender stereotypes can become true not because of inborn, biological factors but due merely to interpersonal processes. In sum, both stereotype threat and self-fulfilling prophecies can reinforce stereotypes by limiting the success of people who violate gender rules.

Self-fulfilling prophecy: Interpersonal process in which a perceiver's expectation about a target influences the target's behavior in such a manner that the target's behavior fulfills the perceiver's expectation.

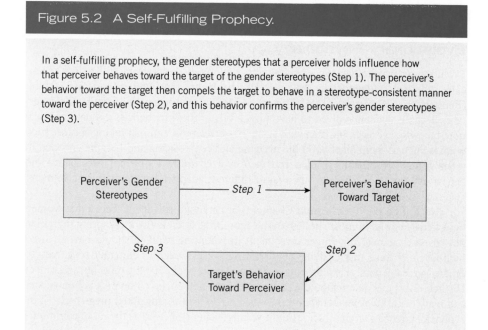

Figure 5.2 A Self-Fulfilling Prophecy.

In a self-fulfilling prophecy, the gender stereotypes that a perceiver holds influence how that perceiver behaves toward the target of the gender stereotypes (Step 1). The perceiver's behavior toward the target then compels the target to behave in a stereotype-consistent manner toward the perceiver (Step 2), and this behavior confirms the perceiver's gender stereotypes (Step 3).

Perceiver's Gender Stereotypes — Step 1 → Perceiver's Behavior Toward Target

Step 3 · Step 2

Target's Behavior Toward Perceiver

Generate another example of a self-fulfilling proph-ecy that follows the three steps outlined in Figure 5.2. What negative consequences might come from the *self-fulfilling prophecy in your example? What are some ways to prevent your self-fulfilling prophecy from happening?*

Where Do Gender Stereotypes Come From?

Uncovering the origins of gender stereotypes proves to be a perplexing and difficult task. How do we come to associate people of different sexes with specific qualities, tenden-cies, and roles? In this section, we will consider three perspectives on this topic that differ in the degree to which they emphasize biological versus social explanations. Note that you encountered two of these theories—evolutionary psychology and biosocial constructionist—in Chapter 3 ("The Nature and Nurture of Sex and Gender"). While evolutionary psychology explains gender stereotypes as arising from evolved sex differ-ences, social role theory views gender stereotypes as arising from the roles that women and men occupy. The biosocial constructionist model integrates ideas from evolutionary and social role approaches.

Evolutionary Psychology

Evolutionary psychology suggests that our stereotypes derive from and reflect geneti-cally inherited differences in the traits and behaviors that women and men exhibit (Kenrick, Trost, & Sundie, 2004). That is, we associate women with warmth and domes-ticity because women evolved to have high levels of these tendencies via natural selec-tion. Likewise, we associate men with agency, assertiveness, and risk-taking because such traits facilitated men's likelihood of surviving and reproducing and became encoded in men's genes. Presumably, women and men evolved to have different personality and behavioral tendencies because they faced different adaptive problems during humans' ancestry.

Recall from the discussion in Chapter 3 of parental investment theory that women (and female adults in most species) invest more time and energy in offspring than men do. Given their relatively larger investment in parenting, women should have evolved high levels of traits that facilitate child-rearing success, such as empathy, sensitivity to others, agreeableness, and nurturing (Christov-Moore et al., 2014; Costa, Terracciano, & McCrae, 2001). Women should also have evolved tendencies to be picky about mates and wary of casual sexual encounters, which could lead to unwanted pregnancy. These evolved tendencies would then result in women being perceived as the more communal and sexually reserved sex. In contrast, men are stereotyped as being promiscuous and unwilling to "settle down," qualities that may reflect their lower parental investment (Buss & Kenrick, 1998).

Because women are relatively selective in their choice of mates, ancestral men who demonstrated especially desirable qualities would have had the most success in attracting mates. (As you may recall, this is the principle of intersexual selection.) Such qualities include agentic traits such as status, social dominance, and competitiveness, as these traits reflect an ability to achieve status, acquire resources, provide for offspring, and offer protection. Recall also the principle of intrasexual selection, which states that male members of most species typically have to compete with each other for access to female mates. Ancestral men who had traits such as aggressiveness and strength would have been more likely to win intrasexual competitions and climb to the top of social dominance hierarchies. Because their social status should have made them attractive to women, they may have reproduced many times while men at the bottom of dominance hierarchies, who lacked desirable mating features, may not have reproduced at all (Buss & Kenrick, 1998). In this manner, men may have evolved a tendency toward high levels of agentic traits. Again, these traits would then result in men being stereotyped as the more agentic sex.

Social Role Theory

Social role theory views gender stereotypes as arising from and reflecting large-scale sex differences in the types of social roles that women and men typically occupy (Eagly, 1987; Eagly & Steffen, 1984). Across cultures and times, women and men have historically occupied different social roles, with women more often performing domestic and child-rearing duties and men more often performing physically demanding and risky duties, such as hunting, warfare, and herding. In contemporary Western cultures, this traditional division of labor manifests in at least two ways: First, women are more likely than men to be homemakers while men are more likely than women to be employed outside the home. Second, women in the paid workforce are more likely than men to occupy low-status positions while men in the workforce are more likely than women to occupy high-status positions. According to social role theory, this distribution of women and men into different types of roles then drives gender stereotypes. As Eagly and Steffen (1984) put it, "Gender stereotypes, like other social stereotypes, reflect perceivers' observations of what people do in daily life" (p. 735). Thus, if people observe women (more often than men) performing child-rearing activities, they should infer that women possess high levels of the traits necessary for childcare, such as warmth, nurturance, and selflessness. Similarly, if people observe men (more often than women) occupying high-status workplace roles, they should infer that men possess qualities essential for success in these roles, such as agency, competence, and assertiveness.

In a classic test of these ideas, Eagly and Steffen (1984) asked participants to consider either "an average woman" or "an average man," who was either employed full-time or a stay-at-home homemaker and parent; in a third condition, participants did not receive any information about the woman's or man's occupation. When people

Social role theory: Theory that gender stereotypes stem from people's observations of the social and occupational roles that women and men typically perform.

did not receive any information about the target person's occupation or role, they relied on gender stereotypes to rate the average woman as higher on communion and lower on agency than the average man. When they had information about the targets' occupations, however, people's ratings of communion and agency followed from the occupations rather than from the targets' sex. Both female and male homemakers were rated equally high in communion, and female and male employees were rated equally high in agency.

More recently, Koenig and Eagly (2014) presented participants with sets of occupations in which Black women, White women, Black men, and White men are actually overrepresented in the United States. For instance, Black men are overrepresented as athletes, laborers, and bus drivers, and White women are overrepresented as homemakers, teachers, and nurses (U.S. Bureau of Labor Statistics, 2005). Participants rated the communal and agentic traits associated both with the occupations and with the sex and race groups, and these correlations were very strong (rs ranging from .68 to .90). This means that stereotypes of different sex and race groups on communion and agency correspond very closely with the traits needed for the groups' typical occupations. Interestingly, these researchers also found that people expect stereotypes about sex and race groups to change in the future as the representation of social groups in different occupational roles changes over time.

Biosocial Constructionist Theory

As you read in Chapter 3, biosocial constructionist theory is an extension of social role theory that draws on both evolutionary and social approaches (W. Wood & Eagly,

2012). According to this perspective, all human societies benefit from dividing labor activities, such as infant care, hunting and gathering, and building, in a manner that maximizes efficiency. In some cases, this means using sex to determine labor suitability because some activities are more (or less) efficiently performed by members of one sex. For instance, the biological fact of women's role in childbearing and nursing means that women can more efficiently perform infant care responsibilities. Conversely, with greater size and strength on average, men can more efficiently perform labor activities requiring strength, endurance, and risk-taking, such as hunting, building, exploring, and fighting off predators. Thus, while not all women bear children, and not all men are big and strong, labor divisions based on sex generally offer practical and efficient solutions.

Two outcomes follow from this sex-based labor division. First, following the logic described in the prior section, people's gender stereotypes reflect their observations of what women and men do in their daily lives. Second, societies socialize children to adopt the traits and preferences that will facilitate performance of their future labor activities. While girls are encouraged to be kind, emotionally responsive, and tidy—qualities essential to childcare and home management—boys are encouraged to be brave, confident, and active in preparation for competitive workplace roles. This should remind you of the earlier discussion of gender rules: Cultural gender stereotypes serve as gender rules, in that people teach children that they ought to display certain traits and avoid others as a function of their sex.

To summarize, evolutionary psychology emphasizes genetically encoded differences between women and men that fuel cultural stereotypes, and social role theory emphasizes how stereotypes emerge from sex-based divisions of labor. The biosocial constructionist theory combines ideas from both of these approaches but refrains from suggesting that women and men are genetically predisposed to display different personality traits (e.g., communion and agency). Instead, the biosocial model suggests that physical differences between men and women account for sex-based divisions of labor, which then produce gender stereotypes and fuel gender socialization practices.

One interesting way in which these approaches differ is in the prospects for change that they offer. If, as evolutionary theories posit, gender stereotypes reflect genetic differences between women and men, then stereotypes will only change as fast as our genes do. In contrast, if gender stereotypes reflect common, sex-based divisions of labor, then they can change rapidly, as economic and sociocultural factors shift. However, think back to the findings we described earlier that showed that communal and agentic gender stereotypes have not changed substantially in the United States since 1983 (Haines et al., 2016), despite women assuming increasingly more agentic roles over time. Does the lack of changes in gender stereotypes over the past 30 years suggest that the social roles approach is wrong? Not necessarily. As you will read in Chapter 11 ("Work and Home"), the distribution of women and men into sex-typed occupations has not changed as much since the early 1990s as it did between the 1960s and 1980s. Perhaps the changes that occurred over the past 30 years have not been dramatic enough to produce noticeable differences in our gender stereotypes.

Postindustrial societies are shifting from jobs that require physical strength (like factory work and manufacturing jobs) to jobs that require intellectual abilities (like computer engineering). Consequently, there may be less sex segregation of occupations in the future.

What would evolutionary psychologists predict about changing gender roles and their relationship to gender stereotypes? What would social role theorists and the biosocial constructionist theorists predict?

Are Gender Stereotypes Accurate?

People sometimes assume that stereotypes are *inaccurate* by definition. You may have heard someone say, "Oh, that's not true; it's just a stereotype," as if a stereotype is nothing more than a myth. In fact, some psychologists do view gender stereotypes as inherently inaccurate, oversimplified, and exaggerated. However, others claim that stereotypes are actually pretty good representations of reality. So which is it? We explore this issue here, as well as in "Debate: Are Gender Stereotypes Accurate?"

Challenges: Defining "Reality" and Accuracy

Testing the accuracy of gender stereotypes is difficult, in part because of several measurement challenges (Jussim et al., 2016). First, researchers must decide what criterion will serve as the index of "reality." The central issue of stereotype accuracy is whether people's stereotyped beliefs correspond to social reality. But measuring that social reality can be tricky. To resolve this dilemma, researchers often rely on actual sex differences in traits, behaviors, cognitive abilities, and other factors, as reported in meta-analyses and large-scale survey studies. In these studies, sex differences are often reported as effect sizes, or statistics that convey the size of the difference between groups. (Refer back to Chapter 2, "Studying Sex and Gender," for a refresher on effect sizes.)

Direction accuracy:
Accuracy regarding the direction of a sex difference.

Discrepancy accuracy:
Accuracy regarding the specific size (and direction) of a sex difference.

Second, researchers must decide which type of accuracy to assess. One type, **direction accuracy**, refers to which group has more of a given quality than the other. For instance, if we stereotype men as stronger than women, and the average man actually outperforms the average woman on tests of physical strength, then the stereotype would be considered accurate for direction. A second, related type, **discrepancy accuracy**, conceptualizes accuracy in absolute terms—that is, how close to or far from reality is the stereotype? To assess this type of accuracy, researchers compute discrepancy scores between people's beliefs about the size of a sex difference and the actual size of the sex difference. For example, we could ask people to rate how "warm" both women and men are and use those ratings to calculate an effect size for the stereotyped sex difference in warmth. We could then subtract this effect size from the effect size for the actual sex difference on warmth. The resulting value would reveal the degree to which people's stereotypes overestimate, underestimate, or match the actual sex difference. Note that this way of measuring accuracy also encapsulates direction accuracy but takes it one step further by considering its distance from the real size of the sex difference.

Researchers have assessed both direction accuracy and discrepancy accuracy for a large number of traits, behaviors, and abilities, and we will summarize some of these results here. We will not, however, cover the accuracy of transgender or sexual minority stereotypes, as no studies have examined the accuracy of these stereotypes using the methods described here.

Cognitive Stereotypes

The topic of sex differences in cognitive abilities has a long and controversial history. Because of the value that people place on intelligence and the links between intelligence and achievement, gender stereotypes about cognitive ability can have powerful consequences for the outcomes of women and men. For example, if members of a given culture stereotype boys as more skilled at science than girls, then that culture might structure educational settings and opportunities in a manner that more effectively fosters science abilities in boys than in girls (recall our discussion of self-fulfilling prophecies). Over the long run, as a result of such educational practices, men might enter the workforce generally better prepared than women for careers in science.

To assess the accuracy of cognitive gender stereotypes, Diane Halpern and her colleagues asked participants to estimate the performance of male and female children and adults on 12 different cognitive tasks in domains of math, science, language and reading, social sciences, and humanities (Halpern, Straight, & Stephenson, 2011). On most of the cognitive tasks, stereotypes accurately reflected the direction of real sex differences. For example, stereotypes accurately placed girls and women ahead of boys and men on 3 of 4 verbal tasks, and they accurately placed boys and men ahead of girls and women on 3 of 5 math and science tasks. Moreover, stereotypes also accurately assumed no sex difference on tasks that showed no real sex difference. Thus, Halpern et al. concluded that gender stereotypes about cognitive abilities are largely accurate for direction. However, on 8 of the 12 tasks, stereotypes *under*estimated the size of the real sex difference, meaning that sex differences in some cognitive domains are larger than people's stereotypes suggest.

Personality Stereotypes

Researchers in one study asked respondents from 26 different countries to rate the typical male and female member of their nation on traits reflecting extraversion, neuroticism, agreeableness, conscientiousness, and openness to experience (the **Big Five personality dimensions**; Löckenhoff et al., 2014). As indices of reality, these researchers used sex difference effect sizes derived from people's self-reports of their own personalities as well as from observer ratings of women and men on the five factors.

Big Five personality dimensions: Five dimensions that many researchers agree capture most of the important variance in personality (extraversion, neuroticism, agreeableness, conscientiousness, and openness to experience).

Consistent with the stereotypes that we have discussed in this chapter, respondents stereotyped women as higher than men on the *warmth* and *positive emotions* facets of extraversion as well as on the *trust, altruism, compliance, modesty,* and *tender-mindedness* facets of agreeableness. Men were stereotyped as higher than women on the *assertiveness* and *excitement-seeking* facets of extraversion and on the *impulsiveness* facet of neuroticism. On all but one of these facets, the stereotypes were correct for direction, and in most cases, stereotypes were close in distance to the real effect sizes for the sex differences.

Nonverbal and Verbal Communication Stereotypes

Similar evidence of stereotype accuracy exists for nonverbal communication. Briton and Hall (1995) asked participants to rate the frequency with which women and men demonstrated 20 different nonverbal behaviors (e.g., interrupts others and uses hands while speaking) and communication skills (e.g., can read others' emotions from nonverbal cues) and then compared these with real sex differences as reported in meta-analyses. These researchers also examined stereotype accuracy separately for female and male perceivers and found no differences: Women's and men's stereotypes were accurate for direction on almost all of the behaviors. Interestingly, however, Shannon Holleran and her collaborators found evidence of stereotype *inaccuracy* in one important communication domain: general talkativeness (Holleran, Mehl, & Levitt, 2009). Despite the stereotype that women talk more than men, these researchers found no sex differences in talkativeness.

Stereotypes Across Multiple Domains

While the stereotype accuracy findings summarized thus far examined accuracy within single domains (e.g., personality or cognitive abilities), Janet Swim (1994) took a different approach. She examined the accuracy of people's gender stereotypes across 17 different domains, including cognitive abilities, leadership potential, helpfulness, nonverbal communication, happiness, and susceptibility to persuasion. This allowed Swim to test whether people understand that sex differences in some domains (e.g., leadership) are generally larger than sex differences in other domains (e.g., happiness). This type of accuracy, called **rank-order accuracy**, is examined by computing correlations between stereotyped and actual sex differences across several dimensions; high correlations mean that stereotypes accurately reveal which sex differences are larger than others. Overall, Swim found a very large correlation between stereotyped and real sex differences across the 17 domains ($r = .79$), suggesting that gender stereotypes offer reasonably accurate information about the relative sizes of sex differences across domains (see Figure 5.3).

In sum, much of the research presented here indicates that gender stereotypes are fairly accurate. Nonetheless, as the issues raised in the debate make clear, it may be premature to conclude that the accuracy issue is fully resolved (see "Debate: Are Gender Stereotypes Accurate?").

Rank-order accuracy: Accuracy regarding the relative sizes of sex differences across different domains.

Figure 5.3   Correlation Between Stereotyped and Real Sex Differences.

Across 17 domains, people's stereotypes about the sizes of sex differences reasonably accurately reflect the real sizes of these sex differences.

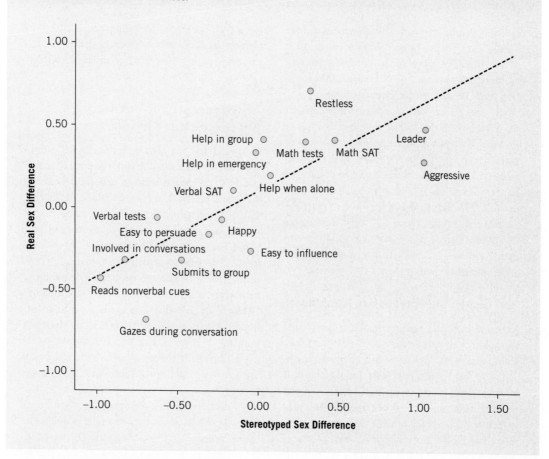

Source: Swim (1994).

Stop and Think

Which type of accuracy—direction, discrepancy, or rank-order—do you think is most important when it comes to measuring the accuracy of stereotypes? What are the strengths and weaknesses of each? If you were going to measure the accuracy of stereotypes, what type of accuracy would you focus on? Why?

Debates over the accuracy of social stereotypes have a long history in psychology. While some theorists debate the appropriate methods for determining accuracy, others debate the very value of the question itself. Because people often use stereotypes to justify unequal systems of power, some consider the question of their accuracy a dangerous one. For example, if women really *are* warmer and less competitive than men, perhaps it makes sense to expect women to become homemakers instead of business leaders. As you can imagine, this conclusion is not one that many gender researchers wish to promote. Despite the controversy of this topic, researchers do examine stereotype accuracy. We will first summarize evidence indicating that gender stereotypes are accurate and then consider a counterview.

Yes, Gender Stereotypes Are Accurate

As you read in this chapter, researchers have tested the accuracy of gender stereotypes about personality traits, verbal and nonverbal communication, cognitive abilities, and happiness. By and large, this research suggests that gender stereotypes are pretty accurate. Whether we consider direction accuracy (which sex exceeds the other?), discrepancy accuracy (how closely do stereotyped sex differences match real sex differences?), or rank-order accuracy (which sex differences are larger than others?), gender stereotypes reflect reality to an impressive degree. There are exceptions, of course, but the overall trend favoring the accuracy of gender stereotypes outweighs these exceptions. For example, when comparing people's beliefs about the size of sex differences with the actual size of sex differences, people are quite accurate on average (Swim, 1994). In fact, Lee Jussim and his colleagues called

stereotype accuracy (including the accuracy of stereotypes about gender) "one of the largest and most replicable effects in all of social psychology" (Jussim et al., 2016, p. 31).

No, Gender Stereotypes Are Not (Necessarily) Accurate

To understand the argument that gender stereotypes are not accurate, it is important first to understand the distinction between **generic beliefs** and **statistical beliefs** (Cimpian, Brandone, & Gelman, 2010). Generic beliefs pertain to categories as wholes, without any reference to numbers or proportions. For example, the statement "Women are friendly" expresses a generic belief. In contrast, statistical beliefs pertain to proportions or numbers, such as the statements "Most women are friendly" "Women are friendlier, on average, than men." Importantly, because generic beliefs are detached from numbers or statistics, their accuracy is virtually impossible to test. What criteria could you use to test whether it is accurate that "Women are friendly"?

Therefore, when measuring stereotype accuracy, researchers exclusively examine people's statistical beliefs about sex categories. For example, Löckenhoff et al. (2014) asked respondents to rate the personalities of a typical woman and man on 5-point scales while Janet Swim (1994) had respondents indicate the percentages of women and men whom they expected to display certain traits or tendencies. In these and other cases, researchers asked participants to report their statistical beliefs about gender, not their generic beliefs about gender. Thus, as Bian and Cimpian (2016) suggest, research on stereotype accuracy only tells us that people's statistical beliefs about gender are fairly accurate. This work, however, reveals nothing about the accuracy of people's generic beliefs about gender.

So the issue of stereotype accuracy boils down to the question of whether stereotypes are more like statistical beliefs or more like generic beliefs. According to Bian and Cimpian (2016), most stereotypes align more with generic beliefs than statistical ones. In other words, stereotypes link groups with traits in a generic way, such as "Men are aggressive" and "Women are pretty." If this is true, then we do not know whether gender stereotypes are accurate or not because we have not yet conducted the right tests. The very act of measuring accuracy forces respondents to express their gender stereotypes in a manner (i.e., as statistical beliefs) that differs from how they usually think about them (i.e., as generic beliefs).

Further, there are reasons to suspect the inaccuracy of generic beliefs about social groups. For instance, generic beliefs tend to be unrelated to statistical facts (Cimpian et al., 2010) and resistant to counterevidence (Chambers, Graham, & Turner, 2008). This means that people cling to their generic beliefs even when confronted with facts or evidence that should cause them to question these beliefs. As an example, suppose you believe that "women are bad drivers" (a generic belief), but you also have several female friends who are good drivers (counterevidence). If you consider these friends "exceptions to the rule," and you do not adjust your stereotype about women drivers, then you are ignoring the counterevidence. If generic beliefs are both unrelated to facts and resistant to counterevidence, they are unlikely to be good reflections of reality. Therefore, if gender stereotypes are more like generic beliefs than statistical beliefs, then they are probably inaccurate.

Now that you have read both sides of this debate, what do you think? Are gender stereotypes accurate or not? Which side of the debate seems more compelling? Which evidence do you find most and least convincing? Why?

So How Universal Are Gender Stereotypes, Really?

Earlier in this chapter, you read that stereotypes about women's communion and men's agency are consistent across cultures. And in fact, J. E. Williams and Best's (1990) cross-cultural data bear this out, when viewed from a "big-picture" perspective. However, when Amy Cuddy and her colleagues examined the data more closely, they observed some subtle but interesting cultural differences (Cuddy et al., 2015). These researchers wondered whether gender stereotypes might differ as a function of core cultural values because dominant social groups are often attributed high levels of culturally valued traits (Ridgeway, 2001). In **individualistic cultures**, such as the United States and many Western European nations, core values prioritize the individual's goals over the group's goals; thus, valued traits include agentic qualities, such as independence, autonomy, and self-reliance. In **collectivistic cultures**, including many East Asian, Middle Eastern, and African nations, core values prioritize the needs of the group over the needs of individuals. In these cultures, valued traits include communal qualities, such as social sensitivity, connectedness to others, and nurturance. Based on

Generic beliefs: Beliefs about categories as wholes, without reference to numbers or proportions.

Statistical beliefs: Beliefs about categories that involve numbers or proportions.

These children are members of the Samburu tribe of Kenya, a highly collectivistic culture that prioritizes group harmony over individual goals.

Source: © iStockPhoto.com/Bartosz Hadyniak

this distinction, Cuddy and her colleagues predicted that members of individualistic nations would stereotype men (the dominant group) as high in individualistic traits while collectivistic nations would stereotype men as high on collectivistic traits. To test this, the researchers reanalyzed Williams and Best's (1990) original data but looked only at those traits (out of 300) that most clearly captured individualism (21 traits) and collectivism (27 traits). When looking only at this subset of traits, a new pattern emerged: The more individualistic a nation was, the more people in that nation associated individualistic traits with men; the more collectivistic a nation was, the more people in that nation associated collectivistic traits with men.

What do you make of this finding? One take-home message is that gender stereotypes may not be as universal as once thought. In a finding that turns much of this chapter on its head, highly collectivistic nations stereotype men as the more other-oriented sex and women as the more self-reliant sex. But think about what this means in terms of core cultural values and dominant social groups. While the *contents* of gender stereotypes may not be as universal as once thought, the tendency to attribute the most culturally valuable traits to the dominant sex category (i.e., men) does appear to be universal. In a sense, this suggests that gender stereotypes may serve as a means by which high-status groups maintain their power over lower-status groups. Turn to Chapter 6 ("Power, Sexism, and Discrimination") for a deeper discussion of how stereotypes not only reflect but also perpetuate systems of status and power.

CHAPTER SUMMARY

5.1 Describe the contents and structure of gender stereotypes, especially in terms of the dimensions of communion and agency.

Of the many specific traits, roles, occupations, and physical attributes that people use to describe groups of female and male people, most fall along two core important dimensions: communion and agency. Communion reflects traits related to warmth, nurturance, and emotional sensitivity (qualities usually associated with girls and women), and agency reflects traits of competence, assertiveness, and status (qualities usually associated with boys and men). The content of gender stereotypes is generally consistent across cultures and, at least in the United States, the strength of people's gender stereotypes has not changed over the past 30 years, perhaps because female and male social roles have not changed as rapidly since the early 1990s as they did from the 1960s to the 1980s.

Despite the universality of broad gender stereotypes, subgroups of men and women have unique stereotypes associated with them. For instance, stereotypes of career women cast them as more competent but less warm than stereotypes of housewives. Furthermore, when considering an individual's standing on multiple social categories (e.g., sex, race, class, and sexual orientation) simultaneously, unique stereotypes emerge. As an example, Middle Eastern women are stereotyped as quiet, which is not a stereotype associated with either women or Middle Eastern people in general. Stereotypes about transgender people portray MtF women as similar to cisgender women while stereotypes of FtM men portray them as more androgynous than cisgender men. Stereotypes about gay men and lesbians largely portray them as similar to members of the other sex. Stereotypes of heterosexual people held by sexual minority individuals tend to contain traits such as "intolerant" and "close-minded," perhaps reflecting intergroup tensions.

5.2 Discuss the social consequences of violating prescriptive and proscriptive gender stereotypes.

Gender stereotypes do not merely describe the traits, roles, and behaviors associated with women and men, but they also prescribe how members of each sex ought to be (e.g., women should be warm, and men should be self-reliant). In contrast, gender proscriptions describe traits that women and men should not have (e.g., women should not be arrogant, and men should not be emotional). According to the status incongruity hypothesis, gender rules justify the gender hierarchy that affords men more status than women. Thus, women who violate gender rules are penalized for being too dominant because they challenge the gender hierarchy, and men who violate gender rules are penalized for appearing too low in status. People reminded of negative stereotypes about their gender group tend to experience stereotype threat, which can lead them to underperform. Gender stereotypes may also result in self-fulfilling prophecies. Stereotype threat and self-fulfilling prophecies both reinforce stereotypes by limiting the success of people who violate gender rules.

5.3 Evaluate the major theories of gender stereotypes.

Theories that seek to explain the origins of gender stereotypes offer different views of how malleable these beliefs are. Evolutionary psychologists view gender stereotypes as arising from genetically encoded sex differences, suggesting that these stereotypes are firmly entrenched and slow to change. In contrast, the social role and biosocial constructionist theories propose that sex-based labor divisions and occupations produce gender stereotypes. These latter approaches imply that stereotypes can shift more rapidly, as sex-based labor divisions change with time. The biosocial constructionist theory also notes that gender rules are adaptive because they prepare children for the roles that they will likely occupy as adults.

5.4 Analyze research and perspectives on the accuracy of gender stereotypes.

Cognitive approaches view stereotyping as part of a natural tendency to simplify a complex social world by reducing it into meaningful categories. Although this can lead to errors and overgeneralizations, stereotypes are not necessarily inaccurate. Some psychologists argue that gender stereotypes are accurate, in terms of direction (which sex exceeds the other?), discrepancy (how large is the sex difference?), and rank-order accuracy (which sex differences are larger than others?). People's reports of gender stereotypes about cognitive skills, personality, communication tendencies, and helpfulness tend to map accurately onto actual sex differences in these domains. Despite this, some argue that the accuracy question remains unanswered because the way that researchers assess stereotypes (as statistical beliefs) does not reflect how people actually hold stereotypes (as generic beliefs).

Test Your Knowledge: True or False?

5.1. The contents of gender stereotypes tend to vary a lot from one culture to another. (False: The contents of gender stereotypes are largely consistent across cultures, with some exceptions.) [p. 152]

5.2. In the United States, the strength of people's gender stereotypes has not weakened over the past several decades. (True: Gender stereotypes are endorsed just as strongly today as they were in the mid-1980s.) [p. 154]

5.3. Being reminded of a negative gender stereotype can cause people to behave consistently with the stereotype. (True: When people are reminded of negative stereotypes about their gender group, this can cause anxious arousal and preoccupation that causes them to confirm the stereotype.) [p. 166]

5.4. Gender stereotypes largely map onto the types of social roles and occupations that women and men perform. (True: Social role theory argues and finds that gender stereotypes accurately reflect the distributions of women and men into sex-based labor and role divisions.) [p. 169]

5.5. Most of the evidence indicates that widely held gender stereotypes are inaccurate. (False: Much evidence indicates that people's gender stereotypes are generally accurate in terms of direction, discrepancy, and rank-ordering.) [p. 173]

Test Your Knowledge: True or False?

6.1 When women outnumber men on college campuses, heterosexual men put less effort and commitment into their college dating relationships.

6.2 Individuals who are members of one subordinate group tend to experience the same amount of discrimination as individuals who are members of two subordinate groups.

6.3 People who endorse hostile attitudes toward women also tend to endorse benevolent attitudes toward women (i.e., beliefs that women should be cherished and protected).

6.4 The United States typically ranks in the top 10 countries in the world in terms of gender equality (measured in terms of gaps between women and men in health, education, political representation, and economic participation).

6.5 Women's intentions to confront gender discrimination match their actual rates of confronting gender discrimination.

Power, Sexism, and Discrimination

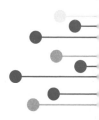

Key Concepts

How Do Power and Privilege Relate to Sex and Gender?
Patriarchal and Matriarchal Social Structures
Structural Versus Dyadic Power
Ways of Exerting Power
    Force
    Resource Control
    Cultural Ideologies
Privilege
Intersectionality, Double Jeopardy, and Invisibility

What Is Sexism, and Why Does It Persist?
Ambivalent Sexism Toward Women
Ambivalent Attitudes Toward Men
Journey of Research: Measuring Gender Role and Sexist Attitudes
Social Dominance and System Justification Theories
Why Do Sexist Attitudes Matter?
Debate: Do Men Experience Sexism?

What Is Gender Discrimination?
Overt Discrimination and Microaggressions
Global Gender Discrimination in Education and Politics

How Can We Resist and Reduce Gender Discrimination?
Affirmative Action: It's the Law
Confronting Gender Discrimination: Individual Efforts
Resisting Gender Discrimination: Collective Action
Being an Ally

Learning Objectives

Students who read this chapter should be able to do the following:

6.1 Explain how social structures are organized by sex across cultures and how power and privilege shape the experiences of individuals and groups.

6.2 Evaluate different theoretical perspectives on sexism and gender inequality.

6.3 Explain the types and consequences of gender discrimination.

6.4 Evaluate the difficulties of recognizing and confronting discrimination and the methods that individuals and groups use to resist and reduce discrimination.

Power, Sexism, and Discrimination

On April 15, 1912, the RMS *Titanic* hit an iceberg in the Atlantic Ocean on its trip from Southampton, England, to New York City. Over the course of the 2 hours and 15 minutes that it took for the ship to sink, 1,500 people died, making it one of the most deadly maritime events in history. Interestingly, women and men did not have equal survival rates: While 75% of the women on board survived the accident, only 17% of the men did. Why? The *Titanic's* captain enforced a code known as the *Birkenhead drill* that dictates that women and children should be saved first in times of emergency. This meant that women and children filled the limited number of lifeboats on the *Titanic* before the captain allowed men to board them.

To many, the word *sexism* conveys hostility toward women, inappropriate attention to women's physical appearance, or negative assumptions about women's competence. From this perspective, rescuing women before men on a sinking ship may not seem like sexism—in fact, it may seem chivalrous. But as Peter Glick and Susan Fiske explain in their *ambivalent sexism theory*, chivalry toward women constitutes a type of sexism (called benevolent sexism) that often coexists alongside the negative and more commonly recognized hostile sexism (Glick & Fiske, 1996). And, in fact, benevolent sexism has negative consequences for women that are just as harmful as—and sometimes more harmful than—treating women with openly sexist hostility. We will consider these consequences in greater detail throughout this chapter.

This chapter tackles broad issues of power, status, sexism, and discrimination. Unlike the last chapter, which focused on the specific contents of gender-relevant stereotypes, this chapter steps back and looks at the bigger picture of group relations. We will examine how sex interacts with other social group memberships to influence levels of group power and how dominant groups maintain power over subordinate groups. We will also take a detailed look at several theories (including ambivalent sexism theory) that contribute to our understanding of gender relations and examine some concrete evidence of gender discrimination and its consequences. Finally, we will discuss why members of disadvantaged groups often do not confront personal discrimination and what positive steps can be taken by those who wish to resist and reduce discrimination.

How Do Power and Privilege Relate to Sex and Gender?

Patriarchal and Matriarchal Social Structures

All human societies have hierarchical structures, with dominant groups enjoying more power and resources than subordinate groups. Specifically, dominant groups have more political and decision-making power and better access to education, desirable jobs, good food, housing and protection, quality medical care, and leisure activities than subordinate groups (Pratto, Sidanius, & Levin, 2006). As far as we know, all known human societies have been *patriarchal*, meaning that men constitute the dominant group, organize the society, and control how it operates. In contrast, we lack evidence of any true *matriarchal* societies, or societies in which women constitute the dominant group. In her famous book *Sex and Temperament in Three Primitive Societies*, anthropologist Margaret Mead (1935) asserted that the Chambri people of Papua New Guinea were a true matriarchal society, with women serving as the primary breadwinners and traders. But later studies of Chambri society revealed that Mead's original analysis overlooked some subtle but important gender dynamics. While Chambri women were the primary fishers and traders, they did not ultimately hold more political power than Chambri men (Gewertz, 1983).

Although social scientists generally view male- rather than female-dominated societies as a human universal, many people still believe in the *myth of matriarchy*, which is the idea that dominant women governed early societies (Eller, 2001). According to the myth, ancestral women ruled over peaceful, cooperative, and nature-loving societies, and people worshipped goddesses instead of gods. As the story goes, matriarchies disappeared gradually over time as patriarchies, which emphasize status, competition, war, and wealth acquisition, rose in prominence and became the dominant human social structure.

Matrilineal society: A society that traces descent through the mother's kinship line and passes inheritance down from mothers to their offspring.

Stop and Think

Why do you think people find the myth of matriarchy *so intriguing? Why is it compelling to envision a past where women held power over men? If truly* *matriarchal societies did exist, how (if at all) might they differ from patriarchal ones?*

Sidebar 6.1: Matriarchal Apes?

While we lack concrete evidence of matriarchal societies in our human ancestry, the nonhuman primate world offers an example in Bonobo chimpanzees, who share about 99% of their genes with humans. Dominant female apes govern Bonobo groups and control their activities (Herdt & Polen-Petit, 2014). Not only are they cooperative and largely peaceful, but Bonobo groups are also quite sexual, with about 75% of their sexual activity being nonreproductive. Primatologists believe that this sexual activity, which includes same-sex sexual activity, promotes strong social bonds and facilitates tendencies to cooperate, share, and live together peacefully (Parish & de Waal, 2000).

Patrilineal society: A society that traces descent through the father's kinship line and passes inheritance down from fathers to their offspring.

Matrilocal society: A society in which husbands typically live near their wives' families.

In addition to patriarchies and matriarchies, there are several other types of gender-related social structures. For instance, **matrilineal societies** trace descent through the mother's kinship line and pass inheritance down from mothers while **patrilineal societies** trace descent and pass inheritance through fathers. Numerous matrilineal societies, such as the Navajo of North America, the Garo of India, and the Tuareg of Northern

Patrilocal society: A society in which wives typically live near their husbands' families.

Africa, have been documented throughout history. Similarly, societies can be **matrilocal**, in which husbands typically live near their wives' families, or **patrilocal**, in which wives typically live near their husbands' families (Koratayev, 2003). Although matrilineal and matrilocal societies are not matriarchies—because women in these societies hold less overall political and decision-making power than men—they do grant women certain power. For instance, the Tuareg of the Sahara Desert are a seminomadic Muslim society in which women have the same sexual rights as men, are free to take lovers before marriage and to divorce without shame, and keep their property and rights after divorce (P. B. Williams, 2015).

Structural Versus Dyadic Power

Thus far, we have discussed power without defining it. **Power** refers to the capacity to determine not only one's own outcomes but the outcomes of others as well. Multiple types of power exist. Patriarchal power is, by definition, **structural**. This means that it

Bonobos live in matriarchal groups governed by dominant females.

Source: © iStockPhoto .com/USO

manifests by shaping how society operates and determining which groups of people have (or lack) access to resources, education, autonomy, jobs, and so on. In contrast, **dyadic power** refers to the capacity to choose intimate partners and relationships and to control the interactions and decisions that occur within those relationships. Thus, those who hold more structural power control the society at large while those who hold more dyadic power control the home and family. This distinction is important because although men hold more political and economic power than women in public domains, women sometimes have more "behind-the-scenes" dyadic power, exerting influence over private matters

ters in relationships and the household (Guttentag & Secord, 1983). The dyadic power of women is not absolute, however, since men can and do use their structural power to limit women's dyadic power. The ability of women to control their own relationship outcomes also depends on factors such as their age, ethnicity, income, and education level (Wingood & DiClemente, 2000). Thus, not all women have the same amount of dyadic power over decisions about things like housework, childcare, and sexual activity (Albarracin & Plambeck, 2010).

The sex ratio, or ratio of men to women in a given environment, also influences the levels of dyadic power that the sexes hold. According to *sex ratio theory* (Guttentag & Secord, 1983), when men outnumber women, women should hold more dyadic power because they have a larger pool of potential partners and more alternatives to choose from if they grow dis-

A Tuareg woman.

Source: Courtesy of Alain Elorza

satisfied with current partners. As their dyadic power increases, heterosexual women should become more selective, placing more emphasis on high-quality male mates who exhibit signs of status, commitment, and financial resources. Heterosexual men, who must attract partners from a relatively small pool, should become motivated to display more desirable qualities—such as relationship commitment—to increase their appeal as mates.

To what extent does the evidence support sex ratio theory? The answer is complicated. In contrast to the theory, we lack evidence that women's mate preferences are more selective when men outnumber them (Stone, Shackelford, & Buss, 2007). In support of the theory, however, men do tend to show more relationship and family commitment when they outnumber women, resulting in lower divorce rates (Barber, 2003). Further, since the value that people place on women's traditional work (e.g., child-rearing and domestic labor) increases under these conditions, women tend to marry younger and have more children. With their life options more constrained by traditional labor arrangements, women tend to achieve lower rates of literacy, education, and labor force participation, which can reinforce their relatively low structural power (South & Trent, 1988). Thus, structural and dyadic power levels are interconnected, with women's levels of dyadic power impacting how much structural power they have.

Not all women, however, experience increases in dyadic power when men outnumber them. Consider current sex ratios in India. Due to the long-term practice of sex-selective abortion (disproportionate abortion of female fetuses), men substantially outnumber women, particularly in the Northern Indian states of Punjab and Haryana. While sex ratio theory would predict that women in this situation should see straightforward increases in their dyadic power, many rural women across India instead are at risk of "bride purchase" in a growing bride trade, due to their general lack of structural power (Samal, 2016). Thus, lower-status and vulnerable women in any given context may see decreases, rather than increases, in dyadic power when men outnumber women.

Power: The capacity to determine one's own and other people's outcomes.

Structural power: The power to shape societies and social systems.

Dyadic power: The power to choose intimate partners and relationships and to control the interactions and decisions that occur within those relationships.

Sidebar 6.2: Sex Ratios and "Leftover" Women

With a sex ratio of about 115 males per 100 females (from birth to age 24), China is an interesting case. Given that China has the largest population of any country in the world (1.38 billion), this sex gap is significant. Depending on the age range, there are about 50–100 million more men than women in China (*CIA World Factbook*, 2016). China's skewed sex ratio has roots in its one-child policy, in effect from 1979 to 2015, when the rates of sex-selective abortion and female infanticide increased as parents tried to ensure having male offspring. With men substantially outnumbering women in China, women should have greater dyadic power in comparison with men. But what does the research show? High sex ratios (meaning men outnumber women) are associated with most Chinese women marrying younger (before age 25) and engaging in more premarital and extramarital sex (Trent & South, 2011). Further, some educated, professional Chinese women delay marriage to establish their careers, despite being stigmatized by family and the general public as unmarriageable and "leftover" women (Ji, 2015). Thus, we do see displays of dyadic power as Chinese women increasingly choose the terms of their intimate relationships even in the face of stigmatization.

What happens when women outnumber men, as they do in former Soviet Republics like Kazakhstan and Kyrgyzstan (Smirnova & Cai, 2015)? In these cases, men tend to have more dyadic power because they have a larger pool of potential mates. According to sex ratio theory, the availability of numerous female partners should encourage male promiscuity and discourage male commitment to any one partner, so heterosexual marriage rates will decline, people will marry later, and divorce rates will climb. College campuses in the United States constitute an environment in which these hypotheses can be tested because women outnumber men with a ratio of approximately 57% women to 43% men (National Center for Education Statistics, 2016). As members of the scarcer sex, heterosexual men on U.S. campuses should be able to get more out of their college relationships while giving less. Research findings support this. When women are in the majority on college campuses, heterosexual women report expecting and receiving less from their male dating partners (Uecker & Regnerus, 2010). Moreover, even though college women outnumber college men across ethnic groups, the sex gaps are approximately two times larger for Black and Latino students than they are for White students. Given this, how do you think heterosexual college relationship dynamics might differ across different ethnic groups?

Ways of Exerting Power

People can wield power in many different ways, and these different types of power have relevance for understanding relations not only between sex groups but also between groups who differ on race, ethnicity, sexual orientation, and gender identity. In Western cultures, dominant groups tend to be White, wealthy, heterosexual, able-bodied, Christian, cisgender men, whereas subordinate groups are those that lack power based on sex, race, ethnicity, socioeconomic status, sexual orientation, gender identity, physical ability, religion, and the intersections of these categories. Though we could discuss many different types of power, we will focus on three types identified by Pratto and Walker (2004)—force, resource control, and cultural ideologies—due to their relevance to sex and gender.

Force. Force refers to the capacity to inflict physical or psychological harm on another (Pratto & Walker, 2004). Examples of force, by which dominant groups wield power over subordinate groups, include domestic abuse, emotional abuse, rape, sexual harassment, murder, child abuse, slavery, human trafficking, imprisonment, and capital punishment. Force need not always involve actual harm because threats of violence can serve as effective forms of control. Given the greater average size, strength, and physical aggressiveness of men relative to women, men, as a group, have universally used force more often and more effectively than women to exert social and political power over others (Brown, 1991).

As an example, consider that men's use of sexual violence against women correlates directly with the amount of structural power that men hold over women. One correlational, cross-national study found that national levels of male-to-female sexual violence were associated with national gender inequality (larger power disparities favoring men over women) and more fear on the part of women (Yodanis, 2004). Of course, we cannot conclude from these correlational findings that men's use of sexual violence *causes* their greater relative power over women, but they at least suggest that sexual violence may serve as a means of force by which men maintain power over women (for further discussion of sexual violence, see Chapter 14, "Aggression and Violence").

Stop and Think

Given that the link between national levels of male-to-female sexual violence and gender inequality is correlational, *how might it be interpreted? What are some possible third variables that might explain this association?*

Men use force to exert power over other men as well. Most violent crimes, such as assault and murder, are committed not only by men but against men as well (Daly & Wilson, 1988). In the United States and Europe, men are twice as likely as women to be victims of aggravated assault and at least three times more likely than women to be murdered. Around the world, men die in battle far more often than women. Additional examples of men's use of force against men include imprisonment and capital punishment (state-sanctioned execution). Across countries, the percentages of male (versus female) prisoners range from 78% to 98%, with 92% of prison inmates in the United States being men. Capital punishment rates show even more gender disparity: In recent years, women made up less than 1% of those legally executed worldwide, and men made up more than 97% of those executed in the United States (Benatar, 2012).

Group-based dominance and power play substantial roles in men's use of force against men. Men of color are by far the most frequent targets of imprisonment and capital punishment while White men in the United States—and men of dominant ethnic groups in other cultures—most commonly represent the state that sanctions such punishment (Pratto & Pitpitan, 2008). Note that the higher incarceration rates

of racial and ethnic minority men in the United States do not necessarily reflect higher criminality among these men, as men of color face higher arrest rates, harsher sentencing, and higher incarceration rates than White men do for the same crimes (Pettit & Western, 2004). Similarly, gay men are disproportionately likely to be victims of violent hate crimes by other men (Federal Bureau of Investigation, 2015b). These patterns suggest that dominant male groups regularly use force to exert power over subordinate male groups.

Ethnic minority men are vastly overrepresented among prison inmates.

Source: © iStockPhoto .com/sakhorn38

Resource control. A second type of power, **resource control**, refers to controlling the creation or distribution of essential and desirable goods, such as money, land, food, and other valued commodities (Pratto & Walker, 2004). Resource control gives power to dominant groups because having access to more resources correlates with safety, health, freedom, and quality of life. In contrast, those who lack resources must depend on others. On average, men—in comparison with women—have greater resource control. Cross-culturally, men tend to make more money, on average, than women for the same work (International Labour Organization, 2007), though the size of this wage gap—at least in the United States—varies significantly by race and ethnicity (as we discuss further in Chapter 11, "Work and Home"). Men also hold high-paying, socially valued jobs more often than women. For example, one study of more than 21,000 firms in 91 different countries found that women hold only 14% of all top executive jobs, and they constitute only 4.5% of all CEOs worldwide (Noland et al., 2016). Historically, laws in many countries have given (and still give) men ownership of household property and possessions, leaving women economically dependent on men (Coontz, 2006).

Although men tend to control resources more often than women do, men of color and gay men have less control over resources than do White and heterosexual men. As an example, heterosexual people regularly attempt to limit sexual minority individuals' access to resources, for instance, through legislation that prevents same-sex couples from adopting children or that allows businesses to deny services to sexual minority individuals (Phillips, 2016). Furthermore, White and Asian people in the United States have access to more wealth, better jobs and education, and higher-quality health care than do Black and Latino people (American Psychological Association, 2017). Worldwide patterns indicate that members of dominant ethnic groups receive more desirable jobs, earn more money, own more land, control more natural resources, and claim more rights and freedoms than do members of subordinate ethnic groups (Pratto & Pitpitan, 2008).

One exception to the general pattern of men's greater resource control is that of child custody following divorce. Men gain sole custody of children in only about 10% of divorce cases in the United States, and this trend is similar across many cultures (Benatar, 2012). Compare this with women, who gain sole custody in about 70% of divorce cases. Likely due to stereotypes about women's superior parenting skills, custody decisions tend to favor mothers over fathers. (You will read more about parenting stereotypes in Chapter 10, "Interpersonal Relationships.") David Benatar (2012) argues that custody decisions favoring mothers constitute an important—but largely ignored—source of systematic sex bias against men. Moreover, he suggests that the lack of daily contact with their children contributes to men's worse mental health following divorce. Though women often suffer more financially from divorce, they generally report being happier than men following a divorce (A. E. Clark & Georgellis, 2013). We explore the possibility of systemic discrimination against men further in "Debate: Do Men Experience Sexism?"

Cultural ideologies. **Cultural ideologies** are sets of beliefs and assumptions about groups that explain and justify unequal social hierarchies. They serve as a means of exerting power because the values that they promote reflect and protect the interests of those in power (Pratto & Walker, 2004). In other words, cultural ideologies represent reality the way dominant groups see it, and they justify the privileged position of dominant groups. For example, as discussed in Chapter 2 ("Studying Sex and Gender"), the cultural ideology of **androcentrism** defines men and their experiences as the universal or default for the species and treats women and their experiences as deviations from the male norm. As one vivid example, the field of psychology largely ignored women's viewpoints and experiences until the 1970s. Researchers assumed that findings from studies with only male participants would generalize to all people, and both the topics of investigation and the definitions of key variables within psychology reflected primarily male interests (Crawford & Marecek, 1989). Though the field has become less androcentric over time, androcentrism is still a powerful ideology that both reflects and perpetuates men's dominant social status.

Other ideologies relevant to discussions of group-based power include ethnocentrism and heterocentrism. **Ethnocentrism** portrays dominant ethnic groups as universal and "normal," and **heterocentrism** portrays heterosexual people as universal and "normal." Just as with androcentrism, these ideologies reflect the perspectives and narratives of dominant groups and largely ignore the perspectives of subordinate groups, thereby communicating that subordinate groups are less normal and less important. Just as mainstream psychology has been androcentric, it is also ethnocentric and heterocentric by assuming that the experiences of primarily White, heterosexual samples will generalize to ethnic and sexual minority individuals (Cole, 2009).

Stereotypes are elements of cultural ideologies. Widespread, cross-cultural gender stereotypes that portray men as "assertive leaders" and women as "caring nurturers" help to justify the traditional division of labor in which men earn money by working outside the home and women occupy unpaid child-rearing and homemaking roles. Ethnic stereotypes, such as stereotypes of Black men as more aggressive than White men or of Latino men as less educated than White men, serve to justify power inequities in which White men have higher social status, better access to lucrative jobs, and lower incarceration rates than ethnic minority men (Pratto & Pitpitan, 2008). Stereotypes of gay men as promiscuous and sexually predatory and of lesbians as deviant and abnormal help to fuel resistance to marriage, adoption, and employment rights for sexual minority individuals.

Importantly, cultural ideologies sometimes encourage members of subordinate groups to accept their own lower status, as in the case of women who appreciate the benefits of protection and chivalry that their female status earns them. (We will return to this idea later in the section "Resisting Gender Discrimination: Collective Action.") In fact, across cultures, the less structural power women have relative to men, the more they embrace cultural ideologies that justify and perpetuate their relative lack of power (Glick et al., 2004).

Androcentrism:
A cultural ideology that defines men and their experiences as universal and treats women and their experiences as deviations from the male norm.

Ethnocentrism:
A cultural ideology that defines the dominant ethnic group as universal and treats other ethnic groups as deviations from the norm.

Heterocentrism:
A cultural ideology that defines heterosexuality as universal and treats sexual minority groups as deviations from the norm.

Stop and Think

We discussed androcentrism, ethnocentrism, and heterocentrism as three cultural ideologies that reflect and privilege the perspectives of dominant groups over subordinate groups. What other cultural ideologies can you think of that privilege dominant groups? What other "-isms" shape how people think about the relations between social groups, and how do they operate?

Privilege

Privilege:
Automatic, unearned advantages associated with belonging to a dominant group.

Double jeopardy hypothesis:
Hypothesis that individuals who belong to two or more subordinate groups face more discrimination than individuals who belong to only one subordinate group.

The concept of **privilege**, which you may recall from Chapter 1, relates to power. As an automatic, unearned advantage associated with belonging to a dominant group, privilege removes the barriers and stressors that members of subordinate groups encounter regularly (Case et al., 2014). In the United States, privilege is typically associated with being White, male, heterosexual, cisgender, able-bodied, Christian, and middle class or wealthy. For instance, concrete examples of male privilege include "higher pay for equal work," "lower risk of sexual harassment," and "lower chance of being interrupted in conversation." Examples of heterosexual privilege include "not having to worry about being disowned by family or losing one's job because of one's sexual orientation" and "being able to share public displays of affection without fear." Since dominant group members experience these privileges routinely and automatically, they may fail to notice them. However, members of dominant groups can develop greater awareness of their privilege through educational activities, such as class discussions (Case et al., 2014).

Intersectionality, Double Jeopardy, and Invisibility

As you learned in previous chapters, all individuals occupy social locations at the intersections of major social categories, such as sex, race, ethnicity, sexual orientation, physical ability, religion, and socioeconomic class (Collins, 2000). Members of subordinate groups often experience discrimination, and the **double jeopardy hypothesis** states that individuals who belong to two or more subordinate groups will experience more discrimination than individuals who belong to one subordinate group. For instance, this hypothesis may explain the finding that Black female victims of domestic violence are blamed more for their situation than are White female victims of domestic violence (Esqueda & Harrison, 2005). Furthermore, women of color tend to experience

Latina women in STEM fields experience heightened levels of backlash from coworkers when they behave assertively.

Source: © iStockPhoto .com/julief514

more frequent workplace harassment than White women, men of color, and White men (Berdahl & Moore, 2006). This occurs because many racial and ethnic minority women encounter both sexual harassment *and* racial harassment at work, leading to higher levels of overall discriminatory treatment. In a related vein, the specific types of gender bias experienced by women in STEM fields differs as a function of their ethnicity. For instance, Black women—compared with Latina, Asian, and White women—report having their competence questioned more frequently while Asian women and Latinas report experiencing more backlash from others when they behave assertively

(J. C. Williams, Phillips, & Hall, 2014). You will read more about workplace bias in Chapter 11, "Work and Home."

In contrast to the double jeopardy hypothesis, the **intersectional invisibility hypothesis** proposes that the experiences of people with multiple subordinate identities are sometimes ignored or disregarded, leading them to feel socially invisible. To understand why this occurs, think back to the cultural ideologies discussed earlier. Ideologies of androcentrism, ethnocentrism, and heterocentrism reinforce the idea that members of dominant groups are the cultural default, or prototype. For instance, men are the prototypical sex while women are nonprototypical, White people are the prototypical race while people of color are nonprototypical (in the United States and many modern Western contexts), heterosexual people are the prototypical sexual orientation while sexual minority individuals are nonprototypical, and so on. See Table 6.1 for some examples of prototypical and nonprototypical group members. Because prototypes come to mind more easily than nonprototypical examples do, people tend to assume prototypicality unless otherwise specified. Therefore, "women" are automatically assumed to be White and straight (the prototypical race and sexual orientation) while "gay people" are assumed to be White and male (the prototypical race and sex). As a result, people who belong to two or more subordinate social groups tend to be more socially "invisible" relative to those who belong only to one subordinate social group (Purdie-Vaughns & Eibach, 2008).

Intersectional invisibility manifests in various ways. Perceptually, people with multiple subordinate identities tend to go unnoticed and have their contributions overlooked in some contexts. To illustrate this, Amanda Sesko and Monica Biernat tested people's memory for faces and statements made by Black women. In one experiment, participants viewed faces of Black women, White women, Black men, and White men. After a break, participants viewed the same faces again, along with some new faces that also differed by race and sex, and made quick decisions about whether the face was "old" (appeared in the first series) or "new" (did not appear in the first series). Participants made more recognition errors with faces of Black women than they did with any of the other groups (see Figure 6.1). In a second experiment, participants listened to a conversation among a group that included both Black and White women and Black and White men. Later, when asked to match each speaker's face with his or her statements, participants made

Intersectional invisibility hypothesis: The prediction that people with multiple subordinate identities are noticed less than those with one subordinate identity.

Table 6.1 **Examples of Ideologies, Prototypes, and Subordinate Group Members.**

Ideology Type	Androcentrism	Ethnocentrism	Heterocentrism
Prototype	Man	White person	Heterosexual person
Example of a *prototypical* subordinate group member	Ethnic minority heterosexual man	White gay man	White heterosexual woman
Example of a *nonprototypical* subordinate group member	Ethnic minority heterosexual woman	Ethnic minority gay man	White gay woman

Source: Content adapted from Purdie-Vaughns and Eibach (2008).

more errors recalling statements made by Black women than by speakers from the other three groups (Sesko & Biernat, 2010). In real-world contexts, this might translate into women of color feeling like others disregard or ignore them, and they may fail to receive credit for contributions that they make to joint projects or collaborations.

While these findings offer an experimental illustration of the invisibility of people with multiple subordinate identities, history offers numerous other examples. Black and Latino women's contributions to both the U.S. civil rights and feminist movements of the 1960s and 1970s have been downplayed, and gay Black men's stories have been left out of both African American and gay histories (Purdie-Vaughns & Eibach, 2008). Similarly, not all men enjoy the experience of male privilege, leaving some (e.g., working-class feminist Latinos) to develop their own unique understandings of manhood (Hurtado & Sinha, 2008). The experiences of individuals with multiple subordinate identities are routinely ignored in psychology research, in cultural discussions of oppression and discrimination, and even in the work of advocacy organizations (Strolovitch, 2006).

Despite these negative consequences of intersectional invisibility, Purdie-Vaughns and Eibach (2008) provocatively suggest that invisibility can serve a protective function as well. Because nonprototypical group members receive less notice and attention from others, they may escape some of the more direct and extreme forms of discrimination that other subordinate group members face. For instance, gay men (prototypical with regard to sex) are the targets of more negative attitudes and more aggressive hate crimes than are lesbian women (nonprototypical with regard to sex). Black men

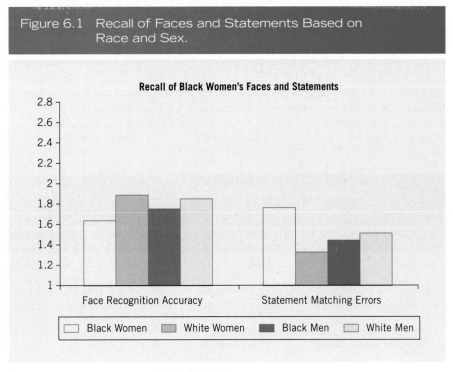

Figure 6.1 Recall of Faces and Statements Based on Race and Sex.

Source: Adapted from Sesko and Biernat (2010).

(prototypical with regard to sex) experience disproportionate rates of incarceration and employment discrimination while incarceration and employment biases against Black women (nonprototypical with regard to sex) are relatively smaller (Sidanius & Pratto, 1999). These trends suggest that having two subordinate identities can shield people from some forms of oppression that are more likely to befall those with only one subordinate identity.

Stop and Think

We have discussed some seemingly contradictory findings. Some evidence shows that individuals who have multiple subordinate identities (e.g., Latina women) face worse outcomes than individuals who have only one subordinate identity (e.g., Latino men), a phenomenon known as double jeopardy. *Other evidence shows that individuals with multiple subordinate identities are shielded from some forms of discrimination, reflecting intersectional invisibility. How might you reconcile these discrepant sets of findings?*

What Is Sexism, and Why Does It Persist?

Sex-based power differences can foster sexism. **Sexism** refers to negative attitudes toward individuals based solely on their sex, combined with institutional and cultural practices that support the unequal status of different sex categories (Swim & Hyers, 2009). Discussions of sexism often lead to disagreement and debate about what it is, especially centering on the concepts of power and privilege. To many feminist psychologists, sexism and sex-based discrimination are two separate constructs, with sexism, by definition, involving structural power differences. From this perspective, since men, as a group, have more structural power than women, they cannot be targets of sexism. However, men can be targets of sex-based discrimination, which refers to negative or unfair treatment based on sex. That said, people do not unanimously agree on whether or not men can be the targets of sexism, an issue we address in the chapter debate.

Some examples of sexism are relatively obvious, such as when a male boss routinely passes over more qualified women to promote less qualified men. But what about when a man behaves chivalrously toward a woman by offering to carry her groceries for her? Does that qualify as sexism? In this section, we will review theories that define and explain the nature and underlying causes of sexism.

Sexism: Negative attitudes toward individuals based solely on their sex, combined with institutional and cultural practices that support the unequal status of women and men.

Ambivalent Sexism Toward Women

> The relationship between women and men as social groups is unique. No other groups have endured so long a relationship of status inequality coupled with such close physical and psychological intimacy. (Glick & Fiske, 1999, p. 520)

Think back to the chapter opening, when we introduced the distinction between hostile sexism and benevolent sexism. This distinction lies at the heart of **ambivalent sexism theory**, which offers a framework for understanding gender relations and sex-based power differences across cultures. According to this theory, a combination of hostile and benevolent attitudes characterizes the relations between women and men across time and cultures. Men, as a group, tend to be the dominant sex worldwide—politically, economically, and interpersonally. This unequal gender hierarchy is supported by hostile sexism, a cultural ideology that justifies men's dominance over women by portraying women as inferior to men. **Hostile sexism** consists of antagonistic and derogatory beliefs about women and their roles. As examples, consider the beliefs that women are less competent than men, that women are moody and untrustworthy, that women manipulate and control men sexually, and that women use their gender to their advantage and complain about sexism when they are outperformed fairly by men.

In addition to being dominant over women, however, men depend on women in many ways. As the quote that begins this section notes, women and men share more "physical and psychological intimacy" than any other pair of social groups. Women's roles in heterosexual intimacy and reproduction, as well as their substantial contributions to labor and childcare, are invaluable for men's survival and functioning. Men's dependence on women gives rise to benevolent sexism, a cultural ideology that justifies men's need for women by portraying women as wonderful, pure, and worthy of protection. Thus, **benevolent sexism** consists of subjectively positive and well-intentioned beliefs about women and their importance, but it also patronizes women because it portrays them as weak and in need of protection. In the chapter opener, we saw benevolent sexism in action with the tendency to save "women and children first" in an emergency.

Hostile sexism directly insults women, making it pretty obvious and easy to identify, whereas benevolent sexism flatters women, making it more socially acceptable. In fact, people may not recognize benevolent sexism as a form of gender bias. In one experiment, Kristen Salomon and collaborators randomly assigned women to experience hostile sexism, benevolent sexism, or no sexism from a male experimenter (Salomon, Burgess, & Bosson, 2015). In the hostile sexism condition, the male experimenter expressed annoyance over women's lack of competence on a difficult test while in the benevolent sexism condition he expressed patronizing sympathy for women who disliked the test. In the control condition, the male experimenter made no comment about women's reactions to the test. Later in the experiment, women rated how sexist the experimenter was. As shown in Figure 6.2, women rated the experimenter as more sexist in the hostile than in the benevolent condition, and more sexist in the benevolent than in the control condition. This indicates that benevolent sexism from a stranger comes across as more subtle than hostile sexism but less subtle than no sexism. Moreover, in some contexts—for instance, romantic and dating contexts—many women respond favorably to men who show benevolent sexism by opening doors and offering to pay for them (Viki, Abrams, & Hutchison, 2003).

Since benevolent sexism often sounds positive on the surface, many people underestimate its harmful nature. For instance, benevolent sexism has an unexpectedly long impact on women's emotional and cardiovascular functioning (Bosson, Pinel, & Vandello, 2010; Salomon et al., 2015). Moreover, exposure to benevolent sexism tends to have a pacifying effect on women, suppressing their motivations to fight against unfair

---

Ambivalent sexism theory: Theory proposing that gender relations are characterized by both negative (hostile sexism) and seemingly positive (benevolent sexism) attitudes toward women.

Hostile sexism: Negative, antagonistic attitudes toward women who violate traditional gender role norms.

Benevolent sexism: Subjectively positive but patronizing attitudes toward women who conform to traditional gender role norms.

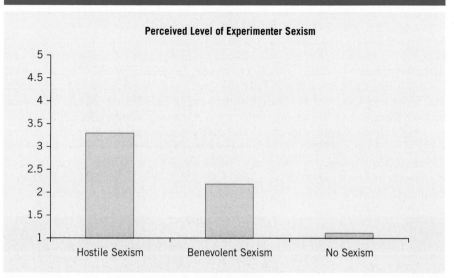

Figure 6.2 Women's Reports of Hostile Versus Benevolent Sexism.

Perceived Level of Experimenter Sexism

Source: Salomon, Burgess, and Bosson (2015).

treatment (J. C. Becker & Wright, 2011). And holding benevolently sexist attitudes correlates with having less sympathy for and more controlling attitudes toward female abuse victims. Both women and men who are higher in benevolent sexism assign less blame and recommend shorter sentences to perpetrators of rape (Viki, Abrams, & Masser, 2004). Similarly, those higher in benevolent sexism assign more blame to victims of rape and domestic violence (Abrams, Viki, Masser, & Bohner, 2003; Yamawaki, Ostenson, & Brown, 2009), and they report less support for traumatic abortion (e.g., abortion of pregnancies that result from rape or where the health of the fetus or mother is in jeopardy; Osborne & Davies, 2012).

While hostile and benevolent ideologies may seem contradictory, they actually complement one another. Moreover, they work jointly to maintain and perpetuate a gender hierarchy in which men wield more power than women but simultaneously depend on women (Glick et al., 2000). This works in a couple of ways. First, people typically direct hostile and benevolent sexism at different types of female behaviors. People most often direct hostile sexism at women who seek status and power or who reject traditional gender role norms and attempt to move into male-dominated spheres. Hostilely sexist beliefs cast such women as manipulative, untrustworthy, and "seeking to control men." Thus, hostile sexism exerts social pressure on women when they attempt to disrupt the gender hierarchy. In contrast, people most often direct benevolent sexism at women who embrace traditional gender roles as homemakers, caregivers, and low-status workers. Such women are idealized, cherished, and protected (think back to the *women-are-wonderful effect* that we discussed in the last chapter). Thus, benevolent sexism "rewards" women who accept traditional female roles without fuss, whereas hostile sexism punishes women who reject these roles.

Second, holding both hostilely and benevolently sexist beliefs simultaneously may serve an important psychological purpose by helping people to view the unequal gender hierarchy as fair. That is, feelings of resentment aroused by reminders of men's unfair dominance over women (hostile sexism) may be soothed, to some degree, by the promise of men's flattery and chivalrous treatment (benevolent sexism). In support of this idea, hostile and benevolent sexism tend to be positively correlated, as measured by the Ambivalent Sexism Inventory (ASI; Glick & Fiske, 1996). See Table 6.2 for the items of the ASI. Using the ASI, Glick and Fiske and their collaborators measured both hostile and benevolent sexism in 16 different nations and found that the average correlation between them was $r = .33$ among men and $r = .44$ among women (Glick et al., 2004). Also, higher levels of both types of sexism at the national level negatively predict national levels of gender inequality across cultures: Women have less power, fewer rights, and a lower standard of living in countries in which women and men have higher levels of both hostile and benevolent sexism (Glick et al., 2000). Thus, when they work together, hostile and benevolent sexism effectively maintain men's dominance over women.

Table 6.2 Items From the Ambivalent Sexism Inventory (ASI).

Hostile Sexism
Women often exaggerate problems they have at work.
Most women interpret innocent remarks or acts as being sexist.
Women are too easily offended.
Most women fail to appreciate fully all that men do for them.
When women lose to men in a fair competition, they typically complain about being discriminated against.
Many women are actually seeking special favors, such as hiring policies that favor them over men, under the guise of asking for "equality."
Women seek to gain power by getting control over men.
Feminists are not seeking for women to have more power than men. [R]
Feminists are making entirely reasonable demands of men. [R]
Once a woman gets a man to commit to her, she usually tries to put him on a tight leash.
There are actually very few women who get a kick out of teasing men by seeming sexually available and then refusing male advances. [R]

Benevolent Sexism
No matter how accomplished he is, a man is not truly complete as a person unless he has the love of a woman.
People are often truly happy in life without being romantically involved with a member of the other sex. [R]

Benevolent Sexism
Every man ought to have a woman whom he adores.
Men are complete without women. [R]
In a disaster, women ought not necessarily to be rescued before men. [R]
Women should be cherished and protected by men.
A good woman should be put on a pedestal by her man.
Men should be willing to sacrifice their own well-being in order to provide financially for the women in their lives.
Many women have a quality of purity that few men possess.
Women, compared to men, tend to have a superior moral sensibility.
Women, as compared to men, tend to have a more refined sense of culture and good taste.

Source: Glick and Fiske (1996).

Note: Items are scored such that higher numbers indicate higher levels of sexism. [R] indicates a reverse-scored item.

Ambivalent Attitudes Toward Men

The ASI focuses on attitudes about women, but what about men? Men report frequent encounters with prejudice directed toward them and other men—for example, hostile or negative comments—and both men and women convey this prejudice (Brinkman, Isacco, & Rosen, 2016). In fact, Glick and Fiske (1999) find evidence that people hold ambivalent attitudes about men that mirror their ambivalent attitudes toward women. Hostile attitudes toward men consist of resentment toward men who are viewed as arrogant, power-hungry, unable to care for themselves, and immoral sexual predators. Benevolent attitudes toward men consist of positive attitudes about men's roles as protectors and providers and beliefs that men ought to be cared for domestically by women. These attitudes are measured with Glick and Fiske's Ambivalence Toward Men Inventory (AMI; see Table 6.3).

Just as with ambivalent sexism toward women, hostile and benevolent attitudes toward men correlate positively with each other. Glick and his colleagues (2004) found that the correlation between hostility and benevolence toward men was $r = .46$ among both men and women across 16 different countries. Moreover, across these same cultures, people who more strongly endorsed hostile and benevolent sexism toward women also endorsed more hostile and benevolent attitudes toward men, with correlations ranging from $r = .34$ to $r = .69$. Finally, higher national scores on hostility and benevolence toward men negatively predict national gender equality indices. This suggests that ambivalent attitudes toward both women and men reflect the same underlying ideology that sustains and perpetuates the unequal gender hierarchy across cultures.

Table 6.3   Items From the Ambivalence Toward Men Inventory (AMI).

Hostility Toward Men

Men will always fight to have greater control in society than women.

Even men who claim to be sensitive to women's rights really want a traditional relationship at home, with the woman performing most of the housekeeping and childcare.

Most men pay lip service to equality for women, but can't handle having a woman as an equal.

When it comes down to it, most men are really like children.

Men would be lost in this world if women weren't there to guide them.

Men act like babies when they are sick.

Most men sexually harass women, even if only in subtle ways, once they are in a position of power over them.

A man who is sexually attracted to a woman typically has no morals about doing whatever it takes to get her in bed.

When men act to "help" women, they are often trying to prove they are better than women.

Men usually try to dominate conversations when talking to women.

Benevolence Toward Men

Even if both members of a couple work, the woman ought to be more attentive to taking care of her man at home.

Men are mainly useful to provide financial security for women.

Women ought to take care of their men at home, because men would fall apart if they had to fend for themselves.

Men are more willing to put themselves in danger to protect others.

Men are more willing to take risks than women.

Men are less likely to fall apart in emergencies than women are.

Every woman needs a male partner who will cherish her.

A woman will never be truly fulfilled in life if she doesn't have a committed, long-term relationship with a man.

Every woman ought to have a man she adores.

Women are incomplete without men.

Source: Glick and Fiske (1999).

Consider the language that Glick and Fiske use when describing ambivalent attitudes toward women versus men. Specifically, they use the term sexism *when describing hostile and benevolent attitudes toward women, but* *they do not use this term when describing hostile and benevolent attitudes toward men. Why do you think Glick and Fiske only refer to* sexism *when describing attitudes toward women? For more on this topic, see the Debate.*

Journey of Research

Measuring Gender Role and Sexist Attitudes

Gender role attitudes are beliefs about the roles that women and men ought to occupy in society. Within psychology, attempts to measure gender role attitudes began in the early 1970s as one strand of the American feminist movement brought women's rights to the forefront of cultural awareness. As the first of its kind, Spence and Helmreich's (1972) Attitudes Toward Women Scale (AWS) measured beliefs about the rights and roles of women and men in the community, workplace, and home (e.g., "The intellectual leadership of a community should be largely in the hands of men"; "A woman should be as free as a man to propose marriage"). While the AWS is one of the most widely used gender role scales in psychology (McHugh & Frieze, 1997), some of its items are outdated in both wording and tone (e.g., "It is ridiculous for a woman to run a locomotive and for a man to darn socks"). Perhaps more importantly, as attitudes about gender equality grew increasingly favorable in the United States since the 1970s (Donnelly et al., 2016), scores on the AWS started to demonstrate *ceiling effects*. That is, most people's AWS scores cluster at the high (more egalitarian) end of the scale, which reduces the scale's usefulness as a statistical predictor (Buckner, 2009).

The next generation of measurements included scales that assess both traditional and egalitarian beliefs about gender roles across a range of domains, such as employment, education, marriage, parenting, social activities, sexuality, and emotional expression. Examples of such scales include the Sex Role Egalitarianism Scale (Beere, King, Beere, & King, 1984) and the Traditional–Egalitarian Sex Role Scale (Larsen & Long, 1988). These scales cover a comprehensive set of gender role attitudes but, like the AWS, they tend to elicit ceiling effects.

In 1995, Janet Swim and colleagues published the Modern Sexism (MS) scale in an effort to capture sexist beliefs that people may be reluctant to reveal on scales such as the AWS (Swim, Aiken, Hall, & Hunter, 1995). Swim reasoned that the ceiling effects commonly observed on the AWS and other gender role scales might not reflect *real* declines in sexist attitudes but rather people's concerns about appearing sexist to others. Therefore, the MS scale measures a more socially acceptable way to express sexism toward women: denial that discrimination against women still exists (e.g., "Discrimination against women is no longer a problem in the United States"). People high in **modern sexism** might acknowledge that gender discrimination was a problem in the past but assert that women and men now have equal opportunities. Importantly, scores

(Continued)

(Continued)

on MS predicted people's voting preferences for a male over a female candidate for senator while scores on a more overt measure of gender role attitudes did not (Swim et al., 1995). This finding lends credence to the idea that overt measures of gender role attitudes may have some statistical shortcomings.

Taking a slightly different approach, Glick and Fiske (1996)—as discussed in the "What Is Sexism" section of this chapter—proposed that sexist attitudes are often ambivalent, meaning that they simultaneously reflect both hostile and benevolent beliefs about women and their roles. Based on this logic, they developed the Ambivalent Sexism Inventory (ASI) to assess hostile and benevolent attitudes toward women (Glick & Fiske, 1996) and the corresponding Ambivalence Toward Men Inventory (AMI) to assess hostile and benevolent attitudes toward men (for scale items, see Tables 6.2 and 6.3). Importantly, across cultures, scores on the benevolent and hostile sexism subscales of both the ASI and the AMI are positively correlated, indicating that both positive and negative beliefs jointly fuel sexism and gender inequality.

More recently, researchers have become interested in gender role attitudes toward people who do not fit cleanly into the gender binary. For example, the Genderism and Transphobia Scale, developed by D. B. Hill and Willoughby (2005), assesses beliefs about the "naturalness" of gender identities that fall outside the male–female binary (e.g., "God made two sexes and two sexes only"). Unlike past measures of gender role attitudes, this scale does not assess attitudes about the roles that transgender people ought to occupy. Instead, it taps into something even more fundamental: attitudes about the very legitimacy of transgender identity.

What do you envision as the next generation of gender role and sexist attitudes measures? If you were a researcher, how would you measure gender role attitudes?

Social Dominance and System Justification Theories

Modern sexism: Socially acceptable form of sexism consisting of a denial that women still face gender discrimination, coupled with resentment toward women who seek social change.

Social dominance orientation (SDO): The belief that inequality among social groups is right and fair because some people and groups should have more status than others.

In addition to ambivalent sexism theory, which specifically addresses gender relations between women and men, social dominance and system justification theories are useful for explaining more generally how unequal group hierarchies persist within societies. According to social dominance theory, some people have a **social dominance orientation (SDO)**, which is a belief that inequality is right and fair because some people and groups should have more status than others. This orientation then helps to legitimize hierarchies based on sex and ethnicity. To measure SDO, researchers use items such as "Some people are just more worthy than others" and "It is not a problem if some people have more of a chance in life than others" (Pratto, Sidanius, Stallworth, & Malle, 1994). There are several interesting findings to note about SDO. First of all—perhaps not surprisingly—members of dominant groups tend to score higher on SDO than do members of subordinate groups. Second, SDO correlates with cultural ideologies that legitimize unequal hierarchies, such as sexism, racism, and prejudice against sexual minority individuals. Third, people higher in SDO tend to seek and prefer occupations (such as law, politics, and business) that protect the interests of high-status groups while those lower in SDO tend to prefer occupations (such as social work, counseling, and special education) that benefit members of subordinate groups. Thus, group hierarchies are maintained via a combination of individual differences in SDO, cultural ideologies that justify inequality,

and individuals' self-selection into occupations that perpetuate power differences
between groups.

While it may make sense that dominant groups defend the system that
benefits them, why would members of
subordinate groups defend a system
that denies them power? Social dominance theory proposes that as long as
the social hierarchy is perceived as stable
and unchanging, subordinate groups will
generally internalize cultural ideologies
that justify their own low status. However, when the hierarchy gets disrupted,
subordinate groups begin to withdraw
their support for ideologies that portray them as less deserving of status (Sidanius &
Pratto, 1999). Taking this idea even further, **system justification theory** posits that all
people have a powerful motivation to justify the sociopolitical system in which their
lives are embedded. Because feelings of uncertainty and unfairness threaten people's
needs for security, people are motivated to accept the current social system as legitimate, even if it denies them access to resources (J. T. Jost et al., 2012). Thus, system
justification theory proposes that members of subordinate groups endorse legitimizing cultural ideologies out of a need to view the hierarchy as fair. Curiously, this need
sometimes results in subordinate group members endorsing more favorable stereotypes about the dominant group than about their own group (J. T. Jost, Kivetz, Rubini,
Guermandi, & Mosso, 2005).

In order to legitimize the social hierarchy, people rely on *complementary stereotypes*,
or stereotypes that link the same group to both positive and negative qualities. People
are motivated to believe that if a group has a clear disadvantage, it also has some com-
pensatory positive attributes that make the disadvantage seem less unfair. For example,
hostile and benevolent sexism contain complementary stereotypes by portraying women
as simultaneously less competent and more virtuous than men. And, in fact, people
exposed to the stereotype that women are low in agency but high in warmth perceive
the unequal gender hierarchy as more fair (J. T. Jost & Kay, 2005). Another legitimizing ideology, the *Protestant work ethic*, refers to the notion that all groups have an equal
chance for success if they just work hard enough (Katz & Hass, 1988). Embracing this
ideology allows people to ignore systematic, group-based inequities and instead attribute
individuals' lack of success to their own failings.

Those who are low in social dominance orientation tend to prefer occupations that allow them to help disadvantaged individuals and serve the community.

Source: © iStockPhoto.com/FatCamera

System justification theory: Theory proposing that people are motivated to justify the sociopolitical system that governs them (even if it treats them unfairly) because doing so reduces uncertainty.

Why Do Sexist Attitudes Matter?

We end this section of the chapter by asking why sexist attitudes matter. What real-world
consequences do they have? Some research indicates that widespread sexist attitudes
shape societal conditions for women and men on a large scale. In one nationally representative, longitudinal study of 57 different countries from every major world region,
Mark Brandt (2011) tracked the association between nation-level endorsement of sexist

beliefs and national indices of gender equality over a 3-year time span. At Time 1, over 82,000 respondents rated their agreement with two statements reflecting sexist beliefs: "On the whole, men make better political leaders than women do" and "On the whole, men make better business executives than women do." Brandt used these ratings to predict national gender equality indices 3 years later (Time 2), controlling for both Time 1 national gender equality and other important variables, such as levels of national educational and economic development. His findings showed that sexist attitudes at Time 1 predicted decreases in national gender equality at Time 2. Interestingly, when Brandt examined these associations separately by sex, he found no differences. This indicates that sexist attitudes held by both women and men predict decreases in women's opportunities and status at the national level. In a very real sense, then, sexist attitudes likely do translate into large-scale societal restrictions on women's opportunities.

Debate

When people hear the term *sexism*, they typically think of bias against women and not against men. Sexism involves institutional and cultural practices that contribute to inequality between women and men. Because men generally have more power than women to determine these institutional practices, it follows that women would be the primary—and perhaps only—targets of sexism. But some take issue with this stance, arguing that men can experience systemic sexism as well. Furthermore, some argue that men face far more violent and damaging forms of sex bias than women. Here, we cover both sides of this issue.

No, Men Do Not Experience Sexism

Across all human cultures, men are disproportionately represented among political leaders, decision-makers, business executives, and owners of land, wealth, and other valued resources. In contrast, women in all cultures are disproportionately denied access to desirable positions of power and wealth. This captures the very definition of sexism: Because of their sex and lack of structural power, women have fewer opportunities in comparison with men. Though men certainly do experience gender discrimination, they cannot experience sexism, given their relatively higher levels of structural power.

Even when women have more dyadic power than men and even in matrilineal societies that trace kinship and inheritance lines to mothers, women as a group do not have as much structural power as men. Widespread cultural ideologies reinforce and perpetuate men's group-based interests, too, by portraying men as well suited for competitive leadership positions and women as better suited for lower-status and homemaker roles (Pratto & Pitpitan, 2008).

For these reasons, some argue that there is no such thing as "sexism against men." In other words, sexism refers to a systemic pattern of cultural practices that supports men's power over women. Of course, many people hold negative beliefs about men, and men as a group experience some negative outcomes that women do not. But to claim that men experience sexism against them ignores the fact that men, the world over, have dominance over women.

Yes, Men Experience Sexism

Prejudice and discrimination against men often get overlooked. Though it is true that men, as a group, have more power than women, this comparison of group averages ignores the reality of many men, particularly those who occupy the lower rungs of the social hierarchy. As Roy Baumeister (2007) notes, because human societies are organized hierarchically, only the most dominant and privileged men at the top of the hierarchy possess structural power. In contrast, the opportunities of men at the bottom of the social hierarchy tend to be just as limited as those of women—and sometimes even more limited. Therefore, arguing that only women can be the targets of sexism ignores the experiences of many low-status men.

Most societies exploit low-status men by using them for high-risk activities, such as fighting in wars or doing dangerous, physically demanding work (Baumeister, 2007). Though some men may reap benefits from these risky activities in terms of status and power, many men end up losing. For instance, men die in war or in workplace accidents much more often than women. In addition, men are much more likely to be incarcerated than women, and they receive harsher prison sentences than women for the same crimes (Benatar, 2012).

Men are also much more likely than women to be victims of homicide. Dying in violent altercations, wars, or workplace accidents may not seem like obvious sexism, but cultural expectations can create strong pressures to conform, leaving men feeling like they have little choice but to perform dangerous roles. In short, societies often treat men as expendable.

Gender bias against men can extend to opportunities and resources as well. For example, women in the United States now enter and graduate college at higher rates than men do, and this sex gap is particularly pronounced for students of color (National Center for Education Statistics, 2016). Men also make up the majority of the U.S. homeless population (U.S. Department of Housing and Urban Development, 2015), and they confront substantial bias when it comes to child custody decisions, which heavily favor mothers over fathers (Benatar, 2012). Whether you use the word *sexism* to refer to these patterns, there is no question that men—and especially low-status men—are targets of some types of systematic gender bias.

What do you think? Do men experience sexism against their group in the same way that women do? Which side of the debate seems more compelling? Which evidence do you find most and least convincing? Why?

What Is Gender Discrimination?

Discrimination refers to unjust treatment based solely on a person's group membership. Thus, **gender discrimination** is unjust treatment based solely on one's sex, sexual orientation, or gender identity. Unlike the concept of sexism, structural power imbalances need not figure centrally in the definition of discrimination. This means that discrimination can be directed toward members of any social group, including dominant groups. Discrimination can take many forms, ranging from blatant and obvious to subtle and ambiguous. Rates and types of gender discrimination also vary widely across the globe, which we will highlight by presenting current examples from the domains of education and politics.

Gender discrimination: Unjust treatment based solely on one's sex, sexual orientation, or gender identity.

Sidebar 6.3: Who Experiences More Bias?

A substantial proportion of men in the United States believe that men experience gender discrimination as much as or more than women do. In one study, U.S. adults rated how much gender bias both women and men experienced in American society in 2012, as well as during past decades in American history (e.g., the 1950s). While men agreed that women's gender bias in the 1950s far outweighed men's, about 44% of men reported that men in 2012 experienced gender bias that was either equal to or greater than women's (Bosson, Vandello, Michniewicz, & Lenes, 2012). Thus, if we take men's own perceptions of discrimination seriously, then discrimination against men appears to be a common, if overlooked, phenomenon. What do you think? Do men have a valid point here?

Overt Discrimination and Microaggressions

Overt gender discrimination is obvious and easy to recognize—examples of this type of discrimination abound. It occurs when an employer refuses to consider well-qualified women for management positions or does not allow men to take parental leave upon the birth of a child. It occurs when girls are denied access to formal education that is open to boys (as they were under Taliban rule in Afghanistan). We see it in Saudi Arabia where women have been forbidden from driving cars (though this will change as of June 2018) and in Yemen where women cannot testify in cases of adultery, sodomy, or theft (Dewey, 2013). In Michigan, Virginia, and North Dakota, state-licensed child welfare agencies can deny joint adoptions to same-sex couples for religious reasons (Family Equality Council, 2017). "Bathroom bills" have been proposed or enacted in several U.S. states to restrict transgender individuals' public bathroom use to that of their assigned sex instead of the gender with which they identify (E. Green, 2016).

In contrast to these overt examples, negative group-based treatment can also be subtle, leading to some disagreement about what qualifies as discrimination. **Microaggressions**, one type of subtle discrimination, are common, everyday insults and indignities directed toward members of subordinate social groups. They can be verbal or behavioral and need not be intentional on the part of the perpetrator (Sue et al., 2007). Researchers have analyzed microaggressions targeting men of color, women of all racial and ethnic groups, and gay and transgender individuals (Nadal, 2013; Owen, Tao, & Rodolfa, 2010). Consider these examples: A woman asks her gay male coworker to oversee decorations for the office party because "you're probably good at that sort of thing." A patient mistakes a female physician who is wearing scrubs for a nurse. A man explains something to a woman that she already knows, a phenomenon referred to as *mansplaining*. A man tells his female coworker that she should smile more. In these examples, there may not be an explicit intent to cause harm on the part of the perpetrator. But these subtle behaviors may be detrimental precisely because they appear trivial or harmless, which can make targets feel uncomfortable about speaking up against them, or even guilty for finding them annoying.

Microaggressions: Common, everyday insults and indignities directed toward members of subordinate social groups.

The construct of microaggressions came under criticism recently because the term describes such a wide range of phenomena that it lacks coherent meaning (Lilienfeld, 2017). This conceptual muddiness makes it difficult to study the effects of microaggressions on their targets, as empirical studies require precise definitions of constructs. Moreover, as you will read in Chapter 14 ("Aggression and Violence"), many psychologists define aggression as behavior that is *intended* to harm another person. Since microaggressions are often not intended to be hurtful but instead reflect insensitivity or unawareness on the part of the perpetrator, this raises an interesting question: How essential is "intent to harm" in the determination of whether a given act qualifies as a microaggression? Moving forward, research on microaggressions will benefit from clearer definitions, as well as a thorough examination of the adverse effects of these acts.

Mansplaining refers to a phenomenon in which a man explains to a woman something that she already knows or corrects her in front of others to demonstrate that he has more expertise. Not only is mansplaining annoying to its target, it can take up valuable time during a busy workday!

Source: © iStockPhoto .com/Georgijevic

Global Gender Discrimination in Education and Politics

The World Economic Forum (WEF; 2016) reports a Global Gender Gap Index, which attempts to capture the degree of equality between men and women in 144 countries by examining measures of health and survival, educational attainment, economic participation and opportunity, and political participation. In 2016, countries with the highest gender equality (in order) were Iceland, Finland, Norway, Sweden, and Rwanda, and countries with the lowest gender equality were Chad, Saudi Arabia, Syria, Pakistan, and Yemen. The United States ranks 45th, with gender equality scores most closely matching those of Laos, Trinidad and Tobago, Australia, Panama, and Serbia. These rankings indicate that there is wide variability in gender equality around the globe. Here, we will examine the specific areas of education and political representation more closely.

Around the world, girls and boys have somewhat different levels of access to education, with 32.1 million girls and 28.9 million boys of primary-school age not attending school. This translates into a global gender gap in which 1.6% more girls of primary-school age are out of school than their male counterparts. However, the gender gaps in out-of-school rates vary widely by region of the world. While the Middle East, Oceania (the islands of the central Pacific Ocean), and sub-Saharan Africa show gender gaps two to four times larger than the global gender gap, East and Southeast Asia show virtually no gender gap (UNESCO, 2016). The countries with the highest percentages of impoverished girls who have never been to school, with rates ranging from 77% to 95%, are Somalia, Niger, and Liberia (UNESCO, 2013). Why does this matter? Cross-nationally, the educational status of women negatively correlates with rates of sexual violence, meaning that countries' violence rates decrease as girls' education levels increase (Yodanis, 2004). Educating girls also delays the age of marriage and childbirth and improves health outcomes for mothers and their children. There are economic benefits of educating girls as well, with a country's average GDP (an indicator of economic health) increasing by 3% with every 10% increase in girls who receive an education (Bourne, 2017).

Malala Yousafzai—first introduced in Chapter 1—is a well-known advocate for girls' education. After winning Pakistan's National Youth Peace Prize for her advocacy, Yousafzai suffered an assassination attempt by the Taliban for promoting secular, anti-Taliban values. She survived the attack and continued her advocacy by establishing the Malala Fund, an organization that works to realize a vision where all girls worldwide will have access to 12 years of quality education. In 2014, at the age of 17, Yousafzai became the youngest ever recipient of the Nobel Peace Prize for her work (https://www.malala.org).

The balance of political representation between women and men is another indicator of national gender equality. In most countries, women are vastly underrepresented in politics. In 2016, only two countries (Rwanda and Bolivia) had 50% or more women in national legislative bodies. Although the percentages of women in legislative bodies around the globe have almost doubled in the past 20 years, the average representation of women is currently at only 22% (UN Women, 2016b). This global percentage accurately captures the current representation of female members of the U.S. House of Representatives (20%) and the U.S. Senate (21%).

Malala Yousafzai, a Pakistani education activist, is the youngest recipient of a Nobel Prize.

Source: Wikimedia Commons

Women are also less likely than men to be heads of state or government. In 2017, there were 15 women serving as their country's head of state or government, with 8 of these (including Angela Merkel of Germany) being their country's first female leader. Although some countries elected their first female leaders approximately 50 years ago (e.g., Indira Gandhi in India in 1966 and Golda Meir in Israel in 1969), the United States lags behind in this regard. Hillary Rodham Clinton, however, came close to winning the U.S. presidency as the Democratic Party nominee in the 2016 presidential election, and she won the popular vote by more than 2.8 million votes. Interestingly, hostile sexism toward women predicted more negative attitudes toward Clinton and more positive attitudes toward Donald Trump among voters in the United States, even after controlling for political affiliation (Ratliff, Redford, Conway, & Smith, 2016).

Given women's ongoing underrepresentation in politics and education around the globe, we will likely see organizations like the Malala Fund continue to advocate for greater gender equality, and progress will come incrementally. For example, when Justin Trudeau became prime minister of Canada in 2015, he appointed the first gender-balanced cabinet (15 women and 15 men) in Canada's history. When asked why this was important to him, he replied, "Because it's 2015" (Austen, 2015).

How Can We Resist and Reduce Gender Discrimination?

Efforts to resist and reduce sexism and gender discrimination come in many forms. Individuals can confront perpetrators of sexism in their daily lives, groups of like-minded people can organize to agitate for social change, and legal reforms can prohibit discrimination at the institutional level. In this section, we consider all of these ways of combatting discrimination. Along the way, we also consider factors that act as barriers to social change and that make the ultimate goal of eliminating discrimination a challenging one.

Affirmative Action: It's the Law

In the domain of employment, sex- and race-based discrimination have been illegal in the United States since the passage of Title VII of the 1964 Civil Rights Act. According to affirmative action laws, employers who do business with the U.S. government must hire qualified women and racial and ethnic minority individuals at rates equal to their representation in the population. Such laws have reduced—but not eliminated—sex and race disparities in employment and earnings since the 1960s (Snipp & Cheung, 2016).

Although it has been law for more than 50 years, affirmative action remains a controversial issue. The belief in *meritocracy* represents one source of opposition to affirmative action. This refers to the belief that individuals should achieve or fail on their own merits and hard work and not receive any advantages due to special hiring "quotas." Individualist cultures like the United States tend to hold strong values of meritocracy, which can make it difficult to enforce antidiscrimination laws. Dominant group members in particular oppose affirmative action when they view such policies as biased against their own group (Wellman, Liu, & Wilkins, 2016).

Modern sexism, which you encountered in the "Journey of Research," is a form of opposition to affirmative action for women. People high in modern sexism deny that gender discrimination still exists, and they oppose policies that benefit women because they view such policies as unfair (Swim et al., 1995). From a modern sexism perspective, if women fail to achieve the level of success that men enjoy, it is not because discrimination suppresses women's achievements but rather because women lack the appropriate levels of effort or skill.

Confronting Gender Discrimination: Individual Efforts

If someone treated you in a discriminatory manner, how would you react? Would you shrug it off, make a joke about it, confront the perpetrator, or do something else? When asked to imagine their responses to a hypothetical episode of gender discrimination, 28% of women claimed that they would confront the perpetrator directly. However, when they were later exposed to actual gender discrimination, no women spoke up (Woodzicka & LaFrance, 2001). Thus, what people think they would do and what they actually do may be quite different.

What makes confronting discrimination so difficult? According to the Confronting Prejudiced Responses Model (see Table 6.4), individuals must overcome several hurdles before they will actively confront discrimination (Ashburn-Nardo, Morris, & Goodwin, 2008). One hurdle, **attributional ambiguity**, refers to the difficulty that people have in attributing negative treatment to discrimination when other possible explanations are present. To illustrate, imagine being a woman enrolled in a seminar in which the male instructor smiles and nods encouragingly in response to comments made by a particular male student. In contrast, when you speak up, the instructor averts his eyes and remains expressionless. Why does your instructor react this way? Perhaps he is sexist and does not respect women. But what if he acts this way because the quality of your discussion contributions is poor? Or what if the instructor was preoccupied by personal concerns during your comments? How can you know which of these explanations is correct?

In fact, members of subordinate groups often cannot know for sure whether negative treatment from others reflects discrimination versus some other cause(s). After all, when people treat you poorly, they rarely explain the rationale for their behavior. Interestingly, this leads to a phenomenon in which women perceive that gender discrimination occurs at the societal level more often than it occurs to them personally. Why might this occur? It may simply be easier to observe large-scale phenomena in the aggregate than in a piecemeal (case-by-case) fashion. Isolated instances of undesirable treatment can be open to interpretation, as we have discussed, making it difficult to know whether discrimination has occurred. In contrast, when viewing evidence and statistics in an aggregated form, patterns of systematic bias become easier to perceive and interpret. To illustrate this, Faye Crosby and colleagues exposed undergraduate men to statistics regarding the salaries of women and men at a fictitious organization in two different formats, piecemeal and aggregated (Crosby, Clayton, Alksnis, & Hemker, 1986). In the piecemeal format, participants saw female and male salaries for each of 10 different departments separately, one department at a time. In the aggregated format, participants saw salary data for the entire company at once, aggregated across all 10 departments and summarized in a single table. Overall, participants perceived more gender discrimination and rated it as more serious when viewing the information in an aggregated versus piecemeal format. Given that people almost always experience personal episodes of discrimination in a piecemeal (rather than aggregated) fashion and that it often assumes subtle forms, people have difficulty knowing with certainty whether the unfavorable treatment they receive reflects discrimination or some other cause.

The tone in which discriminatory comments are delivered also contributes to attributional ambiguity. For instance, jokes that convey insulting stereotypes may mask the speaker's intent and make listeners less likely to attribute the sentiment to discrimination.

Attributional ambiguity: Difficulty in attributing negative treatment to group-based discrimination when other possible explanations for the treatment are present.

Table 6.4   The Confronting Prejudiced Responses Model.

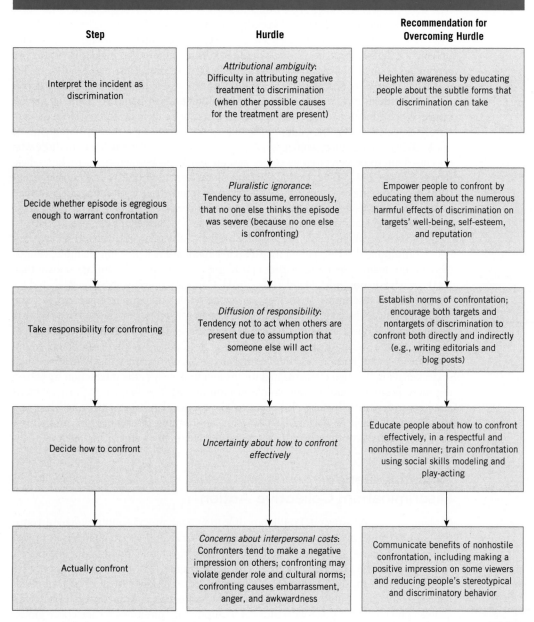

Step	Hurdle	Recommendation for Overcoming Hurdle
Interpret the incident as discrimination	*Attributional ambiguity*: Difficulty in attributing negative treatment to discrimination (when other possible causes for the treatment are present)	Heighten awareness by educating people about the subtle forms that discrimination can take
Decide whether episode is egregious enough to warrant confrontation	*Pluralistic ignorance*: Tendency to assume, erroneously, that no one else thinks the episode was severe (because no one else is confronting)	Empower people to confront by educating them about the numerous harmful effects of discrimination on targets' well-being, self-esteem, and reputation
Take responsibility for confronting	*Diffusion of responsibility*: Tendency not to act when others are present due to assumption that someone else will act	Establish norms of confrontation; encourage both targets and nontargets of discrimination to confront both directly and indirectly (e.g., writing editorials and blog posts)
Decide how to confront	*Uncertainty about how to confront effectively*	Educate people about how to confront effectively, in a respectful and nonhostile manner; train confrontation using social skills modeling and play-acting
Actually confront	*Concerns about interpersonal costs*: Confronters tend to make a negative impression on others; confronting may violate gender role and cultural norms; confronting causes embarrassment, anger, and awkwardness	Communicate benefits of nonhostile confrontation, including making a positive impression on some viewers and reducing people's stereotypical and discriminatory behavior

Source: Adapted from Ashburn-Nardo, Morris, and Goodwin (2008); Czopp, Monteith, and Mark (2006); E. H. Dodd, Giuliano, Boutell, and Moran (2001).

In one study, college women chatted online with a male partner named Mike (really an experimenter) who made either a joke or a serious statement that conveyed the stereotype that "household chores are a woman's job." When the stereotype came in the form of a joke, women rated Mike as less sexist, and they were less likely to confront or challenge him via instant message than when the stereotype came in the form of a serious statement (Mallett, Ford, & Woodzicka, 2016). Thus, humor can make discriminatory sentiments seem more palatable and less like "real" discrimination.

Even with clear and unambiguous discrimination, confrontation does not always occur. Individuals must decide to disregard any potential personal costs that might result from the confrontation. Those who confront discrimination tend to be perceived negatively, especially when they adopt a hostile or accusatory tone (Czopp, Monteith, & Mark, 2006). For instance, women who confront sexism—in comparison with those who do not—tend to be perceived as colder and are liked less by men (J. C. Becker, Glick, Ilic, & Bohner, 2011; E. H. Dodd, Giuliano, Boutell, & Moran, 2001). This may occur because confronting discrimination violates female gender role norms that direct women to avoid conflict with others. In fact, women who endorse such gender norms tend to confront discrimination less frequently (Swim, Eyssell, Murdoch, & Ferguson, 2010).

Fortunately, when people successfully overcome the interpersonal and social barriers to confronting discrimination, they tend to experience benefits. For example, women (though not men) have more respect and liking for women who confront sexism than for those who do not (E. H. Dodd et al., 2001). Confrontation can also effectively reduce stereotypic and discriminatory behaviors. In one set of studies, White participants who were confronted (via computer) about their apparently racist responses to a word task subsequently showed less stereotypical responding and lower racial prejudice scores than those who were not confronted (Czopp et al., 2006). Another experiment found that when a female research assistant confronted male participants in person about their sexist behavior, the men compensated for the awkwardness of the interaction by behaving more positively and seeking common ground with the woman. Ultimately, men's attempts to repair their image led them to like the woman better and to use less sexist language (Mallett & Wagner, 2010). Thus, confronting discrimination can increase people's awareness of their own biases and motivate them to repair their actions.

Resisting Gender Discrimination: Collective Action

On January 21, 2017, over 4.5 million people in more than 165 countries demonstrated the power of collective action by participating in a series of Women's Marches in protest of President Donald Trump's divisive rhetoric regarding women, immigrants, and people of color (Chenoweth & Pressman, 2017). By some counts, this was the biggest collective act of protest in history. What makes collective action unique? In contrast to individual efforts aimed at improving one's own plight, **collective action** consists of behavior enacted on behalf of a group with the goal of improving conditions for the entire group.

Two key factors must be present before people will engage in collective action: (1) recognition that a subordinate group is unfairly disadvantaged and (2) anger on behalf of the group (S. C. Wright, 2010). But now recall what you read earlier about system justification theory, which states that members of disadvantaged groups are often

Collective action: Behavior enacted on behalf of a group with the goal of improving conditions for the entire group.

motivated to view their situation as fair. In general, the need to legitimize the relatively low status of one's group works against the likelihood that subordinate group members will view their plight as unfair. Thus, a group's level of perceived unfairness must exceed a certain threshold, and the resulting anger must be felt intensely before people are willing to disrupt their lives and join collective action efforts.

As we have discussed, benevolent sexism reduces women's tendency to view their group as unfairly disadvantaged. In fact, even brief reminders of benevolent sexism temporarily reduce women's motivation to fight for gender equality. One set of experiments showed that reading brief descriptions of benevolently sexist beliefs (e.g., "Men are incomplete without women") reduced women's collective action behavior (e.g., signing petitions and distributing flyers promoting gender equality) relative to a condition in which they read gender-neutral beliefs (e.g., "Tea is healthier than coffee"). Moreover, this effect emerged because reading about benevolent sexism increased women's perceptions that the gender hierarchy was fair and that they personally benefited from being a woman (J. C. Becker & Wright, 2011).

How can we motivate people to engage in more collective action against discrimination? Interestingly enough, one answer lies in hostile sexism. While women often feel more satisfied with the status quo after reminders of benevolent sexism, they feel less satisfied with the status quo after reminders of hostile sexism. Episodes of hostile sexism increase women's anger, disgust, and even their physiological arousal: One experiment found that women's heart rate, blood pressure, and other indices of cardiovascular arousal showed a sharp spike several minutes after they were treated in a hostilely sexist manner by a male experimenter (see Figure 6.3; Salomon et al., 2015). Importantly, anger arouses and motivates people to confront and challenge the source of their anger. In fact, women engaged in more collective action behavior after reading descriptions of hostilely sexist beliefs than they did after reading gender-neutral beliefs, and this effect

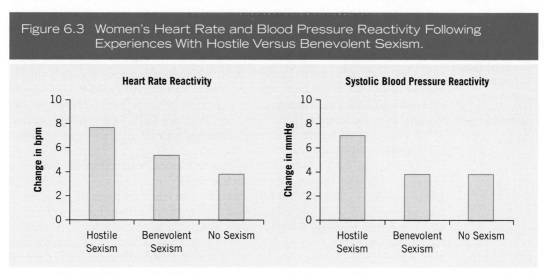

Figure 6.3 Women's Heart Rate and Blood Pressure Reactivity Following Experiences With Hostile Versus Benevolent Sexism.

Source: Salomon, Burgess, and Bosson (2015).

was driven by increases in anger and decreases in the perceived fairness of the gender hierarchy (J. C. Becker & Wright, 2011).

Encouraging greater awareness of the unfair disadvantage that sexism perpetuates also motivates collective action. In a series of studies, J. C. Becker and Swim (2011) asked women and men to record the numbers and types of sexist events they observed or experienced in their lives each day for a week. In the control condition, participants kept records of their daily communications. At the end of the week, the researchers offered participants an opportunity to sign a petition supporting the implementation of anti-sexism programs in schools. Both women and men who spent the week focusing on sexism were more likely to sign the anti-sexism petition than those who did not. Thus, focusing people's attention on sexism can increase their awareness of its unfair consequences and thereby motivate them to take action against it.

Being an Ally

Of course, you do not need to belong to a subordinate or disadvantaged social group in order to resist discrimination and advocate for equality. **Allies** publicly support and promote the rights of marginalized group members, despite not belonging to the group. For example, heterosexual LGBT allies stand up for LGBT communities and issues, gender-egalitarian men advocate for greater political and economic rights for women, and White allies show their public support for anti-racism efforts.

Allies:
Individuals who publicly support and promote the rights of disadvantaged group members but who are not themselves part of the disadvantaged group.

One barrier that allies encounter is stigmatization. For example, people tend to stereotype men who advocate for gender equality and women's causes as high in femininity and low in masculinity (Rudman, Mescher, & Moss-Racusin, 2012). But allies also report experiencing benefits, such as promoting values of social justice, gaining knowledge, and meeting needs for belonging and community (Rostosky, Black, Riggle, & Rosenkrantz, 2015). For many, the benefits of aligning themselves with valued social causes outweigh the potential interpersonal costs.

As you read the chapters to come, you will learn about numerous domains—education, language, sexuality, the workplace, health, and violence—in which some groups experience systematic disadvantages relative to others. In digesting this information, you may wish to consider creative ways to get involved and become an ally for those who lack certain privileges that you possess, whether it be based on sex, race, religion, class, sexual orientation, physical or cognitive ability, or mental health (or the intersections of these categories). Discrimination will be dismantled more readily through the combined efforts of all, including those who enjoy certain privileges and those who do not.

CHAPTER SUMMARY

6.1 Explain how social structures are organized by sex across cultures and how power and privilege shape the experiences of individuals and groups.

Human societies are organized hierarchically, with some groups (dominant groups) having more power and access to resources than other groups (subordinate groups). Patriarchal social structures, in which men are dominant and women are subordinate, appear to be the universal norm. Patriarchal power is structural, meaning that it manifests on a large scale and shapes the entire society. While there are no known human societies controlled by women (matriarchies), societies do vary in terms of how much power women have over inheritance, lineage, and economic decisions. Women also often have dyadic power (the power to choose close relationships and control the decisions that occur within those relationships), although the amount of dyadic power they hold depends on their demographic characteristics (e.g., age and education level) and on men's levels of structural power.

Dominant groups exert power in many ways, including through force, resource control, and cultural ideologies. Men, on average, have more power than women, but power is not distributed evenly among men, with dominant group men routinely maintaining power over ethnic minority, sexual minority, transgender, and poor men. Privilege is an automatic, unearned advantage associated with belonging to a dominant group. Becoming aware of privilege can motivate dominant group members to reduce their own prejudice toward less privileged groups.

All individuals occupy locations at the intersections of major social categories, such as sex, race, ethnicity, sexual orientation, physical ability, religion, and socioeconomic class. The double jeopardy hypothesis states that individuals who belong to two or more subordinate groups face more discrimination than individuals who belong to only one subordinate group because disadvantage accumulates across subordinate identities. In contrast, the intersectional invisibility hypothesis argues that people with multiple subordinate identities receive less attention than those with a single subordinate group identity, which means that they likely escape some of the more extreme forms of discrimination that other subordinate groups face.

6.2 Evaluate different theoretical perspectives on sexism and gender inequality.

Sexism refers to negative attitudes toward individuals based solely on their sex, combined with institutional and cultural practices that support the unequal status of women and men. Ambivalent sexism theory explains sexism as consisting of both hostile sexism and benevolent sexism. These beliefs complement one another and contribute jointly to the unequal gender hierarchy. While hostile sexism punishes women who seek status and power and reject traditional gender role norms, benevolent sexism "rewards" women who embrace traditional gender roles as homemakers, caregivers, and low-status workers. Similarly, ambivalent attitudes toward men consist of hostility and benevolence. Across cultures, hostile and benevolent attitudes toward women and toward men correlate positively with each other, and they correlate negatively with indices of national gender equality.

Social dominance theory argues that unequal group hierarchies are maintained via an ideology called social dominance orientation—the belief that some groups rightly have more status than others. System justification theory proposes that people are motivated to defend the status quo, regardless of their dominant or subordinate group status. To do this, they embrace ideologies and stereotypes that legitimize unequal group hierarchies. For example, complementary stereotypes that portray women as low in agency but high in warmth help the gender hierarchy seem fair and just.

6.3 Explain the types and consequences of gender discrimination.

Gender discrimination refers to unfair treatment of individuals based solely on their sex, sexual orientation, or gender identity. Since gender discrimination does not necessarily involve structural power imbalances, anyone can experience gender discrimination, including members of dominant groups. Discrimination varies in form from subtle to overt, with overt discrimination being obvious and easy to identify. In contrast, micro-aggressions are a more subtle form of discrimination consisting of brief, everyday slights directed toward members of less privileged groups. The consequences of gender discrimination are seen in the domains of education and politics. Around the globe, girls—compared with boys—have less access to primary and secondary education and are more likely to be illiterate. In the political arena, women make up about 22% of legislators worldwide, and only 15 countries currently had a female head of state or government in 2017.

6.4 Evaluate the difficulties of recognizing and confronting discrimination and the methods that individuals and groups use to resist and reduce discrimination.

In the United States, antidiscrimination laws enacted in the mid-1960s led to gradual declines in sex- and race-based employment discrimination. However, affirmative action is controversial, in part because some perceive it as violating values of meritocracy. Modern sexism is a form of opposition to affirmative action for women. People high in modern sexism deny that gender discrimination still exists and oppose policies that benefit women because they view such policies as unfair.

While many women believe that they would confront a person who treated them in a sexist manner, actual confrontation rates are low. People must overcome several hurdles before they will confront the source of a sexist comment or act. Attributional ambiguity refers to the difficulty that people have in knowing whether negative treatment reflects discrimination or some other cause. People tend to incur interpersonal costs when confronting sexism, such as making a bad impression on others and being disliked. If these hurdles can be overcome, confrontation often results in reducing other people's stereotypical and sexist behavior.

Collective action on behalf of a group is unlikely unless people surpass a threshold of perceived unfair disadvantage combined with anger. Experiencing hostile sexism increases women's anger, cardiovascular reactivity, and motivation for collective action. In contrast, benevolent sexism suppresses women's motivation to fight for equality by reminding them of the benefits of being a woman.

Allies are members of dominant groups who publicly support and promote the rights of members of subordinate groups, such as straight and cisgender people who support the rights of LGBTQIA+ individuals. Allies may be negatively stereotyped because they choose to align themselves with subordinate groups, but allies also experience benefits, such as promoting social justice values, gaining knowledge, and meeting needs for belonging.

Test Your Knowledge: True or False?

6.1. When women outnumber men on college campuses, heterosexual men put less effort and commitment into their college dating relationships. (True: When women outnumber men, men are less committed to college relationships.) [p. 188]

6.2. Individuals who are members of one subordinate group tend to experience the same amount of discrimination as individuals who are members of two subordinate groups. (False: Members of two subordinate groups often experience mistreatment based on both of their subordinate statuses.) [p. 192]

6.3. People who endorse hostile attitudes toward women also tend to endorse benevolent attitudes toward women (i.e., beliefs that women should be cherished and protected). (True: Hostile and benevolent sexism are positively correlated.) [p. 197]

6.4. The United States typically ranks in the top 10 countries in the world in terms of gender equality (measured in terms of gaps between women and men in health, education, political representation, and economic participation). (False: The United States ranks 45th out of 144 nations in gender equality.) [p. 207]

6.5. Women's intentions to confront gender discrimination match their actual rates of confronting gender discrimination. (False: Women tend to report that they will confront sexism at higher rates than they actually do.) [p. 210]

UNIT

IV

Cognition, Emotion, and Communication

Chapter 7   Cognitive Abilities and Aptitudes

Chapter 8   Language, Communication, and Emotion

Test Your Knowledge: True or False?

7.1 Most sex differences in cognitive abilities map directly onto sex differences in specific brain structures.

7.2 Girls and boys do not differ significantly in average levels of general mental ability (intelligence).

7.3 Countries with greater gender equality show smaller sex differences in verbal abilities.

7.4 Reminding women about negative stereotypes about women's math abilities can lower their math test performance.

7.5 Women's underrepresentation in careers in science, technology, engineering, and math (STEM) is due, at least to some degree, to lifestyle choices and demands placed on them to rear children and manage homes.

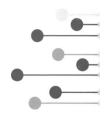

CHAPTER 7

Cognitive Abilities and Aptitudes

Key Concepts

What Is Cognitive Ability?
  Journey of Research: Measuring the Brain From Phrenology to fMRI
  Sex Differences in General Mental Ability

What Are the Sex Differences and Similarities in Cognitive Abilities?
  Verbal Performance
    Vocabulary and Verbal Fluency
    Reading and Writing
    Verbal Reasoning
  Quantitative Performance
  Visual-Spatial Performance
    Mental Rotation
    Spatial Perception and Visualization
    Spatial Location Memory
  Sex Differences in the Variability of Cognitive Abilities

How Do Individual Differences and Context Influence Cognitive Performance?
  Culture
  Stereotype Threat
  Willingness to Guess on Tests
  Achievement Motivation and Sensitivity to Feedback

How Do Sex and Gender Matter in Educational Systems and STEM Fields?
  Education and School Performance
    Cultural Influences
    Home and Classroom Dynamics
  Debate: Do Children Fare Better in Single-Sex Classrooms?
  Sex, Gender, and STEM Fields
    Discrimination
    Interests, Values, and Expectations
    Gendered Family Responsibilities

Learning Objectives

Students who read this chapter should be able to do the following:

7.1 Explain the historical origins of research on sex differences in cognitive abilities.

7.2 Analyze the specific domains of cognitive performance that show sex similarities and differences.

7.3 Evaluate contextual and individual difference factors that can influence cognitive performance.

7.4 Apply research on gender and cognitive performance to real-world issues, such as gender disparities in educational systems, school performance, and STEM disciplines.

Cognitive Abilities and Aptitudes

Of all the topics studied by psychologists interested in gender, sex differences in cognitive abilities are among the most controversial. For evidence of the strong passions that this topic ignites, consider the following cases.

In 2005, Harvard University hosted a conference, attended by some of the world's most eminent scientists, to discuss the underrepresentation of women in the sciences and engineering. The conference organizers invited Lawrence Summers, then president of Harvard, to make some remarks; they encouraged him to be provocative, and he was. Summers's remarks offended many of the conference attendees and drew substantial public criticism (S. Dillon, 2005). What did he say to generate such controversy? Summers (2005) suggested three potential explanations to account for women's relatively low numbers in science and engineering: the intense work demands of these fields, the greater natural aptitude of men at the highest levels of math and science, and sex-based patterns of socialization and discrimination. After emphasizing his first two explanations, Summers then discounted the role of discrimination.

The reaction was intense, with some supporting Summers and others denouncing him. Nancy Hopkins, a prominent MIT biologist, walked out of the talk, later stating, "When he started talking about innate differences in aptitude between men and women, I just couldn't breathe because this kind of bias makes me physically ill. Let's not forget that people used to say that women couldn't drive an automobile" (S. Dillon, 2005). Denice Denton, former chancellor of the University of California, Santa Cruz, criticized Summers for making assertions that could easily be refuted by examining the latest scholarship in the field—scholarship that was, in fact, the very focus of the conference where Summers made his remarks (Bartindale, 2005). Summers later issued a written apology to the Harvard faculty and community, stating that he wrongly oversimplified a very complex matter and should have put more emphasis on the roles of socialization and discrimination. Nonetheless, the damage was done. Summers resigned from Harvard the next year.

In 2006, Aarhus University in Denmark temporarily suspended psychologist Helmuth Nyborg after he published a paper in a reputable journal that showed a significant sex difference in general intelligence favoring men (Nyborg, 2005). Despite the paper passing through the peer review process for publication, it attracted enough controversy that it led to a university investigation. The investigation committee found Nyborg innocent of fraud but guilty of "grossly negligent behavior." The university later revoked Nyborg's suspension but gave him a severe reprimand.

In this chapter, we critically examine the controversial, politically charged topic of sex differences in cognitive abilities. The stakes are high, in part because of how some kinds of cognitive abilities link to occupations with high societal value, such as those in fields of science, technology, engineering, and math. To what extent does women's underrepresentation in STEM occupations reflect sex differences in cognitive abilities, defined as mental skills such as paying attention, reasoning, remembering, solving problems, speaking, and interpreting speech? The research findings in this area are inconsistent. While some specific types of cognitive abilities show moderate to large sex differences, others show small or nonexistent sex differences. Further, while the average performance of adolescent boys on standardized math tests in the United States

Cognitive abilities: Mental skills, such as paying attention, reasoning, remembering, solving problems, speaking, and interpreting speech.

exceeds that of girls (Lindberg, Hyde, Peterson, & Linn, 2010), girls consistently outperform boys when it comes to school math grades (Kenney-Benson, Pomerantz, Ryan, & Patrick, 2006). This chapter attempts to shed light on these complicated issues by examining two related questions. First, what are the sex differences and similarities in cognitive abilities, and why do these patterns emerge? And second, what accounts for gender disparities in educational systems and careers, particularly those involving STEM?

In addressing these questions, we examine the roles of three factors: (1) innate sex differences, (2) discrimination, and (3) sex differences in variables other than cognitive ability, such as preferences, expectations, confidence, or competitiveness. Note that these factors map roughly onto the three explanations that Lawrence Summers covered in his controversial talk. They also run the gamut from nature to nurture: Whereas assumptions about innate sex differences imply biological factors, or nature, as the primary cause, explanations involving discrimination imply social factors, or nurture, as the primary cause. And sex differences in things like preferences, expectations, confidence, and competitiveness are likely caused by a combination of nature and nurture. This may remind you of the theme of Chapter 3 ("The Nature and Nurture of Sex and Gender"), the notion that nature and nurture often cannot easily be separated. Before discussing explanations for sex differences in cognitive abilities, however, we begin with some definitions.

Intelligence (or general mental ability): The general capacity to understand ideas, think abstractly, reason, solve problems, and learn.

What Is Cognitive Ability?

Research on the origins of sex differences in cognitive ability has roots in the scientific study of **intelligence (or general mental ability)**, which is the general capacity to understand ideas, think abstractly, reason, solve problems, and learn. Note that intelligence is a broad capacity to process information and engage in mental activities rather than a specific type of knowledge or expertise, as reflected in this description:

> Intelligence is a very general mental capability
> that . . . involves the ability to reason, plan, solve problems,
> think abstractly, comprehend complex ideas, learn quickly,
> and learn from experience. It is not merely book learning, a narrow academic
> skill, or test-taking smarts. Rather it reflects a broader and deeper capability
> for comprehending our surroundings. (Gottfredson, 1997, p. 13)

The study of sex differences in intelligence dates back to at least the early 19th century. As you read in Chapter 2 ("Studying Sex and Gender"), women in the 19th century were commonly believed to be less intelligent than men. For instance, Charles Darwin (1871), otherwise fairly revolutionary in his thinking, argued that "the chief distinction in the intellectual powers of the two sexes is shown by man attaining to a higher eminence, in whatever he takes up, than woman can attain—whether requiring deep thought, reason, or imagination, or merely the use of the senses and hands" (p. 327).

Charles Darwin was a revolutionary thinker and well ahead of his time in many ways, but he harbored the same 19th-century biases about women's intelligence as many of his peers.

Source: © iStockPhoto.com/rolbos

With the birth of scientific psychology toward the end of the 19th century, some scholars attempted to build a scientific case to justify women's inferior position in society (Shields, 1975). For instance, researchers measured the shape, mass, and volume of male and female brains, arguing that women's smaller brains explained their intellectual inferiority (Fine, 2010). These methods, however, were rooted in questionable assumptions, as you will read about in "Journey of Research: Measuring the Brain From Phrenology to fMRI." Also, as you may recall from Chapter 3, sex differences in brain structure (such as shape and mass) do not map cleanly onto sex differences in brain function (such as processes and capacities). Gender biases in brain measurement studies led psychologist Helen Thompson Woolley, an early pioneer of gender research, to conclude in 1910 that "there is perhaps no field aspiring to be scientific where flagrant personal bias, logic martyred in the cause of supporting a prejudice, unfounded assertions, and even sentimental rot and drivel, have run riot to such an extent as [the psychology of sex differences]" (p. 340). Not surprisingly, the study of sex differences in cognitive abilities still arouses strong opinions and suspicions today, given this long history of bias in the field.

Stop and Think

Science, as a systematic method for asking and answering questions about the world, requires that researchers strive for objectivity and transparency. Given this, what do you make of the gender bias displayed by prominent scientists, such as Charles Darwin? What implications does this bias have for the credibility of science in general and scientific findings in the long run? Does science have ways of correcting itself when human bias creates distortions? If so, how?

Journey of Research

Measuring the Brain From Phrenology to fMRI

Do the brains of women and men differ? As we discussed in Chapter 3 ("The Nature and Nurture of Sex and Gender"), researchers in the field of neuroscience study the structure and function of the brain in order to understand mental processes and behaviors. Scientists and philosophers refer to the distinction between physical matter (the brain and body) and consciousness (the mind) as **dualism**. Although our understanding of the brain's relation to the mind is still incomplete, the study of the brain spans over 200 years, and the tools and theories used to understand the brain have become increasingly sophisticated.

Early methods of studying the brain were crude. In 1796, Franz Joseph Gall introduced a technique he called *cranioscopy,* or **phrenology**, which measured the size of lumps on the surface of the skull to infer various intellectual and psychological attributes. Phrenologists assumed that various areas of the brain had specific cognitive functions, with larger areas indicating greater cognitive and personality strengths. Although popular in the first half of the 19th century, phrenology was eventually dismissed as **pseudoscience**, or beliefs and practices that are presented as scientific despite lacking a factual basis and not being subjected to proper scientific scrutiny (Ioannidis, 2012).

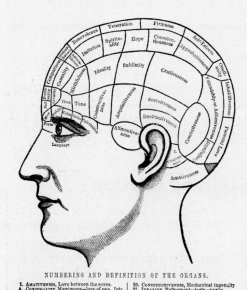

NUMBERING AND DEFINITION OF THE ORGANS.

1. **Amativeness**, Love between the sexes.
A. **Conjugality**, Matrimony—love of one. [etc.
2. **Parental Love**, Regard for offspring, pets, &c.
3. **Friendship**, Adhesiveness—sociability.
4. **Inhabitiveness**, Love of home.
5. **Continuity**, One thing at a time.
E. **Vitativeness**, Love of life.
6. **Combativeness**, Resistance—defense.
7. **Destructiveness**, Executiveness—force.
8. **Alimentiveness**, Appetite—hunger.
9. **Acquisitiveness**, Accumulation.
10. **Secretiveness**, Policy—management.
11. **Cautiousness**, Prudence—provision.
12. **Approbativeness**, Ambition—display.
13. **Self-Esteem**, Self-respect—dignity.
14. **Firmness**, Decision—perseverance.
15. **Conscientiousness**, Justice, equity.
16. **Hope**, Expectation—enterprise.
17. **Spirituality**, Intuition—faith—credulity.
18. **Veneration**, Devotion—respect.
19. **Benevolence**, Kindness—goodness.

20. **Constructiveness**, Mechanical ingenuity
21. **Ideality**, Refinement—taste—purity.
B. **Sublimity**, Love of grandeur—infinitude.
22. **Imitation**, Copying—patterning.
23. **Mirthfulness**, Jocoseness—wit—fun.
24. **Individuality**, Observation.
25. **Form**, Recollection of shape.
26. **Size**, Measuring by the eye.
27. **Weight**, Balancing—climbing.
28. **Color**, Judgment of colors.
29. **Order**, Method—system—arrangement.
30. **Calculation**, Mental arithmetic.
31. **Locality**, Recollection of places.
32. **Eventuality**, Memory of facts.
33. **Time**, Cognizance of duration.
34. **Tune**, Sense of harmony and melody.
35. **Language**, Expression of ideas.
36. **Causality**, Applying causes to effect. [tion.
37. **Comparison**, Inductive reasoning—illustra-
C. **Human Nature**, Perception of motives.
D. **Agreeableness**, Pleasantness—suavity.

A phrenology diagram illustrating the regions on the skull that presumably mapped onto specific locations in the brain where distinct skills and traits were regulated.

Source: © iStockPhoto.com/cjp

In another early method, researchers estimated the size of male and female brains by measuring head circumference or brain weight and volume postmortem. These methods proved unreliable, with questionable connections to intelligence (Fine, 2010), and yet, scientists used them to support the common assumption of women's intellectual inferiority. When theories at the time held that the frontal cortex was the brain region responsible for intelligence (it isn't), scientists began reporting that men had larger frontal lobes than women. When the evidence revealed that there were no actual sex differences in frontal cortex size, the scientific focus shifted to the parietal lobes as the seat of intelligence, and scientists began finding evidence for superior parietal lobes among men (Shields, 1975). In short, the strong belief in men's intellectual superiority seemed to drive the research methods and findings, in contrast to how science should proceed. This underscores the importance of critical evaluation when consuming research, as discussed in Chapter 2 ("Studying Sex and Gender").

Researchers' fascination with measuring brain structures and activity continues today. Sophisticated techniques now allow accurate estimates not just of total brain size but of the size of specific brain regions (Cahill, 2014), cortical thickness, percentages of gray and white matter (Taki et al., 2011), length of **dendrites** (neuronal structures that receive information from other neurons; Griffin & Flanagan-Cato, 2012), and degree of interconnectivity between the cerebral hemispheres (Ingalhalikar et al., 2014). One of the most common brain imaging techniques used today is *functional magnetic resonance imaging* (fMRI), which allows researchers to measure brain activity and to visualize where such activity occurs within specific brain regions. Using such methods, some researchers find sex differences in size and density in certain brain regions (Ruigrok et al., 2014). Others, in contrast, note a great deal of overlap in female and male brains (Joel et al., 2015). And even when sex differences are found, it is hard to know how to interpret them. Despite their

(Continued)

(Continued)

sophistication, neuroscience methods are fraught with the same problem of dualism that plagued thinkers since the 18th century: How do the physical structures of the brain relate to the cognitive processes of the mind? Thus, whether sex differences in the brain manifest as sex differences in cognitive abilities is not at all clear.

As the tools of neuroscience become more sophisticated, the discovery of new sex differences in the brain should invite critical reflection about the meaning and importance of these differences. Recall that, due to neuroplasticity, sex differences in the brain likely emerge through a complex interaction of nature and nurture, as gendered environments shape newborn brains. As past research shows, researchers can use neuroscience findings to sustain false beliefs about *essentialism* (Bluhm, 2013a). We encourage you to keep these ideas in mind when you encounter research that shows sex differences in the brain.

Dualism: The scientific and philosophical position that the physical body and the mind (consciousness) are two fundamentally different entities.

By the turn of the 20th century, scientists moved beyond simply measuring the brain to developing tests that measure intelligence. Alfred Binet and Theodore Simon developed the first modern intelligence test in France in the early 1900s (Binet & Simon, 1908), which led other researchers to popularize the concept of the **intelligence quotient (IQ)**. The IQ is a standardized score that represents an individual's level of intelligence relative to his or her same-age peers. Tests of IQ shifted consensus on the supposed superiority of male intelligence when Lewis Terman, a pioneer of early IQ testing in the United States, demonstrated that boys and girls did not differ in intelligence scores (Terman, 1916).

Phrenology: The discredited study of how the size and shape of the cranium (skull) relates to mental abilities and personal attributes.

Pseudoscience: Beliefs and practices that are presented as scientific despite lacking a factual basis and not being subjected to proper scientific scrutiny.

Dendrites: Branch-like structures of neurons that receive neural messages from other neurons.

Sidebar 7.1: Are We Getting Smarter?

Over a century of intelligence testing reveals a curious pattern. People's average performance on intelligence tests has risen steadily and substantially over time, a phenomenon known as the **Flynn effect** (J. R. Flynn, 1987). The gains in IQ appear across many nations and amount to about three IQ points per decade (Pietschnig & Voracek, 2015). Note that IQ test scores are standardized based on a population mean of 100 and a standard deviation of 15. Three points per decade may not sound like much, but consider those gains stretched across long time spans. As cognitive psychologist Steven Pinker (2011) pointed out, if a teenager with an average IQ of 100 today traveled back in time 100 years and took an IQ test, she would obtain an IQ score of 130, placing her at the 98th percentile relative to her same-age peers.

The Flynn effect likely reflects the joint operation of multiple causes, including better nutrition, reductions in infectious diseases, improvements in schooling, and cognitive stimulation from television and video games (Pietschnig & Voracek, 2015). Although the Flynn effect shows no difference by sex, consider what it suggests about the genetic versus sociocultural causes of cognitive ability. Genes cannot account for such substantial gains in IQ scores over a relatively short time period because species-level genetic changes take too long to evolve (Woodley, 2011). This suggests that environmental factors must play an important role in shaping IQ scores.

Sex Differences in General Mental Ability

Psychologists have long debated whether intelligence consists of a single, general factor or a number of different factors. Many now agree that intelligence consists of several separate yet correlated components that all feed into a superordinate general intelligence (N. Brody, 1992). Given this distinction, we will first examine sex differences in general intelligence and then turn to sex differences in distinct cognitive abilities.

Researchers have been measuring general mental ability for over 100 years, dating back to Charles Spearman (1904). Spearman argued that individuals possessed a general mental ability that related to their performance on all cognitive tasks and was identifiable statistically through a procedure called **factor analysis**, which identifies clusters of related scores. Due to the generality of mental ability, a person with good reading comprehension skills, for example, should also demonstrate good working memory and strong pattern recognition. Consistent with this assumption, general mental ability does predict important outcomes, such as academic performance (Gagne & St. Pere, 2002), job performance (Schmidt & Hunter, 2004), and even health and longevity (Deary, 2009). It also appears to be stable over the lifespan (Deary, Whaley, Lemmon, Crawford, & Starr, 2000) and genetically heritable (Bouchard, 1998), though environmental factors also play an important role. For instance, children adopted from working-class into middle-class homes exhibit IQs that are 12–18 points higher than their siblings raised by their working-class birth parents (Nisbett et al., 2012).

Are there sex differences in general mental ability? Recall the controversial paper by Helmuth Nyborg mentioned in the chapter opening. Although Nyborg (2005) found a significant IQ advantage favoring men, and a few other researchers find a modest male advantage (D. N. Jackson & Rushton, 2006), most studies find negligible sex differences in scores on measures of general mental ability (Colom, Juan-Espinosa, Abad, & García, 2000; Savage-McGlynn, 2012). Overall, the bulk of research suggests that sex differences in general mental ability are small and do not consistently favor one particular sex. However, looking for sex differences in general mental ability presents a challenge because most standardized intelligence tests are intentionally constructed to show no difference in overall female and male scores (Neisser et al., 1996). That is, items that consistently produce sex differences are replaced with items that do not produce differences. Gender neutral by design, these tests cannot be used reliably to examine sex differences in mental ability.

Intelligence quotient (IQ): A score representing an individual's level of intelligence, as measured by a standardized intelligence test. IQ is calculated such that the average for an individual's same-age peers is always set to 100.

Flynn effect: The increase of about three points per decade in average population performance on IQ tests over time (across generations).

Factor analysis: A statistical procedure used to identify clusters of related scores or items.

Stop and Think

Just as researchers design standardized intelligence tests to be gender neutral, they take a similar approach with items that produce ethnic, racial, or cultural differences in responses. Why do you think test designers *intentionally strive to create gender-, race-, and culture-neutral tests? What is the logic behind this strategy? How might this increase or decrease the validity of intelligence tests?*

What Are the Sex Differences and Similarities in Cognitive Abilities?

While the evidence does not consistently support sex differences in overall intelligence, some sex differences do emerge in research on more specialized cognitive abilities. These specific cognitive abilities are often grouped into verbal, quantitative, and spatial abilities, dating back to the groundbreaking work of Thurstone and Thurstone (1941). The Thurstones gave 60 different intelligence tests to a sample of eighth graders and found, using factor analysis, that the test items grouped into these three clusters of abilities. In the mid-1970s, Maccoby and Jacklin (1974) published a comprehensive and influential review of research on sex differences and concluded that the sexes indeed differed in verbal, quantitative, and spatial abilities. This conclusion quickly became the dominant understanding in the field.

By the 1980s and 1990s, however, a more complex picture began to emerge. Janet Hyde and her colleagues conducted several large meta-analyses to update Maccoby and Jacklin's (1974) findings (Hyde, Fennema, & Lamon, 1990; Hyde & Linn, 1988). These and more recent studies reveal a fairly consistent pattern of sex differences, though the size of the difference often depends on factors such as the type of cognitive skill measured, the publication date of the study, and the age or cultural background of the participants (Else-Quest, Hyde, & Linn, 2010). One large study of adults even revealed that health and health habits play a role in some cognitive sex differences. Specifically, Anthony Jorm and colleagues assessed various verbal, perceptual, and memory tasks and found that, after controlling for physical and mental health variables, sex differences disappeared in cases of male advantage and increased in cases of female advantage (Jorm, Anstey, Christensen, & Rodgers, 2004). That is, men's better health on some dimensions, such as pulmonary functioning, depression, and exercise frequency, accounts for their advantages on some cognitive tests, but health variables do not account for female advantages on other cognitive tests.

Recall from Chapter 2 that researchers measure the size of sex differences by calculating d value *effect sizes*, or estimates of the average difference between groups expressed in standardized units. As a reminder, d values are interpreted as reflecting differences that range from *close to zero* to *very large* in magnitude, and Table 7.1 provides you with a refresher of how to interpret d values. Also recall that positive d values indicate effect sizes favoring boys and men, and negative d values indicate effect sizes favoring girls and women. Finally, note that we will first focus on sex differences in average cognitive performance, and then we will consider variability in performance.

Verbal Performance

In their 1974 review article, Maccoby and Jacklin concluded that research consistently showed a female advantage on verbal tasks. Does research conducted since then support this conclusion? In an early meta-analysis, Hyde and Linn (1988) found a very small female advantage in verbal skills ($d = -0.11$), and a later meta-analysis revealed only close-to-zero effect sizes in verbal abilities (Hedges & Nowell, 1995). However, verbal abilities are not a unitary construct, and the size of the difference depends on the area being measured (e.g., vocabulary, verbal fluency, reading, writing, and verbal reasoning). As shown in Table 7.2, when sex differences do emerge, they are relatively small and tend to favor girls and women. Let's take a closer look at sex differences in these specialized verbal domains.

Table 7.1 **A Refresher on Effect Sizes.** The column on the right provides descriptive labels to accompany various ranges of *d* values (column on the left). This helps researchers interpret the magnitude of effects.

d value (absolute value)	Description of size
0.00–0.10	Close to zero
0.11–0.35	Small
0.36–0.65	Medium
0.66–1.00	Large
> 1.00	Very large

Source: Hyde (2005).

Table 7.2 **Sex Differences in Cognitive Performance.** Sex differences in quantitative abilities tend to be close to zero or small; sex differences in verbal abilities tend to be small to moderate; and sex differences in visual-spatial abilities tend to be moderate to large. The size and direction of sex differences, however, differ across the specific cognitive ability of interest.

Variable	*d*	Type of Sex Difference	Size
Verbal ability[a]	−0.11	F > M	Small
Vocabulary[b]	0.06	None	Close to zero
Verbal fluency[c]	−0.24 to −0.45	F > M	Small/moderate
Reading comprehension[a, d]	−0.03 to −0.44	F > M	Variable
Writing[b]	−0.57	F > M	Moderate
Verbal reasoning[e]	0.15	M > F	Small
Quantitative ability[f]	0.00	None	Zero
Computation[g]	−0.14	F > M	Small
Understanding math concepts[g]	−0.03	F > M	Close to zero
Complex problem solving[f, g]	0.07 to 0.32	M > F	Small/close to zero
Visual-spatial ability[h]	0.40	M > F	Moderate

(Continued)

Table 7.2 (Continued)

Variable	d	Type of Sex Difference	Size
Mental rotation[i, j]	0.47 to 0.73	M > F	Moderate/large
Spatial perception[h]	0.33 to 0.48	M > F	Moderate
Spatial visualization[h]	0.19	M > F	Small
Spatial location memory[k]	−0.27	F > M	Small

a. Hyde and Linn (1988), b. Hedges and Nowell (1995), c. Weiss et al. (2003), d. Reilly (2012), e. Strand et al. (2006), f. Hyde et al. (2008), g. Hyde et al. (1990), h. Voyer et al. (1995), i. Lippa et al. (2010), j. Linn and Peterson (1985), k. Voyer et al. (2007).

Vocabulary and verbal fluency. On average, girls learn to talk younger and their vocabularies bloom earlier than boys' do, although the effect sizes are small (Bornstein, Hahn, & Haynes, 2004). By later childhood, however, sex differences in vocabulary generally disappear (Wallentin, 2009). In contrast, tests of verbal fluency tend to show consistent sex differences. **Verbal fluency** is the ability to generate words, and tests of this ability require people to generate as many words as possible that belong to a certain category (e.g., birds) or that begin with a specific letter (e.g., M) in a short period of time (usually 1 minute). In one meta-analysis, Hyde and Linn (1988) reported a small sex difference for verbal fluency (d = −0.33). More recent studies reveal similar effect sizes (ds = −0.24 and −0.45; Weiss, Kemmler, Deisenhammer, Fleischhacker, & Delazer, 2003) and show that the female advantage in verbal fluency is present across ages and sexual orientations (Maylor et al., 2007).

Verbal fluency: The ability to generate words.

Reading and writing. The earliest meta-analysis of reading comprehension found no overall sex difference (d = −0.03; Hyde & Linn, 1988). More recent studies—some conducted across many cultures—find some evidence of a reading advantage for girls. For example, Hedges and Nowell (1995) found an average effect size of d = −0.18 across tests of reading comprehension in the United States. And in a large-scale study of the reading performance of 15-year-olds from 40 countries, including Brazil, Poland, Finland, Indonesia, and New Zealand, girls scored higher than boys in every country (Guiso, Monte, Sapienza, & Zingales, 2008). Similarly, analyzing the 2009 reading data from the Programme for International Student Assessment (PISA), Reilly (2012) found a moderate sex difference favoring girls (d = −0.44). Interestingly, Reilly found that the size of the sex difference in reading correlates with national indices of gender equality: In countries where girls have more educational and economic opportunities, they tend to outperform boys by the widest margins. For example, the largest sex differences in reading ability emerged in Finland (d = −0.64), which has the second-highest level of gender equality in the world, according to the World Economic Forum (2016). By way of comparison, the United States ranks 45th in gender equality and shows a smaller female advantage in reading (d = −0.26).

In terms of writing ability, most research shows that girls again have an advantage, with Hedges and Nowell (1995) reporting a moderate effect size (d = −0.57).

More recent evidence indicates that American girls outperform boys, on average, in tests of writing proficiency administered at Grades 8 and 12 (U.S. Department of Education, 2011). Thus, girls tend to outperform boys in reading and writing, but the sex difference is somewhat larger in writing.

Verbal reasoning. **Verbal reasoning,** or the ability to understand and analyze concepts, offers an exception to the general trend toward a female advantage in verbal abilities. As an example of a test item that measures verbal reasoning, try to solve this analogy: *Remembering* is to *forgetting* as *happy* is to _____. Now consider this word problem: "If Bob is taller than Juan, and Juan is taller than Marcus, which person is the shortest of the three?" Instead of a female advantage on verbal reasoning tasks, studies find either a small male advantage (*d* = 0.15; Strand, Deary, & Smith, 2006) or no sex difference (Feingold, 1988). Some researchers argue that the typical female verbal advantage does not emerge on this type of task because verbal reasoning tasks often require people to transform verbal information mentally (Colom, Contreras, Arend, Leal, & Santacreu, 2004). In other words, to solve the problem about Bob, Juan, and Marcus, you have to visualize the separate elements and then compare across them—perhaps by imagining Bob towering over Juan and Juan towering over Marcus. In general, men tend to outperform women in tasks that use this sort of visual-spatial processing. (We will return to this in the section on "Visual-Spatial Performance.")

Summarizing across what we have just discussed, the female advantage in verbal abilities that was claimed by Maccoby and Jacklin (1974) must be qualified. As shown in Table 7.2, girls outperform boys on some tests of verbal ability but not others, and the sex differences are small to moderate in magnitude. The size of the sex difference also depends on the age of the sample and the culture from which the sample is drawn (Reilly, 2012; Wallentin, 2009).

Countries high in gender equality, such as Finland, show the largest reading advantages for girls in comparison with boys.

Source: © iStockPhoto .com/gpointstudio

Verbal reasoning: The ability to understand and analyze concepts, often tested with analogies or word problems.

Quantitative Performance

Janet Hyde and her colleagues conducted large meta-analyses of sex differences in math performance in 1990 and more recently in 2008 (see Table 7.2). Both meta-analyses summarized data from millions of respondents in the general population and yielded no sex differences in overall math performance or math skills (Hyde et al., 1990; Hyde, Lindberg, Linn, Ellis, & Williams, 2008). Another recent meta-analysis that included data from over two million people also showed little evidence of an overall sex difference (*d* = 0.05), and 64% of the effect sizes fell in the close-to-zero range (Lindberg et al., 2010). However, even though no sex differences emerge in overall math performance, small sex differences do appear in some specific math domains, just as we saw with verbal abilities. In their 1990 meta-analysis, Hyde and colleagues found a small female advantage for computational ability ($d = -0.20$) at ages 5–10 that disappeared by ages 15–18, and they also found a modest male advantage for complex math problem solving ($ds = 0.29$ and 0.32) at ages 15–18 and 19–25 that was absent in the younger age groups. However, the male advantage in complex math problem solving was less evident in more recent meta-analyses, which found only close-to-zero ($d = 0.07$) and small ($d = 0.16$) effect sizes (Hyde et al., 2008; Lindberg et al., 2010).

Cross-culturally, there is evidence of variability across nations in the magnitude of sex differences in math performance. For example, a meta-analysis of the math test scores of nearly 500,000 adolescents from 69 countries found sex differences that ranged from a moderate advantage favoring girls ($d = -0.42$) in Bahrain to a moderate advantage favoring boys ($d = 0.40$) in Tunisia (Else-Quest et al., 2010). Halpern (2004) also found variability in the standardized math test performance of eighth graders across 30 countries, including Canada, Denmark, Iran, Japan, and New Zealand. Though the overall pattern showed boys outperforming girls in most of the countries, statistically significant differences emerged in only seven countries.

Why do you think the relative math performance of girls and boys differs across cultures? Just as we saw with reading abilities, the gender equality of a culture may play a role. Specifically, as the gender equality of a given nation increases, the size of men's advantage in math ability decreases (Guiso et al., 2008; Reilly, 2012), suggesting that sociocultural factors influence sex differences in quantitative performance. In countries in which girls' educational opportunities equal those of boys and more women have careers in science, sex differences in math performance tend to disappear.

Overall, as summarized in Table 7.2, the research shows little difference in the average math performance of girls and boys. Small differences favoring boys sometimes emerge in complex math problem solving among older children (Lindberg et al., 2010), but these gaps in math performance tend to disappear in countries with greater gender equality (Reilly, 2012).

Visual-spatial abilities: Cognitive skills that help individuals understand relationships between objects and navigate three-dimensional space.

Visual-Spatial Performance

Visual-spatial abilities allow people to understand relationships between objects and navigate three-dimensional space. They include the abilities to rotate figures mentally, predict the trajectories that moving objects will follow, and remember the locations of objects. People use these skills any time they navigate through a three-dimensional world in a video game, building structures or fighting off enemies. As with verbal and

---

Stop and Think

Consider the finding that sex differences in cognitive performance correlate with national indices of gender equality. Why might greater gender equality predict smaller male advantages in math and larger female advantages in reading? What do these trends suggest about the extent to which nature and nurture contribute to gender differences in cognitive abilities?

math performance, visual-spatial performance is measured in a number of ways, and the size of the sex difference depends on the specific task used and the age of the target population (Voyer, Voyer, & Bryden, 1995). Sex differences in visual-spatial tasks may also be influenced by factors such as time pressure and prior experience with the task. In general, sex differences favoring boys and men are larger and more consistent in visual-spatial performance, particularly in mental rotation tasks (see Figure 7.1a), than in other cognitive domains.

Figure 7.1   Visual-Spatial Tasks.

Example of a mental rotation, spatial perception, and spatial visualization task. Mental rotation consistently shows one of the largest sex differences (favoring boys and men) in cognitive abilities. Spatial perception shows a moderate sex difference, and spatial visualization shows a small sex difference (both favoring boys/men).

Look at this object: Two of these four drawings show the same object. Can you find the two?

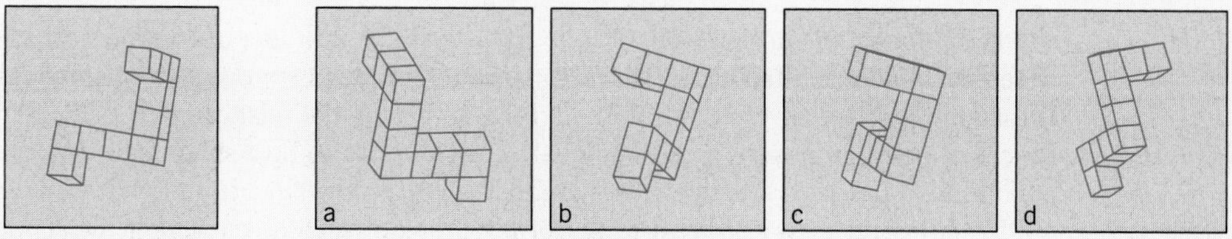

(a) Mental Rotation

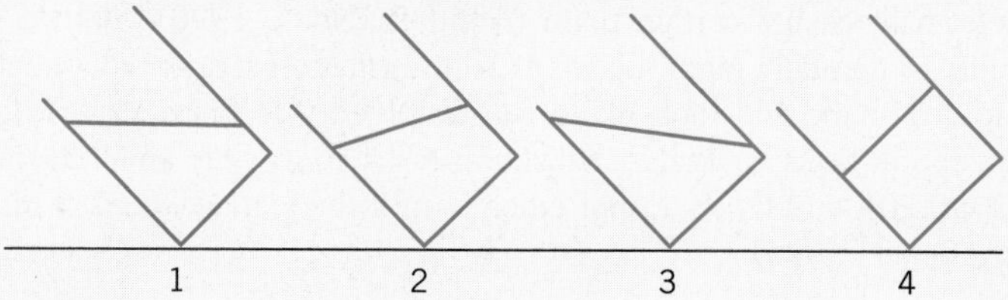

(b) Spatial Perception

Which tilted glass has a horizontal water line?

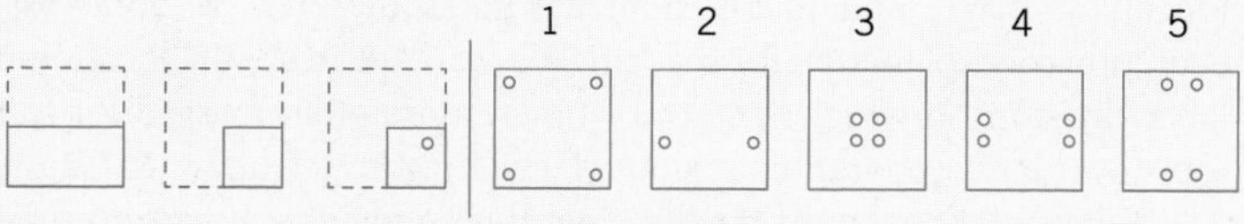

(c) Spatial Visualization

If this paper were folded and hole-punched, as shown, which of the five images would it match when unfolded?

Source: (a) Shepard and Metzler (1971); (b) Linn and Peterson (1985); (c) Chu and Kita (2011).

Mental rotation. Gender researchers show great interest in sex differences in **mental rotation ability**—the ability to rotate an object in one's mind—in part because this skill is essential for success in prestigious, male-dominated occupations such as engineering and architecture. As summarized in Table 7.2, an early review of mental rotation tasks revealed a large sex difference favoring boys and men ($d = 0.73$; Linn & Peterson, 1985), although this difference decreased somewhat over time ($d = 0.47$; Lippa, Collaer, & Peters, 2010). The male advantage in mental rotation appears in infancy (P. C. Quinn & Liben, 2014) and emerges consistently across cultures. For instance, the moderate effect size in mental rotation that we just mentioned ($d = 0.47$) derived from a study of over 200,000 participants in 53 countries (Lippa et al., 2010). Men exceeded women in mental rotation ability in every country, with larger sex differences in countries with greater gender equality and economic development. Interestingly, though, simple experimental manipulations can reduce this sex difference. For example, activating feelings of power by having students sit at a professor's desk improved Israeli women's performance on a mental rotation task (Nissan, Shapira, & Liberman, 2015). Similarly, activating stereotypes about men prior to the mental rotation task erased the sex difference in mental rotation ($d = 0.01$) among Austrian college students, compared with activating stereotypes about women ($d = 0.59$; Ortner & Sieverding, 2008).

Spatial perception and visualization. How well can you identify a true horizontal water level line in a tilted glass? This ability is an example of **spatial perception**, which is the ability to perceive, understand, and remember spatial relations between objects. In spatial perception tasks (see Figure 7.1b), there tends to be a small male advantage in childhood ($d = 0.33$) that increases to moderate ($d = 0.48$) in adulthood (Voyer et al., 1995). Boys and men also tend to perform better on tasks of movement perception, such as judging velocity (Law, Pellegrino, & Hunt, 1993) or estimating when a moving target will reach a certain point (Schiff & Oldak, 1990). **Spatial visualization** is the ability to mentally manipulate spatial information sequentially, such as imagining what a folded shape will look like when unfolded (see Figure 7.1c). In contrast to spatial perception tasks, spatial visualization tasks show only small average male advantages ($ds < 0.20$), and these do not emerge until the teenage years (Linn & Petersen, 1985; Voyer et al., 1995).

Spatial location memory. At least one type of spatial task shows a reverse of the typical male advantage: Women tend to have better **spatial location memory** than men do, which means that women are better than men at remembering where objects are, although the sex difference is small ($d = -0.27$; Voyer, Postma, Brake, & Imperato-McGinley, 2007) and inconsistent across studies (C. M. Jones & Healy, 2006). An evolutionary explanation for the female advantage in spatial location links it to sex-based labor divisions in which ancestral women more often foraged for fruits, vegetables, and roots over large geographic regions (New, Krasnow, Truxaw, & Gaulin, 2007).

What might account for the overall tendency for boys and men to display advantages in visual-spatial skills? Some suggest that play preferences in childhood contribute to boys' enhanced abilities. Boys, as compared with girls, tend to play more games that involve hand–eye coordination, such as throwing and catching balls (Cherney & London, 2006), and they immerse themselves more often in video games that

Mental rotation ability: The ability to rotate an object in one's mind.

Spatial perception: The ability to perceive, understand, and remember relations between objects in three-dimensional space.

Spatial visualization: The ability to represent and manipulate two- and three-dimensional objects mentally.

Spatial location memory: The ability to remember the location of objects in physical space.

require them to manipulate and navigate three-dimensional worlds (Terlecki & Newcombe, 2005). Demonstrating that life experience shapes abilities in these sorts of tasks, one study showed that training participants on an action video game for just 10 hours eliminated sex differences in spatial attention and mental rotation performance (Feng, Spence, & Pratt, 2007). It makes sense, then, that people who get more training with these sorts of games on a regular basis will score higher on measures of visual and spatial abilities. However, recall that the male advantage in mental rotation appears in infancy, before children gain experience with video games. Thus, play preferences may contribute to and enlarge sex differences in visual-spatial skills, but they likely cannot fully explain these sex differences.

Sex differences in spatial attention and mental rotation ability (favoring boys) can be reduced by training participants to play action video games.

Source: © iStockPhoto .com/Chris Ryan

The aforementioned studies suggest that nurture (the different life experiences of girls and boys) contributes to sex differences in spatial abilities, but what about nature? Some preliminary evidence suggests that prenatal exposure to certain hormones and hormone levels can influence the brain in ways that can later shape cognitive abilities. For instance, one study found that female fetuses exposed to unusually high levels of androgens (masculinizing hormones) later exhibited better spatial performance and mental rotation ability than those exposed to normal levels of androgens (Berenbaum, Bryk, & Beltz, 2012). However, this finding should be interpreted with caution because not all studies find effects of prenatal hormone exposure on later cognitive performance (Valla & Ceci, 2011).

In summary, some spatial abilities, such as mental rotation, show moderate to large sex differences favoring boys and men (see Table 7.2). It is likely that biological factors contribute to these sex differences, given the cross-cultural consistency and early appearance of these differences in development. However, some evidence suggests that environmental experiences, such as prior experience and learning, can also influence spatial abilities (Feng et al., 2007).

Sex Differences in the Variability of Cognitive Abilities

Thus far, we have focused on average sex differences in cognitive performance. By shifting the focus to variability, we can examine **outliers**—that is, people at the extreme ends of distributions. Two groups that show no average difference in ability can still differ in the concentrations of people who score very high (or low) on that ability. Consider Figure 7.2, which represents the hypothetical distributions of scores of women (the solid line) and men (the dashed line) on some cognitive test. Note that for both groups, the

Outliers: Values at the extreme ends of a statistical distribution.

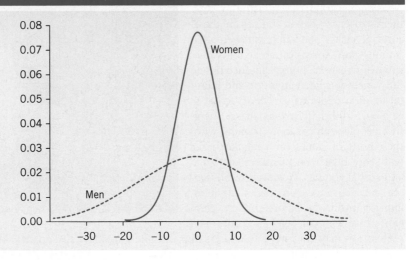

Figure 7.2   Differences in Within-Group Variance.

Source: Chu and Kita (2011).

Note: Although these two distributions have the same mean, the men's distribution has much more within-group variance than the women's distribution.

Greater male variability hypothesis: The prediction that men show more variability than women in their distributions of scores on cognitive performance measures, leading them to be overrepresented in the very bottom and very top of score distributions.

average score is 100. Thus, if we only examined mean differences, we would conclude that the groups have the same level of ability. But looking at Figure 7.2, it is clear that the distributions for women and men are not identical. Men's scores have much more *within-group variance* than women's scores do. Recall from Chapter 2 that within-group variance is an index of how spread out the values are among people within a group. In other words, the men's distribution has more very low and very high scores while the women's scores more tightly cluster around the mean.

The possibility that men show greater variability in cognitive performance is aptly named the **greater male variability hypothesis**. Though first formally proposed by Havelock Ellis in 1894, this hypothesis dates back to Charles Darwin (Shields, 1982). If this hypothesis has merit, sex differences will be more pronounced in the high and low

Stop and Think

With the greater male variability hypothesis in mind, imagine that you took samples of female and male high achievers in math (from the right tails of each distribution). What would you likely find, in terms of the size and direction of the sex difference? How would this *differ if you took samples from the lower, left tails of each distribution or if you took samples from the middle of each distribution? If a sex difference researcher is unaware of this phenomenon, how could it bias the conclusions drawn?*

tails of distributions. In other words, *where* in a distribution a researcher draws a sample will impact the size and direction of the sex difference found.

In support of the greater male variability hypothesis, men are disproportionately represented at both ends of cognitive ability distributions (Bergold, Wendt, Kasper, & Steinmayr, 2017; Hyde et al., 2008). This means that the top scorers on many cognitive tests are more likely to be men than women, but so are the lowest scorers. As early as the 19th century, researchers noted the disproportionate numbers of men in homes for the intellectually challenged (H. Ellis, 1894). Similarly, boys are more likely than girls to receive diagnoses of learning disabilities and developmental disorders, such as dyslexia (J. M. Quinn & Wagner, 2015), autism spectrum disorders (Volkmar, Szatmari, & Sparrow, 1993), and Down syndrome (Verma & Huq, 1987).

How does the hypothesis fare across cultures, race, and time? In a cross-cultural study of over 40 countries, Machin and Pekkarinen (2008) found greater male variance in math performance in most (88%) of the countries examined. However, the male-to-female ratio of top-scoring test-takers in the United States has declined with time, changing from 13 boys to every 1 girl in the early 1980s to about 3:1 by the mid-2000s (Spelke, 2005). Additional research suggests that the greater male hypothesis does not hold consistently for people in every racial and ethnic group. For example, Hyde et al. (2008) found greater male than female variability in math performance for White students but not for Asian students.

What might account for the greater variability in men's cognitive performance? Note that simply finding evidence of greater male variability does not indicate which factors—biological or sociocultural—cause the greater variability. As with most outcomes, both nature and nurture likely play roles. On the nurture side, greater male variability in math ability does not emerge in some countries (e.g., Denmark and The Netherlands), and it tends to decrease as countries show greater evidence of gender equality (Hyde & Mertz, 2009). On the nature side, research suggests that alleles, or variant forms of genes, on the X chromosome can explain sex differences in the lower tails of ability distributions, such as the disproportionate numbers of boys and men with intellectual disabilities (Turkheimer & Halpern, 2009). To date, however, there are no known genetic variations that can account for differences in variability at the high end of the distribution. This brings us back to the chapter opener and the controversial comments that Lawrence Summers made in which he attributed men's disproportionate representation in STEM fields to their greater "natural aptitude" at the highest levels of achievement. Contrary to Summers's position, we lack evidence that nature alone can explain women's underrepresentation in STEM majors and fields. We will return to this issue shortly.

Dyslexia: A learning disability characterized by impairments in reading, including problems with word recognition and spelling.

Autism spectrum disorders: Developmental disorders typically characterized by difficulties with communicating and interacting with others, limited interests or activities, and repetitive behaviors.

Down syndrome: A genetic disorder characterized by physical growth delays, mild to moderate intellectual impairment, and distinct facial features.

Allele: A variant form of a gene.

How Do Individual Differences and Context Influence Cognitive Performance?

Thus far, we have noted several times that nature and nurture interact in complex ways to produce sex differences in cognitive performance. In fact, this assumption lies at the heart of Diane Halpern's (2004) biopsychosocial model, which addresses a range of biological and environmental factors that contribute to cognitive performance (see Figure 7.3). Halpern argues that biology (e.g., genetic predispositions and prenatal hormones) and environment (e.g., culture and learning experiences) are inextricably linked and mutually shape each other to produce cognitive abilities. In other words, cause and effect are circular, and each factor both influences and is influenced by the other. This model fits the evidence well and echoes the point we made in Chapter 3 about the inseparability of nature and nurture. People's learning experiences influence the structure and growth of their neurons, and the structure of the brain, in turn, leads people to develop certain skills and aptitudes and to select experiences that reinforce and strengthen the brain's architecture. Learning is both biological and environmental, "as inseparable as conjoined twins who share a common heart" (Halpern, 2004, p. 138).

To get a fuller picture of how sex and gender relate to cognitive performance, it is important to examine various contextual factors and individual difference variables that can impact performance. For instance, some people approach high-stakes

Figure 7.3 A Biopsychosocial Model of Cognitive Ability.

Halpern's (2004) model of cognitive ability assumes that biological factors (e.g., genes and hormones), psychological variables (e.g., learning), and social factors (e.g., culture) are inextricably linked and mutually shape each other.

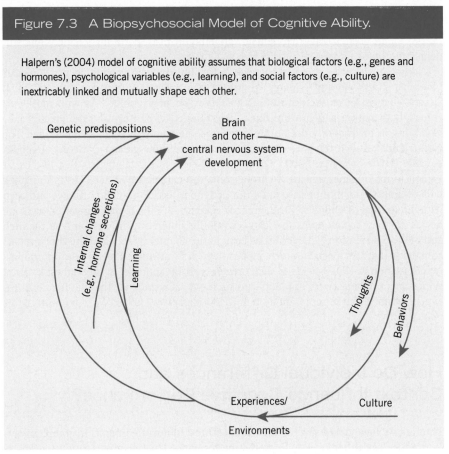

Source: Halpern (2004).

testing situations as an exciting challenge and prepare for them accordingly while others freeze up. Or a person may feel perfectly at ease taking a standardized test but have little motivation to put in sustained effort on a daily basis in school, resulting in high test scores but poor grades. In what follows, we review several variables that may contribute to sex differences in cognitive test performance. While reading this material, consider where each factor might enter the circle of Halpern's (2004) biopsychosocial model of cognitive ability (see Figure 7.3). If you find this task difficult, that's because it is—disentangling whether factors are biological, cultural, social, or psychological often poses a real challenge.

Culture

What can cross-cultural evidence tell us about gender and cognitive ability? If boys have an innate cognitive advantage in quantitative skills, or girls have an innate advantage in verbal skills, it should hold across cultures. The evidence here is mixed and depends on the cognitive ability domain. On the nurture side, several large cross-cultural studies, representing hundreds of thousands of people, find a fair amount of cross-cultural variation in the size of some cognitive sex differences. As noted earlier, the size of these differences often correlates with measures of gender equality, suggesting that some sex differences stem less from biology and more from cultural, structural, and economic features of societies (Hyde & Mertz, 2009; D. I. Miller & Halpern, 2014). Of all the cognitive domains, math performance shows the greatest variability in sex differences from culture to culture (Else-Quest et al., 2010). Moving more toward the nature side, verbal and visual-spatial sex differences generally show less (though still some) cross-cultural variation (Halpern, 2004; Lippa et al., 2010; Reilly, 2012). As of yet, there is no consensus regarding why girls consistently outperform boys in reading or why boys consistently outperform girls in mental rotation across cultures.

Stereotype Threat

You may recall the concept of *stereotype threat* from Chapter 5 ("The Contents and Origins of Gender Stereotypes"). Stereotype threat is the anxiety people feel when they risk confirming a negative stereotype about their group. For example, consider the stereotype that Lawrence Summers espoused in the chapter opener: that girls and women lack STEM aptitude relative to men. Now imagine that you are a woman who is taking a difficult but important math exam that will determine whether you can get college math credit. Many people experience anxiety in these situations, but if you are a woman who is reminded about gender stereotypes before the exam, you may notice an extra little voice of doubt in your head, adding to your anxieties: "What if the stereotypes are true? Maybe I'm not cut out for this." In fact, reminding women about negative gender stereotypes before a math exam can lower their test performance.

Almost two decades ago, Spencer, Steele, and Quinn (1999) proposed that stereotype threat anxiety accounts for at least part of the sex difference in math performance at the high end of achievement. Not only do experiments demonstrate that women's math performance suffers if they are reminded of negative gender stereotypes before an exam, but a large body of evidence indicates that girls and women have more math anxiety in general than boys and men. Boys across the globe report somewhat more positive attitudes and feelings about math than girls (ds from 0.10 to 0.33), and girls in the United States tend to have lower math self-confidence ($d = 0.27$) and greater math anxiety ($d = -0.23$) than boys (Else-Quest et al., 2010).

How exactly does stereotype threat impair performance? Being reminded of a negative stereotype about one's group can disrupt working memory capacity (Rydell, McConnell, & Beilock, 2009; Schmader & Johns, 2003). This can be especially detrimental when trying to solve complex math problems because such problems often require people to hold several pieces of information in memory simultaneously. So nagging doubts about the poor math abilities associated with one's sex can cause lapses in concentration that disrupt performance. Consistent with this explanation, stereotype threat effects diminish for women who have a greater working memory capacity (Regner et al., 2010).

By now, researchers have conducted hundreds of studies on stereotype threat. Meta-analyses indicate that the effects of stereotype threat on women's cognitive test performance fall in the small to moderate range, with ds from 0.18 to 0.36 (Nguyen & Ryan, 2008; Picho, Rodriguez, & Finnie, 2013; Walton & Spencer, 2009), but the type of threat makes a difference. For instance, researchers can manipulate stereotype threat using either subtle cues (e.g., merely reminding people of their sex by having them write it down on a form prior to an exam) or blatant cues (e.g., telling people before a math exam that "women tend to perform worse than men on this test"). Subtle cues tend to elicit stronger stereotype threat effects than blatant cues, perhaps because blatant reminders of stereotypes are easier to attribute to discrimination (recall the material on attributional ambiguity from Chapter 6, "Power, Sexism, and Discrimination"). Moreover, women who identify moderately strongly with math generally experience the most negative effects of stereotype threat on math test performance. For women who identify very strongly with math, confidence in their math abilities likely helps them to overcome the threat of negative stereotypes, and women who do not identify with math at all may not feel threatened by negative stereotypes. Summarizing across many studies, Walton and Spencer (2009) estimated that stereotype threat anxiety likely reduces the average Scholastic Aptitude Test (SAT) math performance of girls by 19 to 21 points. (Boys typically outperform girls by an average of 32 points on the SAT math test.) And as we noted in Chapter 5, some researchers estimated that having students indicate their sex after—instead of before—they take the Advanced Placement calculus exam could result in an additional 4,700 women receiving college calculus credit each year (Danaher & Crandall, 2009).

Is there anything that women can do to overcome the negative effects of stereotype threat? Miyake and colleagues (2010) suggested an interesting intervention. They recruited women enrolled in college-level physics courses and asked them to do a brief exercise at the beginning of the semester in which they wrote about their most important values. This exercise provided women with feelings of integrity and self-worth that buffered them against the negative effects of stereotype threat and subsequently raised their physics grades, especially among those who held the stereotype that men are superior to women in physics. Thus, when feeling anxious or troubled about negative gender stereotypes, it may help to shift attention to unrelated topics that boost self-esteem. Stereotype threat effects also diminished in an experiment when researchers told some

Sidebar 7.2: You've Come a Long Way, Barbie

In July 1992, Mattel released a talking Barbie that was programmed to utter several canned phrases. One of Barbie's phrases—"Math class is tough!"—raised the ire of the American Association of University Women for its negative portrayal of girls' math abilities. By October 1992, Mattel responded to the controversy by removing the offensive phrase from Barbie's lexicon. Almost a generation later, following a poll of fans, Mattel introduced computer engineer Barbie in 2010 and scientist Barbie in 2016.

Unlike the Barbie of the early 1990s, who struggled to keep up in her math class, today's Barbie is more likely to pursue a career as a computer engineer or scientist.

Source: © iStockPhoto.com/ivanastar

women that sex differences in math result from life experiences rather than genes (Dar-Nimrod & Heine, 2006). By default, people often assume that sex differences are rooted in biological causes, so messages that counter this belief can relieve women's anxiety and improve their performance.

Willingness to Guess on Tests

If you were taking an important test, and you did not know an answer, would you guess or leave the item blank? Some tests impose penalties for guessing incorrectly by subtracting points for errors. This is true of the SAT, which is used by many U.S. colleges to make admissions decisions. Since boys, on average, outperform girls on the math portion of the SAT, it is worth considering whether boys and girls differ in their willingness to guess on this test. Baldiga (2013) conducted an experiment in which people answered practice questions from the SAT under one of two conditions: either there was or was not a penalty for incorrect answers. In the "no penalty" condition, everyone answered every question, but in the penalty condition, women were less likely than men to take guesses. This is important because skipping questions on the SAT hurts performance: People tend to do better when guessing rather than simply leaving answers blank. This may help explain why women tend to score slightly lower on the SAT than men do but still get better grades than men in college. That is, the SAT underpredicts women's college performance, perhaps in part because of women's reluctance to guess on the SAT when they do not know the correct answers. If so, then sex differences in willingness to take risks may account for some test performance differences.

Achievement Motivation and Sensitivity to Feedback

Achievement motivation: An individual's need to meet goals and accomplish tasks.

Some question whether differences in **achievement motivation**—or individuals' need to meet goals and accomplish tasks—can explain girls' (sometimes) lower performance in complex math reasoning tests. When it comes to math, perhaps girls feel less motivated to succeed or persist in the face of failure than boys do. However, Jacquelynne Eccles has been studying this issue for many years (Eccles, 1984, 2005; Eccles, Adler, & Meece, 1984), and she finds no evidence that girls are more likely to give up after academic failures. In fact, some studies find that girls show higher intrinsic motivation for school in general while boys show greater work avoidance (Spinath, Eckert, & Steinmayr, 2014). This may explain why, despite roughly equal cognitive ability and generally small differences on standardized test scores, girls tend to get better school grades than boys.

If there are no sex differences in achievement motivation, then perhaps there are sex differences in the effects that feedback has on people's confidence? Imagine struggling as a student to learn some challenging new material. Your teacher gives you mixed feedback on your performance, communicating that you could be doing much better. How do you react? Tomi-Ann Roberts (1991) reviewed evidence indicating that women and men tend to respond differently to evaluative feedback about their performance. In general, women's self-evaluations tend to be more responsive than men's to the feedback that they receive, both good and bad. This may be because women, more so than men, tend to approach performance situations as a way of gaining information about their abilities. In contrast, men tend to approach performance situations as opportunities to compete, more often adopting a self-confident approach that makes them relatively impervious to others' evaluations of them. Thus, men are more inclined than women to respond to feedback by acknowledging positive comments and denying negative ones. While neither approach is necessarily better than the other, they may produce differences in how women and men develop—and then update—their beliefs about their abilities.

Stop and Think

Consider the pros and cons of these different strategies for dealing with evaluative feedback about cognitive performance. In what ways might it be beneficial to remain responsive to others' feedback? In what ways *might it be costly or detrimental? How about the strategy of ignoring negative performance evaluations? How might this approach be beneficial or detrimental in the long run?*

How Do Sex and Gender Matter in Educational Systems and STEM Fields?

Education and School Performance

Cultural influences. As you may recall from the previous chapter, girls and boys do not have equal access to education around the globe, with some areas of the world such as the Middle East and sub-Saharan Africa showing the largest gender gaps favoring boys (UNESCO, 2016). Increasing educational access for girls not only has psychological and physical health benefits for individual girls, but it has economic benefits for entire communities as well. As girls' level of education (and hence earning potential) increases within a community, the degree of poverty in the community decreases (Bourne, 2014).

For girls and boys with access to education, sex and culture may interact to shape educational outcomes. East Asian cultures, such as Taiwan and Japan, tend to stress *effort-based learning* in which teachers and other adults expect students to put effort into their studies regardless of their personal interest in the subject matter. In contrast, Western cultures, such as the United States, tend to emphasize *interest-based learning* in which adults encourage students to channel their efforts into particular domains of interest. How do these different educational emphases relate to outcomes? To answer this, E. M. Evans, Schweingruber, and Stevenson (2002) examined academic interest and knowledge levels in representative samples of 11th-grade girls and boys in Taiwan, Japan, and the United States. Overall, regardless of sex, students in Taiwan and Japan performed better in math than their U.S. counterparts. Moreover, sex differences (favoring boys) in math were larger in Taiwan and Japan than in the United States, but East Asian girls still outperformed both girls and boys in the United States. This occurred even though East Asian girls reported lower levels of interest in math as compared with U.S. boys. That is, their culture's emphasis on effort-based learning led girls to achieve better math performance. This suggests that cultural values may play a more powerful role in shaping school performance than gender roles do.

Home and classroom dynamics. Children's academic interests are malleable, making them susceptible to influence by specific home and school environments. For instance, Edward Melhuish and his colleagues followed English children over time and found that children's math achievement at age 10 was predicted less strongly by their sex than it was by factors such as their home learning environment at ages 3–4, their mother's education level, and the effectiveness of their primary school (Meluish et al., 2008). Just as more stimulating home environments can enhance children's academic performance, parents can also behave in ways that decrease their children's performance. Erin Maloney and her colleagues conducted a longitudinal study of first and second graders' math achievement and found that the children of parents higher in math anxiety learned less math and showed increases in math anxiety over the course of the school year, but this occurred only when parents frequently helped with math homework (Maloney, Ramirez, Gunderson, Levine, & Beilock, 2015). Thus, math-anxious parents may unintentionally pass their math anxiety onto their children while helping them with math. However, when math-anxious parents are trained in how to complete structured, interactional math activities with their children, it can increase the children's math achievement across the school year (Berkowitz et al., 2015). This intervention works regardless of sex, but since girls and women show higher levels of math anxiety compared with boys and men (as discussed earlier), the intervention holds the potential to decrease sex differences in math anxiety.

Just as with home environments, school environments can shape children's academic expectations and interests. The domain of math is again relevant here. As discussed, girls often have more negative attitudes toward math than boys do, which has bearing on girls' math performance and their choices regarding math-related courses and careers (Gunderson, Ramirez, Levine, & Beilock, 2012). To what degree are children's math attitudes shaped by their teachers' attitudes? The findings in this area are mixed. For instance, some evidence suggests that teachers' gender stereotypes about math can spill over and influence their students' gender stereotypes about math (Keller, 2001). However, teachers' perceptions of their own students' math abilities tend to be accurate rather than based merely on gender stereotypes (Jussim & Eccles, 1992). Finally, although teachers' beliefs about their students' math potential in kindergarten predict students' interest in math across the elementary school years, this pattern holds for both female and male students (Upadyaya & Eccles, 2014). Thus, while teachers' gender stereotypes can influence their students' gender stereotypes, there is less evidence that teachers' expectations directly drive sex differences in their students' math performance.

In some cases, school performance can be impacted by the more troubling issue of overt discrimination. For instance, one study of over 250 primarily Latino, Black, and White sexual minority youth at urban high schools in the United States found that students who reported more daily experiences with homophobic or transphobic discrimination also had worse school performance, more absenteeism, and more discipline problems at school (Craig & Smith, 2014). Given the role of high school performance in predicting future life outcomes, it will be important for researchers to examine how best to meet the unique needs of sexual minority youth within schools. In a related vein, some advocate that educating girls and boys in single-sex classrooms would be an effective strategy to minimize the negative consequences of gender-biased school environments. The key question here centers on the relative effectiveness of single-sex versus mixed-sex learning environments, which we explore in "Debate: Do Children Fare Better in Single-Sex Classrooms?"

Debate

Given the nature of the topic and the uneven and sometimes contradictory state of the research findings, people often have quite passionate opinions about gender and cognitive abilities. Here, we will consider a relevant real-world social issue: whether single-sex or mixed-sex classrooms produce better learning outcomes. The public push for single-sex education is fairly recent. In 2002, the United States had only about a dozen public schools that offered single-sex classrooms, but by 2011, this number had grown to over 500 (Hartmann, 2011). Advocates of single-sex schooling believe that traditional mixed-sex classrooms can harm children's learning and socialization, while others argue that the evidence does not support this claim. What are the arguments for and against single-sex classrooms, and what does the evidence suggest?

Yes, Children Fare Better in Single-Sex Classrooms

Single-sex schooling advocates, such as the National Association for Single Sex Public Education, argue that the current environment in schools is sexist and narrows children's expectations. They further argue that single-sex classrooms can dissolve gender stereotypes and allow children to flourish (Hartmann, 2011). In addition, these groups argue that boys and girls should be separated due to differences either in cognitive learning or in temperaments and social needs.

In a longitudinal study of Canadian high school students, Shapka and Keating (2003) found that girls who received math and science instruction in single-sex classrooms in the 9th or 10th grade later took more math and science classes and made better grades in these classes than girls who received math and science instruction in mixed-sex classrooms. Furthermore, Kessels and Hannover (2008) randomly assigned German eighth graders to single-sex versus mixed-sex physics classes and found that girls in single-sex classes reported having more positive perceptions of their physics ability than girls instructed in mixed-sex classrooms.

Evidence also suggests that because boys and girls tend to behave differently, teachers treat them differently in classrooms. For example, one study (Cornwell, Mustard, & Van Parys, 2013) found that elementary teachers factor children's behavior into grades, and girls exhibit better classroom behavior than boys, on average. Girls tend to be more attentive, more persistent, more independent, less disruptive, and less fidgety than boys. These sex differences in temperaments lead some to argue that most of today's classrooms are not designed with boys in mind. Lessons that require sitting quietly for long periods of time are not ideal for boys' greater activity levels. Single-sex classrooms would allow teachers to tailor learning to the unique learning styles and behavior patterns of boys and girls.

The effectiveness of single-sex versus mixed-sex classrooms may depend on the cultural setting. For cultural and religious regions, education is often segregated by sex in Muslim cultures, and in many Muslim countries that score relatively low on measures of gender equality, girls actually outperform boys on math tests. This may occur because in countries with rigid gender roles and high gender inequality, mixed-sex classrooms may harm girls by reinforcing their subordinate status (Ellison & Swanson, 2010; Fryer & Levitt, 2010). This suggests that the effectiveness of single-sex versus mixed-sex education may depend on complex cultural factors.

No, Children Do Not Fare Better in Single-Sex Classrooms

Rather than erasing gender stereotypes, single-sex classrooms may actually reinforce stereotypes because the contrast between the single-sex classroom and the outside (mixed-sex) world simply highlights how the world is organized by sex. Furthermore, educating children in single-sex classrooms can leave them unprepared for a world in which they must interact with people of all sexes and genders (Halpern et al., 2012).

In a recent meta-analysis of the effects of single-sex versus mixed-sex schooling on performance, researchers examined cross-cultural data from more than 1.6 million students in Grades K–12 (Pahlke, Hyde, & Allison, 2014). They looked at sex differences in science and math performance, as well as in attitudes toward school, gender stereotyping, aggression, body image, and victimization. The evidence did not support the superiority of single-sex classrooms, showing no significant differences overall in performance or attitudes for boys or girls in single-sex versus mixed-sex classrooms. A 2012 report in *Science* published by leading cognitive psychologists argued that the push for single-sex education is "deeply misguided, and

(Continued)

(Continued)

often justified by weak, cherry picked, or misconstrued scientific claims rather than valid scientific evidence" (Halpern et al., 2012, p. 1706).

Rather than single-sex schooling, some advocate for attending more closely to the unique temperaments and cognitive styles of boys when developing school curricula. For instance, some countries (e.g., Australia, Canada, and the United Kingdom) are experimenting with programs to make schools more "boy friendly" by, for instance, increasing physical activity and recess time, selecting more male-oriented reading assignments, instituting campaigns to increase male literacy, and recruiting more male teachers (Hoff Sommers, 2013).

Now that you have read both sides of this debate, where do you fall on the issue? Which evidence do you find most convincing and which conclusions most reasonable?

Women are underrepresented in math-intensive STEM fields. For example, women constitute only about 25% of computer programmers in the United States. Given few sex differences in cognitive abilities, why do you think so few women pursue programming careers?

Sex, Gender, and STEM Fields

The evidence reviewed in this chapter suggests that, overall, women and men do not differ in intellectual ability, which challenges the notion that women lack the ability to compete for careers in science and math. And yet, consider the following: Although women represent about half the U.S. workforce, only 26% of workers in STEM fields were women in 2011 (Landivar, 2013). In 2006, women earned about 40.2% of all doctorates in the sciences and engineering, but they constitute only 5.0% of full professors in engineering, 17.4% in computer science, 26.2% in life sciences, 8.3% in physical sciences, and 8.6% in mathematics (Burrelli, 2008). What's going on here? Is there a gender bias in STEM disciplines? In the following sections, we consider some possible explanations for gender disparities in STEM fields.

Discrimination. Women's underrepresentation in STEM fields may result from discrimination, either overt or subtle. As we discussed in Chapter 6, gender biases that curtail women's options can occur at many stages and take many forms. For instance, one study found that U.S. undergraduate women encountered more benevolent sexism (such as paternalistic offers of extra assistance) than hostile sexism (such as overtly insulting comments about their competence) in their STEM courses. Moreover, women who experienced more benevolent sexism—and who were weakly identified with STEM fields—also reported lower confidence in their STEM abilities and weaker intentions to major in a STEM field (Kuchynka et al., 2017). Thus, experiences with sexism in their college courses may discourage women from pursuing STEM as a major, especially if they do not identify especially strongly with STEM as a major.

Even among women who succeed in STEM at the college level, there may be hiring biases that work against them. In one study, science faculty evaluated a fictitious undergraduate student—portrayed as either a woman or a man—who applied for a job as a laboratory manager. Both female and male science professors viewed the male applicant—in comparison with the female applicant—as more competent and hirable, even though the applicants varied only in their sex (Moss-Racusin, Dovidio, Brescoll, Graham, & Handelsman, 2012). In another study, when participants considered candidates for a job that required math, they were twice as likely to recommend hiring male candidates as compared with female candidates, even when the groups had identical math skills (Reuben, Sapienza, & Zingales, 2014). In fact, male scientists at top universities employ more male than female graduate students and postdoctoral students in their labs (Sheltzer & Smith, 2014). Finally, once hired, women face discrimination in STEM workplaces. In one study of over 500 women in science, more than a third reported experiencing sex-based harassment in the workplace (J. C. Williams, Phillips, & Hall, 2014). Women of color may be especially likely to face discrimination in STEM workplaces. Their experiences range from having their competence questioned, to having to prove themselves repeatedly, to receiving backlash when they behave assertively.

However, some findings challenge the notion of widespread discrimination against women in STEM. Consider the fact that women now earn 53% of PhDs in biology, 48% of medical degrees, and 78% of veterinary degrees (National Center for Education Statistics, 2012). These statistics indicate that women equal or even surpass men in some areas of STEM. Moreover, one review concluded that female professors in math-intensive STEM disciplines earn as much as men, receive tenure and promotion at comparable rates, and persist equally at their jobs (Ceci, Ginther, Kahn, & Williams, 2014). This review also concluded that women with PhDs now get hired for math-intensive academic jobs at rates comparable to men, suggesting recent changes to the long-standing patterns of gender bias in STEM disciplines, at least in academia. Similarly, in another study, faculty asked to evaluate hypothetical job candidates for STEM faculty positions preferred female applicants 2:1 over equally qualified male candidates (W. Williams & Ceci, 2015). In short, the evidence for overt sexism in STEM disciplines is mixed and suggests that factors other than cognitive abilities may be important in explaining women's underrepresentation.

Interests, values, and expectations. Another potential explanation for the relative lack of women in STEM disciplines is that such careers simply appeal to them less. Supporting this explanation, the values and preferences of men and women differ in ways that can steer them to pursue different careers. For example, women tend to prefer activities and jobs that emphasize interactions with others and that require interpersonal skills while men tend to prefer activities and jobs that emphasize working with machines or computers (Lippa, 2001; Su, Rounds, & Armstrong, 2009). In one study, Amanda Diekman and her colleagues asked college students about their interests in various careers, as well as how much they endorsed communal goals (e.g., helping others and working with people) and agentic goals (e.g., power over others and mastery). The results showed that the more people endorsed communal goals, the less interest they had in STEM careers (Diekman, Brown, Johnson, & Clark, 2010).

This suggests that women may lack interest in STEM careers because they do not view them as offering opportunities to meet communal goals. Note that sex differences in communal and agentic goals, as well as beliefs about whether STEM careers offer opportunities to meet communal goals, emerge early in childhood. Researchers find that the beliefs and values of girls and boys start to differentiate along gender-stereotyped lines in the first grade (Eccles et al., 1993). Thus, by the time they enter high school and college, girls may undervalue STEM careers because they do not view them as "helping" careers (Eccles, 2007).

Sidebar 7.3: Getting Girls Interested in Computer Programming

Even young children in the United States believe that boys are better at computer programming and robotics than girls. How can we improve girls' computer technology self-efficacy? Allison Master and colleagues recruited first-grade girls and boys to an experiment in which they programmed robots. In a control group of nonprogrammers, boys showed more interest and self-efficacy in programming than girls did. But among the group that had the programming lesson, the gender gap in interests and self-efficacy disappeared (Master, Cheryan, Moscatelli, & Meltzoff, 2017). Providing girls with early positive technology experiences may be critical to closing the gender gap in STEM.

Other research looks more closely at how children's academic attitudes and beliefs predict their pursuit of specific STEM disciplines. As noted, among adolescents, boys, compared with girls, have more positive math self-views and expectations of success. These sex differences emerge among White, Latino, Black, and Asian American adolescents, with effect sizes in the small to moderate range (ds ranging from 0.16 to 0.62; Else-Quest, Mineo, & Higgins, 2013). Accordingly, male students are more likely than female students to take classes in computer and information science, engineering, science technologies, and physics, all of which are math intensive. In contrast, girls (particularly White and Asian American girls) tend to place more value than boys do on science, with moderate effect sizes ($ds = -0.43$ and -0.49; Else-Quest et al., 2013). Moreover, female students are more likely than male students to take classes that are more science oriented and less math intensive, such as chemistry, advanced biology, health science, algebra II, and precalculus (B. Cunningham, Hoyer, & Sparks, 2015). These patterns suggest that it may not make sense to consider STEM disciplines as a block when talking about sex differences because women may outnumber men in some of these disciplines while men outnumber women in others.

Gendered family responsibilities. Thus far, our analysis of sex differences in STEM focuses on factors that attract girls and women to—or repel them from—STEM fields.

Consider the finding that people's interests in STEM disciplines are shaped by their assumptions about whether or not STEM fields allow opportunities for helping others versus achievement and mastery. Is it true that STEM disciplines are not "helping" disciplines? Can you think of ways in which careers in

STEM can help others, improve quality of life, and fulfill communal goals? Imagine that you were tasked with designing an educational campaign to change widespread beliefs about the lack of communal opportunities in STEM fields. What examples or messages might you include?

But what about outside factors that might pull women in other directions? One interesting hypothesis states that women's underrepresentation in STEM fields has less to do with how women feel about STEM than it does with the gendered family responsibilities that fall disproportionately to women. Ceci and Williams (2009) argue that women often opt out of competitive STEM careers at a young age due to desires for and responsibilities of family. To examine this idea, Kimberly Robertson and her colleagues tracked top-performing math and science students from youth through adulthood and found sex differences in work hours and preferences by the time the students reached their mid-30s (Robertson, Smeets, Lubinski, & Benbow, 2010). Specifically, women willingly worked fewer hours per week than men due to increased family obligations. Moreover, women in science fields who have children are less likely to be promoted than men who have children (Ceci, Williams, & Barnett, 2009). Thus, even when women have STEM careers, they may not advance to the highest ranks of their field at the same rates that men do because of sex-based labor divisions in which the bulk of childcare and household management falls to them.

In summary, women's underrepresentation in STEM fields may have more to do with lifestyle choices and the demands placed on career women to rear children and manage homes than with sex differences in cognitive ability. The same tug of war between family and career that pulled at two-time Nobel Prize–winning physicist and chemist Marie Curie 100 years ago still operates today. In Chapter 11 ("Work and Home"), we examine in greater detail how the clash between career demands and gendered expectations for family obligations can impact women's career paths.

We now have the benefit of over 100 years of research on gender and cognitive abilities. Although little evidence exists for consistent sex differences in overall general mental ability or IQ, some research indicates small to moderate sex differences in specific cognitive abilities, although the size of these differences varies across time, place, and population. There may also be differences in the variability of cognitive performance that leads men to outnumber women at both the very high and very low ends of cognitive test distributions. Rather than drawing a conclusion about what all of this means, we instead raise a provocative question: Is it possible that we, as a culture, place too much importance on raw intelligence? Perhaps so. Intelligence is not the only—or even the most important—predictor of academic and career success. Other behavioral and personality

Sidebar 7.4: "It Has Not Been Easy"

French physicist Marie Curie won the Nobel Prize for science not once but twice. First, in 1903, she and her husband Pierre Curie shared the Nobel Prize in Physics, and second, in 1911, Curie won the Nobel Prize in Chemistry. Curie had this to say about gendered family responsibilities:

"I have frequently been questioned, especially by women, of how I could reconcile family life with a scientific career. Well, it has not been easy."

—Marie Curie (1867–1934)

factors, such as self-discipline (Duckworth & Seligman, 2005) and conscientiousness (Conrad, 2006), predict performance in school, often better than performance on standardized tests, like IQ exams or the SAT. Of course being smart has its advantages, but intelligence is only part of what leads to academic and career success.

CHAPTER SUMMARY

7.1 Explain the historical origins of research on sex differences in cognitive abilities.

Research on cognitive ability, or intelligence, began at the end of the 18th century with crude studies measuring the bumps on people's heads to predict various mental capabilities. By the early 20th century, researchers began developing tests to measure intelligence and IQ. Much of this early research started with an assumption of female intellectual inferiority, and researchers often selectively sought and interpreted evidence to support this biased view. Over the next 100 years, researchers employed increasingly sophisticated cognitive tests and brain scanning techniques. In addition to improvements in the methods

used for measuring cognitive abilities, there have also been reductions in blatant gender biases in the study of cognitive abilities. Research demonstrates no sex differences in general mental ability, and interestingly, both sexes are consistently increasing in IQ over time. However, there are some differences in more specialized cognitive abilities.

7.2 Analyze the specific domains of cognitive performance that show sex similarities and differences.

Cognitive psychologists examine performance on tests of verbal, quantitative, and visual-spatial abilities. Both the size and consistency of sex differences in cognitive abilities varies across specific tests, methods, and populations. Some verbal abilities, like speech production, reading comprehension, and writing, appear to favor girls over boys, but the size of the differences is generally small to moderate. In contrast, data do not support the stereotype of male superiority in math. Some studies find sex differences favoring boys on complex math problem solving, but these differences vary across time and culture. Boys in most cultures do report somewhat more positive attitudes about math, and girls often report less confidence and more anxiety about math.

One domain that produces reliable sex differences is visual-spatial abilities. This includes skills such as rotating figures mentally, determining relationships between objects, predicting trajectories of moving objects, and remembering locations of objects. Boys and men tend to outperform girls and women on most visual-spatial tests, with the exception of spatial location memory, which shows a slight female advantage.

In addition to average differences in cognitive performance, some researchers focus on sex differences in variability of performance. The cognitive performance of boys and men is typically more variable than that of girls and women. Thus, disproportionately more boys and men are at both the high and low extremes of performance. However, the causes of this greater variability—whether biological, environmental, or some combination of the two—are not well understood.

7.3 Evaluate contextual and individual difference factors that can influence cognitive performance.

Sex differences in cognitive performance, which seem to be decreasing over time, show inconsistency across studies and methods. They also vary in magnitude across cultures based on factors such as gender equality. When sex differences emerge, we do not fully understand the cause(s) of these differences—that is, whether they are "innate" and biological or products of culture, learning, and life experiences. Phenomena such as the Flynn effect (increases in population IQs over generations) suggest that cognitive ability is flexible and influenced by contextual factors. Even if there are intrinsic aptitude differences, we lack definitive evidence for differences in brain structures or hormones that would explain them. Furthermore, performance in testing situations is affected by contextual and motivational factors, such as stereotype threat, willingness to guess, achievement motivation, and sensitivity to feedback.

7.4 Apply research on gender and cognitive performance to real-world issues, such as gender disparities in educational systems, school performance, and STEM disciplines.

Boys tend to have greater access to education around the globe, but increasing educational access for girls can lead not only to psychological and physical health benefits for girls but also to economic benefits for communities. Moreover, cultural values can predict school performance. Even though East Asian girls report lower levels of interest in math as compared with U.S. boys, their cultural emphasis on effort-based learning leads them to achieve higher levels of math performance. Children have malleable academic interests, which means that parents, teachers, and learning environments—both at home and at school—can shape them in significant ways. Parents with math anxiety can pass this along to their children, but doing regular math activities together at home can increase children's math achievement. Gender-based discrimination at school can decrease academic performance of sexual minority and gender identity minority high school students. Researchers disagree about whether single-sex or mixed-sex school environments are more effective for learning, with each side offering unique advantages and disadvantages.

Women tend to be underrepresented in STEM disciplines. In contrast to the mostly small and inconsistent sex differences in cognitive abilities, sex differences in interests, values, and expectations appear to be larger. Some theorists propose that women's underrepresentation in some STEM disciplines has less to do with differences in cognitive aptitude and more to do with factors such as discrimination and different interests and family responsibilities.

Test Your Knowledge: True or False?

7.1. Most sex differences in cognitive abilities map directly onto sex differences in specific brain structures. (False: It is unclear whether or how sex differences in brain structures map onto sex differences in cognitive abilities.) [p. 225–226]

7.2. Girls and boys do not differ significantly in average levels of general mental ability (intelligence). (True: There are no consistent sex differences in average intelligence, although there are some small to moderate sex differences in specific cognitive abilities.) [p. 227]

7.3. Countries with greater gender equality show smaller sex differences in verbal abilities. (False: In countries that have more gender equality, girls tend to outperform boys in reading performance by the widest margins.) [p. 230]

7.4. Reminding women about negative stereotypes about women's math abilities can lower their math test performance. (True: When reminded of negative stereotypes about women's math abilities, women experience stereotype threat, which can interfere with their performance on math tests.) [p. 239]

7.5. Women's underrepresentation in careers in science, technology, engineering, and math (STEM) is due, at least to some degree, to lifestyle choices and demands placed on them to rear children and manage homes. (True: Women opt out of STEM careers at higher rates than men, at least in part, because of family obligations.) [p. 249]

Test Your Knowledge: True or False?

8.1 Gendered word choice can influence people's thoughts and perceptions.

8.2 On average, women talk more than men.

8.3 Sex differences in language use emerge consistently, regardless of variables such as culture, race, social status, and education level.

8.4 On average, girls and women smile more than boys and men.

8.5 Compared with women, men tend to be better at identifying and managing their own emotions and the emotions of others.

CHAPTER 8

Language, Communication, and Emotion

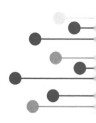

Key Concepts

How Does Gender-Related Language Influence Social Perception?

Gendered Features of Language

The Generic Masculine

Grammatical Gender

Diminutives and Gender Labels

The Influence of Gendered Language on Perceptions

What Roles Do Sex and Gender Play in Verbal Communication?

Sex Differences in *How* People Communicate

Who Talks More?

Who Interrupts More?

Sex Differences in *What* People Communicate

Gossip

Social Media

Beyond Sex Differences: Intersectionality in Communication

Verbal Communication: What's the Big Picture?

What Roles Do Sex and Gender Play in Nonverbal Communication?

Smiling and Eye Contact

Personal Space and Touch

Body Posture and Gait

Nonverbal Communication: What's the Big Picture?

How Do Sex and Gender Shape the Experience, Expression, and Identification of Emotions?

Emotional Experience and Expression

Debate: Are Women More Emotional Than Men?

Display Rules

Encoding and Decoding Accuracy

Empathy and Emotional Intelligence

Journey of Research: Understanding Empathy, From Darwin to Mirror Neurons

Learning Objectives

Students who read this chapter should be able to do the following:

8.1 Describe how gender-related words and language shape perceptions.

8.2 Analyze sex similarities and differences in verbal and nonverbal communication.

8.3 Evaluate how status, power, and culture shape sex differences in communication.

8.4 Analyze how sex and gender shape the experience and expression of emotion.

Language, Communication, and Emotion

In 2002, Moshe Koppel and his colleagues created a computer program that allowed them to test whether men and women use language differently. They fed the program samples of text, both fiction and nonfiction, from 566 authors. By analyzing the writings of men and women, the computer taught itself to recognize sex differences in word usage and sentence structure, and it correctly identified the author's sex 80% of the time (Koppel, Argamon, & Shimoni, 2002). This suggests that male and female authors use language differently, but how? What cues did Koppel's program rely on to determine writers' sex? It turns out that sex differences in written communication are not obvious and tend to be more about grammar than content. For example, female writers use communal prepositions (e.g., *with*) and write in the present tense more than male writers, who more frequently use words that quantify nouns (e.g., *two* and *more*).

So computers can recognize a person's sex fairly accurately just by reading text, but what about humans? People certainly *think* that they can tell the difference between the writing of men and women. Nobel Prize–winning author V. S. Naipaul once claimed that female authors write in a "sentimental" style that he could easily identify within a few paragraphs (Fallon, 2011). But what does the research show? Anthony Mulac and his colleagues have studied this topic for decades, and their findings reveal that humans fall short of computers when it comes to detecting sex differences in communication. For example, people cannot accurately guess sex based on verbal or written descriptions of landscape photos, nor can they identify the sex of fourth, eighth, or 12th graders based on their written essays (Mulac, 2006). Research by Kristine Nowak corroborates these findings. Nowak (2003) had participants engage in an online, text-based interaction with a "partner" to discuss a neutral topic. Unbeknownst to participants, their partners' responses were written in advance by male and female research assistants. Nowak found that participants were no better than chance at guessing whether their "partner" was male or female. Taken together, these studies suggest that spoken and written language does not differ by sex in ways that humans can detect readily. In fact, despite V. S. Naipaul's claims regarding women's easily identifiable, "sentimental" writing style, women writers have sometimes used pseudonyms to pass successfully as men. The English novelist George Eliot, for instance, was actually Mary Ann Evans, and American science fiction writer James Tiptree Jr. was really Alice B. Sheldon.

English novelist Mary Ann Evans wrote under the name George Eliot.

Source: Wikimedia Commons. George Eliot by Samuel Laurence

This chapter addresses gender and communication in a broad sense, focusing on words and language, verbal and nonverbal communication, and emotional expression. Given how accurately the computer program designed by Koppel and his colleagues (2002) distinguished between the writing of male and female authors, there may in fact be gender "fingerprints" in communication. But sex differences in communication do not always map onto common gender stereotypes, as we will discuss in this chapter. Before considering sex differences in communication, we will examine whether language itself reflects and perpetuates gender biases.

How Does Gender-Related Language Influence Social Perception?

Cultural debates often arise around word choice. Sometimes cultural attitudes change faster than language, which can create a period of ambiguity about acceptable word usage. Is it preferable to say *Mrs.* or *Ms.*? *Homosexual* or *gay*? *Sex change surgery* or *genital reconstruction surgery*? Using nonpreferred terminology can lead to awkward interactions if certain terms carry offensive or outdated meanings. For example, while the word *homosexual* may seem acceptable to some, many gay people find it alienating due to its association with an era during which people pathologized same-sex sexuality (Gingold, Hancock, & Cerbone, 2006).

These kinds of debates about language may strike some as unnecessary **political correctness**, or overblown pressure to avoid offending members of socially disadvantaged groups. Others, however, propose that word choice is important because words have the power to shape social perceptions and attitudes. According to linguist Benjamin Whorf (1956), the structure of language determines the nature of thought. The **Whorfian hypothesis (or linguistic relativity hypothesis)** proposes that a person who uses one set of words or speaks one language may actually see the world differently than a person who uses a different set of words or speaks a different language. In the sections to follow, we discuss the ways in which words and language can influence people's ideas about sex and gender.

Political correctness: The social norm—often viewed as taken to an extreme—that people should avoid language or acts that might offend, marginalize, or exclude members of socially disadvantaged groups.

Whorfian (linguistic relativity) hypothesis: Hypothesis stating that the structure of language determines the nature of the speaker's thoughts and worldviews.

Stop and Think

People frequently use the term the opposite sex *to refer to the sex binary. How might this term influence how people think about sex differences and similarities? Are women and men "opposite" to one another? What other terms might be used in place of the* opposite sex *that would convey similar meaning?*

Gendered Features of Language

The generic masculine. The **generic masculine** refers to the tradition of using male-gendered terms to refer to mixed-sex groups, sex-unspecified groups, or people in general. Examples include using words such as *mankind, chairman, forefathers, brotherhood,* and *manpower* to refer to both men and women and using male pronouns to refer to mixed-sex groups (e.g., a teacher announcing, "Each student should

Generic masculine: The use of male-gendered terms to refer not only to men but to mixed-sex groups, to human beings in general, or to individuals whose sex is unknown or unspecified.

sharpen his pencil before the exam"). Consider another example: using the phrase "Hey, guys!" to refer to a mixed-sex group or even a group of all women. While this might not strike you as odd, think about how it differs from saying, "Hey, gals!" to a group of all men.

The generic masculine is imprecise and can obscure meaning. Consider this statement: "Most congressmen oppose the Equal Rights Amendment." Does this mean that most members of Congress oppose the Equal Rights Amendment or just that most male members of Congress oppose it? The use of the generic masculine makes it hard to know. The generic masculine also tends to render girls and women invisible. Consistent with the Whorfian hypothesis, several experiments demonstrate that generic masculine language (versus gender-inclusive language) produces gender-biased thoughts in adults and children (Hyde, 1984; Vainapel, Shamir, Tenenbaum, & Gilam, 2015). In one experiment, women who took part in mock job interviews heard either generic masculine (*he*), gender-inclusive (*he or she*), or gender-neutral (*one*) language from the interviewer. For instance, the interviewer said, "We usually know a good employee when we see *him*" versus ". . . when we see *him or her*" or ". . . when we see *one*." Women in the generic masculine condition reported a lower expected sense of belonging, lower motivation, and less identification with the job than those exposed to inclusive language (Stout & Dasgupta, 2011). In contrast, as shown in Figure 8.1, men's expected sense of belonging in the job was unaffected by the language that the interviewer used.

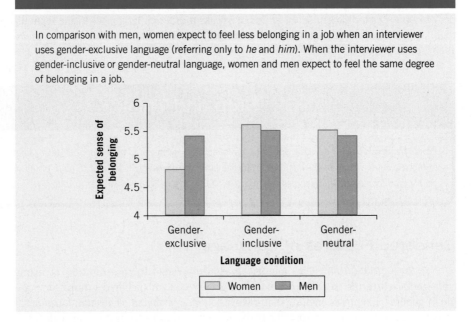

Figure 8.1   Gendered Language and Sense of Belonging in a Job.

In comparison with men, women expect to feel less belonging in a job when an interviewer uses gender-exclusive language (referring only to *he* and *him*). When the interviewer uses gender-inclusive or gender-neutral language, women and men expect to feel the same degree of belonging in a job.

Source: Stout and Dasgupta (2011).

Sidebar 8.1: Does the Term *Men* Mean *Men and Women*?

Consider two books that shaped British intellectual thought: Thomas Paine's (1791/1999) *Rights of Man* and Mary Wollstonecraft's (1792) *A Vindication of the Rights of Woman*. The latter is clearly about women, but the former is presumably about humankind more generally. (Or is it?) In a related vein, consider the Dictionary Act, which the U.S. Congress passed in 1871 to make the generic masculine refer to both men and women in all federal laws. When late-19th-century suffragists argued that laws phrased in the generic masculine giving *men* the right to vote also gave women the right to vote, their appeals were denied (Baron, 2016). These examples illustrate that the generic masculine tends to be ambiguous and selectively applied.

Norms are changing and generic masculine language has been increasingly replaced by more gender-neutral language in English-language academic texts and popular discourse over the past few decades (Earp, 2012). Moreover, the American Psychological Association (2010) now recommends using gender-inclusive language in its *Publication Manual*, an influential writing style resource not just for psychologists but for authors in other fields, such as nursing, sociology, and education. Table 8.1 offers several examples of gender-inclusive language that can be used in place of the generic masculine.

What about nonbinary individuals who identify as neither male nor female? What language options are inclusive of nonbinary people? Some use *they* as a singular, for instance, saying, "They are running late," to refer to the fact that Ana is running late. Others, however, have difficulty adjusting grammatically to the use of plural pronouns to describe singular targets. As gender-neutral language becomes more common, new gender-neutral pronouns emerge (e.g., using *ze/zir* instead of *she/her* and *he/him*). In 2012, Sweden introduced the gender-neutral pronoun *hen* to be used in place of *hon* (she) and *han* (he) when an individual is transgender or when sex is unknown or irrelevant. One study showed that from 2012 to 2015, everyday usage of the word *hen* increased in Sweden, and attitudes toward this pronoun shifted from negative to positive (Sendén, Bäck, & Lindqvist, 2015).

Table 8.1 Gender-Exclusive and Gender-Inclusive Language.

Gender Exclusive	Gender Inclusive
Mailman, policeman, chairman	Mail carrier, police officer, chairperson
Mankind, brotherhood	Humanity, friendship
He, his, him, you guys (to refer to mixed-sex groups)	He or she, hers or his, her or him, you all
Diminutive, Trivializing Language	**Gender Neutral, Higher-Status Language**
Actress, authoress, stewardess	Actor, author, flight attendant
Girls (to refer to adult women)	Women

Language evolves continually, with new words regularly introduced into the lexicon (e.g., emoji, hangry, and bromance). As gender-neutral pronouns become more common, do you think they will be accepted as readily as words like mansplain *are? Or will people resist adopting gender-neutral pronouns? Why or why not?*

Grammatical gender: A type of classification system in certain languages, such as French and Hindi, in which most nouns are assigned a gender (masculine, feminine, and sometimes neutral).

Diminutive: A form of a word used to indicate a smaller, less powerful, or more familiar version (e.g., booklet, duckling, mommy, and daddy).

Grammatical gender. Some languages, such as Arabic, Hindi, Russian, Spanish, and French have **grammatical gender**, which means that nouns are classified as masculine, feminine, and sometimes neutral. Other languages, such as English, Finnish, Turkish, Korean, and Maori do not have grammatical gender. For example, *table* and *bread* do not have genders in English, but table is feminine in Spanish (*la mesa*) and French (*la table*), whereas bread is masculine in Spanish and French (*el pan, le pain*). What might be some consequences of speaking a language that uses gendered nouns? Does this relate to gender role attitudes at the cultural level? Some findings point to this possibility. Nations that have gendered languages have lower levels of gender equality compared with nations that speak genderless languages (Prewitt-Freilino et al., 2012). This may be because referring to objects as masculine or feminine enhances gender distinctions within a culture (Boroditsky, Schmidt, & Phillips, 2003). Of course, we cannot draw a causal conclusion from this correlation because perhaps the gender equality of cultures drives gendered language customs (rather than the other way around). However, some experimental research supports the idea that gendered language can increase sexist beliefs. When bilingual students were randomly assigned to complete a survey on sexist attitudes in Spanish or French (gendered languages), they reported more sexist attitudes than when they completed the same survey in English, a relatively nongendered language (Wasserman & Weseley, 2009). This finding is consistent with the Whorfian hypothesis (discussed earlier in the chapter) that language can affect the way people think.

Diminutives and gender labels. Adding gendered suffixes or labels to neutral words also introduces gender into language. Nouns become feminized with gendered suffixes, such as when *hero* becomes *heroine*, *actor* becomes *actress*, and *host* becomes *hostess*. Sometimes people add unnecessary qualifiers to a role, such as *female scientist* or *male nurse*. These suffixes and qualifiers imply and spotlight gender role norm violations. Gender suffixes and qualifiers can also suggest subtle power differences, for example, by implying that a female scientist differs somehow from a "regular scientist" (Crawford, 2001). Gender labels can also be used as **diminutives**. A common example of this occurs in the United States when people refer to adult women as *girls*. Technically speaking, since a *girl* is a female child, calling grown women *girls* can be a way of reducing their social status and infantilizing them.

Several decades ago in the United States, people commonly referred to married women using only their husbands' name (e.g., this would be like calling Beyoncé "Mrs. Shawn Carter"). This type of labeling stems from the 17th-century principle of *coverture*, which was a common law that transferred a woman's legal rights and property to her husband upon marriage (Cullen-DuPont, 2000). In essence, coverture erased a woman's identity and subsumed it under that of her husband. Of course, much has changed since coverture was abolished in the late 19th century. In fact, women in the United States have become increasingly likely since the 1980s to keep their own last names upon marriage (C. C. Miller & Willis, 2015).

The Influence of Gendered Language on Perceptions

How does gendered language affect perceptions? We have already discussed how people report more sexist attitudes in gendered versus nongendered languages. As another example, language can reinforce gender stereotypes. In an analysis of adjectives from a repository of millions of words from English-language fiction and nonfiction texts published between 1990 and 2012, linguist Nic Subtirelu found that authors used the trait *pushy* far more often to describe women than men and the trait *condescending* far more often to describe men than women (Khazan, 2014). Think about the different meanings of these words. To condescend is to look down on someone; thus, calling men condescending implies that they are in a position of relative power. In contrast, calling women pushy implies that they attempt to assert more power than they legitimately have. In this sense, word use reinforces stereotypes about sex differences in power.

Additional evidence for the Whorfian hypothesis is found in the language that people use to describe sexual and domestic violence. Henley, Miller, and Beazley (1995) analyzed the content of over 1,500 newspaper articles and found that the verbs *raped* and *murdered* were more likely to be stated in the passive voice (e.g., "X was raped") in comparison with other verbs, such as *thanked* and *robbed*, which were more likely to be stated in the active voice (e.g., "X robbed Y"). Furthermore, people use passive voice more frequently to describe instances of domestic violence with male, rather than female, perpetrators (Frazer & Miller, 2008). For example, written descriptions of male-to-female partner violence more frequently include wordings such as "She was beaten," while descriptions of female-to-male partner violence more frequently include wordings such as "She beat him." These wordings directly affect how people attribute harm and blame to victims and perpetrators. When people read passive-voice (versus active-voice) accounts of rape, they perceive less harm to victims, more responsibility to victims, and less responsibility to perpetrators (Bohner, 2001; Henley et al., 1995). Likely without realizing it, crime reporters may describe rape and domestic violence in ways that heighten the blame associated with female victims and reduce the blame associated with male perpetrators.

People sometimes intentionally invent words to give legitimacy to experiences or to raise awareness about social issues. As Gloria Steinem (1983) famously quipped, "We have terms like *sexual harassment* and *battered women*. A few years ago, they were just called *life*" (p. 149). Giving names to experiences like *sexual harassment* and *marital rape* can bring attention to unacknowledged problems and thereby initiate change (C. A. Smith, Johnston-Robledo, McHugh, & Chrisler, 2010). People also sometimes transform the meaning of words, which happens when members of a stigmatized group reclaim a derogatory label and use it in an empowering way. For example, when critics called Hillary Clinton a "bitch," *Saturday Night Live* cast member Tina Fey responded by saying, "So am I. Know what? Bitches get stuff done" (Clark-Flory, 2008). Similarly, LGBT individuals reappropriate terms like *queer*, *queen*, *dyke*, and *fag* as positive self-labels. Experimental evidence shows that when members of stigmatized groups label themselves with derogatory words, they feel more powerful, and observers perceive them and their group as more powerful, too (A. D. Galinsky et al., 2013). Thus, adopting derogatory self-labels can empower people and lessen stigma.

What Roles Do Sex and Gender Play in Verbal Communication?

Different cultures approach: The belief that boys and girls are socialized to use language so differently that they may as well come from different "cultures," which leads to miscommunication.

In the chapter opener, we addressed a topic widely debated among researchers: whether women and men communicate differently. On one side, sometimes called the **different cultures approach**, researchers view difference as the rule and male–female miscommunication as inevitable. Proponents of this approach suggest that boys and girls are socialized within different "cultures" and accordingly develop different and nonoverlapping communication styles (Maltz & Borker, 1982; J. T. Wood, 2015). Specifically, girls and women develop an affective communication style that is emotionally expressive and oriented toward maintaining relationships, whereas boys and men develop an instrumental communication style that is informational and oriented toward problem solving and completing tasks. On the other side, researchers view similarity as the rule and find sparse evidence of substantive differences in male and female communication patterns (Crawford, 2001; Dindia, 2006). So which perspective is accurate? In this section and the next one ("What Role Do Sex and Gender Play in Nonverbal Communication?"), we examine this question.

Sidebar 8.2: Mars and Venus?

Even though the evidence generally shows small sex differences in emotional and assertive language, some authors profit greatly from portraying sex differences in communication styles as large. This might remind you of our discussion of minimalist versus maximalist approaches to interpreting sex differences in Chapter 2 ("Studying Sex and Gender"). John Gray, a maximalist who espouses the different cultures thesis, wrote a series of pop psychology books about gender, including *Men Are From Mars, Women Are From Venus* (1992). Gray argues that women and men are so different that they could come from different planets (not simply different cultures), which leads to miscommunication and relationship problems. Though Gray's work has wide popular appeal, his ideas about male–female differences are not grounded in scientific research.

Sex Differences in *How* People Communicate

The study of oral communication can be approached from different angles. You can examine *how* people communicate (e.g., how much or how fast they talk, how many hesitations they use). You can also examine the *contents* of communication, such as the topics people discuss and the types of words they typically use. We will first examine how women and men communicate before moving to the contents of gendered communication.

Who talks more? Proverbs from both Western and Eastern cultures reflect a common stereotype of women as talkative:

> *"Women's tongues are like lambs' tails—they are never still."*
>
> —Old English proverb

> *"Where there are women and geese, there is noise."*
>
> —Japanese proverb

This stereotype implies not only that women are talkative but that the contents of their speech are unimportant, comparable to the "noise" made by geese. Conversely, a well-known male stereotype is of the "strong, silent type." Picture the gunslinger in any number of westerns, such as Clint Eastwood as Blondie in *The Good, the Bad, and the Ugly* or Denzel Washington as Sam Chisolm in *The Magnificent Seven*. Men like these seem to derive power from their lack of frivolous conversation. But does research support the stereotype that women talk more than men? To find out, Shannon Holleran and her collaborators recorded people's spontaneous conversations in their daily lives using small digital voice recorders (Holleran, Mehl, & Levitt, 2009). When they compared the word use of women and men, they found no significant sex difference: Both women and men spoke about 16,000 words per day, on average. However, there were huge individual differences. One person spoke an estimated 795 words a day while another spoke 47,000 words. Both were men.

Classic Hollywood westerns often portrayed the gunslinger as a strong, silent loner. His gun did the talking for him.

Source: © iStockPhoto.com/YinYang

The findings of Holleran and her colleagues (2009) align with meta-analyses showing that sex differences in talkativeness are often small and depend on contextual factors. For example, Leaper and Ayres (2007) found that men, on average, were slightly more talkative than women ($d = 0.14$). Another meta-analysis of children showed that girls, on average, were slightly more talkative than boys ($d = -0.11$), but this difference only held for very young children between the ages of 1 and 2.5 (Leaper & Smith, 2004). Recall from Chapter 7 ("Cognitive Abilities and Aptitudes") that girls tend to talk earlier than boys, which could account for this sex difference in very young children. When it comes to parental communication, mothers, on average, talk more to their children than fathers do ($d = -0.26$; Leaper, Anderson, & Sanders, 1998). Women also tend to be more talkative in small, collaborative groups but not in noncollaborative settings (Onnela, Waber, Pentland, Schnorf, & Lazer, 2014). Finally, men tend to talk more than women in formal task-oriented, mixed-sex groups (D. James & Drakich, 1993).

Who interrupts more? In one of the earliest studies of interruptions, Zimmerman and West (1975) unobtrusively tape-recorded conversations of male–male, female–female, or female–male pairs in public places (coffee shops, drug stores, etc.). The results were striking. Interruptions were 10 times more frequent in mixed-sex conversations than in same-sex ones, and in mixed-sex dyads, men initiated 96% of the interruptions. In contrast, in same-sex pairs, men and women were equally likely to interrupt. This suggests that men may use language to dominate—and particularly to dominate women. However, subsequent research did not always find that men interrupt more. One review of 21 studies concluded that, overall, there was little evidence that men interrupted more, either in same-sex or mixed-sex groups (D. James & Clarke, 1993). Another meta-analysis of 43 studies by K. J. Anderson and Leaper (1998) found again that men *were* more likely to interrupt than women, although the effect size was small ($d = 0.15$) and depended on the context. These discrepancies across studies may partly reflect differences in how researchers define interruptions. Some researchers consider only negative instances of simultaneous talking, such as when one speaker talks over another in a disrespectful and undermining manner. This sort of interruption can be interpreted as a way of showing dominance. However, others propose that simultaneous, overlapping talk can also be a supportive, cooperative type of speech that signals interest and affirms the speaker's meaning (Coates, 2004/2016).

When distinguishing the type of interruption, research finds that boys tend to use more intrusive interruptions than girls in mixed-sex pairs (Leman, Ahmed, & Ozarow, 2005), and female doctors tend to use more supportive interruptions than male doctors (Menz & Al-Roubaie, 2008). Further, when K. J. Anderson and Leaper (1998) restricted their meta-analysis to studies that examined intrusive interruptions only, they found that the effect size (favoring men) more than doubled ($d = 0.33$). Though most research in this area is conducted with English speakers in the United States, Itakura and Tsui (2004) examined conversational patterns in mixed-sex dyads of Japanese university students and found a similar pattern. Male students tended to use more self-oriented interruptions that controlled the development of the conversation, whereas female students tended to use more supportive, other-oriented interruptions that helped to reinforce male conversational dominance. Thus, while women tend to interrupt more often in ways that build rapport, men tend to interrupt more often in ways that dominate conversation. Men may be especially likely to interrupt in high-stakes, competitive contexts. For example, a study of interruptions among U.S. Supreme Court justices found that female justices were disproportionately interrupted by their male colleagues during oral arguments, in comparison with the reverse pattern (Jacobi & Schweers, 2017).

Sex Differences in *What* People Communicate

Gossip. Many think of gossip—defined as conversation, often of a personal nature, about someone who is not present—as primarily negative. Some researchers believe, however, that gossip serves important functions, such as enforcing a group's moral norms (Feinberg, Willer, Stellar, & Keltner, 2012) and enhancing social bonds (McAndrew, 2008). For instance, gossip serves as a primary means of learning who likes (and does not like) whom. This type of social information can help people to form alliances and bond with others (Bosson, Johnson, Niederhoffer, & Swann, 2006). That said, gossip can also be used as a form of **relational aggression**, a subtle form of aggression that is intended to harm the target's social relationships or status (for more on relational aggression, see Chapter 14, "Aggression and Violence"). People who lack social status may use gossip as a way of gaining power when they are blocked from other routes to power. This may explain why gossip is typically associated with women more than men (Wert & Salovey, 2004). Although research on gender and gossip is somewhat limited, one set of researchers analyzed tape recordings of conversations among friends and found more negative gossip between female friend pairs than between male friend or cross-sex pairs (Leaper & Holliday, 1995). A recent review supports this, suggesting that girls and women—compared with boys and men—show more interest in information about same-sex others and more often use gossip as a form of relational aggression (McAndrew, 2014).

Relational aggression: Subtle aggression, usually committed when the target is not physically present, that is intended to harm the target's social relationships or status.

Social media. Social media offers an interesting window into everyday communications because it provides a rich source of conversational word use. Andrew Schwarz and colleagues sampled 700 million words, phrases, and topics in Facebook messages in an effort to identify whether and how English-speaking women and men use language differently (Schwarz et al., 2013). They created "word clouds" to visually represent male and female communication (see Figure 8.2). A few things immediately stand out. For instance, men use profanity more frequently than women do. This corroborates other research showing that men tend to swear more than women across cultures and times (Ginsburg, Ogletree, & Silakowski, 2003), though the sex gap seems to be narrowing in Western cultures (Jay, 2009). Women use more emotion words (e.g., *excited*) and more social words and symbols (e.g., "love you" and "<3"). Men use the possessive *my* when mentioning their significant other (e.g., *wife* or *girlfriend*) more often than women do. Men are also more likely than women to talk about objects (e.g., xbox).

Another Facebook study found that women talked about friends and family more often than men did, whereas men used argumentative language more often than women did (G. Park et al., 2016). Women also used warmer, more compassionate, and more polite language than men did, but women and men did not differ in the assertiveness of their language. These social media findings largely mimic those of an earlier meta-analysis, which found a close-to-zero effect size for assertive speech that slightly favored men ($d = 0.09$) and a small tendency for women to use more affiliative speech than men

(d = −0.12; Leaper & Ayres, 2007). Other meta-analyses show that women tend to self-disclose slightly more than men (d = −0.18; Dindia & Allen, 1992) and that women use more tentative (hesitant, uncertain) speech than men do (d = −0.23; Leaper & Robnett, 2011).

Table 8.2 summarizes these sex differences in assertive speech, affiliative speech, self-disclosure, and tentative speech. Note that most of the effect sizes are small and that the findings are complex. For example, even though women tend to self-disclose more than men on average, the sex of the interaction partner makes a difference: Women disclose more than men do to female partners (d = 0.35) and to same-sex others (d = 0.37), but there is no sex difference in self-disclosure to male partners (d = 0.00), and men disclose slightly more than women do to other-sex partners (d = 0.13). Furthermore, the sex difference in disclosure is larger when interacting with familiar others than with strangers (Dindia & Allen, 1992).

Figure 8.2 Facebook "Word Clouds."

These word clouds represent words and phrases that most highly distinguish male and female Facebook users. The larger the word, the more strongly it is correlated with the corresponding sex.

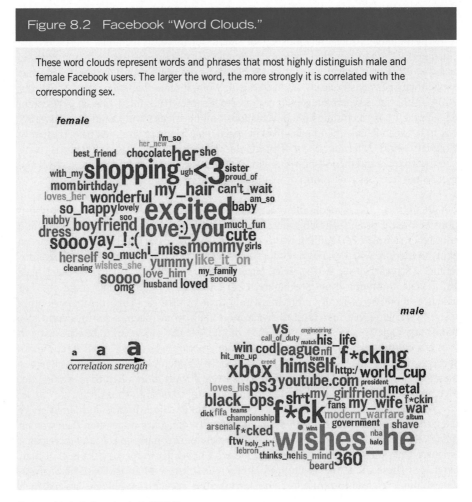

Source: H. A. Schwartz et al. (2013).

Table 8.2 **Sex Differences in Verbal Communication.** Researchers study sex differences in verbal communication in terms of how much people talk, how assertively and tentatively they speak, how affiliative they are, and how much they self-disclose. As you can see, most sex differences are in the small and close-to-zero ranges, with a few moderate effect sizes.

Variable	d	Size
Talkativeness[a]	0.14	Small
Total speaking turns	−0.40	Moderate
Total words spoken	−0.01	Close to zero
Rate of speaking	0.14	Small
Duration of speaking	0.24	Small
Total statements	0.28	Small
Mean utterance length	0.37	Moderate
Assertive speech	0.09	Close to zero
Criticism[a]	−0.13	Small
Disagreement[a]	−0.06	Close to zero
General interruptions[b]	0.15	Small
Intrusive interruptions[b]	0.33	Small
Directives (e.g., "Turn that off now.")[a]	0.00	Zero
Information[a]	0.07	Close to zero
Suggestions[a]	0.27	Small
Affiliative speech[a]	−0.12	Small
Active understanding	−0.41	Moderate
Support	−0.16	Small
Agreement	−0.08	Close to zero
Acknowledgment	0.01	Close to zero
General socioemotional (combination of solidarity, affection, and support)	−0.35	Small–moderate
Self-disclosure[c]	−0.18	Small
Tentative speech[d]	−0.23	Small
Uncertainty (e.g., "I could be wrong, but . . .")	−0.33	Small
Hedges (e.g., "I guess" or "kind of")	−0.15	Small

(Continued)

Table 8.2 (Continued)

Variable	d	Size
Tag questions (e.g., "Great weather today, *isn't it?*")	−0.23	Small
Intensifiers (e.g., *very*, *so*, and *really*)	−0.38	Moderate
General (combination of tags, hedges, and qualifiers)	−0.31	Small

Source: a. Leaper and Ayres (2007); b. K. J. Anderson and Leaper (1998); c. Dindia and Allen (1992); d. Leaper and Robnett (2011).

Note: Positive *d* values indicate that boys and men score higher than girls and women; negative *d* values indicate that girls and women score higher than boys and men.

Beyond Sex Differences: Intersectionality in Communication

Not all women are the same, nor are all men. Many of the communication findings discussed so far—for example, that women use more tentative language and that men argue more and show less warmth in their speech—gloss over this within-sex variability. Furthermore, because studies that compare across sex categories use ex post facto designs and not true experiments (see Chapter 2, "Studying Sex and Gender"), findings that appear to reflect sex differences in communication may actually reflect the operation of third variables that are associated with sex. For example, in a sample of Iranian men and women, individuals with more education raised more topics (a sign of dominance) in mixed-sex conversations than individuals with less education, regardless of sex (Samar & Alibakhshi, 2007). It is thus important to examine the roles of factors such as education level, class, race, ethnicity, sexual orientation, and gender identity in communication patterns.

As discussed in earlier chapters, intersectional approaches acknowledge that multiple, interconnected identities—each associated with different levels of power and privilege—shape people's experiences. In a review of the intersections of sex and race in language use, Nancy Henley found that the speech of Black women and men in the United States did not differ in politeness, tentativeness, or argumentativeness. Moreover, studies comparing college-educated Black and White women show that Black women tend to use more assertive language than White women (Henley, 1995b).

Individuals with different language or dialect options across multiple identities (e.g., across identities associated with culture, race, class, sexual orientation, and gender) tend to show communicative flexibility and engage in **code switching** (Houston & Scott, 2006). Code switching means strategically switching back and forth between languages and their different cultural meanings. For example, Besnier (2003) describes the language patterns of the **fakaleiti**, who are Tonga natives assigned male at birth who assume a relatively feminine manner. In a largely monolingual culture that primarily speaks Tongan and associates English with status and prestige, the fakaleiti use English (and code switch strategically between Tongan and English) as a means of expressing

Code switching:
The process by which bilinguals and multilinguals switch back and forth between languages and their different cultural meaning systems.

Fakaleiti:
Transgender individuals from Tonga, an archipelago nation in the South Pacific, who are assigned male at birth but assume a relatively feminine manner. Similar to the fa'afafine in Samoa.

resistance to their marginal identities. Similarly, Moroccan women commonly use code switching between Berber, Moroccan Arabic, and French as a means of empowerment in a relatively patriarchal society. Code switching to French, which is associated with status and prestige, allows Moroccan women to gain attention and talking time in mixed-sex conversations (Sadiqi, 2003).

Code switching also occurs between dialects of the same language. For example, many Black children in the United States grow up speaking both a vernacular Black English and a more formal English that is considered standard by linguists. Research by Karla Scott shows that Black female college students sometimes use standard English to establish their credibility and intelligence in the classroom, but they code-switch to vernacular Black English outside the classroom to emphasize and substantiate their distinct experiences as Black Americans (Houston & Scott, 2006; K. D. Scott, 2000). In this way, Black women show communicative flexibility as they negotiate complex identities. More broadly, some propose that girls, women, and gender-nonconforming individuals use their voices and language as a means of countering typical gender expectations (F. L. Johnson, 2006).

Sidebar 8.3: When the "Best Woman" Is a Gentleman

Before announcing the challenges in each episode of *RuPaul's Drag Race*—a reality television program in which drag queens compete for the title of "America's Next Drag Superstar"—show host RuPaul (or "Mama Ru") inspires the contestants with the rallying cry "Gentlemen start your engines. And may the best *woman* win!" This phrase, as well as many others used on *Drag Race*, subverts sex and gender norms and challenges the gender binary by suggesting that the same individuals can be both *gentlemen* and *women*.

Contestants from *RuPaul's Drag Race Allstars* participate in the LGBT Pride March in New York City in 2016.

Source: © iStockPhoto.com/scarletsails

Verbal Communication: What's the Big Picture?

What overall conclusions can we draw about sex differences in verbal communication? Do women and men seem to be from "different cultures," or are they more similar? As we have discussed, sex differences do sometimes emerge when comparing the contents and topics of female and male speech. Women tend to use more emotional and warm language and talk about others more often, whereas men tend to be more argumentative, use more intrusive interruptions, and discuss objects more often. But we also see a great deal of complexity and nuance, with findings varying from study to study based on the demographic characteristics of the samples and the specific language features and contextual variables assessed.

Note also that proponents of the different cultures thesis typically draw their evidence from small studies, personal anecdotes, or the media (Burleson & Kunkel, 2006). Further, meta-analyses on sex differences in communication reveal average effect sizes in the small range (ds from 0.24 to 0.26), leading Dindia (2006) to suggest that women and men may come from neighboring states (such as South Dakota and North Dakota) rather than from different cultures or planets. Thus, although stereotypes paint female speech as expressive and relational and male speech as instrumental and assertive, the evidence does not strongly support these stereotypes. Instead, the differences are generally small, and the similarities often outweigh the differences.

Stop and Think

If the evidence indicates that women and men show more similarity than dissimilarity in communication, what specific factors might account for the popularity of the "different cultures" or "different planets" perspectives? Why have John Gray's Mars and Venus books sold millions of copies worldwide? What strategies could psychologists use to get the wider public to understand the true nature of sex differences in communication? How effective would these strategies be?

What Role Do Sex and Gender Play in Nonverbal Communication?

Beyond verbal communication, people also use a rich repertoire of nonverbal behaviors to convey meaning. Nonverbal communication occurs through nonlinguistic channels. Try muting the TV and watching two people interact. You will probably find that you can still understand a good deal of their communication. In fact, one early researcher of nonverbal behavior estimated that people express no more than about one-third of the social meaning of a conversation through words, with the rest conveyed through nonverbal channels (Birdwhistell, 1970). People can communicate power through their posture, eye contact, or facial expressions. A person may use a subtle touch, extended eye contact, or a coy smile to communicate romantic interest. And as every child knows, a parent can convey disapproval with a stern look. Note also that nonverbal behavior can influence speech, as when a speaker raises her voice at the end of a sentence to signify disbelief. Speech tone, pitch, and inflection count as nonverbal behavior because they use sound, but not language per se, to convey meaning.

Just as with verbal communication, people have gender stereotypes about nonverbal behaviors, with women stereotyped as more nonverbally expressive than men (Briton & Hall, 1995). In fact, research reveals some consistent differences in the nonverbal communication patterns of men and women. In addition to sex, culture shapes nonverbal behaviors in important ways. In this section, we consider some specific sex differences in nonverbal behavior, acknowledging cultural differences where relevant.

Smiling and Eye Contact

Girls and women tend to smile more than boys and men, with a meta-analysis revealing a medium effect size ($d = -0.41$; LaFrance, Hecht, & Paluck, 2003). David Dodd and his colleagues examined thousands of yearbook photos from students in kindergarten through college and found that, starting around fourth grade, girls smiled more than boys on average (Dodd, Russell, & Jenkins, 1999). This effect replicates in photos of adults as well, although the difference emerges only for lower-status women in posed (but not candid) photos (J. A. Hall, LeBeau, Reinoso, & Thayer, 2001). The finding that women smile more than men also holds across cultures and ethnicities, though substantial cross-cultural differences emerge in both the amount that people smile and the size of the sex difference. For example, Jeanne Tsai and her colleagues found that in cultures that place more value on excited emotional expressions (e.g., the United States and France), political leaders show more pronounced smiles in their official photos than do leaders in cultures that place less value on displays of excitement (e.g., China and Japan; Tsai et al., 2016).

If girls and women tend to smile more, does this indicate greater happiness? Not necessarily. People smile for many reasons other than joy; for example, social tension, embarrassment, and nervousness can trigger smiling. In fact, larger sex differences in smiling emerge when people engage in social interactions, feel social tension, or believe others to be observing them. Interestingly, however, sex differences in smiling decrease when people occupy caretaker roles, such as parent, doctor, or therapist (LaFrance et al., 2003).

Eye contact, another type of nonverbal communication, conveys rich meaning. Women tend to gaze at their interaction partners more than men do. People also gaze *at* women more than men. Accordingly, the highest amount of mutual eye contact tends to

Political leaders in cultures that value displays of excitement smile more than leaders in cultures that place less value on excited displays. The facial expressions of Japanese prime minister Shinzo Abe and former U.S. president Barack Obama show this cultural difference as they pose for the camera.

Source: Retrieved from the White House Archives

occur among pairs of women (LaFrance & Vial, 2016). Men and women also differ in eye contact in mixed-sex dyads. Men tend to look at their female interaction partners more while speaking to them and to look away more while listening to them, a pattern known as **visual dominance**. In contrast, women look at their male interaction partners more when listening than they do when speaking (Dovidio, Ellyson, Keating, Heltman, & Brown, 1988). In this sense, men's eye contact behavior is often interpreted as a dominance display because people higher in power tend to use the visual dominance pattern more.

Note also that cultures vary in their norms regarding eye contact. In Western cultures, eye contact often conveys a sign of respect while averting the eyes may signify disrespect or dishonesty. In contrast, in East Asian cultures, too much eye contact conveys disrespect or even threat, and people avert their eyes as a sign of respect (A. McCarthy, Lee, Itakura, & Muir, 2008). Subcultural differences in perceptions of eye contact exist as well. For instance, when shown photographs of unfamiliar Black and White men, White college students rated the Black men with a direct gaze (e.g., those making eye contact) as more threatening than both the Black men with an averted gaze and the White men with either type of gaze (Richeson, Todd, Trawalter, & Baird, 2008). How do you interpret this pattern of findings?

Personal Space and Touch

Personal space refers to the zone around people that provides an invisible "buffer" between the self and others. Intrusions into their personal space often make people feel uncomfortable. In general, men in Western cultures tend to have larger personal space zones than women, meaning that they stand farther away from others—and especially from other men—during social interactions. In addition, both men and women stand closer to women than to men (J. A. Hall, 1984; Ozdemir, 2008). Why might men adopt larger personal space zones around other men? Some suggest it could demonstrate dominance by increasing personal territory. In one study, researchers measured male and female participants on agentic traits (e.g., dominant, assertive, and forceful) and communal traits (e.g., affectionate, loyal, and warm) and then videotaped them unobtrusively while they interacted with either a same-sex or other-sex partner. Pairs in which both partners possessed high levels of agentic traits maintained the largest interpersonal distances, regardless of sex (Uzzell & Horne, 2006). Thus, larger personal space seems to correspond with having a more dominant personality. Of course, the personal distance with which people feel comfortable depends on culture as well. People from Mediterranean and Latin cultures prefer smaller personal space zones than do people from Britain (Beaulieu, 2004), and men interacting in Arab cultures prefer smaller personal space zones than men interacting in the United States (Hewitt & Alqahtani, 2003).

What about touch? In studies of touch, many of which have been conducted with heterosexual samples in the United States, girls and women tend to touch more (Major, 2012)—and report greater comfort with being touched—than their male counterparts. But variables such as the closeness of the relationship play a role. In mixed-sex, nonintimate dyads, men tend to initiate touch more than women, but in heterosexual marriages, wives touch their spouses more than husbands do (J. C. S. Smith, Vogel, Madon, & Edwards, 2011). One cross-cultural study presented people in England, Finland, Italy, France, and Russia with computerized silhouettes that represented the self and asked them to identify

Visual dominance: A pattern of eye contact in which a person looks at others when speaking and looks away when listening.

where they would allow various others who differed in closeness (e.g., romantic partner, father, sister, acquaintance, and stranger) to touch them. Not surprisingly, the closer the relationship, the more body areas were reported as acceptable to touch. In addition, women allowed more touches in general than men did, except from female acquaintances and female strangers (Suvilehto, Glerean, Dunbar, Hari, & Nummenmaa, 2015).

The sex of the interaction partner plays a role as well. Girls and women generally touch each other more when interacting than boys and men do (Major, 2012), and same-sex touch may be considered more acceptable among women than men, at least in Western contexts (Derlega, Catanzaro, & Lewis, 2001). Exceptions to this general rule do occur, however. In sports, fans readily accept male–male touch in the form of long hugs or pats on the rear (Kneidinger, Maple, & Tross, 2001). In fact, sports teams that touch each other more (e.g., high fives and chest bumps) also tend to have better season records, possibly because affiliative touch releases **oxytocin**, a neurotransmitter that facilitates bonding and coordination (Kraus, Huang, & Keltner, 2010). Cultures outside of the United States also more commonly accept male–male touch. In many Latin American, European, and Middle Eastern countries, men commonly kiss each other in greeting. Further, in Southeast Asia, India, and the Middle East, men often walk in public holding hands without any romantic overtones (Fattah, 2005).

> **Oxytocin:** A neurotransmitter that facilitates bonding, connectedness, and coordination.

Stop and Think

Why do you think that the United States prohibits male–male touch in public more strongly than some other countries? What consequences might the disapproval of public expressions of male–male touch have? Have U.S. attitudes about this changed over time? If so, how?

Of course, not all meanings of touch are positive. Touch can be used to harass, objectify, and demean. Often in these cases, more powerful individuals use touch to control, objectify, or harm less powerful others. We will return to this topic in Chapter 13, "Gender and Psychological Health," and Chapter 14, "Aggression and Violence."

Body Posture and Gait

Certain aspects of body posture—the way people hold their bodies—can communicate things such as mood, status, and dominance. For instance, people perceive those who assume an expansive posture that takes up space (e.g., spreading the legs and stretching arms out or clasping them behind the head) as more socially dominant (J. A. Hall, Coats, & LeBeau, 2005). Adopting an expansive "power pose"—standing tall with legs spread apart and hands on hips—may even foster feelings of power and confidence that translate into better performance (Cuddy, Wilmuth, Yap, & Carney, 2015). Perhaps not surprisingly, men tend to assume this sort of expansive body posture more often than women (J. A. Hall, 1984; Vrugt & Luyerink, 2000). The tendency for men to spread out while sitting even inspired a neologism: **manspreading**. Men's tendency to

> **Manspreading:** The tendency for some men to spread out and adopt an expansive posture while sitting, thus taking up more space.

Use of manspreading and restrictive body posture while waiting for a job interview.

Source: © iStockPhoto .com/Neustockimages

spread their legs into a "V" shape became such a nuisance on crowded public subways—where manspreading can fill two or three seats—that the New York City Department of Transportation started a public ad campaign in 2014 to stop the practice (Fitzsimmons, 2014). In contrast, women more frequently assume a restrictive body posture, which means sitting or standing in ways that take up little space (e.g., crossing one's legs or folding one's arms close to the chest).

Manspreading might seem rude, but it may also have benefits. Tanya Vacharkulksemsuk and her colleagues ran people through a "speed dating" study in which single people met multiple different potential dates in very brief face-to-face interactions. The researchers coded whether individuals sat in restricted or expansive body postures during their dates. Even more than smiling and laughing, expansive postures made women and men seem more attractive and desirable as dates (Vacharkulksemsuk et al., 2016). Therefore, both women and men may benefit from manspreading, especially when trying to attract or impress others. Finally, women tend to use more body posture behaviors that socially engage their partners. For instance, they tend to orient their bodies toward, lean toward, and nod at their interaction partners more than men do (Helweg-Larsen, Cunningham, Carrico, & Pergram, 2004).

Sidebar 8.4: When Dominance Hurts Math Performance

Some research finds that simply witnessing male dominance behaviors can undermine women's confidence and impair their math performance. Katie Van Loo and Robert Rydell (2014) had participants watch a video of female and male actors discussing a math study group. In one version of the video, the man displayed nonverbal dominance behaviors (increased eye contact, gesturing, and open, relaxed postures) while the woman displayed nondominant behaviors. In another version, the woman displayed dominant behaviors while the man displayed nondominant behaviors. Then, participants took a math test. The videos did not affect men, but women who watched the dominant man performed worse on the test and reported greater unease about confirming a negative stereotype.

Beyond body posture, researchers also study gait (a person's manner of walking). You might not think of gait as a form of nonverbal communication, but the way people walk can convey information. People tend to perceive walking with swaying hips as feminine and walking with swaggering shoulders as masculine (K. J. Johnson & Tassinary, 2005). In fact, the gaits of women and men tend to differ, and people can usually tell the sex of a walker even with very minimal cues. To study this, researchers strip away almost all information about people except their gait by attaching sensors to their joints and recording their movements as they walk. A computer then interprets the sensors and presents a minimal animated figure called a **point-light display** (see embedded image). Even from these minimal displays, viewers can accurately determine a walker's sex (Pollick, Kay, Heim, & Stringer, 2005).

People can also identify a walker's sexual orientation based on gender-atypical gaits (swaying hips in men and swaggering shoulders in women), with accuracy above chance levels (K. L. Johnson, Gill, Reichman, & Tassinary, 2007). Why might some gay men and lesbians display gender-atypical gaits? Because sexual minority status is a concealable identity that is linked historically with prejudice and violence, some lesbian and gay individuals may use subtle nonverbal cues, such as walking style, as a means of communicating with and identifying one another (Carrol & Gilroy, 2002). Supporting this logic, gay men and lesbians have higher accuracy than heterosexual men and women when it comes to identifying others' sexual orientation based on nonverbal cues (Ambady, Hallahan, & Conner, 1999). Eye contact, in particular, is an important cue used by gay men and lesbians to identify one another (Nicholas, 2004).

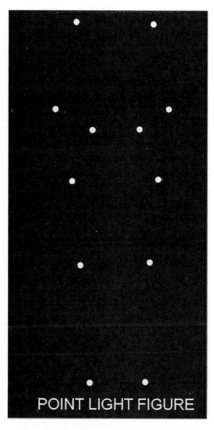

POINT LIGHT FIGURE

A point-light display. Can you identify the sex of this figure?

Source: Gurnsey, Roddy, and Troje (2010).

Nonverbal Communication: What's the Big Picture?

Sex differences in nonverbal behaviors, which are summarized in Table 8.3, tend to be fairly consistent with gender role stereotypes and expectations. In general, women show more other-oriented behaviors that indicate concern for and attention to interaction partners, such as smiling and nodding. Men tend to show more dominant and self-promoting nonverbal behaviors, such as expansive posture and visual dominance. Though sex differences in nonverbal communication are not large in an absolute sense, they do tend to be larger than sex differences in verbal communication (J. A. Hall, 2006).

Why might this pattern of sex differences in nonverbal communication emerge? According to the subordination hypothesis, sex differences in nonverbal communication result from status and power differences between the sexes (Henley, 1995a). But the empirical evidence does not fully support this hypothesis. If it were true, we would expect a match between male-typical and higher-status nonverbal behaviors and a match between female-typical and lower-status nonverbal behaviors. Instead, many of the nonverbal behaviors that distinguish high- and low-status individuals differ from those that

Point-light display: A minimal animated figure represented by points of light, which is created by a computer that reads sensors attached to the joints of a moving person.

Table 8.3 Sex Differences in Nonverbal Behavior. Girls generally display the nonverbal behaviors in the left-hand column more frequently than do boys and men, with the reverse true of the nonverbal behaviors in the right-hand column.

Girls/Women > Boys/Men	Boys/Men > Girls/Women
Gazing	Visual dominance
Smiling	Speech volume
Nodding	Filled pauses (*ah, um*)
Gesturing	Interpersonal space
Restrictive body postures	Expansive body postures
Hip sway	Shoulder swagger
Forward leaning	Body movements (fidgeting)
Posture mirroring	
Touching	

Source: Adapted from LaFrance and Vial (2016), Table 6.1.

distinguish men and women (J. A. Hall et al., 2001; Mast & Sczesny, 2010). This is particularly true for female-typical nonverbal behaviors, such as nodding and smiling, which do not differ between high- and low-status individuals. In contrast, male-typical nonverbal behaviors (e.g., expansive posture and visual dominance) more consistently relate to status and power. Thus, the findings reveal a great deal of complexity, which is also evident in the cross-cultural variation in behaviors such as eye contact, personal space, and touch (Matsumoto, 2006).

Stop and Think

The subordination hypothesis predicts that men should show the same nonverbal behaviors as higher-status individuals and women should show the same nonverbal behaviors as lower-status individuals. But female-typical nonverbal behaviors, such as smiling and nodding, do not predict status. Why do you think the typical nonverbal behavior of men relates to status when the typical nonverbal behavior of women does not?

How Do Sex and Gender Shape the Experience, Expression, and Identification of Emotions?

Experiencing, expressing, and identifying **emotions** are separate capacities. Feeling an emotion does not necessarily mean being able to express it clearly, nor does seeing a friend's emotional expression guarantee that one can identify it accurately. Keeping these three emotion abilities separate is key in a discussion of sex differences in emotionality. In this section, we will explore sex differences in the experience, expression, and recognition of emotions. We will also examine **display rules** that govern when emotions should and should not be expressed, noting whether and when culture and sex interact to shape emotionality.

> **Emotion:** A complex, internal, subjective reaction to an event or stimulus that includes physiological, psychological, and behavioral components. Basic emotions, such as joy, anger, and fear, are thought to be innate and universally expressed and recognized.

> **Display rules:** Culture-specific norms that regulate how, when, and whether individuals should express particular emotions.

Sidebar 8.5: How Basic Are the Basic Emotions?

Going back to Darwin (1872), researchers often seek to identify basic emotions that are innate and universally expressed and recognized (Ekman, 1972). While a great deal of research finds evidence of six basic emotions (happiness, fear, disgust, surprise, anger, and sadness), debate about the true universality of these emotions continues. In a meta-analysis of studies from 42 different nations, Elfenbein and Ambady (2002) found that the recognition of these basic emotions from facial expressions occurred at better-than-chance levels of guessing. But recognition accuracy ranged from 47% to 88% across nations, and accuracy was higher when people judged emotions of their own in-groups and when judging happiness and anger (relative to the other emotions). In another cross-cultural meta-analysis, Merten (2005) found that women, compared with men, recognized the basic emotions more accurately and that sex differences were greater in countries with more economic and political equality. Given this variability across cultures, some researchers view emotions as having a spontaneous, universally expressed biological component that can also be shaped culturally to conform to local standards (Hwang & Matsumoto, 2015).

Emotional Experience and Expression

Who is more emotional: women or men? This seemingly simple question is actually quite complicated due to the multifaceted nature of emotionality. On the one hand, it may refer to how people *feel* emotions, meaning the intensity, frequency, or range of emotions that they privately experience. On the other hand, it may refer to how openly or frequently people *express* emotions. Of these two different meanings of emotionality, researchers find sex differences in private emotional experiences more difficult to study, in part because emotion is a subjective phenomenon, and self-reports are an imperfect means of accessing it. In general, while girls and women report experiencing more affiliative emotions (e.g., warmth and love) and vulnerable emotions (e.g., sadness and anxiety), boys and men report experiencing more anger and pride (Brebner, 2003; L. R. Brody & Hall, 2010). However, these sex differences do not always hold up when researchers use different methods, such as physiological indices or naturalistic observations. This suggests that people's self-reports may be influenced by gender roles and stereotypes rather than actual differences in subjectively experienced emotions. For more detail on this topic, see the chapter debate, "Are Women More Emotional Than Men?"

Debate

Women have long been stereotyped as the more emotional sex. For instance, 19th-century scholars believed that the biological energy spent in developing their reproductive systems limited women's intellectual capacity, leaving them more subject to emotionality. Men, in contrast, were seen as more capable of using reason to harness their emotions (Shields, 2007). Though scientists no longer believe that reproduction usurps women's intellectual abilities, the stereotype of women as more emotional than men still persists today. Is it accurate? Let's examine the evidence on each side.

Yes, Women Are More Emotional

A number of research findings show greater emotionality in women. Girls and women report experiencing a greater frequency and intensity of affiliative emotions, such as love, affection, and warmth, compared with boys and men. Girls and women also report more vulnerable and self-conscious emotions, such as sadness, fear, anxiety, and embarrassment (Brebner, 2003). Starting around the age of 2, girls cry more than boys. In adulthood, women report greater crying frequency, crying intensity, and crying proneness (the likelihood of crying in response to specific situations) than men (Vingerhoets & Scheirs, 2000). In fact,

girls and women consistently show more expressiveness than boys and men across most emotions (LaFrance & Banaji, 1992), and they tend to convey emotions more accurately. This could stem from women having more experience with emotions.

Finally, girls and women—in comparison with boys and men—tend to use more emotional language. For example, the autobiographical narratives of girls contain more emotional content than those of boys (Fivush & Buckner, 2003), and women in heterosexual dating relationships tend to communicate more emotion than men, particularly when discussing difficult topics (Vogel, Wester, Heesacker, & Madon, 2003). Taken collectively, these findings indicate that women are more emotional than men.

No, Women Are Not More Emotional

Because most people believe that men and women differ in emotionality, they may "see" more evidence of this difference than is actually there. For example, people rate facial photographs (digitally altered to appear male or female) as sadder when they perceive the face as female, despite the expression being identical (Plant, Kling, & Smith, 2004). In one classic study, participants who watched the same video of an infant becoming startled and agitated in response to a jack-in-the-box labeled the reaction as "fear" more frequently when they thought the baby was a girl and as "anger" more frequently when they thought the baby was a boy (Condry & Condry, 1976). These findings suggest that people may perceive sex differences in emotionality that do not exist.

Researchers also often use biased definitions of emotion. As Stephanie Shields (2002) argues, people maintain the idea of the inexpressive male, in part, because they fail to label certain emotional expressions in men as *emotionality*. For instance, if people exclude anger from their definition of emotion, this may reinforce the stereotype of men as less emotional than women.

In reality, women and men are similarly emotional, but they tend to express different emotions.

Though oversimplifying a bit, women generally report experiencing more happiness, sadness, and fear, whereas men report experiencing more anger, contempt, and pride (L. R. Brody & Hall, 2010; Fischer, Rodriguez Mosquera, van Vianen, & Manstead, 2004). To complicate matters, while men facially display anger more than women (Coats & Feldman, 1996), women report getting more intensely angry than men (Chentsova-Dutton & Tsai, 2007), suggesting that women may mask their facial expressions of anger.

Finally, measuring emotions poses a challenge, in part due to the weaknesses of self-report methods. Self-report measures require individuals to recall and aggregate past emotional experiences, a task that allows gender stereotypes to influence people's responses. To address this, Reed Larson and his colleagues employed a pager method to

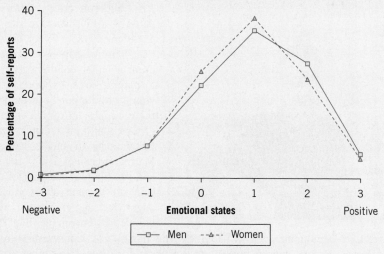

Figure 8.3 Positive and Negative States Reported by Men and Women.

Women and men reported their positive and negative emotion states on a daily basis over a week. As you can see, the sexes experienced positive and negative states at very similar frequencies.

Source: Larson and Pleck (1999). Data drawn from Larson and Richards (1994).

(Continued)

assess emotional states in real time (paging participants seven to eight times per day for 1 week). As shown in Figure 8.3, they found obvious similarity in the positive and negative emotional states reported by women and men (Larson & Richards, 1994). Moreover, physiological measures of emotion, such as heart rate and skin conductance, show no clear pattern of sex differences in emotions, such as sadness, anger, and happiness (Neumann & Waldstein, 2001). Thus, even though men may express certain emotions less than women do, they do not appear to experience these emotions less strongly.

Which side of this debate seems more compelling to you? Which evidence do you find most and least convincing? Why?

When it comes to the *expression* of emotions, consistent sex differences tend to emerge. Leslie Brody (1999, 2000) proposes that these sex differences in emotional expression result from a combination of biological and sociocultural factors, with socialization playing the primary role. Biologically, girls and boys tend to display differences in temperament early in infancy, with boys often showing higher arousal and activity levels and girls often showing better impulse control and attention. These differences, in turn, affect how parents, peers, and teachers respond to children's emotional states. Socialization agents may encourage boys—more than girls—to dampen their emotions as a way of regulating their high arousal and activity levels. In this way, boys may gradually learn to suppress the expression of emotions. Similarly, girls may receive encouragement to express affiliative emotions, such as sympathy and warmth, and to avoid conflict by directing negative emotions inward (e.g., sadness, guilt, and anxiety) because these emotional expressions are consistent with the female gender role. (We will return to the topic of inward-directed emotions in Chapter 13, "Gender and Psychological Health.")

Who has higher status?

Source: © iStockPhoto .com/Jaykayl; © iStockPhoto.com/ feedough

Children's peer groups and play patterns also encourage the expression of different emotions for boys and girls. Recall from Chapter 4, "Gender Development," that children generally prefer to play in same-sex groups for much of young childhood. Boys tend to display more rough-and-tumble play in larger groups while girls display more cooperative play in smaller groups (Fabes, Martin, & Hanish, 2003). In turn, rough-and-tumble play encourages the expression of competitive emotions, such as anger and aggressiveness, while cooperative play encourages the expression of relational emotions, such as happiness and nurturance. Consistent with these play patterns, a meta-analysis revealed that girls tend to show more other-oriented positive emotions (e.g., sympathy) and inward-focused negative emotions (e.g., fear and shame) than boys, whereas boys tend to show more outward-focused emotions (e.g., anger) than girls (Chaplin & Aldao, 2013). Still, these sex differences are quite small.

Display rules. Violating display rules—culture-specific norms that regulate how, when, and whether individuals should express particular emotions—can bring social penalties. For example, because women are generally expected to display positive emotions (Stoppard & Gunn Gruchy, 1993), they may be criticized or seen as unfriendly when they do not. Any woman who has ever been told to "smile more" will recognize this rule. Consistent with this display rule, P. A. Simpson and Stroh (2004) found that female managers expressed more positive emotions and suppressed negative emotions while male managers suppressed positive emotions and expressed more negative emotions. Expressing anger, in particular, can be costly for women. In the workplace, women who express anger are seen as having lower status and are recommended for lower salaries in comparison with men who express anger (Brescoll & Uhlman, 2008). Interestingly, the display rule prohibiting anger expressions in women may depend on race. In a study examining perceptions of managers, White women managers were conferred lower status when expressing dominance, but Black women (and White men) managers were not (Livingston, Rosette, & Washington, 2012). Although dominance differs from anger, it does involve toughness and willingness to express disappointment at subordinates, which can come across as anger.

Display rules also dictate that men should express powerful emotions like anger and avoid low-power emotions like sadness. In fact, others view men who express anger in a professional context as having higher status than men who express sadness (Brescoll & Uhlman, 2008). In one study, Larissa Tiedens had U.S. participants watch videotapes of then president Bill Clinton's testimony during the Monica Lewinsky scandal in which he expressed either anger or sadness (Tiedens, 2001). Participants expressed more approval for Clinton and stronger belief that he should remain president after watching the angry clip. Further demonstrating the penalties that men receive for expressing sadness, people tend to evaluate depressed men more negatively than they evaluate depressed women (L. R. Brody, 1999).

Here again, though, display rules may depend on race. Since Black men tend to be stereotyped as more aggressive than White men in the United States, they may face penalties for expressing anger that White men do not face. In fact, ratings of photographs of Fortune 500 CEOs reveal that Black male CEOs are seen as more "baby-faced" and warmer than White male CEOs (Livingston & Pearce, 2009). Robert Livingston labeled this phenomenon the **teddy bear effect**, arguing that Black men who appear physically nonthreatening may have an advantage in seeking high-status positions because they do not activate people's stereotypes about Black men as aggressive. Perhaps it is not a coincidence that former president Barack Obama gained a reputation for being emotionally calm and rarely expressing anger.

Prominent Black male leaders like Barack Obama often have "baby-faced" features. Such features may counter stereotypes of Black men as aggressive, which can help Black men advance to high-status positions.

Source: Retrieved from the White House Archives

Not only do emotional display rules differ across racial and subcultural groups within a single country, they vary cross-culturally as well. One large-scale study found that, in comparison with people from collectivistic cultures (e.g., Indonesia, South Korea, and China), people from individualistic cultures (e.g., United States, Canada, and Australia) believe that it is more acceptable to express emotions (particularly negative emotions) to members of their in-groups (Matsumoto et al., 2008). But the greater permissibility of emotional expressions in individualistic cultures may primarily extend to women because these same cultures also often have a display rule that restricts men's expressions of certain emotions. For example, Agneta Fischer and colleagues examined cross-cultural sex differences in the expression of powerful emotions (anger and disgust) and powerless emotions (fear, sadness, shame, and guilt). Their findings indicated that men from Western cultures with higher levels of gender equality reported the lowest levels of powerless emotions, suggesting that the male gender role in Western cultures restricts men's expression of these low-power emotions (Fischer et al., 2004).

Stop and Think

In the United States, research typically shows that women are more emotionally expressive than men. However, in some cultures, both women and men are expected to temper their expression of emotions (especially negative emotions) among their in-groups. What are some of the benefits and costs of being less emotionally expressive? What are some of the benefits and costs of being more emotionally expressive? How might the cultural context change these benefits and costs?

Encoding and Decoding Accuracy

Communicating emotion effectively through nonverbal behavior involves both accurate encoding and decoding of emotional content. **Encoding accuracy** refers to the nonverbal communication of emotion (and other types of content) in a clear manner that others can easily interpret, and **decoding accuracy** refers to the correct deciphering of nonverbal emotion (and other content) that others express. As you will see, women tend to have an advantage over men in both types of accuracy.

On average, women are more expressive than men in nonverbal behavior and facial expressions (Kring & Gordon, 1998), and they demonstrate more skill in producing nonverbal behaviors that observers read as intended (LaFrance & Vial, 2016). These sex differences in encoding accuracy seem to reflect the tendency for men to suppress their nonverbal expressions while women more often amplify their expressions.

In comparison with boys and men, girls and women also show greater facility at decoding emotions expressed by others (J. A. Hall & Matsumoto, 2004). These sex differences emerge early in life, with female infants slightly outperforming male infants ($d = -0.18$), and the differences remain consistent (although small) throughout childhood and adolescence ($d = -0.13$; McClure, 2000). By adulthood, the effect size for sex differences in decoding accuracy is medium ($d = -0.40$; J. A. Hall, 1984). In one study, women outperformed men at judging the emotion (e.g., anger, fear, and happiness) conveyed by point-light display figures who engaged in a variety of behaviors, such as walking, jumping, or kicking a ball (Alaerts, Nackaerts, Meyns, Swinnen, & Wenderoth, 2011). However, women's superior decoding accuracy may not reflect sex per se but, instead, their greater likelihood of possessing gender-typed personality traits. Both men and women who are higher in female-typed traits (e.g., warmth and kindness) show better decoding accuracy (Trommsdorff & John, 1992).

Empathy and Emotional Intelligence

Charles Darwin was among the first to view emotion expression as having an important purpose as a form of communication (see "Journey of Research: Understanding Empathy, From Darwin to Mirror Neurons"). Emotions connect individuals, and reading the emotions of others helps all social animals navigate their worlds successfully. But beyond mere decoding accuracy, humans also benefit from the ability to feel empathy for others. **Empathy** refers to the tendency to feel what others feel and to see the world from the vantage point of others (i.e., to "put yourself in someone else's shoes"). Empathy has both cognitive and affective components because it involves both understanding and feeling emotions. Humans are not alone in their capacity for affective forms of empathy. As discussed in the "Journey of Research," other animals mimic the distress of their species mates, for instance. But more cognitive aspects of empathy, such as the capacity to understand the minds of others, require higher-order cognitive processing abilities that are likely rare among nonhuman animals and may be unique to humans (Heyes, 2015). Empathy plays a key role in the bonds that humans form as highly social creatures.

Empathy: The tendency to feel the emotional state of another person and to see the world from another person's vantage point. Empathy has both affective and cognitive components.

Journey of Research

Understanding Empathy, From Darwin to Mirror Neurons

Have you ever winced in pain while watching someone else hurt themself? Or cried watching a sad movie? Why do we have emotional reactions to events that happen to other people? This question has long interested philosophers and scientists. In the 18th century, Scottish economist and philosopher Adam Smith (1759/1966) noted the curious human tendency to imagine ourselves in the situation of others and mimic their emotional states. Scientists have long attempted to understand why we have empathy and what purpose it serves.

Darwin was the first scientist to study human emotions systematically. In 1872, he published *The Expression of the Emotions in Man and Animals*, an influential book that shaped the psychological study of emotions for decades to come. Darwin noted parallels in displays of emotion between humans and other animals, and he assumed that they had the same origins and functions, which was quite a radical notion at the time. Darwin contended that emotions went beyond self-expression to serve as a means of communication. He observed, for instance, that many animals mimic the

(Continued)

distress of others in pain or danger. This type of emotional mimicry is automatic, suggesting that empathy may be wired into our brains.

Darwin saw an important connection between the subjective feeling of an emotion and the physical expression of that emotion. One of the founding figures of psychology, William James (1884), built on Darwin's ideas and argued that our physical bodies *produce* our feelings: "We feel sorry because we cry, angry because we strike, afraid because we tremble," wrote James. The notion that physical motor movements, such as turning up the corners of the mouth into a smile, can produce a corresponding emotion in the brain was provocative but required testing. In fact, evidence does suggest that people find cartoons funnier if they hold their mouth in the shape of a smile versus a frown (Strack, Martin, & Stepper, 1988) and that people injected with Botox (a toxin that paralyzes facial muscles to remove wrinkles) report less intense emotions after the injection compared with before the injection (Hennenlotter et al., 2008).

Empathy takes this mind–body connection one step further by linking other people's emotional experiences to our own. For instance, some studies show **emotional contagion** effects, in which one person's emotions directly trigger similar emotions in others (Hatfield, Cacioppo, & Rapson, 1993). Other studies

document a tendency for humans to mimic the facial expressions of others in pain, just as Darwin observed in monkeys decades earlier (Bavelas, Black, Lemery, & Mullett, 1986). Still others document how people unconsciously tend to imitate others' speech inflections and gestures, such as foot tapping or face touching (Chartrand & Bargh, 1999). These behaviors may lay the foundation of empathy and facilitate interpersonal interactions and bonding.

In the early 1990s, neuroscientists discovered a potential neurological marker of empathy while studying macaque monkeys. Some neurons—dubbed **mirror neurons**—fired both when monkeys performed a behavior and when they watched others perform the same behavior (di Pellegrino, Fadiga, Fogassi, Gallese, & Rizzolatti, 1992). Later research documented mirror neuron regions in human brains (Rizzolatti & Craighero, 2004). Although neuroscientists still debate the precise purpose of mirror neurons, many argue that they serve as the neural basis of empathy (Marshall, 2014).

Darwin could never have anticipated the technological advances in the fields of psychology and neuroscience. But the theoretical groundwork he laid over a century ago still guides the study of empathy, and his insights still resonate strongly today. No doubt he would smile at the progress made, and we might smile watching him.

Emotional contagion: The tendency for people to synchronize their emotions automatically with the emotions of others, without necessarily being aware of it happening.

So what does empathy have to do with sex and gender? One answer has to do with stereotypes. Many people stereotype women as more attuned to the emotions of others, better able to "read" people (think of the notion of "women's intuition"), and more concerned about others (Fischer & Evers, 2013). In short, people believe that women have more empathy than men. As noted earlier, women also display better decoding accuracy than men, meaning that they interpret the emotions expressed by others more accurately. But does this translate into women truly being higher in empathy than men?

The answer to this depends on the way that researchers conceptualize and measure empathy. For instance, on self-report measures (see Table 8.4), girls and women report more empathy than boys and men (Baron-Cohen & Wheelwright, 2004), though sex differences in empathy decrease with age (Schieman & Van Gundy, 2000). In contrast to self-report measures, empathic accuracy tests measure the ability to infer the thoughts or feelings of others correctly. For example, in one test, participants watch videos of actual interviews and try to infer the interviewee's thoughts at various points. The results of a meta-analysis revealed that women do slightly better on tests of empathic accuracy, but larger sex differences emerge when participants know they are being evaluated on empathy (Ickes, Gesn, & Graham, 2000). This suggests that sex differences in empathy might have as much to do with motivation as they do with ability.

Researchers also study sex differences in empathy by examining emotional contagion. As discussed in the "Journey of Research," emotional contagion occurs when people automatically (and often without awareness) synchronize their emotions with the emotions of others (Hatfield et al., 1993). Imagine seeing a stranger cry in response to her dog's death and beginning to cry along with her. Even watching a video of someone crying or smiling can trigger a similar response in watchers. In fact, women tend to show higher levels of emotional contagion than men (Doherty, Orimoto,

Mirror neurons: Neurons that fire both when performing an action and when observing another individual perform the action.

Table 8.4 **How Empathic Are You?** The items below were taken from two widely used self-report measures of empathy.

Think about how much each of the statements below describes you, using the following scale:

Does not describe me well   Describes me very well

| 1 | 2 | 3 | 4 | 5 |

1. I often have tender, concerned feelings for people less fortunate than me.
2. When I see someone being taken advantage of, I feel kind of protective towards them.
3. I sometimes find it difficult to see things from the "other guy's" point of view.
4. I try to look at everybody's side of a disagreement before I make a decision.
5. I really get involved with the feelings of the characters in a novel.
6. When I watch a good movie, I can very easily put myself in the place of a leading character.
7. Being in a tense emotional situation scares me.
8. When I see someone who badly needs help in an emergency, I go to pieces.
9. I can easily tell if someone else is interested or bored with what I am saying.
10. I am quick to spot when someone in a group is feeling awkward or uncomfortable.
11. It upsets me to see animals in pain.
12. I tend to get emotionally involved with a friend's problems.

The first eight items were drawn from the Interpersonal Reactivity Inventory (M. H. Davis, 1983), and the last four items were drawn from the Empathy Quotient (Baron-Cohen & Wheelwright, 2004), two of the most widely used measures of empathy. Higher scores on all items, except Item 3, indicate higher levels of empathy. To calculate your final score, subtract your response to Item 3 from the value 6, and then sum across all of your ratings. Total scores can range from 12 to 60, with higher scores indicating greater empathy.

Singelis, Hatfield, & Hebb, 1995). But does mimicking the emotions of others mean that one actually feels them? Though it is difficult to measure genuine feelings, studying brain activity may offer some insight. Here, the evidence is mixed. Some studies use **electroencephalogram (EEG)** technology to measure electrical activity in the brain, and they find that women show higher empathic responding than men to others' suffering (C. Y. Yang, Decety, Lee, Chen, & Cheng, 2009). However, other studies that use **functional magnetic resonance imaging (fMRI)** to map brain activity with magnetic fields find no overall evidence for a sex difference in empathy when observing others in pain (Lamm, Decety, & Singer, 2011).

The concept of **emotional intelligence** relates to empathy. Emotionally intelligent people show awareness of their own and others' emotions, manage their own and others' emotions well (e.g., by cheering others up or calming them down), and use their emotions effectively to solve problems and facilitate actions (Mayer, Roberts, & Barsade, 2008). As the name implies, people high in this tendency are intelligent about emotions in general. Curiously, in comparison with women, men estimate their emotional intelligence as higher (Petrides & Furnham, 2006), but women score higher than men on various measures of emotional intelligence. One review found a moderate sex difference favoring women ($d = -0.47$) for performance-based measures of emotional intelligence (Joseph & Newman, 2010).

In sum, compared with men, women appear somewhat more empathic and show moderately higher levels of emotional intelligence. But some of the sex differences in empathy may reflect motivation rather than ability. Of course, you may be wondering why this matters. What purpose do empathy and emotional intelligence serve? In fact, empathy helps people be moral, motivates them to help others, and prevents them from hurting others (N. Eisenberg, Spinrad, & Sadovsky, 2005). People who score high on empathy-related measures have better mental health, better interpersonal relationships (J. A. Hall, Andrzejewski, & Yopchick, 2009), and higher marital satisfaction (Mirgain & Cordova, 2007). Imagine what problems might diminish across the globe if people in general could develop more empathy.

Electroencephalogram (EEG): A brain imaging technique that reads electrical activity in the brain with the use of sensors on the scalp.

Functional magnetic resonance imaging (fMRI): A brain imaging technique that uses magnetic field and radio waves to map brain activity.

Emotional intelligence: The ability to identify and manage one's own emotions and the emotions of others, and to use emotions to solve problems.

CHAPTER SUMMARY

8.1 Describe how gender-related words and language shape perceptions.

According to the Whorfian hypothesis, the structure and content of language determines people's cognitions and perceptions. Gendered language has a number of consequences. The use of the generic masculine (male-gendered words to refer to mixed-sex or sex-unspecified individuals or groups) is problematic due to its ambiguity and selective application. Some languages assign gendered articles to nouns, which may lead to gender-typical thinking more generally. Language can also reinforce gender and status differences through the use of diminutives (e.g., calling women *girls*) and unnecessary labeling (e.g., *male nurse*). At the same time, language can empower and transform by bringing cultural visibility and legitimacy to experiences (e.g., sexual harassment or date rape) that were previously ignored. Similarly, members of stigmatized groups may derive power from labeling themselves with reclaimed, derogatory terms (e.g., "bitch" and "fag").

8.2 Analyze sex similarities and differences in verbal and nonverbal communication.

Despite cultural stereotypes of talkative women and silent men, men and women talk about the same amount. Men may intrusively interrupt conversations more often than women. Girls and women gossip about others more than boys and men, but the sex difference is not large. Recent studies of social media use find that men more often use profanity and argumentative language, whereas women more often use warm, polite, and emotional language. Women talk more about friends and family, and men talk more about objects. These sex differences in language and verbal communication are generally small.

Stereotypes portray women as more nonverbally expressive than men, and research reveals sex differences that are consistent with these stereotypes. Girls and women tend to smile more—and gaze at their interaction partners more—than do boys and men, and they also show greater ability to read the emotional cues of others accurately (decoding accuracy).

Men stand farther away from others, especially from other men, during social interactions. Gender norms about touching show substantial cultural differences, but women tend to touch and get touched in social interaction more than men do. Men tend to sit and stand in more expansive postures than women, which may communicate status and dominance. Gait provides cues about both sex and sexual orientation.

8.3 Evaluate how status, power, and culture shape sex differences in communication.

Communication can establish and reinforce status and power. Some individuals with marginalized identities (e.g., the fakaleiti in Tonga) strategically code switch between different languages to express resistance to their marginalization. Moroccan women also commonly code switch between different languages as a means of empowerment in a patriarchal society. Some gender-nonconforming individuals use language to challenge the gender binary and disrupt

gender expectations. Emotion can also convey different levels of power. Anger and disgust signal and reinforce high power, whereas shame and sadness signal low power. Emotional display rules, socialized early in life, tend to allow men to express power emotions more than women and may prohibit men from expressing low-power emotions.

Cross-cultural variation exists in channels of nonverbal communication. In Western cultures, eye contact signifies respect while averting the eyes can signify disrespect or dishonesty. In contrast, averting the eyes in East Asian countries signifies respect while too much eye contact may be perceived as disrespectful or threatening. Unlike the United States, many countries in the Middle East are generally accepting of male–male touch in public. Men kiss each other in greeting and walk in public holding hands, without romantic overtones.

8.4 Analyze how sex and gender shape the experience and expression of emotion.

Stereotypes depict women as more emotional than men. Girls and women do express some emotions (happiness, affection, fear, sadness, and embarrassment) more than men, but men express some emotions (anger, contempt, and pride) more than women. In contrast, physiological measures of emotion and studies that track people in their daily lives find no consistent sex differences in the experience of emotion. This suggests that women amplify certain emotional expressions, or men suppress them.

Women tend to score higher than men on measures of empathy (the capacity to feel, understand, and decode the emotional state of another) and emotional intelligence (the ability to identify and manage one's own emotions and the emotions of others and to use emotions to solve problems and facilitate action). However, with sex differences in the small–moderate range, they are not as large or consistent as stereotypes suggest, and they tend to differ according to motivational and social factors.

Test Your Knowledge: True or False?

8.1. Gendered word choice can influence people's thoughts and perceptions. (True: Consistent with the Whorfian hypothesis, word choice can influence thoughts by making gender categories more or less salient, by reinforcing gender stereotypes, and by influencing perceptions of blame associated with perpetrators and victims of violence.) [p. 261]

8.2. On average, women talk more than men. (False: Men are slightly more talkative than women, but the effect size is small and differs depending on contextual factors.) [p. 263]

8.3. Sex differences in language use emerge consistently, regardless of variables such as culture, race, social status, and education level. (False: Language use differs greatly by culture, race, social status, and education level, and these variables interact with sex in complex ways to influence whether and when sex differences emerge.) [p. 268]

8.4. On average, girls and women smile more than boys and men. (True: This is a fairly robust sex difference found across cultures.) [p. 271]

8.5. Compared with women, men tend to be better at identifying and managing their own emotions and the emotions of others. (False: While men estimate their emotional intelligence as higher than women do, women score higher on measures of emotional intelligence.) [p. 286]

Sexuality, Relationships, and Work

Chapter 9   Sexual Orientation and Sexuality

Chapter 10   Interpersonal Relationships

Chapter 11   Work and Home

Test Your Knowledge: True or False?

9.1 Approximately 10% of the U.S. population identifies as gay, lesbian, or bisexual.

9.2 Many asexual people report difficulty in understanding their internal experiences of their sexuality because they lack the language to describe these experiences.

9.3 Although we usually assume that love follows desire (we fall in love with people after first finding them sexually attractive), it is just as possible for desire to follow love (we can become sexually attracted to someone after first falling in love with them).

9.4 Genital reconstructive surgery typically makes it difficult for transgender people to have orgasms.

9.5 While men experience their sexual peak between the ages of 19 and 25, women reach their sexual peak around the ages of 30–35.

CHAPTER 9

Sexual Orientation and Sexuality

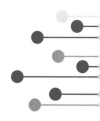

Key Concepts

How Do Understandings of Sexuality and Sexual Orientation Differ Across Time and Culture?
Journey of Research: Sexual Orientation Change Efforts

What Is Sexual Orientation?
Sexual Identity
Motivation: Desire and Love
Sexual Behavior
Complexity of Sexual Orientation

How Does Sexual Orientation Develop?
Phase Models of Sexual Identity Development
Milestone and Narrative Models of Sexual
Minority Identity Development

Why Do People Differ in Sexual Orientation?
Biological Theories
Evolutionary Theories
The Integrative Approach
Evaluation of Theories

How Do Sex and Gender Contribute to the Experience of Sexuality?
Sexual Behavior and Attitudes
Debate: Do Men Have a Stronger Sex Drive Than Women?
Orgasm Frequency and Sexual Satisfaction
Sexual Fluidity

How Does Sexuality Change Over the Life Course?
Sexual Trajectories
The Medicalization of Sexual Changes

Learning Objectives

Students who read this chapter should be able to do the following:

9.1 Locate current understandings of sexuality and sexual orientation within social, cultural, and historical contexts.

9.2 Describe the multiple dimensions of sexual orientation, and analyze different models of sexual identity development.

9.3 Evaluate biological, evolutionary, and integrative theories of sexual orientation.

9.4 Explain sex differences in sexuality, including attitudes and behaviors, orgasms and sexual satisfaction, and sexual fluidity.

9.5 Understand issues in sexuality across the life course, such as sexual peaks and the medicalization of sexual changes.

Sexual Orientation and Sexuality

In some ways, Roy and Silo were like many other same-sex male couples. Residents of the same urban community, they met in 1998, hit it off, and soon became inseparable. As their intimacy grew, Roy and Silo began to desire a family, but, of course, they could not conceive a child together. Instead, they adopted an infant girl named Tango and raised her in a safe and caring environment.

In other ways, Roy and Silo were very unique. For one thing, they were chin-strap penguins living in New York City's Central Park Zoo. For another thing, their keeper never witnessed Roy and Silo engaging in sexual acts with one another, although the two did exhibit other penguin mating rituals, such as building a nest, intertwining their necks, and serenading one another with mating calls. Despite being penguins—and penguins that possibly never performed sexual acts with each other—Roy and Silo were labeled "gay" in a *New York Times* article (D. Smith, 2004).

Controversy ensued. Advocates of LGB rights heralded Roy and Silo's union as proof that same-sex sexuality is both natural and normal. "If Roy and Silo can do it, why can't humans?" asked *Newsweek* columnist Gersh Kuntzman (2004). Inspired by the penguins' love story, Peter Parnell and Justin Richardson wrote a children's book titled *And Tango Makes Three* that depicted a close-knit penguin family unit consisting of two dads and their adopted daughter. But traditional marriage advocates pushed back. Some viewed *And Tango Makes Three* as an attempt to indoctrinate children into a worldview that promoted same-sex sexuality. Parents in several U.S. states, concerned that the book would expose their children to controversial issues of sexuality, requested that school and public libraries either remove or restrict access to the book. Between 2006 and 2010, the picture book describing Roy and Silo's family was consistently either the first- or second-most-challenged book in the United States.

Why all the fuss over a couple of penguins who hatched an egg together? As this example illustrates, same-sex sexuality is a controversial issue for some, and the passions that people feel about it run deep. While some are anguished by the stigmatization and prejudice faced by sexual minority individuals, others are outraged by the increasing societal expectation that they accept what they perceive as an immoral lifestyle. Although these issues are clearly human ones, Roy and Silo's partnership nonetheless became a metaphor for an emotionally charged cultural war. The penguins' egg-hatching behavior served as a cultural Rorschach test, with people on both sides of the issue projecting their own hopes and fears onto the event.

And what about Roy and Silo? Were they really gay? Does it even make sense to talk about nonhuman animals as having a sexual orientation? As we will discuss in this chapter, sexual orientation is a complex phenomenon shaped by a combination of genes, neurology, hormones, culture, and social factors. We define **sexual orientation** as an enduring pattern of cognitive, motivational, and behavioral tendencies that regulates the experience, conduct, and expression of **sexuality**, which is the capacity for sexual responses and experiences. Thus, sexual orientation describes not only the sex(es) of the persons toward whom individuals direct their romantic and sexual feelings but also

Sexual orientation: A complex, enduring pattern of cognitive, motivational, and behavioral tendencies that shapes how people experience and express their sexuality. Often framed more simply as the sex or sexes toward whom an individual feels attracted.

Sexuality: The capacity for sexual responses and experiences.

the self-labels they adopt and the sexual behavior they enact. Given these definitions, it seems clear that nonhuman animals like penguins have sexuality but less clear that they have sexual orientation.

In this chapter, we offer a broad overview of the concept of sexual orientation, from its historical origins in 19th-century Western medicine to current ways of thinking about it. Along the way, we also address the complexity of sexual orientation, including coverage of the most updated knowledge of what it is, why people differ on it, and how it develops. The second half of the chapter considers how sex and gender relate to sexuality and how people's experiences of their sexuality change over the life course.

Note that sexual orientation is typically defined in terms of the sexes of its primary objects, which means discussions of it often reinforce the sex binary. Thinking or talking about sexual orientation often involves assumptions that the world consists of people who are either female or male and that our sexuality orients us toward one or more of these sexes. Therefore, much of this chapter uses the sex binary as a framework. However, not everyone experiences sexuality in this manner. When possible, we draw your attention to alternative ways of experiencing sexuality that do not involve carving the world into female and male. In this spirit, consider this quotation from gender researcher Sandra Bem (1993):

> Although some of the (very few) individuals to whom I have been attracted . . . have been men and some have been women, what those individuals have in common has nothing to do with either their biological sex or mine—from which I conclude, not that I am attracted to both sexes, but that my sexuality is organized around dimensions other than sex. (p. vii)

How Do Understandings of Sexuality and Sexual Orientation Differ Across Time and Culture?

The idea that people have a stable, internal drive that orients them, sexually, toward members of a particular sex emerged relatively recently from Western cultures. The earliest known references to sexual orientation appeared in a letter written by the Hungarian journalist Karl-Maria Kertbeny in the late 1860s (Fone, 2000). Kertbeny used the word *Homosexualität* to describe erotic desire toward persons of the same sex and the word *Normalsexualität* to describe erotic desire toward persons of the other sex (note that the *normal* in Normalsexualität was not meant as a morality judgment but merely signified that this was the more common form of desire). In English-language texts, the word *homosexual* was first used in 1892 by American psychiatrist James Kiernan, who defined "a homosexual" as an individual whose "general mental state is that of the opposite sex." By the 1930s, both *homosexuality* and *heterosexuality* were used widely.

These early references to heterosexuality and homosexuality reflected a new way of thinking about sexuality. Whereas people have always had sexuality, it did not become popular to classify people into groups based on the sex of the people they desire until the 1860s. This new labeling did more than create categories of sexuality types; it shifted how people thought about sexuality. Prior to the mid-1800s, sexual behavior was seen primarily as something that people *did*. Now, sexuality was something that people *had*. Thus, humans' understanding of our own propensity for sexuality has changed over time and may continue to change as cultural values shift and awareness of diversity increases.

Stop and Think

To the extent that sexual orientation guides people's attractions to specific types of people, are those attractions based on other people's sex, or are they based on other people's gender identity? Because most people are cisgender, their sex and gender identity are the same. But what about transgender, genderqueer, or nonbinary individuals? Suppose a cisgender man pursues a relationship with an MtF woman. Is the man "straight" (because his partner identifies as a woman), or is he "gay" (because his partner was assigned male at birth)? Does sexual orientation always fit cleanly into one or the other category?

Prior to the mid-1800s, to the extent that members of Western cultures made assumptions about people's sexuality, these pertained to the specific sexual acts or roles (e.g., penetrative versus receptive) that people performed rather than the sex(es) of the partners that people preferred. In ancient Greece, for example, adult men and adolescent boys commonly formed temporary, same-sex couplings, or *pederastic relationships*, in which men offered education, socialization, and protection in exchange for sexual favors from their younger partners. In such pairings, meaning was derived not from either man's assumed orientation toward same-sex partners but, instead, from the sexual role played by each partner, with the penetrative role conveying maturity and higher social status and the receptive role conveying youth and lower social status (Fone, 2000).

Similarly, in non-Western cultures, sexual behavior often has meanings that have little to do with sexual orientation. Consider the Sambian people of Papua New Guinea.

Among these people, pubescent boys undergo a manhood ritual that involves fellating and ingesting the semen of adult male tribe members (Herdt, 1982). Sambian people believe that only through ingesting semen can boys gain the strength and bravery to become warriors, and once they have transitioned to manhood, they maintain heterosexual relationships. This cultural practice is not thought to reflect same-sex desire but, instead, gender role socialization.

Why did people's thinking about sexual orientation change? Some scholars argue that 19th-century Western medical and scientific fields developed the idea of sexual orientation as a means of control-ling people's erotic behavior (Foucault, 1978). Categorizing and labeling sexuality gave scientific credibility to the notion that some kinds of sexual attractions were "natural" and "normal," whereas others were "deviant." Moreover, defining sexual orientation as a stable aspect of people's characters, rather than merely a form of behavior, allowed for harsher criminal penalties for those who committed "deviant" sexual acts. Consistent with this logic, this new medicalized way of thinking about sexual orientation corresponded with the adoption of more stringent sexual laws in Germany in the latter half of the 19th century (Hutter, 1993). Regardless of why people started to conceptualize and label distinct sexual orientations, the tendency to do so remains popular today, although cultures vary widely in the labels and meanings that they give to different sexual orientations. We will consider these and other sexual orientation labels in the next section.

Detail from an ancient Greek fresco depicting an adult man (at right) and his younger male lover (at left). From the Tomb of the Diver, Paestum, Italy, circa 480 BC.

Source: © iStockPhoto .com/peuceta

Journey of Research

Sexual Orientation Change Efforts

Sexual orientation change efforts (SOCEs; sometimes called *conversion therapies*) have a controversial and troubling history within psychology. In the late 19th century, Sigmund Freud and his daughter Anna treated gay and lesbian clients who wished to change their sexual orientation, although Freud was skeptical about the likely success of this treatment: "To undertake to convert a fully developed homosexual into a heterosexual is not much more promising than to do the reverse" (S. Freud, 1920, p. 129).

What does the research say about the outcomes of SOCEs? Some early accounts portrayed them as effective.

(Continued)

(Continued)

Anna Freud, for example, claimed to have "successfully" treated several gay male patients using psychoanalysis (A. Freud, 1949, 1951). Her evidence was based solely on *case studies*, however, which tend to lack generalizability and fall prey to observer bias (recall these topics from Chapter 2, "Studying Sex and Gender").

In 1962, Irving Bieber reported on the results of psychoanalysis with 106 gay men, concluding that 27% of them shifted to exclusive heterosexuality following treatment (Bieber et al., 1962). Over the next decades, other psychoanalysts reported comparable rates of "success"—defined as a change to exclusive heterosexuality—ranging from 18% to 44% (Throckmorton, 1998). However, the clients most likely to report changes in sexual orientation were those who were strongly motivated to change and who had prior histories of heterosexual experiences or leanings. This raised questions about the generalizability of the findings.

From the 1960s to the 1980s, research examined the effectiveness of behaviorism-based SOCEs, which often used aversion therapy to condition gay male clients to associate sexual stimuli (such as images of attractive nude men) with pain, nausea, or negative mental imagery (M. P. Feldman, MacCulloch, & Orford, 1971). Other behavioral methods included assertiveness training or reinforcement of heterosexual behaviors (Greenspoon & Lamal, 1987). Again, mixed findings emerged, with reports of conversion to heterosexuality ranging from 0% to 65%.

Comparatively little systematic research examines the effectiveness of SOCEs that use cognitive therapy, group therapy, or religion-based approaches (Haldeman, 1994). The existing research in these areas often relies on single case studies or very small samples, and the same individuals who conduct the therapy also interpret and report the results, raising the possibility of observer bias. Moreover, almost all of the evidence regarding the effectiveness of SOCEs relies on self-reports by clients, many of whom are strongly motivated to pursue a heterosexual life for religious or cultural reasons. People who want to change might claim that their treatment was effective because they are in denial about their true leanings or because they feel pressured to portray themselves in a particular manner.

In 1973, the American Psychiatric Association declassified same-sex sexuality as a psychological disorder, and shortly thereafter, the American Psychological Association urged "all mental health professionals to take the lead in removing the stigma of mental illness that has long been associated with homosexual orientations" (Conger, 1975, p. 633). Given that same-sex sexuality was no longer considered a disorder, it became professionally unethical to conduct SOCEs, so research on their effectiveness declined (APA, 2009a). Though religion-based SOCEs remain prevalent, the people who conduct these therapies often lack professional training in psychology and do not follow the ethical codes of the APA. Further, when conducted with minors against their will, religion-based SOCEs may harm their recipients by increasing the risk of depression, anxiety, drug use, and suicide (Human Rights Campaign, 2017).

To offer a conclusive answer about the effectiveness of SOCEs, an APA task force conducted a systematic review of 83 published, peer-reviewed studies on SOCEs in the mid-2000s (APA, 2009a). The task force determined that the research does not offer a sound basis for concluding that SOCEs reduce same-sex attraction or behavior or increase other-sex attraction or behavior. Moreover, many people suffer harm from SOCEs. Given these outcomes, the task force concluded that SOCEs are not likely to be effective and strongly opposed their use. Similarly, most major medical and psychological organizations, including the World Health Organization, the American Medical Association, and the American Academy of Pediatrics, discredit the effectiveness of SOCEs and take official positions against their practice. By now, over 20 U.S. states have introduced legislation to prevent licensed mental health providers from using SOCEs with minors (Human Rights Campaign, 2017). However, since they are difficult to regulate legally, privately operated, religion-based SOCEs are still practiced on vulnerable sexual minority youth today.

What Is Sexual Orientation?

What exactly is sexual orientation? Since the earliest origins of the concept of sexual orientation, different scholars have offered different definitions of it. As we discussed earlier, James Kiernan defined same-sex sexuality in terms of an individual's "mental state," implying that sexual orientation is a psychological phenomenon. Almost 60 years later, Alfred Kinsey defined sexual orientation in terms of both sexual feelings and sexual experiences, thus adding a behavioral component to the definition (Kinsey, Pomeroy, & Martin, 1948). Others propose even more complex definitions. Herek (2000), for instance, lists five dimensions of sexual orientation, including sexual attraction, sexual behavior, personal identity, romantic relationships, and community membership. Given the complexity of sexual orientation, people do not necessarily agree about how best to define it. Here, we talk about three primary dimensions of sexual orientation: identity, motivation, and behavior.

Sexual Identity

Identity refers to one's recognition of the self as belonging to a given social group or category, along with the emotional significance that one attaches to this group membership. Thus, **sexual identity** refers to both the label that a person uses to describe her sexual orientation and the emotional reactions that she has to this label. Most people use the terms that we have already encountered in this chapter, including *heterosexual* or *straight*, *lesbian*, *gay*, and *bisexual*. How frequently are these sexual identities represented in the population? Ask anyone what percentage of people identifies as gay or lesbian, and they are likely to answer "10 percent." This widely touted statistic stems from Kinsey's research of the late 1940s in which he concluded that "10 percent of the [White] males are more or less exclusively homosexual . . . for at least three years between the ages of 16 and 55" (Kinsey et al., 1948, pp. 650–651). Members of the gay rights movement of the 1970s later popularized the "10 percent" statistic to convince the public that "We [gay men and lesbians] Are Everywhere" (Voeller, 1990), and it remains firmly entrenched in the popular psyche today.

> **Sexual identity:**
> The label used to describe a person's sexual orientation and the emotional reactions that the person has to this label.

A popular slogan in the gay rights movement of the 1970s.

Source: http://democratsforequality.org/wp-content/uploads/2015/01/We-Are-Everywhere.jpg

In fact, this percentage overestimates the number of people who identify as sexual minority individuals in the United States. Kinsey and his collaborators arrived at the 10% statistic by using convenience sampling to collect their data, and this sampling method can give a biased view of reality. In *convenience sampling*, researchers locate readily available respondents who are likely to possess the particular features of interest. In contrast, in *probability sampling*, researchers collect data from members of a given population randomly, meaning that every member of the population has the same chance of being surveyed. Using probability sampling, Laumann and his colleagues found that 2.0% of men and 0.9% of women identified as gay and lesbian, respectively, while 0.8% of men and 0.5% of women identified as bisexual; the remainder (97.2% of men and 98.6% of women) identified as heterosexual (Laumann, Gagnon, Michael, & Michaels, 1994). Herbenick et al. (2010) found comparable numbers, with 4.2% of men and 0.9% of women identifying as gay or lesbian, 2.6% of men and 3.6% of women identifying as bisexual, 92.2% of men and 93.2% of women identifying as heterosexual, and 1.0% of men and 2.3% of women selecting "Other."

What identities fall into this "Other" category? Recall from Chapter 1 that *pansexual* individuals experience romantic or sexual attractions to people of all sexes and gender identities while *polysexual* individuals are attracted to others of multiple (but not necessarily all) sexes and genders. For example, Sandra Bem's description of her sexuality as an attraction to people based not on their sex but on some other dimension seems consistent with the polysexual label. Also mentioned in earlier chapters, Native American *two-spirit* people possess both a male and female spirit and may have same-sex attractions, Indian *hijras* are assigned male at birth but live as nonbinary and have sex with men, and *māhūwahine* (in Hawaii) and *fa'afafine* (in Samoa) are men who identify as women and primarily have sex with men. Finally, people who identify as *asexual* lack sexual interest in other people. In a large, national probability survey of British residents, Anthony Bogaert found that 1% of respondents indicated never having felt sexual attraction to another person (Bogaert, 2004). These individuals may still experience romantic love, however, and some of them engage in sexual activity with partners despite their lack of sexual interest. Others, who identify as *aromantic*, lack all romantic interest in others, although they may experience sexual desire.

Once people categorize themselves into a given social group, they tend to incorporate the traits, behaviors, and values associated with this group into their self-concept (J. C. Turner, Hogg, Oakes, Reicher, & Wetherell, 1987). Thus, people often come to view themselves as similar to other members of their sexual orientation group and as sharing similar experiences and outcomes. Accordingly, many people view their sexual identity as a central and important part of themselves and associate it with positive feelings. There are exceptions to this, however. Given the stigmatization and prejudice that sexual minority individuals face in many cultures, some experience negative, shameful, or fearful emotions associated with their sexual identity. For example, some Latino gay men who are raised with values of *familism*, or strong family interdependence, report experiencing feelings of regret, sadness, and conflict surrounding their sexual identity if relatives interpret their same-sex sexuality as a family betrayal (A. A. Eaton & Rios, 2017). Some sexual minority individuals also experience *internalized homophobia*, which occurs when LGB people internalize the negative messages that they receive about same-sex sexuality from the larger culture. People higher in internalized homophobia tend to feel less positive about their sexual identity and less connected to other LGB individuals (Szymanski, Kashubeck-West, & Meyer, 2008).

Finally, some people do not identify with a sexual orientation label at all. Some may avoid a label due to uncertainty about which one best applies to them. Others may consider themselves *fluid*, view sexual identity labels as overly simplistic, or avoid labeling themselves because they do not consider their sexuality a core feature of the self that connects them to others within a social category. In an upcoming section, we will go into more detail about the phases that characterize the development of sexual identity (see "How Does Sexual Orientation Develop?").

Sidebar 9.2: Saying "No" To Labels

Actress and musician Carrie Brownstein and pop star Miley Cyrus have dated both men and women but do not label themselves bisexual. "I never think of sexuality as an identifier," wrote Brownstein (Talbot, 2012). Similarly, Cyrus said, "For me, I don't want to label myself as anything. . . . We love putting people in categories, but what I like sexually isn't going to label me as a person" (Dockterman, 2015).

Motivation: Desire and Love

People experience the motivation components of sexual orientation as feelings of desire and love, both of which consist of longing for and impulse to seek proximity to a given target. Evolutionary theorists describe desire (lust) and love (attachment) as distinct but overlapping systems that regulate reproduction and mating (H. E. Fisher, 1998; Hazan & Zeifman, 1994). Although desire and love are often directed toward the same partner or person, they do not need to be. Moreover, each of them can be directed toward persons of the same or another sex. That is, a person may feel sexual desire primarily toward persons of the other sex while typically falling in love with persons of the same sex. Below, we consider these motivations in turn (see Table 9.1 for a summary).

Sexual desire (lust)—or a yearning to engage in sexual activities—is characterized by heightened physiological arousal and regulated by gonadal hormones (*estrogens* and *androgens*) and neurotransmitters, including *oxytocin* (Diamond, 2003). Serving an adaptive function, sexual desire presumably motivates sexual union for the purpose of reproduction (H. E. Fisher, 1998). According to this logic, the mating system likely codes for an intrinsic orientation to feel lust toward other-sex persons, at least for most people, as this type of mating behavior most frequently produces offspring. Nonetheless, as noted by Lisa Diamond (2003), same-sex sexual desire can and often does coexist with other-sex sexual desires without impeding reproductive success.

Sexual desire may motivate people to seek out sexual union, but love motivates people to direct their attentions toward a specific other person who is cherished above others. **Love (attachment)** consists of strong feelings of affection and attachment that go beyond mere warmth. The early stage of love (sometimes called passionate love) consists

Sexual desire (lust): A wish or urge to engage in sexual activities.

Love (attachment): Strong feelings of affection and attachment that go beyond mere warmth.

Passionate love: An early stage of love characterized by arousal, urgent longing, and exhilaration.

Dopamine: A neurotransmitter that is associated with feelings of reward, positive arousal, and intentional control of voluntary movement.

Table 9.1 **Motivational Components of Sexual Orientation.** Evolutionary theorists view desire and love as part of larger behavioral systems that regulate mating, reproduction, and parenting. As you can see, these systems are associated with specific goals, feelings, behaviors, and neurological substances.

Motivation	System	Goal	Feelings	Behaviors	Neurology
Lust (sexual desire)	Mating	Sexual gratification	Arousal, craving	Sexual union	Estrogens, androgens, oxytocin
Attraction (romantic love)	Reproduction	Creating bond with specific other	Arousal, exhilaration, preoccupation	Seeking and maintaining proximity	Dopamine, norepinephrine
Attachment (companionate love)	Parenting	Raising vulnerable infants	Warmth, caring, emotional intimacy	Maintaining proximity, sharing resources, coordinating activities	Oxytocin, vasopressin

Norepinephrine:
A neuropeptide that is associated with sympathetic arousal and the "fight-or-flight" response.

Companionate love: A later stage of love characterized by calm feelings of warmth and emotional closeness.

Pair-bonding system: A system in which two adult members of a species remain bonded to one another for the purpose of producing and raising offspring.

of arousal, urgent longing, feelings of exhilaration, and obsessive thinking about the love object. Such feelings are associated with elevated levels of neurotransmitters, including **dopamine** (which regulates feelings of reward and positive arousal) and **norepinephrine** (which plays a role in sympathetic arousal and the "fight-or-flight" response; Bartels & Zeki, 2000). The later stages of love (sometimes called **companionate love**) consist of calm, warm, and emotionally close feelings of intimacy toward a familiar other. Oxytocin and *vasopressin*, a neuropeptide related to intimacy and bonding, regulate this type of love (Carter, DeVries, & Getz, 1995).

Cross-cultural evidence indicates that passionate love toward mating partners is a universal or near-universal human experience (Jankowiak & Fisher, 1992). According to evolutionary approaches, passionate love encourages individuals to focus their mating efforts on a specific, preferred love object for the purpose of raising offspring. More specifically, the mammalian tendency to become attached reflects the operation of the **pair-bonding system**, which presumably evolved to motivate coparenting behaviors (Hazan & Shaver, 1994). The logic goes like this: Compared with many other animals, human infants are vulnerable at birth and dependent on extended caregiving by willing adults. For example, human infants cannot hunt or prepare their own food, escape from predators, seek shelter and safety, or perform many other survival-relevant acts that infants of other species can do shortly after birth. Moreover, because human infants wean at much younger ages than members of many other primate species, human adults can have babies at relatively short intervals. As a result, humans can have multiple, highly dependent offspring at the same time, a challenge best met through *biparental care*, or consistent and reliable parenting by two adults who coordinate activities and pool resources (Pillsworth & Haselton, 2005). Thus, love motivates adult mates to remain together in biparental units for long enough to see their offspring through a vulnerable infancy and childhood. Feelings of love make it difficult, after all, to abandon one's family in search of other options. Note, however, that biparental care need not be provided by parents of different sexes, as any adults can work together to raise offspring. Based on this logic, Lisa Diamond (2003) argues that the evolved tendency to fall in love and form pair bonds does not orient people to experience romantic love primarily toward other-sex people. Moreover, some take issue with the evolutionary suggestion that children need two parents to thrive, noting that plenty of single parents successfully raise healthy and well-adjusted children (Silverstein & Auerbach, 1999). We will return to this issue in Chapter 10, "Interpersonal Relationships."

Unlike humans, baby sea turtles can run, seek safety, and find food as soon as they hatch from their eggs. They do not need parents to assist them, and it's a good thing, too—sea turtle moms leave their babies before the babies even hatch.

Source: © iStockPhoto .com/Karliux_

According to some theorists, adult mates experience essentially the same love that infants form for their caregivers within the first few months of life (Hazan & Shaver, 1994). For instance, the same neurological circuits regulate both types of love relationships, and people experience and describe both kinds of love similarly: as a desire for proximity to the loved one, accompanied by feelings of warmth, intimacy, and caring. Given this, Lisa Diamond (2003) argues that an attachment system that genetically coded for an orientation to prefer one sex over others would be maladaptive. For example, a male baby who could only grow attached to female adults would be at a disadvantage if his mother died or left the family unit. In fact, infants readily form attachments to parents of all sexes (Kochanska & Kim, 2012). Therefore, adults should also have the capacity to fall in love with others of any sex. This capacity may underlie the tendency for people to sometimes "fall in love" with a person of the sex that does not usually attract them, such as when a woman who identifies as heterosexual experiences a novel, unexpected romantic attraction to another woman. We will return to this topic later.

Stop and Think

Evolutionary theory offers a framework for making sense of universally observed behavioral patterns, such as pair bonding. However, exceptions to pair bonding are found in every human culture. For instance, more U.S. families are now headed by single parents than ever before. Can evolutionary theory explain this change in the traditional family structure? If so, how might evolutionary theory explain this trend? If not, what implications does this have for the explanatory power of evolutionary theory?

Sexual Behavior

Sexual behavior includes anything that can be considered an erotic act, including behavior performed alone (e.g., masturbation and viewing of pornography) or with others (e.g., intercourse and oral sex), as well as acts performed with others who are not physically present (e.g., cybersex and sexting). So what exactly do people do sexually, and with whom do they do it? As you might imagine, sexual behavior can be difficult to measure accurately because many people consider it extremely private. Still, we can get a rough look at the relative rates of various sexual behaviors by using random sampling techniques. In one nationally representative sample of over 5,800 U.S. adults, solo masturbation and vaginal intercourse were the most frequent sexual behaviors reported, with 62% of men and 39% of women reporting masturbation in the past month and 59% of men and 58% of women reporting vaginal intercourse in the past month (Herbenick et al., 2010). All other behaviors measured, including partnered masturbation, oral sex, and anal sex, were reported relatively less frequently by adults in this age range. Further, those ages 18–59 years old reported higher rates of most sexual behaviors than did adolescents younger than 18 and adults ages 60 and older.

Individuals report same-sex sexual behavior relatively less frequently. For example, whereas 86% of men ages 18–59 reported having vaginal sex at least once in their lifetime, only 8% reported experiencing receptive anal sex (penetrative anal sex with another man was not measured in this study), and 10%–11% reported oral sex with a man (Herbenick et al., 2010). Among women, while 91% reported having had vaginal sex during their lifetime, only 10%–12% reported having oral sex with a woman. These rates roughly match those obtained in the study conducted by Edward Laumann and his colleagues, who found that just over 9% of men and 4% of women reported engaging in any type of sexual activity with a same-sex partner (Laumann et al., 1994).

What about same-sex sexual behavior in non-Western cultures? In a classic anthropological investigation of preliterate societies around the world, Ford and Beach (1951) found evidence of male–male sexual behavior in 64% of the societies they studied and female–female sexual behavior in 22% of societies. Broude and Greene (1976) reviewed ethnographic data collected in 69 non-Western cultures and found evidence of same-sex sexual behavior in 41% of them. Taken as a whole, these data suggest that same-sex behavior, while rarer than male–female sexual behavior, is likely not limited to any particular type of culture.

Some scholars propose that exposure to Western ideas, norms, and attitudes can have an impact on the sexual behaviors of non-Western societies. For instance, one large-scale survey in Thailand showed substantial differences in sexual behaviors as a function of rapid urbanization (Techasrivichien et al., 2016). Younger respondents, compared with older generations, reported engaging in sexual activity at a younger age, had sex with more partners, and had more sexual intercourse outside of marriage. Moreover, among the older generations, men consistently displayed more permissive sexual behavior (e.g., more sex partners and more sex outside marriage) than women, but these sex differences shrank substantially or disappeared among the younger respondents. This suggests that exposure to urbanization corresponded with reductions in *sexual double standards* (norms that allow greater sexual freedom in men than in women). Why do you think that increases in urbanization correlate with the adoption of less conservative sexual attitudes and behaviors?

Complexity of Sexual Orientation

Why distinguish between identity, motivation, and behavior when defining sexual orientation? Most discussions of sexual orientation in popular media and academic literature refer solely to people's identity as gay, straight, or bisexual, without considering the different dimensions of sexual orientation separately. But the use of these three category labels implies that people experience their sexual orientation in a unified, consistent manner, which is not necessarily true. For instance, in Laumann et al.'s (1994) study, among respondents who reported *any* same-sex sexuality, there was little correspondence among the dimensions of identity, desire, and behavior. While about half of these people reported same-sex desire without corresponding same-sex behavior or same-sex identity, about a fifth of them reported same-sex behavior without same-sex desire or same-sex identity. Think about what this means. Some heterosexual-identified people feel same-sex desire without acting on it while others experience same-sex sexual behavior without adopting a same-sex sexual identity. Similarly, some gay-, lesbian-, and bisexual-identified people report (a) same-sex desire without same-sex behavior, (b) other-sex behavior with or without other-sex desire, or (c) some other combination of desire and behavior. Thus, people who report same-sex sexuality on any dimension commonly experience incongruity among the dimensions.

To examine the complexity of sexual orientation further, Weinrich and Klein (2002) asked over 1,400 U.S. adults to rate themselves on seven dimensions. These dimensions were (1) their own sexual identity, (2) the sexual identity of people they spend time with, and the sex or sexes of people (3) toward whom they feel sexual attraction, (4) about whom they have sexual fantasies, (5) with whom they share sexual behavior, (6) with whom they fall in love, and (7) with whom they socialize. Their findings revealed five distinct subtypes of sexual orientation: heterosexual, gay/lesbian, bi-heterosexual, bi-bisexual, and bi-gay/lesbian. Each of these subtypes comprised a unique and specific pattern of identity, motivation, and behavior. Other examinations yield similar distinct subtypes of sexual orientation that fall somewhere between gay and straight (Worthington & Reynolds, 2009). Finally, Lisa Diamond finds evidence for sexual orientation subtypes that reflect the fluidity versus stability of the identity rather than the sex or gender of the people toward whom attraction is directed. For instance, Diamond finds distinctions between stable lesbians, fluid lesbians, fluid bisexual women, and unlabeled bisexual women (L. M. Diamond, 2005, 2008). These analyses highlight the need for more nuanced understandings of sexual orientation that go beyond a simple, three-category system.

Stop and Think

How do you think researchers should define sexual orientation? Should they rely on people's self-labels alone? Or their behaviors or desires? Does one of these aspects more clearly represent sexual orientation than the others? Should researchers measure all of them? Why or why not?

How Does Sexual Orientation Develop?

Given the complexity of sexual orientation, how do people come to think of themselves as gay, straight, polysexual, asexual, or something else? At what age do people start to develop a sense of themselves as sexual beings, and how do they make sense of these experiences? According to phase models, most people proceed sequentially through a similar series of phases as they discover and internalize a sexual identity. In these sections, we will summarize these phase models as well as other models that focus more on milestones or narrative themes.

Phase Models of Sexual Identity Development

Phase models of sexual identity development: Models that posit distinct phases of emotional, psychological, social, and behavioral experiences that mark transitions in self-knowledge as people develop a sexual identity.

According to **phase models** (summarized in Figure 9.1), sexual identity development consists of distinct emotional, psychological, social, and behavioral phases that mark important transitions in self-knowledge and self-definition. Note, however, that these phases do not occur in the same order for all people, nor does everyone experience all phases. That said, many sexual minority individuals experience an early phase of *awareness* during which they recognize a sense of differentness from others and first realize that people can differ in sexual orientation (Fassinger & Miller, 1997; Worthington, Navarro, & Savoy, 2002). The awareness phase may be accompanied by feelings of confusion, fear, or bewilderment as sexual minority individuals seek to understand their private feelings and anticipate rejection or stigmatization by others. Interestingly, some heterosexual people bypass the awareness phase of identity development if their socialization within a heteronormative culture never inspires feelings of difference. In such cases, heterosexual individuals may instead experience a phase of *unexplored commitment* characterized by a lack of conscious thought about whether to adopt a heterosexual identity and, for some, an unquestioning acceptance of the privileges of heterosexuality (Worthington, Savoy, Dillon, & Vernaglia, 2002).

In the *exploration* phase, some sexual minority individuals explore same-sex attractions and erotic feelings, learn about other sexual minority people and communities, and continue to acquire more complex self-knowledge. For others, the exploration phase does not produce clear awareness and self-knowledge, perhaps due to internal or external resistance to same-sex sexuality. These individuals may then experience a phase of *identity uncertainty* during which their sexual orientation remains unclear. Heterosexual individuals in the exploration phase may actively explore and gain awareness of their attractions, sexual preferences, desired partner characteristics, and modes of sexual expression (Worthington et al., 2002). In this phase, some heterosexual people become aware of their heterosexual privilege and either question its fairness or accept it as right and just. As shown in Figure 9.1, however, some heterosexual individuals bypass the exploration phase altogether and remain in a prolonged phase of unexplored commitment.

During the *deepening and commitment* phase, information and experiences acquired through exploration lead to an increasing commitment to one's sexual identity, greater self-knowledge, and active choices about how to relate to others sexually. For sexual minority individuals, this phase often involves further involvement in an

Figure 9.1   Phase Models of Sexual Identity Development.

Phase models of sexual identity development identify distinct emotional, psychological, social, and behavioral phases that mark important transitions in self-knowledge and self-definition. Here, you can see that the phases differ slightly for lesbian, gay, and bisexual individuals; heterosexual individuals; and asexual individuals.

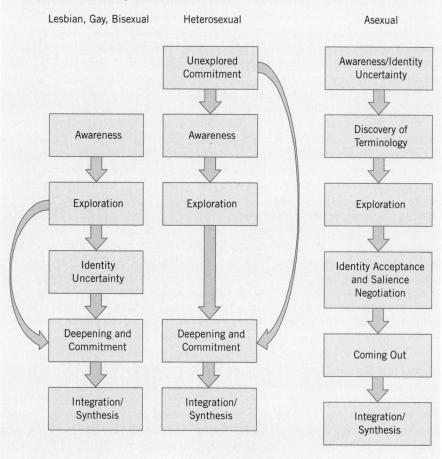

LGBTQIA+ community. For heterosexual people, this stage may involve the refinement of conscious attitudes and moral values regarding heterosexual privilege and societal treatment of sexual minority individuals. During the final phase of *integration and synthesis*, sexual identity becomes fully integrated into an overall sense of self. Individuals who reach this phase experience their sexual identity as coherent, volitional, and integrated with other valued identities, such as race and ethnicity, religious orientation, gender, physical ability, and so on.

Asexual individuals often report experiencing a comparable but slightly more elaborate series of developmental phases (Robbins, Low, & Query, 2016). Like other sexual minority individuals, many asexual people recall an awareness phase during which they realized their difference from others. However, because asexuality is not well understood and people often lack language for describing it, asexual people may experience the awareness phase as identity uncertainty (see Figure 9.1). Initially, they may pathologize their own experiences and assume that something is wrong with them. Many asexual individuals then recall a distinct *discovery of terminology* phase during which they first encounter the language with which to describe their experiences. The Internet typically plays an important role in this phase, as asexual people search out online communities (such as the Asexual Visibility and Education Network, or AVEN; http://www.asexuality.org) that validate their experiences and contribute to self-awareness. This phase then leads to the exploration phase, characterized by expanding knowledge, connections to other people and communities, and—for some asexual individuals—a tendency to embrace and internalize their asexual identity.

In the phase of *identity acceptance and salience negotiation*, asexual individuals may acknowledge and accept asexuality as a legitimate orientation and assess the centrality of asexuality to their sense of self. Some feel a strong sense of connection to this identity and derive meaning from it, while others view it as unimportant to their self-concept. Some asexual individuals may decide at this point to enter a *coming-out* phase in which they publicly label themselves and discuss their identity with others. Coming out may be especially important for those asexual individuals who are or desire to become involved in a romantic relationship. For instance, revealing their asexuality can help people to negotiate the terms of their relationships and discuss with partners whether or how much sexual activity is acceptable. Other asexual people, however, feel no need to reveal their identity to others and may therefore bypass the coming-out phase. These negotiations and decisions continue to the integration and synthesis phase, during which individuals integrate sexual identity into the self-concept as either a central or relatively peripheral aspect.

Most of the research on phase models of sexual identity development assesses primarily White samples of respondents. What about people who experience multiple oppressions associated with disadvantaged identities? One qualitative study of Middle Eastern sexual minority individuals living in the United States illustrates how religious and cultural factors can complicate the development of sexual identity. For instance, these individuals noted that Middle Eastern cultures tend to deny and erase same-sex sexuality, making it very difficult for them to understand and interpret their own private experiences during the awareness phase. Because Islam strictly prohibits same-sex sexuality, some individuals felt such incompatibility between their sexual minority identity and their Muslim identity that they underwent a prolonged phase of identity uncertainty. One woman noted being especially anxious about revealing her sexual minority status to other Middle Easterners, whom she viewed as being liable to "out" her to others for breaking strict rules about sexuality. The phases of exploration and deepening and commitment may also be complicated for many Middle Eastern sexual minorities by the lack of a visible and supportive LGBTQIA+ community with whom to connect. Several individuals described the Middle Eastern sexual minority community as invisible, small, and disjointed. For others, however, their dual identities as sexual

Milestone models of sexual identity development: Models that identify the timing, sequence, and tone of different milestones that many sexual minority individuals experience.

and ethnic minority individuals gave them a sense of resilience and strength. For instance, developing an ethnic identity as Middle Eastern in the United States helped one gay man cope with adversity as he gained awareness of his sexual minority identity. Finally, several people mentioned pride about bridging two seemingly unconnected worlds, excitement about their unique perspective on life, and a sense of responsibility to advocate for others (Ikizler & Szymanski, 2014).

Milestone and Narrative Models of Sexual Minority Identity Development

Rather than identifying phases of identity development, **milestone models** instead identify the timing, sequence, and tone of different milestones that many sexual minority individuals experience. Such milestones may include awareness of first same-sex attraction, labeling the self as a sexual minority individual, first same-sex sexual contact, and first disclosure of identity to others (Savin-Williams & Diamond, 2000). By tracking the ages and orders in which these milestones occur, researchers observe some interesting sex differences. For example, as shown in Table 9.2, sexual minority girls generally become aware of same-sex attractions, experience their first same-sex sexual contact, and label their sexual identity at a slightly older age than boys. Moreover, girls—relative to boys—more frequently experience their first same-sex attraction in emotional terms (e.g., falling in love) and have their first same-sex sexual experience in the context of a dating relationship. In contrast, boys—relative to girls—more frequently experience their first same-sex attraction as primarily sexual and have their first same-sex sexual contact with a friend or stranger. Finally, women are more likely to label themselves as sexual minorities and disclose this identity to others *before* their first same-sex sexual contact, whereas men are more likely to label themselves and disclose to others *after* their first sexual contact. These sex differences may reflect gender socialization patterns that encourage girls to prioritize the emotional components of sex and to confine sexual activity to relationship contexts while boys experience greater freedom to prioritize the pleasurable (e.g., purely physical and nonemotional) aspects of sex and to pursue sex without love.

Finally, the **narrative approach** to sexual identity development broadly considers how multiple sources of oppression and pride interact to shape identity within specific contexts. For instance, one qualitative analysis within this approach groups relevant life experiences into classes of *socializing structures* (SSs) and *individual decisions and actions* (IDAs). SSs include social contexts and institutions that either empower or disempower sexual identity development, including family, friends, workplaces, community, religion, and culture. Within such contexts, sexual minority individuals often report experiencing contradictory forces, such as invisibility and support or hostility and celebration. IDAs include private experiences, such as discovering one's sexuality, labeling the self and

Some Muslim sexual minority individuals feel that their religious and cultural background erases and silences their sexual minority identity. Here, Muslim people participate in the Gay Pride Parade in London in 2011 to bring visibility to their intersecting identities.

Source: Fæ [CC BY-SA 3.0 (http:// creativecommons.org/ licenses/by-sa/3.0)], via Wikimedia Commons

Narrative approach to sexual identity development: An approach that broadly considers how multiple sources of oppression and pride interact to shape sexual identity within specific contexts.

Table 9.2 **Sexual Identity Milestones.** Developmental psychologists note sex differences in the ages and contexts of various milestones among sexual minority youths. Girls tend to experience same-sex sexuality at somewhat older ages than boys, and girls' first same-sex experiences tend to occur in more emotional and romantic and less purely sexual contexts than boys'.

Milestone	Girls/Women	Boys/Men
First same-sex attraction	9.0 years	7.7 years
First same-sex sexual contact	16.4 years	14.1 years
First self-labeling	17.6 years	16.4 years
First disclosure	17.9 years	17.9 years
Self-label occurred before first sexual contact	80%	49%
First sexual contact occurred before self-label	20%	51%
First same-sex attraction was sexual	44%	69%
First same-sex attraction was emotional	40%	7%
First same-sex sexual contact was with a stranger	0%	20%
First same-sex sexual contact was with a friend	33%	64%
First same-sex sexual contact was with a romantic partner	62%	5%

Source: Savin-Williams and Diamond (2000).

disclosing to others, acquiring and sharing knowledge, becoming an activist, and finding inspiration through creative works. These classes of experiences jointly influence each other in a nonlinear and flexible manner, with both of them shaped strongly by national and racial background (D. N. Shapiro, Rios, & Stewart, 2010).

Stop and Think

While phase models identify common phases that presumably unfold sequentially for most people, milestone models identify the timing of important turning points, and narrative models focus on broad themes of similarity and difference within specific contexts. Which of these approaches do you think does the best job of describing sexual orientation development? If you identify with a sexual orientation, how did you experience the development of this part of yourself? Do you view your own development more in terms of phases, milestones, or contextual themes? If you were going to study sexual identity development, which approach would you adopt? Why?

Why Do People Differ in Sexual Orientation?

Why do people differ in sexual orientation? Are people born with an unchangeable sexual orientation, or do life experiences shape our sexuality? The truth is we do not yet have a definitive answer to these questions, but there is no shortage of theories. Most contemporary approaches view biology and genes as playing essential roles while also considering the roles of social factors, such as environments and life experiences. In the following sections, we cover several influential theories of sexual orientation. (These are also summarized for you in Table 9.3.)

Table 9.3 **Theories of Sexual Orientation.** Theories of sexual orientation range from primarily biological to integrative (combining biological and sociocultural factors).

Theoretical Approach	Main Concepts	Primary Assumptions	Evaluation of Evidence
Behavioral genetics	Genes, heritability estimates	Genetic differences among people account for a moderate proportion of the population variance in adults' sexual orientation, and heritability of sexual orientation is somewhat stronger among men than women.	There is strong empirical support for a role of genes in sexual orientation differences, but no evidence of any nongenetic factors that must also contribute.
Neurohormonal theory	Testosterone, estradiol, sexual differentiation	Fetuses of any sex that are exposed prenatally to male-typical levels of sex hormones will prefer female partners at puberty; those exposed to female-typical levels of sex hormones will prefer male partners at puberty.	Most research supporting the theory comes from animal studies, but the little available human data are consistent with the theory.
Fraternal birth order effect	Older male siblings, antigens	The more older biological brothers a man has, the higher his likelihood of identifying as gay. Male fetuses emit antigens that evoke a maternal immune response, which grows stronger with each male fetus. Eventually, the mother's immune response disrupts typical male fetal development.	There is strong evidence of the birth order effect itself, but little evidence for its explanation (male fetuses emit antigens that evoke maternal immune responses).
Alliance formation hypothesis	Genes, reciprocal altruism	Same-sex sexual activity between primate friend pairs increases likelihood of friends assisting and defending each other, which increases likelihood of passing on genes that code for same-sex sexual behavior.	Evidence is based on nonhuman primates, and relevance to humans is speculative.

(Continued)

Table 9.3 (Continued)

Theoretical Approach	Main Concepts	Primary Assumptions	Evaluation of Evidence
Kin selection theory	Genes, altruism	Gay men provide above-average levels of child-rearing assistance to their siblings, thus increasing the survival of nephews and nieces and passing along genes that code for male same-sex orientation.	The theory explains male but not female same-sex orientation, and evidence is largely speculative.
Fecundity hypothesis	Genes, fecundity (tendency to bear children)	Biological mothers and aunts of gay men bear more children than do mothers and aunts of heterosexual men, thus passing along genes that code for male same-sex orientation.	Evidence of increased fecundity among female relatives of gay men is strong, but the theory does not explain why this occurs, and it only addresses male (not female) same-sex orientation.
Tipping point theory	Genes, communal traits	Groups of genes that code for same-sex sexuality also code for communal traits (in men) and agentic traits (in women). These traits increase the likelihood that genetic relatives of gay men and lesbians will have mating success, thus passing along genes that code for same-sex orientation.	There is solid evidence that men with more communal traits and women with more agentic traits have more sexual partners, but genetic evidence that personality traits are linked to sexual orientation is lacking.
Biobehavioral model	Love, desire, passionate friendships	The biological and behavioral links between love and desire are bidirectional, meaning that love can lead to desire and desire can lead to love. Conditions of prolonged sex segregation combined with proximity, intimacy, and touch can lead people to develop passionate friendships that evolve into novel sexual desires.	Most research supporting the theory comes from animal studies, but the available human data are consistent with the theory.

Biological Theories

Early sexologists Richard von Krafft-Ebing (1886/1998) and Havelock Ellis (1915) theorized a biological basis of sexual orientation, but it would be decades before scientific methods advanced to the point where researchers could test these ideas in a rigorous manner. Now, we have substantial evidence that biological factors shape the emergence and direction of sexual orientation. In terms of genes, a large body of evidence indicates that sexual orientation is moderately heritable—and somewhat more so among men than

Sidebar 9.3: Can Family Dynamics Shape Sexual Orientation?

For the first half of the 20th century, Sigmund Freud's psychoanalytic theory was the "go-to" theory for explaining sexual orientation. The theory stated that family dynamics that occurred during a critical phase early in life (between the ages of 3 and 5) shaped a person's sexual orientation. In most cases, family experiences during this phase lead children to develop as heterosexual through a process of *identification* with the same-sex (presumably heterosexual) parent. In some cases, however, a boy might develop a same-sex orientation if he has a domineering mother and an absent or passive father; a girl might develop a same-sex orientation if her father disappoints her deeply (S. Freud, 1920). In support of the psychoanalytic perspective, Irving Bieber and his colleagues (1962) reported that larger proportions of gay than straight adult men recalled overcontrolling mothers and detached or rejecting fathers in childhood. However, critics noted flaws in Bieber's work, and many attempts at replication over the years failed to offer any evidence that family dynamics early in a child's life play a role in sexual orientation (Hooker, 1969; Whitam & Zent, 1984). While Freud's ideas about the causes of sexual orientation are creative and provocative, those who seek evidence-based explanations will have to look elsewhere.

among women. Heritability estimates for sexual orientation suggest that genes account for 14%–67% of the population variance in men's sexual orientation and 8%–30% of the population variance in women's sexual orientation (J. M. Bailey, Dunne, & Martin, 2000; Burri, Spector, & Rahman, 2015). Any remaining variance in sexual orientation, beyond that accounted for by genes, must reflect nongenetic factors.

Another biological approach—the neurohormonal approach—posits that fetal exposure to sex hormones, particularly *testosterone* and *estradiol*, plays an important role in the development of sexual orientation (L. Ellis & Ames, 1987). As you may recall from Chapter 3 ("The Nature and Nurture of Sex and Gender"), the fetal brain and nervous system undergo a process of sexual differentiation between the second and fifth months of gestation, and this relies heavily on production of and exposure to sex hormones. Genes that code for biological sex guide the levels of these hormones, but other factors can also influence whether a fetus gets exposed to female-typical or male-typical levels of hormones. The neurohormonal approach proposes that fetuses (of any sex) that get exposed to female-typical hormone levels will display a preference for male sexual partners at puberty, and those exposed to male-typical levels will display a preference for female partners at puberty. In most cases, this process results in heterosexual orientations, but in some cases, it results in same-sex orientations.

The **fraternal birth order effect**, another biological approach, posits prenatal causes of sexual orientation. This effect refers to the positive correlation that exists between the number of older brothers a man has and his own likelihood of identifying as gay. In over a dozen different samples, Ray Blanchard and his colleagues observed that a man's odds of identifying as gay in adulthood increase by about 33% with every additional older,

Fraternal birth order effect:
Positive correlation between the number of older brothers a man has and his likelihood of identifying as gay.

biological brother that he has (Blanchard, 2001). Interestingly, this effect is exclusive to men: Older sisters are not associated with the sexual orientation of later-born sons, and lesbian identification does not correlate with the number of older siblings of any sex that a woman has. The effect also does not apply to adopted older male siblings, indicating that it does not reflect primarily environmental factors. Blanchard's explanation is that male—but not female—fetuses emit an *antigen* (a foreign substance) that evokes a maternal immune response, and this response grows stronger with each subsequent male fetus that a mother carries. In other words, the mother's body treats each male fetus as a foreign invader and activates an immune response against it. After carrying a certain number of male fetuses, the mother's body produces enough antibodies to prevent the fetal brain from developing in a male-typical fashion, resulting in male same-sex sexuality. But why would this happen? Some speculate that this maternal immune response evolved because it reduces the likelihood that later-born sons will compete against their brothers for access to limited mates (E. M. Miller, 2000). While provocative and interesting, this hypothesis remains speculative.

Evolutionary Theories

As discussed in previous chapters, evolutionary theories seek to identify how tendencies observed today might reflect genetically heritable adaptations to ancestral environments. While evolutionary and biological theories both focus on the role of genes in transmitting human traits, evolutionary approaches tend to focus more on big-picture explanations for why people inherit certain tendencies in the first place. Because people with a same-sex orientation reproduce at lower rates than heterosexual people (Iemmola & Ciani, 2009), some question how the genes that code for same-sex sexuality get transmitted. And yet, both female–female and male–male sexual behavior is evident in over 450 animal species around the world (Bagemihl, 1999), including 33 different primate species. So how do same-sex orientations get passed on?

One evolutionary explanation, termed the **alliance formation hypothesis**, argues that same-sex sexual activity promotes beneficial friendship bonds between unrelated primate pairs. For instance, friend pairs who bond through same-sex sexual activity are more likely to display *reciprocal altruism*, meaning that they more frequently risk their own safety or expend their own resources to assist and defend one another (Vasey, 1993). If such behavior increases survival rates, then it should get transmitted genetically from one generation to the next (provided that these individuals also engage in heterosexual mating). Although this hypothesis derives from studies of nonhumans, Kirkpatrick (2000) proposes that the same logic applies to human same-sex sexual activity as well. This hypothesis remains speculative, however.

Another evolutionary hypothesis explains male same-sex sexuality as a form of **kin selection**. In this view, male same-sex sexuality persists in the gene pool because the benefits that same-sex-oriented individuals bestow on their genetic relatives offset the costs to them of not reproducing. Specifically, if a gay man provides larger-than-average amounts of child-rearing assistance to his siblings, thereby increasing the likelihood that his nieces and nephews will survive and pass on their genes, then the genes that code for same-sex sexuality will get transmitted. This hypothesis receives no support in Western cultures, including the United States, United Kingdom, and Canada (Bobrow & Bailey, 2001;

Alliance formation hypothesis: The hypothesis that same-sex sexual activity is adaptive because it promotes emotional bonds and facilitates survival and resource sharing between pairs of friends.

Kin selection: Helping behavior that is costly to the helper in the short term but beneficial in the long term because it increases the survival likelihood of the helper's genetic relatives.

Rahman & Hull, 2005). However, Vasey and his colleagues find support for it among the fa'afafine of Samoa. As we have discussed, the fa'afafine—individuals who are assigned male at birth but display female-typical interests and play preferences in childhood—are socialized to fill a female gender role. In adulthood, they show higher levels of altruism toward nieces and nephews than do heterosexual men and women (Vasey & VanderLaan, 2009). Note that fa'afafine individuals are generally culturally valued and respected, whereas gay men raised in Western cultures often face stigma, and this difference

Two fa'afafine friends.

Source: Education Images/Universal Media Group/Getty Images

may help to explain why the kin selection hypothesis receives support in Samoa but not in Western cultures. Male same-sex sexuality could have evolved via kin selection if ancestral societies typically responded to impending male homosexuality—that is, childhood cues such as female-typical play preferences—by socializing boys to fulfill unique and valued social roles (VanderLaan, Ren, & Vasey, 2013). In other words, because growing up gay in a Western culture that devalues and stigmatizes one's sexual identity is relatively less likely to foster the sort of consistent, family-oriented altruism that we observe in Samoa, it is difficult to detect evidence of the kin selection hypothesis in Western cultures.

Genes for male same-sex sexuality may also pass down if the relatives of sexual minority individuals are especially *fecund*, or likely to reproduce. Consistent with this **fecundity hypothesis**, the biological mothers and aunts of gay men tend to have more children than the biological mothers and aunts of heterosexual men (Iemmola & Ciani, 2009). Since men share many genes with their mothers and aunts, these women's heightened fecundity likely keeps the genes that code for same-sex sexuality in the population.

The **tipping point theory** uses a similar logic. This theory posits a group of genes that together code for same-sex sexuality in men and that genes in this group also code for communal personality tendencies, such as kindness and sensitivity. Some men inherit the genes for communal personality but remain heterosexual, and because communal traits are desirable to women, these men have a reproductive advantage over their peers: Their desirable personalities increase their mating opportunities, and they pass on their genes with relative success. Men who inherit many of these genes, however, reach a tipping point at which their own mate preferences become reversed, and they demonstrate a same-sex orientation (E. M. Miller, 2000). In partial support of this theory, heterosexual men who possess more communal traits do tend to have more female sexual partners (Zietsch et al., 2008), suggesting that they are highly attractive to women.

Tipping point logic may also explain female same-sex sexuality. Andrea Burri and her colleagues found that reports of having more agentic personality traits in childhood predicted both same-sex attraction and larger numbers of sexual partners in adult women (Burri et al., 2015). Moreover, Burri proposes that common genetic factors influence all three of these factors (personality, adult same-sex attraction, and number of

Fecundity hypothesis: The hypothesis that genes for same-sex sexuality get passed on genetically because the female relatives of gay men produce many offspring.

Tipping point theory: The theory that genes for same-sex sexuality get passed on because the same-sex relatives of gay and lesbian people have personalities that increase their likelihood of engaging in reproductive sex.

sexual partners). Thus, genes that code for lesbian sexual orientation may also code for agentic personalities and a tendency to pursue more sexual partners. Importantly, the links between agentic personality and more sexual partners emerge among both lesbian and heterosexual women. If heterosexual women who share genes with lesbians (such as their sisters) have more reproductive sex with men, then the genes that code for same-sex sexuality in women will remain in the gene pool.

Stop and Think

Note that most (though not all) of the theories summarized in this section focus on explaining same-sex sexual orientation rather than heterosexuality. Why do you think this is? What (if anything) does this reveal about the perspectives and assumptions of the researchers? Do you think that heterosexuality requires as much explanation as same-sex sexuality does? Why or why not?

The Integrative Approach

Biobehavioral model: A model that proposes that the links between romantic love and sexual desire are bidirectional and that prolonged proximity and touch in sex-segregated environments can lead people to develop novel sexual attractions.

Integrative approaches—reflecting a theme you have seen throughout this book—consider how biological and social-environmental factors jointly contribute to the development and experience of sexual orientation. For example, Lisa Diamond's (2003) **biobehavioral model** proposes that the links between love and desire are bidirectional, meaning that just as people can fall in love with others for whom they first feel sexual desire, people can also develop sexual desire for people with whom they first fall in love. This model particularly helps explain how people develop novel sexual attractions, as in the case of a woman who identifies as heterosexual but develops feelings of sexual desire for another woman at some point past puberty. According to Diamond, this type of novel sexual attraction is relatively rare but may occur under conditions of prolonged physical proximity, social intimacy, and touch. These conditions often present themselves in sex-segregated environments during adolescence and early adulthood, such as in boarding schools, sororities, fraternities, athletic teams, prisons, and the military. In such environments, people may form intense, *passionate friendships* with same-sex peers that are indistinguishable—in terms of behavior, emotion, and neurological processes—from romantic love. Historians and anthropologists have noted these passionate friendships between heterosexual youth in ancient Greece, Native American cultures, Africa, Melanesia, Samoa, Guatemala, and contemporary Western cultures.

According to Lisa Diamond (2003), passionate friendships reflect the operation of the attachment system, which helps people become attached to others with whom they share closeness and touch. However, since the attachment system is not intrinsically oriented toward persons of any particular sex, and the attachment and sexual mating systems share similar underlying neurological mechanisms (see Table 9.1), passionate same-sex friendships can grow into feelings of sexual desire. Diamond proposes that this model can help explain the experiences of both heterosexual and gay- or lesbian-identified people who unexpectedly develop feelings of sexual attraction toward persons of the sex that does not typically attract them.

Evaluation of Theories

So which theory does the best job of explaining sexual orientation? Unfortunately, there is no simple answer to this question. Both biological and environmental factors shape the development of sexual orientation, but researchers do not fully understand the precise ways in which these factors interact. And while some of the theories summarized here have empirical support, none of them explains all of the variance in sexual orientation. Moreover, although most of these theories assume that social and environmental factors explain at least some of the variance in sexual orientations, none of them—save for Lisa Diamond's (2003) biobehavioral model and Freud's outdated and debunked psychoanalytic explanation (see Sidebar 9.3)—specifies what these social and environmental factors might be. Finally, you may have noticed an overall tendency for many theories to focus more on explaining male than female sexual orientation. Why might this be? Do you think this pattern reflects the androcentric bias that plagues much of psychology's history? Or alternatively, perhaps male sexual orientation is easier to explain than female sexual orientation for some reason?

How Do Sex and Gender Contribute to the Experience of Sexuality?

People commonly believe that women—compared with men—desire fewer sexual partners, have less interest in casual sex, and are more selective in choosing sexual partners and mates. Recall from our discussions of *parental investment theory* (see Chapter 3, "The Nature and Nurture of Sex and Gender," and Chapter 5, "The Contents and Origins of Gender Stereotypes") that evolutionary theories locate the origins of this sex difference in evolved tendencies. Because women invest more than men do in gestating and caring for offspring, they should have evolved a tendency to be sexually reserved, highly selective, and uninterested in casual sexual encounters that might leave them pregnant.

But are women less interested than men in casual sex? Terri Conley and her collaborators think not. In fact, Conley considers many popular beliefs about gender and sexuality to be myths that do not hold up to scrutiny (Conley, Moors, Matsick, Ziegler, & Valentine, 2011). Think about the stereotype that men are relatively unselective when it comes to choosing sexual partners. According to this view, the average heterosexual man who walks into a room full of potential dates will find more of them desirable as sexual partners than will the average heterosexual woman. But Finkel and Eastwick (2009) questioned whether this really reflects an evolved, biological sex difference or whether it can be explained by gender norms. Specifically, they asked whether the simple act of approaching a potential partner, as opposed to being approached, might explain men's attraction to a wider range of partners. To examine this, the researchers randomly assigned women and men at heterosexual "speed-dating" events to play the roles of either rotators (daters who walked from date to date) or sitters (daters who remained seated and got approached by multiple dates). Each person had 4-minute dates with approximately 12 different other-sex partners, after which they rated their sexual attraction to each partner. When men rotated and women did not, men reported more sexual attraction to their partners than women did. However, as shown in Figure 9.2, when women rotated and men did not, the sex difference in sexual attraction disappeared—women and men reported equal attraction to their partners. Thus, given the social norm that men rather than women should approach potential dates, men may exhibit greater sexual interest than women because of their role as "the suitor" in dating contexts and not because of an evolved tendency.

In a similar vein, Conley and her collaborators describe several sex differences in sexuality that people commonly accept as fact, and then, they systematically debunk each "fact" by pointing out conditions under which it fails to emerge (Conley et al., 2011). These are summarized in Table 9.4. What do you think about these beliefs and their alternative interpretations? In the sections that follow, we will consider several aspects of sexuality for which sex differences do—and do not—emerge.

Sexual Behavior and Attitudes

Petersen and Hyde (2010) conducted a meta-analysis of sex differences in sexuality from 1993 through 2007 to determine whether men truly are the more sexual sex. They reviewed research on 14 different sexual behaviors (e.g., vaginal, anal, and oral sex; masturbation; pornography use; and cybersex), and 16 sexual attitudes (e.g., attitudes about casual sex, extramarital sex, and same-sex sexuality). Overall, men reported more

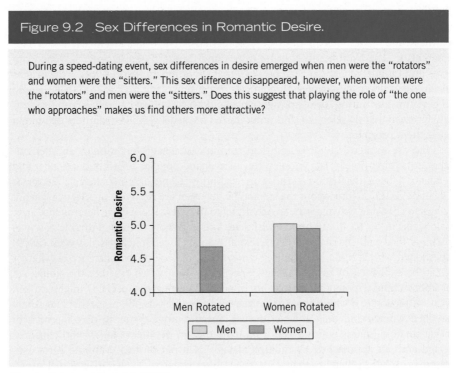

Figure 9.2   Sex Differences in Romantic Desire.

During a speed-dating event, sex differences in desire emerged when men were the "rotators" and women were the "sitters." This sex difference disappeared, however, when women were the "rotators" and men were the "sitters." Does this suggest that playing the role of "the one who approaches" makes us find others more attractive?

Source: Finkel and Eastwick (2009).

Table 9.4 **Sex Differences in Sexuality?** Terri Conley and her collaborators summarized several sex differences in relationship preferences and sexuality that have been widely replicated and are commonly accepted as fact (Conley et al., 2011). They then systematically debunked each "fact" by pointing out conditions under which it fails to emerge. What do you think about these beliefs and alternative interpretations?

Common Belief	Alternative Finding/Interpretation
Women and men have sex-specific preferences for qualities in long-term mates.	Sex differences in preferences for attractiveness and status disappear when considering actual (rather than ideal) partners.
Men desire more sexual partners than women do over their lifetime.	Sex differences in desire for sexual partners disappear when you look at *median*, rather than *mean*, number of desired partners. This suggests that the sex difference that is typically observed reflects outliers—that is, relatively few men who report unusually large numbers of desired sex partners drive up men's mean desired partners.
Men actually have more sexual partners than women do over their lifetime.	Sex differences in reported numbers of actual sex partners disappear when respondents believe they are connected to a lie detector.
Women orgasm less frequently than men do, reflecting a weaker biological sex drive than men's.	Women orgasm substantially less than men in casual hookups, but the sex difference in orgasm rates is vastly reduced in the context of established relationships in which male partners are more likely to provide clitoral stimulation to women during sex.
Men are more open to casual sex than women are, reflecting their greater interest in sex.	Sex differences in willingness to have casual sex disappear when the casual sex partner is believed to be "good in bed" and when women do not expect to be "slut shamed" for having casual sex.
Women are choosier than men in picking mates.	Sex differences in pickiness disappear when women play the role of "suitor" (approaching men in a dating context), suggesting that pickiness is less about one's biological sex than it is about gender norms that typically cast men in the "suitor" role.

Source: Conley, Moors, Matsick, Ziegler, and Valentine (2011).

sexual experience than women did on 13 of the 14 behaviors, but most of the effects were in the small range ($ds < 0.37$), and 28% of the differences were in the close-to-zero range. Men also reported more permissive attitudes about sex than women on 9 of 16 measures, but again, the effects were mostly small, and 31% of them were close to zero. The only medium effects that emerged were for men reporting greater frequency of casual sex, masturbation, and pornography use and more favorable attitudes toward casual sex. In contrast, women were more likely than men to report same-sex sexual experiences (with a close-to-zero effect size, $d = -0.05$) and more favorable attitudes about sex accompanied by emotional commitment. They also reported stronger support for sexual minority rights and same-sex marriage. Again, however, these effects were small. Finally, sex differences in adolescents' reported rates of sexual intercourse have decreased somewhat over time, due primarily to decreases in adolescent boys' reports of intercourse. Summarizing across all of these patterns, Petersen and Hyde concluded that the sexes are more similar than different when it comes to sexual behavior and attitudes, and this similarity increases with time. This may remind you of the finding described earlier, in which young women and men in Thailand show smaller sex differences in sexual behavior than the older generations do (Techasrivichien et al., 2016).

Debate

Who do you think has a stronger sex drive, men or women? Stereotypes usually portray men as the more lustful sex, but researchers disagree on whether men actually have a stronger sex drive or whether women and men have similar sex drives. Here we define sex drive as the motivation or desire to engage in sexual activity (Baumeister, Catanese, & Vohs, 2001). Let's consider the arguments for both positions.

Yes, Men Have a Stronger Sex Drive

Evidence for a stronger male sex drive comes from a variety of sources. Men self-report having a stronger sex drive than women do, and this pattern emerges across cultures (Lippa, 2009; Schmitt, 2005). Men also report thinking about sex more often than women do (Fischtein, Herold, & Desmarais, 2007). In one study, college men and women reported all of their sexual thoughts and fantasies over 7 days (J. C. Jones & Barlow, 1990). Men reported an average of eight thoughts per day while women reported about five thoughts per day.

On average, men report wanting to have sex more often than women do. Heterosexual men report desiring sex more frequently than heterosexual women do, in both dating and marriage relationships (Willoughby, Farero, & Busby, 2014; Willoughby & Vitas, 2012). Same-sex couples show the same pattern, with gay male couples reporting more frequent sex than lesbian couples (Blair & Pukall, 2014). Men also tend to seek greater sexual variety. When questioned about their ideal number of sexual partners, men report wanting more partners than women, on average (Pedersen, Miller, Putcha-Bhagavatula, & Yang, 2002). Men also tend to have more positive attitudes toward casual sex compared with women, and they report masturbating more frequently than women (Petersen & Hyde, 2010). Across the world, men are much more likely than women to pay for commercial sexual services, prostitutes, and other erotic entertainment (Hakim, 2015). Taken as a whole, these studies provide compelling evidence that men have a stronger sex drive than women.

No, Men Do Not Necessarily Have a Stronger Sex Drive

Much research on sexual attitudes and behaviors relies on people's self-reports. Because a pervasive double standard exists, such that people tend to admire men for being sexual and stigmatize women for it, women may be reluctant to acknowledge the strength of their sex drive. Thus, women likely underreport their sexual desires, fantasies, and behavior while men may exaggerate theirs. To test this, one study asked people to report the frequency of various sexual behaviors, such as masturbation and watching pornography. When people thought that the experimenter might view their responses, men reported substantially more sexual behavior than women. But when people thought that they were connected to a "lie detector" that could determine the truthfulness of their answers, women and men reported more similar rates of sexual behavior (M. G. Alexander & Fisher, 2003).

Although men do report thinking about sex somewhat more often than women do, they also report thinking more often than women do about other bodily needs, such as food and sleep (T. D. Fisher, Moore, & Pittenger, 2012). This indicates that men may focus more on their bodily needs in general. In contrast, women may be more inclined to ignore their bodily needs, possibly due to widespread experiences with objectification (T. A. Roberts & Pennebaker, 1995; you'll read more about this in Chapter 13, "Gender and Psychological Health").

What about men's reported desire for more partners than women? While true that, on average, men report wanting more sexual partners than women do, this is misleading. The distributions of desired sexual partners are highly skewed,

meaning that a small number of men report extremely high numbers, and this inflates the statistical mean for men. When we look at the median values instead—the values that fall at the 50th percentile of each distribution—we see that women and men both claim to desire just one partner over the next 30 years (Pedersen et al., 2002). Thus, most men and women have similar desires.

The findings that men want more sexual activity and more casual sex than women may also be misleading. For example, while gay male couples do report having sex more frequently than lesbian couples, lesbian couples report having sexual encounters that last longer than those of gay male and heterosexual couples (Blair & Pukall, 2014). Thus, if one considers not just frequency but duration of sex, men's tendency toward more sexual activity goes away. Furthermore, women express as much willingness to accept casual sex offers as men if they believe that the potential sex partner is "a great lover" (Conley, 2011). Also, women may turn down casual sex offers to avoid slut shaming, not because of a low sex drive (Conley et al., 2011).

In short, many of the findings of greater male sex drive are based on potentially unreliable self-reports. Furthermore, sex differences can be diminished or eliminated when researchers look at median values rather than means or take into account factors like duration of sexual encounters, expected pleasure, and concerns about stigma.

What do you think? Which evidence do you find most and least convincing? Why?

Orgasm Frequency and Sexual Satisfaction

Having an orgasm during sexual activity is a strong predictor of overall sexual satisfaction (Haning et al., 2007), and orgasm frequency predicts not only sexual satisfaction but also relationship satisfaction for heterosexual, lesbian, and bisexual women, as well as for heterosexual men (Frederick, St. John, Garcia, & Lloyd, 2017). Orgasm rates do not appear to differ between White, Latino, Black, Asian, or Native American young adults (A. M. Galinsky & Sonenstein, 2011), but they differ consistently by sex: Women orgasm less frequently than men in the context of heterosexual sexual activity, a phenomenon referred to as the **orgasm gap** . For example, in an investigation of over 2,600 college students reporting on their most recent *hookup* (defined as a casual sexual encounter with someone who is not one's relationship partner), 70% of men and 34% of women had an orgasm during vaginal intercourse (England, Shafer, & Fogarty, 2008). As shown in Figure 9.3, the size of the orgasm gap during hookups differs by type of sexual activity, but in each case, men orgasm at higher rates than women do.

Several factors, both biological and social, affect orgasm frequency. For instance, some research indicates that genes explain about 31% of the population variance in women's rates of orgasm during sexual intercourse (Dawood, Kirk, Bailey, Andrews, & Martin, 2005). This may occur because genes affect the distance between the clitoris and the vaginal opening (Wallen & Lloyd, 2011). For women with a larger distance, the clitoris receives less stimulation during heterosexual intercourse, and clitoral stimulation directly relates to orgasm for women.

In terms of social factors, the sex of women's sexual partners also plays a role in orgasm rates. Reports that they "usually or always" orgasm during sexual intimacy are made by 65% of heterosexual women, compared with 86% of lesbian women, 95%

Orgasm gap: The tendency for women to have lower rates of orgasm than men during heterosexual sexual encounters.

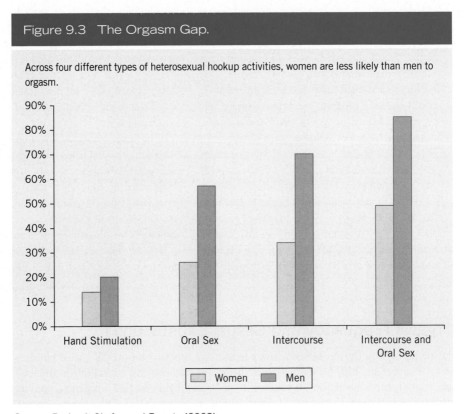

Figure 9.3   The Orgasm Gap.

Across four different types of heterosexual hookup activities, women are less likely than men to orgasm.

Source: England, Shafer, and Fogarty (2008).

of heterosexual men, and 89% of gay men (Frederick et al., 2017). In other words, women orgasm relatively less frequently during sexual encounters with men than during sexual encounters with other women. However, the heterosexual orgasm gap is smaller in the context of established relationships than in hookups because men in relationships more frequently engage in foreplay activities that produce clitoral stimulation (Armstrong, England, & Fogarty, 2009). For instance, receiving oral sex predicts orgasm among heterosexual, lesbian, and bisexual women (Frederick et al., 2017), but women receive oral sex less often than men do from hookup partners. Similarly, for heterosexual and bisexual (but not lesbian) women, the duration of sexual encounters correlates positively with orgasm frequency. Therefore, if sexual activity during the average hookup does not last very long, then the likelihood of women orgasming will be decreased. Finally, women who know the location of their clitoris more frequently orgasm during masturbation than women who lack such knowledge (L. D. Wade, Kremer, & Brown, 2005). Thus, women's knowledge of their clitoris and both the time and attention that their partners spend on this body part contribute significantly to women's orgasm likelihood. But in the context of casual sexual relationships, women may be reluctant to share their sexual needs or request stimulation that will lead to orgasm. For instance, heterosexual women in one qualitative interview study reported not requesting clitoral stimulation during sexual activity out of fear of damaging their partner's ego (Salisbury & Fisher, 2014).

Stop and Think

Given the biological and social factors that contribute to the orgasm gap, what steps might people take to close this gap? Who bears the greatest responsibility in increasing women's orgasm rates: women, their partners, or society? Do you interpret the orgasm gap as unfair? Why or why not?

One interesting question concerns the effects (if any) of *genital reconstructive surgery* (GRS) and hormone treatments on the orgasm rates and sexual desire of transgender individuals who undergo these procedures. Small sample sizes and large variance in the findings across relevant studies make drawing conclusions about this question difficult. Moreover, many studies lack comparable data from both before and after individuals undergo treatments. However, one review of the literature concluded that MtF (male-to-female) women generally report high orgasm rates following GRS (C. Klein & Gorzalka, 2009). For instance, in a study of 232 MtF women, 85% reported achieving orgasm from either masturbation or sexual intercourse after surgery. However, the findings regarding spontaneous sexual desire, such as fantasies or thoughts about sex, vary a lot for MtF women: Some report an increase following surgery, some report a decrease, and some report no change. In contrast, FtM (female-to-male) men tend more consistently to report an increase in sexual desire, likely resulting from testosterone treatments, as well as high rates of orgasm after surgery: Between 78% and 100% of FtM men report reaching orgasm during either masturbation or intercourse after GRS.

Sexual Fluidity

As discussed earlier in this chapter, people sometimes change how they experience their sexuality or develop novel romantic or sexual feelings toward individuals of a sex that does not usually attract them. In one longitudinal study of sexual minority women, Lisa Diamond (2008) found that 67% of them exhibited **sexual fluidity** by changing how they identified their sexual orientation over a 10-year period. Another large study of transgender and gender-nonconforming adolescents found that 58% reported changes in their sexual attractions over their lives (Katz-Wise, Reisner, Hughto, & Keo-Meier, 2016). In contrast to these studies that used convenience samples, a large, nationally representative sample of emerging adults found much lower rates of sexual orientation change over time: While 7.4% of young adults changed to a more same-sex-oriented identity over time, 4.4% changed to a less same-sex-oriented identity, and 88.2% reported no change (Everett, 2015).

Interestingly, some evidence suggests that women demonstrate sexual fluidity more frequently than men. Roy Baumeister (2000) reviewed evidence collected from thousands of respondents over several decades. He found that—in comparison with men—women's sexual orientation tends to change more over their lives, and women more frequently exhibit sexual behaviors that differ from their private attitudes and feelings. For example, lesbian women consistently report more heterosexual sexual experiences than gay men, and heterosexual women report more same-sex sexual desires and experiences than heterosexual men. In general, women—more often than men—exhibit discrepancies between the identity, motivation, and behavior components of sexual orientation (Norris, Marcus, & Green, 2015). In fact, some data suggest that, relative to men, women show greater sexual response to both male and female sexual stimuli regardless of their sexual orientation. For instance, heterosexual and lesbian women become genitally aroused in response to both female *and* male sexual stimuli while heterosexual and gay men become genitally aroused only in response to the type of sexual stimuli that corresponds with their sexual orientation (Chivers, Rieger, Latty, & Bailey, 2004). Similarly, among heterosexual women, stronger sex drive predicts increased sexual attraction to both women and men, whereas among heterosexual men, stronger sex drive predicts sexual attraction to women only (Lippa, 2006).

Why might this be the case? Baumeister (2000) offers the provocative thesis that women's greater sexual fluidity reflects an adaptive response to a gender hierarchy in which they wield less power, strength, and status than men. Because men typically are stronger, more aggressive, and more dominant than women, it may have been adaptive for women to become somewhat sexually malleable in response to men's greater power. Put another way, if women have historically had less control over when and with whom they had sex, an ability to adapt fluidly to salient sexual cues may have facilitated women's survival. While intriguing, this explanation would be difficult to test empirically. How might you design a study that would definitively test its validity?

Sexual fluidity:
The tendency for people's sexual orientation or sexual identity to change across time.

How Does Sexuality Change Over the Life Course?

Sexual Trajectories

At what age do women and men reach their **sexual peak**, or the height of their interest in and enjoyment of sexual activity? People commonly assume that men reach their peak approximately 10 years younger than women. For instance, both college students and middle-aged adults estimated that men peak sexually between the ages of 19 and 24, while women peak sexually between the ages of 28 and 34 (Barr, Bryan, & Kenrick, 2002). This belief has roots in the classic work of Albert Kinsey, who wrote that men desire sexual contact most strongly in their early years while women's sexual interest grows with age (Kinsey, Pomeroy, Martin, & Gebhard, 1953). But how valid is this assumption? The answer is complicated and depends on how researchers define *sexual peak*. On a biological level, there is little evidence that the hormone levels of women and men follow different trajectories or that men's hormones peak at a younger age than women's (Baldwin & Baldwin, 1997). Moreover, in terms of sexual behavior, women and men both show similar, gradual increases in sexual activity from puberty through midlife, a plateau between the ages of 45 and 55, and then gradual declines over the next several decades (Mercer et al., 2013). This again contradicts the notion that the sexes reach their peaks at different, nonoverlapping ages.

What about in terms of sexual desire? Here, some evidence suggests that men (at least in the United States and Canada) peak slightly younger than women. As shown in Figure 9.4, men report their highest levels of lust in their late 20s, and women report their highest levels of lust a few years after that, in their early to mid-30s (Schmitt et al., 2002). Moreover, women between the ages of 27 and 45, compared to those ages 18–26 and those ages 46 or older, report stronger motivation to engage in sexual intercourse, more frequent and intense sexual fantasies, and greater willingness to have casual sex (Easton, Confer, Goetz, & Buss, 2010). These findings point to a small sex difference in sexual trajectories, with women experiencing their highest levels of sexual desire in an age range (27–45) during which fertility declines. But the pattern depicted in Figure 9.4 hardly indicates the large, 10-year gap in sexual peaks that many people presume, and some scholars caution against putting too much stock in these self-report data given that they come exclusively from Western cultures.

Regardless of when people reach their sexual peak, sexual activity tends to be highest between the ages of 16 and 44, followed by a plateau and then a gradual decline over

> **Sexual peak:**
> The height of a person's interest in, enjoyment of, or engagement in sexual activity over time.

Stop and Think

Given that there is not strong evidence of a 10-year gap in the sexual peaks of women and men, why do you think people believe this so widely? What factors contribute to perpetuating this belief, and what consequences might result from it?

Figure 9.4 Sex Differences in Lust Across Ages.

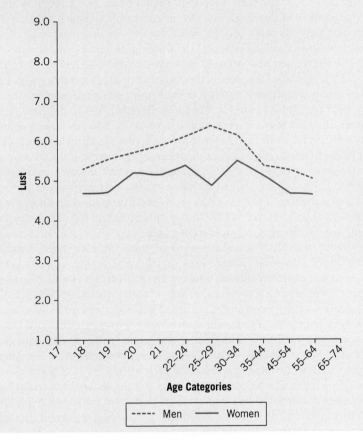

Do women and men experience a sexual peak at different ages? If we define sexual peak as self-reported lust, then men seem to peak at a slightly younger age (their late 20s) than women do (their early 30s).

Source: Schmitt, Shackleford, Duntley, and Tooke (2002).

the next several decades (Mercer et al., 2013). For instance, one longitudinal study of Singaporean couples found that rates of sexual activity declined from five to six times per month before age 55 to three times per month after the age of 55 (Goh, Tain, Tong, Mok, & Ng, 2004). Men also become less likely to orgasm during sex as they get older, regardless of sexual orientation (Frederick et al., 2017).

Corresponding to this trajectory of sexual activity over the life course, the importance of sexual health to people's overall quality of life follows a similar pattern: As people age from their 20s to early 40s, sexual health plays an increasingly important role in general quality of life. However, the importance of sexual health for quality of life declines for women and men between the ages of 50 and 80. That said, sexual satisfaction correlates with both physical and mental health across adults of different ages (K. E. Flynn et al., 2016). Moreover, studies that track adults through their 60s and 70s, across both Western and Eastern cultures, find that people who have regular sexual activity, more frequent orgasms, and more enjoyable sex also have lower mortality rates (L. M. Diamond & Huebner, 2012). Thus, while people may experience declines in sexual activity as they age, engaging in regular sexual activity still correlates with good health.

The Medicalization of Sexual Changes

Around the middle of life, adults begin to experience hormonal changes that can influence their sexual behavior and their experiences of sexuality. For women, **menopause**—the cessation of menstruation and fertility, accompanied by stable declines in estrogen levels—usually occurs between the ages of 45 and 55 (although this can vary a lot). *Perimenopause*, the phase prior to menopause, usually occurs in the early-to-mid 40s. In this phase, fertility begins to decline, estrogen levels rise and fall, and menstrual periods and ovulation may become irregular. Women's sexual desire often declines with the onset of menopause, although many people continue to have satisfying sexual activity well beyond menopause. Also, around the age of 50, men tend to lose erectile function and often report having more difficulty either achieving or maintaining an erection, a condition commonly referred to as **erectile dysfunction**. Both of these phases—menopause and the loss of erectile function—are natural and normal (if sometimes frustrating and unpleasant) physiological process. And yet, the term erectile *dysfunction* portrays men's transition as a medical illness. Similarly, the pervasive treatment of menopause with drug therapies encourages a perception of menopause as unnatural and medically problematic.

Feminist scholars have long written about the **medicalization** of sexuality, or the process whereby societies view normal, natural conditions and transitions as medical illnesses that require diagnoses and treatments. Medicalization can be problematic because it increases people's reliance on unnecessary and sometimes ill-advised treatments, makes people feel like there is something wrong with them, and casts healthy people into the role of medical patients. For instance, the medical view of menopausal women as "hormone deficient" encourages women to use hormone replacement therapies (HRTs), often consisting of estrogen or progesterone in pill or skin patch form. While members of the medical community recommend HRTs based on the claim that menopausal declines in estrogen put women at an increased risk of illnesses like heart disease, large-scale epidemiological studies instead show that some HRTs increase women's risk of developing breast cancer (V. Meyer, 2003; Million Women Study Collaborators, 2003).

The medicalization of sexuality also focuses attention on biological factors that underlie sexuality and ignores social, emotional, and cultural factors. Consider Viagra, the wildly successful "impotence drug" that hit the market in 1998. Viagra presumably solves the "problem" of erectile dysfunction through physiological means, by increasing blood flow to the penis. And yet, erections are not only a physiological phenomenon—they also reflect psychological arousal, mood and emotion, context, stimulation, culture,

Menopause: The cessation of menstruation and fertility, accompanied by stable declines in estrogen levels, that usually occurs between the ages of 45 and 55.

Erectile dysfunction: A condition characterized by loss of erectile function and difficulty achieving or maintaining an erection.

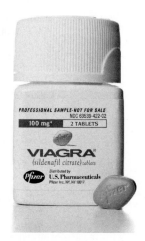

Viagra is commonly prescribed for erectile dysfunction.

Source: © iStockPhoto.com/jfmdesign

Medicalization:
The process whereby normal, natural physical conditions and transitions are viewed as medical illnesses that require diagnoses and treatments.

Sidebar 9.4: The Age-Old Search for Impotence Cures

The search for impotence cures is nothing new. Over the centuries, men have tried to improve the vigor of their sexual functioning with various remedies. Some examples include chewing on garlic and leeks (ancient Rome); drinking the secretion of Spanish fly beetles (ancient Greece); roasting and eating wolf penises (medieval Europe); having goat testicles surgically implanted into their scrotum (U.S., early 20th century); and using radium suppositories (U.S., the 1920s). Alas, none of these remedies proved reliably effective, and some—such as radioactive suppositories—likely did serious damage to men's health (Paulus, 2016).

partners, sexual techniques, and life stage (Tiefer, 2006). Not only does the medicalization of impotence reduce the complexity of erections to a single, physiological cause (i.e., blood flow), it also reduces men's sexuality to the rigidity of their erections (Tiefer, 1994). This focus on penile rigidity as the essence of men's sexuality ignores other ways in which men can and do experience sexual gratification, both with and without partners.

Declines in sexual interest and activity later in life are normal. While some people may wish to seek medical treatments to help ease them through midlife transitions, such treatments are often unnecessary, may bring health risks, and can subtly influence how people think about their own sexuality. Moreover, sexual activity—with or without medical interventions—can contribute to overall well-being and physical health well into the later decades of life. In fact, researchers now recognize the importance of positive sexual activity for a healthy and happy life (L. M. Diamond & Huebner, 2012). And self-acceptance appears to be a key component of healthy sexuality, regardless of what (if any) sexual identity label one adopts, whom one loves and desires, and what sexual behaviors one pursues.

CHAPTER SUMMARY

9.1 **Locate current understandings of sexuality and sexual orientation within social, cultural, and historical contexts.**

Psychologists define sexual orientation as an enduring pattern of cognitive, motivational, and behavioral tendencies that guides how people experience and express their sexuality. Sexuality refers to the capacity for sexual experiences. The concept of sexual orientation is a relatively recent, Western development. In different cultures and times, same-sex sexuality has meanings that have little to do with sexual orientation. The tendency to define and label sexual orientation may have emerged as a means of controlling people's erotic behavior.

9.2 Describe the multiple dimensions of sexual orientation, and analyze different models of sexual identity development.

Sexual identity refers to the label that people use to describe their sexual orientation and the emotional reactions that they have to this label. Most people identify as gay/lesbian, straight, or bisexual, but there are many other categories and labels whose prevalence differs across cultures. Evolutionary theories view love (attachment) and sexual desire (lust) as motivational states that compel people to seek proximity to and mate with others. Sexual desire presumably encourages reproductive mating, and love encourages both pair bonding (attachment to a mate for the purpose of raising infants) and attachment to infants. The behavioral component of sexual orientation consists of the sexual acts that people perform both alone and with others. Importantly, not all people experience the cognitive, motivational, and behavioral components of sexual orientation in a unified, consistent manner.

Phase models of sexual identity development describe distinct phases that mark important transitions in self-knowledge as people develop a sexual identity. While gay, lesbian, and bisexual individuals usually go through phases of awareness, exploration, deepening and commitment, and integration and synthesis, they may also go through an identity uncertainty phase. Heterosexual individuals may bypass the awareness and exploration phases and experience a prolonged unexplored commitment phase. Asexual individuals may experience unique phases of terminology discovery, coming out, and identity acceptance and salience negotiation. Instead of phases, milestone models identify the timing, sequence, and tone of different sexual identity milestones while narrative approaches broadly consider how sources of oppression and pride interact to shape sexual identities within specific contexts.

9.3 Evaluate biological, evolutionary, and integrative theories of sexual orientation.

Biological theories propose that sexual orientation is moderately heritable, associated with fetal exposure to sex hormones, and predicted (among men) by having more older, biological brothers. Evolutionary theories posit that carrying the genes for same-sex

sexuality confers an advantage by increasing altruism and helping among friends and genetic relatives or by increasing the attractiveness and fecundity of one's genetic relatives. Integrative approaches, such as the biobehavioral model, consider how biological and social environments shape sexual orientation and can explain how people sometimes develop novel sexual attractions that follow from romantic love. Sexual orientation is a complex phenomenon that likely reflects many underlying causes, and no single theory fully accounts for the differences in sexual orientation across all people.

9.4 Explain sex differences in sexuality, including attitudes and behaviors, orgasms and sexual satisfaction, and sexual fluidity.

People commonly assume that women are less sexual and hold less permissive sexual attitudes than men. However, meta-analyses show that most sex differences in sexual behavior and attitudes are in the small and close-to-zero ranges. As one exception, women have orgasms less often than men in the context of casual heterosexual sex and hookups (the orgasm gap). The orgasm gap is smaller, however, in committed heterosexual relationships and when male partners engage in more stimulation of the clitoris. Both male-to-female (MtF) and female-to-male (FtM) individuals report high rates of orgasm after genital reconstructive surgery, although FtM men consistently report higher rates of orgasm and sexual desire than MtF women. Women tend to show more sexual fluidity than men, meaning that they more frequently experience changes in sexual orientation or sexual identity across time.

9.5 Understand issues in sexuality across the life course, such as sexual peaks and the medicalization of sexual changes.

For both women and men, sexual interest increases from puberty through midlife and then gradually declines from age 55 through the next several decades. While women and men do not appear to "peak" at very different ages, either in terms of hormones or behavior, men tend to report their highest levels of sexual desire in their late 20s, and women report their highest levels in their early 30s. Thus, little evidence supports the 10-year gap in the sexual peaks of women and men that many people assume. Women also report stronger motivation to engage in sexual intercourse during the perimenopause phase, which is the phase preceding menopause. Menopause marks the end of menstruation and women's fertility, a period when estrogen levels and women's sexual interest typically decline. Men around this age may also lose erectile function and have fewer orgasms. The diagnosis of erectile dysfunction in men reflects the medicalization of sexuality, whereby society views normal changes in sexual functioning as medical illnesses that require treatments. Physicians often encourage menopausal women to take hormone replacement therapy, but this can increase the risk of breast cancer. Men may be encouraged to take Viagra, which tends to reduce men's sexuality to the rigidity of their erections. Regardless of these physical changes and declines in rates of sexual behavior, women and men can maintain satisfying sexual lives through old age, and sexual activity relates positively to good physical health, well-being, and long life.

Test Your Knowledge: True or False?

9.1. Approximately 10% of the U.S. population identifies as gay, lesbian, or bisexual. (False: The percentage of the population that identifies as gay, lesbian, or bisexual is quite a bit lower than 10%.) [p. 298]

9.2. Many asexual people report difficulty in understanding their internal experiences of their sexuality because they lack the language to describe these experiences. (True: Because asexuality is not well understood, asexual people often lack the language to describe and understand their experiences until they first encounter the relevant terminology.) [p. 306]

9.3. Although we usually assume that love follows desire (we fall in love with people after first finding them sexually attractive), it is just as possible for desire to follow love (we can become sexually attracted to someone after first falling in love with them). (True: The links between love and desire go in both directions.) [p. 314]

9.4. Genital reconstructive surgery typically makes it difficult for transgender people to have orgasms. (False: Transgender people report relatively high rates of orgasm following surgery.) [p. 321]

9.5. While men experience their sexual peak between the ages of 19 and 25, women reach their sexual peak around the ages of 30–35. (False: There is little evidence that men and women "peak" sexually at such disparate ages.) [p. 323]

For many, the term "traditional marriage" likely conjures an image of a White, middle-class, heterosexual couple with two children, where the man is the breadwinner and the woman is the homemaker.

Source: © iStockPhoto.com/George Marks

Test Your Knowledge: True or False?

10.1 College students who are in "friends-with-benefits" sexual relationships report that the quality of their friendship declines after they introduce sex into the mix.

10.2 In surveys of romantic partner preferences, men tend to rate physical attractiveness as more important in a mate than women do, and women tend to rate good financial prospects as more important in a mate than men do.

10.3 Arranged marriages—in which a relative or family friend selects the marriage partners—are the most common form of marriage worldwide.

10.4 In the context of heterosexual romantic relationships, men tend to experience more jealousy than women do regarding the possibility of their partner falling in love with someone else.

10.5 In general, relationship satisfaction decreases after couples have children.

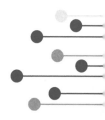

CHAPTER 10

Interpersonal Relationships

Key Concepts

What Roles Do Sex and Gender Play in Social Networks and Friendships?
Social Networks
Friendships
Sex Differences in Friendship Intimacy
Cross-Sex Friendships
Friends With Benefits
LGBT Friendships

What Roles Do Sex and Gender Play in Interpersonal Attraction?
Mate Preferences: Similarities and Differences
Mate Selection: Whom Do We Choose?
Dating Relationships
Dating Scripts and Paternalistic Chivalry
Experiencing Love and Romance

What Is the Nature of Marriage—Past and Present?
A Brief Social History of Marriage
Contemporary Marriage-Like Relationships
The Changing American Family
Arranged Versus Autonomous Marriages
Polygyny and Polyandry
Consensual Nonmonogamy and Polyamory

What Roles Do Sex and Gender Play in Committed Relationships?
Happy Relationships: Equity and Love
Making Decisions
Dividing Labor and Childcare
Showing Love
Relationship Struggles: Jealousy and Conflict
Jealousy
Dealing With Conflict
Debate: Did Women and Men Evolve Different Jealousy
Reactions?
Separation and Divorce

**What Roles Do Sex and Gender Play in Parenting
and Family Relationships?**
Parent to Parent: Gender and Parental Relationships
Parent to Child: Gender and Caring for Children

Learning Objectives

Students who read this chapter should be able to do the following:

10.1 Analyze the roles of sex, gender, and LGBT status in social networks, friendships, and friendship intimacy.

10.2 Evaluate major theoretical perspectives on sex similarities and differences in mate preferences and mate choices.

10.3 Explain the roles of gender and gender norms in dating relationships and romance.

10.4 Describe diverse marital arrangements across sociohistorical contexts, races and ethnicities, cultures, and sexual orientations.

10.5 Analyze sex differences and similarities in the factors that contribute to relationship satisfaction, conflict, and separation.

10.6 Describe the roles of sex and gender in parenting and family relationships.

Interpersonal Relationships

In 2015, the U.S. Supreme Court ruled the Defense of Marriage Act (DOMA) unconstitutional and, in doing so, paved the way for the legalization of same-sex marriage across the country. During the time leading up to this ruling, people widely discussed how the Supreme Court decision might affect the institution of "traditional marriage" in the United States. While advocates of DOMA feared that same-sex marriages would destroy traditional marriage, marriage equality supporters viewed the very term "traditional marriage" as heterosexist and exclusionary. But what exactly did people *mean* by "traditional marriage"?

For many, the term "traditional marriage" calls to mind an image of a (typically White) 1950s-style couple composed of a breadwinner husband and a homemaker wife. This couple married out of love after a romantic (but sexually chaste) courtship and then had two or three children together. Happy to divide work and family roles along typical gender lines, they remained faithful to one another and did not divorce, even when the going got tough. In short, their relationship had all of the components typically associated with the mid-20th-century Western ideal of marriage: romantic love between two middle-class individuals, a single-income household, gendered labor divisions, sexual fidelity, biological offspring, and longevity.

As historian Stephanie Coontz (2006) notes, however, this form of marriage is far from traditional. Instead, this marital arrangement was unique to a specific location and time in history, reaching its heyday in the 1950s and early 1960s in Western Europe and North America and then morphing into something different. It was not just short-lived but exclusive as well, for only people of certain economic means could comfortably support a family on a single income. The iconic image of the single-earner, traditional marriage did not represent poor, working-class, and racial and ethnic minority individuals. Thus, while marriage has existed in every known human society since before the time of recorded history, it has only rarely looked like the Western traditional marriage of the 1950s.

From this perspective, same-sex marriage poses no threat to traditional marriage, for the 1950s version of traditional marriage has not been the norm in the United States for more than four decades. Taking an even broader look, we see that marriage has assumed many different forms throughout history, continually being shaped and reshaped by the unique cultural and social conditions in which it occurs. But if the specific details of marriages differ across time and culture, the purposes of marriage have remained largely unchanged: Marriage expands family networks, builds community, merges resources, supports offspring, and legitimizes inheritances. In other words, marriage helps us to meet core needs by connecting us to one another.

In this chapter, we start with the assumption that humans are a social species, hardwired to form connections with one another. These connections take many forms, including large, extended networks of acquaintances, small friend groups, domestic partnerships, parent–child attachments, and extended family relationships. Moreover, regardless of pressures to conform to dominant cultural and historical traditions, people have always demonstrated flexibility and creativity in how they structure their relationships, networks, and families. Here, we will cover a diverse range of relationship types and family structures. With each type of relationship, we will consider how sex and gender shape the types of connections we seek, the manner in which we bond with others, and the outcomes of these relationships for health and well-being.

What Roles Do Sex and Gender Play in Social Networks and Friendships?

People have a powerful need to feel connected to others. According to social psychologists, meeting our **need to belong** aids survival and well-being in the same way that meeting our needs for air, food, and water does (Baumeister & Leary, 1995). Having frequent, emotionally positive interactions with a small number of other people can help to satisfy the need to belong. When people do not meet their need to belong, a host of maladies ensues, including disease vulnerability, depression and mental illness, criminality, and even premature death. People often meet the need to belong by developing social networks and friendships. While the study of social networks yields insight into the *quantity* of social connections that people have, the study of friendships allows insight into the *quality* of people's connections.

Need to belong: The fundamental need for a small number of close relationships that offer frequent, positive interactions.

Social network: The extended circle of people with whom there are regular interactions.

Social Networks

Social networks are the extended circles of people with whom we interact regularly, whether or not we know them well or feel close to them. Larger social networks can indicate better social integration, which predicts positive psychological and physical health outcomes (Cable, Bartley, Chandola, & Sacker, 2013). For example, in one classic study of randomly sampled households in California, Berkman and Syme (1979) tracked people over time and found that those with smaller social networks died earlier, from all causes of death, than those with more social connections, even controlling for things like initial health status, smoking, and exercise. Moreover, this pattern emerged at all age groups, from ages 30 through 70. This likely occurs because more socially integrated people have better access to social support, which predicts better cardiovascular, neuroendocrine, and immune functioning (Uchino, 2006). Thus, in a very real sense, our survival and well-being depend on our connections to others.

What role does gender play in social networks? As you read in Chapter 4 ("Gender Development"), sex differences in network size emerge in early and middle childhood. Boys tend to form larger social networks consisting of multiple extended connections while girls tend to prefer smaller peer groups. Both boys and girls have mostly (about 85%) same-sex peers in their social networks on average, although Black children tend to have more cross-sex peers in their networks than White children do (Kovacs, Parker, & Hoffman, 1996). By adolescence, sex differences in network size tend to disappear (Neal, 2010), and by adulthood, women's social networks tend to be richer (if not larger) than men's. Compared with men, women tend to spend more time with their networks, view their networks as more emotionally available to them, and get more emotional support from their networks (Pines & Zaidman, 2003). Women also tend to offer more responsive and attentive support to network members than men do (Monin & Clark, 2011), a finding that may remind you of our discussion of sex differences in supportive communication from Chapter 8 ("Language, Communication, and Emotion"). Thus, people benefit by having more women in their social networks.

Another sex difference lies in the importance of having a spouse or romantic partner in one's social network. Living with a romantic partner or spouse predicts mental health better for men than for women. For example, whereas unpartnered men in their 40s have lower well-being in their 50s in comparison with partnered men, women's romantic partnership status in their 40s does not predict their well-being in their 50s (Cable et al., 2013). This pattern means that intimate partnerships tend to have more bearing on the health of men than women, a finding we will revisit in later sections.

Finally, social network composition often differs by race and ethnicity. For instance, in the United States, extended family and kin tend to play a larger role in the social networks of Latino, Black, and Native American people than they do in the networks of White people (Pernice-Duca, 2010). The social networks of White people generally contain more domestic partners and nonrelative friends, as compared with the social networks of people of color (MacPhee, Fritz, & Miller-Heyl, 1996).

Friendships

What do people want in their friendships? For the most part, women and men both want trustworthy and dependable friends who are similar to them and with whom they can share activities (J. A. Hall, 2011). Women and men also both value warmth, kindness, expressiveness, openness, and a sense of humor in friends (Sprecher & Regan, 2002), and they both desire closeness and intimacy in their same-sex friendships (Sandserson, Rahm, & Beigbeder, 2005). And yet, despite wanting these same things, women and

Women's friendships tend to involve more shared emotions and self-disclosure while men's tend to involve more shared activities.

Source: © iStockPhoto.com/Portra; © iStockPhoto.com/technotr

men seem to do friendship somewhat differently. Women's same-sex friendships involve higher levels of shared emotions, personal disclosure, and social support. In contrast, men's same-sex friendships tend to involve higher levels of shared activities and conversations about relatively nonpersonal topics, such as sports or work. This sex difference is puzzling. If women and men both desire friendships that involve more intimacy, why might these sex differences in same-sex friendships emerge?

Sex differences in friendship intimacy. One hypothesis is that the male gender role discourages certain forms of same-sex closeness. For example, boys and men learn to restrict expressions of emotions—and especially vulnerable emotions that might make them appear weak or needy. Moreover, the male gender role discourages intimate bonds with other men because these may raise suspicions about same-sex sexuality. These two factors—*emotional restraint* and *homophobia*—explain some of the sex differences in friendship intimacy (Bank & Hansford, 2000). For instance, men with greater concerns about being perceived as gay also disclose less personal information with their same-sex friends, and this partially explains their lower levels of friendship closeness and satisfaction (Morman, Schrodt, & Tornes, 2012). Thus, although men recognize that emotional self-disclosure can lead to intimacy in friendships, some men may avoid it because it violates male gender role norms.

However, another hypothesis is that men's and women's same-sex friendships do not actually differ in intimacy levels. By equating emotional intimacy with self-disclosure and treating shared activities and self-disclosure as mutually exclusive, researchers might incorrectly attribute more intimacy to female friendships than to male friendships. In fact, women do tend to self-disclose somewhat more than men ($d = -0.18$), but this sex difference is small (Dindia & Allen, 1992). Moreover, Radmacher and Azmitia (2006) found that the use of self-disclosure to attain closeness in friendships increased with age, from adolescence to early adulthood, and was equally important for young women and men. Thus, by the time they reach young adulthood, women and men equally report relying on self-disclosure and shared emotions as routes to intimacy with their best friends. Behavioral evidence bears this out as well: Among young adults, there are no sex differences in the amount of personal information that people self-disclose on Facebook (Farber & Nitzburg, 2016). Finally, for young men (but not young women), sharing more activities predicts stronger feelings of emotional closeness, especially with their best male friend (Radmacher & Azmitia, 2006). Thus, perhaps men and women do have similarly close friendships, but they achieve closeness in somewhat different ways.

The **homosocial perspective** espouses this view and seeks to understand the unique ways in which men achieve intimacy with one another. This perspective notes that men often organize their relational life by forming *comradeships*, or cohesive units characterized by shared goals, joint activities and teamwork, and adherence to group norms. For example, think of leagues that men form to play sports like basketball, flag football, or soccer. Within comradeships, power and status are structured hierarchically, and interactions often contain seemingly opposite emotional experiences, such as competition and affection, aggression and humor, and homophobia and male–male intimacy. Through this interplay of opposing emotions, men form intensely emotional bonds with one another that meet their needs for affiliation. Moreover, friendships initially formed within comradeships may persist

Homosocial perspective: An approach that proposes that men achieve friendship intimacy in the context of cohesive, hierarchical units that share goals and joint activities and contain opposing emotions (e.g., competition and affection).

outside the context of the hierarchy, as in the case of close friends who share emotional intimacy based on having spent their young adulthood together in the same military unit (D. Kaplan & Rosenmann, 2014).

The homosocial perspective thus proposes that women's and men's friendships both allow for intimacy but via different social dynamics. While men's intimacy tends to stem from larger, hierarchically organized groups and interactions containing opposing emotions, women tend to achieve intimacy in the context of dyadic relationships, with a few close friends, involving high levels of self-disclosure. The profile pictures that people post to social networking sites reveal this sex difference in friendship preferences. As you may recall from Chapter 4 ("Gender Development"), an analysis of over 112,000 Facebook profile pictures from accounts in all world regions found that men were more likely than women to appear in photos of large all-male groups while women were more likely than men to appear in photos of two women (David-Barrett et al., 2015). The cross-cultural consistency of these patterns suggests that these sex differences in friendship patterns may be universal.

Stop and Think

In your view, who has more intimate friendships: women or men? Why? Is it reasonable to define intimacy in terms of self-disclosure? Can intimacy develop through shared activities? If so, how? Are self-disclosure and shared activities mutually exclusive in friendships? In your view, what is the best way to define intimacy?

Cross-sex friendships. Cross-sex friendships between women and men—while relatively rarer in early and middle childhood—become quite common by the time people reach college age, at least in Western cultures. One study found that U.S. college women and men both reported an average of about four close cross-sex friends (Bleske & Buss, 2000). To a large degree, people desire and appreciate the same things in cross-sex friends as they do in same-sex friends, including kindness, honesty, humor, companionship, and openness. One difference, however, is that cross-sex friends can offer unique insight into the romantic preferences of the other sex. Young heterosexual adults seek more advice from cross-sex than same-sex friends about the mating desires of the other sex (Bleske & Buss, 2000), and they feel less competition in cross-sex than in same-sex friendships (Rawlins, 2009).

While women and men perceive many of the same benefits of having cross-sex friends, a couple of key differences stand out. First, women are more likely than men to report initiating cross-sex friendships for the physical protection that male friends can offer (e.g., walking them to their car at night and looking out for them in dangerous situations; $d = -0.45$). Second, heterosexual men are more likely than women to report initiating cross-sex friendships in the hopes that the relationship will become sexual ($d = 0.37$) or will lead to a long-term romantic relationship ($d = 0.26$; Bleske-Rechek & Buss, 2001). However, because cross-sex friends often do not explicitly define the status or terms of their friendship (Guerrero & Chavez, 2005), complications may arise if one friend does not reciprocate the romantic or sexual interest of the other.

The **audience problem** occurs when others assume that two friends are romantically involved. Cross-sex friends more frequently encounter the audience problem than same-sex friends do, likely due to the pervasiveness of heterocentrism. For example, gossip websites such as TMZ and Perez Hilton feature "New Couple Alert" posts that contain pictures of platonic cross-sex friends accompanied by coy speculation about the romantic nature of their friendship (McDonnell & Mehta, 2016). These types of media images reinforce the notions that women and men cannot be platonic friends, that cross-sex friends are more likely than same-sex friends to be lovers, and that it is appropriate and "normal" to speculate about the ulterior (romantic or sexual) motives of cross-sex friends.

In some cases, however, audiences who assume a romantic connection between cross-sex friends may be responding to genuine cues of attraction. For instance, people who actually do feel more romantic and sexual desire for a cross-sex friend and who have sex with their cross-sex friend experience the audience problem more often (Schoonover & McEwan, 2014). In strictly platonic cross-sex friendships, in which neither partner desires a romantic or sexual connection, audiences less frequently assume that the relationship is romantic.

Cross-sex friendships between straight women and gay men also reduce the likelihood of the audience problem. Both members of these friend pairs view these friendships as especially useful because they allow for an exchange of valuable mating advice without concerns about sexual interest, competition, or ulterior motives. In fact, straight women rate dating advice from a gay man as more trustworthy than advice from either a straight woman or a straight man, and gay men rate dating advice from a straight woman as more trustworthy than dating advice from a lesbian or a gay man (E. M. Russell, DelPriore, Butterfield, & Hill, 2013).

Friendship patterns vary across cultures, particularly in terms of cross-sex friendships. In general, adolescents in Western relative to Eastern cultures more frequently have cross-sex friends and engage in casual dating with other-sex partners (Z. H. Li, Connolly, Jiang, Pepler, & Craig, 2010). However, this may be changing due to the spreading reach of Western ideas and media. For instance, one study measured the cross-sex friendships of South Asian Indian college students in three settings that differed in their exposure to Western culture: same-sex Indian schools with minimal Western exposure (*traditional*), coeducational Indian schools with some Western influences (*transitioning*), and Canadian schools with full immersion in Western culture (*diaspora*). The proportions of students who spent time with mixed-sex peers and casually dated an other-sex partner were highest among students in the diaspora group and lowest among those in the traditional group. Similarly, students in the diaspora group reported more cross-sex friendships than those in the transitional and traditional groups (Dhariwal & Connolly, 2013).

Friends with benefits. The latter half of the 20th century in the United States saw large changes in attitudes about the permissibility of premarital sex. From the early 1970s through 2012, the percentages of adults who called premarital sex "not at all wrong" climbed from 29% to 58% (Twenge, Sherman, & Wells, 2015). In fact, many young

Audience problem: The tendency for observers to assume that platonic friends are romantically involved; especially likely to occur in cross-sex friendships.

Friends-with-benefits relationships: Arrangements in which two friends have occasional, casual sexual interactions without the expectation of a romantic relationship.

Chosen families: The friend circles of many LGBT individuals that offer many of the resources and benefits of biological families but that consist largely of individuals who understand the unique challenges of being LGBT.

Passionate friendships: Friendships characterized by intense longing for proximity, high levels of affection, and large amounts of physical touch (e.g., cuddling and hand holding). For some sexual minority women, these friendships provide the context for their first same-sex sexual experiences.

adults today report engaging in casual sexual relationships ("hookups") with members of their social networks. In **friends with benefits relationships** (FWBs), two friends have occasional, casual sexual interactions without the expectation of a romantic relationship. While it is difficult to estimate precisely what percentage of friendships offers such benefits, one study found that 54% of men and 43% of college women reported at least one FWB relationship in the past year (Owen & Fincham, 2011). These rates may differ by race and other factors, though: Among college students, rates of FWBs tend to be higher among students who are White, younger, and less religious (Kalish & Kimmel, 2011). What about same-sex friendships? Relatively little is known about FWB arrangements between same-sex friends, although one study found that 62.5% of gay men and 33.6% of lesbians reported ever having had sex with a casual friend (Nardi & Sherrod, 1994).

Research identifies several different types of FWBs that vary in the degree to which the sexual contact is truly "expectation free." In one study, about one-third of FWBs contained at least one partner who desired to shift their friendship to a romantic relationship (Mongeau, Knight, Williams, Eden, & Shaw, 2013). Just as with cross-sex friendships, FWBs can bring with them a unique set of complications, especially when partners do not explicitly define the nature of their friendship. Nonetheless, in one study of college students, about two-thirds of students who reported FWBs said that the quality of the friendship actually improved following sex (Afifi & Faulkner, 2000).

LGBT friendships. Historically, sexual and gender identity minority individuals have had less supportive families than heterosexual individuals. While this may be changing as awareness and acceptance of LGBT people increases, troubled family relationships remain a theme for many sexual and gender identity minority individuals. For this reason, members of the LGBT community often place special importance on their social networks and friendships to meet their belonging needs. Moreover, LGBT individuals often befriend each other. For example, same-sex-attracted high school students tend to seek out other same-sex-attracted students, forming reciprocal friendships that may shield them from some of the negative consequences of stigmatization (Martin-Storey, Cheadle, Skalamera, & Crosnoe, 2015). In adulthood, LGBT individuals often gravitate toward intentional communities of sexual minority and gender identity minority friends. Such friend communities may serve as **chosen families**, or friend circles that stand in for biological families but that consist largely of individuals who understand the unique challenges of being LGBT (Weston, 2005). Chosen families are often an important source of social support for LGBT individuals. One study found that LGB individuals relied on other LGB people for most of their everyday support needs (Frost, Meyer, & Schwartz, 2016). Interestingly, some research indicates that transgender adults tend to have larger and more diverse friend networks than do LGB individuals (Erosheva, Kim, Emlet, & Fredriksen-Goldsen, 2016). This may reflect the fact that transgender friendship communities often develop online, allowing large groups of people to connect across large geographical distances (Beemyn & Rankin, 2011).

When it comes to close friendships, sexual minority women, in particular, more frequently form intense friendships with other women that sometimes skirt the boundaries between friendship and romance. Lisa Diamond (2002) studies what she calls **passionate friendships** between sexual minority women. As you may recall from Chapter 9 ("Sexual Orientation and Sexuality"), passionate friendships tend to contain elements usually associated with romantic relationships, such as intense longing for proximity, high levels of affection and emotionality, and large amounts of physical touch (e.g., cuddling and hand-holding). Moreover, for some sexual minority women, these friendships do become sexual and may serve as these women's first same-sex sexual experiences. Despite the presence or absence of sexual contact, enduring feelings of intimacy often characterize the close friendships between lesbian women: Lesbians are more likely than gay men to list ex-lovers among their current closest friends (Nardi & Sherrod, 1994).

Sexual minority women in passionate friendships tend to share a lot of physical touch.

Source: © iStockPhoto .com/mauro_grigollo

What Roles Do Sex and Gender Play in Interpersonal Attraction?

What do women and men ideally want in romantic relationship partners? What roles do sex and gender play in attraction, dating, romance, and love? In this section, we will address all of these questions, identifying both similarities and differences in how people of different sexes experience attraction and love.

Mate Preferences: Similarities and Differences

When it comes to **mate preferences**—the qualities that people claim to desire in mates—women and men share many similarities. Most adolescents and young adults desire partners who love them, who have favorable traits (dependability, emotional stability, intelligence, and sociability), and who are similar to them and want the same things that they want (Boxer, Noonan, & Whelan, 2015). These mate preferences do not differ much by sex or sexual orientation (Toro-Morn & Sprecher, 2003).

Mate preferences: Qualities that people claim to desire in a potential sexual or romantic mate.

Figure 10.1 shows U.S. college undergraduates' ratings of the importance of 18 different qualities, arranged according to their average importance ratings (Boxer et al., 2015). What do you notice about Figure 10.1? Note that although women tend to rate most of the qualities as more important than men do, the sex differences are generally small in magnitude. Furthermore, the three most important qualities desired by both women and men are those that reveal a dependable, stable, and loving partner. That said, the sex differences that emerge on some partner qualities attract a great deal of research attention, so let's consider these.

Women and men differ in the importance that they place on a partner's physical attractiveness, domestic (homemaking and childcare) competence, and earning potential (e.g., social status, resources, and ambition). As you can see in Figure 10.1, men tend to rate "good looks" and "good cook, housekeeper" as more important in a mate than

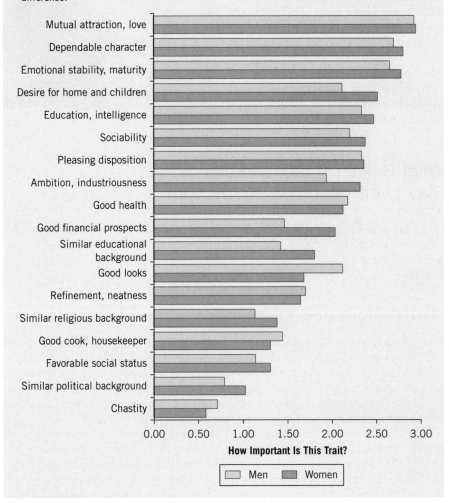

Figure 10.1 U.S. Undergraduates' Mate Preferences by Sex.

U.S. undergraduate women and men rated the importance of several different mate qualities, which appear below in declining order of overall importance. Where in this figure do you see sex similarities? Where do you see sex differences? Is there more evidence of similarity or difference?

How Important Is This Trait?

Legend: Men, Women

Source: Boxer, Noonan, and Whelan (2015).

Notes: Ratings were made on scales of 0 = *unimportant/irrelevant in a mate* to 3 = *essential in a mate*.

women do, and women tend to rate "good financial prospects" and "ambition, industriousness" as more important than men do. These average sex differences emerge time and time again in self-reports of mate preferences, and they replicate across cultures that otherwise differ a great deal, including the United States, Singapore, Japan, Bulgaria, Sweden, India, Nigeria, and Zambia (N. P. Li, Valentine, & Patel, 2011; Shackelford, Schmitt, & Buss, 2005). Moreover, gay and straight men alike both prioritize the looks of potential mates more than lesbian and straight women do (Lawson, James, Jannson, Koyama, & Hill, 2014; Lippa, 2007). However, lesbians prioritize earning potential less than straight women do, instead emphasizing personality traits such as honesty (C. A. Smith, Konik, & Tuve, 2011).

This pattern of sex differences in mating preferences depends on the type of relationship that people consider when indicating their preferences. The pattern just described, with men prioritizing looks over earning potential and women prioritizing earning potential over looks, emerges when people consider long-term mates with whom they might raise a family. In contrast, when considering short-term ("one-night stand") partners, both women and men prioritize physical attractiveness over other qualities (N. P. Li & Kenrick, 2006).

The size of these sex differences also differs by race. One study found that Black women were more likely than White women to say that they would marry someone without a steady job, and White women were more likely than Black women to say that they would marry someone who was not attractive (Sprecher, Sullivan, & Hatfield, 1994). Some theorists propose that Black women prioritize the economic benefits of marriage less than White women do, given that Black men—because of long-standing structural racism—generally have lower earning potential than White men (South, 1991). If heterosexual Black women depend less economically on husbands than heterosexual White women do, they may be freer to prioritize their mates' attractiveness.

Two theoretical approaches can explain sex differences in mate preferences. According to *parental investment theory* (which you encountered in Chapter 5, "The Contents and Origins of Gender Stereotypes"), female members of many species are especially picky when choosing mates because they invest more than males do in each offspring (Trivers, 1972). Because mating with a low-quality partner carries more risk for women than it does for men, women display a stronger preference for partners who can offer resources and protection. In contrast, men should show a stronger preference for partners who are attractive because physical attractiveness indicates reproductive and genetic health. Furthermore, men should desire female partners who display childcare and homemaking capacities, as these qualities enhance the survival of offspring. In short, the evolutionary perspective argues that women's emphasis on resource provision and men's emphasis on attractiveness and domesticity enhanced our ancestors' reproductive success. Moreover, these preferences should not differ across sexual orientations, because they are assumed to have evolved as sex-linked traits (Kenrick, Keefe, Bryan, Barr, & Brown, 1995). Supporting this theory, the sex differences summarized previously emerge in dozens of cultures across six continents (Shackelford et al., 2005).

In contrast, the sociocultural perspective views sex differences in mate preferences as a product of social roles and labor divisions rather than genes. When women primarily perform unpaid domestic labor and have access to fewer economic resources than men, they benefit from selecting partners who can offer financial support. In contrast, when men primarily occupy wage-earning roles outside the home, they benefit from selecting female partners who can perform domestic duties. Moreover, having greater economic flexibility allows men the luxury of prioritizing attractiveness—a desirable but not necessary trait—in their mates. In support of this theory, the tendency to prioritize earning potential over attractiveness in mates reverses among financially independent women (Moore, Cassidy, Law Smith, & Perrett, 2006). Similarly, as noted before, Black women prioritize earning potential in male partners less than White women, which may reflect their reduced economic dependence on male partners. Sex differences in mate preferences are also consistently weaker—and sometimes reversed—among men and women who reject traditional gender role ideologies (Eastwick et al., 2006) and in nations with higher gender equality scores (Zentner & Eagly, 2015). For instance, women rate a partner's good housekeeping skills as more important than men do in Finland and Germany, two countries with very high gender equality indices. Finally, sex differences in mate preferences have declined over time, as the domestic and employment roles of women and men have grown increasingly similar (Buss, Shackelford, Kirkpatrick, & Larsen, 2001). These patterns suggest that sex differences in mate preferences partly reflect sex differences in social roles and women's access to economic resources.

Mate Selection: Whom Do We Choose?

Surveys about the qualities that people desire in a partner are an efficient way to gather data, but they may not be realistic. Do the qualities we think are important translate into actual preferences when meeting real people in face-to-face encounters? To test this, Eastwick and Finkel (2008) used a speed-dating venue to assess the links between people's reported mate preferences and their actual interest in strangers. In this venue, heterosexual women and men met in pairs for 4-minute "dates" and then rotated until they had met every other-sex person in the room. After each "date," people indicated their interest in dating the person they just met and rated the person's physical attractiveness and likely earning potential. General mate preferences, measured before the speed-dating event, showed the typical patterns, with men rating "physical attractiveness" as more important than women and women rating "earning potential" as more important than men. However, the desire to date actual partners was similarly predicted—among both women and men—by their ratings of the partners' attractiveness and (to a lesser degree) by their beliefs about the partners' earning potential. Thus, both sexes showed more interest in dating people they just met when they perceived them as more attractive and more likely to earn good money. This suggests that the sex differences often observed in studies of mate preferences may not strongly guide reactions to real, in-the-flesh, potential mates.

So what does guide people's choice of mates? There are several factors that predict interpersonal attraction, and these are summarized in Table 10.1. One especially influential factor, however, is similarity. **Partner homogamy** refers to the strong, cross-cultural tendency for people to bond and mate with similar others on variables such as age, race and ethnicity, religion, socioeconomic status, personality, intelligence, education, interests, attitudes,

Partner homogamy: The tendency for people to bond and mate with others who are similar to them on demographic, personality, background, and physical attributes.

Table 10.1 What Attracts Us to Others? Research on liking and attraction identifies all of these as factors that predict attraction to others and choice of specific others as mates.

Factor That Predicts Attraction/Mate Choice	Description
Similarity	Having things in common
Reciprocal liking	Mutually felt and conveyed interest and attraction
Familiarity	Repeated or prolonged exposure to the other; spending time with the other
Appearance	Physical attractiveness
Personality	Attractive personality traits (e.g., intelligence, kindness, and sense of humor)
Social influence	Approval or disapproval of the other by family and/or friends
Filling needs	The other fulfills needs; makes me happy; and makes me feel cared for, respected, protected, and valued
Arousal	Having a strong physiological reaction to the other (e.g., racing heart and rapid breathing)
Readiness	Feeling ready for a romantic relationship
Isolation	Spending time alone with the other
Mysteriousness	Feeling intrigued by the other, wanting to know more about the other
Specific cues	Particular characteristics or features of the other that hold personal importance for the self

Source: Summarized from Riela, Rodriguez, Aron, Xu, and Acevedo (2010).

attractiveness, and even mental health symptoms (Figueredo et al., 2015; McCrae et al., 2008). Homogamous partners are familiar, they validate people's worldviews, and they reduce the likelihood of interpersonal conflicts. Interestingly, members of same-sex couples tend to show less partner homogamy on dimensions such as age, race/ethnicity, and educational attainment than members of heterosexual couples (C. R. Schwartz & Graf, 2009). Why do you think this occurs? Some suggest that the smaller total pool of potential partners for gay men and lesbians reduces their likelihood of meeting highly similar partners. Moreover, same-sex-attracted individuals are less likely than heterosexual people to meet their partners in settings characterized by high levels of homogamy, such as schools and workplaces (Kalmijn & Flap, 2001). Instead, sexual minority individuals more often meet potential partners in urban settings where they tend to encounter large numbers of people from diverse backgrounds.

Source: © iStockPhoto
.com/bluegame

Dating Relationships

Suppose you meet someone you like and want to date. What happens next? In this section, we will discuss one dating domain in which gender seems to play a pretty powerful role (gendered expectations regarding power and chivalry) and another in which gender makes little difference (experiences of love and romance).

Dating scripts and paternalistic chivalry. Social norms about heterosexual dating dictate that men should play the more powerful and active role while women should passively await male attention. In fact, a review of studies published from 1980 through 2010 found that young women's and men's **dating scripts** for first dates did not differ much over a 20-year period (A. A. Eaton & Rose, 2011). Dating scripts are stereotyped, cognitive representations of the sequences of events and behaviors that occur during dates. Both women and men expect men to plan first dates, select the venue and activities, pick their date up, and pay for the date. If sexual contact occurs, men are expected to initiate it. Interestingly, dating scripts for same-sex couples parallel those for heterosexual couples in terms of the expected events (discuss plans, get dressed, see a movie, go to eat or get a drink; Peplau & Fingerhut, 2007), although they, of course, lack the same expectation of sex differences in who controls the date.

Paternalistic chivalry, another dating norm that has not changed much over the past several decades, refers to the expectation that men should be both protective and polite toward women in romantic contexts, treating dates like "ladies" and offering to pay for them (A. A. Eaton & Rose, 2011). As you may recall from Chapter 6 ("Power, Sexism, and Discrimination"), paternalistic chivalry reflects benevolent sexism, the belief that women are more virtuous than men and ought to be cherished and protected. Women and men both view paternalistic chivalry favorably in dating contexts, although those who score higher in benevolent sexism endorse this dating norm more strongly (Viki, Abrams, & Hutchison, 2003).

The principle of partner homogamy refers to the powerful tendency for people to bond with others who are similar in appearance, background, personality, interests, and attitudes.

Dating scripts: Stereotyped, cognitive representations of the sequences of events that take place during dates.

Paternalistic chivalry: The norm that dictates that men should be protective of women and treat them as if they are special and virtuous.

Sidebar 10.1: Dating Double Standards?

Consider some common heterosexual dating norms. Should men hold open doors for women? Is it okay for women to ask men out for a first date? Who should pay on a first date? Should a man or a woman propose marriage? If a couple marries, should the woman adopt her male partner's last name? When Paynter and Leaper (2016) asked college students these questions, they found evidence of some relationship double standards. That is, both men and women were more comfortable with men paying for first dates and proposing marriage, and they were more comfortable with women adopting their partner's last name. Women and men also expected men to ask women out on a first date rather than the reverse, although men held this expectation less strongly than women did. Men also expected men to hold doors open for women rather than the reverse while women felt that both men and women should hold doors for the other.

What about "hookups" and FWBs? As noted earlier, young adults today in countries like the United States report engaging in more casual sexual relationships with members of their social networks than in the past (Bogle, 2008). Does this form of dating still follow traditional norms and scripts? To some degree, it does. As A. A. Eaton and Rose (2011) noted, "hookup" scripts afford men more power than women over the initiation of physical contact. Moreover, men perceive themselves as gaining status from hookups while women more frequently feel that they lose status, and women report more guilt and regret about hookups than men do. These patterns reflect traditional gender role norms that afford men more sexual freedom than women.

Stop and Think

Over the past half of a century, women have pushed for equal treatment to men in domains of work, academics, athletics, and legal rights, among others. Given this, why do you think women still tolerate—and even appreciate—inequitable treatment when it comes to dating and romance? Why are traditional gendered dating scripts so persistent? Are there benefits to women and/or men of following traditional scripts in the domains of dating and romance? If so, what might these be?

Experiencing love and romance. Who do you think is more romantic about love and falls in love more easily: women or men? Despite stereotypes of women as the more romantic sex, the findings regarding sex differences in love and romance are mixed. On the one hand, women's personalities do tend to be more oriented toward love and romance than men's. Women rate themselves higher than men do across a set of traits known collectively as *emotional investment* (loving, lovable, romantic, affectionate, cuddlesome, compassionate, and passionate), and this sex difference emerges almost universally across cultures (Schmitt et al., 2009). On the other hand, having a "loving" personality does not necessarily mean that women experience love and romance more intensely than men. In fact, women and men generally think of and experience love in similar ways, as an affectionate feeling of deep attachment to another (Fehr, 2006). Moreover, several studies fail to find sex differences in how frequently or easily people fall in love (Galperin & Haselton, 2010; Riela, Rodriguez, Aron, Xu, & Acevedo, 2010). College-age women and men also want similar types of "love acts" from romantic partners: They both want partners to show them love by verbalizing affection, sharing sexual intimacy, and performing caring actions. Women do, however, report a stronger desire than men for partners to show love by focusing on the relationship and being emotionally supportive (Perrin et al., 2011). Interestingly, counter to gender stereotypes, some research shows that American and Chinese men endorse some romantic beliefs more strongly than women (Sprecher & Toro-Morn, 2002), but the sex differences are small and do not consistently replicate. In short, the sexes may be more similar than different when it comes to how they experience love and romance.

What Is the Nature of Marriage—Past and Present?

Marriage—the practice of formalizing a domestic bond between individuals—has long been a central part of human societies. However, marriages and marriage-like relationships have changed a great deal over time. In this section, we will summarize the social history of marriage to offer a context for understanding contemporary marital and family arrangements.

A Brief Social History of Marriage

Throughout human history, marriage has rarely been about the romantic desires of the individual marriage partners (Coontz, 2006). Instead, marriage has served the primary purposes of expanding family networks, sharing resources, and increasing the family labor source. In line with these practical goals of marriage, decisions about who should marry whom have rarely been based on romance or love. Most marriages throughout history have been arranged, often negotiated by parents and other kin, neighbors, judges, or priests.

Marriages historically have also tended to afford men more authority, power, and freedom than women. Throughout history, women have had relatively little say in their choice of partners, and once married, they have often been considered property of their husbands. For example, among the peasant and merchant classes of the Middle Ages—and even as late as 18th-century British colonial America—a woman became a **feme covert** when she married, transferring her identity to that of her husband and losing most, if not all, of her legal rights and standings in the process (Gundersen & Gampel, 1982). Laws like these have consistently upheld husbands' rights to their wives' belongings and earnings, as well their bodies: Men have been legally allowed to beat their wives, demand sex from them, and divorce them if no children are produced (Coontz, 2006). In other words, marriage has largely been a patriarchal arrangement that institutionalized men's power over women.

Feme covert: The legal status of married women in British common law and American colonial law, whereby women transferred their identities and rights to their husband upon marriage.

Over time, both of these themes have changed, at least in Western cultures. The practice of marrying for love originated in Western Europe sometime between the 16th and 18th centuries (Coontz, 2006), and by the end of the 1700s, love-based marriage was the cultural ideal in Western Europe and North America (although arranged marriages remain the norm in many other cultures, as you will read later). At the same time, women's status improved within marriages over time, largely as a result of feminist efforts. For example, women began earning voting rights in Europe, North America, Australia, and New Zealand in the late 19th century, and they earned full suffrage in the United States in 1920. In 1960, the birth control pill became commercially available, giving women more control over their reproductive activities. In the 1970s, a cascade of groundbreaking legal decisions in the United States curtailed gender discrimination in educational and financial contexts, criminalized domestic violence, and guaranteed women the right to abortion. Over the past several decades, the work and family roles of women and men became increasingly similar in theUnited States, Europe, Canada, and Australia (Bianchi, Robinson, & Milkie, 2006). How have these shifts changed the face of marriage?

Contemporary Marriage-Like Relationships

As noted in the chapter opening, the traditional marriage configuration of the 1950s and 1960s was short-lived. Since the 1960s, social and economic changes in the United States led to several major changes in American families (summarized in Figure 10.2). Let's examine these further.

The changing American family. Americans today are marrying at lower rates than ever before. Whereas only 9% of American adults ages 25 or older had never been married in 1960, the percentage today is now 20% (W. Wang & Parker, 2014). These rates differ by race, with larger percentages of Latino and Black adults, relative to Asian and White adults, reporting "never married" status. While most adults do marry, they marry later today than they did in the 1960s (see Figure 10.3), and more couples are cohabiting, divorcing, and remarrying than ever before. The American family has been declining in size, too. Women are having fewer children, and they are having their first child at older ages (Pew Research Center [PRC], 2015). More women are also having children outside of marriage. Whereas only 5% of births occurred outside of marriage in 1960, this percentage rose to 40% by 2015. As shown in Figure 10.2, racial and ethnic differences emerge in the prevalence of women having children outside of marriage. These differences likely reflect race and ethnicity differences in socioeconomic status. Latinas and Black women tend to have fewer economic resources and lower education levels compared with Asian and White women, and people with fewer resources and less education are less likely to marry and more likely to have children outside of marriage (Fry, 2010; Musick, 2002). But having a child outside of marriage then decreases the likelihood of marrying by age 40—and especially so for Latinas and Black women (Graefe & Lichter, 2002).

In 1960, 73% of children under the age of 18 in the United States lived in a family with two married parents in their first marriage. Today, due to increases in divorce, single parenthood, nonmarried cohabitation, and remarriage, only 46% of children

Figure 10.2 Race and Ethnicity Differences in American Family Variables.

These trends reflect marked changes in American family arrangements since the 1950s. Where race and ethnicity differences exist, these often reflect differences in socioeconomic status, with members of wealthier groups (White and Asian people) being more likely to marry, less likely to have children outside of marriage, and less likely to be single parents.

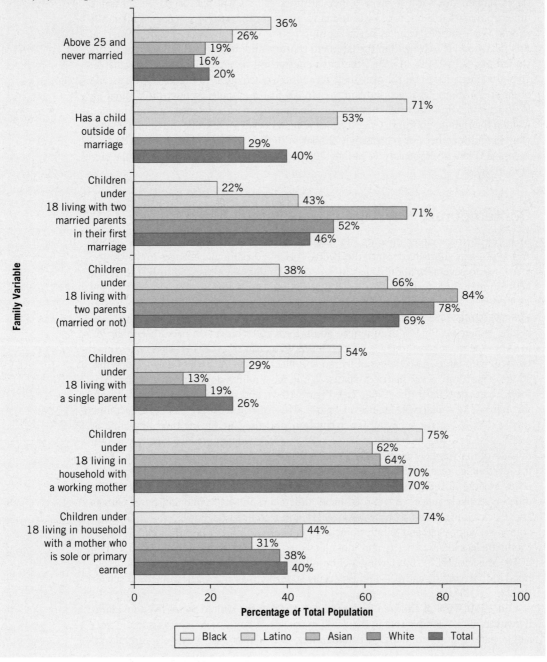

live in this type of family (PRC, 2015). In fact, fewer children than ever before (62%) live in households with two married parents today. In 1960, only 9% of children lived with a single parent; today, 26% do. These statistics differ by race, with more than half of Black children and relatively fewer Asian, White, and Hispanic children living in single-parent households (see Figure 10.2). In contrast to other racial and ethnic groups, children in Black families are more likely to have grandparents—and especially maternal grandmothers—who contribute substantially to child-rearing (Hirsch, Mickus, & Boerger, 2002). Black, as compared with White, children and adolescents also often have a larger number of strong ties to nonparental adults, such as uncles and older brothers.

Married women in the United States today have more education than their husbands, and most mothers—regardless of race or ethnicity—are in the labor force. Today, mothers are the primary or sole breadwinners in 40% of families with children living at home, up from only 11% in 1960. Among Black mothers, 74% are either the primary or sole family earner.

Arranged versus autonomous marriages. Most marriages throughout human history have been **arranged**, meaning that third parties, such as parents or relatives of the couple, select pairings based on an assessment of similarity, compatibility, and

Arranged marriage: Marriage in which third parties, such as parents or relatives, select potential marriage partners, with both partners having the right to refuse.

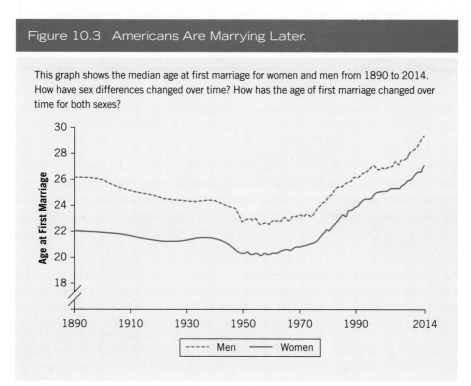

Figure 10.3 Americans Are Marrying Later.

This graph shows the median age at first marriage for women and men from 1890 to 2014. How have sex differences changed over time? How has the age of first marriage changed over time for both sexes?

Source: U.S. Census Bureau (2015a).

Autonomous (love) marriage: Marriage in which individuals select their own partners.

Polygyny: Marriage between one husband and multiple wives; polygyny is more common than polyandry and is practiced today in some Muslim-majority countries in Africa, the Middle East, and South Asia.

mutual benefit. Counter to some misconceptions, arranged marriages are typically voluntary, with both partners having the right to refuse the pairing. In contrast, human rights organizations generally oppose *forced marriages*, or arranged marriages in which the partners have no say. In **autonomous marriages** (sometimes called **love marriages**), individuals select their own partners based on attraction, love, or other personal factors, without formal permission or approval from parents or guardians.

Today, just over 53% of all marriages worldwide are arranged (Statistic Brain, 2012). While autonomous marriages predominate in Europe and North America, arranged marriages are common in collectivistic cultures in Africa, Asia, the Middle East, and Latin America, as well as among some religious groups in Europe and North America, such as the Amish and Orthodox Jewish people (Myers, Madathil, & Tingle, 2005; Zaidi & Shuraydi, 2002). Autonomous marriages end in divorce far more often than arranged marriages (50% versus 6%). However, this does not necessarily mean that arranged marriages are happier than autonomous marriages because people in arranged marriages may be unlikely to divorce for social or cultural reasons.

Stop and Think

Why do you think autonomous marriages end in divorce much more often than arranged marriages? Is it better to arrange marriages or to allow people to choose their relationship partners? What are some of the pros and cons of both types of marital arrangements?

Polyandry: Marriage between one wife and multiple husbands; polyandry is very rare historically.

Consensual nonmonogamy (CNM): A relationship arrangement in which all partners agree that it is acceptable to pursue sexual and/or romantic relationships with others.

Polygyny and polyandry. In polygamous marriages, one individual is married to more than one other spouse at a time. **Polygyny** refers to marriage between a husband and multiple wives, while **polyandry** refers to marriage between a wife and multiple husbands. Throughout history, polygyny has been a common marital arrangement; polyandry, in contrast, is rare. For example, while 82% of human societies have permitted polygyny, 1% have permitted polyandry, and the remainder (17%) permit only monogamous marriage (Marlowe, 2000). Many Muslim-majority countries in Africa, the Middle East, and South Asia practice polygyny today, although only a minority of men in polygynous societies marry more than one woman. Polygynous cultures more frequently have strict hierarchical political structures, unequal distributions of wealth, higher ratios of women to men, and high levels of infectious diseases (Barber, 2008). These conditions allow small numbers of high-status, physically healthy men to control disproportionate levels of resources, which enables them to support multiple wives and many offspring. Women in such societies may benefit from the protection afforded by joining large, resource-rich households, and in cultures with high disease levels, a healthy male partner who exhibits pathogen resistance improves the likelihood of passing on good genes to offspring. That said, some research finds that women have poorer mental health and relationship satisfaction in polygynous than in monogamous marriages (Shepard, 2012).

Consensual nonmonogamy and polyamory. **Consensual nonmonogamy** (CNM) refers to relationship arrangements in which all partners agree that it is acceptable to pursue sexual and/or romantic relationships with more than one other partner (Conley, Moors, Matsick, & Ziegler, 2013). CNMs can be structured in many different ways, reflecting the specific needs and desires of the individuals involved. For instance, partners may designate specific times when it is okay for them to have sex with others, or they may agree that all of them must be present during nonmonogamous encounters (e.g., threesomes or group sex). **Polyamory**, a specific type of CNM, refers to relationships in which adults have more than one other adult intimate relationship partner, with the knowledge and consent of all parties. Polyamorists (sometimes referred to as *polys*) typically view polyamory as a responsible and ethical form of nonmonogamy that differs from casual sex (Klesse, 2006).

Some estimates place the number of people involved in CNMs in the United States at about 4% (Conley et al., 2013) and the number of polyamorous individuals in the United States between 1.2 and 9.8 million (Sheff, 2013). However, because many people in Western cultures view monogamy as the ideal relationship form, CNMs tend to be stigmatized, and people in CNMs may remain closeted about their status. Thus, accurate prevalence rates are difficult to determine. Moreover, relatively little research examines CNMs and polyamory, as compared with monogamous relationships. The existing research is largely based on studies of gay men because gay male couples more frequently participate in CNMs than lesbian and heterosexual couples (LaSala, 2005). For the most part, research finds no noticeable differences in well-being, relationship satisfaction, or relationship longevity between people in monogamous versus CNM relationships (Rubel & Bogaert, 2015). However, one source of dysfunction in CNMs occurs when partners stray from their unique relationship agreements. Time management is another source of stress in some polyamorous relationships because of the challenges of creating a schedule that allows everyone the time they desire in specific pairings, groups, or as a whole family (Emens, 2004).

Writer and actor Dan Savage uses the term "monogamish" to describe the type of consensually nonmonogamous relationship he has with his husband.

Source: By Dan Savage - Provided by the subject., CC BY-SA 3.0, https://commons.wikimedia.org/w/index.php?curid=4810559

Polyamory: A type of consensual nonmonogamy in which adults have more than one other adult intimate relationship partner, with the knowledge and consent of all parties.

Sidebar 10.2: Practicing the Principles of Polyamory?

Polyamory, or the practice of forming intimate relationships with more than one other adult, can take many different forms. Some examples include these: A woman is in love with and has sex with two men; the two men are best friends but do not share a sexual relationship. A four-person family consists of a married male–female couple and two other men who are lovers of the husband and of each other; all four of them have outside sexual relationships that they disclose to

(Continued)

(Continued)

each other. A woman has a primary female lover and an occasional female lover; she and her primary lover sometimes have group sex with others, but the primary lover often feels jealousy and anger when the woman spends time alone with her occasional lover. To deal with this, the woman and her primary lover talk regularly and openly about their feelings. Despite their differences, these arrangements all share an emphasis on the core principles of polyamory: honesty, self-knowledge, consent, self-possession, and the prioritizing of love over negative emotions such as jealousy (Emens, 2004).

What Roles Do Sex and Gender Play in Committed Relationships?

As we have seen, marriages and committed relationships can assume many forms. However, one thing seems clear: A happy marriage is good for your health. Married people, on average, have better physical health and lower rates of mortality than unmarried people (R. M. Kaplan & Kronick, 2006). As noted earlier, however, men generally experience more positive health benefits from marriage than do women. In contrast, the costs of unhappy marriage tend to be worse for women than for men. While men in unhappy marriages still tend to have better outcomes than single men, women in unhappy marriages experience higher risk of depression and alcoholism, poorer immune functioning, and increased risk of stroke and cardiovascular disease than do happily married and never-married women (Balog et al., 2003). So what makes a marriage happy or unhappy? How do people show and maintain love, deal with conflict, and adapt to separation and divorce? In the upcoming sections, we will consider how gender relates to these aspects of committed relationships.

Happy Relationships: Equity and Love

Making decisions. Members of Western cultures tend to value egalitarian relationships in which partners share power and contribute to decisions equally. This is especially true among same-sex (and particularly lesbian) couples, who rate equality as more essential for their relationships than heterosexual couples do (Peplau & Fingerhut, 2007). When couples share equally in decisions that affect their relationship, they report higher levels of relationship satisfaction (Worley & Samp, 2016). In contrast, unequal decision making in relationships predicts lower satisfaction for both partners, and in extreme cases, female partners who lack decision-making power face greater risk of domestic violence and higher mortality rates (Hibbard & Pope, 1993; Kaura & Allen, 2004).

That said, almost half of couples studied report at least some power imbalance in their relationships (J. A. Simpson, Farrell, Orina, & Rothman, 2015). When imbalances occur within heterosexual relationships, partners usually agree that the man has more control over decisions. As one interesting exception to this trend, in a study of unmarried Black professionals who were dating, women reported having more power over relationship decisions than men did (L. E. Davis, Williams, Emerson, & Hourd-Bryant, 2000). Davis and his collaborators attributed this pattern to the fact that Black women in the United States have historically worked outside the home, often as primary breadwinners, to a greater degree than have White women.

Of course, couple members may not always agree about the balance of decision-making power in their relationship. Sprecher and Felmlee (1997) found that men tended to view themselves as having more decision-making power than their female partners while women viewed themselves and their partners as contributing more equally to decisions. Moreover, even when inequalities exist, couples may still view decision making as fair if they each wield more power in different domains. For example, if one partner has more say over financial decisions, and the other has more say over parenting decisions, they may both maintain feelings of fairness (Kulik, 2011). These findings suggest that perceived fairness of decision making (equity)—in comparison with actual equality—may be more important for relationship functioning.

Dividing labor and childcare. Most marriages today in the United States consist of dual-earner couples, so it is no wonder that fairness of household and childcare labor divisions plays a large role in marital satisfaction. Couples who share domestic labor more equally report the highest relationship satisfaction, and this holds for both heterosexual and same-sex couples (Gilbert, 1993; Kurdek, 2006; Saginak & Saginak, 2005). As with decision making, however, perceived fairness (equity) may be more important than actual equality. As you will read in more detail in Chapter 11 ("Work and Home"), members of many heterosexual couples divide labor according to traditional gendered patterns, with wives logging more hours on housework and childcare than husbands. This pattern holds even when women work full-time outside the home. Nonetheless, if traditional gender beliefs shape people's views of labor divisions, then couples may still perceive these arrangements as fair. One study of dual-earner heterosexual couples found that both wives and husbands perceived their labor division as fairer to the extent that they spent a larger proportion of their total work hours on gender-typical tasks (i.e., domestic labor for wives and paid labor for husbands). In turn, perceived fairness of labor divisions predicted relationship satisfaction for both couple members (J. R. Wilkie, Ferree, & Ratcliff, 1998).

If perceptions of labor division fairness are rooted in traditional gender roles, then do nontraditional couples divide labor more equally? Perhaps so. As shown in Figure 10.4, lesbian couples report the most egalitarian divisions of labor, followed by gay and heterosexual cohabiting couples, childless married heterosexual couples, and, finally, married heterosexual parents (Kurdek, 2006). Other factors that may contribute to equal divisions of labor include socioeconomic status and job flexibility. For instance, one study found that the couples with the most egalitarian labor divisions were those who could pay someone else to clean for them and whose jobs allowed for more scheduling flexibility (Carrington, 1999). Thus, regardless of their ideals, lower-income couples with highly demanding or inflexible job schedules may have difficulty achieving truly equal labor divisions in the home.

Figure 10.4 Household Labor Divisions by Couple Type.

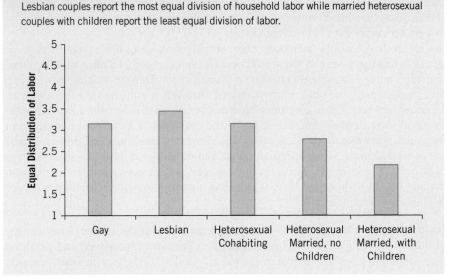

Lesbian couples report the most equal division of household labor while married heterosexual couples with children report the least equal division of labor.

Source: Kurdek (2006).

Note: Scores range from 1 (one partner does this all the time) to 5 (we do this equally).

Showing love. When asked to describe the typical ways that people of their own sex show love, heterosexual men are more likely than women to mention acts that involve displaying resources, such as "buying expensive gifts" or "treating her to dinner." In contrast, heterosexual women are more likely than men to list acts that assure commitment and sexual exclusivity, such as "displaying affection in public" or "performing sex acts for him" (T. J. Wade, Auer, & Roth, 2009). So do these stereotypes map onto real sex differences in how people show love? Not exactly. When Elizabeth Schoenfeld and her colleagues tracked couples over 13 years of marriage (Schoenfeld et al., 2012), they found that both wives' and husbands' feelings of love for their spouses were positively correlated with affectionate behaviors, such as saying "I love you," showing approval, and affectionate touching (e.g., hugging and holding hands). However, for wives only, those who reported greater love for their partners also showed less negativity (e.g., less criticizing and less complaining). For husbands only, those who reported greater love for partners also initiated sex more frequently and did more couple-centered leisure activities and a larger percentage of daily housework with their wives. These sex differences in "love acts" may remind you of the sex differences we noted earlier regarding friendships: Women may be especially likely to show affection by regulating the emotional tone of close relationships while men may be more likely to show affection by engaging in joint activities.

Relationship Struggles: Jealousy and Conflict

Jealousy. In small doses, jealousy can be adaptive because it motivates actions that fend off rivals, which can help to protect the bond between romantic partners. However, in larger amounts, jealousy can be corrosive. Jealously correlates strongly with anger, and it surfaces as one of the most often cited motives for intimate partner violence committed by both women and men, in both heterosexual and same-sex relationships (Goldenberg, Stephenson, Freeland, Finneran, & Hadley, 2016; Langhinrichsen-Rohling, McCullars, & Misra, 2012; Mason, Lewis, Gargurevich, & Kelley, 2016). Jealousy can undermine trust, erode satisfaction, and increase stress and conflict.

While women and men do not differ in the frequency or intensity of jealousy that they experience, some researchers argue that there are sex differences in the types of partner behaviors that activate jealousy. On average, men tend to react with more jealousy to a partner's *sexual infidelity* (having sex with someone else) than they do to a partner's *emotional infidelity* (falling in love with someone else). In contrast, women tend to experience more jealousy in response to emotional than sexual infidelity. This sex difference has been replicated several times and across dozens of different cultures (Kaighobadi, Shackelford, & Goetz, 2009). Evolutionary psychologists explain these sex differences as resulting from the unique adaptive problems that ancestral women and men faced early in humans' history. As we first discussed in Chapter 3 ("The Nature and Nurture of Sex and Gender"), ancestral men faced the problem of *paternity uncertainty*. This means that because fertilization occurs internally to women, men could not know with 100% certainty that any given offspring carried their genes. A man who jealously guarded his female mate to prevent her from having sex with other men would therefore have reduced his own risk of supporting offspring who did not carry his genes, a situation referred to as *cuckoldry*. Thus, men may have evolved a tendency to feel strong jealousy at the prospect of female partners' sexual infidelity (Kaighobadi et al., 2009).

The adaptive problem faced by ancestral women, in contrast, involved securing a mate who would remain committed to the family unit. Because of female humans' greater parental investment (the amount of time and energy necessary to produce offspring physically), ancestral women would have benefited from seeking mates who offered dependable assistance and resources (Trivers, 1972). Thus, women should have evolved a tendency to react with strong jealousy to cues that a male partner was in love with someone else because this meant he would likely abandon the family unit and take his resources elsewhere. Despite the neatness of this logic, some scholars view the evolutionary account of sex differences in jealousy as flawed while others propose that evolutionary psychologists exaggerate the size and reliability of these sex differences. For more on this, refer to "Debate: Did Women and Men Evolve Different Jealousy Reactions?"

Dealing with conflict. What do couples fight about? Across cultures, common sources of conflict include sex and physical intimacy, money, divisions of labor, and parenting (L. M. Dillon et al., 2015). These important issues require decision making and negotiation, making them ripe for disagreements. But now let's consider another answer to this question. When asked, "What do couples fight about?" during an interview with Anderson Cooper, psychologist Dr. John Gottman replied, "Absolutely nothing. Couples

While many scholars agree that women and men evolved different jealousy reactions to a mate's infidelity, others question many of the assumptions behind this position. Here, we consider both sides of this debate.

Yes, Sex Differences in Jealousy Are Evolved

Over a dozen studies find that men experience more sexual than emotional jealousy, whereas women experience more emotional than sexual jealousy. This sex difference emerges both in people's self-reports and on physiological measures, with men showing more central nervous system arousal when imagining a partner's sexual versus emotional infidelity, and women showing more arousal when imagining emotional versus sexual infidelity (Buss, Larsen, Westen, & Semmelroth, 1992). Moreover, men react with stronger jealousy to hypothetical cues indicating a partner's sexual infidelity ("She suddenly refuses to have sex with you") than to cues indicating emotional infidelity ("She does not say 'I love you' anymore"; Schützwohl, 2005). These sex differences appear in archival records and across dozens of cultures. For instance, one investigation of 160 societies found that divorce more frequently follows a wife's than a husband's sexual infidelity (Betzig, 1989). In other words, across cultures, men tend to be less accepting than women of a partner's sexual infidelity. When a tendency appears universally like this, it can suggest that the tendency is evolved.

Evolutionary psychologists propose that these sex differences emerge due to the different mating problems that ancestral women and men faced. For men—but not women—genetic paternity was not assured, and cuckoldry imposes substantial reproductive costs for men. Men who unwittingly raise another man's offspring invest time, energy, and resources on children who do not carry their genes; furthermore, they lose out on other mating opportunities. Many other animal species exhibit anticuckoldry mechanisms, and it makes sense that humans would have evolved such a mechanism as well (Buss et al., 1992). If so, sexual jealousy is a likely candidate.

No, Sex Differences in Jealousy Are Not Evolved

Just because a sex difference exists, it does not necessarily make it a product of evolution. In fact, sex differences in jealousy can just as easily be explained as stemming from sociocultural factors, such as men's desire to control and suppress women's sexuality. From this perspective, a female partner's sexual infidelity is threatening because it indicates a level of sexual autonomy that challenges male dominance over women (Travis & White, 2000). Thus, men may experience more sexual than emotional jealousy because of the need to control women's bodies, not because of paternity uncertainty. Conversely, a male partner's emotional infidelity—and the prospect of abandonment that it foretells—may be especially distressing to women because patriarchal gender inequities, such as the gender wage gap, ensure that women tend to remain economically dependent on men (Hyde & Oliver, 2000).

Moreover, sex differences in jealousy are not as reliable and consistent as some scholars claim. Christine Harris (2003) notes that much of the research on sex differences in jealousy uses forced-choice, hypothetical scenarios in which people imagine their reactions to infidelity. These studies often use college student samples in which large subsets of people lack personal experience with serious, committed relationships. Such studies cannot necessarily reveal how people actually react when faced with an unfaithful partner and may reflect people's gender stereotypes rather than evolved tendencies. Harris also notes that using a forced-choice method (in which participants must choose which would bother them more: emotional or sexual infidelity) produces the previously described sex differences. However, when people rate how much each type of infidelity bothers them on a seven-point rating scale, for example, both sexes report being equally bothered by both kinds of infidelity. Thus, men may only report more sexual than emotional jealousy when forced to choose.

Finally, Christine Harris's (2003) review indicates that there is a great deal of within-sex variance, and many men rate emotional infidelity as more troubling than sexual infidelity. In fact, gay men—similar to heterosexual and lesbian women—report being more distressed by emotional than sexual infidelity (Sheets & Wolfe, 2001). This reversal of the expected sex difference raises questions about whether sexual jealousy is an evolved, sex-linked tendency.

What do you think? Do men display a clear tendency toward sexual jealousy as an evolved mechanism? Or is the evidence for evolved sex differences in jealousy too unclear to allow for firm conclusions? Which evidence do you find most convincing, and why?

fight about nothing" (April 18, 2002). In other words, fights often arise due to temporary annoyances, knee-jerk reactions, or misunderstandings that spiral out of control. If this is the case, then it may be more important to understand *how* couples fight than *what* they fight about.

Imagine that you got married within the past 6 months (congratulations!), and you and your spouse agree to participate in a study of "newlywed interactions" at Dr. Gottman's research laboratory. Upon arriving at the laboratory, you and your spouse generate a list of problems that create disagreements in your relationship. You then select two or three of your most problematic issues and discuss these issues for 15 minutes while being videotaped. Seems pretty simple, right? What you likely do not realize (and might not want to know) is that Gottman and his collaborators can predict, with impressive accuracy, the likelihood of your marriage ending in divorce based on this procedure. Moreover, they can predict the likelihood of you getting divorced within a 6-year period based on the *first 3 minutes* of your videotaped discussion (Carrère & Gottman, 1999), and they can predict whether you will divorce earlier or later in your marriage, over a 14-year period, with a 93% accuracy rate (Gottman & Levenson, 2000).

What is Gottman's secret? It all has to do with the emotions and interaction patterns that couple members express during conflicts. For example, most heterosexual couples show a decrease in nonverbal expressions of positive emotions (e.g., joy, humor, and affection) and an increase in expressions of negative emotions (e.g., defensiveness and anger) during discussions of tense topics, and this is true for both wives and husbands. However, husbands' changes in emotional expressions over time hold an important key to predicting heterosexual couples' longevity: In unstable marriages (e.g., those that end in divorce), husbands show a more rapid escalation of negative emotion and a more rapid decline of positive emotion during the first few minutes of conflict discussions.

In contrast, although husbands in stable marriages show a small increase in negative emotions during conflict discussions, they also maintain a moderately high level of positive emotions throughout such discussions. In other words, when newlywed husbands maintain moderate levels of nonverbal joy, affection, and humor during tense conflict discussions, the couple is more likely to stay together (Carrère & Gottman, 1999).

Another gendered interaction pattern that predicts divorce is termed the **demand–withdraw pattern**. In this pattern, one couple member makes a demanding or critical remark, and the other partner responds by withdrawing from the interaction, either emotionally or physically. This withdrawal reaction shuts down further communication and can leave the first partner feeling as though she or he is talking to a "stone wall" (hence the term *stonewalling* to refer to this withdrawal behavior). Gottman and his collaborators find that the demand–withdraw pattern predicts divorce but primarily when the wife demands and the husband withdraws (Gottman & Levenson, 2000). This may be because women generally initiate discussions about conflict topics more often than men do. Moreover, women tend to display more hostility during conflicts than men do ($d = -0.16$), and men tend to stonewall during conflicts more than women do ($d = 0.16$; Woodin, 2011). Note that these effect sizes are small, however.

What about same-sex couples? In one study, same-sex couples expressed more positive and fewer negative emotions than heterosexual couples when first initiating conflict discussions (Gottman et al., 2003). Moreover, same-sex couples—and lesbians, in particular—continued to display positive emotion throughout the duration of conflict discussions. Gottman and his collaborators speculated that the positive interactions maintained by same-sex couples during conflict discussions may reflect the emphasis that these couples place on relationship equality.

For both heterosexual and same-sex pairings, couples who show higher levels of hostility (anger, demanding, and dominating) during conflict discussions are lower in satisfaction, and those who show more intimacy (humor and self-disclosure) and problem solving (offering solutions and requesting clarification) during conflict discussions are more satisfied. Distress and withdrawal during conflict discussions also predict lower relationship satisfaction, although these associations are relatively weaker (Woodin, 2011). In sum, it appears that *how* couples fight is very important when it comes to relationship functioning.

Demand–withdraw pattern: An interpersonal relationship pattern in which one couple member criticizes or demands, and the other partner responds by withdrawing emotionally or physically.

Separation and Divorce

The vast majority of people end up marrying, and research consistently finds that married people report greater happiness and life satisfaction than unmarried people (Wadsworth, 2016). Yet one seeming paradox of romantic relationships is that about 40% of first-time marriages in Western countries end in divorce (Aughinbaugh, Robles, & Sun, 2013). And divorce is not simply a modern, Western phenomenon. Divorce rates are 37% over the first 5 years of marriage among the !Kung, a hunter-gatherer society of the Kalahari Desert (Howell, 1979), and 39% among the Hadza, an indigenous group from Tanzania (Blurton Jones, Marlowe, Hawkes, & O'Connell, 2000). What about the success of same-sex relationships? Because same-sex marriage was only recently legalized throughout the United States (and remains illegal in much of the world), official marriage and divorce rates are lacking. Some research suggests that same-sex couples—and particularly gay men—have higher rates of breakups than other-sex couples (Lau, 2012). However, Rosenfeld (2014) found similar breakup rates across same-sex and other-sex couples when considering couples who were married or had marriage-like commitments. Moreover, as mentioned, staying together does not necessarily mean that a couple is happy. Some of the barriers to divorce that keep unhappy couples together, such as children or financial dependence on a spouse, are less common in same-sex than other-sex relationships (Kurdek, 2004).

Why do people end relationships? Do women and men end relationships for similar reasons? Across cultures, women report relationship problems more often (L. M. Dillon et al., 2015) and initiate divorce more often (Hewett, Western, & Baxter, 2006) than men. Moreover, gender plays a role in several of the reasons that people give for ending relationships. First, women more often blame declines in the quality of communication while men more often blame declines in joint activities (Riessman, 1990). Second, as discussed previously, inequities in housework and childcare contribute to relationship tension. Finally, infidelity commonly leads to relationship dissolution, and men tend to report being unfaithful more often than women do. In the United States, about 25% of men and 15% of women admit to marital infidelity, and these rates do not differ by race or ethnicity (Blow & Hartnett, 2005).

Most couples find relationship dissolution painful. But who suffers more? The answer depends on the metric we use. Financially, women tend to suffer more than men from divorce (Tach & Eads, 2015). Psychologically, however, men may fare worse. Men show a larger dip in happiness following divorce than women (Lucas, 2005), and mortality rates are higher for men than women following divorce (Shor, Roelfs, Bugyi, & Schwartz, 2012). This ties back to the idea we raised earlier: that romantic relationships have more bearing on the health of men than women.

Stop and Think

Throughout this chapter, we have discussed evidence suggesting that men, as compared with women, suffer more in terms of mental and physical health when they lack or lose a close, marriage-like partnership. Why do you think this is the case? How would the evolutionary and sociocultural perspectives explain this finding?

What Roles Do Sex and Gender Play in Parenting and Family Relationships?

At some point in their lives, most people become parents. In the United States, by the age of 40, 85% of women and 76% of men have had at least one child (Martinez, Daniels, & Chandra, 2012). Parenting often, although not always, involves at least two important relationships: one between coparents (if there are two parents) and the other between parent and child. In this section, we will consider how gender shapes both of these relationships.

Parent to Parent: Gender and Parental Relationships

Although parents often anticipate the birth of a new child with joy and excitement, parenthood is typically associated with declines in relationship satisfaction. On average, parents report lower levels of relationship satisfaction than nonparents do (Twenge, Campbell, & Foster, 2003). New children introduce several factors that can strain relationship quality, including financial burdens, restrictions of freedom and leisure time, disrupted sleep, reduced sexual activity, and role conflicts (e.g., having to juggle competing demands of job and parenting).

So how does gender fit in? Although both parents become less satisfied with their relationship following the introduction of new children to the family, mothers generally suffer a larger decline in happiness than fathers, especially when children are infants. One meta-analysis found that the effect size for the difference in relationship satisfaction between parents and nonparents is larger for mothers of infants than it is for mothers of older children or for fathers of any-age children (Twenge et al., 2003). While much of the research summarized in this meta-analysis drew from Western samples, similar sex differences emerge in Eastern samples as well (Lu, 2005). Mothers also experience **postpartum depression** more often than fathers do. One study found that 9.3% of mothers versus 3.4% of fathers received new diagnoses of depression within 3 months of their infant's birth (Escribà-Agüir & Artazcoz, 2011).

Postpartum depression: Depression following (or associated with) childbirth.

You might think of postpartum depression as something that only affects women, but men can develop it too.

Source: © iStockPhoto .com/tommaso79

These sex differences in relationship satisfaction and depression may occur, in part, because mothers usually shoulder more of the parenting responsibilities than fathers do, at least in heterosexual relationships. Still, even in couples that split parenting chores more evenly, parenthood predicts reductions in relationship satisfaction. For example, same-sex couples report more equitable divisions of childcare than heterosexual couples do (Farr & Patterson, 2013), and lesbian mothers feel more satisfied than heterosexual mothers do with their partner's contributions to parenting (Bos, van Balen, & van den Boom, 2004). Nonetheless, members of lesbian and gay couples report declines in relationship happiness and increases in conflict after becoming parents (Goldberg, Smith, & Kashy, 2010).

The reality may be that parenting—and especially new parenting—is a stressful process that poses unique challenges for relationships. Many parenting stressors (e.g., financial burdens and reductions in leisure time) hit both parents equally hard, but others are gendered, such as norms that place more childcare responsibility on women than men. As another gendered source of dissatisfaction, fathers sometimes feel "left out" and disconnected from the family unit as mothers bond with a new infant (Nyostrom & Ohrling, 2004). Moreover, the negative impact of parenthood on relationship satisfaction appears to be increasing over time (Twenge et al., 2003), likely due to growing expectations that parents will spend more time with children and less "child-free" time with their partners (see Chapter 11, "Work and Home," for more details about these trends).

Sidebar 10.3: Child-Free by Choice?

In the past several decades, the number of people in Western cultures choosing to remain child-free (**child-free by choice**) has grown at a rapid pace (Agrillo & Nelini, 2008). Some of the reasons that people give for this decision include lack of desire (e.g., lack of parenting drive and belief that childhood is too difficult), personal advancement (e.g., ability to focus on career and desire to avoid financial burden), health concerns (e.g., desire not to pass on a hereditary disease), and concerns for humanity and the earth (e.g., concerns about overpopulation and the environment and belief that the world is too full of human suffering). While both members of heterosexual couples who remain child-free elicit feelings of moral outrage in others (Ashburn-Nardo, 2017), the bulk of the responsibility for being child-free often falls to women: Others assume, when a heterosexual couple is child-free by choice, that the decision not to have children lies more with the woman than with the man (Koropeckyj-Cox, Romano, & Moras, 2007).

Child-free by choice: The status of an individual or couple who decides not to have children.

In the face of all these negative impacts, is there any good news about parenting? Absolutely! First, although many parents experience declines in relationship satisfaction, this is not universal—relationship satisfaction remains stable or even increases after the transition to parenthood among a sizeable minority of couples (A. F. Shapiro, Gottman, & Carrère, 2000). Second, even when declines in satisfaction occur, satisfaction often rebounds over time as couples adjust to the changes in their lives (Cox, Paley, Burchinal, & Payne, 1999). Third, although relationship satisfaction often decreases after the birth of a child, individual happiness often increases: Compared with nonparents, parents report higher levels of personal happiness and meaning in life (S. K. Nelson, Kushlev, English, Dunn, & Lyubomirsky, 2013). Fourth, active father involvement and coparenting correlates with greater relationship satisfaction, particularly for mothers (McLain & Brown, 2017). And finally, the most obvious "good news" about parenting is that most people genuinely love their children and feel happy to have them around, even if it means that their marital happiness takes a (hopefully temporary) hit.

Parent to Child: Gender and Caring for Children

Have you ever encountered the term *maternal instinct*? How about the claim that "a mother's intuition is always right"? These reflect common folk wisdom about the natural caregiving talents that presumably come with being a woman. As the story goes, being a woman means possessing a biological drive to bear and care for children (the *maternal instinct*), as well as an inborn, almost supernatural ability to intuit an offspring's needs without the help of language (a *mother's intuition*). In psychological terms, both of these concepts reflect **essentialist beliefs** about parenting. Recall from past chapters that essentialist beliefs are assumptions that observed sex differences reflect inherent, natural, biological differences between women and men. According to these beliefs, the biological capacities of pregnancy, childbirth, and lactation imbue women with a natural instinct to nurture offspring and an intuitive, "gut-level" understanding of children's needs (B. Park, Banchefsky, & Reynolds, 2015).

Essentialist beliefs: Assumptions that observed sex differences reflect inherent, natural, biological differences between women and men.

The flip side of these assumptions is that men lack a strong parenting instinct. Compared with women, men are stereotyped as relatively uninterested in becoming fathers, disinclined to take responsibility for their children, and low in natural caregiving talent. And yet, those who adopt essentialist beliefs about parenting also view fathers as playing a unique and critical role in children's development. For instance, from an essentialist perspective, sons need a strong father figure to develop a normal, "healthy" masculine gender identity. Table 10.2 summarizes these essentialist beliefs about mothers and fathers.

Essentialist beliefs about parenting are firmly entrenched. In one study of Black and White U.S. adults, respondents were much more likely to attribute sex differences in nurturance—as compared with sex differences in violence or math ability—to genetic factors (Cole, Jayaratne, Cecchi, Feldbaum, & Petty, 2007). However, these beliefs

Table 10.2 Essentialist Beliefs About Mothers and Fathers. Essentialist beliefs link sex differences to underlying biological causes. Endorsing essentialist beliefs about parents is associated with valuing some types of family arrangements (e.g., heterosexual, two-parent) over others and with negative beliefs about working mothers.

Essentialist Beliefs About Mothers	Essentialist Beliefs About Fathers
Biological experiences of pregnancy, childbirth, and lactation imbue women with a natural instinct toward parenting and nurturing offspring.	Men lack a biological parenting instinct and are not driven to nurture offspring.
Women's biology affords them an intuitive understanding of their children's needs.	Men lack natural parenting skills and are unable to care for children unless they are given specific instructions.
Children need mothers more than they need fathers.	Children (especially boys) need fathers in order to develop in a healthy manner.
Parenting provides women with a deep sense of reward and satisfaction.	Men are not naturally motivated to parent but can be induced to do so through the institution of marriage.

Source: Liss, Schiffrin, Mackintosh, Miles-McLean, and Erchull (2013); Silverstein and Auerbach (1999).

should be evaluated critically because they can shape people's attitudes about "appropriate" family structures and practices. For example, people who endorse essentialist parenting beliefs are more inclined to view heterosexual, two-parent families as superior to other types of family structures. Furthermore, people who more strongly endorse essentialist beliefs about mothering also tend to assume that mothers of young children cannot excel in the workplace (B. Park et al., 2015), a belief that might subtly shape employers' work evaluations of their female employees.

So what do the data say about these essentialist assumptions? When psychologists first began examining the caretaking behaviors of new mothers and fathers, they were surprised to discover no sex differences in parenting quality. In fact, women and men, on average, show similar levels of competence (or incompetence) in meeting the needs of new infants. As Lamb (1987) noted, "Parenting skills are usually acquired 'on the job' by both mothers and fathers" (p. 11). However, because the primary caretaker in heterosexual couples is usually the mother, women often receive more "on-the-job" training in parenthood than fathers do. By spending more time with infants, mothers may develop greater sensitivity to infants' needs and a better ability to interpret infants' nonverbal communications. This may explain why mothers sometimes seem to have intuitive parenting skills. However, when men are the primary caregivers of infants, they parent just as well as women do (Lamb, 1997).

Regardless of the sex of the parent, the predictors of good parent–child relationships and good outcomes for children are the same: Children fare best when parents demonstrate *warmth*, *sensitivity*, and *consistency* (Lamb, 1997). While warmth is probably self-explanatory, sensitivity and consistency can use some explaining. In the context of parenting, *sensitivity* means being able to evaluate or interpret a child's needs and respond appropriately while *consistency* means responding in a predictable, reliable manner so that infants come to expect that their needs will be met. According to **attachment theory**, caregivers who consistently and reliably offer warm, sensitive responses to their infants will develop strong attachment relationships with children, and vice versa (Bowlby, 1980). Moreover, children who receive this type of parenting tend to have the best outcomes in terms of social and emotional competence, cognitive functioning, and physical and mental health (Ranson & Urichuk, 2008).

Attachment theory: A theory that describes the processes by which adults and infants become attached and develop strong emotional bonds.

Children can thrive with parents of any sex, as long as parents provide warmth, sensitivity, and consistency.

Source: © iStockPhoto .com/Juanmonino

From this perspective, the sex or gender identity of a parent makes little difference for children's outcomes. In other words, children do not need both a mother and a father to thrive. In fact, studies that compare same-sex versus heterosexual parents find no differences across couple type in the quality of relationship that parents have with children, children's attachment to parents, children's behavioral problems at school, or children's relationships with peers (Erich, Kanenberg, Case, Allen, & Bogdanos, 2009; Farr &

Patterson, 2013). Moreover, children can thrive with a single parent, provided that the parent offers warm, sensitive, and consistent caretaking (Silverstein & Auerbach, 1999). Of course, given the difficulty of parenting, successful caregiving may be more likely to occur if two adults share the task. Even so, high-quality parenting is possible for single parents to achieve.

Stop and Think

Why do you think essentialist beliefs about parenting, such as the notions of a mother's instinct *and* a mother's intuition, *are so appealing? Are you surprised to learn that there are no real sex differences in* "natural talent" *at parenting? Why or why not? We mentioned a couple of possible negative consequences of essentialist beliefs about parenting—what are some others?*

CHAPTER SUMMARY

10.1 Analyze the roles of sex, gender, and LGBT status in social networks, friendships, and friendship intimacy.

People have a fundamental need to belong, which they can meet through social networks and close friendships. Social networks are an important source of social support, and people benefit from having richer, larger networks. Perhaps because women tend to give more and higher-quality emotional support than men do, men derive unique benefits from having a female romantic partner in their social network. LGBT people, in particular, rely on networks of friends for support and companionship with similar others who understand their experiences.

Women and men both want emotional intimacy in their close friendships, but women's friendships often appear more intimate than men's, perhaps due to gender role socialization or differences in how researchers conceptualize *intimacy*. On average, women tend to pursue dyadic friendships centered on shared emotions, and men tend to pursue group friendships centered on shared activities, leading them to achieve friendship intimacy through different paths. Cross-sex friendships, which become more common in young adulthood, can offer unique benefits while also inviting unique complications. Many adolescents and young adults in the United States today pursue casual sexual relationships with their friends (e.g., friends with benefits). Among lesbian friend pairs, intense romantic attractions (passionate friendships) may develop into first loves or first same-sex sexual experiences.

10.2 Evaluate major theoretical perspectives on sex similarities and differences in mate preferences and mate choices.

Women and men desire many of the same traits in their ideal mates. Where differences exist, they tend to be small. However, theorists have long debated the interpretation of sex differences in a small set of mate preferences: Women tend to rate a partner's ambition and earning potential as more important than men do, and men tend to rate a partner's attractiveness and homemaking skill as more important than women do. These differences emerge across cultures, but there are exceptions. Lesbians and Black women place less emphasis on earning potential than do heterosexual and White women, respectively. While evolutionary psychologists explain this difference using parental investment theory—that is, women should prioritize a mate's resources because women invest more in reproduction—sociocultural psychologists propose that women's restricted access to economic resources forces them to seek mates who offer financial support. In face-to-face encounters, both women's and men's attraction to dating partners is equally predicted by the partners' attractiveness and perceived earning potential. One of the best predictors of actual mate selection is partner homogamy, or overall similarity.

10.3 Explain the roles of gender and gender norms in dating relationships and romance.

Dating scripts have not changed much over time and still seem to dictate that men should play a more active role than women in the events of the date. Many also expect men to display paternalistic chivalry by treating their date like a "lady," paying for her, and being protective and polite. Some of these norms persist even in the context of more casual, hookup-type relationships. Despite the persistence of behavioral gender norms, there are few consistent sex differences in how women and men define romantic love, experience love, or show love to their dating partners.

10.4 Describe diverse marital arrangements across sociohistorical contexts, races and ethnicities, cultures, and sexual orientations.

Historically, most marriages were arranged and afforded men more power than women. Today, autonomous marriages are more common in Europe and North America, although arranged marriages predominate in many collectivistic cultures. In the United States, people today marry later, delay childbirth, and have fewer children than ever before. Relative to past decades, more children in the United States today live in single-parent households or in households with a stepparent or two same-sex parents. These trends differ by race, with Black women being more likely than White, Asian, and Hispanic women to be single parents. While marriage usually involves only two individuals, this is not always the case. Many Muslim-majority cultures practice polygyny, in which one man marries multiple wives. Consensual nonmonogamous

arrangements (CNMs) are somewhat more common among gay men than among lesbians and heterosexual partners. CNMs assume many forms, however, and do not always involve same-sex sexuality. Polyamorous arrangements are a form of CNM in which adults have more than one other adult intimate relationship partner, with the knowledge and consent of all parties.

10.5 Analyze sex differences and similarities in the factors that contribute to relationship satisfaction, conflict, and separation.

People benefit from being married in terms of both mental and physical health. However, men seem to benefit more from marriage than women do while women suffer more than men do from unhappy marriages. Two predictors of marital happiness are perceived equity of decision making and perceived equity of labor divisions. When inequities in decision making occur, they tend to favor men, although this may differ by race. In heterosexual couples, women tend to do more housework and childcare than men. Same-sex couples, especially lesbian couples, value egalitarian labor divisions more than heterosexual couples do. Women and men show love to their partners in similar ways, by being affectionate, showing approval, spending time together, and sharing sexual intimacy. However, women (more than men) show love by refraining from expressing negativity while men (more than women) show love through joint activities.

Jealousy is both adaptive—in that it motivates actions to restore a relationship—and corrosive, in that it predicts conflict, abuse, and relationship dissatisfaction. Some propose that men evolved to feel more jealousy over a partner's sexual infidelity while women evolved to feel more jealousy over a partner's emotional infidelity. However, the size and reliability of this sex difference is widely disputed. Across cultures, couples tend to experience conflict about similar topics, but the *way* that couples fight may be more important than what they fight about. Couples who maintain higher levels of positive emotions during conflict discussions and who keep negative emotions from escalating too abruptly are less likely to divorce. Same-sex couples, especially lesbian couples, show more positive emotion than heterosexual couples during tense discussions. In heterosexual couples, one predictor of divorce is a particular demand–withdraw pattern in which wives make a critical remark and husbands shut down. Divorce is common worldwide, with inequitable labor divisions and infidelity as two common causes of separation. Following divorce, women tend to suffer financially more than men, but men tend to suffer psychologically more than women.

10.5 Describe the roles of sex and gender in parenting and family relationships.

Parenthood correlates with declines in relationship satisfaction, for both heterosexual and same-sex couples. In heterosexual couples, women tend to suffer sharper declines in satisfaction and greater risk of postpartum depression than men, likely because women often shoulder the bulk of childcare. For many couples that become less satisfied after parenthood, satisfaction often rebounds after time.

Essentialist beliefs about parenthood cast women as "naturally" and "instinctively" maternal and fathers as lacking natural parenting skills. The evidence does not support the validity of these beliefs, showing instead that both mothers and fathers learn how to parent from experience, and neither sex has greater natural parenting skills. Children do not need both a mother and a father and can thrive with one parent or with two parents of the same sex. The best predictors of strong parent–child relationships and of adaptive outcomes for children are parental warmth, sensitivity, and consistency. Research that compares the well-being of children with heterosexual versus same-sex parents finds no overall differences.

Test Your Knowledge: True or False?

10.1. College students who are in "friends-with-benefits" sexual relationships report that the quality of their friendship declines after they introduce sex into the mix. (False: The majority of students in "friends-with-benefits" arrangements report that the friendship improves after it becomes sexual.) [p. 338]

10.2. In surveys of romantic partner preferences, men tend to rate physical attractiveness as more important in a mate than women do, and women tend to rate good financial prospects as more important in a mate than men do. (True: This pattern emerges across cultures.) [p. 339]

10.3. Arranged marriages—in which a relative or family friend selects the marriage partners—are the most common form of marriage worldwide. (True: Slightly more than one-half of marriages worldwide are arranged.) [p. 349]

10.4. In the context of heterosexual romantic relationships, men tend to experience more jealousy than women do regarding the possibility of their partner falling in love with someone else. (False: Depending on the methods used, men either report identical levels of emotional jealousy or less emotional jealousy than women.) [p. 355]

10.5. In general, relationship satisfaction decreases after couples have children. (True: This pattern emerges for most couples, whether they are heterosexual, lesbian, or gay.) [p. 360]

Test Your Knowledge: True or False?

11.1 In the United States, since the 1960s, mothers have doubled and fathers have tripled the amount of time per week, on average, that they spend on childcare.

11.2 In households in which women make more money than their husbands, wives tend to do less housework than husbands.

11.3 Women hold fewer top executive positions than men, in part because of gender stereotypes that contribute to biases in hiring and career advancement.

11.4 Once you account for differences in the occupations that women and men choose, the gender wage gap disappears.

11.5 Flexible work policies, such as telecommuting and flexible hours, correlate with less worker productivity and generally negative outcomes for organizations.

CHAPTER 11

Work and Home

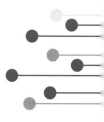

Key Concepts

How Have Work and Home Labor Divisions Changed?

How Do People Divide Housework and Childcare at Home?

Trends and Inequities

Who Does What?

Childcare

Predictors of the Division of Domestic Labor

Time Availability

Relative Income

Gender Role Ideology

Maternal Gatekeeping

How Does Gender Operate in the Workplace?

Gender and Leadership

Glass Ceilings, Glass Cliffs, and Sticky Floors

Bias Against Women

Sexual Orientation, Gender Identity, and Race

Bias Against Men

How Can We Explain the Gender Wage Gap?

What Is the Gender Wage Gap?

Debate: Is the Gender Wage Gap a Myth?

Possible Explanations for the Gender Wage Gap

Education and Occupational Segregation

Occupational Feminization

Salary Negotiation

Relocations and Career Interruptions

Overwork

Conclusions About the Gender Wage Gap

How Do Work and Family Roles Interact?

Journey of Research: From Work–Family Conflict to Work–Life Enrichment

Conflict and Enrichment

Flexible Work and Family Leave Policies

Learning Objectives

Students who read this chapter should be able to do the following:

11.1   Evaluate factors that influence the gendered division of labor in the home.

11.2   Describe subtle workplace gender biases that create and reinforce status differences between dominant and subordinate groups.

11.3   Explain the gender wage gap and the various theories that account for it.

11.4   Analyze the challenges and benefits of work–life balance and relevant factors, such as parental leave and flexible work arrangements.

Work and Home

Visit any public park in Sweden during midweek, and you will likely see men pushing babies in strollers and playing with their children. This is the result of over 40 years of top-down social engineering. In 1974, Sweden became the first country in the world to include fathers in work–family legislation, replacing *maternity leave* with the more inclusive *parental leave*. This legislation granted parents 6 months of paid leave after the birth of a child, with each parent entitled to half of that time. Gender roles can be resistant to change, however, and fathers did not take full advantage of parental leave at first. Most gave their leave days to their wives. In the first decades of Sweden's new work–family practice, 90% of the leave days were taken by women (Rangecroft, 2016).

To combat this trend, Sweden changed the legislation to increase fathers' involvement by instituting "daddy quotas" in 1995. These were nontransferable paid leave days that had to be taken by fathers, or else the couple would lose them. At first only 30 days, daddy quotas increased to 90 days by 2016. Fathers now take about 25% of the total paid leave among Swedish parents. As of 2016, Swedish parents got 480 days of paid parental leave, with 390 of these paid at 80% of their salary (and the rest at lower rates). In fact, Sweden boasts some the most progressive parental leave legislation in the world. It also consistently ranks among the most gender-egalitarian countries in the world (World Economic Forum, 2015).

The Swedish model stands in sharp contrast to the U.S. model. In 2015, the United States remained the only developed, industrialized nation in the world that did not have any national laws guaranteeing paid parental leave (ABC News, 2015). Despite the fact that both partners are employed in most American married couples, fathers still spend about half as much time as mothers on childcare (Parker, 2015). In contrast, Swedish fathers spend about two-thirds as much time as mothers do on childcare (Evertsson, 2012).

This chapter focuses on work both outside and inside the home. Both types of work play central roles in how people define themselves. Work outside the home not only involves making money, but people form work identities as well. Similarly, people's roles as homemakers, parents, or partners (for those who choose to adopt these roles) are often central to their sense of self. Recall from past chapters that most societies divide the two domains of work—outside and inside the home—along gendered lines. On average, women around the world work less and earn less than men outside of the home, and they do a greater share of household labor and childcare inside the home. People universally associate unpaid domestic labor with womanhood and femininity and paid labor in the workforce with manhood and masculinity. But as the Swedish and American examples make clear, work life and home life are not independent of one another. Personal decisions and organizational and government policies in one domain can affect outcomes in the other domain. Prioritizing paid work, for instance, necessarily means that a person will have less time to devote to home and family. As you read this chapter, keep in mind how gendered experiences in the domains of work and home intersect and mutually influence one another.

How Have Work and Home Labor Divisions Changed?

Many of you reading this book are likely to be unmarried students who have not yet chosen a career. What does the future hold for you after college? You may have thought about if and when you will get married, whether you will pursue a full-time career, whether or not you will have children, and, if so, when you will have them. Today, in the United States and most Western, industrialized nations, the choices that people make regarding work and family differ in many ways from the choices that people made in the mid-20th century. We covered several of these differences in Chapter 10 ("Interpersonal Relationships"), but we will review them briefly here.

In 1950, the average woman was married by about age 20 and the average man by about 23. By 2015, those ages had increased to 27 and 29, respectively (U.S. Census Bureau, 2015a). Not surprisingly, the age of first-time parents also rose. Over the past 45 years, the age at which women have their first child increased from 21 to 26, for example (T. J. Mathews & Hamilton, 2016), and more couples opt not to have children and remain *child-free by choice*. Single and same-sex parents head many more households today than in the past. For instance, in 1960, about 9% of children lived in single-parent households; by 2015, the percentage was 26% (U.S. Census Bureau, 2015b). In 1990, census data indicated that same-sex couples headed about 145,000 households in the United States while 2010 data suggest about 902,000 such households (U.S. Census Bureau, 2012).

What about divisions of labor? In 1965, American woman with children typically spent about 32 hours a week doing housework and about 8 hours doing paid work. By 2011, mothers, on average, did 18 hours of housework and 21 hours of paid work (Parker, 2015), though note that this pattern did not apply to all women. Recall from Chapter 10 that poor women, working-class women, and women of color in the United States have always worked in the paid labor force at relatively high rates (Kessler-Harris, 2003). In 1960, men were the sole breadwinners in 70% of American married couples, whereas 60% of married couples were dual-earners by 2012 (Parker, 2015). In 1960, mothers were the primary or sole providers in about 11% of U.S. households with children, and that number rose to 40% by 2011 (Pew Research Center [PRC], 2015). Many adults in industrialized nations now engage in both paid employment and unpaid family work, with fathers' contributions to housework increasing from 4 hours per week in 1960 to 10 hours, on average, today (Parker, 2015). However, there are exceptions to these patterns: Women constitute only 16%–20% of the paid labor force in Afghanistan, Iran, and Saudi Arabia, for example (World Bank, 2015).

Thus, by some measures, work and family trends have generally moved toward greater gender equality. Women's labor force participation steadily increased over the past half-century, and many occupations have become less gender segregated. The gender wage gap has narrowed from several decades ago (American Association of University Women, 2017). In many societies, people expect men to be active parents and contribute to housework. By other measures, however, progress toward full gender equality seems to have stalled. Worldwide, women hold only 14% of top executive positions and 4.5%

of CEO positions (Noland, Moran, & Kotschwar, 2016), and men still resist entering traditionally female-dominated occupations, such as nursing and elementary education. A gender wage gap remains in virtually every nation, and women still do the majority of housework and childcare the world over. In the sections that follow, we will take a closer look at divisions of labor in both the home and the workplace, carefully considering both their causes and consequences.

How Do People Divide Housework and Childcare at Home?

Let's begin by considering domestic labor, or the unpaid work that people do in their homes, from laundry and cleaning to meal preparation, childcare, and yard work. Social scientists have tracked people's domestic labor for decades, so we can examine how much people are doing, what they are doing, and how these variables have changed over time.

Trends and Inequities

On average, women do more domestic labor (housework and childcare) than men, a pattern that holds true across ethnicity, culture, and time and persists regardless of whether both members of the couple are employed. Figure 11.1 shows how the amount of time spent on housework changed over the past several decades in the United States for both members of heterosexual couples. Note that two main trends stand out. First, people do much less housework overall now than in the past (except childcare). This is probably largely the result of middle-class women being much more likely to be in the workforce today than in years past. Second, the gender gap in housework is shrinking. Women continue to do most of the housework, but the disparity in female and male contributions is smaller today than it used to be. The slopes of the trend lines reveal the main reason for the shrinking gap. Women do much less housework now, about half of what they did in 1965, whereas men do about twice what they did in 1965, even though their rate of change is still lower than women's (Bianchi, Sayer, Milkie, & Robinson, 2012). And these figures may actually underestimate the work that women do in the home. Not only do women in heterosexual couples do the majority of physical housework, they also do the majority of "mental" housework—remembering and reminding their partners and children about tasks such as household errands or doctor visits (Ahn, Haines, & Mason, 2017). Though usually not captured in counts of housework hours, this type of work can be time-consuming and mentally taxing.

Another trend suggests that over the course of heterosexual marriage, husbands' contributions to housework tend to decline. For instance, a longitudinal study in Germany found that while many new couples began by sharing housework duties fairly evenly, the husbands decreased their share over the next 14 years, even when the wife made more money or worked longer hours than the husband outside the home (Grunow, Schulz, & Blossfeld, 2012). The fact that most women continue to do the majority of housework, combined with women's increased levels of employment, suggests that women

Figure 11.1 Hours Spent on Housework in the United States.

Since 1965, women in the United States have decreased and men have increased the hours per week they spend on housework. Still, women spend about 6 more hours per week on housework than men.

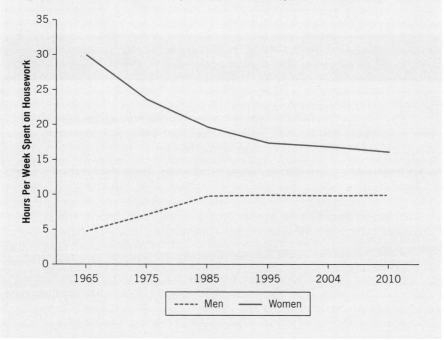

Source: Bianchi, Sayer, Milkie, and Robinson (2012).

experience ever-increasing pressures on their time. Women's increased commitment to paid employment has not been matched by a parallel commitment among men to divide housework and childcare equally in the home. In a sense, then, many women work what sociologist Arlie Hochschild (1989) aptly labeled a "second shift" at home following their work outside the home. This can have implications for psychological and relational health because, as you read in Chapter 10, the perceived fairness of labor divisions inside the home (housework and childcare) contributes to both individual well-being and marital satisfaction (Gilbert, 1993).

Some theorists propose that men's unequal contributions to labor on the home front led to a trend called the **stalled gender revolution** (England, 2010). Between the 1960s and the late 1980s, the United States saw steady gains in women's participation in economic, educational, workplace, and political domains. More and more women sought employment outside the home, got college and advanced degrees, and entered previously male-dominated fields of work and study. As mentioned, however, shifts in women's time from inside to outside the home were not matched by equal shifts in men's time from outside to inside the home: Men did not pick up an hour of housework and childcare for every hour of paid employment that women added to their schedules. As a result, the gender revolution that

Stalled gender revolution: A historical trend in the United States in which women made large gains in the workforce between the 1960s and 1980s, but this began to plateau in the early 1990s.

characterized the decades of the 1960s, 1970s, and 1980s stalled at the beginning of the 1990s. Women's increasing gains plateaued as their workplace advancement was limited by the realities of housework and childcare that fell largely on their shoulders. For this reason, some scholars propose that unequal divisions of labor at home now represent one of the last and most stubborn barriers to true gender equality (J. C. Williams, 2010).

Stop and Think

We noted here and elsewhere in this book that men's social roles, attitudes, and behaviors have been slower to change than women's social roles, attitudes, and behaviors. What psychological and structural reasons do you suspect might account for this, and what might be done to overcome these barriers? How might cultures like the United States increase men's involvement with housework and childcare?

Thus far, we have focused on the division of household labor within heterosexual couples. What about same-sex couples? Interestingly, same-sex couples—in contrast to heterosexual couples—generally share household responsibilities more equally (Goldberg, 2013). Why might this be the case? First, as you read in Chapter 10, same-sex couples tend to place great value on equality in their relationships (Peplau & Fingerhut, 2007). Second, members of same-sex couples often report dividing housework based on personal preferences and abilities.

Who Does What?

Even when women and men share household labor, they tend to divide it in gender-typical ways. Consider how typical "male" and "female" housework differs. Women tend to do more cooking, laundry, cleaning, and childcare, all of which are ongoing, essential, and time-consuming tasks. These sorts of activities also tend to occur inside the home. In contrast, typical male tasks can be performed occasionally rather than every day, and they therefore allow for more choice and flexibility in terms of scheduling (Lachance-Grzela & Bouchard, 2010). For example, male-typical tasks include home repairs or taking out the garbage. Male-typed jobs also tend to be more dangerous, such as climbing on the roof, cutting wood, and doing electrical repairs, and they often occur outdoors (e.g., lawn maintenance, grilling, and washing the car).

As mentioned, same-sex couples more frequently share household responsibilities equally, in part because they base their allocations on personal preferences or abilities rather than on traditional gender roles. For example, one study found that 74% of same-sex couples—but only 38% of other-sex couples—share routine childcare responsibilities equally (Matos, 2015). Similarly, compared with other-sex couples, larger proportions of same-sex couples share laundry and household repair responsibilities equally.

Men tend to do more outdoor, flexible household chores while women tend to do more indoor, daily chores.

Source: © iStockPhoto .com/amadea; © iStockPhoto.com/ sturti

Childcare

As with other domestic duties, women do the majority of childcare in heterosexual relationships, but the sex difference has narrowed over recent decades. *Time use diary* studies tracking childcare from the 1960s to the first decade of the 21st century show that despite women increasing their time in paid labor, they are not spending less time with their children. In fact, in the United States since the 1960s, women have doubled and men have tripled the hours per week they spend on childcare (Bianchi, Robinson, & Milkie, 2006). These trends are similar in other countries as well. One analysis of 20 Western, industrialized nations from 1965 to 2003 found increases in time spent on childcare among married, employed fathers in all nations (Hook, 2006). In short, a norm of intensive parenting emerged in recent decades. Compared with parents in past generations, both men and women today increasingly devote substantial time to their children.

Of course, parents are not the only adults responsible for childcare. Particularly in non-Western, collectivistic cultures—and among racial and ethnic minority families and those lower in socioeconomic status in Western cultures—other relatives, such as aunts, uncles, grandparents, and older siblings, take an active role in raising children. Recall from Chapter 10 ("Interpersonal Relationships") that maternal grandmothers, uncles, and older siblings often contribute substantially to child-rearing in Black families in the United States (Hirsch, Mickus, & Boerger, 2002). Moreover, cultural norms regarding the expected degree of parental involvement differ both across countries and across time. In some Asian cultures, such as China and Korea, the Confucian code of *genpu jibo* (or "strict father, affectionate mother") describes a parenting norm in which fathers, relative to mothers, should be authoritarian, strict, and emotionally distant from children. Although guided by the genpu jibo code until World War II, Japan appears to be changing as attitudes become more gender egalitarian and the government implements social policies, such as subsidized paternity leave, to encourage greater father involvement (Nakazawa & Schwalb, 2013).

Sidebar 11.1: Men Who Do Child-Rearing

Since the late 1980s, the Japanese government has initiated several social programs to change norms about parenting and encourage more parental involvement among fathers. For example, a poster distributed by the government in 1999 showed a young father holding his laughing infant with a caption that read, "A man who is not involved in child-rearing is not really a father." Today, the *ikumen* project (*ikumen* means "men who do child-rearing") tracks information about childcare leave programs, offers advice and stories about parenting, and seeks to improve society by helping men become more active parents (Nakazawa & Schwalb, 2013).

In Japan, the ikumen movement encourages fathers to take a more active role in parenting and childcare.

Source: By Jorge Hernández Valiñani [CC BY 2.0], via Wikimedia Commons

Stop and Think

Why do you think parenting norms are changing around the world? What sorts of factors might explain these changes?

What consequences—good or bad—might increases in parenting time have for child and family outcomes?

Predictors of the Division of Domestic Labor

What determines how couples divide household labor? Why do some couples divide housework evenly while one partner does the vast majority in others? And how do couples decide exactly which tasks they will do?

Time availability theory: The theory that the partner who spends less time in paid work will do more housework.

Time availability. One early theory, referred to as **time availability theory**, proposed that couples decide how much time to spend on housework based on how much time they have available. That is, the partner with the most free time at home assumes more responsibility for housework. In support of this theory, both men and women who spend more time in paid employment spend less time on housework (Aassve, Fuochi, &

Mencarini, 2014). However, this theory cannot explain why women in heterosexual relationships continue to do the bulk of housework regardless of their share of the couple's combined paid work hours (Sullivan, 2006). In fact, employed women do more than half of the housework even when their male partners are unemployed (Brines, 1994). Moreover, time availability theory is limited because it assumes that people have some choice about when they do housework and childcare, but for many working-class families, couple members work on opposite shifts. Regardless of his total number of work hours, a husband who works an overnight shift may have to cook meals and take care of children during the day if his wife is at work (Usdansky, 2011). In such cases, *when* time is available becomes more important than *how much* time is available.

Relative income. According to the **relative income hypothesis**, couple members trade off income for housework such that whoever makes more money does less housework (Aassve et al., 2014). Because men typically earn more money than women, they do less housework. However, this model receives only mixed support. Some research shows that women's relative income has no bearing on the proportion of housework they do (Artis & Pavalko, 2003). Other research shows that when husbands depend financially on their wives, they become *less*, not more, willing to do housework (Brines, 1994). Yet another study found that women decrease their relative contribution to household labor the more money they make but only up to the point where they make as much as their husbands. Between the point where women's paid employment contributes about half of the household income to the point where women are the sole earners, their housework also *increases* by about 5–6 hours per week. In other words, as men become more dependent on the incomes of their breadwinner wives, women do more—not less—housework (Bittman England, Sayer, Folbre, & Matheson, 2003). Why might this happen? The answer may have to do with gender roles and the gendered meaning of housework, as we discuss in the next section.

Gender role ideology. In both workplace and home environments, people can demonstrate their gender identities symbolically. That is, some people derive an important sense of identity from their sex-based labor. If so, then we might predict that beliefs about gender largely drive people's willingness to do housework. The **gender role ideology hypothesis** holds that a couple's beliefs about gender roles influence the division of housework. How well does the gender role ideology hypothesis hold up? Several studies find that people with more gender-egalitarian attitudes tend to divide housework equally, whereas those with more traditional attitudes about gender tend to divide housework along gendered lines, with women doing more overall (Aassve et al., 2014). Similarly, looking across cultures, couples divide housework more evenly in countries with more egalitarian attitudes about gender (Treas & Drobnic, 2010).

The gender role ideology hypothesis can also help to explain the paradox identified in the previous section: When a husband depends more on his wife for economic support, he does less housework, whereas women tend to do more housework the more they outearn their husbands. These patterns cannot be explained easily by either the time availability theory or the relative income hypothesis. Instead, they fit better with the view that some men experience their economic dependence as a threat to their gender identity, and they attempt to restore their masculinity by avoiding "feminine" housework. Because being financially dependent on a woman violates traditional male role norms, men whose wives outearn them may feel inadequate. In fact, perceivers view

Relative income hypothesis: The hypothesis that the partner who contributes proportionally less to the household income will do more housework.

Gender role ideology hypothesis: The hypothesis that a couple's beliefs about gender roles influence the manner in which they divide housework and childcare.

such men as lacking masculinity and as relatively powerless in their marriage (Hettinger, Hutchinson, & Bosson, 2013). Resisting housework may therefore offer men a means of displaying power and masculinity. Consistent with this idea, when men feel subordinated and powerless at work, they also tend to do fewer female-typed household tasks at home (Arrighi & Maume, 2001).

Maternal gatekeeping. It would be easy to look at the unequal division of household labor and chalk it up to men's unwillingness to help or to their incompetence in the domestic arena. This implies that women would ideally like responsibilities to be shared equally, and in fact, many people do desire such egalitarian arrangements. But women sometimes express reluctance to give up household and childcare work to men, a phenomenon referred to as **maternal gatekeeping** (S. M. Allen & Hawkins, 1999). This may be especially likely to occur among women who derive a strong sense of identity from their expertise in housework and childcare and who view home management as their domain.

You may recall from Chapter 10 that many couples perceive the division of housework and childcare as fair and equitable even when women do the bulk of it (J. R. Wilkie et al., 1998). The phenomenon of maternal gatekeeping may help to explain this pattern. Women do up to about 66% of the domestic work before they start reporting that the allocation is unfair; for men, the division starts to feel unfair when they do about 36% of the domestic work (Lennon & Rosenfeld, 1994). Women also tend to report liking housework more than men, and both women and men believe women to be more competent at housework (van Hooff, 2011). In fact, to demonstrate their unsuitability for housework, some men perform *strategic incompetence* with domestic chores (Biernat & Wortman, 1991). For example, men may burn the dinner, dress the kids in mismatched socks, or do a sloppy job with the laundry to demonstrate that they cannot handle the housework. Thus, couples may rationalize inequalities by endorsing the belief that women show greater aptitude for domestic labor than men. This may remind you of the material discussed in Chapter 6 ("Power, Sexism, and Discrimination") on *cultural ideologies* that justify sex-based labor divisions.

In sum, work life and home life are intimately connected. If we want to understand how men and women think about and divide housework, we need to consider their time commitments to the workplace, their relative incomes, and, perhaps most importantly, their gender ideologies. All of these factors seem to influence how decisions about labor division get made in the home. Importantly, however, although unequal divisions of household labor persist and work for some couples, this does not mean that they are appropriate for all couples. More balanced divisions of housework correlate with positive outcomes for women, in particular, including lower levels of depression and higher marital satisfaction (Coltrane, 2000).

Maternal gatekeeping: Behaviors and attitudes by women that discourage men's involvement in domestic labor and childcare.

Stop and Think

If women in heterosexual couples are satisfied with somewhat unequal divisions of labor, do these inequalities matter? Given that, on average, men work more hours than women outside the home, is it fair to expect divisions of labor within the home to be equal? Why or why not?

How Does Gender Operate in the Workplace?

Just as housework allows individuals to demonstrate and perform gender, so too does paid employment. In many ways, the world of work has been, and remains, a "man's world." The breadwinner role is central to men's gender status in many cultures (Gilmore, 1990; Thebaud, 2010), and the workplace offers a context for men to demonstrate masculinity. But what happens when women enter this male domain, as they have done over the past 60 years?

Gender and Leadership

Women make up 40% of the world's workforce, but they hold only a small percentage of upper-management positions. Although women now outnumber men in mid-level management positions (J. C. Williams, 2010), relatively few rise to top of the corporate ladder. As we noted earlier, women around the world hold only 4.5% of CEO positions and 14% of top business executive positions (Noland et al., 2016). Why might this be? Some argue that women lack the specific abilities or traits that make effective leaders, but research does not support this explanation (Carli & Eagly, 2011). For instance, intelligence correlates modestly with leadership effectiveness, but as we discussed in Chapter 7 ("Cognitive Abilities and Aptitudes"), there are no sex differences in general intelligence. Some personality traits (e.g., extraversion, conscientiousness, low neuroticism, and openness) also correlate modestly with leadership effectiveness, but women and men differ little in these traits, and when they do, which sex possesses more of the trait varies.

Researchers have measured sex differences in leadership effectiveness fairly extensively. Two large meta-analyses show no sex difference in overall leader effectiveness (Eagly, Karau, & Makhijani, 1995; Paustian-Underdahl, Walker, & Woehr, 2014). However, men tend to be rated as more effective leaders in male-dominated settings, such as the military, and women tend to be rated as more effective leaders in female-dominated settings, such as elementary and primary schools and social service agencies. This may reflect actual sex differences in leadership competence in these different settings, but it might also result from gender stereotypes about these gendered environments.

How do organizations fare financially under leaders of different sexes? One massive global study of companies in 91 countries found that companies with more female executives and board members have higher profits (Noland et al., 2016). Other studies, however, paint a more complex picture. For instance, one study of publicly traded firms from 1996 to 2003 found that in weaker performing firms, having more women board members positively predicts firm financial performance, but in stronger performing firms, having more women board members negatively predicts firm financial performance (Adams & Ferreira, 2009). The authors attributed this to the finding that boards with more women tend to display stricter governance (e.g., more board meetings and fewer attendance problems), which may benefit otherwise weak firms and hurt strong ones. Similarly, a meta-analysis found a positive association between female board representation and market performance in more gender-egalitarian countries, whereas a negative association emerged in countries with lower gender equity (Post & Byron, 2015). Thus, the links between women's representation in leadership roles and financial performance are not straightforward and may depend on other factors, such as firm performance and broader cultural values. Moreover, keep in mind that these findings are correlational, and we therefore cannot conclude that the sex composition of leadership roles *causes* increases or decreases in firm financial performance.

Sidebar 11.2: *More* Gender Equality or *True* Gender Equality?

A study of more than 21,900 firms in 91 countries found that in about one-third of all firms, women hold fewer than 5% of executive positions and board seats (Noland et al., 2016). In 77% of all firms, women hold fewer than 30% of executive positions and board seats. There are only 11 firms in the world (0.05% of all firms) in which women hold *all* executive positions and board seats. Outside of these 11 firms, the highest proportions of female corporate board members are in firms in Norway (40% female) and Iceland (51% female). This means that even in the most gender-egalitarian corporations in the world, it is relatively rare for women to make up even half of the top-level positions. Thus, studies showing the outcomes associated with *more* gender equality in leadership roles do not reveal the potential outcomes of *true* gender equality.

Transformational leadership style: A style of leading that involves active mentorship, inspiring trust in subordinates, and encouraging others to develop to their full potential.

Laissez-faire leadership style: A hands-off leadership style in which workers are allowed to complete responsibilities however they want, as long as the job gets done.

Beyond effectiveness, some evidence suggests that women and men may lead somewhat differently. Female leaders tend to adopt more interpersonally oriented, democratic, collaborative, and less directive leadership styles than male leaders (Eagly, Johannesen-Schmidt, & van Engen, 2003; van Engen & Willemsen, 2004). Women also tend to use a **transformational leadership style** somewhat more than men, which means that they lead through mentoring actively, inspiring trust, and encouraging others to develop their full potential. Transformational leadership correlates moderately with organizational performance and worker satisfaction (Judge & Piccolo, 2004). Female leaders also more frequently reward workers for satisfactory performance, whereas male leaders more often use a **laissez-faire** (or "hands-off") **leadership style** and wait until problems become severe before addressing them. However, effect sizes for these sex differences in leadership all fall in the close-to-zero and small ranges.

Given the lack of clear evidence of a leadership advantage for men, why are there so few women leaders? The answer may lie in gender stereotypes and biases, to which we turn next. Although overt, intentional gender bias certainly exists in the workplace, not all employers or workers consciously discriminate against women. Many employers care about their workers and strive for inclusive environments free from gender bias and sexism. However, subtle, indirect, and unintentional forms of bias can sometimes make gender bias in the workplace difficult to detect and even more difficult to prove to others.

Women, relative to men, are slightly more likely to demonstrate a democratic, collaborative form of leadership.

Source: © iStockPhoto.com/Rawpixel

Glass Ceilings, Glass Cliffs, and Sticky Floors

The **glass ceiling** refers to the invisible barriers that keep women (and other under-represented individuals) from rising to the upper rungs of the corporate ladder, regardless of their qualifications or achievements (Hymowitz & Schellhardt, 1986). Through this metaphorical glass ceiling, women can see the elite positions but not reach them, and the barriers to progress are not obvious. Some argue that the glass ceiling reflects the persistent stereotype that since being a manager is a masculine role, men are more qualified than women for upper-level management positions. You may recall our discussion of this stereotype, deemed the *think manager–think male* effect (Schein, 1973), in Chapter 5 ("The Contents and Origins of Gender Stereotypes"). Evidence of the think manager–think male effect emerges in cultures around the world, although more strongly in men and in members of Eastern cultures. Moreover, even though this stereotype has generally decreased in strength over time (Koenig et al., 2011), it still contributes to biased gender dynamics in the workplace, including the dismissal of women's accomplishments, the exclusion of women from inner decision-making circles (or **old boys' networks**), and sex-based harassment (for more on this, see Chapter 14, "Aggression and Violence").

When women do rise to the top, it sometimes occurs under less-than-ideal circumstances. For instance, women get called upon more often than men to help save companies in decline, a phenomenon known as the **glass cliff effect** (M. K. Ryan & Haslam, 2005). The term *glass cliff* refers to a leadership position fraught with risk, which occurs

Glass ceiling: Invisible barriers in the workplace that prevent women from rising to top corporate positions.

Old boys' networks: Informal, inner circles of men who exclude women from decision making and use their influence to help other men.

Glass cliff effect: The tendency to place women into leadership positions under risky, precarious circumstances in which the likelihood of failure is high.

when a company needs to be saved from failure or from a high-profile scandal. Evidence for the glass cliff effect is widespread. Companies more often select female over male leaders under risky, unfavorable conditions; female lawyers get assigned more often than male lawyers to lead high-risk, controversial cases; and female politicians get recommended more often than their male counterparts for "unwinnable" seats (Bruckmuller, Ryan, Floor, & Haslam, 2014). And the predictable outcome of taking over a sinking ship is, of course, a greater chance of failure.

Whereas the glass ceiling refers to barriers that keep women from top positions, the **sticky floor** refers to barriers that keep low-wage workers from ascending from the bottom (Booth, Francesconi, & Frank, 2003). Not only are women disproportionately concentrated in low-wage, low-mobility positions in clerical, service work, health care, and childcare occupations, but they also—in comparison with men—get paid less in the same jobs and have fewer opportunities to advance to better positions. Similarly, people of color disproportionately get "stuck" at the floor level of organizations (Yap & Konrad, 2009). This low-level, sticky-floor discrimination shows up widely in research across cultures (Chi & Li, 2008; Duraisamy & Duraisamy, 2016).

Bias Against Women

Joan Williams and Rachel Dempsey (2014) identified four pervasive biases against women in the workplace. The first, dubbed the **prove-it-again bias**, reflects doubts about women's competence. Because women are less represented in some jobs—particularly in positions of leadership and power—they may not seem as well suited for these jobs. As a result, women often have to provide extra evidence of competence in order to seem as competent as men. For example, even when women's work accomplishments are identical in quality to men's, others perceive women's work as inferior. Similarly, people tend to attribute a man's success in the workplace to his natural ability (a presumably stable quality) while attributing a woman's success to hard work or luck (relatively temporary and ephemeral factors). Consider how these attributions can differently impact the impressions that men and women make in the workplace. If a man makes an error or displays poor performance, others may give him the benefit of the doubt because his natural competence presumably remains intact. If a woman performs poorly, however, it may be easier to blame her for not working hard enough. Thus, women often have to prove themselves over and over in order to be taken as seriously as men.

A second bias, called the **maternal wall**, reflects the challenges that employed women face as mothers. Women suffer a *motherhood penalty*, whereas no parallel "fatherhood penalty" exists. Amy Cuddy and her colleagues demonstrated this by having participants rate the profiles of fictitious employees of a consulting firm who either did or did not have children. Perhaps not surprisingly, participants rated working mothers as more warm and likeable than their child-free counterparts. However, they also rated working mothers as less competent than child-free women and expressed more reluctance to hire and promote them. What about fathers? Working fathers suffer no penalties in the workplace comparable to those experienced by working mothers. In fact, fathers were seen as warmer than men without children, and the two groups were rated equally high in competence (Cuddy, Fiske, & Glick, 2004). So people view working parents of

Sticky floor: Barriers that keep low-wage workers, who are disproportionately likely to be women and racial and ethnic minority individuals, from being promoted.

Prove-it-again bias: Gender bias in which stereotypes about women's unsuitability for high-status positions result in women having to work harder than men to prove their competence.

Maternal wall: Gender bias in which working mothers—but not working fathers—are perceived as less competent at their jobs.

both sexes as warmer than child-free workers, but mothers also take a hit in perceived competence that fathers somehow escape.

J. C. Williams and Dempsey (2014) called the third type of bias the **tightrope**. Some types of jobs require masculine qualities of agency and assertiveness, but people stereotype women as lower in agency than men. As a result, women who occupy male-dominated jobs may find themselves caught in a bind: If they behave assertively, which may be required for job performance, they violate gender role norms and are viewed as less likable. If they behave warmly, which is expected for their sex, they may undermine their own job performance and appear lacking in competence. This tightrope bias manifests as a backlash against agentic women. For instance, people view women who succeed in male-typed jobs as successful and competent, but they tend to like them less than equally successful men (Heilman, Wallen, Fuchs, & Tamkins, 2004). And as you may recall from Chapter 5, research on the *status incongruity hypothesis* finds that people dislike agentic women because they seem "too high" in dominance (Rudman et al., 2012).

Finally, women show the **tug of war** against other women. Perhaps not surprisingly, given the pressures and restrictions that we have discussed here, women sometimes feel like they have to compete with other women for access to limited jobs, promotions, and workplace rewards. This can lead women to dissociate themselves from each other, a phenomenon called the **queen bee syndrome**. As one example, consider a Dutch study of senior female police officers (Derks, Van Laar, Ellemers, & de Groot, 2011). When primed to think about gender bias during their careers, the officers who identified weakly with their gender demonstrated a queen bee response by describing themselves in more masculine terms and distancing themselves from other women. This suggests that gender biases in work environments can make it difficult for women to support other women, which may explain why women sometimes evaluate highly successful female employees more harshly than men do (Benard & Correll, 2010).

Sexual Orientation, Gender Identity, and Race

Investigations of workplace bias based on sexual orientation and gender identity find consistently high levels of discrimination. One national U.S. survey found that 42% of LGB-identified individuals experienced employment discrimination, and 35% experienced harassment at work (Gates, 2010). Similarly, 57% of transgender respondents in a U.S. sample reported experiencing different types of bias and discrimination at work, including being fired, being denied employment or promotion, and being harassed (Badgett, Lau, Sears, & Ho, 2007). In particular, transgender people who transition to their felt gender identity can experience difficult workplace experiences. In one qualitative study of transgender employees, the majority described their transition process as awkward and uncomfortable for their coworkers (Brewster, Velez, Mennicke, & Tebbe, 2014). For a few, the process was easier than anticipated, but the majority experienced discrimination, including job termination, sabotage by management, harassment and intimidation, stigmatization, and ostracism. Given these alarmingly high rates of workplace discrimination, some scholars call for dramatic improvements in how organizations meet the needs of sexual and gender identity minority employees (Ozturk & Tatli, 2016).

Tightrope: Gender bias in which employed women are viewed as less likable if they are assertive and as less competent if they are warm.

Tug of war: Gender bias in which women feel like they have to compete against one another for access to limited positions, promotions, and workplace rewards.

Queen bee syndrome: A phenomenon in which women who hold authority positions in male-dominated professions dissociate themselves from other women and treat women employees more critically.

You may recall the concept of intersectionality and the related *double jeopardy hypothesis* discussed at length in Chapter 6 ("Power, Sexism, and Discrimination"). According to the double jeopardy hypothesis, people who occupy two or more dis advantaged social groups face more discrimination than those who occupy one disadvantaged group. In line with this hypothesis, ethnic minority women face more overall harassment in the workplace than do White women or ethnic minority men because they experience both sex-based harassment and racial harassment (Berdahl & Moore, 2006). One qualitative study of Black women's workplace experiences documented some of the unique race-based struggles that they face, including subtle racism, a lack of mentorship, feelings of isolation and exclusion, and pressure to *code switch*, or change how they express themselves in front of White people (J. C. Hall, Everett, & Hamilton-Mason, 2012). Some of these types of treatment fall under the label of microaggressions, which (as you may recall from Chapter 6) are casual, subtle, and offensive comments or actions directed at marginalized group members. A coworker's comment that "You don't look gay" or a request of "Can I touch your hair?" to a Black woman may sound well intended to the speaker, but these sorts of comments can reinforce stereotypes, make people feel singled out, and cause workplace stress (Sue, 2010). Moreover, because many types of microaggressions are not illegal, they remain difficult to document and fight against. They can thus add up and contribute to a challenging work environment.

An additional source of workplace bias associated with intersectionality has to do with perceptions of job fit for people of different sexes and racial groups. Research shows that gender stereotypes vary by race, with Asian people stereotyped as more feminine than White people, and Black people stereotyped as more masculine than White people. Thus, when considering the intersections of race and sex, a complex pattern of gender stereotypes emerges. As shown in Figure 11.2, others tend to view Asian women as highly feminine, Black men as highly masculine, and White women and White men as moderately feminine and masculine, respectively. In contrast, people do not strongly associate Black women and Asian men with either femininity or masculinity. This pattern of stereotyping has consequences for perceived job fit: Asian women tend to be perceived as unsuited for male-type jobs, such as security officers, while Black men tend to be viewed as unsuited for female-type jobs, such as librarians (E. V. Hall, Galinsky, & Phillips, 2015). These gender stereotypes may thus create unfair barriers that affect hiring decisions for some people with marginalized identities. Moreover, when members of racial and ethnic groups hold jobs that do not seem to match the gender stereotypes about their groups, they may encounter heightened levels of harassment and microaggressions.

Interestingly, some members of historically disadvantaged groups appear especially *well* suited for certain jobs given their unique group memberships. For example, recall our discussion of the *teddy bear effect* from Chapter 8 ("Language, Communication, and Emotion"). This effect refers to the tendency for Black men with "baby-faced" features to have an advantage when seeking leadership positions because they are viewed as masculine but not aggressive (Livingston & Pearce, 2009). Similarly, gay Black men may have an advantage when it comes to their perceived leadership abilities. To demonstrate this, Wilson and his colleagues showed people 108 different facial images of gay and straight Black and White men and asked them to rate each man on

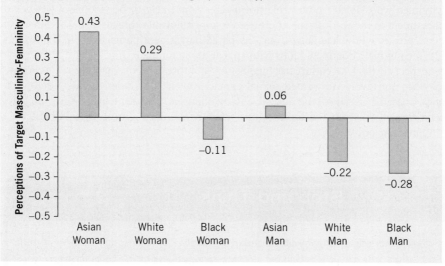

Figure 11.2   Gender Stereotypes of Sex and Race Categories.

Asian and White women are stereotyped as relatively high in femininity, Black women and Asian men are stereotyped as relatively gender neutral, and White and Black men are stereotyped as relatively high in masculinity. (Scores are calculated by subtracting ratings of masculinity from ratings of femininity for each group. Thus, positive scores mean that a group is stereotyped as more feminine than masculine, scores near zero mean that a group is not sex-typed, and negative scores mean that a group is stereotyped as more masculine than feminine.)

Source: E. V. Hall, Galinsky, and Phillips (2015).

leadership ability. Participants did not know the sexual orientation of the people they rated, but they nonetheless rated gay Black men overall as higher in leadership ability than both gay White men and straight Black men. Other ratings indicated that gay Black men's leadership advantage may occur because their faces appear high in both warmth and masculinity, an especially appealing combination for leaders (J. P. Wilson, Remedios, & Rule, 2017).

Bias Against Men

Though most research on gender bias in the workplace focuses on women, men face bias at work as well. Think for a moment about the type of man most likely to be a target of gender bias or discrimination. Who comes to mind? Like women, men who conform less to typical gender role expectations are most frequently targeted (Berdahl, Magley, & Waldo, 1996). Consider the following examples: Men who succeed in traditionally female jobs tend to be disrespected and perceived as "wimpy" (Heilman & Wallen, 2010). Men who behave modestly during a job interview encounter more prejudice than comparably modest women (Moss-Racusin et al., 2010). Even working for a female boss can make men seem less masculine (Brescoll, Uhlmann, Moss-Racusin, & Sarnell, 2011). And as we will detail later in this chapter, men who signal their commitment to their families by requesting family leave can face penalties at work.

While some might assume that sexual interest serves as the primary motivation behind sexual harassment in the workplace, Jennifer Berdahl (2007) instead views such harassment as a means by which people (usually men) assert their gender status and power over others. (In fact, Berdahl refers to sexual harassment as *sex-based harassment* because the latter phrasing more clearly conveys the notion that this treatment is based on a person's sex and need not be sexual.) This perspective can help to explain why men who violate gender role norms are more likely to be victims of sex-based harassment in the workplace—their gender nonconformity threatens the legitimacy of men's greater workplace power, and sex-based harassment punishes them. For example, men in male-dominated jobs who appear too feminine or insufficiently masculine are especially likely to endure teasing, insults, and threats from coworkers. This behavior does not involve unwanted sexual contact, but it falls under the legal definition of sex-based harassment because it entails offensive treatment based on a person's sex. We will consider the topic of sex-based harassment more fully in Chapter 14 ("Aggression and Violence").

Stop and Think

Why do you think so many workplaces struggle with issues of gender bias? Do you view all of the various types of gender bias—against women, against LGBT individuals, against people who occupy multiple subordinate groups, and against men—as reflecting a common,

underlying purpose? Or do these different types of gender bias serve distinct purposes? Given these pervasive gender biases in the workplace, what strategies might people use to overcome them? And how might these strategies differ based on the specific type of gender bias?

How Can We Explain the Gender Wage Gap?

In the United States, the Equal Pay Act of 1963 made sex-based wage discrimination illegal. And yet, every year the U.S. government reports an annual gender wage gap (see Figure 11.3 for a comparison of women's and men's relative earnings over the years). Almost every industrialized country now has laws mandating equal pay regardless of sex, and still, women earn less than men in every country (Blau & Kahn, 2003). How can a gender gap in wages persist if it is illegal? In part, this may occur because the discrimination that contributes to the gap is subtle and difficult to detect and prosecute. Alternatively, perhaps factors other than discrimination account for the gender wage gap.

Figure 11.3   The Changing Gender Wage Gap.

This figure displays women's median annual earnings as a percentage of men's median annual earnings for full-time, year-round workers in the United States. The gender wage gap has been closing slowly but steadily since 1990. Do you think it will disappear entirely some day?

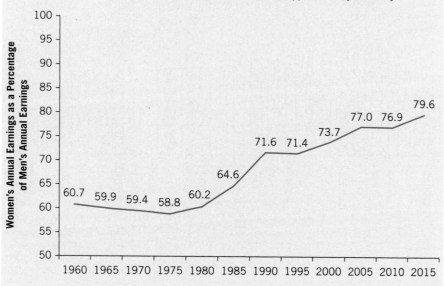

Source: Institute for Women's Policy Research (2016).

Finally, some label the gender wage gap a myth and assert that it no longer exists (see "Debate: Is the Gender Wage Gap a Myth?").

What Is the Gender Wage Gap?

Stated simply, the **gender wage gap** is the difference in earnings between men and women. It is usually expressed as a ratio of women's earnings to men's earnings—specifically, women's median yearly earnings for full-time, year-round work as a percentage of men's earnings. So a ratio of $0.50 would mean that women earn 50% of what men earn while a ratio of $1.00 would indicate perfect pay equality. In 2014, the gender earnings ratio in the United States was $0.80, meaning that women earned, on average, 20% less than men (Institute for Women's Policy Research, 2016). The United States is not alone: Women earn less than men in every country around the world (see Figure 11.4). As you can see in Figure 11.4, South Korea has the largest gender wage gap ($0.63), and Italy has the lowest ($0.94), but in no country do women earn as much as men (OECD, 2016).

Gender wage gap: The difference in earnings between men and women, usually expressed as a ratio (or percentage) of women's to men's median yearly earnings for full-time, year-round work. A gender wage gap of 1.00 would reflect gender parity.

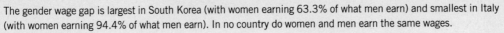

Figure 11.4 The Gender Wage Gap Around the World.

The gender wage gap is largest in South Korea (with women earning 63.3% of what men earn) and smallest in Italy (with women earning 94.4% of what men earn). In no country do women and men earn the same wages.

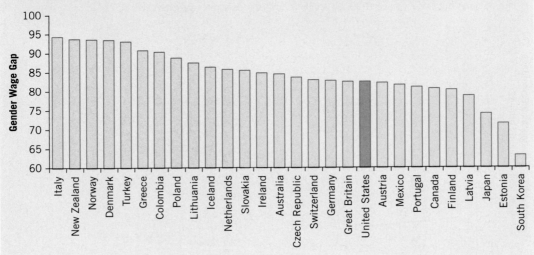

Source: OECD (2016).

Sidebar 11.3: A Day of Equal Pay?

Have you heard of Equal Pay Day? This is the day of each year on which women's earnings in the United States (theoretically) "catch up" to men's earnings from the prior year. In other words, Equal Pay Day represents how far women would have to work into the following year to earn what men earned in the previous year. So the closer Equal Pay Day is to January, the better for women. Equal Pay Day was April 12th in 2016 and April 4th in 2017, and it will fall on April 10th in 2018.

The gender wage gap holds across race and ethnicity as well. Black, Latina, Asian American, Native American, and White women all earn less than men of their race group. A different picture emerges, however, when comparing the pay of women of color to that of White men in the United States: Latina women make 54% of what White men earn, Native American women earn 58% of what White men earn, and Black women make 63% of what White men earn. In contrast, White women's earnings are 75% of White men's, and Asian women have the smallest wage gap, earning 85% of what White men earn (AAUW, 2017). Sexual orientation also relates to the size of the wage gap in an interesting way. Lesbian women earn on average about 9% more than heterosexual women (although they still earn less than men do) while gay men earn about 11% less than heterosexual men do (Klawitter, 2014).

According to a frequently cited statistic from the Bureau of Labor Statistics (BLS), women engaged in full-time employment in the United States earn about 80 cents for every dollar men earn (Institute for Women's Policy Research, 2016). Similar gaps exist in virtually every country around the world—sometimes a little smaller, sometimes a little larger, but always present. Yet some express skepticism that the gender wage gap actually exists. Consider these headlines: "The 'Wage Gap' Myth That Won't Die" (Ketterer, 2015), "The Gender Wage Gap Lie" (Rosin, 2013), and "No, Women Don't Make Less Than Men" (Hoff Sommers, 2014). Which is it? Is there a substantial and persistent gap between the earnings of women and men, or are the statistics that purport to show a wage gap misleading? In this debate section, we introduce you to the basic arguments and perspectives of the two competing sides so you can consider which side makes more sense on the surface. We then use the remainder of this section to examine in finer detail the evidence that both sides utilize to build their cases.

The Wage Gap Is a Myth

Critics describe the 80 cents statistic as crude and meaningless because—in their view—it does not consider factors that may account for the gap, such as the types of occupations in which men and women work, job experience, and hours worked. Even limiting the wage gap statistic to full-time workers (as the BLS does) creates the false sense of a level playing field. In fact, even among full-time workers (that is, anyone working over 35 hours a week), men tend to work longer hours than women. Also, women choose low-paying jobs more frequently than men. For instance, women gravitate toward college majors that lead to relatively low-paying careers (social work and early childhood education), whereas men gravitate toward more lucrative majors (engineering and computer science; Carnevale & Cheah, 2013).

Once you control for relevant lifestyle factors, the gap diminishes significantly. Therefore, the wage gap does not reflect sex-based discrimination, but instead, it reflects men's occupational choices and greater time spent in paid employment. And it is only fair that these factors should lead to greater pay for men.

The Wage Gap Is Real

Gender wage gaps are pervasive. They exist widely in nations across the globe, and they exist regardless of race or marital status. While it is true that men and women tend to pursue different occupations, the gap persists even when examining pay within the same occupations and when controlling statistically for variables such as education level and time investment in work.

Moreover, evidence that the wage gap is partially explained by men working in more lucrative careers or putting in longer work hours would not suggest that the gap is not real. The wage gap need not be caused by intentional discrimination. Although many employers try to be fair and unbiased, subtle institutional barriers and cultural biases can reinforce different expectations for men and women. For instance, the lack of extended paid maternity leave forces many women (more than men) to interrupt their careers when children arrive, which contributes to sex differences in pay.

(Continued)

(Continued)

Bringing these biases to light may help matters. Some research suggests that just requiring companies to report their gender wage gaps publicly can make people aware of biases and motivate efforts to reduce them (Lipman, 2015).

Having been introduced to both sides of the debate, what is your initial position about the validity of the wage gap? As you read further, you will encounter more detailed evidence in support of each position. Consider which evidence you find most persuasive, and evaluate whether you think the gender wage gap reflects gender discrimination, individual lifestyle choices and priorities, or some combination of these factors.

Although workplace gender discrimination is illegal in most countries, many subtle, structural biases can keep women from attaining high-paying jobs or advancing in their careers. As you read earlier, glass ceilings, glass cliffs, and sticky floors can impact the way employers view women and how women view themselves. Women may even be expected to do extra homemaking and secretarial tasks at work that are not expected of men. Known as *office housework*, these tasks include things like arranging office parties, buying cards for sick coworkers, baking cupcakes for a coworker's birthday, or taking notes during office meetings (Kolb & Porter, 2015). While not illegal, expecting women instead of men to perform these tasks does constitute differential treatment that can slow women's advancement. Thus, while both subtle and overt discrimination likely contribute to the wage gap, other nondiscrimination factors also may play a role. What are some of these factors?

Lilly Ledbetter (center), with U.S. Secretary of Labor Thomas Perez (left) and Principal Deputy Assistant Secretary for Policy Sharon Block (right) at the White House United State of Women Summit, June 15, 2016.

Source: By US Department of Labor CC BY 2.0 via Wikimedia Commons

Sidebar 11.4: Lilly Ledbetter

Lilly Ledbetter, a Goodyear plant supervisor for almost two decades, filed a sex discrimination suit against Goodyear in 1998 for paying her substantially less than her male counterparts. After almost a decade, she lost her case when the Supreme Court rejected her appeal in 2007. Ledbetter was honored in 2009 when President Obama signed the Lilly Ledbetter Fair Pay Restoration Act into law, making it easier for workers to sue employers for pay discrimination.

Possible Explanations for the Gender Wage Gap

Education and occupational segregation. Some argue that the wage gap exists because men are more educated than women. However, the pay gap exists at all levels of education (AAUW, 2017). Men with a high school education receive higher pay than women with a high school education, and men with college and advanced degrees receive higher pay than women with these degrees. Furthermore, while men in the United States had more education than women in the past, this sex difference no longer exists, and yet, the pay gap persists.

If different education levels cannot explain the wage gap, perhaps men earn more than women because men work in high-paying occupations more frequently than women. If Roberto the surgeon makes more than Maria the nurse, should this be surprising? Table 11.1 shows the top-20 most commonly held jobs for men and women in the United States. As you can see, very little overlap exists between the lists, showing that occupations are indeed highly sex segregated. Though **occupational segregation** likely contributes to the gender wage gap (Hegewisch & Hartmann, 2014), note that the gap exists in both male-dominated and female-dominated jobs, and there is only one occupation—that of stock clerk—for which women make more money than men (see Table 11.1).

Occupational segregation: The segregation of occupations by sex, such that men primarily work in occupations dominated by men, and women primarily work in occupations dominated by women.

Table 11.1 **The Gender Wage Gap.** This table shows the gender wage gap for the 20 most common occupations for women and men in the United States in 2014. The wage gap numbers are calculated as women's earnings as a percentage of men's. Values lower than 100 indicate that women earn less than men, and values above 100 indicate that women earn more than men. Missing values reflect occupations in which there are too few female workers to calculate the gap.

Women's Most Common Occupations	Wage Gap	Men's Most Common Occupations	Wage Gap
Secretary/administrative assistant	84.5	Driver/sales worker and truck driver	73.7
Elementary & middle school teacher	87.2	Manager, all other	81.7
Registered nurse	90.4	Supervisor of retail sales workers	75.0
Nursing, psychiatric, & home health aide	88.3	Construction laborer	—
Supervisor of retail sales workers	75.0	Janitor, building cleaner	76.9
Customer service representative	86.8	Laborer & freight, stock, & material mover	87.2
Manager, all other	81.7	Retail salesperson	70.3

(Continued)

Table 11.1 (Continued)

Women's Most Common Occupations	Wage Gap	Men's Most Common Occupations	Wage Gap
Cashier	93.9	Software developer	83.9
Accountant, auditor	80.8	Sale representative, wholesale & manufacturing	77.9
Receptionist, information clerk	86.4	Grounds maintenance worker	—
Office supervisor	83.0	Chief executive	70.0
Office clerk, general	94.6	Carpenter	—
Bookkeeping, accounting, auditing clerk	90.2	Cook	97.4
Retail salesperson	70.3	Automotive service tech, mechanic	—
Maid, housekeeping cleaner	99.0	Production worker	72.8
Financial manager	67.4	Stock clerk, order filler	102.0
Social worker	94.1	Supervisor of production and operating workers	70.0
Secondary school teacher	88.8	Electrician	—
Waitress/waiter	82.8	Police and sheriff's patrol officer	71.2
Personal care aide	91.4	Miscellaneous assembler, fabricator	79.9

Source: Hegewisch and Ellis (2015).

Sex differences in occupational preferences may develop early. One study of the career aspirations of U.S. high school valedictorians found that female valedictorians planned to pursue careers with a median salary of $74,608 while male valedictorians planned to pursue careers with a median salary of $97,734 (York, 2008). These sex differences then carry over into choice of college majors. Table 11.2 shows the top-10 highest- and lowest-paying college majors in the United States, along with the percentages of women and men in these majors (Carnevale, Strohl, & Melton, 2014). Notice that men dominate the top-paying majors, whereas women dominate the lowest-paying majors. Women concentrate in the lowest-paying professions as well. In the United States, more than twice as many women as men work in jobs that pay poverty-level wages (Hegewisch & Ellis, 2015), and as noted earlier, this pattern emerges across cultures as well.

Women's tendency to occupy low-paying jobs cannot fully explain the gender wage gap, however. Even within the same low-paying occupations, men make more than women (see Table 11.1). An analysis of wage gaps in 116 occupations in the

Table 11.2 Highest- and Lowest-Paying U.S. College Majors. As you can see, with some exceptions, men tend to dominate the 10 highest-paying U.S. college majors while women tend to dominate the 10 lowest-paying U.S. college majors.

10 Highest-Paying College Majors	Percentage Male	10 Lowest-Paying College Majors	Percentage Female
Petroleum engineering	87%	Counseling psychology	74%
Pharmaceutical sciences & administration	48%	Early childhood education	97%
Mathematics & computer science	67%	Theology & religious vocations	34%
Aerospace engineering	88%	Human services & community organization	81%
Chemical engineering	72%	Social work	88%
Electrical engineering	89%	Drama & theater arts	60%
Naval architecture & marine engineering	97%	Studio arts	66%
Mechanical engineering	90%	Communication disorders sciences & services	94%
Metallurgical engineering	83%	Visual & performing arts	77%
Mining & mineral engineering	90%	Health & medical preparatory programs	55%

Source: Carnevale, Strohl, and Melton (2014).

United States found only one occupation (health care technicians) in which women and men earn equal salaries and one (stock clerks) in which women earn slightly more than men (Hegewisch & Ellis, 2015). In the remaining occupations, women earn less than men regardless of whether the occupation is female typed, male typed, or gender neutral. Thus, female truck drivers and police officers earn less their male counterparts but so do female nurses and elementary school teachers.

Occupational feminization. Perhaps women do not choose low-paying jobs so much as jobs become low paying when (or because) women choose them. When women enter previously male-dominated fields in large numbers—a phenomenon termed **occupational feminization**—the pay for these jobs tends to decline (Levanon, England, & Allison, 2009). One study of the links between occupational feminization and pay found that male-typed occupations that experienced the largest feminization between 1970 and 2007 also experienced the largest decreases in men's wages, and these declines were

Occupational feminization: The entrance of women in large numbers into a previously male-dominated occupation.

larger in higher-paying occupations (Mandel, 2013). Another cross-national study found that moving into or remaining in a feminizing occupation correlates with losses in individual earnings ranging from 3% in Germany to 12% in Britain (Murphy & Oesch, 2015). In other words, women's entrance into jobs corresponds with a societal tendency to devalue those jobs and accordingly compensate them less.

What about the reverse? Do occupations pay more as men enter them in higher numbers (a phenomenon termed **occupational masculinization**)? As we mentioned earlier, men generally have not entered female-dominated occupations and domains as readily as women have entered male-dominated ones. Thus, examples of occupational masculinization are relatively hard to find. Software programming, however, offers an interesting example. When the first digital computers were developed in the United States during World War II, women held most software programming jobs because so many men were fighting abroad (Abbate, 2012). Until the mid-1960s, programming remained a popular career choice among women. However, as the computing industry ballooned and the demand for programmers exploded over the next decades, the field of programming began to masculinize. Today, women constitute only 21% of computer programmers and 18% of software developers (U.S. Bureau of Labor Statistics, 2015a).

Occupational masculinization: The (relatively rare) entrance of men in large numbers into a previously female-dominated occupation.

ENIAC (Electronic Numerical Integrator and Computer) programmers Betty Jean Jennings (left) and Fran Bilas (right) operate the ENIAC's main control panel in 1945.

Source: By United States Army, Public Domain, https:// commons.wikimedia .org/w/index .php?curid=978783

Did wages increase as the field masculinized? Indeed, they did. Today, software programming is a highly lucrative career. In 2015, the average annual salary for programmers was $97,930 (compared with the national average salary of $48,320 across all occupations; U.S. Bureau of Labor Statistics, 2015a). While "it is" difficult to know whether the high salaries in this field reflect masculinization or other factors (such as a high demand for workers driven by a fast-growing industry), some scholars propose that the masculinization of programming was directly tied to the increasing valuation and prestige of this occupation (Ensmenger, 2010).

Thus, the occupational choices that men and women make cannot fully explain the gender wage gap. Even if occupational choices account for some of the wage gap, "choice" can be a loaded term because people's choices can be constrained by gender expectations. Why do men choose riskier but higher-paying occupations? Why do men choose to work more hours while women more often chose to work part time? These life choices are often shaped by factors that do not reflect personal desires.

Salary negotiation. Although the pay gap increases as workers get older, it is evident among young people just beginning their careers. One year out of college, women working full time earn less than their male peers, even those majoring in the same fields (Corbett & Hill, 2012). This suggests that some wage gaps begin at the bargaining table, the moment one accepts a job. In fact, women tend to negotiate less often than men for higher salaries. Linda Babcock and her colleagues asked recent MBA graduates if they initiated a job negotiation and found that 51.9% of men negotiated their job offer, whereas only 12.5% of women did (Babcock, Gelfand, Small, & Stayn, 2006). Women also received average annual starting salaries that were 8.5% lower than those of men. An experimental study shed further light on this sex difference. In this experiment, volunteers learned that they would receive anywhere from $3 to $10 for playing a word game (Small, Gelfand, Babcock, & Gettman, 2007). When offered only $3 and told it was "negotiable," men requested additional money more frequently than women did. However, this sex difference went away when researchers told participants that they could "ask for more" money. In other words, framing the situation as a "negotiation" may be intimidating for women because it runs counter to female gender role norms of politeness. However, framing the situation as simply "requesting more" does not violate gender role norms.

Not only do women negotiate less often, but people evaluate women who negotiate—in comparison with men who negotiate—more negatively (Bowles, Babcock, & Lai, 2007). This may remind you of the *tightrope bias* that we discussed earlier, in which assertive women are penalized for appearing too aggressive. The possibility of negative evaluations can inhibit women from initiating salary negotiations. In addition, experimental evidence shows that negotiators offer less money to women than to men because they expect women to be satisfied with smaller salary offers (Solnick, 2001). Unfortunately, real costs result from not negotiating a first job offer. What might seem like a small disadvantage can accumulate over time and become a large loss over a career. Babcock and Laschever (2009) provide an example of two 30-year-old business graduates, a man and a woman, who receive job offers of $100,000 a year. The woman accepts the offer, but the man negotiates and raises his offer to $111,000. Even if they both receive identical 3% annual raises for the rest of their careers, by the time they retire at age 65, the difference between their annual salaries will have widened to $30,953. Over the course of 35 years, that initial $11,000 difference amounts to about $1.6 million at retirement.

Relocations and career interruptions. Employers may pay women less than men because they believe women to be less likely to leave their current position for a higher salary elsewhere. In fact, women do express more reluctance than men to relocate (Baldridge, Eddleston, & Veiga, 2006). In one study that asked employees if they would be willing to take a much better job in a city 100 miles away, 57% of men and 89% of women reported reluctance to move, with particular reluctance in women whose husbands made more money than they did (Bielby & Bielby, 1992). This suggests that husbands' potential salary loss may deter wives from pursuing higher-paying jobs elsewhere, but wives' potential salary loss does not similarly deter men from pursuing such opportunities.

Regardless of sex, income grows with job experience. But since society expects women to take on the lion's share of domestic and childcare responsibilities, it becomes harder for them to build this job experience without career interruptions. This might help explain why the gender wage gap becomes larger with age. In the United States, for people 35 and under, women earn about 90% of men's pay, but for people 35 and older, women earn between 74% and 82% of men's pay (AAUW, 2017). A study that tracked graduates from a prestigious law school examined the role of career interruptions in the widening gender wage gap. During the first year after graduation, women earned 93% of men's wages. Fifteen years later, this small wage gap was a big gap—with women earning only 62% of men's wages—and having children explained nearly half of this larger gap (R. G. Wood, Corcoran, & Courant, 1993). This reflects a phenomenon called the **motherhood penalty**, in which working mothers pay a significant wage penalty for having children, and the more children they have, the greater the penalty (Budig & England, 2001; Kahn, García-Manglano, & Bianchi, 2014). A report from the U.S. Bureau of Labor Statistics (2009) showed that while unmarried women earn 94.2% of what their unmarried male counterparts earn, married women earn only 75.5% as much as married men. This can be explained, in part, by mothers being more likely than fathers to work part time and thus lose out on job experience. As shown in Figure 11.5, employed mothers interrupt their careers more often than employed fathers in order to care for a child or another family member (PRC, 2013). However, even accounting for part-time work, a gender wage gap still remains. Note that this is not a *parenthood* penalty because men experience no wage penalty when they become fathers. If anything, fatherhood enhances wages for many men (Killewald, 2012).

Motherhood penalty: The wage penalty that working women—but not working men—experience following the birth of a child.

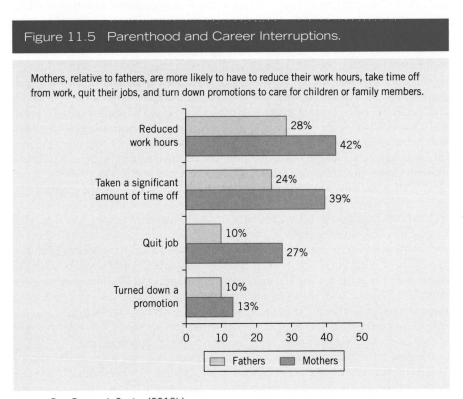

Figure 11.5 Parenthood and Career Interruptions.

Mothers, relative to fathers, are more likely to have to reduce their work hours, take time off from work, quit their jobs, and turn down promotions to care for children or family members.

Reduced work hours — Fathers 28%, Mothers 42%
Taken a significant amount of time off — Fathers 24%, Mothers 39%
Quit job — Fathers 10%, Mothers 27%
Turned down a promotion — Fathers 10%, Mothers 13%

Source: Pew Research Center (2013b).

Note: Based on those who have ever worked, *fathers* and *mothers* include those with children of any age, including adult children (*n* = 1,254).

Overwork. In contrast to the expectation that women should curtail their career ambitions for family, the traditional breadwinner role for men carries with it expectations that they should work a lot—and particularly when they have a family to support. This norm can have powerful consequences for how men think about and approach their work (J. C. Williams, 2010). Consider the Silicon Valley engineers studied by Marianne Cooper (2000), who turned long hours into a demonstration of masculinity. Said one father, "There's a kind of machismo culture among the young male engineers where you just don't sleep. He's a real man; he works 90-hour weeks. He's a slacker; he works 50 hours a week" (p. 382).

Defined as working 50 or more hours per week, **overwork** is on the rise, especially among men. One analysis found that the percentage of employed Americans who overwork rose from 13% of men and 3% of women in the early 1980s to 19% of men and 7% of women by 2000. Overwork occurs more often in professional and managerial occupations, and it perpetuates the gender wage gap in these occupations. In fact, some estimate that overwork—and its financial rewards—account for about 10% of the total gender wage gap (Cha & Wheedon, 2014). Moreover, parenthood exacerbates the gender gap in overwork: Men who have children work 50-plus hours a week more frequently than men without children, but women who have children are less likely to work 50-plus hours per week (J. C. Williams & Dempsey, 2014). While the male role norm of devotion to work and overwork may seem relatively harmless, some evidence suggests that it can be dangerous. Consider the growing problem in Japan of *karoshi*, which means "death by overwork." Karoshi describes sudden deaths, typically due to heart attack or stroke, among people (usually men) who work long hours in stressful jobs. A related phenomenon, *karojisatsu*, refers more specifically to "suicide from overwork" (Harden, 2008). And even when overwork does not kill people, it can undermine their happiness and well-being. J. C. Williams (2010) notes that the vast majority of men who overwork report a strong preference to work fewer hours per week and spend more time with their children and families.

Overwork: Working 50 or more hours per week in paid employment.

Conclusions About the Gender Wage Gap

Given all of the complicated factors that go into determining people's wages, what can we conclude? A gender wage gap exists in all nations, but explaining why it occurs poses a challenge. No single cause has been identified, and the wage gap likely results from many different factors. The choices that people make—about occupations, negotiations, and parenting—contribute to the gap, but bear in mind that what might seem like personal choices may, in fact, be constrained by gender norms and expectations. Certain college majors and occupations might be seen as more "appropriate" for women than men. Taking time off from work after the birth of a child might be acceptable or even expected for women but frowned upon for men. Finally, the wage gap persists even when we take into account different career choices and time investments in work. Thus, at least part of this gap can likely be explained by the various gender biases we discussed earlier in the chapter.

How Do Work and Family Roles Interact?

Given what you have read so far, one thing is clear: We cannot understand how sex and gender influence labor divisions in the home without also considering how sex and gender influence workplace dynamics and vice versa. Until recently, however, most researchers examined work and home life separately, without considering their overlap. This changed in the 1980s, when research on the *work–family interface* took off (J. C. Williams, Berdahl, & Vandello, 2016). Researchers in this area study how work, family, and home life interact and how their interaction relates to health, well-being, job satisfaction, and employee productivity, as well as to organizational outcomes. For an overview of the history of work and family, see "Journey of Research: From Work–Family Conflict to Work–Life Enrichment."

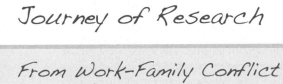

Journey of Research

From Work-Family Conflict to Work-Life Enrichment

In the first half of the 20th century, many households comprised a single-earner husband and a homemaker wife (although, as you may recall from Chapter 10, this was less true for racial minority and working-class families). Then, as women in most industrialized societies began to enter the workforce in increasing numbers in the second half of the century, the normative family model shifted to that of a dual-earner family.

Today, in over 60% of two-parent families with children, both parents work outside the home, and men have generally increased their involvement in domestic labor and childcare. As a result of these shifts, researchers began to study the ways in which work life and family life impact each other. Scholars from many disciplines—including industrial-organizational (I-O) and social psychology, sociology, and business—study the work–family interface (J. C. Williams et al., 2016). As a main focus, they ask whether having multiple roles (employed worker and family member) comes with more benefits or drawbacks.

The earliest research on work and family began in the 1960s, and *work–family conflict* was the dominant theme. One of the earliest theories of work and family, William Goode's (1960) *scarcity hypothesis*, proposed that having multiple roles will necessarily create tension, conflict, and a sense of overload. From the 1960s through the 1990s, a great deal of research documented the negative consequences of work–family conflict for personal well-being and interpersonal relationships (Byron, 2005).

By the turn of the 21st century, work–family researchers began studying the alternate possibility that work roles and family roles can enhance one another. The *expansion hypothesis*, reflecting this *work–family enrichment* perspective, proposes that the self-esteem and fulfillment provided by one role can spill over and have positive consequences for other roles (Barnett & Hyde, 2001). Note that the conflict and enrichment perspectives are not mutually exclusive, and both are supported by research. In fact, when studies measure both feelings of work–family conflict and enrichment, the two constructs often do not correlate very strongly (Greenhaus & Powell, 2006), meaning that they can both exist independently of each other.

What lies ahead for work–family research? First, researchers have been studying more diverse populations, considering how race, culture, and social class influence the work–family interface (J. C. Williams et al., 2016). In addition, researchers have begun to consider how *flexible work arrangements* (such as flexible work hours, telecommuting, or paid family leave) can affect people's sense of balance between their work and home lives. As more and more people incorporate both work and family roles into their identities, this field of research will likely gain importance.

Conflict and Enrichment

Researchers who study the work–family interface primarily focus on how people's **work–life balance**—the manner in which people prioritize these two domains of life—predicts various personal and organizational outcomes. As you read in the "Journey of Research," early work on this topic was largely influenced by the scarcity hypothesis, which views time and energy as finite resources, such that time spent in one domain (work vs. home) will necessarily detract from contributions to the other domain (Goode, 1960). In fact, to the extent that people perceive more **work–family conflict**, they do experience more negative mental and physical health outcomes, and this holds true regardless of people's sex (Byron, 2005). Moreover, women and men tend to report similar levels of work–family conflict, although men's feelings of conflict have been increasing faster than women's, at least in the United States (Aumann, Galisnky, & Matos, 2011). This may be due, in part, to men's increasing overwork, as discussed earlier. Another factor may be the expanding role of communication technologies (e.g., computers, e-mail, and smartphones) that blur the boundaries between work and home and make it harder to for some people to disconnect psychologically from their work when they are at home.

Note that the work–life conflict perspective frames work and family as incompatible. This perspective has been criticized because it reinforces the belief that parents—and especially mothers—who work outside the home will necessarily show declines in their parenting abilities (Ruderman, Ohlott, Panzer, & King, 2002). In fact, focusing solely on the incompatibility of work and home can be shortsighted because evidence suggests

Work–life balance: The manner in which people prioritize work and home life.

Work–family conflict: Feelings of stressful conflict between work life and home life, in which time spent in each domain detracts from contributions to the other domain.

that work and home roles are often mutually beneficial. Having a fulfilling, rewarding job can produce positive spillover into the home, and having a satisfying, happy home life can produce positive spillover into work (McNall, Nicklin, & Masuda, 2010). This effect, referred to as **work–life enrichment**, correlates with positive outcomes such as marital satisfaction, sleep quality, and job satisfaction (T. D. Allen, 2012). Interestingly, women tend to experience higher levels of work–family enrichment than men do (van Steenbergen, Ellemers, & Mooijaart, 2007).

Stop and Think

Why do you think that the positive spillover effects between work and home life are stronger for women than they are for men? What factors have you encountered so far in this book that might help to explain this sex difference in work–life enrichment?

Sidebar 11.5: The Benefits of a Working Mom?

Early work–family conflict research suggested that the outside employment of mothers might have detrimental effects on their children. In fact, this does not seem to be the case. A meta-analysis of 69 studies of working mothers found that children whose mothers worked when they were young did not suffer cognitively or behaviorally (Lucas-Thompson, Goldberg, & Prasue, 2010). And a cross-cultural study of adults from 25 nations found that women whose mothers worked outside the home when they were young earned more money and had more advanced positions than women who grew up with stay-at-home mothers. Moreover, men raised by working mothers spent nearly twice as many hours on household and childcare (McGinn, Ruiz Castro, & Long Lingo, 2015).

Work–life enrichment: Feelings of positive enrichment between work life and home life, in which a fulfilling job produces positive spillover into the home, and a satisfying home life produces positive spillover into work.

Flexible work arrangements: Arrangements in which employees control the location or timing of their work (e.g., flexible schedules and telecommuting).

Flexible Work and Family Leave Policies

As diverse family arrangements become common—and the number of dual-earner families continues to increase—a key to achieving ideal work–life balance may lie in flexible work arrangements. In **flexible work arrangements**, employees control the location or timing of their work. Some examples include the following: flexibility in the scheduling of hours worked (*flex time*), such as compressed workweeks or alternative work schedules; flexibility in the numbers of hours worked, such as part-time work, job shares, or parental leave; and flexibility in the physical location of work, such as telecommuting. In general, research shows positive benefits to workers who use flexible work arrangements, including increased productivity and job satisfaction and lower absenteeism (Baltes, Briggs, Huff, Wright, & Neuman, 1999; Gilbert, 1993; Gilbert & Rader, 2001). These worker outcomes can then have positive consequences for organizations because organizations profit from greater worker productivity and lower rates of absenteeism. Flexible work arrangements also reduce work–life conflict, but the effects are modest (T. A. Allen, Johnson, Kiburz, & Shockley, 2013). Note also that flexible work arrangements generally benefit women more than men, likely because women bear responsibility for the majority of family management activities, such as scheduling doctor appointments and meeting with teachers (T. D. Allen, 2012).

Flexible work arrangements, such as working from home, correlate with increased productivity and work satisfaction.

Source: © iStockPhoto .com/ranckreporter

Despite the benefits of flexible work arrangements—and the desire of most employees for flexibility in work arrangements—relatively few people take advantage of them (Weeden, 2005). Why do workers avoid desirable arrangements that can benefit them and their families? One explanation lies in the hidden costs to pursuing flexible work, such as negative evaluations from others, or **work flexibility stigma**. For example, people rated women on flexible work schedules as lower in career dedication and advancement potential than women on traditional schedules (Rogier & Padgett, 2004). Similarly, male and female accountants who used flexible work arrangements were seen as less likely to advance and more likely to leave their jobs (J. R. Cohen & Single, 2001).

Men, in particular, may be vulnerable to work flexibility stigma. While both men and women who pursue flexible work are evaluated relatively negatively and recommended for smaller raises, men who use such arrangements face the added penalty of being seen as less masculine (Rudman & Mescher, 2013; Vandello, Hettinger, Bosson, & Siddiqi, 2013). When Vandello and colleagues asked college students about their intentions to use flexible work arrangements in their future careers, men reported valuing workplace flexibility and work–life balance just as strongly as women did. However, men anticipated a relatively low likelihood of actually using work flex arrangements, and they reported believing that others would view them as less masculine for doing so (Vandello, Hettinger, Bosson, & Siddiqi, 2013). Think back to the story about parental leave in Sweden that opened this chapter. Even in Sweden, one of the most gender-egalitarian nations in the world, men resisted taking parental leave until the government instituted "daddy quotas."

Thus, organizations should strive to institute flexible work policies that meet the needs of employees without stigmatizing them. Some organizations have begun to address this problem through creative interventions. For example, Leslie Perlow (2012) worked with employees at the Boston Consulting Group (BCG) to help identify and resolve their high levels of work–family conflict and job burnout. Perlow found that unpredictable schedules were a major cause of the problem. Working with a BCG team, Perlow gave them a collective goal of scheduling predictable time off (PTO). Each team member got one night of PTO each week (no phone, e-mail, or work of any kind)

Work flexibility stigma: Negative evaluations that workers receive for pursuing flexible work arrangements.

starting at 6:00 p.m. The team monitored whether people took their PTO, and if not, they discussed what to do differently next time. This intervention was so successful that BCG subsequently used PTO scheduling with over 2,000 employees in 14 countries.

At Best Buy, Cali Ressler and Jody Thompson developed another a beneficial workplace intervention—the results-only work environment (ROWE)—which Gap subsequently implemented as well. Under the strategy, employees get paid for their results rather than the number of hours they work. Employees can work from home when they want, and they do not need to take sick days or vacation time as long as they perform their tasks. Meetings are optional. Work flexibility is the norm. Studies of the ROWE model show that it decreases work–family conflict, negative spillover, and job turnover (Kelly, Moen, & Tranby, 2011; Moen, Kelly, & Hill, 2011).

Nations vary in the degree to which their governments mandate flexible work policies. As we mentioned at the opening of the chapter, the United States stands alone among modern, industrialized nations in lacking paid parental leave. Examining how national paid leave policies affect work–family conflict can shed light on their effectiveness. One recent study comparing national paid leave policies across 12 industrialized nations found that having paid sick leave correlates with somewhat less work–family conflict. However, having paid parental leave or paid annual leave had little association with work–family conflict (T. D. Allen et al., 2014). Overall, the results suggest that paid leave policies understandably do not solve all the problems of working parents and that national policies, while helpful, will not be a magic solution to creating work–life balance.

That said, some findings do suggest that parental leave can have important benefits for children. Longitudinal data collected in several European nations indicate that more generous paid parental leave programs correlate with lower high school dropout rates and higher earnings by age 30 among children of working parents (Carneiro, Loken, & Salvanes, 2015). Even more striking, links exist between parental leave and infant and child mortality: Across nations, a 10-week increase in parental leave correlates with a 2%–3% reduction in the likelihood of infant death and a 4.5%–6.6% decrease in rates of child death between the ages of 1 and 5 (Ruhm, 2000). This may occur due to the simple fact that high-quality parenting is time-intensive. For instance, breastfeeding helps ensure infants' nutritional health during the first 6 months of life and correlates with reduced infant mortality from various common causes (M. S. Kramer et al., 2001). But mothers who work full time without flexible arrangements have more difficulty breastfeeding. In light of such findings, continued research on the effects of parental leave and flexible work policies is essential.

CHAPTER SUMMARY

11.1 Evaluate factors that influence the gendered division of labor in the home.

In heterosexual relationships, women, on average, do more housework than men, even among dual-earner couples. Some point to working women's greater time investment in housework and childcare as the cause of the "stalled gender revolution." The types of domestic work that heterosexual men and women do often falls along gendered lines, with women doing more daily routine work (e.g., cooking and laundry) and childcare and men doing more outdoor and non-daily work (e.g., lawn care). Same-sex couples tend to share household responsibilities more equally than heterosexual couples. Explanations for gendered divisions of labor include the time availability hypothesis, which asserts that more time spent in employment should equal less time on housework, and the relative income hypothesis, which asserts that whoever makes more money will do less housework. These explanations receive only mixed support. For instance, when wives outearn husbands, husbands do less housework. Gender role ideology tends to be a relatively good predictor of the division of labor. Because people may invest their identities into gendered labor divisions, some women resist men's contributions to household labor (e.g., maternal gatekeeping).

11.2 Describe subtle workplace gender biases that create and reinforce status differences between dominant and subordinate groups.

Women and men do not differ in their natural leadership abilities or success as leaders, although they display slightly different leadership styles. A host of workplace biases exist that may keep women from reaching workplace equality with men. The glass ceiling refers to invisible barriers that keep women from being promoted to high-level positions, while the glass cliff refers to a phenomenon in which women get promoted to top positions under precarious circumstances. The sticky floor keeps women concentrated in low-paying, low-mobility positions. These biases may result in women needing to prove themselves repeatedly, having difficulty advancing after they have children, walking a tightrope between being liked (but disrespected) or respected (but disliked), and feeling tension from other women due to competition for limited positions. Sexual orientation and gender identity minority individuals face even higher rates of gender bias in the workplace. Racial and ethnic minority women and men experience unique types of bias, including microaggressions, subtle stigmatization, and perceived unsuitability for certain jobs. Men who violate gender role norms also experience gender bias at work, including insults and threats.

11.3 Explain the gender wage gap and the various theories that account for it.

Gender wage gaps persist across all countries. Identifying the reasons for these gaps is challenging because there is no single cause. Gender biases and discrimination likely play roles in the wage gap, but probably the largest factor contributing to sex differences in workplace status is the expectation that women should be responsible for the majority of home and family care. This expectation can influence the types of occupations that men and women enter, the number of hours they work, whether or not they negotiate for higher salaries, their willingness to relocate for better jobs, whether they interrupt their careers to care for family, and the amount of time they devote to nonwork activities. The occupations most popular with women tend to pay less than the occupations most popular with men, but evidence also suggests that as women enter previously male-dominated fields, the salaries in these fields decline. Conversely, when men enter occupations at higher rates, salaries tend to increase.

11.4 Analyze the challenges and benefits of work–life balance and relevant factors, such as parental leave and flexible work arrangements.

Having an ideal work–life balance correlates with health, well-being, job satisfaction, and employee productivity, as well as with positive organizational outcomes. Work–life conflict continues to rise in the United States, particularly among men, as the number of hours worked increases and communication technologies make it harder to disconnect from work. However, having a fulfilling, rewarding job can produce positive spillover into the home, and having a satisfying, happy home life can produce positive spillover into work. Women tend to experience more of this work–life enrichment than men do. Workplaces have begun to address the reality of diverse families and the importance of work–life balance by offering more paid parental leave and flexible work arrangements, such as telecommuting or compressed workweeks. Despite the benefits of flexible work arrangements, many workers resist taking advantage of them, in part due to the anticipated and actual stigmatization that people face when they pursue these arrangements. Men, in particular, may be viewed as less masculine when pursuing flexible work arrangements, and this predicts their decreased intentions to pursue flexible work. Generous national paid leave policies only weakly predict reduced work–family conflict, but such policies may have important long-term benefits for children of working parents.

Test Your Knowledge: True or False?

11.1. In the United States, since the 1960s, mothers have doubled and fathers have tripled the amount of time per week, on average, that they spend on childcare. (True: The past half-century has seen large increases in the amount of time that parents spend on childcare, and this is true both in the United States and around the world.) [p. 375]

11.2. In households in which women make more money than their husbands, wives tend to do less housework than husbands. (False: Some research finds that women do relatively less housework the more they earn but only up until the point where they earn as much as husbands. From that point on, men do *less* housework the more their wives outearn them.) [p. 377]

11.3. Women hold fewer top executive positions than men, in part because of gender stereotypes that contribute to biases in hiring and career advancement. (True: There are numerous workplace gender biases that prevent women from advancing in the workplace.) [p. 382–383]

11.4. Once you account for differences in the occupations that women and men choose, the gender wage gap disappears. (False: Men do tend to select higher-paying jobs, but men earn more than women in both high- and low-paying occupations.) [p. 391]

11.5. Flexible work policies, such as telecommuting and flexible hours, correlate with less worker productivity and generally negative outcomes for organizations. (False: Flexible work arrangements correlate with greater productivity and tend to benefit both employees and organizations.) [p. 400–401]

Health and Well-Being

Chapter 12   Gender and Physical Health

Chapter 13   Gender and Psychological
             health

Chapter 14   Aggression and Violence

Susannah Mushatt Jones on her 113th birthday, with her 72-year-old niece, Lois Judge.

Source: Debbie Egan-Chin/NY Daily News/Getty Images

Test Your Knowledge: True or False?

12.1 Women tend to live longer than men in wealthier countries, but men live longer than women in poorer countries.

12.2 In surveys, men generally report being in better health than women.

12.3 Men in most societies, including the United States, smoke tobacco and drink alcohol more than women do.

12.4 Heart disease is the leading cause of death for women in the United States, but physicians less often test and prescribe medicine for heart disease in women than in men.

12.5 In health care surveys, most transgender adults say that it is not necessarily important for their doctor to know their gender identity status.

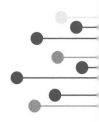

CHAPTER
12

Gender and Physical Health

Key Concepts

How Have Understandings of Health and Longevity Changed Over Time?

Changes in Life Expectancy

Mortality (Death) and Morbidity (Sickness)

Debate: Do Women or Men Experience Better Physical Health?

How Do Biological Factors Shape Sex Differences in Health?

Genetic Factors

Hormonal Influences

An Evolutionary Theory of Health and Longevity

How Do Social Factors Contribute to Sex Disparities in Health?

Health-Relevant Behavior: Things That People *Do*

    Accidents and Risky Sex

    Smoking, Alcohol Use, and Diet

    Physical Activity and Exercise

Health-Relevant Traits: Ways That People *Are*

Accessing Health Care

    Seeking Health Care

    Receiving Health Care

Gender-Egalitarian Communities and Health

How Do Multiple Systems of Discrimination Shape Health and Health Care?

Race, Ethnicity, and Sex

Socioeconomic Status, Sex, and Race/Ethnicity

Sexual Orientation and Gender Identity

How Has Reproductive Health Been Medicalized?

Journey of Research: Pregnancy and Childbirth Advice Through the Centuries.

Learning Objectives

Students who read this chapter should be able to do the following:

12.1 Describe the major causes of mortality for men and women and how they have changed over time.

12.2 Explain biological and social causes for gender gaps in health and longevity.

12.3 Analyze the roles of race, social class, sexual orientation, gender identity, and intersectionality in physical health.

12.4 Explain key issues that result from the medicalization of sexual and reproductive health.

Gender and Physical Health

Before New Yorker Susannah Mushatt Jones died in 2016 just shy of her 117th birthday, she was the oldest living American. Born in Alabama into a poor family of sharecroppers, Jones moved to Harlem as a young woman. Asked about the key to a long life, she claimed that abstaining from alcohol and tobacco kept her going. This may be true to a degree, but a more important factor likely contributed to Jones's longevity. Topping the list of the oldest people who have ever lived are Jeanne Calment (age 122), Sarah Knauss (age 119), and Lucy Hannah (age 117). Notice anything similar about these people? They're all women. In fact, 96% of the 50 oldest people alive in 2016 were women (Margolis, 2016).

Women swell the ranks of the elderly. Among all people in the United States, women constitute 55% of those who are in their 70s, 62% of those in their 80s, 72% of those in their 90s, and 83% of those over the age of 100 (U.S. Census Bureau, 2010). Moreover, women outlive men in every country in the world, by an average of 4.7 years worldwide (World Health Organization [WHO], 2017a). Not a new phenomenon, we have known that women outlive men for as long as there have been reliable death records. Data from 1751 to 1790 in Sweden, the first country to collect national death records, show that the average life expectancy for women was 36.6, compared with 33.7 for men (Perls & Fretts, 1998).

It may not surprise anyone who has visited a nursing facility that women tend to live longer than men. But have you ever wondered why this is so? Are women just "naturally" likely to outlive men? Are the sex differences in longevity due to something biological or are there social factors in play? As is the case with many questions about sex and gender, both types of factors interact to influence sex differences in longevity.

But longevity tells only part of the story of health. That women outlive men does not necessarily mean that they experience better health than men do. In fact, in comparison with men, women tend to report higher rates of illness. Health, illness, wellness, and longevity are all complicated concepts, and our understandings of them continually evolve. In this and the next chapter, we attempt to shed some light on the roles that sex and gender play in health. We focus on physical health in this chapter and on mental health and well-being in the next chapter. Of course, physical and mental health do not operate independently of each other. Physical health influences mental health, and mental health influences physical health. At the end of this chapter, we will consider the connection between the two.

How Have Understandings of Health and Longevity Changed Over Time?

From a health perspective, you live at the best possible time in human history. Our understandings of disease and medicine, along with improved safety standards, have radically transformed humanity in a relatively short time period. If you lived at the turn of the 20th century, you would likely die much younger and from a different cause, as compared with today.

Changes in Life Expectancy

Figure 12.1 shows the average **life expectancy**, or length of time a person is expected to live, based on year of birth over the past century. Note that life expectancy was 46.3 for men and 48.3 for women in 1900, and this increased to 76.9 for men and 81.6 for women by 2015 (WHO, 2017b). This near doubling of the average life span in just over a century may be one of the most remarkable achievements in human history. But now note the sex difference depicted in Figure 12.1. Although women's life expectancy exceeds men's across the entire century, the gap grew over time, reached a peak sex difference of 7.6 years in 1970 and then shrunk somewhat (currently at 4.7 years). Why might the gender gap in longevity have gotten larger and then smaller over the past century? A number of reasons account for this fluctuating longevity gap, and we will discuss them throughout this chapter, but changes in smoking patterns over time played a substantial role. Men have always smoked more than women, but that gap has narrowed (Centers for Disease Control and Prevention, 2015a).

When it comes to health and longevity, not all groups are equal. Due to unique stressors (e.g., discrimination, poverty, and lack of health insurance), members of groups that are marginalized on the basis of race, ethnicity, sexual orientation, and gender identity tend to have lower life expectancies than dominant group members. For instance,

Life expectancy: The average length of time a person is expected to live, based on year of birth.

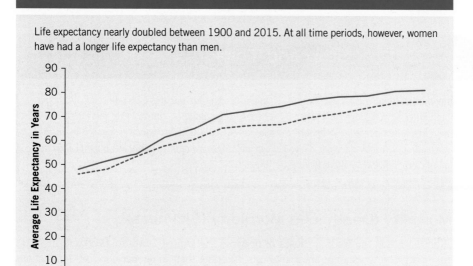

Figure 12.1 Estimated U.S. Life Expectancy at Birth.

Life expectancy nearly doubled between 1900 and 2015. At all time periods, however, women have had a longer life expectancy than men.

Source: E. Arias (2015).

in the United States, White people tend to outlive Black people by about 3.6 years, and Latino people tend to outlive Black people by about 6.6 years (National Center for Health Statistics [NCHS], 2015). Note that Latino people in the United States also outlive White people by an average of 3 years; for more on this, see Sidebar 12.1. Moreover, gay, lesbian, and bisexual people who live in communities characterized by high levels of antigay prejudice have a life expectancy that is 12 years shorter than that of gay, lesbian, and bisexual people who live in more welcoming communities (Hatzenbuehler et al., 2014).

Latino paradox:
A phenomenon in which Latino Americans in the United States have health outcomes as good as, if not better than, those of non-Latino White people in the United States, despite tending to have a lower average income and less education.

Sidebar 12.1: The Latino Paradox

Since the mid-1980s, health researchers have been interested in the **Latino paradox**, which refers to the tendency for Latino Americans in the United States to have health outcomes as good as, if not better than, those of non-Latino White people in the United States, despite tending to have a lower average income and less education. This is considered a paradox because lower income and education generally correlate with worse health outcomes worldwide. While several hypotheses (regarding diet, smoking, exercise, and family ties) have been offered to explain this paradox, researchers still do not fully understand it. Of note, the Latino health advantage correlates negatively with degree of acculturation, meaning that the health advantage decreases as Latinos become more acculturated to the U.S. lifestyle (Gonzalez, 2015).

Stop and Think

Consider the finding that LGB individuals who live in high-prejudice communities have a shorter life expectancy than those who live in low-prejudice communities. This link is correlational, which does not allow for a determination of cause and effect. What factors might account for this link? Do you think that exposure to stigmatization causes early mortality, and if so, how? Could this association be caused by a third variable? If so, what third variable(s) might be operating here?

Mortality (Death) and Morbidity (Sickness)

Table 12.1 lists the leading causes of death in the United States in 1900 and in 2010. Take a minute to examine these two lists and note their differences. In 1900, infectious diseases such as pneumonia and tuberculosis topped the list. Over the decades, discoveries and developments like vaccines, antibiotics, refrigeration (which slows the growth of bacteria in food), and mosquito control (mosquitos transmit many fatal diseases), along with improved understandings of health and health care, led people to become healthier and live longer. As longevity increased, "diseases of old age" replaced infectious diseases among the top causes of death. For instance, people die of heart disease, cancer, and Alzheimer's disease more frequently now than they did a century ago.

Table 12.1	**Leading Causes of Death in the United States.** Compare the top-10 leading causes of death in the United States. in 1900 and 2010 (note that number of deaths is per 100,000 people). What differences do you notice?		
1900	**Number of Deaths**	**2010**	**Number of Deaths**
Pneumonia or influenza	202.2	Heart disease	192.9
Tuberculosis	194.4	Cancer	185.9
Gastrointestinal infections	142.7	Noninfectious airways diseases	44.6
Heart disease	137.4	Cerebrovascular disease	41.8
Cerebrovascular disease	106.9	Accidents	38.2
Kidney disease	88.6	Alzheimer's disease	27.0
Accidents	72.3	Diabetes	22.3
Cancer	64.0	Kidney disease	16.3
Senility	50.2	Pneumonia or influenza	16.2
Diphtheria	40.3	Suicide	12.2

Source: D. S. Jones, Podolsky, and Greene (2012).

Moreover, for every one of the top causes of death in 2010, except Alzheimer's disease, men die at higher rates than women (Kruger & Nesse, 2006). So men suffer from life-threatening conditions more often than women. Women, however, tend to suffer from chronic, nonfatal, debilitating conditions—such as arthritis, osteoporosis, and autoimmune disorders—more often than men (Needham & Hill, 2010). These sex differences underlie the **morbidity-mortality paradox**, the phenomenon in which women tend to have higher rates of morbidity (sickness) but lower rates of mortality (death) than men.

Women's relatively higher rates of chronic, nonfatal illnesses and health conditions are evident in their self-reports of health. Researchers interested in self-reported health usually measure health broadly, by asking questions such as, "For your age, in general, would you rate your health as excellent, good, fair, poor, or bad?" In response to such questions, women report poorer health than men do at all ages and in all world regions, although the gender gap in self-reported health is smaller in European and sub-Saharan African countries and larger in Latin American and South Asian countries (Boerma, Hosseinpoor, Verdes, & Chatterji, 2016).

Some suggest that women may overinflate their self-reported ill health, but this does not seem to be the case. For example, one study investigated the links between sex, self-reported health, and chronic conditions in over 29,000 women and men and found that

Morbidity-mortality paradox: A phenomenon in which women have higher rates of morbidity (sickness and disability) than men while men have higher rates of mortality (death) than women.

women's poorer self-reported health was fully explained by women's higher likelihood of suffering various chronic pain conditions (Malmusi, Artazcoz, Benach, & Borrell, 2012). Specifically, in comparison with men, women more frequently suffer from musculoskeletal disorders (such as arthritis and neck or back pain) and chronic pain conditions (headaches), and these chronic, discomfort-causing conditions fuel women's reports of poorer health. But why would these sex differences in painful conditions occur? Some propose that women's traditional role of serving as caretakers for others contributes to their poorer health because being a caretaker can increase stress and make people vulnerable to various debilitating conditions. In addition, taking care of others may reduce the likelihood of taking care of oneself (Helgeson, 2003). These factors may explain why women experience more conditions of chronic discomfort than men do.

It might also be possible that men overinflate their reports of physical health, perhaps because they are either unaware of—or unwilling to admit to—physical shortcomings. Sex differences in reported health could also reflect differences in the populations surveyed. For example, women outnumber men at older ages, and health surveys of older men (obviously) only take into account those still living. Thus, older men who outlive their peers may perceive themselves as pretty healthy in comparison, and this perception may inflate their ratings of health compared with women's. For more on the topic of mortality versus morbidity, turn to "Debate: Do Women or Men Experience Better Physical Health?"

Debate

Who is generally healthier: women or men? Women undeniably live longer than men in most every culture around the world, often by several years. But although living a long life is one way to measure health, it is not the only way. What if a person lives a long life but suffers a painful debilitating condition for a large portion of it? Some argue that while men have higher rates of *mortality* (death) than women, women have higher rates of *morbidity* (sickness) than men. Let's consider both sides of the debate.

Men Are Healthier

If we use self-reported health as a guide, men are healthier. Despite women living longer, men report better health than women do. Women report poorer health than men do at all ages and in all world regions (Boerma et al., 2016). Asking people to report their own health status might not seem like a very valid indicator of health, but in fact, self-reported health strongly predicts subsequent mortality (Schnittker & Bacak, 2014).

Women's health-related behaviors are consistent with these self-reports. Women use more health-related services, make more doctor visits, and spend more out-of-pocket money on health care and prescriptions than men do. Women also take more sick days from work than men (Jenkins, 2014; NCHS, 2015).

Similarly, women suffer more than men from several chronic, debilitating conditions, including joint, abdominal, and chest pain; irritable bowel syndrome; headaches and migraines; widespread body pain; and fibromyalgia (LaResche, 1999). Women are also more likely than men to develop autoimmune diseases (when the immune system attacks healthy cells by mistake), such as multiple sclerosis, rheumatoid arthritis, and lupus (Lockshin, 2005). Thus, women's advantage in longevity does not necessarily mean an advantage in overall health.

Women Are Healthier

Women's greater life expectancies across cultures suggest that women are, in fact, healthier than men. In developed nations, men's rates of death from nearly all major causes exceed women's (Kruger & Nesse, 2006). Although women self-report worse health than men, this may be due to gender role norms that pressure men to suppress any signs of weakness while allowing women to express their vulnerabilities and seek help. Thus, if women appear sicker than men, this may be because they go to the doctor more often and admit to their illnesses.

Stereotypes portray women as the physically weaker sex, but girls and women are actually heartier and more robust biologically than boys and men. Although slightly more baby boys than girls are born each year, boys die at higher rates than girls at every age (T. J. Mathews & Hamilton, 2005). By their first birthday, baby boys are about 24% more likely to die than girls (Drevenstedt, Crimmins, Vasunilashorn, & Finch, 2008). The higher male mortality rate may reflect the fact of a stronger female immune system: Compared with girls and women, boys and men get more infections and have more difficulty clearing them (Zuk, 2009).

Now that you have read both sides of the debate, which evidence seems more compelling? Do you think it makes more sense to conceptualize health in terms of mortality or morbidity? Why?

How Do Biological Factors Shape Sex Differences in Health?

Humans are not the only species in which females outlive males. In most animal species, from mollusks to mice to macaques, females have a longer average lifespan than males (Perls & Fretts, 1998). The cross-species generality of female animals' longer lifespan suggests biological bases for this sex difference. In this section, we examine how various biological factors shape health and contribute to sex differences in health and longevity.

Genetic Factors

As we discussed in Chapter 3 ("The Nature and Nurture of Sex and Gender"), genetic sex is determined by the sex chromosomes, termed X and Y. Individuals who carry an X and a Y chromosome usually become boys, whereas those who carry two X chromosomes usually become girls. Interestingly, having two X chromosomes may provide a health advantage to girls and women. How so? The sex chromosomes can sometimes carry genetic mutations that code for diseases, such as muscular dystrophy or hemophilia (Perls & Fretts, 1998). However, most sex-linked diseases are passed down

From mollusks to mice to macaques, and, of course, humans, female members of many animal species outlive male members.

Source: © iStockPhoto.com/nono57; © iStockPhoto.com/CreativeNature_nl; ©iStockPhoto.com/JodiJacobson; © iStockPhoto.com/hadynyah

through the X chromosome, which contains far more genes than the much smaller Y chromosome. Among people who have two X chromosomes, if they carry a recessive, disease-producing, abnormal gene on one X chromosome, the normal gene on the other X chromosome can override the abnormal gene and prevent the expression of the disease. In this case, the individual will be a carrier of the defective gene, but she will not experience the disease. In contrast, among people who have only one X chromosome, if they carry a disease-producing, abnormal gene on that X chromosome, they do not have another X chromosome to overcome the abnormality, thus making them more likely to develop the disease. In this way, males, relative to females, are more vulnerable to X-linked diseases.

Telomeres:
Disposable DNA sequences at the ends of chromosome strands that protect the remaining genes on the chromosomes during cell division.

The discovery of **telomeres** represents an exciting breakthrough in the genetics of aging. Telomeres are deoxyribonucleic acid (DNA) sequences at the ends of chromosome strands that protect genetic data and allow for cells to divide. Think of them as the caps at the tips of shoelaces that keep the laces from fraying. Each time a cell divides, the telomeres get shorter, until eventually the cell can no longer divide, and it dies. Although the telomeres of male and female chromosomes are the same length at birth, male telomeres shorten faster than female telomeres, suggesting that male cells age faster (Barrett & Richardson, 2011). Thus, sex differences in telomeres appear linked to sex differences in aging and longevity. Much remains unknown, but research on telomeres may one day unlock the secrets of sex differences in aging and life expectancy.

Hormonal Influences

Sex hormones, including testosterone and estrogen, play well-documented roles in health and longevity. Testosterone, which is much higher, on average, in men than women, boosts male fertility by increasing aggression and risk taking, as well as by contributing to sex drive and regulating sperm production. However, testosterone also has negative consequences for long-term health. For instance, testosterone decreases levels of "good" cholesterol (high-density lipoprotein, or HDL) and increases levels of "bad" cholesterol (low-density lipoprotein, or LDL), thereby increasing the risk of cardiovascular disease (Herbst, Amory, Brunzell, Chansky, & Bremner, 2003). Testosterone also suppresses the body's immune system, which can help to explain why women have more robust immune responses than men (Furman et al., 2014). In fact, male members of most species, including humans, generally show greater susceptibility to infections from parasites, bacteria, viruses, and fungi than their female counterparts (Zuk & McKean, 1996). This may reflect the suppressing effects of testosterone on male animals' immune system.

Conversely, estrogen, which is typically much higher in women than men, provides health benefits. Premenopausal women, who have higher levels of estrogen than menopausal women, have lower blood pressure and a reduced incidence of cardiovascular disease compared with age-matched men, and this may be due, in part, to their higher estrogen levels (Xue, Johnson, & Hay, 2013). Estrogen also increases cardiac output during the menstrual cycle, which some liken to a "jogging female heart" because it mimics the effects of exercise (Eskes & Haanen, 2007). Finally, estrogen increases the expression of longevity-associated genes (Viña, Borrás, Gambini, Sastre, & Pallardó, 2005). However, it also can increase the risk of certain forms of cancer, such as breast, uterine, and ovarian cancers.

Stop and Think

You have encountered several different types of evidence suggesting that women have a physical health advantage over men. Women are more resistant to infections, inherit fewer sex-linked genetic diseases, age *more slowly, and produce more health-promoting hormones than men. Why do you think women's biology imbues them with a health advantage over men? How might evolution play a role in these patterns?*

An Evolutionary Theory of Health and Longevity

Stepping back a bit, we can ask why female and male members of species even differ at all in ways that contribute to health and longevity. To answer this question, evolutionary theorists point to the different mating challenges that men and women faced in their ancestral past. Recall from our discussion of sexual selection in Chapter 3 ("The Nature and Nurture of Sex and Gender") that traits and behaviors that increase the likelihood of reproduction more frequently get passed on genetically. Because male and female members of many species presumably faced different mating challenges in their ancestral past, they should have adapted by evolving different features (e.g., hormone levels, traits, and behaviors) that allowed them to overcome these challenges. Since gestation occurs internally in the female in most mammalian species, females invest more in each offspring than males do and tend to be more discriminating than males in choosing mates. In contrast, male animals of many species, including humans, typically compete for access to female mates by performing aggressive and risky behavior. At the same time that risky and aggressive tendencies give some males a reproductive advantage over others, they also increase the likelihood of death. Thus, evolutionary theorists propose that men evolved to pursue a "live hard, die young" strategy because this strategy results in more offspring, even if it means an earlier average age of death for men than women (Zuk, 2009).

How does this relate to health and longevity? Consider testosterone. Men have higher concentrations of testosterone than women. This may be the result of evolutionary pressures on men to compete aggressively for mates because such aggressive competition increases men's reproductive success. However, while having high levels of testosterone may pay off in terms of passing on their genes, it may also, as we discussed, have the cost of suppressing men's immune systems and making them more vulnerable to infection. In other words, testosterone is good for reproduction but bad for long-term survival. According to the evolutionary hypothesis, men's bodies evolved to prioritize procreation over the development of immunity (Zuk, 2009).

Next, evolutionary theorists propose that women's bodies evolved to invest more energy into repairing themselves. People age because the body's cells naturally produce tiny damaging mistakes from time to time. Bodies work constantly to repair this cell damage, but some cells survive unrepaired. Over time, these damaged cells accumulate, which accounts for physical aging. Although genes get passed on to offspring, the individual body itself is disposable, but some evolutionary theorists hypothesize that the female body is less disposable than the male body (Kirkwood, 2010). Why? The physical health of a pregnant woman's body plays a critical role in the success of reproduction, fetal growth, and infant nourishment while the physical health of men's bodies is less critical to successful reproduction and fetal health. So the female body may have evolved to repair itself more effectively—that is, age less slowly—than the male body. In fact, for the male body, the costs of expending resources on cell repair may be outweighed by the advantages of diverting those resources elsewhere (e.g., competition for mates and hunting food). In short, evolutionary theorists argue that what makes our bodies great machines for passing on our genes does not always help us live a long time. Moreover, the different physical roles played by the bodies of women and men in reproduction can help to explain sex differences in risk taking, immune response, aging, and longevity.

How Do Social Factors Contribute to Sex Disparities in Health?

As the preceding section illustrates, biological factors undoubtedly play a role in sex differences in health and longevity. But our behavior matters as well, as reflected in the dramatic increase in life expectancy and the changes in leading causes of death over the past century. Turning back to Table 12.1, you will notice that most all leading causes of death in 2010 can be influenced, to some extent, by people's behaviors. Things like diet, exercise, alcohol, smoking, and drug use can influence rates of heart disease, cancers, diabetes, and kidney disease. Accidents, suicides, and homicides have obvious behavioral influences. In fact, the more that behavioral factors contribute to a given cause of death, the larger the sex difference in rates of death from that cause (Kruger & Nesse, 2006). In this section, we will consider social factors that contribute to sex disparities in health. These include behaviors that can improve health and those that can impair health. What kinds of things do women and men do—and *not* do—that influence their health in positive and negative ways?

Health-Relevant Behavior: Things That People *Do*

Accidents and risky sex. One of the most promising explanations for sex differences in physical health is men's proclivity toward risky behaviors, which undoubtedly contributes to their lower survival rates. For instance, accidental deaths are the fourth leading cause of death in the United States for men but only seventh for women. In the workplace, men account for an astonishing 93% of fatal injuries (U.S. Bureau of Labor Statistics, 2015b). At home, men account for 83% of accidental deaths, likely due to engaging in riskier tasks, such as repairing electrical problems, climbing on roofs, and so on (Driscoll et al., 2003). Men also engage in more risky and accident-prone leisure activities and sports than women, such as rock climbing, whitewater rafting, cliff diving, skydiving,

scuba diving, motorcycle racing, and bungee jumping (Schrader & Wann, 1999). In the United States, in comparison with women, men are three times more likely to own a personal firearm (Pew Research Center, 2013) and six times more likely to die from an unintentional firearm injury (Centers for Disease Control and Prevention, 2015b).

On the road, men drive more recklessly than women. In the United States, men account for about 71% of motor vehicle fatalities, including 92% of motorcycle deaths (IIHS, 2016), and European men are three times more likely than women to die in road traffic accidents (White et al., 2011). Men drive more than women, which could explain these findings, but even controlling for miles driven, men account for more deaths. In other words, the *way* that men drive plays a role in their vehicle accident deaths. In comparison with women, men less frequently wear seat belts and more frequently speed and drive under the influence of alcohol or other drugs (IIHS, 2016).

Men tend to take more physical risks than women, on average.

Source: © iStockPhoto .com/Grigorev_Vladimir

Another form of risky behavior, sexual activity, reveals a somewhat different pattern. Not all sex is risky, but unprotected sex, sex with a stranger, and sex while intoxicated or under the influence of other drugs can increase the risks of sexually transmitted diseases, pregnancy, and violence. One meta-analysis of 47 studies found almost no sex differences in risky sexual behavior overall ($d = 0.07$), but some sex differences emerged as a function of age. While male teenagers tend to engage in riskier sex than female teenagers, women are slightly more likely than men to engage in risky sexual activity during the postcollege years ($d = -0.11$; Byrnes, Miller, & Schafer, 1999). Not surprisingly, some kinds of risky sex (e.g., intoxicated sex) go hand in hand with other kinds of risky sex (e.g., unprotected sex). One study of college students found that for both women and men, alcohol consumption during their most recent episode of sex with a nonregular partner correlated with a lower likelihood of condom use (Connor, Psutka, Cousins, Gray, & Kypri, 2013).

One of the most devastating consequences of risky sex—for both women and men— is infection by the **human immunodeficiency virus (HIV)**. In the United States, 81% of new HIV cases each year are among men (Centers for Disease Control and Prevention, 2017), but globally, women account for about half of all HIV cases among adults (UN Women, 2016a). As shown in Figure 12.2, the types of sexual activity associated with HIV infection show large sex differences: Among men, most cases of HIV transmission (77%) occur during same-sex sexual activity, while among women, most cases (86%) occur during heterosexual activity.

HIV/AIDS also disproportionately affects Black and Latino people in the United States. While Black and Latino people represent about 12% and 17% of the U.S. population, respectively, they account for 45% and 25% of new HIV diagnoses (Centers for Disease Control and Prevention, 2017). These race and ethnicity disparities in HIV infection rates are not well understood. They do not appear to reflect differences in risky behaviors, such as numbers of sexual partners, frequency of risky sexual practices, or tendency to use substances during sex. However, some researchers have made headway by analyzing **risk networks**, which are extended networks of individuals with whom people have sexual contact or engage in other risky practices, such as intravenous drug use. According to the logic of risk networks, the likelihood of HIV infection increases as a function of both individual risks (e.g., having unprotected sex) and the proportion of infected sexual partners in a person's risk network. Thus, even if Black and Latino people do not take more individual risks than White people, they may still exhibit higher rates of HIV infection than White people if they have higher concentrations of HIV-infected sexual partners in their risk networks than White people do (Mustanski, Birkett, Kuhns, Latkin, & Muth, 2015).

Despite advances in new **highly active antiretroviral therapies (HAARTs)** that greatly reduce the risk of dying from HIV-related causes, only about 41% of those living with HIV across the world can afford these therapies (Avert.org, 2016). Moreover, at the same time that HAARTs can offer hope in fighting HIV/AIDS to those who can afford them, they can also have the unintended and ironic effect of increasing people's tendencies to engage in risky sex. One study tracked a sample of HIV-negative gay men over 3 years and measured both their concerns about contracting HIV and their tendency to engage in *unprotected receptive anal intercourse* (URAI), the sex act that carries the single highest probability of HIV transmission (Beyrer et al., 2012). While most men in the

Human immunodeficiency virus (HIV): A virus that attacks the body's immune system and makes it difficult for the body to fight diseases.

Risk networks: Extended networks of individuals with whom people have sexual contact or engage in other risky practices (e.g., intravenous drug use) that can transmit disease.

Highly active antiretroviral therapies (HAARTs): Drug treatments, usually consisting of a combination of at least three drugs, that suppress HIV replication.

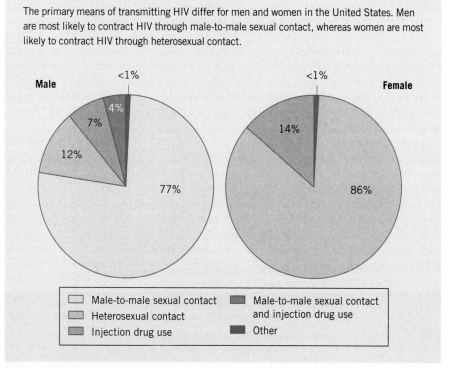

Figure 12.2 Transmission of HIV.

The primary means of transmitting HIV differ for men and women in the United States. Men are most likely to contract HIV through male-to-male sexual contact, whereas women are most likely to contract HIV through heterosexual contact.

Male
<1%
4%
7%
12%
77%

Female
<1%
14%
86%

- ☐ Male-to-male sexual contact
- ☐ Heterosexual contact
- ☐ Injection drug use
- ■ Male-to-male sexual contact and injection drug use
- ■ Other

Source: National Institute on Drug Abuse (2010).

sample remained highly concerned about the possibility of contracting HIV, those who reported that the availability of HAARTs made them less concerned about HIV were also more likely to have URAI with casual sex partners (Stolte, Dukers, Geskus, Coutinho, & de Wit, 2004). This suggests that the availability of HAARTs may give some people a false sense of security that can increase their risky sexual activity.

Smoking, alcohol use, and diet. Globally, nearly five times as many men as women smoke (Guindon & Boisclair, 2003). Though relatively smaller, this sex differences exists in the United States, where 18.8% of men versus 14.8% of women smoke (Jamal et al., 2015). Smoking is now widely recognized as one of the riskiest health habits, but this was not always the case. In the United States, smoking rates rose steadily between 1900 and the mid-1960s, at which point the rates leveled off and then slowly declined. The decrease likely stemmed from research published in the 1940s and 1950s that convincingly linked smoking to lung cancer, which then spawned several decades of anti-smoking health campaigns in the United States (U.S. Department of Health and Human Services, 2000). These health campaigns paid off: Whereas nearly half of Americans smoked at the middle of the 20th century, only about 17% of adults smoke today.

Table 12.2 shows not only the declining rates of smoking in the United States over the past several decades but also the shrinking sex difference in smoking rates. In 1955, men were about twice as likely as women to smoke, but today, men are only 1.27 times as likely as women to smoke. As noted earlier, this declining sex difference in smoking helps explain why the overall gender longevity gap decreased over the past few decades. Specifically, deaths from smoking-related diseases, such as lung cancer, chronic obstructive pulmonary disease (COPD), and heart disease, have become more evenly distributed across men and women. However, despite smoking less than men, women often have more difficulty quitting than men do (P. H. Smith et al., 2015). This may be because women are more likely than men to use smoking to control their weight based on the belief that smoking suppresses the appetite (Pomerleau & Snedecor, 2008).

Like smoking, alcohol abuse used to be mainly a male problem, but the sex difference narrowed in recent years. In the United States, 60% of men, compared with 44% of women, drink alcohol regularly (Blackwell, Lucas, & Clark, 2014), which may be partly due to the association of alcohol consumption with masculinity. Drinking modest amounts of alcohol (one drink per day for women and two drinks per day for men) does not seem to have negative effects, but drinking more than that can be a danger to health by increasing risks of hypertension, heart disease, liver disease, and various cancers, not to mention increasing risks for violence and accidents. When it comes to excessive, dangerous drinking, men outnumber women.

Table 12.2 **Percentages of U.S. Adults Who Smoke.** Both men and women have decreased their smoking rates since 1955. Men have always smoked at higher rates than women, but the sex difference has gotten much smaller over the decades.

Year	Overall	Men	Women	Sex Difference
1955	—	56.9	28.4	28.5
1965	42.4	51.9	33.9	18.0
1970	37.4	44.1	31.5	12.6
1980	33.2	37.6	29.3	8.3
1990	25.5	28.4	22.8	5.6
2000	23.3	25.7	21.0	4.7
2010	19.3	21.5	17.3	4.2
2013	17.8	20.5	15.3	5.2
2014	17.0	18.8	14.8	4.0

Source: Centers for Disease Control and Prevention (2015a); Jamal et al. (2015).

For instance, men are more likely than women to **binge drink**, which is defined as consuming four or more alcoholic drinks in 1–2 hours for women and five or more drinks in 1–2 hours for men. In one large, representative sample of U.S. adults, nearly twice as many men (24.6%) than women (12.5%) reported binge drinking over the past month (Kanny, Liu, Brewer, & Lu, 2013).

Men also become dependent on alcohol more frequently than women do. In one survey of people in the United States, nearly twice as many men (4.5%) than women (2.5%) met diagnostic criteria for alcohol dependence (Esser et al., 2014), a psychological disorder in which alcohol use becomes habitual and difficult to control and interferes with normal functioning (for more on this, see Chapter 13, "Gender and Psychological Health"). Not surprisingly, given their more risky and excessive use of alcohol, men die from alcohol-related causes more often than women do (Minino, Heron, Murphy, & Kochanek, 2007).

In addition to drinking more alcohol than women, men generally eat less healthy diets than women. Women tend to eat more fruits, vegetables, and fiber and to limit salt, whereas men tend to eat more meat and high-fat foods (Prattala et al., 2007; Wardle et al., 2004). Most major health organizations propose that the risks of chronic diseases, including diabetes, cancer, and car-diovascular disease, can be reduced by adopting a diet high in fruits, vegetables, and whole grains, moderate in lean proteins and dairy products, and low in saturated fatty acids, fried foods, sodium, and sugar (World Heart Federation, 2014). While most people could likely ben-efit from an improved diet, men in particular often resist adopting such changes. This may partly be due to the existence of powerful, cross-cultural gender stereotypes about food and diets. For example, men and masculinity are associated with red meat and alcohol while women and femininity are associated with fruits, vegetables, and fish (O'Doherty & Holm, 1999; Rozin, Hormes, Faith, & Wansink, 2012). More generally, stereotypes associate healthy diets with femininity and unhealthy diets with masculinity (Oakes & Slotterback, 2004). Thus, eating healthy and low-fat foods can be threatening for men because it may lead others to view them as feminine or insufficiently masculine. Conversely, going out of their way to eat unhealthy foods can signal men's masculinity to others. Consider the appeal of the Heart Attack Grill in Las Vegas, Nevada, which markets itself as a manly restau-rant for thrill-seekers. Its menu advertises such options as a 9,000-calorie Quadruple Bypass Burger and Flatliner Fries cooked in pure lard. The restaurant gained notoriety in recent years when at least two male customers suffered heart attacks while eating there (Jaslow, 2012).

As we have discussed in these sections, robust links exist between being male and taking health risks. In fact, some theorists propose risk taking as a core element of the male gender role. Men often learn to use risky behavior as a means of

Binge drinking: Consuming four or more alcoholic drinks within 1–2 hours for women and five or more drinks within 1–2 hours for men.

Men are more likely than women to make a show of eating high-calorie, fatty foods.

Source: © iStockPhoto .com/Stormcab

demonstrating masculine competence, knowing full well the associated perils. As you read in Chapter 4 ("Gender Development"), many cultures around the world subject adolescent boys to physically demanding manhood rituals in which they earn the status of "real men" through public performance of risky and painful acts. Thus, there may be a powerful cultural incentive for men to take risks with their health: Should they survive, they prove their manhood—at least until the next time.

Physical activity and exercise. In contrast to the trends discussed so far, boys and men demonstrate somewhat healthier habits than girls and women in the domains of physical activity and exercise. A sedentary, nonactive lifestyle contributes to the development of noncommunicable diseases, whereas regular activity and exercise contribute to good physical and mental health and quality of life. To meet recommended guidelines for physical activity, adults should engage in at least 30 minutes of moderate-intensity physical activity at least 5 days per week, or 20 minutes of vigorous activity at least 3 days per week. Moreover, this physical activity can take many forms, including leisure activities, work/housework, and transportation (e.g., biking to work). In most countries around the world, including the United States, girls and women are less physically active, on average, than boys and men (Hallal et al., 2012). One large-scale study tracked the physical activity of 9- and 15-year-old European children over 4 days and found that boys showed higher levels of physical activity than girls at both ages (Riddoch et al., 2004). Similarly, women across the globe are slightly more likely than men (33.7% vs. 27.9%) to be classified as *physically inactive* by not meeting minimum activity guidelines. Across all ages, girls and women walk less and engage in less vigorous physical activity than do boys and men (Hallal et al., 2012).

Percentages of physical inactivity differ by world region as well, ranging from 17.0% in Southeast Asia to 27.5% in Africa, 34.8% in Europe, and 43.3% in North and South America (Hallal et al., 2012). Interestingly, inactivity increases with the income of a country, likely because wealthier countries tend to be more industrialized and technologically advanced, which means that people's jobs typically entail less physical labor, and public transportation is more widely available. Thus, while wealth obviously improves quality of life in many ways, it can also discourage healthy levels of physical activity. For instance, in one study that tracked physical activity among U.S. residents of various ages throughout the day, fewer than 12% of men and 6% of women over the age of 12 met minimum guidelines for sufficient daily activity (Troiano et al., 2007).

Physical activity also declines with age, both in the United States and worldwide (Hallal et al., 2012). While about 42% of children (ages 6–11) in the United States meet minimum guidelines for physical activity, activity generally declines across adolescence. The 20s and 30s tend to be somewhat more active than other ages for both women and men, but physical activity then declines steadily from the 40s to the 70s and beyond (Troiano et al., 2007). One study found that the most sedentary U.S. adults—specifically, older adolescents and adults aged 60 and older—spent about 60% of their waking hours in sedentary pursuits (C. E. Mathews et al., 2008). Not only does a sedentary lifestyle increase people's likelihood of developing chronic illnesses and medical conditions, it also contributes to rising rates of obesity.

Sidebar 12.2: A Global Obesity Epidemic?

Changes in diet and physical activity over the past several decades led to alarming increases in the prevalence of overweight and obese people. According to some health officials, we are in the midst of an obesity epidemic. Worldwide, obesity rates doubled since 1980 (WHO, 2017c). About 39% of adults in the world are overweight, and in the Americas, the rate exceeds 60%. Physicians typically identify people as overweight or obese based on the **body mass index (BMI)**, which is a person's weight in kilograms divided by the square of his or her height in meters. In wealthy, developed countries, more men than women meet criteria for being **overweight**—defined as a BMI between 25 and 30—but in many countries, more women than men are **obese**, defined as a BMI over 30 (Kanter & Caballero, 2012). Tackling this epidemic will be a challenge, as many cultures must confront sedentary lifestyles and calorie-dense, processed foods.

Body mass index (BMI): A person's weight in kilograms divided by the square of height in meters.

Overweight: Having a body mass index between 25 and 30.

Obese: Having a body mass index over 30.

Stop and Think

Imagine that you are in charge of developing a public health campaign to increase Americans' physical activity levels. What strategies would you use to increase physical activity? Would your health campaign use different strategies to appeal to people of different sexes? Why or why not? People often cite a lack of time as a primary impediment to exercise. How would you convince people to work more regular activity into their daily routine? Keep in mind that activity can include transportation (e.g., walking or bicycling instead of driving) and housework.

Health-Relevant Traits: Ways That People *Are*

Aside from the things people *do* that contribute to or impair physical health, the ways that people *are*, such as their levels of agency and communion, may also enhance or impair physical health. For instance, regardless of sex or gender identity, people higher in agentic traits, such as competitiveness, assertiveness, and leadership, tend to have fewer physical symptoms and better adjustment to illnesses than those lower in agency (Helgeson, 2003). At the same time, people who display stronger preferences for male-typical occupations are also more likely to die at any given age (Lippa, Martin, & Friedman, 2000). In contrast, no consistent links emerge between physical health and communal traits, such as warmth, cooperativeness, and nurturance.

According to Vicki Helgeson (2003), more extreme and dysfunctional versions of agentic and communal traits—known as **unmitigated agency** and **unmitigated communion**—play a central role in physical health. While unmitigated agency is a focus on the self to the exclusion of others, unmitigated communion is a focus on others to the neglect of the self. Both of these tendencies are bad for physical health but for

Unmitigated agency: A tendency to focus on the self to the neglect of other people.

Unmitigated communion: A tendency to focus on others to the neglect of the self.

different reasons. Consider unmitigated agency. People high in unmitigated agency often behave inappropriately with others—they are arrogant, boastful, dominating, vindictive, and self-absorbed. They also have a mistrusting, negative view of others. These qualities lead to interpersonal conflict and make it difficult for people to rely on others for social support. People high in unmitigated agency also engage more often in negative health behaviors, such as smoking, drinking, and drug use, and they tend to disregard the advice of doctors. For example, Helgeson writes about a cardiac patient, high in unmitigated agency, whose doctor told him to limit his intake of eggs; instead, the man *increased* the number of eggs he ate, perhaps out of a need to feel in control or a sense of invulnerability. Finally, people high in unmitigated agency lack social skills, which means that they have difficulty seeking social support or accepting it when it arrives. Via these four paths—poor health behaviors, interpersonal behavior that leads to conflict, negative views of others, and poor social skills—unmitigated agency correlates with negative physical health outcomes as well as increased depression, hostility, and tension (see Figure 12.3).

Figure 12.3   Links of Unmitigated Agency and Communion to Health.

Unmitigated agency and unmitigated communion both predict poor health outcomes but via somewhat different paths. Some features that they both share, however, are inappropriate interpersonal behaviors that lead to conflict and a lack of social support from others.

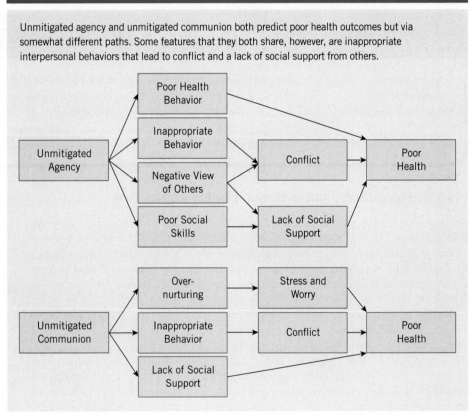

Source: Helgeson (2003).

Similarly, unmitigated communion predicts increases not only in physical symptoms but in psychological symptoms (anxiety and depression) as well (Helgeson, 2003). This occurs via several paths. First, people high in unmitigated communion chronically overnurture, exerting a great deal of energy to support others. Intensive support provision often becomes stressful and taxing, which then compromises the immune system and increases the likelihood of illness. Moreover, those high in unmitigated communion tend to take on the problems of others as their own, which compounds their stress and worry. Next, they behave inappropriately with others by being intrusive, overly concerned, and controlling, which leads to relationship imbalance and conflict. Finally, people high in unmitigated communion avoid focusing on themselves and ignore their own health, often failing to seek and accept social support from others. Figure 12.4 shows the three paths—overnurturance of others that causes stress and worry, inappropriate behavior that creates conflict, and failure to benefit from social support—through which people high in unmitigated communion suffer poorer health outcomes.

Keep in mind that while unmitigated agency and unmitigated communion are associated with sex, the correlation is not perfect. That is, both women and men can be high in either unmitigated agency or unmitigated communion, and these tendencies sometimes override sex in predicting health problems. For example, in one study, Helgeson and Fritz (1996) found that sex differences in depression were fully explained by people's levels of unmitigated communion. Therefore, although gender socialization processes likely encourage more men than women to exhibit unmitigated agency and more women than men to exhibit unmitigated communion, these tendencies are bad for people's health regardless of their sex.

Accessing Health Care

Maintaining good health requires being proactive, which means not just treating illnesses when they arise but also scheduling regular visits to monitor health and prevent problems from arising in the first place. Perhaps not surprisingly, men do not attend to these routine health care needs as conscientiously as women. In addition to this sex difference in people's tendency to seek health care, sex and gender also influence the quality of health care that people receive from doctors. In this section, we will consider both of these patterns.

Seeking health care. In the United States, women are more likely than men to visit doctors, they visit doctors more frequently, and they are also more likely to have a personal physician or a regular place where they receive health care (Blackwell et al., 2014). How should we interpret these findings? It could be an indicator that women are sicker, which aligns with women's tendency to self-report worse health than men. However, women are more likely than men to schedule regular checkups even when they are well. The sex difference in health care utilization could also reflect women's use of routine doctor visits to address reproductive health needs, such as Pap smears, mammograms, contraception, and prenatal care. In fact, these types of visits account for a sizeable proportion of women's health care use (Owens, 2008).

Sex differences in health care utilization could also reflect gender role norms that discourage men from seeking help, even if they experience pain or illness symptoms.

People expect men to be self-reliant, tough, and stoic, and these qualities discourage men from attending to their health (Addis & Mahalik, 2003). Moreover, men who endorse more traditional beliefs about masculinity are more likely to postpone seeking medical help for physical problems (Himmelstein & Sanchez, 2016). These men are also more likely to choose male doctors, even though they communicate less openly with male than female doctors. This can have important consequences for men because disclosures to doctors about emotional problems during routine health visits serve as a primary route through which individuals receive effective help for mental illness (for more on this topic, see Chapter 13, "Gender and Psychological Health").

As a participant in the Tuskegee Syphilis Study, Herman Shaw believed that he was receiving treatment for syphilis when he was not. Here, at age 94, Shaw embraces President Bill Clinton after receiving a public apology at the White House on May 16, 1997.

Men's underutilization of health care also differs by race, with Black and Latino men in the United States being less likely than White men to have a regular doctor or health care provider. For instance, while 23% of White men have no regular doctor, 30% of Black men and 49% of Latino men have no regular doctor (McFarlane & Nikora, 2014). For Black men, mistrust of the health care industry may pose an additional barrier to routine doctor visits that goes beyond male gender role norms (Hammond, Matthews, Mohottige, Agyemang, & Corbie-Smith, 2010). Relative to White Americans, Black Americans tend to view medical doctors as more distant and uncaring and as less trustworthy in their intentions. These views may stem, in part, from historical events such as the Tuskegee Syphilis Study that took place from 1932 to 1972 in Alabama (Gamble, 1997). As part of this study, researchers gave hundreds of poor, illiterate Black men with syphilis a placebo drug instead of penicillin, a known treatment for the disease, so that they could study the natural progression of untreated syphilis. While this study was eventually shut down for ethical reasons, and a class action lawsuit awarded $9 million to the families of the men who participated, it is understandable that Black men's feelings of medical mistrust still linger.

Unfortunately, men's lower rates of health care use may become self-reinforcing. Conversely, establishing a routine with a regular doctor can increase comfort levels and make future visits more likely. Routine visits can also increase the likelihood that doctors detect problematic health issues early. For instance, during a routine doctor visit, a physician might ask about other health issues, which can prompt a patient to disclose a condition that might otherwise go untreated. Thus, by seeking routine health care more frequently, women have more opportunities for health problems to be detected and treated.

Receiving health care. Of course, while deciding to visit a doctor may be under people's control, the treatment that they receive from the doctor is less so. Sex and gender influence the health care that people receive in a couple of ways. First, the sex of the physician may play a role in how patients are treated. Female, as compared with male, primary care physicians tend to have longer visits with their patients, and they engage in more patient-centered communication, such as positive talk and psychosocial counseling (Roter, Hall, & Aoki, 2002). As mentioned earlier, men who hold more traditional beliefs about gender tend to prefer male over female doctors, which means that they are less likely to benefit from the increased time and attention that female doctors tend to provide.

Second, doctors may (likely unknowingly) treat their male and female patients differently, even when they present with similar symptoms. **Implicit physician biases** refer to automatic, nonconscious judgments and behaviors exhibited by doctors that are elicited by features of patients, such as sex, race, or social class. Essentially, these biases occur when doctors rely on stereotypes to make judgments or decisions about specific individuals under their care. Once activated, implicit physician biases can perpetuate health disparities between groups (E. N. Chapman, Kaatz, & Carnes, 2013). For example, imagine a man who visits a doctor complaining of stress, lack of appetite, and fatigue. Now, imagine a woman presenting with the same symptoms. Doctors may be more likely to diagnose the woman as suffering from depression because stereotypes link depression to women more than to men. In some cases, this may result in a man's depression going untreated because of the influence of stereotypes on doctor's judgments.

To measure implicit physician biases, researchers present physicians with hypothetical cases of either female or male patients who display identical sets of symptoms. The findings reveal that physicians more often diagnose COPD in a "middle-aged former smoker with a persistent cough" when the patient is male compared with when she is female (K. R. Chapman, Tashkin, & Pye, 2001). Similarly, when orthopedic surgeons read about either a male or a female patient with moderate knee pain and osteoarthritis, they more frequently referred the male than the female patient for a total knee replacement (Borkhoff et al., 2008). In addition to sex, implicit physician biases occur with regard to race, age, and obesity status. For example, medical students recommend breast reconstruction following mastectomy more often for younger than older patients (Madan, Cooper, Gratzer, & Beech, 2006). Moreover, physicians with greater implicit race bias recommend appropriate treatments less often for a Black patient who presents with heart attack symptoms than for a White patient who presents with the same symptoms (Green et al., 2007). In each of these cases, some groups of people systematically receive lower-quality health care than others due to physician biases.

These biases can have major consequences. For example, because stereotypes link heart disease with men, physicians tend to test women for heart disease less often than they test men (McKinlay, 1996), even though heart disease is the leading cause of death for women in the United States. Moreover, when women present with symptoms of heart disease, physicians are less likely to prescribe them essential cardiovascular drugs (Koopman et al., 2013). Factors such as these that reduce the quality of health care that women receive for heart disease symptoms can mean the difference between life and death.

Gender-Egalitarian Communities and Health

Summarizing over the past several sections, we see that many aspects of the male gender role work against men's physical health. Men, relative to women, more frequently engage in unhealthy behaviors (smoking and excessive drinking) and take unnecessary risks (reckless driving and dangerous hobbies), they show less concern for their health and

Implicit physician biases: Automatic, nonconscious judgments and behaviors, based on stereotypes, that influence how physicians evaluate or treat patients.

diet, and they tend to avoid routine health services and delay seeking help when sick. All of this suggests that the male gender role can be toxic for physical health and may help explain the shorter life expectancies of men. At the same time, women's expected roles as caregivers may account for their overall higher levels of chronic pain conditions and poorer self-reported health. If these aspects of male and female gender roles account for sex differences in mortality and morbidity, then the sex differences should decrease or disappear in cultures that do not enforce traditional gender role norms. What happens in places that do not enforce strict gender roles?

Israeli kibbutz societies tend to have similar roles for women and men. **Kibbutzim** are collective agricultural communities in Israel that base work and social life on socialist principles, and community members commit to gender-egalitarian lifestyles. Men and women engage in similar daily activities and social roles, and everyone contributes equally to decision making. Studies of gender and health among kibbutz members find no sex differences in health status or illness behaviors, such as doctor visits and medications (Anson, Levenson, & Bonneh, 1990). Also, the sex differences in life expectancy found in most cultures around the world are much smaller on kibbutzim (Leviatan & Cohen, 1985).

Some groups of Catholic nuns and monks also live in environments that minimize sex differences in behavior. Women and men in these religious groups have similar diets, stressors, and lifestyles. They take a vow to live in poverty and chastity and have the same daily routine of sleeping, working, and recreation. One study of nuns and monks in Germany compared this group with age-matched samples from the general population and found much smaller sex differences in mortality between nuns and monks (Luy, 2003). Finally, studies of Seventh-day Adventists in the United States and the Netherlands suggest a similar relationship between gender roles and health. Seventh-day Adventists are a religious community that advocates a number of specific healthy behaviors, including vegetarian diets, no tobacco or alcohol, and regular exercise. The environmental conditions and lifestyles of Seventh-day Adventist men and women are fairly similar, although they do engage in some different occupational and gender roles. Seventh-day Adventists have an average life expectancy of 86 years (Fraser & Shavlik, 2001) and show smaller sex differences in mortality than the general population (Berkel & de Waard, 1983).

These studies of different communities suggest that social behaviors and lifestyles can influence the size of sex differences in health and longevity. At the same time, given that women outlive men even among these populations, they reinforce the idea that biological differences also play a role. This brings us back to a recurring theme in this book: that nature and nurture interact in complex ways to shape the attributes and outcomes of women and men.

Kibbutzim: Collective agricultural communities in Israel in which work and social roles reflect socialist principles, and community members pursue gender-egalitarian lifestyles.

Stop and Think

Consider the notion that the male gender role is "toxic for physical health." Do you believe this proposition? If male-typed behaviors and norms undermine men's physical health, why do you think men continue to behave this way? We mentioned one domain in which men exhibit healthier behavior than women: physical activity. This illustrates one positive health behavior associated with the male gender role. What are some others?

How Do Multiple Systems of Discrimination Shape Health and Health Care?

Thus far, we have focused on the links of sex and gender to health, but what about other important identities? By considering the intersections of sex, class, race and ethnicity, sexual orientation, and gender identity, we can ask questions such as these: Do sex differences in mortality rates also differ by race and ethnicity? What unique reproductive health challenges do poor women around the world face? How does LGBT status increase people's vulnerability to illness and poor health?

Race, Ethnicity, and Sex

Just as we see gender gaps in longevity, racial gaps in lifespan exist as well. Even though life expectancy increased since 1970 by 17% for Black people, as compared with increasing by 10% for White people, the average Black American lives nearly 4 years less than the average White American while the average Latino American lives about 3 years longer than the average White American. Black men, in particular, have a relatively short life expectancy of about 72.3 years, compared with the life expectancy of White men (76.5), Black women (78.4), and White women (81.3; Kochanek et al., 2015). One factor that plays a role in the lower life expectancy rates of Black men is homicide. For instance, 45% of all homicide victims were Black men in 2015 while 31% were White men, 13% were White women, and 7% were Black women (FBI, 2015a). In comparison with the life expectancy of White men, homicide accounts for a loss of 0.87 years, heart disease accounts for a loss of 1.12 years, and cancer accounts for a loss of 0.80 years in the life expectancies of Black men. As noted earlier, HIV/AIDS also kills Black people at a higher rate than White people, and the race difference is especially large for men: Black men are over six times more likely than White men to die from HIV/AIDS (Centers for Disease Control and Prevention, 2017).

The factors that shape race differences in life expectancy begin before birth. More likely to be born at low birth weights, Black babies are twice as likely as White babies to die in infancy. Racial and ethnic minority children, including Black, Latino, Asian, and Native American children, also have less regular access to health care than White children (Blackwell et al., 2014), and Black children tend to have less access to nutritious foods in comparison with White children (Kann et al., 2014). For example, studies in Los Angeles, New York City, and New Orleans find that neighborhoods with higher proportions of Black residents also tend to have a higher density of fast-food restaurants and convenience stores that stock canned and processed foods and fewer opportunities to obtain healthy, fresh foods (Hilmers, Hilmers, & Dave, 2012). In fact, people of color in the United States often live in **food deserts**, or neighborhoods in which the lack of nearby grocery stores and easy public transportation limits residents' regular access to fresh, healthy food, especially fruits and vegetables.

Race differences in access to healthful diets may help explain race differences in obesity rates. Table 12.3 shows the percentage of overweight (BMI between 25 and 30) and obese (BMI over 30) adult Americans, broken down by sex and race. As you can see, Latino and Black people are both more likely to be obese than Asian and White people,

Food deserts: Neighborhoods in which the lack of nearby grocery stores and easy public transportation limits residents' regular access to fresh, healthy food.

Table 12.3 **Percentage of Overweight and Obese U.S. Adults.**
In general, men are more likely than women to be overweight and less likely than women to be obese. But note that these sex differences differ by race and ethnicity. Sex differences in being overweight are larger for Asian and White people than they are for Latino and Black people. Sex differences in obesity are larger for Latino and Black people than they are for Asian and White people. What do you think accounts for these interactions of sex with race and ethnicity?

	Overweight			Obese		
	25 ≤ BMI < 30			BMI ≥ 30		
	All	Men	Women	All	Men	Women
Non-Latino White	33.9	39.7	28.2	34.6	34.0	35.3
Black	28.3	31.7	25.5	48.0	37.9	56.5
Latino	35.8	40.5	31.5	42.6	39.1	45.6
Asian	28.5	35.6	22.5	11.8	11.3	11.9

Source: National Center for Health Statistics (2016).

and they are also more likely to reside in food deserts. The story gets a bit more complicated, however, when we examine race differences by sex. As we mentioned in Sidebar 12.2, while men around the world more often meet criteria for overweight, women more often meet criteria for obesity. Although this overall pattern emerges in the United States as well, the size and direction of sex differences in overweight and obesity rates differ by race. For example, the sex difference showing that men tend to be overweight more often than women is somewhat larger for Asian and White people than it is for Latino and Black people. In contrast, the tendency for women to have higher rates of obesity than men emerges only among Latino and Black people (and not among Asian and White people).

Socioeconomic status (SES):
A measure of an individual's (or household's) total income, educational background, and occupation.

Socioeconomic Status, Sex, and Race/Ethnicity

Socioeconomic status (SES)—a measure of an individual's (or household's) total income, educational background, and occupation—consistently correlates with physical health. Across the world, people lower in SES have poorer health and die younger than those higher in SES. Several factors likely account for this. Poor people are less likely to have health insurance and access to quality medical care. Just as with people of color, poor people often live in food deserts, making it difficult for them to access fresh, healthy food. Across developed countries, people lower in SES tend to become overweight or obese more often than those higher in SES (Devaux & Sassi, 2013), which makes them more vulnerable to weight-related physical health problems, such as high blood pressure, coronary heart disease, diabetes, stroke, and chronic pain.

Poor girls and women, in particular, often face acute reproductive health obstacles that can perpetuate their low SES. Across cultures, in comparison with those higher in SES, poor girls and women use contraception less often, receive less education about the prevention of sexually transmitted diseases, and have less access to maternal health services. As a result, they more frequently have children before the age of 18 (Rani & Lule, 2004), and early motherhood reduces the likelihood that young women will get an education, gain financial autonomy, and move out of poverty. In fact, this self-perpetuating cycle likely contributes to the **feminization of poverty**, which refers to the global tendency for women to experience disproportionate rates of poverty (McLanahan & Kelly, 2006).

SES and race are associated in the United States, with Latino, Native American, and Black people typically having lower SES than White and Asian people (D. R. Williams, Priest, & Anderson, 2016). Note, however, that SES does not fully explain race differences in physical health. Instead, SES interacts with race to predict worse health outcomes for people of color who are also low in SES. For instance, Black men who are lower in SES (i.e., who lack a high school degree) are more than 5 times more likely to die from homicide compared with Black men who attended at least some college. But college-educated Black men are still 11 times more likely to die from homicide compared with their similarly educated White male peers, and educated Black men are more likely to die from homicide than the least educated White men. Similarly, when comparing Black and White Americans at the same levels of SES, Black Americans at all SES levels have higher rates of diabetes, cardiovascular disease, and hypertension, and higher mortality rates from coronary heart disease and cancer (D. R. Williams & Jackson, 2005; D. R. Williams, Mohammed, Leavell, & Collins, 2010). This suggests that the health benefits associated with higher SES in the United States are not as apparent for groups that face institutional racism as they are for White Americans. In fact, according to **minority stress theory**, belonging to a stigmatized group creates unique stressors, such as harassment, abuse, and employment discrimination, that combine to increase minority individuals' vulnerability to all types of health problems, regardless of their SES (I. H. Meyer, 2003).

Feminization of poverty: The global tendency for women to experience disproportionate rates of poverty.

Minority stress theory: A theory that proposes that belonging to a stigmatized group can create stressors that are unique to the minority experience.

Sexual Orientation and Gender Identity

On average, lesbian, gay, and bisexual individuals—in comparison with heterosexual individuals—experience higher rates of cardiovascular disease and obesity (lesbian and bisexual women), higher rates of overall poor health (gay and bisexual men), and higher rates of diabetes (bisexual men; Fredriksen-Goldsen, Kim, Barkan, Muraco, & Hoy-Ellis, 2013). Moreover, transgender adults report poorer physical health and higher rates of physical disability than their nontransgender LGB peers (Fredriksen-Goldsen et al., 2014). According to minority stress theory, the chronic stress associated with belonging to a stigmatized group can impact physical health via two routes. First, it increases people's reliance on unhealthy coping behaviors (such as drinking alcohol to cope with anxiety), and second, it overburdens the body's stress response and immune systems, thereby weakening the ability to fight illness (I. H. Meyer, 2003).

Both of these routes can impact the health of sexual and gender identity minority individuals. For instance, in comparison with heterosexual individuals, LGB individuals report more chronic worry and tension, and they tend to engage more often in risky health behaviors, such as smoking, drug use, physical inactivity, and risky sex (Conron, Mimiaga, & Landers, 2010; Saewyc et al., 2006). Similarly, transgender individuals frequently encounter social stressors, such as discrimination, violence, and sexual abuse, that correlate with poorer physical health outcomes (Hughto, Reisner, & Pachankis, 2015). They also report more risky health behaviors, including smoking and physical inactivity, in comparison with their nontransgender LGB counterparts (Fredriksen-Goldsen et al., 2014). Moreover, some research shows that LGB people who experience more extremely stressful events during childhood and adolescence (such as sexual or physical abuse, homelessness, or witnessing violence) also exhibit more biological markers of cardiovascular risk while the same links between stressful life events and cardiovascular functioning are not evident in heterosexual individuals (Hatzenbuehler, Slopen, & McLaughlin, 2014). Consistent with minority stress theory, this shows that belonging to a stigmatized group can increase the body's vulnerability to health problems.

In addition to facing stigma-related social stressors that can lead to impaired health, LGBT individuals often experience barriers to high-quality health care. For one thing, relative to heterosexual individuals, sexual minority individuals are less likely to have health insurance (Dahlhamer, Galinsky, Joestl, & Ward, 2016). Several factors may explain this. Historically, nonrecognition of same-sex partnerships kept many sexual minority individuals from obtaining employer-sponsored insurance coverage through their partners. Even though same-sex marriage is now legally recognized throughout the United States, it will likely take years to close the gaps in health care coverage based on sexual orientation. Furthermore, not all states protect against employment discrimination based on sexual orientation or gender identity. As of this writing, only 20 U.S. states legally protect against employment discrimination on the basis of sexual orientation and gender identity in both public and private sectors. Given that many people get healthcare coverage through their employers, the vulnerability of unprotected LGBT individuals to job loss can put them at risk of losing insurance coverage.

Even when LGBT individuals do have insurance and access to health care, other barriers may prevent them from receiving the same quality of health care that heterosexual and cisgender people enjoy (see Figure 12.4). For example, doctors may lack an understanding of the unique health needs of sexual and gender identity minority individuals. Consider the health needs of FtM (female-to-male) people who identify and present as men but have developed breasts or female genitalia. Like cisgender women, such individuals benefit from standard gynecological care, including cancer screenings, mammograms, and Pap smears. And yet, many FtM men forgo routine gynecological care due to the perception that doctors lack either the competence or the sensitivity to offer them adequate care (Dutton, Koenig, & Fennie, 2008).

Moreover, when transgender individuals choose to undergo hormone therapy to bring their physical appearance into greater alignment with their gender identity, they need ongoing treatment from a doctor who can prescribe and monitor hormone therapy (C. A. Unger, 2014). However, the educational training of doctors, which occurs within a heteronormative and cisnormative academic culture, leaves many doctors unprepared to meet the unique health needs of transgender individuals. In fact, one study of transgender adults found that 20% of them had to educate their doctors about their health needs, and more than 25% of them reported needing—but not having access to—at least one transgender-specific service, such as hormone treatment, gynecological care, or psychotherapy (Bradford, Reisner, Honnold, & Xavier, 2013).

For a variety of reasons, LGBT individuals and their doctors alike may feel uncomfortable discussing sexual orientation or gender identity status (see Figure 12.4). On the one hand, internalized homophobia or transphobia may make some LGBT individuals anxious about disclosing their sexual orientation or gender identity to their doctor. On the other hand, doctors may prefer not to ask patients about their LGBT status because they assume that such questions will make patients uncomfortable (Haider et al., 2017). And yet, most transgender individuals believe that it is important for their primary care provider to know about their gender identity status (Maragh-Bass et al., 2017). When doctors know the sexual orientation and gender identity status of patients, it can increase

Figure 12.4   Barriers to Health Care Faced by LGBT Individuals.

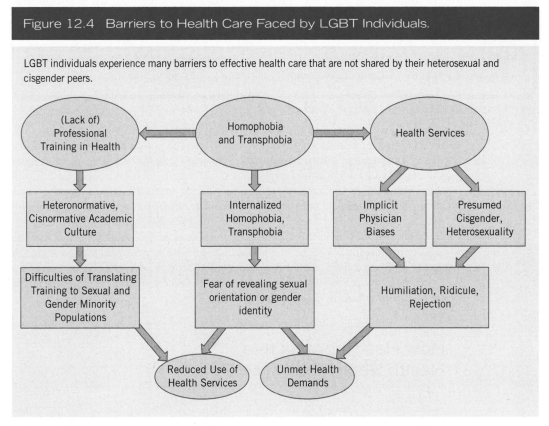

LGBT individuals experience many barriers to effective health care that are not shared by their heterosexual and cisgender peers.

Source: Adapted from Albuquerque et al. (2016).

the likelihood of open doctor–patient communication about risk factors, health screenings, and treatments that can improve health outcomes.

The fear of discrimination still discourages many transgender individuals from seeking medical care when needed (Grant et al., 2010). These fears may be well founded. One study of transgender people found that 41% experienced health care–related discrimination (Bradford et al., 2013). Similarly, another study found that 19% of transgender and gender-nonconforming adults were denied service by a doctor or other provider (due to their identity), 28% were verbally harassed in a doctor's office, and 2% were physically attacked in a doctor's office (Grant et al., 2010). In extreme cases, medical discrimination can result in death, as you may recall from Chapter 1 when we discussed the case of Tyra Hunter. Hunter, a 24-year-old transgender woman, was injured in a car accident and died because paramedics stopped treating her when they discovered that she had male genitals.

Stop and Think

Most transgender people want their doctors to know about their transgender status, but they may experience discrimination and mistreatment if they reveal their status. How can we solve this problem? What sorts of changes might have to occur—at the level of societal attitudes, medical training practices, education, and so on—in order for transgender people to be able to disclose their gender identity status to doctors without fear of discrimination?

Of course, there is a great deal of variety among LGBT people regarding their physical health outcomes, health risk behaviors, and utilization of health care services. Some sexual and gender identity minority individuals thrive despite adversity and stigma. What factors might protect the health of LGBT individuals? Having social resources in the form of an accepting family, extended social networks, and a strong, supportive community can all help insulate sexual and gender identity minority individuals from the negative effects of stigma (Fredriksen-Goldsen, Kim, Shiu, Goldsen, & Emlet, 2015; Hatzenbuehler, 2014). For instance, a study conducted before marriage equality became the law of the land found that same-sex couples who lived in states that legally recognized their relationships experienced better health than those who did not (M. E. Williams & Fredriksen-Goldsen, 2014). We will consider these protective factors for LGBT individuals in the next chapter.

How Has Reproductive Health Been Medicalized?

As we mentioned earlier in this chapter, living today (as opposed to 100 years ago) has its health benefits. Thanks to advances in our understanding of biology, chemistry, and technology, we can now safely and effectively treat hundreds of physical health conditions that, in former days, might have killed us. But at the same time that advances in the fields of health and medicine offer great benefits, they can also create their own set of complicated problems. One such problem is that of *medicalization*, the process whereby normal, natural conditions—such as the menstrual cycle, pregnancy, and childbirth—come to be viewed as medical conditions that require diagnoses and treatments. You may recall our discussion of the medicalization of sexuality from Chapter 9, "Sexual Orientation and Sexuality." Here, we will examine the medicalization of reproductive health and its consequences; these are summarized for you in Table 12.4.

Table 12.4 Medicalization of Reproductive Health. Researchers identify several natural aspects of reproductive health that are medicalized, or viewed as medical conditions that require treatments. Each kind of medicalization brings potential problematic consequences.

Domain of Medicalization	Potential Consequences
Menstruation	
Premenstrual syndrome	Leads to view of women's bodies as regularly sick, bad, or dangerous; fuels cultural stereotypes of "moody, irrational" women; focuses on negative and unpleasant aspects of the menstrual cycle and ignores positive aspects
Pregnancy	
Home pregnancy tests	By allowing for pregnancy detection earlier than is possible through reliance on bodily cues, home pregnancy tests hasten women's transition to the role of "medical patient" and encourage earlier consultation with obstetricians and initiation of pregnancy health regimes
Pregnancy health regimes: diet, exercise, and prenatal vitamins	Heighten concerns about well-being of unborn baby; elicit feelings of guilt; disempower women to make decisions about their own health practices
Ultrasound scans during low-risk pregnancy	Do not consistently improve outcomes; exaggerate women's perceptions of risk and danger associated with pregnancy
Childbirth	
Hospitalized births	Facilitate view of childbirth as a "high-risk" process that requires oversight by experts; render women dependent on medical professionals; reinforce notion of childbirth as "unknown" and "threatening" and lead women to overestimate the likelihood of problems

(Continued)

Table 12.4 (Continued)

Domain of Medicalization	Potential Consequences
Childbirth	
Routine obstetric interventions (episiotomy, labor induction, epidural analgesia, fetal heart monitoring)	Little consensus regarding the necessity of these procedures; they may introduce complications that can then require further intervention; alienate women from their bodies; heighten sense of danger surrounding childbirth
Cesarean sections (20%–30% of all hospital births in several Western cultures)	While sometimes medically necessary for the health of women or infants, Caesarean sections are overused; can increase risks of harm or complication; negatively impact women's experiences of childbirth and bonding with infants

Source: C. Fisher, Hauck, and Fenwick (2006); J. Roberts, Griffiths, Verran, and Ayre (2015); Tone (2012).

The medicalization of natural physiological conditions can change how people think about these conditions, making them seem abnormal and negative. As an example, consider **premenstrual syndrome** (PMS), which is considered a diagnosable illness consisting of aches and pains, bloating, anxiety, anger, depressed mood, and moodiness that occurs monthly before the onset of menstruation (Ussher & Perz, 2013). And yet, it is normal for healthy women to experience these and other changes across the menstrual cycle, corresponding with natural fluctuations in hormone levels. In fact, some estimate that as many as 75% of women in Western cultures would meet diagnostic criteria for PMS if they sought such a diagnosis (Steiner & Born, 2000). As feminist scholars note, the labeling of women's normal reproductive cycle as an illness encourages a view of women's bodies as things that regularly become sick and unable to function. This can then fuel stereotypes of premenstrual women as dysfunctional, incapable of logic, and not to be taken seriously as leaders. Moreover, the medicalization of PMS drives a focus on the negative aspects of women's reproductive cycle, drawing attention away from the positive aspects. In fact, many women notice positive bodily cues and changes that accompany menstruation, such as feelings of elation, energy and creativity, peaks of efficiency, positive body image, and increased sexual interest (King & Ussher, 2012). However, these positive changes are routinely ignored in cultural understandings of PMS.

One of the most controversial consequences of medicalization is the overuse of unnecessary (and sometimes unadvised) interventions and treatments. As one example, doctors in some countries have been performing **Cesarean section (C-section) procedures**—the use of surgery to deliver a baby through the mother's lower abdomen—at ever-increasing rates. In 1970, the rate of C-section births in the United States, Canada, and Australia was about 6%; today, it falls between 25% and 30% in these same countries (Malacrida & Boulton, 2014). Worldwide, C-section rates range from below 2% among the least developed nations to highs of 50% in China and Taiwan

Premenstrual syndrome: A diagnosable illness that some women experience before the onset of menstruation and that consists of symptoms including aches and pains, bloating, anxiety, anger, and moodiness.

Cesarean section (C-section) procedure: The use of surgery to deliver a baby through the mother's lower abdomen.

Sidebar 12.3: PMS Around the World?

Is PMS (premenstrual syndrome) a real biological disorder or a culturally constructed problem? PMS is little known outside of Western cultures (Chrisler & Caplan, 2002). Chinese women, for instance, rarely report negative affect associated with PMS. This is not to say that premenstrual symptoms (e.g., bloating, cramps, and constipation) do not exist in non-Western cultures. However, apparently only people in some Western cultures consider these to be symptoms that require professional help. Non-Western cultures often have more positive attitudes and beliefs about menstruation (Bures, 2016). Moreover, among immigrant women who move to the United States, the longer they live in the United States, the more likely they are to experience depressed mood and mood swings in the week before their period begins (Pilver, Kasl, Desai, & Levy, 2011). This leads some to argue that PMS, as a socially constructed condition, should not be used as a label to pathologize normal hormonal changes in women.

(M. C. Klein et al., 2006; Machizawa & Hayasi, 2012). When performed appropriately in emergency situations, C-sections can and do save the lives of mothers and babies. And yet, the World Health Organization recommends that C-section rates should not exceed 15% in any world region. This suggests that doctors perform a substantial proportion of these procedures unnecessarily, especially in more developed and wealthier nations. As major surgeries, C-sections carry all of the risks of any major surgery and often involve a painful recovery. Moreover, women who have Cesarean births (compared with those who have vaginal births) report less satisfaction with the birth experience, take longer to bond with their infants, are less likely to breastfeed, and interact with their infants less after returning home (DiMatteo et al., 1996).

Labor induction, fetal heart monitoring, ultrasound exams, epidural analgesia, and episiotomies are now conducted routinely during pregnancy and childbirth, even when medically unnecessary (M. C. Klein et al., 2006). In addition to being costly, these procedures may increase the risks of harm and medical complications. Moreover, such procedures can alienate women from their bodies by turning pregnancy and childbirth into one long medical procedure, and the overuse of obstetric interventions can heighten women's sense of danger and uncertainty. For more on how societal views of pregnancy and childbirth have evolved over time, see "Journey of Research: Pregnancy and Childbirth Advice Through the Centuries."

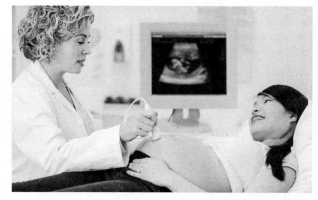

Contemporary Western pregnancies are highly medicalized.

Source: © iStockPhoto .com/FatCamera

Having explored the sex-related dimensions of physical health in this chapter, we will turn our attention to mental health in the next chapter. Though we cover mental and physical health in separate chapters (due to the large amount of material), note that there is a fundamental interconnectedness between mental and physical health. For example, depression correlates with a greater risk of cardiovascular disease, stroke, diabetes, cancer, and HIV/AIDS (D. L. Evans & Charney, 2003). And anxiety disorders correlate with arthritis, migraines, chronic pain, irritable bowel syndrome, coronary heart disease, diabetes, asthma, and COPD (Culpepper, 2009).

Journey of Research

Pregnancy and Childbirth Advice Through the Centuries

How a society views pregnancy and childbirth offers a window into its views about women and about health more generally. For centuries, from ancient Greece to the Middle Ages, Western medical advice to pregnant women changed very little because doctors (who were men) played little role in pregnancies and childbirth. Before the 20th century, nearly everyone delivered at home (Feder, 2014). Lacking scientific knowledge of anatomy and reproduction, advice to women relied on intuition and superstition. Most advice probably came from mothers and midwives, who delivered babies.

Probably the most influential early medical voice was Soranus, a famous second-century Greek physician who wrote a text on gynecology that was consulted for centuries. However, the science behind his advice was lacking. For instance, Soranus advocated against heavy drinking because drunken fantasies (such as thinking about monkeys) could influence the baby by turning it hairy. He also warned against sex during pregnancy, reasoning that it drained women of vital energies that should flow to the child. Following Soranus, early books about women's health were mostly written by monks, who had the advantage of being literate but the disadvantage of being celibate and having little contact with women, making their advice questionable (Hutter Epstein, 2010).

For the most part, science and medicine had little to say on pregnancy and childbirth for centuries.

It was not until the 17th century that the medicalization of pregnancy and childbirth began (Feder, 2014). Medical doctors began replacing midwives as the primary caretakers of pregnant women, and the medical community began to take an interest in prenatal science and nutrition, though with questionable science that reflected insulting stereotypes about women. For instance, people during the Victorian era of the 19th century viewed women as weak, fragile, passive, and highly emotional. Doctors often placed pregnant women, particularly middle-class pregnant women, in near confinement to keep them from anything strenuous or emotional (Malone, 2000). Since society viewed sex and pregnancy as shameful at the time, pregnant women dressed in a manner that hid the pregnancy for as long as possible. Although anesthetics were discovered in the 19th century, religious views of the era dictated that pain and suffering were natural, dutiful parts of childbirth (Hutter Epstein, 2010). Pain relief medicine did not become common for women during childbirth until the 20th century.

By the turn of the century, medical advice still reflected conservative views about women and sexuality. Some doctors, such as John Harvey Kellogg (the inventor of Corn Flakes), advised against sex during pregnancy for fear that the mother's enjoyment would get transmitted to her child, turning it into a lustful pervert. Dubious medical advice to pregnant women persisted throughout much of the 20th century. For instance, doctors advised pregnant women to avoid exercise and to calm their nerves by smoking cigarettes. As late as the 1970s, some medical professionals still doubted the link between mothers' smoking and health risks (such as low birth weight) for the baby (Lumley & Astbury, 1982).

What about today? Medical advice is much more scientifically grounded, although women often do receive questionable advice from friends and family. Most women now recognize that smoking harms both the mother and fetus. Many people, however, still do not understand that excessive weight gain during pregnancy can be harmful, and some advise pregnant women to put on a lot of weight (Verna et al., 2016). Furthermore, people increasingly realize that pregnancy and childbirth are overmedicalized. While medical technologies can reduce infant and mother mortality, the increasing medicalization of childbirth (e.g., epidurals and C-sections) can increase the risks of complications and medical problems.

Stop and Think

What do you think about the medicalization of reproductive health? Do you think increases in C-sections, ultrasounds, and epidurals are signs of a smart society that benefits wisely from advances in health knowledge and technology? Or are they signs that the field of medicine has too much control over a natural and nonmedical process? What about PMS? Do you think that this should be treated as a diagnosable medical condition? Why or why not?

What does this have to do with sex and gender? Psychological disorders can be broadly classified as either *internalizing disorders*—in which negative and problematic emotions and behaviors are directed inward—or *externalizing disorders*, in which these emotions and behaviors are directed outward. So, for instance, depression is an internalizing disorder and alcohol abuse is an externalizing disorder. We will have more to say about these disorders in the next chapter, but for now, we note that mental health professionals tend to diagnose women more often than men with internalizing disorders and men more often than women with externalizing disorders. In addition, women's greater experience of internalizing disorders contributes, at least to some degree, to their tendency to experience more chronic physical health conditions. At the same time, men's greater experience of externalizing disorders contributes to their tendency to experience more frequent life-threatening health conditions (Needham & Hill, 2010). In other words, women live longer than men but report more chronic, nonfatal illnesses partly because women and men experience different types of mental health problems. Although researchers do not fully understand the complex links between psychological and physical health, they have made significant progress in understanding this interconnection in a relatively short period of time. Ultimately, well-being is a product of a healthy mind and body. It will be interesting to see where the next research developments in this area take us.

CHAPTER SUMMARY

12.1 Describe the major causes of mortality for men and women and how they have changed over time.

A century ago, the average life expectancy was much shorter, and the most common causes of death were from infectious diseases (pneumonia, influenza, tuberculosis, and gastrointestinal infections). As people have lived longer, the most common types of death today are diseases of old age (heart disease and cancer). Women, on average, outlive men across time and place, but the longevity gap between men and women in the United States has decreased since the mid-20th century. Today, women outlive men by slightly less than 5 years.

12.2 Explain biological and social causes for gender gaps in health and longevity.

Female members of many animal species tend to outlive males. Sex differences in both genes and hormones may contribute to health and longevity. The presence of two X chromosomes may provide a female advantage when recessive disease-producing abnormalities appear on the X chromosome. In these cases, the disorder will not be expressed if the genes carrying abnormalities appear only on one X chromosome. In addition, protective DNA sequences called telomeres at the ends of chromosome strands degrade faster in men than women, suggesting that men may age faster at the genetic level. At the hormonal level, women's higher levels of estrogen (at least premenopause) may protect them against heart disease, and men's elevated testosterone levels may increase their mortality risks.

Men engage in more health-risking behaviors, and women engage in more health-promoting behaviors. Smoking and alcohol consumption kill more men than women. Heart disease and cancer are the biggest killers in developed countries, and men die more frequently than women from these diseases. Men's relative reluctance to visit doctors also means that they less frequently identify and treat dangerous health conditions in a timely manner. Given that men's relatively risky behaviors often negatively affect health, some argue that the male gender role is toxic.

However, having too much of either male-typical traits or female-typical traits, to the exclusion of the other types of traits, can be bad for health. This occurs either because it reduces help seeking (unmitigated agency) or because it fosters prioritizing others' needs over one's own (unmitigated communion). Studies of subcultures with more egalitarian gender roles find that the usual sex differences in health and longevity are greatly minimized, largely because men tend to live longer.

12.3 Analyze the roles of race, social class, sexual orientation, gender identity, and intersectionality in physical health.

On average, members of stigmatized groups (in terms of race, SES, and sexual orientation) experience worse health outcomes than their less stigmatized counterparts. Factors shaping these negative health outcomes include increased stress associated with prejudice and stigmatization, poorer nutrition, decreased access to health insurance and health care, and fewer positive experiences with health care. For members of marginalized groups, real or perceived stigma can lead to mistrust of the medical establishment and avoidance of preventative health care visits.

12.4 Explain key issues that result from the medicalization of sexual and reproductive health.

A side effect of the rapid advancement of medicine and medical knowledge is the tendency to see natural variations in life experiences through the lens of illness or disease. Common and natural processes such as physical and emotional changes associated with women's monthly menstrual cycle are considered medical problems to be solved. Medical interventions, such as those that often accompany pregnancy and childbirth, may be overused and unnecessary. And complex phenomena are reduced to biological processes, which ignores important social, emotional, and cultural influences. In this way, we would do well to consider and more fully understand the psychological and sociocultural dimensions of physical health.

Test Your Knowledge: True or False?

12.1. Women tend to live longer than men in wealthier countries, but men live longer than women in poorer countries. (False: Women outlive men in every country on the planet.) [p. 408]

12.2. In surveys, men generally report being in better health than women. (True: Around the globe, women consistently report poorer physical health than men do.) [p. 412]

12.3. Men in most societies, including the United States, smoke tobacco and drink alcohol more than women do. (True: The gender gap, however, is shrinking in the United States) [p. 420–421]

12.4. Heart disease is the leading cause of death for women in the United States, but physicians less often test and prescribe medicine for heart disease in women than in men. (True: This may reflect implicit physician biases, in which stereotypes subtly influence physicians' decisions.) [p. 427]

12.5. In health care surveys, most transgender adults say that it is not necessarily important for their doctor to know their gender identity status. (False: Most transgender adults say that it is important for their doctor to know their gender identity status.) [p. 434]

Charles Haley—pictured here in 1992 when he was with the Dallas Cowboys—suffered from undiagnosed bipolar disorder for much of his career. Haley now speaks out publicly on the importance of asking for help.

Source: Stephen Dunn/Getty Images Sport/Getty Images

Test Your Knowledge: True or False?

13.1 Approximately one-quarter (25%) of all people in the United States will meet diagnostic criteria for a mental illness during their lifetime.

13.2 In general, men are more likely than women to suffer from alcohol, drug, and other substance use disorders.

13.3 Eating disorders only occur in Western cultures.

13.4 Sexual and gender minority youths who live in neighborhoods with higher rates of hate crimes against LGBT people are more likely to attempt suicide.

13.5 Across cultures, men generally report higher levels of happiness and positive emotions than women do.

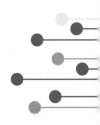

Key Concepts

How Are Mental Illnesses Defined, Classified, and Conceptualized?

The *Diagnostic and Statistical Manual* and the *International Classification of Diseases*

The Transdiagnostic Approach: Internalizing and Externalizing Disorders

Journey of Research: Treatment of Transgender Identity in the DSM

What Factors Contribute to Sex Differences in Internalizing Disorders?

Gender Role Factors

Abuse and Violence Factors

Personality Factors

Biological Factors

What Factors Contribute to Sex Differences in Externalizing Disorders?

Gender Role Factors

Personality Factors

Biological Factors

Debate: Do Women Suffer From Depression More Than Men?

What Roles Do Sex and Gender Play in Eating and Body Image Disorders?

Objectification Theory, Body Image, and Eating Disorders

Links to Women's Mental Health

Roles of Media and Culture

Intersectionality and Eating Disorders Among Women

Gender Identity, Body Dissatisfaction, and Eating Disorders

The Desire for Muscularity

How Do Sexual and Gender Minority Statuses Relate to Mental Health?

Victimization, Discrimination, and Rejection

Homelessness

Institutional Discrimination: A Hostile Environment

Internalized Stigma: Homophobia and Transphobia From Within

What Roles Do Sex and Gender Play in Mental Health Help-Seeking?

Sex Differences in Rates of Help-Seeking

Intersectionality and Help-Seeking

What Roles Do Sex and Gender Play in Happiness and Well-Being?

Subjective Well-Being

Communion, Agency, and Well-Being

Learning Objectives

Students who read this chapter should be able to do the following:

13.1 Define psychological disorders and explain the major approaches to classifying them.

13.2 Analyze the various factors (e.g., gender roles, abuse, personality, and biology) that contribute to sex differences in rates of internalizing and externalizing disorders.

13.3 Explain the roles of gender and self-objectification in eating and body image disorders.

13.4 Describe the unique mental health vulnerabilities experienced by LGBT individuals.

13.5 Evaluate the roles of sex and gender in help-seeking.

13.6 Understand how sex and gender relate to happiness and well-being.

Gender and Psychological Health

In 2015, Charles Haley was inducted into the Pro Football Hall of Fame after a career of unparalleled achievements that included five Super Bowl Championships. During his Hall of Fame acceptance speech, after opening with a brief anecdote, an obviously nervous Haley abruptly switched topics: "[My ex-wife] Karen in 1988, she diagnosed me with manic depression . . . and I never really listened, nor did I step up to the plate and do something about it. My life spiraled out of control for years." During his years as a pro football player, Haley had a reputation for being volatile, aggressive, and uncooperative. Unable to control his temper and moods, Haley punched his fist through windows, got into physical confrontations with other players, and occasionally alarmed his teammates with bouts of uncontrollable sobbing. Haley's undiagnosed and untreated mental illness cost him his marriage, got him traded off his team, and threatened to destroy his career on multiple occasions.

Today, Haley talks openly about his diagnosis of bipolar disorder (formerly referred to as manic depression) and his regrets about not addressing his psychological problems much earlier in his life. As a mentor for young athletes, he works hard to destigmatize mental illness and break down the norm of fierce self-reliance that pervades the hyper-masculine world of professional sports. Haley implores young men who are struggling with mental illness, "You *gotta* ask for help." This message might be a hard one to sell, however. In male-dominated environments—and especially those that value physical strength and toughness—there are powerful pressures against expressing vulnerability and emotional pain. Elite male athletes who internalize hypermasculine norms tend to hold negative attitudes toward both mental illness and help-seeking (T.-V. Jones, 2016). Consider the words of Brandon Marshall, an NFL wide receiver who was diagnosed with borderline personality disorder in 2011 after several years' worth of high-profile arrests, domestic squabbles, and personal conflicts: "Before I [got treatment], if someone had said 'mental health' to me, the first thing that came to mind was mental toughness and *masking* pain, hiding, keeping it in. That's what was embedded in me since I was a kid, you know, never show a sign of weakness."

Despite the stigma surrounding mental illness among professional athletes, things may be changing for the better. In 2014, Marshall cofounded Project 375 (project375.org) to raise awareness and end the stigma surrounding mental illness, particularly for men. He and other professional athletes like Haley are speaking out publicly about their battles with psychological disorders and the need to seek help. However, the stigma of mental illness reaches far beyond the arena of professional sports. Across cultures, male gender role norms of toughness and self-reliance discourage expressions of vulnerability. Men from all races, ethnicities, occupations, and socioeconomic groups who suffer from mental illness may be reluctant to acknowledge and treat it for fear of appearing unmanly. This is especially troubling because of the worldwide prevalence of mental illness. Lifetime rates of mental illness (the percentage of people who will meet diagnostic criteria for a mental illness during their life) range from a low of 12% in Nigeria to a high of 47% in the United States (see Table 13.1; Kessler et al., 2009). In the United States, about 18% of adults and 14% of adolescents experience a mental illness each year (Center for Behavioral Health Statistics and Quality, 2015).

Table 13.1	**Psychological Disorders Around the World.** The lowest lifetime rates of psychological disorders (percentages of people who will develop a disorder in their lifetime) occur in Nigeria and China while the highest rates occur in the United States and New Zealand.		
Country	**Lifetime Percentage of Any Disorder**	**Country**	**Lifetime Percentage of Any Disorder**
Nigeria	12.0	Belgium	29.1
People's Republic of China	13.2	South Africa	30.3
Israel	17.6	Netherlands	31.7
Japan	18.0	Ukraine	36.1
Italy	18.1	France	37.9
Spain	19.4	Colombia	39.1
Germany	25.2	New Zealand	39.3
Lebanon	25.8	United States	47.4
Mexico	26.1		

Source: Kessler et al. (2009).

In this chapter, we will examine questions about mental illness and health through the lens of gender. What does it mean to have a mental illness, and conversely, what does it mean to be psychologically healthy? What forms do mental illnesses take, and do disorders differ by sex? Are there sex differences in help-seeking tendencies? In addressing these questions, our primary emphases will be on internalizing disorders (e.g., mood and anxiety disorders), externalizing disorders (e.g., conduct and substance use disorders), and eating disorders. We will also address psychological disorders among people who identify as gender and sexual minorities, as rates of mental illness are especially high among these groups. To begin, we will cover some of the basics of defining and categorizing mental illness. Note that we will use the terms *mental illness* and *psychological disorder* interchangeably in this chapter.

How Are Mental Illnesses Defined, Classified, and Conceptualized?

Defining mental illness is difficult. How do you know whether someone's behavior is just "quirky" versus a sign of disorder? How can you tell if your feelings are normal sadness versus diagnosable depression? Unfortunately, these questions have no simple answers. Psychologists have debated questions surrounding the definitions, diagnoses, and treatments of mental illness for as long as psychology has existed, and they will likely continue doing so (see the "Journey of Research" for an example). That said, clinical psychologists generally agree that a **psychological disorder (or mental illness)** is a persistent disruption or disturbance of thought, emotion, or behavior that causes significant distress or impairment in functioning. So feeling sad and lonely for several weeks after a breakup would not likely qualify as a disorder. However, if a breakup makes you so sad that you stop spending time with friends, lose interest in your hobbies, and become overwhelmed with self-loathing, then you might meet criteria for a disorder.

The *Diagnostic and Statistical Manual* and the *International Classification of Diseases*

Psychologists recognize over 200 distinct psychological disorders, each of which consists of a unique set of symptoms. To describe and classify these disorders, the American Psychiatric Association publishes the *Diagnostic and Statistical Manual of Mental Disorders* (*DSM*), a resource text that categorizes disorders based on their primary symptom (e.g., depressed mood, anxiety, and substance use). Another similar system is the *International Classification of Diseases and Related Health Problems* (*ICD*), published by the World Health Organization (WHO). Broader than the *DSM*, the *ICD* includes not just psychological but also medical illnesses. Both texts are updated regularly to reflect new scientific knowledge and research findings, with the *DSM* currently in its fifth edition (*DSM-5*) and the *ICD* in its 10th (*ICD-10*).

The Transdiagnostic Approach: Internalizing and Externalizing Disorders

As you will see throughout this chapter, we refer regularly to specific disorders, such as depression, social phobia, and conduct disorder (see Tables 13.2–13.4 for descriptions of these and other disorders discussed in this chapter). However, for much of the chapter, we use an organizing framework that combines the depressive and anxiety disorders together into one group (called **internalizing disorders**) and the antisocial, conduct, substance use, and impulsivity-related disorders into another group (called **externalizing disorders**). This framework reflects the **transdiagnostic approach**, which assumes that most psychological disorders are actually different manifestations of a few core, underlying dimensions (Krueger & Eaton, 2015). Rather than viewing depression and anxiety disorders as separate conditions, the transdiagnostic approach views them as different versions of the same heritable tendency.

Backed by solid empirical research, the transdiagnostic approach offers a useful organizing frame for this chapter because there are persistent sex differences across the internalizing and externalizing disorders. Internalizing disorders consist of problematic emotions and behaviors that are directed inward while externalizing disorders consist of problematic feelings and behaviors that are directed outward. What does it mean to direct feelings *inward* or *outward*? Generally speaking, symptoms of internalizing disorders include things like low self-esteem, social withdrawal, anxiety, restrained eating, and acts of nonsuicidal self-injury, like cutting oneself. In other words, the sufferer experiences symptoms privately and expresses disturbance largely by blaming and punishing the self. In contrast, the primary symptoms of externalizing disorders include things like aggression, impulsivity, interpersonal manipulation, and drug and alcohol abuse. These acts tend to involve either victimizing others or altering one's consciousness in a manner that impairs judgment and reduces inhibitions against harm.

In general, women show higher prevalence rates than men do for internalizing disorders while men have higher prevalence rates than women do for externalizing disorders. One study of U.S. adults found that the effect size for women's higher levels of internalizing disorders was small ($d = -0.23$) while the effect size for men's higher levels of externalizing disorders was medium ($d = 0.52$; M. D. Kramer, Krueger, & Hicks, 2008). Researchers report similar sex differences in Europe, Asia, North and south America, Africa, and the Middle East (Seedat et al., 2009). Moreover, sex differences in internalizing and externalizing behaviors emerge in childhood (Rescorla et al., 2014). In the sections that follow, we will consider several different possible explanations for these persistent sex differences.

Gender dysphoria: A disorder characterized by clinically significant distress arising from the mismatch between one's assigned sex and psychological sense of gender.

Journey of Research

Treatment of Transgender Identity in the DSM

The psychiatric community's understanding of transgender people has a long and complicated history, as evidenced by several changes to the *Diagnostic and Statistical Manual* (*DSM*) over time. In the medical field, the study of transgender individuals emerged in the late 19th century (Krafft-Ebing, 1886/1965), but it was not until the 1950s that the psychiatric community grew increasingly interested in transgender identity as a psychological phenomenon. This interest was sparked, in part, by the high-profile case of Christine (born George) Jorgenson, an American WWII veteran who underwent genital reconstructive surgery in Denmark in 1952 and transitioned from male to female.

From the 1950s through the 1980s, mainstream psychiatry and psychology viewed transgender identity as a mental illness requiring treatment with psychotherapy (Drescher, 2010). Although the first two editions of the *DSM* included no reference to transgender identity, many psychiatrists considered it a form of delusional belief stemming from neuroticism, schizophrenia, or confused homosexuality. This mistaken tendency to equate transgender identity with same-sex sexual orientation should be familiar to you from past chapters (especially Chapters 5 and 9).

By the late 1970s, a substantial body of research existed on the topic of transgender identity, allowing for sufficient psychiatric consensus regarding its nature and characteristics. Reflecting this consensus, the *DSM-III* (APA, 1980) included two diagnoses of *gender identity disorder* (GID). One diagnosis was for adolescents and

(Continued)

adults (transsexualism), and the other applied to children (GID in childhood). For both disorders, symptoms included an intense and persistent identification with the other sex, a belief that one's assigned sex is inconsistent with one's true gender identity, and significant distress caused by the perceived mismatch between sex and gender identity. However, with the publication of the *DSM-IV* in 1994, transsexualism was removed as a separate diagnosis, and GID was expanded to include cross-sex identification among both children and adults.

Critics of the inclusion of GID in the *DSM* argue that transgender identity is a natural variation of gender expression and that calling it a "disorder" unfairly pathologizes it (Drescher, 2010). Moreover, some propose that the feelings of distress associated with transgender identities are caused not by the condition itself but by negative and stigmatizing societal reactions to those who do not fit cleanly into the sex and gender binaries (APA, 2009). In fact, recent data support this proposition. A study of 250 transgender adults in Mexico City found that experiences of social rejection and violence related to being transgender strongly predicted psychological distress, whereas feelings of gender incongruence did not (Robles et al., 2016). In contrast, those who advocate to retain transgender identity in the *DSM* argue that transgender individuals often experience distress associated with inhabiting the "wrong" body and that this distress, by itself, can cause clinical impairment.

Responding to these controversies, the *DSM-5* again revised its treatment of transgender identity in 2013, replacing GID with the label **gender dysphoria** (GD). GD is diagnosed when an individual experiences clinically significant distress because of a "difference between the individual's expressed/experienced gender and the gender others would assign him or her" (APA, 2013). In contrast to GID, the definition of GD emphasizes feelings of distress rather than a mismatch between assigned sex and psychological gender. Moreover, prior *DSM* versions used language that presumed binary gender categories (e.g., "identification with *the other gender*" [italics included]), while the language used to define GD acknowledges a wider range of nonbinary identities. Finally, unlike GID, the GD label does not include the word *disorder*. Although these changes represent an important shift in clinical thinking, many still argue that removing transgender diagnoses from the *DSM* altogether is a necessary step toward destigmatizing transgender identities (Lev, 2013). Considering similar arguments, the WHO is currently evaluating a proposal to remove gender identity disorder from the *International Classification of Diseases*.

Stop and Think

What factors do you think account for changes over time in how the DSM defines disorders? How can something be a disorder at one point in time but not in another? Why has diagnosing disorders of gender identity been *particularly challenging and controversial? Did the DSM-5 get the diagnosis right with gender dysphoria? Do the pros of including the gender dysphoria diagnosis in the DSM outweigh the cons or vice versa? Why?*

What Factors Contribute to Sex Differences in Internalizing Disorders?

As noted, internalizing disorders include mood and anxiety disorders (eating disorders are also considered internalizing disorders, but we will discuss these separately). Table 13.2 summarizes several internalizing disorders and indicates the size of the sex difference for each. Note that of these disorders, only bipolar disorder does not show a consistent sex difference. The remaining internalizing disorders have sex differences that range from small ($d = -0.14$) to medium ($d = -0.53$) in size. Many factors likely contribute to these sex differences, and we consider several of them here. Note, however, that our focus is on factors that contribute to sex differences in disorders, not on factors that cause the disorders themselves.

Table 13.2 **Internalizing Disorders.** These disorders include depressive disorders and anxiety disorders. As you can see, there are sex differences favoring women for lifetime rates of almost all internalizing disorders (except for bipolar disorder), and effect sizes range from small to medium.

Disorder	Description	Effect Size (*d*) for Sex Difference in Lifetime Rates
Major depressive disorder	All-encompassing low mood, low self-esteem, and a loss of interest in normally enjoyable activities that lasts at least 2 weeks	−0.35
Dysthymia (also called persistent depressive disorder)	Chronic low mood and low self-esteem that lasts at least 2 years but is less severe than major depression	−0.35
Bipolar disorder	Episodes of significantly elevated mood, arousal, and energy levels (mania) interspersed with contrasting episodes of low mood (depression)	0.06
Generalized anxiety disorder	Disproportionate worry about everyday things (such as money, health, and relationships) that is ongoing and uncontrollable	−0.29

(Continued)

Table 13.2 (Continued)

Disorder	Description	Effect Size (*d*) for Sex Difference in Lifetime Rates
Panic disorder	Recurring, brief attacks of panic that come on suddenly and are accompanied by racing heart, shortness of breath, dizziness, numbness, and fears of dying	−0.35
Phobic disorder/ social anxiety disorder	Persistent, irrational, extreme fear of a specific object or situation; in social anxiety disorder, extreme fear is of social interaction	−0.38/ −0.14
Posttraumatic stress disorder (PTSD)	Recurring flashbacks, nightmares, panic, and hypervigilance resulting from a traumatic experience (e.g., sexual abuse, physical assault, and wartime experiences)	−0.53

Source: Seedat et al. (2009).

Gender Role Factors

There are several ways in which gender roles may contribute to sex differences in internalizing disorders. One early hypothesis, the *gender intensification hypothesis*, proposed that the pressure to adopt sex-typed traits and behavior intensifies during adolescence as children go through puberty and prepare for adulthood (J. P. Hill & Lynch, 1983). As adolescent girls increasingly adopt stereotypically feminine tendencies, such as emotionality and self-sacrifice, they may develop a helpless coping style that increases depressive tendencies. In contrast, adolescent boys increasingly adopt stereotypically masculine qualities, such as confidence and self-esteem, that can buffer them from depression. This logic may sound reasonable, but the data do not cleanly support it. As you read in Chapter 4, "Gender Development," adolescents in the United States do not appear to undergo an intensification of sex-typed traits (Priess et al., 2009). And while increases in male-typed traits during adolescence correlate with decreases in depression for both boys and girls, adolescent boys and girls in the United States today do not differ much on male-typed traits.

Rumination: Passively and persistently focusing attention on one's negative mood, its causes, and its possible consequences.

That said, sex differences in certain coping styles can contribute to sex differences in mood and anxiety disorders. Susan Nolen-Hoeksema's (1991) *response styles theory* focuses on a coping style called **rumination**, which involves passively and persistently focusing attention on one's negative mood. For example, a woman who has a ruminative style might think repetitively about how upset she feels after an unsuccessful job interview, dwelling on her flaws and wondering why she feels so badly. Women score higher than men in the tendency to ruminate when distressed (Tamres, Janicki, & Helgeson,

2002), and rumination correlates with depression, social phobia, posttraumatic stress disorder (PTSD), and generalized anxiety disorder (Nolen-Hoeksema, 2012). Thus, women's greater tendency to cope passively with negative emotions may prolong and amplify their depressive and anxious moods while men's tendency to cope more actively with negative emotions—by distracting themselves or doing physical activities—may protect them from developing internalizing disorders.

Stop and Think

Simply documenting that women ruminate more than men does not explain why this occurs. What are some possible reasons for this sex difference in the tendency to ruminate? What have you learned in other chapters of this book (e.g., about gender development or about gendered language, communication, and emotion) that might help explain this difference?

Another gender role approach asks whether sex-based labor divisions contribute to sex differences in depression by limiting the number of social roles that women occupy. According to Peggy Thoits (1986) and the **expansion hypothesis** (which you may recall from Chapter 11, "Work and Home"), occupying multiple social roles, such as *spouse, employee*, and *church member*, can buffer people against distress by imbuing their lives with meaning and social connectedness. This hypothesis predicts that women become depressed more frequently than men because traditional sex-based labor divisions restrict them to a relatively small number of home-based roles (e.g., *spouse* and *parent*) while men typically occupy a wider range of roles (e.g., *spouse, parent, employed worker*, and *group member*). Data from two nationally representative samples of U.S. adults supported the expansion hypothesis, but other more recent studies failed to replicate this effect (Weich, Sloggett, & Lewis, 2001). These conflicting findings may reflect the fact that women have been occupying greater numbers of social roles over time.

Expansion hypothesis: The prediction that occupying multiple social roles is associated with psychological and physical health benefits.

Sidebar 13.1: Too Many vs. Too Few Social Roles?

In contrast to Thoits's (1986) expansion hypothesis, the *scarcity hypothesis* (which you may recall from Chapter 11) proposes that occupying multiple roles increases stress due to role overload, or feeling overtaxed by competing demands on time. Though the scarcity hypothesis may seem plausible on the surface, the bulk of the evidence shows that the benefits of occupying multiple roles outweigh the costs (Barnett & Hyde, 2001).

A related gender role approach asks whether widespread devaluing of female-type labor (i.e., childcare and housework) contributes to women's high rates of depression. If this were the case, we should see smaller sex differences in depression in cultures that place more value on female-typical labor. In fact, sex differences in depression are smaller or nonexistent among some subcultures, such as Orthodox Jewish and Amish communities, that honor the homemaker role as a position of great importance (Piccinelli & Wilkinson, 2000). Sex differences in depression also get smaller as gender equality increases within cultures over time. One study of over 72,000 adults in 15 different countries found that increases in nation-level indices of gender equality correlated with decreases in the size of sex differences in depression (Seedat et al., 2009).

Sex differences in depression are relatively small among the Amish, a cultural group in which women's labor is highly valued.

Source: © iStockPhoto .com/Left_Coast_ Photographer

Abuse and Violence Factors

Childhood sexual abuse is a traumatic life experience that has profound consequences for mental health, and it disproportionately affects girls. A meta-analysis of 331 independent samples with over 9.9 million participants worldwide found that 18.0% of girls report sexual abuse, compared with 7.6% of boys (Stoltenborgh, van Ijzendoorn, Euser, & Bakermans-Kranenburg, 2011). Moreover, as you will read in Chapter 14 ("Aggression and Violence"), girls and women are more likely than boys and men to experience many types of sexual violence across all cultures. Does exposure to sexual violence contribute to sex differences in internalizing disorders? To some degree, yes. One review concluded that sex differences in childhood sexual abuse can explain up to 35% of the sex difference in adult depression (Cutler & Nolen-Hoeksema, 1991). That said, sexual abuse in childhood predicts adult depression regardless of victims' sex. Boys may be less likely to experience sexual violence than girls, but when they do, their risk of depression is high.

Personality Factors

Neuroticism:
The tendency to experience high levels of negative emotions.

Sex differences in internalizing disorders may also reflect sex differences in **neuroticism,** defined as the chronic tendency to experience negative emotions. People high in neuroticism worry easily and describe themselves as "moody" and "blue." Not surprisingly, neuroticism correlates very strongly with internalizing disorders (Griffith et al., 2010), and women across cultures tend to score higher in neuroticism than men (Costa, Terracciano, & McCrae, 2001).

Biological Factors

Some research finds that girls and women, as compared with boys and men, respond to stress with more extreme nervous system activity. This elevated stress response then predicts higher levels of depressive and anxious symptoms. Moreover, female sex hormones such as estrogens—whose levels increase dramatically in puberty—enhance the sensitivity of the stress response and heighten young women's vulnerability to the long-term effects of stress. This may account for the dramatic rise in internalizing disorders often observed among girls in early adolescence (Zahn-Waxler, Shirtcliff, & Marceau, 2008).

What Factors Contribute to Sex Differences in Externalizing Disorders?

Externalizing disorders are characterized by deficits in impulse control; patterns of aggression, violence, or criminality; and substance abuse. Table 13.3 summarizes several externalizing disorders and their sex differences. You can see that men experience each of these disorders more frequently than women do, with effect sizes ranging from small ($d = 0.12$) to medium ($d = 0.66$). In what follows, we will cover several factors that may contribute to sex differences in externalizing disorders.

Table 13.3 **Externalizing Disorders.** These disorders include substance use disorders, conduct and antisocial disorders, and attention deficit disorders. Lifetime rates of these externalizing disorders all show sex differences favoring men, with effect sizes ranging from small to medium.

Disorder	Description	Effect Size (*d*) for Sex Difference in Lifetime Rates
Attention-deficit/ hyperactivity disorder (ADHD)	Difficulty focusing attention on a single task paired with a tendency toward hyperactivity	0.28
Conduct disorder	Ongoing pattern of oppositional, defiant, and antisocial behavior and criminal activity (e.g., theft, vandalism, sexual coercion, physical violence, lying, and running away)	0.38
Oppositional defiant disorder	Ongoing pattern of angry disobedience and defiant behavior toward authority figures	0.12
Antisocial personality disorder	Pattern of callous, manipulative, and deceitful treatment of others, combined with tendencies toward hostility, impulsivity, irresponsibility, and risk taking	0.21
Substance use disorder: alcohol use/ drug use	Recurrent use of alcohol and/or drugs that causes significant impairment, such as health problems, disability, or problems meeting responsibilities at work, school, or home	0.66/ 0.51

Source: N. R. Eaton et al. (2012); Seedat et al. (2009).

Gender Role Factors

Just as gender roles can help explain sex differences in internalizing disorders, they may also help explain why boys and men display externalizing disorders at higher rates than girls and women. For instance, as you read in Chapter 8 ("Language, Communication, and Emotion"), boys learn from an early age to avoid displaying emotions that might make them seem vulnerable, like sadness and anxiety (L. R. Brody & Hall, 2010). In contrast, parents and other socialization agents typically consider anger—a relatively powerful emotion—more acceptable for boys to display. Therefore, boys may learn to express negative emotions through angry outbursts instead of sad withdrawal.

Another gender role factor is parental discipline. Parents tend to discipline boys and girls differently, using harsher strategies with sons than daughters. This may help to explain the higher rates of conduct and antisocial disorders among male youth because harsh parental punishment, such as yelling and physical aggression, predicts aggressive behavior, criminality, and delinquency in youth (Meier, Slutske, Heath, & Martin, 2009). Moreover, inconsistent parenting, especially inconsistent use of punishment, predicts increases in children's conduct problems over time, but the reverse is true as well: Children who display more antisocial tendencies elicit more inconsistent discipline from parents (Hawes, Dadds, Frost, & Hasking, 2011). If boys display more antisocial traits than girls (which they do, as we will discuss), then their personalities may further contribute to these sex differences in parental discipline.

Finally, gender role differences in coping strategies may contribute to sex differences in externalizing disorders, and particularly substance use problems. Whereas women tend to ruminate when distressed, men more often distract themselves from stress via alcohol or drugs (Harrell & Karim, 2008). Ultimately, this can become habitual and may lead to substance abuse problems. Moreover, men tend to use distraction as a coping mechanism more often than they use other, healthier means of coping with stress, such as seeking social support (Tamres et al., 2002). We will return to this idea later, when we discuss sex differences in help-seeking.

Personality Factors

Impulsivity and effortful control may contribute to sex differences in externalizing disorders. **Impulsivity** consists of traits such as sensation seeking, novelty seeking, and risk taking while **effortful control** consists of persistence, focus, and inhibitory control. As a group, externalizing disorders correlate with high levels of impulsivity and low levels of effortful control, and both of these personality factors show sex differences. Meta-analyses reveal a very large effect size favoring girls for levels of effortful control ($d = -1.01$; Else-Quest, Hyde, Goldsmith, & Van Hulle, 2006) and medium effect sizes favoring men for sensation seeking ($d = 0.41$) and risk taking ($d = 0.36$; Cross, Copping, & Campbell, 2011). These personality factors predict increases in antisocial and substance use disorders over time (Krueger, 1999), suggesting that they may play a causal role in the development of externalizing disorders.

Another relevant personality factor, **callous-unemotional (CU) traits**, includes low levels of empathy, guilt, and warmth. These tendencies underlie the aggression, criminal behavior, and lack of remorse often present in conduct and antisocial disorders.

Impulsivity: A personality factor that consists of traits such as sensation seeking, novelty seeking, and risk taking.

Effortful control: The capacity for persistence, focus, and inhibitory control.

Callous-unemotional traits: A personality factor consisting of low levels of empathy, guilt, and warmth.

Prefrontal cortex: A brain region involved in impulse control, emotion regulation, and planning behaviors.

Adolescent boys tend to score higher in CU traits than girls ($d = 0.52$), which may help to explain their increased tendencies toward these disorders (Pihet, Etter, Schmid, & Kimonis, 2015). And as noted earlier, boys' higher levels of CU traits may both elicit and result from inconsistent parental disciplinary practices.

Stop and Think

Consider that boys tend to have lower levels of empathy, guilt, and warmth than girls. Does this sufficiently explain sex differences in externalizing disorders, like conduct disorder and antisocial personality disorder? What factors might help to explain
why boys are lower on these traits than girls? What have you learned in other chapters (e.g., about gender development or about gendered language, communication, and emotion) that could help explain this sex difference?

Biological Factors

Recall from Chapter 3 ("The Nature and Nurture of Sex and Gender") that testosterone masculinizes fetuses in utero, affecting both the structure and function of the brain. One brain region affected by prenatal testosterone exposure, the **prefrontal cortex** (PFC), may play a role in the development of externalizing conditions, such as ADHD and substance disorders. Activity of the PFC contributes to impulse control, emotion regulation, and planning, all of which are relevant to externalizing tendencies. Although the PFC develops gradually throughout adolescence in all children, it tends to develop more slowly in boys than girls. Moreover, exposure to larger amounts of prenatal testosterone predicts lower PFC volume among boys aged 8–11

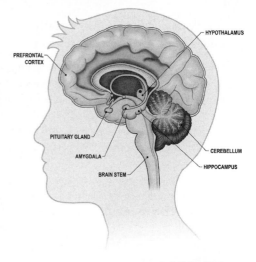

(Lombardo et al., 2012). Decreases in PFC volume, in turn, correlate with increased vulnerability to ADHD and other externalizing disorders.

Dopamine (DA)—a neurotransmitter involved in feelings of reward and control of voluntary movement—may also contribute to sex differences in externalizing tendencies. On average, women tend to show enhanced dopamine functioning compared with men, which may protect them against disorders characterized by poor impulse control, such as ADHD and substance abuse (Martel, 2013). Moreover, recent research examines the role of the dopamine transporter protein (DAT1)—a protein that regulates the brain's use of DA—in externalizing disorders. Among boys and men, a variant of the gene that codes for DAT1 is linked to externalizing and antisocial behaviors (S. A. Burt & Mikolajewski, 2008). Importantly, men may be more likely than women to inherit this genetic variant, which can partially explain their higher rates of externalizing symptoms and disorders.

Activity of the prefrontal cortex (PFC) contributes to impulse control, emotion regulation, and planning and may play a role in the development of externalizing conditions, such as ADHD and substance disorders.

Source: © iStockPhoto .com/jambojam

Depression, the leading cause of disability worldwide, disproportionately affects women: Women receive depression diagnoses at twice the rate of men, in both Western and non-Western cultures. In this chapter, we consider many possible explanations for why women are more prone to depression than men. But what if there isn't actually a sex difference in depression? In the following debate, we consider this possibility.

No, Women and Men Are Equally Likely to Suffer From Depression

Some scholars propose that people of different sexes are equally vulnerable to depression, but they reveal their depression via different symptoms. In other words, depression "looks" different in women and men, and it therefore gets diagnosed at lower rates among men. This perspective holds that classic symptoms of depression, such as sadness, hopelessness, and low self-worth, are inconsistent with male gender role norms of toughness and invulnerability and that men who suffer from depression instead tend to display male-typed symptoms, such as anger attacks, irritability, alcohol and substance use, risk taking, and aggression (Addis, 2008). What do you notice about these symptoms? Typically classified as externalizing symptoms, these are not considered symptoms of depression (an internalizing disorder). In contrast to traditional clinical approaches, then, the male-type depression perspective argues that some externalizing behaviors and symptoms should not be seen as distinct from depression because they reflect male-typical expressions of depression.

In support of this perspective, some research shows that depressed male patients report more anger and aggression, less impulse control, and more substance use than depressed female patients do (Winkler, Pjrek, & Kasper, 2005). Moreover, a *gender-inclusive depression scale* that measured both traditional symptoms (e.g., depressed mood, stress, and indecisiveness) and male-typed symptoms (e.g., anger, substance use, and risk taking) showed similar rates of depression among men and women (30.6% of men vs. 33.3% of women) in a nationally representative sample (L. A. Martin, Neighbors, & Griffith, 2013).

Links between depression, suicide, and sex also support the notion of a male-type depression. Depression increases people's risk of suicide by 20% (E. C. Harris & Barraclough, 1997), and although adolescent girls attempt suicide more frequently than boys (Lewinsohn, Rohde, Seeley, & Baldwin, 2001), men disproportionately die from suicide. Men, especially young men, account for close to 80% of deaths by suicide (Centers for Disease Control and Prevention, 2015c). How can we reconcile the fact of women's higher depression rates with men's higher suicide rates? The male-type depression hypothesis offers a possible solution by suggesting that at least some of men's increased risk of suicide may reflect depression that goes undiagnosed.

Yes, Women Are More Likely Than Men to Suffer From Depression

Decades of research point to higher rates of depression among women than men, and this sex difference emerges across nations and cultures. The notion of a male-type depression that looks different from traditional depression is problematic for several reasons. First, accepting the premise of a male-type depression requires that we change the definition of depression. Clinical psychologists identify a specific set of symptoms that characterize major depressive disorder, and these symptoms clearly occur more frequently among women than among men. Sex differences in depression rates may go away when we include aggression, risk taking, and substance use in our definition of depression—but in doing so, the thing we call *depression* loses some of its meaning.

On a related note, clinical psychologists view many of the symptoms of male-type depression, such as aggression, risk taking, and substance abuse, as symptoms of externalizing disorders, which occur more often in men. The fact that men display these symptoms does not necessarily signify clinical depression; it could mean that they have an externalizing disorder.

Finally, at least some of the symptoms of male-type depression may not occur more commonly among men than women. One large-scale study of people with major depression found that women were more likely than men to experience clinically significant levels of irritability and anger attacks associated with their depression (Judd, Schettler, Coryell, Akiskal, & Fiedorowicz, 2013). This raises questions about whether irritability should be included among the male-type depression symptoms.

Having heard both sides of the debate, which arguments do you find more convincing, and why? Is it possible that both perspectives hold some truth? What do you think is the best way to define major depressive disorder? This question will only become more important with time as rates of depression continue to climb.

Sidebar 13.2: The Gender Paradox of Suicide

The **gender paradox of suicide** refers to the fact that girls and women more frequently exhibit nonfatal suicide behavior, such as suicidal ideation, suicide attempts, and nonsuicidal self-injury, while boys and men more frequently die from suicide in almost all countries (Krysinska, Batterham, & Christensen, 2017). This may reflect sex differences in the suicide methods commonly used, with boys and men being more likely to use violent means, such as firearms. There may also be sex differences in the problems that predict suicidality. For men, work problems, financial problems, substance use problems, and relationship dissolution are stronger predictors of suicide. For women, problems with children, depression and anxiety, and obesity more strongly predict suicide (Branco et al., 2017; R. Evans, Scourfield, & Moore, 2016; Krysinska et al., 2017). For sexual and gender identity minority youths, peer bullying and family rejection are often precursors to suicide (Wolff, Allen, Himes, Fish, & Losardo, 2014).

How do you know if you or someone you know is at risk? Suicidality can be difficult to detect accurately, even for experts, but there are some clear warning signs. If someone threatens to kill themselves, actively looks for ways to kill themselves (e.g., tries to attain a weapon or pills), or talks or writes about suicide or dying, this signals a need for immediate help from an expert (such as those at the National Suicide

Gender paradox of suicide: A pattern in which girls and women more frequently exhibit nonfatal suicide behavior (suicidal ideation, suicide attempts, and nonsuicidal self-injury) while boys and men more frequently die from suicide.

(Continued)

Prevention Lifeline: 1-800-273-8255). Other warning signs include feelings of hopelessness or purposelessness, feeling trapped like "there's no way out," withdrawal and social isolation, dramatic mood changes, agitation, changes in sleeping patterns (either unable to sleep or sleeping all the time), and thoughtlessly reckless or risky behavior (Rudd et al., 2006). For more information on suicide and how to prevent it, visit https://suicidepreventionlifeline.org.

What Roles Do Sex and Gender Play in Eating and Body Image Disorders?

In the United States, approximately 20 million women and 10 million men meet diagnostic criteria for an eating disorder at some point during their lives (T. D. Wade, Keski-Rahkonen, & Hudson, 2011). Eating disorders (summarized in Table 13.4) are serious medical conditions that affect both psychological and physical health. Anorexia nervosa, for example, correlates with the highest mortality rate of all mental illnesses (Arcelus, Mitchell, Wales, & Nielsen, 2011), and it carries a 23% increase in risk of death by suicide (E. C. Harris & Barraclough, 1997).

Girls and women are between 1.75 and 3 times more likely to experience eating disorders than are boys and men (Hudson, Hiripi, Pope, & Kessler, 2007). Moreover, certain populations are especially vulnerable to developing these disorders. Both anorexia and bulimia occur more frequently in Western than non-Western societies and among adolescent and young adult women more frequently than older women (Fairburn & Harrison, 2003). Rates of eating disorders are also higher among transgender than cisgender people (B. A. Jones, Haycraft, Murjan, & Arcelus, 2016), and gay men have higher eating disorder rates than straight men (although rates between gay and straight women do not differ; M. B. Feldman & Meyer, 2007). Athletes in aesthetic sports, such as gymnastics, dancing, and figure skating, also show elevated rates of eating disorders (Bachner-Melman, Zohar, Ebstein, Elizur, & Constantini, 2006).

Sidebar 13.3: Boys and Body Image

Most research on body image and eating disorders focuses on girls and women. However, researchers today are paying more attention to male eating disorders. Male eating disorders may be underdetected because the symptoms often look different for boys and girls. Whereas girls often take measures to lose weight, boys take risky measures to gain muscle mass, including taking supplements, growth hormones, and steroids. One national sample of U.S. adolescents found that 17.9% of boys reported being extremely concerned with their weight and physique, and this group also showed higher rates of drug use and depression (Field et al., 2014).

Table 13.4 Eating and Body Dysmorphic Disorders. While lifetime rates of eating disorders show sex differences that favor women, with small to medium effect sizes, muscle dysmorphia is almost exclusively diagnosed among men. This does not mean that women do not suffer from this disorder, but that valid estimates of its rates among women cannot be calculated.

Disorder	Description	Effect Size (*d*) for Sex Difference in Lifetime Rates
Anorexia nervosa	Distorted self-perception and an irrational fear of gaining weight that result in excessive food restriction and extreme weight loss	−0.61
Bulimia nervosa	Cycles of binging (eating large amounts of food in a short amount of time) followed by purging (ridding oneself of food by vomiting, using laxatives, or exercising excessively)	−0.61
Binge eating disorder	Recurrent episodes of binge eating (i.e., eating rapidly, eating until uncomfortably full, or eating large amounts when not hungry) accompanied by feelings of disgust, guilt, and distress	−0.32
Muscle dysmorphia (a form of body dysmorphic disorder)[a]	Preoccupation with concerns about insufficient muscularity, often accompanied by excessive exercising and dangerous health practices (e.g., anabolic steroid misuse)	—

Source: Hudson, Hiripi, Pope, and Kessler (2007).

Note: a. We were unable to calculate effect sizes for muscle dysmorphia because population rates are not available.

Risk factors for eating disorders include troubled relationships with parents, early sexual abuse, low self-esteem, perfectionism, chronic pressure to be slim, and body dissatisfaction. While these risk factors can help identify which individuals are especially likely to develop eating disorders, they fail to explain the prevalence of eating disorders in the first place or their disproportionate impact on girls and young women. Fortunately, objectification theory helps answer these questions. We will use objectification theory as a framework for evaluating both eating disorders and a subtype of body dysmorphic disorder called muscle dysmorphia that affects men more often than women.

Objectification Theory, Body Image, and Eating Disorders

Objectification theory argues that being raised within a sociocultural context that routinely objectifies and sexualizes the female body has consequences for female mental health. To be objectified is to be "treated as a body (or collection of body parts) valued predominantly for its use to (or consumption by) others" (Fredrickson & Roberts, 1997, p. 174). Objectifying others means seeing them as less than fully human. Objectification theory notes that, as compared with the male body, the female body is more commonly objectified, via media images that sexualize the female form as well as through common daily experiences (e.g., street harassment, unwanted touching, and appearance-related comments). In turn, objectification teaches girls and women that their worth depends more on their appearance than on their actions or accomplishments. It also teaches girls and women to internalize an outsider's perspective on their physical selves, resulting in a chronic preoccupation with their appearance. This constant **self-objectification** increases young women's risk for body dissatisfaction, eating disorders, depression, and substance use problems (Carr & Szymanski, 2011; Moradi & Huang, 2008).

In an early demonstration of objectification theory, Fredrickson and colleagues randomly assigned women to try on either a swimsuit or a sweater in front of a full-length mirror and then measured their feelings of body shame and the number of cookies that they ate as part of a supposed "taste test" (Fredrickson, Roberts, Noll, Quinn, & Twenge, 1998). Women who were self-objectified by wearing the swimsuit reported more body shame than those wearing the sweater, and self-objectified women also consumed fewer cookies than sweater-wearing women. A follow-up study showed that trying on a swimsuit had no effect on men's feelings of body shame or eating behaviors. Similar effects have been found in other experiments, demonstrating that self-objectification increases women's shame about their appearance and decreases their self-esteem (Moradi & Huang, 2008).

Being raised in a culture that routinely objectifies and sexualizes the female body can encourage women to take an outsider's perspective on their own appearance.

Source: © iStockPhoto .com/warrengoldswain

Links to women's mental health. A lot of correlational research links self-objectification to negative mental health outcomes. Across dozens of studies that control for factors such as age, race and ethnicity, body weight, personality, and other risk factors, self-objectification consistently predicts higher levels of eating disorder symptoms (e.g., restricted eating and disordered eating behaviors), lower self-esteem, more depressive symptoms, and reduced psychological well-being (Lindner & Tantleff-Dunn, 2017; Moradi & Huang, 2008).

According to some theories, feelings of body shame drive these links between self-objectification and negative mental health outcomes. That is, chronically evaluating their physical appearance leads women to experience more body shame, which, in turn, increases their vulnerability to eating disorders, depression, low self-esteem, and substance abuse. Other models also consider whether **social comparisons** drive the links between self-objectification and negative outcomes (see Figure 13.1). According to these models, self-objectification leads women to compare their bodies with their peers' bodies. Social comparisons then predict body shame, which predicts eating disorder symptoms (Tylka & Sabik, 2010).

Of course, because the data linking self-objectification with eating disorders are largely correlational, we cannot draw causal conclusions from them. However, studies that use longitudinal designs to track changes in self-objectification and mental health over time find similar links between these variables (B. A. Jones & Griffiths, 2015), and these designs allow for somewhat more confidence regarding causality. Moreover, by linking body image problems and eating disorders to a larger sociocultural cause—that is, regular exposure to media images and experiences that sexualize women's bodies—objectification theory can explain why these disorders occur more often among women than men. On that note, we will consider the role of the media more fully, especially as it pertains to cultural differences in objectification.

Roles of media and culture. Researchers initially developed and tested objectification theory in Western contexts. Reflecting this, 85.5% of all participants in studies of self-objectification have been women from Western cultures including the United States, Australia, and Canada (Loughnan et al., 2015). Do the assumptions behind objectification theory apply similarly to the experiences of non-Western women? According to the theory, the mass media, which include social networks, magazines, television, Internet, and films, are a primary way that people are exposed to objectified (thin, flawless, and sexualized) images of women. And, in fact, young Western women who use more social media, especially social network sites and magazines, also report higher self-objectification (Slater & Tiggemann, 2015). But media depictions of women's bodies vary widely across cultures, reflecting differences in religion, values, gender equality, and economic and political systems. Do the media objectify women in non-Western cultures to the same degree as they do in Western cultures? It seems not. For instance, magazines in Asian countries (such as China, South Korea, Singapore, and Taiwan) show relatively few models in a nude, partially nude, or sexual manner (Frith, Shaw, & Cheng, 2005; M. R. Nelson & Paek, 2005).

Objectification theory: Theory stating that experiencing socialization within a cultural context that objectifies the female body encourages girls and women to internalize an outsider's perspective on themselves and engage in self-objectification.

Self-objectification: Defining the self in terms of how the body appears to others instead of what the body can do or how the body feels.

Social comparisons: Comparisons between the self and another person on a specific domain.

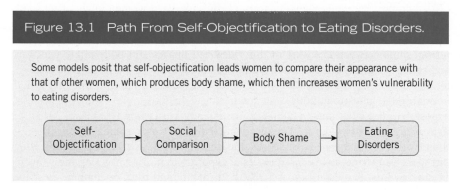

Figure 13.1 Path From Self-Objectification to Eating Disorders.

Some models posit that self-objectification leads women to compare their appearance with that of other women, which produces body shame, which then increases women's vulnerability to eating disorders.

Self-Objectification → Social Comparison → Body Shame → Eating Disorders

Source: Tylka and Sabik (2010).

What about cultural differences in self-objectification? One study compared the prevalence of self-objectification tendencies across seven diverse cultures, including the United States, United Kingdom, Australia, Italy, India, Pakistan, and Japan (Loughnan et al., 2015). Although women scored higher in self-objectification than men did overall, there were cultural differences: People in the United States, United Kingdom, and Australia self-objectified more than those in Italy, Japan, Pakistan, and India. Thus, self-objectification was higher in several Western cultures than in non-Western cultures, which may help explain the lower rates of eating disorders in non-Western cultures.

However, cultural differences in self-objectification may be changing, as people in non-Western countries get exposed to more and more Western media and values of materialism. For instance, one study of young Chinese women found that materialism predicted self-objectification tendencies (Teng et al., 2017). Another study measured self-objectification among two generations of women (mothers and daughters) in Nepal, a country that spent most of its history cut off from Western influences until about the mid-1980s. While both generations of Nepali women were lower in self-objectification than U.S. women, Nepali daughters were higher in self-objectification than their mothers (Crawford et al., 2009), perhaps reflecting their increased exposure to Western, objectified representations of women.

Does exposure to Western media increase non-Western women's eating disorder vulnerability? To answer this question, Anne Becker and her colleagues assessed the prevalence of eating disorders among groups of school girls in a Fijian village both 1 month after and 3 years after Western television was first introduced to the area in 1995. After 3 years of Western television exposure, the percentage of young Fijian women who displayed clinical levels of eating disorder symptoms had more than doubled from 12.7% to 29.2% (A. Becker, Burwell, Herzog, Hamburg, & Gilman, 2002).

Again, all of the findings summarized here are correlational, so we must interpret them with caution. However, the findings do support the idea that a largely Western tendency to objectify and sexualize women's bodies can explain both sex and culture differences in body dissatisfaction and eating disorder tendencies. If so, then we might see increases in eating disorders around the world as the influence of Western culture continues to increase.

Note, however, that not all researchers agree that exposure to thin, idealized images of women affects body image and eating disorders. For example, Christopher Ferguson (2013) argues that while media imagery of thin, idealized women might affect some (but not most) girls and women, other factors, such as genes, also influence eating disorders. The issue is far from settled. One meta-analysis found small to moderate relationships between exposure to thin, idealized images and body image concerns and eating behaviors (Grabe, Ward, & Hyde, 2008). However, another meta-analysis found little to no relationship between women's exposure to thin media images and body image (Holmstrom, 2004). Yet another meta-analysis found little evidence that exposure to muscular images influences men's body satisfaction (Ferguson, 2013). In light of this mixed evidence, Ferguson concluded that only some women—that is, those with preexisting body dissatisfaction and/or genetic tendencies toward eating disorders—suffer negative consequences of exposure to media images of thin women. In other words, Ferguson proposes that both nature and nurture combine to shape eating disorder outcomes.

Intersectionality and Eating Disorders Among Women

Clinical psychologists historically assumed that eating disorders primarily affected White women, but recent studies paint a different picture. One literature review found that White women were more likely than Black, Latina, and Asian American women to develop anorexia while rates of bulimia and binge eating disorder were comparable across racial and ethnic groups (Cachelin, Dohm, & Brown, 2009). These data are summarized in Figure 13.2.

If rates of some eating disorders are similar across racial and ethnic groups, what about the risk factors? This question is important because understanding the risk factors can help clinicians develop interventions and treatments for eating disorders among diverse groups. Interestingly, research suggests that racial and ethnic minority identities can protect against eating disorders in some ways but also create unique vulnerabilities in other ways. For instance, *thin ideal internalization*, or the belief that an ultrathin body is ideal for women, predicts eating disorders among White women. On average, however, Black women tend to score lower in thin ideal internalization than White, Latina, and Asian American women. Moreover, among women of color, having a stronger **ethnic identity**—a sense of connectedness to one's racial or ethnic group—weakens the link between thin ideal internalization and eating pathology (Rakhkovskaya & Warren, 2014).

Ethnic identity: A psychological sense of connectedness to one's racial or ethnic group.

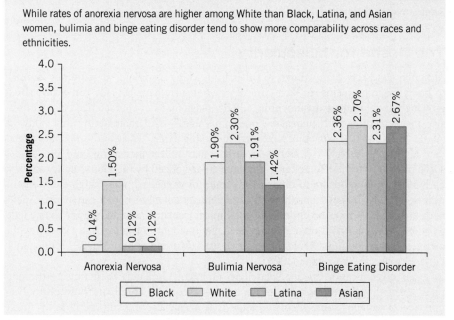

Figure 13.2   Eating Disorders Among U.S. Women.

While rates of anorexia nervosa are higher among White than Black, Latina, and Asian women, bulimia and binge eating disorder tend to show more comparability across races and ethnicities.

Source: Cachelin, Dohm, and Brown (2009).

This suggests that a stronger ethnic identity can buffer women against some types of eating concerns.

At the same time, women of color face a unique source of body shame not shared by White women: racial discrimination. Some research finds that more frequent race-based mistreatment predicts body shame, which predicts eating disorder symptoms among Latina women (Velez, Campos, & Moradi, 2015). Thus, the links between risk factors (e.g., thin ideal internalization and body shame) and eating pathology among women of color are complex, and more research is needed on this topic.

Gender Identity, Body Dissatisfaction, and Eating Disorders

Transgender people are especially vulnerable to developing eating disorders. On average, transmen and transwomen have higher levels of body dissatisfaction and more disordered eating behaviors than their cisgender peers (B. A. Jones et al., 2016). For transgender people, body dissatisfaction may result when certain body parts or physical features remind them of their assigned sex, which differs from their gender identity. In such cases, individuals may use excessive dieting or other disordered eating practices to suppress physical features associated with their birth sex or to accentuate body features consistent with their gender identity. Interestingly, body satisfaction often increases among transgender individuals after they undergo genital reconstructive surgery or hormone treatments, suggesting that the mismatch between assigned sex and gender identity is a primary source of body image problems. We will return to the topic of mental health and transgender identity in a later section ("How Do Sexual and Gender Minority Statuses Relate to Mental Health?").

The Desire for Muscularity

Although less likely than women to suffer from eating disorders, men are not immune to body image problems. In fact, clinical psychologists have become concerned about growing rates of **muscle dysmorphia**, a body image disorder characterized by an obsessive preoccupation with increasing one's muscularity and maintaining low body fat (W. R. Jones, 2010). Sometimes referred to as "bigorexia," muscle dysmorphia affects men almost exclusively (see Table 13.4) and may reflect increasing (and unrealistic) social pressures for men to obtain a physique characterized by high muscularity and low body fat. Just as exposure to objectified images of women's bodies heightens women's feelings of body shame, exposure to objectified images of men's bodies can increase men's body shame. However, the underlying body image concerns that drive body shame tend to differ for women and men. Women feel shame about not being thin enough while men feel shame about not being muscular enough (Murnen & Karazsia, 2017; Olivardia, Pope, Borowiecki, & Cohane, 2004).

Can objectification theory shed light on men's problems with muscle dysmorphia? Even though researchers developed this theory to illuminate how objectification affects women, some theorists argue that it can also explain men's body image concerns, especially due to increasing cultural objectification of the male form.

Muscle dysmorphia: A body image disorder characterized by an obsessive preoccupation with increasing one's muscularity and maintaining low body fat.

In fact, the same processes seem to underlie both women's and men's reactions to objectification. Greater exposure to idealized images of men's bodies encourages men to self-objectify, which increases their body dissatisfaction and heightens their vulnerability to body image disorders (Moradi & Huang, 2008).

Moreover, objectification theory may be especially useful for understanding the development of eating and body image disorders among gay men, who experience stronger pressures to conform to physical attractiveness standards than heterosexual men do. Gay men, compared with heterosexual men, report lower satisfaction with their bodies and muscles (Frederick & Essayli, 2016) and greater self-objectification, drive for thinness, and disordered eating symptoms (Martins, Tiggemann, & Kirkebride, 2007; Siever, 1994). Similar to women, gay men are regularly objectified by men within a patriarchal context, and gay men, relative to straight men, report feeling more objectified by others and more judged based on their appearance (Frederick & Essayli, 2016). In a replication of the swimsuit study described earlier, researchers objectified gay and heterosexual men by making them wear a pair of Speedo briefs (Martins et al., 2007). Their findings showed that self-objectified gay men scored higher in body shame than those who were not self-objectified while the clothing manipulation did not affect heterosexual men's body image. Thus, the root of body image problems may not be objectification by itself but objectification by the **male gaze**, which refers to a voyeuristic and sexual mode of viewing others that reflects men's patriarchal power.

Men may develop an obsessive preoccupation with increasing the size of their muscles while maintaining low body fat, a condition termed muscle dysmorphia.

Source: © iStockPhoto .com/Art-Of-Photo

Stop and Think

This section focused on how the tendency to objectify people's bodies leads to unhealthy outcomes. Suppose you were in charge of a campaign to protect girls and boys from the harmful effects of objectification. What shape would your campaign take? What factors do you think would be the most powerful in countering the effects of objectification? How would your strategies differ, if at all, when addressing female versus male objectification?

How Do Sexual and Gender Minority Statuses Relate to Mental Health?

Sexual minority and transgender people display heightened risks of mental illnesses and symptoms including depression, anxiety disorders, alcohol and substance abuse

Male gaze: A mode of viewing others that is voyeuristic and sexual and that reflects men's patriarchal power over women and other objectified individuals.

problems, self-injury, and suicidality (S. T. Russell & Fish, 2016). What might account for these differences in the rates of mental illness? As you may recall from Chapter 12 ("Gender and Physical Health"), *minority stress theory* proposes that belonging to a stigmatized group can create stressors unique to the minority experience (I. H. Meyer, 2003). These stressors, which include rejection, harassment, abuse, discrimination, and internalized stigma, combine to increase people's vulnerability to all types of mental illness. Here, we will consider several factors that contribute to sexual and gender minority stress.

Victimization, Discrimination, and Rejection

The stressors of victimization (e.g., bullying and threats) and discrimination (e.g., restricted opportunities and denial of services) disproportionately affect LGBT people. Sexual minority and gender-nonconforming youths and adults who experience more victimization and bullying also report more depressive symptoms, suicidality, anxiety and PTSD symptoms, and substance use disorders (Burton, Marshal, Chisolm, Sucato, & Friedman, 2013; N. R. Eaton, 2014).

For LGBT people, victimization sometimes occurs at the hands of close family members, including parents. Unlike racial and ethnic minorities, LGBT individuals often come from families in which relatives do not share their minority status. Accordingly, they experience a heightened risk of being treated as outcasts or rejected by parents or family. Sexual minority adults who experienced more parental rejection of their sexuality (e.g., disparaging comments and anger) during adolescence also report higher rates of attempted suicide, depression, illegal drug use, and risky sex than their peers who experienced less parental rejection (C. Ryan, Huebner, Diaz, & Sanchez, 2009). Similarly, higher levels of family rejection in response to coming out as transgender predict higher rates of attempted suicide and greater substance abuse among transgender adults (A. Klein & Golub, 2016).

While a lack of parental rejection is good, an abundance of parental acceptance is even better. Strong, high-quality parent–child relationships, characterized by connectedness, support, and warmth, can buffer sexual and gender minority youths from the negative consequences of sexual minority stress. Across dozens of studies, LGB young adults who reported more parental support and more positive, warm relationships with their parents in adolescence were less likely to use substances, displayed lower rates of depression and distress, and were at a lower risk of suicide (Bouris et al., 2010). In fact, one study found that positive connections with parents and family were the single best protector against suicidal behavior among both sexual minority and heterosexual adolescents (M. E. Eisenberg & Resnick, 2006). Less research examines the outcomes of parental acceptance among transgender youths, but what little there is suggests similar benefits (C. Ryan, Russell, Huebner, Diaz, & Sanchez, 2010). The importance of positive family relationships for all youths, regardless of sexual orientation and gender identity, cannot be overstated.

Homelessness

Relative to heterosexual and cisgender youth, LGBT youth are at an increased risk of homelessness. Some estimate that LGBT teens make up 20%–40% of the 1.7 million homeless youth in the United States, despite representing only 5%–7% of the youth population (Quintana, Rosenthal, & Krehely, 2010). Furthermore, a disproportionately large number of homeless LGBT youth are Black and Latino/a and thus may experience minority stress related to multiple intersecting identities. Young people become homeless for a variety of reasons, including parental neglect, abuse, and family conflict, but LGBT youth are especially likely to be evicted by parents or run away to escape abuse. Moreover, homelessness, which takes a terrible toll on the mental health of all youths, has an especially harmful effect on LGBT individuals. Homeless LGBT youths suffer more depression, anxiety, conduct problems, and substance use problems compared with both homeless heterosexual youths and nonhomeless LGBT youths (Rosario, Schrimshaw, & Hunter, 2011).

Institutional Discrimination: A Hostile Environment

So far, we have primarily considered minority stressors that involve direct mistreatment from others. However, minority stressors can exist on a larger scale, reflecting environmental conditions that can impact psychological health. One study found that LGBT youths who lived in neighborhoods with higher rates of violent LGBT hate crimes had more suicidal ideation and attempted suicide more frequently compared with both heterosexual youths exposed to LGBT hate crimes and LGBT youths exposed to non-LGBT-based violent crimes (Duncan & Hatzenbuehler, 2014). Moreover, sexual minority adults who live in states that do not provide legal protections based on sexual orientation experience disproportionately high rates of mood and anxiety disorders (Hatzenbuehler, Keyes, & Hasin, 2009). Findings like these indicate that living within a "hostile" environment can impair the mental health of LGBT individuals, perhaps by arousing chronic feelings of anxiety, worry, and hopelessness.

Internalized Stigma: Homophobia and Transphobia From Within

Ironically, sometimes minority stress can come from inside. As you may recall from Chapter 9 ("Sexual Orientation and Sexuality"), **internalized homophobia** consists of self-directed antigay attitudes held by sexual minority persons. Similarly, **internalized transphobia** refers to self-directed antitransgender attitudes held by transgender people. These occur when people internalize the negative, devaluing attitudes and beliefs held about their group by the surrounding culture. Internalized stigma then produces conflicts and stress that can manifest as mental health problems. For instance, internalized homophobia predicts depression, anxiety, and substance abuse problems, with small to medium effect sizes ($d = 0.26$), among the LGB population (Brubaker, Garrett, & Dew, 2009; Newcomb & Mustanski, 2010), and internalized transphobia predicts depression and suicidality among transgender adults (Breslow et al., 2015; Tebbe & Moradi, 2016).

Sexual minority individuals who occupy more than one disadvantaged group may suffer even greater levels of internalized stigma. To illustrate, some findings indicate that internalized homophobia is higher among Black and Latino than White sexual minority individuals (O'Leary, Fisher, Purcell, Spikes, & Gomez, 2007). This may occur because

Internalized homophobia: Self-directed antigay attitudes held by sexual minority persons.

Internalized transphobia: Self-directed transphobic attitudes held by transgender persons.

racial and ethnic minority LGB individuals internalize both homophobia and racism, which can increase their vulnerability to psychological distress (Szymanski & Gupta, 2009). This makes sense from the perspective of minority stress theory: The condition of *double stigma*—being a member of more than one stigmatized group—should be doubly stressful.

Stop and Think

Why do you think some individuals internalize negative attitudes about their sexual orientation or gender identity? What aspects of a person's environment, upbringing, or personality might make them more inclined to *internalize stigmatizing attitudes about their group? Conversely, what factors might protect sexual and gender minority individuals from embracing negative, self-directed attitudes?*

What Roles Do Sex and Gender Play in Mental Health Help-Seeking?

Sex Differences in Rates of Help-Seeking

On average, men are less likely to seek help for mental health problems than women are, just as men are less likely to visit doctors for physical health issues (see Chapter 12, "Gender and Physical Health"). However, this sex difference depends on a couple of factors. First, the type of help provider makes a difference. Sex differences in help-seeking for mental health problems from medical doctors and informal sources (e.g., self-help groups and spiritual providers) are consistently large, but sex differences in help-seeking from mental health professionals (e.g., psychotherapists and social workers) are relatively smaller. This pattern emerges across several large, nationally representative studies of adults who meet diagnostic criteria for mental illnesses in the United States and Europe (Kovess-Masfety et al., 2014; Susukida, Mojtabai, & Mendelson, 2015). Men are thus far less likely than women to bring up emotional or mental health problems during routine doctor visits, which can be an important first step toward getting help. Second, the type of symptoms that people experience can make a difference. For instance, sex differences in utilization of mental health services may be larger for anxiety problems than for depression problems (Mackenzie, Reynolds, Cairney, Streiner, & Sareen, 2012). Finally, although men with mental health problems seek less help than women, women also underutilize professional services. One study found that fewer than 40% of U.S. women who met diagnostic criteria for a mood or anxiety disorder in the past year sought help for it (Susukida et al., 2015). The tendency to underutilize psychological help services clearly does not apply just to men.

That said, many researchers seek to understand—and thereby close—the gender gap in mental health help-seeking. Much of this research focuses on how the male gender role suppresses help-seeking. Seeking help for emotional pain involves expressing emotions and making oneself vulnerable, behaviors that are inconsistent with male role norms of toughness, self-reliance, and stoicism. Men who conform more strongly to these male role norms and who endorse more traditional gender ideologies also tend to hold more negative attitudes toward seeking mental health help (Berger, Levant, McMillan, Kelleher, & Sellers, 2005; Yousaf, Popat, & Hunter, 2015). The surrounding context can also play a role in whether or not people seek help for emotional problems. Male-dominated and hypermasculine environments, such as competitive sports and the military, tend to press for self-reliance and mental toughness and discourage vulnerability and help-seeking. Think back to the stories of Charles Haley and Brandon Marshall that opened this chapter. Socialized from an early age within the tough world of football, both Haley and Marshall resisted seeking help until their mental health problems almost destroyed their careers. Community type (rural versus urban) may also play a role in mental health help-seeking. Men from rural communities less frequently seek help for emotional problems than do men from urban communities, likely because of the strong norms of tough, self-reliance that are especially salient in rural areas (Hammer, Vogel, & Heimerdinger-Edwards, 2013). Note that masculine and male-dominated environments do not only influence the behavior of men. For instance, norms of toughness and self-reliance in the military suppress mental health help-seeking among both women and men (Clement et al., 2015).

Military norms of toughness and self-reliance may discourage people from seeking help for mental health problems.

Source: © iStockPhoto .com/MivPiv

Stop and Think

As we mentioned in the chapter opening, Charles Haley and Brandon Marshall both work to destigmatize mental illness and encourage men to seek help when needed. Do you think their efforts are likely to be successful? Why or why not? Are *messages about the importance of help-seeking more likely to be effective if they come from stereotypically tough male role models? What steps would you take to increase people's use of mental health services?*

Intersectionality and Help-Seeking

As we noted earlier, women do not necessarily seek mental health help when they need it, and Black women may be especially unlikely to do so. Even when controlling for access to insurance, Black women are less likely than White women to utilize professional psychological services (Padgett, Patrick, Burns, & Schlesinger, 1994). To explain this race difference, some researchers look to the **strong Black woman (SBW) schema**, a set of beliefs and attitudes about what it means to be a Black woman. According to the SBW schema, Black women are strong, selfless, resilient, and able to persevere despite oppression and financial hardship (Settles, Pratt-Hyatt, & Buchanan, 2008). Although the SBW schema can be a source of strength and self-efficacy for Black women, it may also hinder their tendencies to seek help because it encourages self-reliance and emotional inhibition in the face of stressors. Consistent with these ideas, Black women who more strongly endorsed the SBW schema were also less willing to acknowledge psychological problems and less open to seeking professional psychological help (Watson & Hunter, 2015). Thus, unique features that arise from the intersection of gender and racial identities may influence help-seeking tendencies.

What Roles Do Sex and Gender Play in Happiness and Well-Being?

Thus far, we have devoted most of this chapter to discussions of mental illness. But what about psychological health? What does it mean to be mentally healthy? Here, we consider two prominent models of mental health and the roles that sex and gender play in each.

Subjective Well-Being

Psychologists who study happiness often examine a variable called **subjective well-being** (SWB). SWB refers to both short-term experiences of positive emotions and longer-term, global judgments of life satisfaction, meaning, and purpose (Diener, Suh, Lucas, & Smith, 1999). Given that women suffer from higher rates of depression than men do, we might suspect that men are higher on SWB than women. However, there is little evidence for a consistent sex difference in SWB. Women do tend to report more negative emotions than men, but the sexes generally do not differ in overall positive emotions. One study that measured the predictors of SWB in 50 countries found no sex differences across cultures either in happiness or in the factors that predicted happiness (Lun & Bond, 2016). Moreover, although women and men report similar frequencies of positive emotions, women report stronger intensities of positive emotions than men do (Lucas & Gohm, 2000). Thus, having a higher propensity for depression does not mean that women report being less happy than men in general.

That said, both age and cultural factors may contribute to sex differences in SWB. For instance, one meta-analysis found that older women—but not younger women—reported lower life satisfaction and happiness than men (Pinquart & Sörensen, 2001). This sex difference was small, however, and driven largely by women's greater likelihood of widowhood, physical health problems, and economic stress. Another study measured sex differences in people's belief that they were living "the best possible life" (a variable that captures the life satisfaction element of SWB) in seven different world regions. Across the globe, women actually reported greater SWB than men in both middle-income and high-income countries, but men had slightly higher SWB than women in the poorest countries, where women are generally less empowered and more economically dependent on men (Graham & Chattopadhyay, 2013).

Of all the factors that seem to have a substantial and lasting influence on happiness, sex and gender do not seem to play much of a role. Some factors that we cannot control, such as genes and personality, contribute to happiness levels, but so do more controllable factors. People can increase their happiness by developing satisfying social relationships, maintaining good physical health and regular exercise, practicing kindness and gratitude, and helping others selflessly (Lyubomirsky, 2008). As shown in Figure 13.3, a meta-analysis of the effects of positive psychology interventions, such as practicing optimistic thinking, writing about gratitude, and thinking about positive experiences, found that these practices increase well-being and decrease depression with small to very large effect sizes (Sin & Lyubomirsky, 2009). Fortunately, people of all sexes and genders can cultivate such practices.

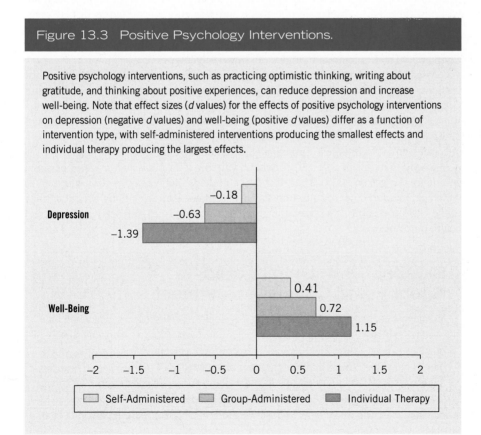

Figure 13.3 Positive Psychology Interventions.

Positive psychology interventions, such as practicing optimistic thinking, writing about gratitude, and thinking about positive experiences, can reduce depression and increase well-being. Note that effect sizes (*d* values) for the effects of positive psychology interventions on depression (negative *d* values) and well-being (positive *d* values) differ as a function of intervention type, with self-administered interventions producing the smallest effects and individual therapy producing the largest effects.

Source: Sin and Lyubomirsky (2009).

Although women and men do not differ much in overall happiness, it is possible that the sources *of happiness differ across sex. Think about the things that make you happy. Can you think of sources of happiness that might differ for women and men? As a researcher, how would you test this?*

Communion, Agency, and Well-Being

Rather than focusing on subjective feelings of happiness and life satisfaction, some researchers instead conceptualize well-being as a balance between communion and agency. As discussed throughout this book, *communion* refers to qualities (e.g., warmth and generosity) that connect and orient people to others, and *agency* refers to qualities (e.g., independence and assertiveness) that distinguish people from others and orient them toward the self. These dimensions are relevant to gender roles because men are typically expected to display agentic traits, and women are expected to display communal traits. Not only do these dimensions underlie sex-typed traits, they also underlie common gender stereotypes (recall the stereotype content model that we discussed in Chapter 5, "The Contents and Origins of Gender Stereotypes").

As we discussed in the last chapter on physical health, extreme and dysfunctional versions of agentic and communal traits—referred to as *unmitigated communion* and *unmitigated agency*—are both associated with deficits in well-being but for different reasons. Unmitigated agency, which consists of extreme self-reliance and negative views of others, correlates with interpersonal difficulties, poor-quality relationships, and a lack of social support from others. Unmitigated communion, characterized by overattentiveness to others and neglect of self, correlates with low self-esteem and a lack of personal autonomy (Helgeson, 2003). Thus, if children undergo highly sex-typed socialization in which parents and other socialization agents encourage them to embody one set of traits to the exclusion of the other, then they may be less likely to experience positive mental health outcomes.

Sidebar 13.4: Unmitigated Agency and Cancer Adjustment

Unmitigated agency can make it difficult for people to seek social support when they need it the most, such as after a cancer diagnosis. In one study of men who survived prostate cancer, unmitigated agency predicted more depressive symptoms, worse mental health, and more intrusive thoughts about cancer 14 months later (Helgeson & Lepore, 2004). Not surprisingly, higher scores on unmitigated agency also correlated with having fewer sources of social support to assist men with coping. In contrast, men who were higher in healthy agency had more social support and better outcomes over time.

In one recent test of these ideas, Yi Wang (2016) proposed that optimal mental health—what he refers to as *balanced authenticity*—requires finding a middle ground between the competing needs for agency and communion. In support of this perspective, people who scored higher on a measure of balanced authenticity also scored higher across several indices of personal mental health (e.g., subjective well-being, self-esteem, and feelings of competence) and social connectedness (e.g., positive relations with others, empathic concern for others, and perspective taking). Thus, from this perspective, one form of optimal mental health involves being able to move flexibly between "feminine" and "masculine" tendencies.

CHAPTER SUMMARY

13.1 Define psychological disorders and explain the major approaches to classifying them.

Psychological disorders (mental illnesses) are persistent disruptions or disturbances in thought, emotion, or behavior that cause significant distress or impairment. Both the APA and WHO publish reference manuals that define and classify psychological disorders. While the APA's reference text—the *DSM*—describes over 200 distinct disorders, the transdiagnostic approach proposes that most of these disorders reflect different manifestations of a few core, heritable dimensions. These dimensions include the internalizing disorders (which consist of symptoms directed inward, toward the self) and the externalizing disorders (which consist of symptoms directed outward, toward others).

13.2 Analyze the various factors (e.g., gender roles, abuse, personality, and biology) that contribute to sex differences in rates of internalizing and externalizing disorders.

Internalizing disorders, which include mood, anxiety, and eating disorders, are cross-culturally more common among women than men, with small to medium effect sizes. Explanations for this sex difference vary, and each one likely accounts for some portion of the overall effect. Gender socialization may teach girls and women to cope passively with negative emotions (ruminate), and traditional labor divisions restrict women to a smaller number of socially devalued, home-based roles. Girls and women experience sexual violence at higher rates than boys and men, which can contribute to depression, and women the world over tend to be higher in neuroticism (negative emotionality) than men. Girls and women also demonstrate a more reactive physiological response to stress, which can increase their vulnerability to internalizing disorders, especially during adolescence.

Externalizing disorders, including impulse control, attention, conduct, antisocial, and substance disorders, are cross-culturally more common among men than women, with medium effect sizes. This sex difference may reflect the operation of multiple factors. Boys often learn to display anger instead of sadness or fear, and parents tend to discipline sons more harshly than daughters. Men are more likely than women to use drugs and alcohol to cope with negative emotions, and they may have personality traits (high impulsivity and callous-unemotional traits and low effortful control) that render them vulnerable to externalizing tendencies. Boys also have lower brain volume in an area of the brain that regulates impulse control (the prefrontal cortex) and may be more likely to inherit dopamine irregularities that underlie poor impulse control.

13.3 Explain the roles of gender and self-objectification in eating and body image disorders.

Women develop eating disorders (e.g., anorexia nervosa and bulimia nervosa) more frequently than men while men develop muscle dysmorphia more frequently than women. Eating disorders have a genetic component, but other factors contribute to their development as well. Objectification theory posits that repeated exposure to objectified, idealized, and sexualized images of women's bodies causes women to engage in self-objectification, which then predicts body dissatisfaction, eating disorders, low self-esteem, depression, and substance use problems. Western media are more likely to depict women in an objectified manner, which may partially explain why eating disorders occur more frequently among Western women. However, increases in self-objectification and eating disorders are observed in non-Western cultures that undergo increasing exposure to Western media (e.g., Nepal and Fiji).

Black women are less likely than White women to internalize the thin ideal, and racial and ethnic minority women with stronger ethnic identities may be buffered from some types of eating disorders. However, experiences of racial discrimination can contribute to body shame and eating disorders among women of color. Transgender individuals display heightened levels of body dissatisfaction and eating disorders, but these symptoms often subside after genital reconstructive surgery or hormone treatment. Rates of muscle dysmorphia among men are on the rise, possibly due to increasing portrayals of highly muscular male images in the media. Gay men experience a relatively high frequency of body image issues, possibly because they—like heterosexual women—are especially likely to be targets of the male gaze, a sexualized and voyeuristic way of viewing others that reflects patriarchal power.

13.4 Describe the unique mental health vulnerabilities experienced by LGBT individuals.

LGBT people have higher levels of internalizing and externalizing disorders than heterosexual and cisgender people. Minority stress theory proposes that belonging to a stigmatized group creates unique stressors that heighten vulnerability to mental illness. Some stressors experienced by LGBT people include discrimination, physical and verbal victimization, parental and family rejection, homelessness, threatening environmental conditions, lack of legal protections, and internalized stigma. Parental acceptance and support offer a considerable buffer against the negative effects of minority stress.

13.5 Evaluate the roles of sex and gender in help-seeking.

Men seek help for mental health problems from medical doctors at much lower rates than women, but sex differences in help-seeking from mental health professionals are smaller. Sex differences in help-seeking may also differ depending on disorder type (e.g., anxiety vs. depression). Most people with mental health problems, regardless of sex, fail to seek adequate help for these problems. Men are especially unlikely to seek mental health help if they endorse male role norms of toughness and self-reliance or if they occupy male-dominated, hypercompetitive environments. Black women who more strongly endorse views of Black women as strong and resilient are also less likely to seek professional mental health assistance.

13.6 Understand how sex and gender relate to happiness and well-being.

Approaches to psychological health that focus on subjective well-being find few consistent sex differences. Women report more negative emotions than men, but they do not consistently report lower happiness than men. In general, the factors that predict happiness seem to be similar for women and men. Approaches to health that focus on communion and agency propose that optimal well-being reflects a balance between these dimensions. Being too extreme on agency (unmitigated agency) can undermine well-being by reducing relationship quality and social support while being too extreme on communion (unmitigated communion) can lead to self-neglect and low confidence. People high in balanced authenticity—a middle ground between agency and communion—tend to score highest in both personal mental health and connectedness to others.

Test Your Knowledge: True or False?

13.1. Approximately one-quarter (25%) of all people in the United States will meet diagnostic criteria for a mental illness during their lifetime. (False: Almost one-half (47%) of all people in the United States will meet diagnostic criteria for a mental illness during their lifetime.) [p. 445]

13.2. In general, men are more likely than women to suffer from alcohol, drug, and other substance use disorders. (True: Sex differences in these types of disorders are in the medium effect size range.) [p. 453]

13.3. Eating disorders only occur in Western cultures. (False: While eating disorder rates tend to be lower in non-Western cultures, increasing exposure to Western, objectified representations of women correlates with increased eating disorders among women in non-Western cultures.) [p. 462]

13.4. Sexual and gender minority youths who live in neighborhoods with higher rates of hate crimes against LGBT people are more likely to attempt suicide. (True: Sexual and gender minority youths who have not personally experienced hate crimes are more likely to attempt suicide if they live in neighborhoods with higher rates of LGBT hate crimes.) [p. 467]

13.5. Across cultures, men generally report higher levels of happiness and positive emotions than women do. (False: There are not persistent sex differences in the amount of happiness that women and men report.) [p. 470]

Passersby on the campus of the University of California at Los Angeles write messages to support survivors of sexual assault on June 4, 2015.

Source: The Washington Post/The Washington Post/Getty Images

Test Your Knowledge: True or False?

14.1   Around the world, young men commit the vast majority of violent crimes.

14.2   Girls use indirect, relational forms of aggression, such as gossip and spreading rumors, much more often than boys do.

14.3   Between one-third and two-thirds of sexual assault victims around the world are age 15 or younger.

14.4   False allegations of rape are common.

14.5   Attractive women who embody ideals of femininity are most likely to be targeted for workplace sex-based harassment.

CHAPTER

14

Aggression and Violence

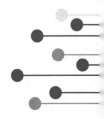

Key Concepts

Are There Sex Differences in Aggression?

    Sex Differences in Perpetrating Aggression

        Physical Aggression

        Verbal Aggression

        Relational Aggression

        Cyberbullying

    Sex Differences in Experiencing Aggression

    What's the Big Picture?

What Are the Major Forms of Gender-Based Aggression and Violence?

    Intimate Partner Violence

        Situational Couple Violence Versus Intimate Terrorism

        Debate: Do Men Perpetrate Intimate Partner Violence More Often Than Women?

    Sexual Violence: Rape and Sexual Assault

        How Common Is Sexual Violence?

        Who Commits Sexual Violence?

        The Aftermath of Sexual Violence

    Sex-Based Harassment

What Explains Gender-Based Aggression and Violence?

    Biological Factors

        Testosterone

        Evolved Jealousy

    Sociocultural Factors

        Honor Cultures

        Precarious Manhood

        Power and Structural Gender Inequality

        I^3 Theory

What Is the Relationship Between Pornography and Sexual Aggression?

    Definitions and Prevalence

    Journey of Research: Science, Politics, and Pornography

    Pornography and Sexual Aggression

Learning Objectives

Students who read this chapter should be able to do the following:

14.1 Analyze research on sex differences and similarities across different types of aggression.

14.2 Evaluate the gender dynamics of intimate partner violence, sexual assault, and sex-based harassment.

14.3 Discuss biological and sociocultural factors that explain sex differences in gender-based aggression.

14.4 Use research findings on gender-based violence to understand the relationship between pornography and sexual aggression.

Aggression and Violence

In 2015, the Association of American Universities (AAU) published the results of a massive study of sexual assaults conducted with over 150,000 students on 27 U.S. college campuses (AAU, 2015). Overall, 27% of female seniors reported experiencing some type of nonconsensual sexual contact perpetrated through incapacitation (by alcohol, drugs, or force) since entering college, and 13% had experienced unwanted penetration, attempted penetration, or oral sex. Less publicized were the results from men: 8.6% of male seniors reported experiencing some kind of unwanted sexual contact, and 2.9% had experienced unwanted penetration, attempted penetration, or oral sex. Transgender students had higher rates of assault than cisgender women and men: 30.8% reported unwanted sexual contact. Furthermore, only 28% of even the most serious incidents were reported to an official law enforcement agency or campus Title IX office.

The AAU report triggered controversy and mixed reactions. Some considered the results disturbing and believed them to reveal clear evidence of an epidemic of sexual violence on college campuses (Pérez-Peña, 2015). Others moved quickly to debunk the numbers. Some critics dismissed the survey claims as moral panic not backed up by reality. They argued that studies like these inflate estimates of sexual assault by lumping together rape with acts that are less serious violations, such as groping and other unwanted touching. Furthermore, they cautioned that the low response rate (only 19.3% of students who received the survey returned it) raised questions about the validity of the numbers (Yoffe, 2015).

The AAU survey highlights how reports of sexual violence can ignite passionate debates. Although few would question that sexual assault is a terrible crime, many disagree about its prevalence, both on and off of college campuses. Due to the sensitive nature of sexual assault, officially reported sexual assault rates are likely unreliable. But relying on self-reports made by sexual assault survivors, as researchers often do, can also be problematic. One the one hand, if individuals who experience sexual assault respond to surveys more often than those who do not, out of a motivation to share their experiences, this could lead to overinflated estimates of sexual assault prevalence. On the other hand, if sexual assault survivors are unlikely to respond to surveys, out of feelings of shame, fear of retaliation, or desire to avoid thinking about the assault, this could lead to underestimates of prevalence. These and other issues make sexual assault a challenging topic of research study.

This chapter will discuss gender and aggression in two ways. First, we will examine sex differences in the prevalence of various types of aggression. As you read in Chapter 5 ("The Contents and Origins of Gender Stereotypes"), men are stereotyped as being more aggressive than women, and here, we will evaluate the validity of this stereotype. Second, we will examine specific forms of aggression through the lens of gender. Intimate partner violence, rape, sexual harassment, and aggressive pornography are gendered acts. To understand why these types of aggression occur, we need to understand how gender contributes to power differences within relationships and in society. But first, we will define some terminology.

Social psychologists define **aggression** as behavior that is intended to cause psychological or physical harm to another person or animal. Note that aggression can—but does not have to—involve physical contact. While **physical aggression** involves

Aggression:
Behavior intended to cause psychological or physical harm to another person or animal.

Physical aggression:
Physical acts intended to cause injury or harm to others.

physical acts intended to cause injury or harm (e.g., hitting, kicking, shoving, or biting), **verbal aggression** involves communications that intend to harm another person (e.g., yelling, teasing, or cyberbullying). Note here that *intention* to harm is key—throwing a book at someone's head with the intention of hurting them is considered an act of physical violence even if you miss your target and hit the wall instead. Aggression can also be direct and "in your face" or less direct and subtle. **Direct aggression** involves overt verbal or physical behaviors aimed directly at another person while **indirect aggression**, sometimes called **relational aggression**, involves acts intended to harm another person's social relationships or status (e.g., spreading rumors and excluding someone socially), and these acts often occur when the victim is not physically present. Though somewhat vaguely defined, **violence** typically refers to severe forms of physical aggression, such as homicide, that have extreme harm as their goal. Violence is a subset of aggression because all violence is aggression, but not all aggression is violence. For instance, researchers do not typically consider verbal and indirect aggression—no matter how cruel—as forms of violence.

Verbal aggression: Communications intended to cause harm to others.

Direct aggression: Overt verbal or physical behaviors aimed directly at another person, with the intention to harm.

Stop and Think

In the next section, we examine sex differences in aggression. Before reading further, try to make predictions about what the research shows. Do you think sex differences in aggression will differ by the type of aggression examined? Do you think society considers some forms of aggression to be more serious than others? If so, why?

Are There Sex Differences in Aggression?

Sex Differences in Perpetrating Aggression

Which sex do you think is more aggressive? Gender stereotypes clearly point to men. And in fact, if we examined only violent crime data recorded by law enforcement agencies, men would indeed emerge as the more aggressive sex. But this does not give a complete picture. In this section, we will examine sex differences in physical, verbal, and relational aggression, as well as in cyberbullying. Research on sex differences in each of these types of aggression reveals a bit more nuance and complexity than gender stereotypes would suggest. Let's examine some of these findings.

Indirect (relational) aggression: Behaviors intended to harm another person's social relationships or status, often performed when the target is not physically present.

Violence: Severe forms of physical aggression that have extreme harm as their goal.

Physical aggression. Analyses of crime data reveal that men commit the vast majority of violent crimes. In 2015, men in the United States accounted for about 80% of overall violent crime arrests and about 88% of arrests for murder and non-negligent manslaughter (Federal Bureau of Investigation, 2015c). This pattern of greater male violence holds up across the globe, in countries such as Bangladesh, Chile, Finland, Japan, Malaysia, Oman, Poland, Russia, and Uganda (Agha, 2009). Moreover, although violent crime rates in the United States began a steady decline in 1993 and have remained relatively stable since 2000, young adult men between 18 and 24 years old still commit a dispro-portionate share of violent crimes (A. Cooper & Smith, 2011). Evolutionary psychologists Margo Wilson and Martin Daly (1985) coined the term *young male syndrome* to capture this phenomenon. After examining homicides across many cultures and time periods, they find a remarkably consistent pattern: Men are much more likely to kill (and be killed) in their late teens and early 20s than at any other time in their lives (as an example of this pattern, see Figure 14.1).

Though men account for the vast majority of violent crime arrests in the United States, the proportion of female arrests for violent crime (20%) is not negligible (Federal Bureau of Investigation, 2015c). Female incarceration rates for both violent and non-violent crimes have grown more rapidly than male incarceration rates since the 1980s (Sentencing Project, 2015). White women largely account for the growth in female incarceration, showing a 56% increase from 2000 to 2014, in comparison with a 7% increase for Latina women and a 47% decrease for Black women. Despite this, Latina and Black women remain overrepresented in the incarcerated population. Regardless of race and ethnicity, there are sex differences in the backgrounds of offenders, with incar-cerated female (as compared with male) offenders more often having a background of physical or sexual abuse, mental illness, substance abuse, and economic marginalization

Figure 14.1   Canadian Homicide Rates by Age and Sex of Offender.

These data show the numbers of men and women, across different ages, who were accused of committing homicides in Canada in 2015. Note that men kill at much higher rates than women at all ages. How do these data show evidence for what Wilson and Daly (1985) refer to as *young male syndrome?*

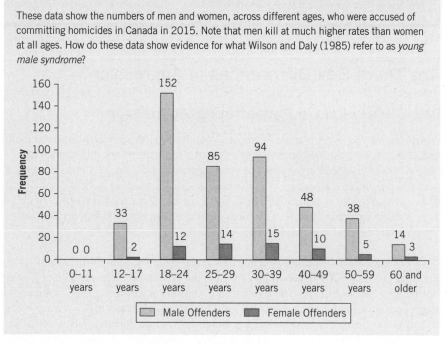

Source: Statistics Canada (2016).

(Sentencing Project, 2007). In fact, the *feminization of poverty*—which, as you may recall, is the tendency for women to experience disproportionate rates of poverty around the world—likely contributes to female crime rates in the United States (Heimer, 2000).

Since extreme physical violence is difficult, if not impossible, to measure in controlled laboratory settings or via surveys, psychologists often focus on less severe forms of physical aggression. Mirroring the violent crime data, boys and men are more physically aggressive than girls and women in both laboratory experiments and real-world settings (Archer, 2004; Knight, Fabes, & Higgins, 1996), and this is true across cultures (Lansford et al., 2012). Though the magnitude of the sex difference in physical aggression varies with contextual factors, it tends to hover in the medium to large range. For instance, an early meta-analysis found a large effect size ($d = 0.72$) for the sex difference in physical aggression (Hyde, 1984b), and a more recent meta-analysis found a medium effect size ($d = 0.59$; Knight, Guthrie, Page, & Fabes, 2002). Sex differences in physical aggression emerge early in life, by about ages 3 to 6, which corresponds with the time that children in most societies begin interacting in organized peer groups.

Sex differences in physical aggression are among the more stable sex differences, showing greater male aggression across direct observation, peer-report, teacher-report, and self-report methods (Archer, 2004). As noted, however, the findings vary based on a number of factors. The sex difference tends to be larger in studies with younger—as compared with older—participants and in studies done in natural—as compared with laboratory—settings (Knight et al., 2002). Moreover, sex differences in lab settings (favoring men) tend to be larger when the aggression is unprovoked than when it is provoked (Bettencourt & Miller, 1996). People may also modify their physical aggression to conform to gender role norms. To illustrate, Jennifer Lightdale and Deborah Prentice (1994) had participants play a video game in which they could drop virtual bombs on an opponent under conditions that either drew attention to their identity (they were singled out and wore a name tag) or did not highlight their identity (they were not singled out and did not wear a name tag). When participants' identity was highlighted, men dropped more bombs than women, presumably to conform to gender norms. However, when participants' identity was not salient, the sex difference vanished, and women behaved just as aggressively as men.

Sidebar 14.1: Young Male Avatar Syndrome?

Playing violent video games is linked with increased aggressive behavior immediately after playing. Does gender matter? Yes, but the character on the screen may matter more than the person playing the game. Researchers assigned college students to play a violent video game (*Street Fighter IV* or *Virtual Fighter 5*) as either a male or female avatar. After gameplay, the participants had an opportunity to aggress against another person in the experiment. Both male and female students who played as male avatars behaved more aggressively than those who played as female avatars (G. S. Yang, Huesmann, & Bushman, 2014).

Verbal aggression. Given that boys and men tend to be physically stronger, on average, than girls and women, it is perhaps not surprising that they display more physical aggression. This does not mean, however, that girls get into fewer conflicts than boys or that girls do not express hostility. In fact, there are no sex differences in tendencies to express anger ($d = -0.04$; Archer, 2004). So when girls and women are motivated by anger to behave aggressively, they may simply rely on more nonphysical means of harming others. For instance, the sex difference found with physical aggression shrinks if we examine direct verbal aggression, such as insults or criticism (see Table 14.1). One meta-analysis found greater male than female verbal aggression, but the effect size was small ($d = 0.19$) for self-reported verbal aggression and even smaller ($d = 0.09$) for observations of

Table 14.1 **Effect Sizes for Sex Differences in Aggression and Anger.** Researchers examine sex differences in physical aggression, verbal aggression, relational aggression, cyberbullying, and anger (an emotion strongly associated with aggression). Most sex differences are close to zero or small, with the exception of the medium effect sizes found for physical aggression.

Type of Aggression (or Anger)	*d*	Size
Physical aggression (Overall)	**0.59**[d]	**Medium**
Self-report	0.59[a]	Medium
Observation	0.55[a]	Medium
Verbal aggression (Overall)	**0.28**[d]	**Small**
Self-report	0.19[a]	Small
Observation	0.09[a]	Close to zero
Relational/indirect aggression (Overall)	**−0.07**[d]	**Close to zero**
Self-report	0.03[c]	Close to zero
Observation	−0.05[c]	Close to zero
Cyberbullying (Overall)	**0.08**[b]	**Close to zero**
Anger (Self-report)	**−0.04**[a]	**Close to zero**

Source: a. Archer (2004); b. Barlett and Coyne (2014); c. Card, Stucky, Sawalani, and Little (2008); d. Knight, Guthrie, Page, and Fabes (2002).

Note: Positive *d* values indicate that boys and men score higher than girls and women; negative *d* values indicate that girls and women score higher than boys and men.

verbal aggression (Archer, 2004). Thus, the sexes use verbal aggression at roughly comparable rates.

Relational aggression. Unlike other animals that rely primarily on direct, physical aggression, humans can use more subtle, sophisticated, and stealthy methods to harm others. With indirect or relational aggression, an individual can harm others through ostracism or social rejection without being identified. Although we do not put people in jail for gossiping about others, indirect aggression can be quite damaging, leading to stress, depression, and even suicide, in extreme cases (Murray-Close, Nelson, Ostrov, Casas, & Crick, 2016).

Relational aggression involves attempts to hurt others using exclusion, gossip, and other social means.

Source: © iStockPhoto .com/Highwaystarz-Photography

As children get older, they tend to rely less on physical aggression and more on indirect means of aggression. Although some early research found that girls used more relational aggression than boys (Björkqvist, Österman, & Lagerspetz, 1994), recent meta-analyses report small or no sex differences in this type of aggression. When small sex differences (favoring women) emerge, they often occur in samples of older participants (e.g., not young children), and with methods other than self-report, such as observation, peer report, and teacher report (Card, Stucky, Sawalani, & Little, 2008; Scheithauser, Haag, Mahlke, & Ittel, 2008). Thus, overall, the evidence does not point to large sex differences in relational aggression. Given the stereotype of "mean girls" who hurt each other with social exclusion and false rumors, does this finding surprise you?

Cyberbullying. With the rise of the digital age, a new way of aggressing has emerged. **Cyberbullying** consists of aggression committed via the Internet, mobile phones, or other types of electronic or digital technologies. One review found that for younger children, girls engaged in more cyberbullying than boys, but after about age 11, boys cyberbullied more than girls. Overall, the sex differences were small ($d = 0.08$; Barlett & Coyne, 2014). Just as with traditional bullying, victimization by cyberbullying correlates with depression, loneliness, low self-esteem, suicidal ideation, and suicide attempts. One study of 2,000 randomly selected middle schoolers found that children who experienced either traditional bullying (e.g., direct verbal aggression) or cyberbullying were almost twice as likely to attempt suicide as those who did not experience bullying (Hinduja & Patchin, 2010). Interestingly, this study also showed that children who bullied others were more likely to attempt suicide than those who did not bully. Given that these are correlational data, we cannot conclude that either bullying or being bullied *causes* negative mental health outcomes. Nonetheless, the take-home point is that any involvement in bullying, either as perpetrator or as victim, is associated with increased suicide risk.

Cyberbullying: Verbal or relational aggression committed via the Internet, mobile phones, or other types of electronic or digital technologies.

Consider the differences between traditional bully-ing and cyberbullying, especially in terms of pre-vention. Which of these types of bullying is more

difficult to address and decrease? Why? What specific strategies might be effective in reducing the rates of cyberbullying?

Sex Differences in Experiencing Aggression

Our attention so far has primarily been on the sex of aggressors, but what about the targets of aggression? Which sex is more likely to experience aggression? Meta-analyses of laboratory studies reveal that both men and women aggress more toward men than toward women (Archer, 2004). Crime statistics also bear this out: Men are more likely than women to be victims of almost all types of violent crimes, including homicides, assaults, and armed robberies (Truman & Langton, 2015).

But do these findings of greater male victimization hold across the board, regard-less of characteristics such as sexual orientation and race or ethnicity? A recent meta-analysis found that male sexual minority individuals experience various forms of aggression (property damage, threats, and verbal harassment) more often than female sexual minority individuals (Katz-Wise & Hyde, 2012). The same meta-analysis also found that sexual minority individuals, in comparison with heterosexual individuals, tend to experience more violence, though most effect sizes were in the small range. The pattern of greater male victimization also holds within race and ethnicity for Black, Latino, and White people, meaning that men in each of these groups tend to experience more violent crime than their female counterparts (Lauritsen & Heimer, 2009). Moreover, since the 1970s, rates of violent crime victimization in the United States have typically been highest among Black people, followed by Latino people, and then White people.

There are two exceptions to the general trend toward greater male victimization, and we will discuss both in more detail later in this chapter: sexual assaults (including rape) and intimate partner violence. Women and girls constitute the vast majority of targets of sexual aggression (Black et al., 2011), and men and women appear roughly equally likely to suffer intimate partner violence (although researchers fiercely debate the evidence for sex differences versus similarities in intimate partner violence). Thus, the overall pattern of greater male victimization is found for many—but not all—types of aggression.

What's the Big Picture?

So what do we conclude about sex differences in aggression? People of all sexes com-mit aggressive acts, but the nature of sex differences in aggression depends on the type of aggression measured, the age of the sample, and the setting in which the aggression takes place. Boys and men exhibit more physical aggression and extreme violence than girls and women, although certain factors can increase or decrease these differences. However, studies of direct verbal and indirect relational aggression show smaller sex differences. When girls and women use aggression, they tend to use less physical forms of it. Finally, many forms of aggression—except sexual aggression and intimate partner violence—target boys and men more than girls and women.

What Are the Major Forms of Gender-Based Aggression and Violence?

In this section, we consider several specific forms of aggression as gendered acts. These forms of aggression, best understood by considering gendered power structures, often reflect male violence against women: rape, honor killings, sexual harassment, and aggressive pornography. Others, such as intimate partner violence, may target men and women equally but still reflect gender dynamics. Please be aware that some of this material is difficult to read, particularly for those who have personal experiences with aggression and violence. Keep in mind, though, that the research described here seeks to increase knowledge so that we can address and reduce the problem of gender-based violence.

Intimate Partner Violence

Intimate partner violence refers to any behavior intended to cause physical harm to a romantic partner. The earliest research on intimate partner violence framed it largely in terms of male violence against women, as reflected in language such as *wife beating* and *battered wives*. Even today, researchers direct most of their attention toward violence against women in heterosexual relationships. The World Health Organization (WHO, 2013) reports that 30% of women around the world experience physical violence by a partner at some point in their lives, and as many as 38% of all murders of women are committed by intimate partners. In the United States, 35.6% of women and 28.5% of men are victims of intimate partner violence at some point in their lives (Breiding, Chen, & Black, 2014). These rates vary by race and ethnicity in the United States, with Native American, multiracial, and Black people experiencing higher average rates of intimate partner violence than Latino, White, and Asian people (see Figure 14.2 for lifetime rates of intimate partner violence by sex and race/ethnicity).

Intimate partner violence tends to occur with similar severity and prevalence in same-sex relationships—both female and male—as it does in heterosexual relationships (Ofreneo & Montiel, 2010). Moreover, as you read earlier, some data indicate that women and men are roughly equally likely to be victims of intimate partner violence. However, the issue of sex differences in intimate partner violence is hotly debated. For more on this, see "Debate: Do Men Perpetrate Intimate Partner Violence More Often Than Women?"

Intimate partner violence: Any behavior intended to cause physical harm to a romantic partner.

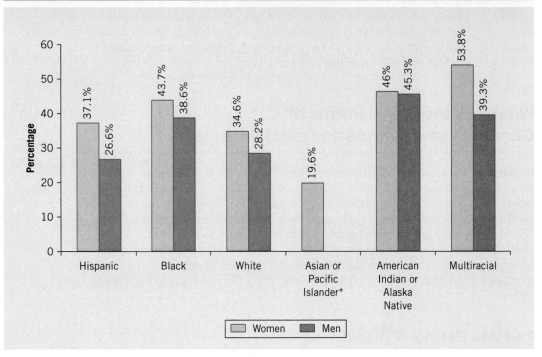

Source: Breiding, Chen, and Black (2014).

Note: No data available for Asian or Pacific Islander males.

Situational couple violence: Intimate partner violence that results when heated conflicts escalate; committed by men and women about equally.

Intimate terrorism: Intimate partner violence in which one partner (usually a man) repeatedly uses violence and fear to dominate and control the other.

Situational couple violence versus intimate terrorism. How can we resolve these conflicting estimates of the frequency of male and female partner violence raised in the debate? According to Michael Johnson (2008), the resolution involves recognizing two distinct forms of intimate partner violence. The most frequent type, called **situational couple violence**, occurs when heated conflicts get out of hand and escalate unpredictably into violence. This type of violence is relatively unlikely to result in serious injury to either partner. In contrast, **intimate terrorism** is relatively rarer and occurs when one partner consistently uses violence and fear to dominate and control the other. In intimate terrorism, aggression tends to escalate in severity over time, sometimes resulting in serious injury. Women perpetrate situational couple violence at slightly higher rates than men, but men perpetrate intimate terrorism far more frequently than women (Archer, 2000). Thus, perhaps the gender symmetry hypothesis better explains situational couple violence while the gender asymmetry hypothesis better explains intimate terrorism.

When you think about violence in intimate relationships, what do you picture? Many people think of the perpetrators as men and the targets as women. We have shelters for abused women, organizations dedicated to eradicating domestic violence against women, and federal laws to combat violence against women, such as the U.S. Violence Against Women Act (1994/2013). However, both men and women perpetrate and experience intimate partner violence. The debate over sex differences in intimate partner violence is unresolved and heated. Let's examine both sides.

Women and Men Commit Intimate Partner Violence in Equal Numbers

Despite the stereotypes of male batterers and female victims, the *gender symmetry* perspective holds that women and men physically assault their partners in roughly equal numbers, with largely parallel risk factors and motivations (Straus, 2009). Research in the United States dating back to the 1970s confirms that women show as much, if not more, physical aggression in intimate relationships as men, with one national survey showing that women initiate intimate partner violence in 53% of cases, compared with men in 42% of cases (Straus, 2005).

To counter this evidence, some argue that women commit aggression in self-defense, but this does not capture the complete picture. While researchers estimate that approximately 25%–30% of women's relationship violence is committed in self-defense (Straus, 2005), women report many other motivations as well, such as responding to verbal provocation, retaliating, and gaining control (Langhinrichsen-Rohling, 2010). Similarly, Whitaker

and colleagues found mutual violence (committed by both partners) to be the most common pattern among U.S. couples, but when it came to nonreciprocal violence (committed by just one partner), women were the perpetrators in 70% of cases (Whitaker, Haileyesus, Swahn, & Saltzman, 2007). This clearly contradicts the perspective that intimate partner violence is an expression of male dominance.

The gender symmetry perspective argues that similar mechanisms drive the violence of men and women and that viewing intimate partner violence as a patriarchal form of control over women both ignores and trivializes violence against men. In fact, men who experience intimate partner violence are at increased risk for posttraumatic stress disorder, depression, and suicidal ideation (Randle & Graham, 2011). Men's rights advocates claim that focusing primarily on heterosexual women as victims of intimate partner violence unjustly misdirects policy efforts.

Men Commit Intimate Partner Violence More Often (and More Extremely) Than Women

Proponents of the *gender asymmetry* perspective often frame the issue of intimate partner violence as one of men's dominative control of women. Because men are larger and stronger than women, and they possess more social power, it follows that they sometimes use violence as a tool of control in relationships. From this perspective, intimate partner violence is a gendered act that reinforces men's power over women (Dobash & Dobash, 1979; recall our discussion of these issues in Chapter 6, "Power, Sexism, and Discrimination").

(Continued)

(Continued)

While survey research in Western, industrialized nations finds that women perpetrate slightly more aggression in heterosexual relationships than men (Archer, 2000), this partly reflects how researchers measure intimate partner violence. For example, studies that find gender symmetry in intimate partner violence often do not measure acts such as stalking and sexual violence, which are perpetrated more frequently by men (Saunders, 2002). Furthermore, simply tallying up how many people report intimate partner violence ignores important information, such as the severity of the physical aggression that people use. For instance, men tend to injure their partners more often than women do. One national U.S. survey found that although men and women reported similar rates of victimization overall, almost twice as many women as men (39% of women and 21% of men) experienced injury in their most recent incident of violence (I. Arias & Corso, 2005). Similarly, women report more fear of their partners than men do (Caldwell, Swan, & Woodbrown, 2012), and women victims of intimate partner violence more frequently end up in emergency rooms and domestic violence shelters. In other words, the meanings and consequences of intimate partner violence differ across the sexes.

Proponents of the gender asymmetry perspective also note that men kill their spouses more than women do, particularly in countries outside of the United States (Dobash, Dobash, Wilson, & Daly, 1992). The motives for male and female spousal homicides differ as well. Men who kill their spouses typically do so after suspecting infidelity, perpetrating long periods of intimidation and abuse, and being left by their spouses. In contrast, wives are more likely to kill their husbands following years of abuse and out of self-defense or fear (Saunders, 2002).

Finally, the gender symmetry in partner violence found in Western nations does not appear to generalize to other nations (Archer, 2006). In countries with less gender equality, women experience more—and men experience less—intimate partner violence. Proponents of the gender asymmetry position argue that it is therefore misguided and dangerous to view intimate partner violence as gender neutral. As long as power differences exist within relationships, women will bear the brunt of partner violence.

Now that you have read both sides of this debate, what do you think? Which evidence do you find most convincing? Why?

Sexual Violence: Rape and Sexual Assault

Sexual assault:
Unwanted sexual contact without the explicit consent of the victim.

Rape:
Nonconsensual penetration of the mouth, vagina, or anus by the penis, fingers, or objects.

Sexual violence can take many forms, and addressing it can be challenging due to varying definitions and understandings of constructs like force, consent, and coercion. Complicating matters further, legal definitions of rape and sexual assault differ from place to place. **Sexual assault** is usually used as a general term to mean unwanted sexual contact without the explicit consent of the victim, whereas **rape** tends to be defined more narrowly as the nonconsensual penetration of the mouth, vagina, or anus by a penis, finger, or object (Koss & Kilpatrick, 2001). Thus, rape is a form of sexual assault, but not all sexual assault is rape. Note, however, that cultures and subcultures differ widely in terms of how readily they tolerate—or even normalize—acts that some would define as rape. For example, some sexual acts, although unwanted by their targets, may occur as part of long-standing cultural rituals. Such customs include arranged child marriages, which involve what many would consider child rape; forced prostitution; and forced virginity examinations (nonconsensual gynecological examinations that assess whether a girl or woman has had vaginal intercourse). We will discuss some of these customs further in a later section (see "Power and Structural Gender Inequality").

Sidebar 14.2: What Is "Consent"?

Consent means that all parties have a clear and unambiguous agreement, expressed outwardly through mutually understandable words or actions, to engage in sexual activity. Consent is thus about communication. To clarify what consent does and does not entail, the Rape Abuse and Incest National Network (RAINN, 2016) offers the following guidelines.

- A person must have the freedom and capacity to give consent.

- A person facing intimidation (like someone in an abusive relationship) or under pressure from a person in power does not have the freedom to give consent.

- A person who is incapacitated by drugs or alcohol, asleep, or unconscious does not have the capacity to give consent.

- Consent can be verbal or nonverbal.

- Consent can be withdrawn at any time.

- Consent to engage in one sexual activity does not mean consent to engage in a different sexual activity, and past consent to engage in a sexual activity does not mean consent to engage in future sexual activities.

- Marriage does not automatically mean consent is given for sexual activity.

- Consent cannot be assumed by the way a person dresses, smiles, or flirts.

How common is sexual violence? Due to its personal, distressing, and stigmatizing nature, sexual violence is among the most underreported crimes, which makes it challenging to estimate its prevalence accurately. Furthermore, many agencies focus solely on reporting sexual violence rates for women. The WHO estimates that one in three women worldwide experiences some form of physical or sexual violence (WHO, 2016) and that 7% of women are sexually assaulted by someone other than a partner (WHO, 2013). The regions of the world with the highest rates of rape include North America, southern Africa, and Oceania, and the regions with the lowest rates of rape include South Asia, the Near and Middle East, and Central Asia (Harrendorf, Heiskanen, & Malby, 2010). Globally, rape rates have been increasing since 1996 (although Canada and the United States show the reverse pattern), and the countries with the highest rates of rape are South Africa, Australia, and Swaziland.

Certain individuals have a higher risk of being raped in their lifetime than others, with race and ethnicity playing a role in these prevalence rates. In the United States, 18.3% of women (about 22 million women) and 1.4% of men (about 1.6 million men) report being raped at least once in their lifetime. Multiracial women in the United States are more likely to be raped (33.5%) than Native American women (26.9%), Black women (22.0%), White women (18.8%), and Latina women (14.6%; Black et al., 2011). The race of male perpetrators also differs with the race of rape victims: Native American women are most frequently sexually assaulted by White men, whereas Black and White women are most frequently assaulted by same-race men (Luna-Firebaugh, 2006). Latinas generally experience lower rates of sexual assault than White, Black, Asian, and Native American women, although U.S.-born Latinas experience higher rates of sexual assault in the United States than foreign-born immigrant or migrant worker Latinas (Hazen & Soriano, 2007).

Women's status as empowered versus marginalized matters as well. Between one-third and two-thirds of sexual assault victims around the world are 15 years old or younger (Heise, Ellsberg, & Gottmoeller, 2002), and girls and women with developmental disabilities experience relatively high rates of sexual assaults (Reiter, Bryen, & Shachar, 2007). Women who live in poverty or experience homelessness have higher rates of sexual assault (Abbey, Jacques-Tiura, & Parkhill, 2010). Sex workers are also at a heightened risk for sexual violence, partly because this work is illegal in many countries, giving workers little protection from the legal system (Deering et al., 2014). Vulnerable undocumented immigrants and refugees similarly experience a heightened risk of sexual assault, often as they flee military conflicts at home, and legal and language barriers may prevent them from seeking or obtaining help (Hynes & Lopes Cardozo, 2000). People living in areas of military conflict become frequent targets as well because soldiers sometimes use rape as a strategy to undermine community bonds and weaken enemy resistance (D. K. Cohen, 2013). In short, being young, female, marginalized, and disempowered places individuals at a higher risk of sexual assault.

Rates of sexual assault also differ across gendered social contexts. For example, military contexts are typically male-dominated settings characterized by strict hierarchies, strong loyalty ties, and values of toughness and aggressiveness (Turchik & Wilson, 2010). In such settings, sexual assault rates of both women and men tend to be relatively high, and powerful norms discourage victims from reporting assaults. One study of over 5,200 students at three U.S. military academies found that 24% of women and 8% of men were sexually assaulted in the past year, and 5% of women and 2% of men were raped in the past year (Snyder, Fisher, Scherer, & Daigle, 2012). Moreover, 45% of female and 12% of male sexual assault victims reported **polyvictimization**, meaning that they experienced more than one type of aggressive victimization (e.g., sexual assault, physical abuse, and bullying). Not surprisingly, polyvictimization predicts more severe trauma symptoms, even in comparison with repeated exposure to the same type of aggression (H. A. Turner, Finkelhour, & Ormrod, 2010).

Polyvictimization: Experiencing more than one type of aggressive victimization.

Sexual assault is also quite common on college campuses, particularly for women. Alcohol intoxication plays a substantial role in this, with approximately 50% of all sexual assaults involving alcohol use by the perpetrator, victim, or both (Abbey, Zawacki, Buck, Clinton, & McAuslan, 2004). Recall from the beginning of the chapter that 27% of U.S. college senior women across 27 different universities reported experiencing nonconsensual sexual contact since entering college (AAU, 2015). These numbers are consistent with those in a 2007 survey of over 6,800 students at two large U.S. universities in which 19.0% of women and 6.1% of men experienced attempted or completed sexual assault

Sidebar 14.3: Rape as a Weapon of War

Chinese and Malaysian girls forced to serve as sexual slaves (known as "comfort women") for Japanese troops during World War II.

Source: By Lemon A E (Sergeant), No 9 Army Film & Photographic Unit

Throughout history and to the present day, rape is often used in war as a weapon to terrorize and demoralize the enemy and as an instrument of ethnic cleansing. Before and during World War II, the Japanese Imperial Army forced "comfort women" from occupied East and Southeast Asian countries into prostitution. In the Kosovo war in the late 1990s, Serbian and Yugoslav forces frequently used rape to terrorize civilians and force ethnic Albanians out of Kosovo. While the Geneva Conventions of 1949 did not mention rape or sexual violence by name, they did classify torture and inhumane treatment as *grave breaches* (war crimes). It was not until the late 1990s, with the Yugoslav and Rwandan Tribunals, that rape was explicitly codified as a crime against humanity, which resulted in more systematic enforcement of rules against rape as a war crime (Paterson, 2016).

since entering college. In comparison with other racial and ethnic groups, Black women in this survey were more likely to be sexually assaulted through physical force, whereas White women were more likely to be sexually assaulted when they were incapacitated with drugs or alcohol (Krebs, Lindquist, Warner, Fisher, & Martin, 2007). Moreover, as mentioned in the chapter opening, gender minority students are particularly vulnerable to sexual assault, with 39.1% of transgender, genderqueer, gender-nonconforming, and "questioning" seniors reporting nonconsensual sexual contact (AAU, 2015).

Note that self-reports of rape underestimate its actual frequency for several reasons. For instance, **unacknowledged rape** is a phenomenon in which individuals have experiences that meet legal definitions of rape without labeling their experience as such. Consider an individual who was intoxicated during a rape, an individual who did not fight back or say "no" despite not giving consent, or an individual who was dating or married to the perpetrator at the time of the assault. Because these scenarios do not match stereotypical scripts for rape (e.g., a stranger forcefully attacking someone who fights back and says "No!"), people who experience them may not identify them as rape. Some estimates indicate that up to 73% of women and 76% of men who experience rape do not label their experiences as rape (Artime, McCallum, & Peterson, 2014; Littleton, Rhatigan, & Axsom, 2007). What accounts for unacknowledged rape? One predictor is endorsement of **rape myths**, or false beliefs about rape, rape victims,

Unacknowledged rape: An experience that meets the legal definition of rape but is not labeled as rape by the victim.

Rape myths: Widely held false beliefs about rape, rape victims, and rapists.

and rapists (Suarez & Gadalla, 2010). People who more strongly endorse rape myths tend to interpret sexual violence as "rape" less often, especially if it involves circumstances that do not match their typical scripts for rape (Sasson & Paul, 2014). See Table 14.2 for some common rape myths.

Table 14.2 Some Common Rape Myths. Rape myths are false beliefs about rape, rape victims, and rapists. People who more strongly endorse these beliefs are less likely to label acts as *rape* even when they meet legal definitions of rape, and they are also more likely to blame rape victims for their own assault.

- Women often make false reports of rape.
- Only "bad" women get raped; therefore, women who get raped must have deserved it.
- Men can't be raped.
- Rape usually occurs between strangers.
- If a woman doesn't resist, it isn't rape.
- Only certain kinds of people get raped.
- A lot of women lead a man on and then cry rape.
- Many women secretly desire to be raped.
- Women are almost never raped by their boyfriends.
- Rapists are usually sexually frustrated individuals.

Source: M. R. Burt (1980); Payne, Lonsway, and Fitzgerald (1999).

Stop and Think

Why do you think that there is sometimes a discrepancy between legal definitions of rape and people's tendency to label their own experiences as rape?

What do you think this gap reflects? What steps could be taken to decrease this discrepancy?

Who commits sexual violence? Some stereotypes about rape and rapists ring true. For instance, most rapists are men. In a nationally representative survey of U.S. residents, men committed 98.1% of rapes of girls and women and 93.3% of rapes of boys and men (Black et al., 2011). But unlike common scripts for rape, most sexual assaults do not involve an armed stranger who surprises his victim. Rapists use weapons in only about 11% of assaults, and rape targets typically know their offenders. In the United States, only 22% of sexual assaults are committed by strangers, in contrast to 38% committed by acquaintances, 34% by intimate partners, and 6% by relatives. Also in the United States, 48% of sexual assault perpetrators are age 30 or older, and 57% are White (Planty, Langton, Krebs, Berzofsky, & Smiley-McDonald, 2013). In a later section ("What Explains Gender-Based Aggression and Violence?"), we will dig deeper into some explanations for sexual violence and gender-based aggression.

The aftermath of sexual violence. Experiencing sexual violence has serious impacts on psychological and physical health in both women and men. In a nationally representative sample of adults in the United States, sexual violence victimization predicted higher rates of depression, anxiety disorders, concentration problems, agitation, sleep problems, and energy loss among both women and men (Choudhary, Smith, & Bossarte, 2012). Another U.S. study of predominantly low-income, Black women veterans found that sexual and intimate partner violence victimization predicted physical symptoms, such as back pain, pelvic pain, fatigue, and nausea (R. Campbell, Greeson, Bybee, & Raja, 2008). In a study of rape in South Africa, a country with one of the highest sexual violence rates in the world, rural women reported elevated levels of depression following rape, which increased over time, especially if their social support systems became critical and disapproving after the rape (Wyatt et al., 2017).

As mentioned, sexual violence is an underreported crime. National surveys in both the United Kingdom and the United States reveal that only 20%–34% of people who experience sexual violence report their assaults to law enforcement authorities (Sinozich & Langton, 2014; Walby & Allen, 2004). A study of female college students in the United States showed that only 5% reported their assault to police or campus authorities, although almost 70% disclosed their victimization informally to someone else, usually a friend. When survivors do not report sexual assault to police, their reasons include fears that they lack adequate proof, police will not take them seriously, their families will find out, and the perpetrators will retaliate. In one sample, Black women—in comparison with Hispanic and White women—were more likely to report their sexual victimization to the police, and people reported more stereotypical incidents of sexual assault (e.g., perpetrated by a stranger or with a weapon) to the police more often than less stereotypical incidents (B. S. Fisher, Daigle, Cullen, & Turner, 2003).

A culture of victim blaming also contributes to the underreporting of sexual assault crimes, and examples of victim blaming permeate the media. Consider this headline from a Montreal newspaper regarding a gang rape of a 15-year-old girl: "Presumed gang-rape victim had consumed too much alcohol" (Drimonis, 2017). Similarly, following a 2012 case in Steubenville, Ohio, in which two high school football players kidnapped and raped a 16-year-old girl, some members of the community blamed the girl for her assault because she had been drinking (Macur & Schweber, 2012). In fact, people judge female rape victims who have been drinking—in comparison with those who have not—as more responsible for their assault (Sims, Noel, & Maisto, 2007). Furthermore, men generally assign more blame to rape victims than women do, and White men assign more blame to Black than to White female rape victims (Donovan, 2007). People also blame gay male rape victims more than heterosexual male rape victims for their assaults (White & Yamawaki, 2009).

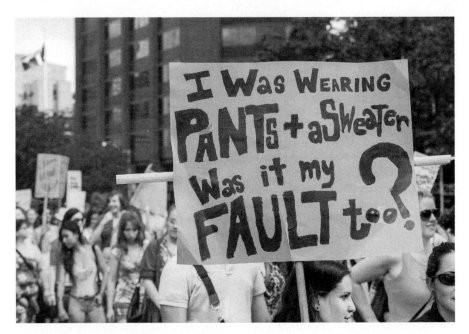

A protest against sexual violence in Toronto. This sign draws attention to the practice of blaming rape victims based on their clothing or appearance.

Source: © iStockPhoto.com/jentakespictures

False rape allegations: Accusations of rape that the accuser knows to be false.

What about **false rape allegations**, in which a person knowingly accuses an innocent individual of rape? How often does this occur? It is difficult to determine the number of false rape allegations accurately because it requires distinguishing between mistaken reports of rape that the accuser believes to be true (involving mistaken identity, for instance) and false allegations that the accuser knows to be false. That said, the results of a recent meta-analysis estimated that 5.2% of rape allegations are false (C. E. Ferguson & Malouff, 2016). Thus, false allegations of rape are quite rare and are comparable to rates of false allegations of other felonies, such as murder (Gross, 2008).

Much more often, rapists get away with their crimes without facing an investigation, trial, or jail time. Only a minority of reported rape cases results in the successful prosecution of the offender (Morris, 2013). However, the race and ethnicity of the perpetrator makes a difference in rates of successful prosecution of rape cases. While more than half of sexual assault perpetrators in the United States are White (Planty et al., 2013), White people are disproportionately less likely to be arrested for rape while Black and Latino people are disproportionately more likely to be arrested for rape (Federal Bureau of Investigation, 2015d). And when White people of privilege are arrested and even convicted of rape, they may receive more lenient sentences than racial and ethnic minority perpetrators. A recent example is found in the case of Brock Turner, a 19-year-old White Stanford student who sexually assaulted an unconscious 22-year-old woman in 2015. Although Turner was convicted of three felony counts of sexual assault and his convictions carried a 2-year minimum sentence, the judge gave him 6 months in county jail out of concern (among other reasons) that his future would be negatively impacted by a prison sentence ("Stanford Sexual Assault," 2016). Thinking back to Chapter 6 ("Power, Sexism, and Discrimination"), the tendency to prosecute and sentence dominant versus subordinate group members differentially for sexual assault may reflect a hierarchical social structure in which White people exert power over racial and ethnic minority individuals through the penal system.

Given the gravity of the sexual assault problem in the United States and around the world, education and prevention efforts are critical. Positive steps are slowly being taken, with an increase in initiatives and organizations addressing sexual assault. For example, in 2005, the Department of Defense formally approved a Sexual Assault Prevention and Response Policy and established the Sexual Assault Prevention and Response Office to oversee the policy. They also trained thousands of sexual assault response coordinators who act as first responders when dealing with sexual assault in the military. In 2014, the Obama-Biden administration launched the It's On Us initiative, an awareness and education campaign to end sexual assault on college campuses. In addition to recruiting celebrities to make public service announcements, the campaign challenged college students across the United States to become active participants in preventing sexual assault. By 2015, over 250,000 college students had signed a pledge to do the following: (a) intervene to prevent sexual assault when it is happening, (b) recognize that if no consent is given, then the act is sexual assault, and (c) create a new culture that supports survivors and rejects sexual assault. Beyond the United States, UN Women, a United Nations organization dedicated to gender equality and the empowerment of women, specifically addresses the problem of sexual violence worldwide. This group launched initiatives around the globe to increase survivors' access to services, influence the adoption of laws and policies that protect survivors and punish perpetrators, and create safe spaces where women and girls can be free from sex-based harassment and violence.

Sex-Based Harassment

Another form of gendered aggression, **sex-based harassment** (or **sexual harassment**), refers to behavior that derogates or humiliates an individual based on the individual's sex, sexual orientation, or gender identity. Sex-based harassment includes unwanted touching, sexual gestures, catcalls, comments, or jokes, as well as bullying and insults. Though not a new phenomenon, sex-based harassment first received a label in the 1970s (Rowe, 1981) and did not gain much attention in organizations and courts in the United States until the 1980s. Although researchers originally used the term *sexual harassment*, we use *sex-based harassment* instead. As you may recall from Chapter 11 ("Work and Home"), Jennifer Berdahl (2007) recommends this label as a way of avoiding confusion because sex-based harassment does not always involve sexual comments or behavior.

Despite the psychological harm it causes, sex-based harassment is frequently tolerated as normal, even in countries where it is illegal, such as the United States. Federal law in the United States recognizes two types of sex-based harassment: quid pro quo and hostile environment. *Quid pro quo harassment* occurs when a person

Sex-based harassment (sexual harassment): Behavior that derogates or humiliates an individual based on the individual's sex, sexual orientation, or gender identity.

with power offers advantages (e.g., a promotion) in exchange for sexual favors. *Hostile environment harassment* refers to negative speech (e.g., sexist jokes) or behavior (e.g., gestures) that creates an intimidating or offensive environment, and it often occurs between individuals of equal status (Maass, Cadinu, & Galdi, 2013). In addition, psychologists typically divide sex-based harassment into three different types of behavior: *gender harassment* (making sexual or sexist remarks or gestures; displaying sexual or sexist materials), *unwanted sexual attention* (initiating unwanted sexual discussions or touching), and *sexual coercion* (compelling sexual favors through job threats or rewards). Note that sexual coercion aligns more with quid pro quo harassment, whereas gender harassment and unwanted sexual attention map more onto hostile environment harassment.

Though sex-based harassment can occur anywhere, it is typically studied in workplace, school, and military settings, where it occurs fairly commonly. In the workplace, estimated sex-based harassment rates for women hover in the 40%–60% range, whereas rates for men range from 10%–20%. These rates vary based on the type of harassment, with sexual coercion being the least frequent type (Berdahl & Raver, 2011; Feldblum & Lipnic, 2016). In middle and high school settings in the United States, approximately 56% of girls and 40% of boys experience sex-based harassment per year, with the most frequent type being unwelcome comments, jokes, and gestures (C. Hill & Kearl, 2011). In the military, 22% of female and 7% of male active service members report experiencing sex-based harassment in the past year (Farris et al., 2016). Sexual jokes are the most common form of harassment of female service members, whereas being accused of not acting masculine enough is the most common harassment of male service members. Despite the higher rates of sex-based harassment reported by girls and women, men tend to underestimate the amount of harassment that the women in their lives experience, as shown in Figure 14.3 (PerryUndem, 2017).

Sidebar 14.4: Street Harassment in the United States

Street harassment:
Uninvited sexual attention or harassment from a stranger in a public space.

Street harassment consists of uninvited sexual attention or harassment from a stranger in a public space. In 2014, a nationally representative survey of 2,000 U.S. adults revealed that 65% of women and 25% of men experienced street harassment in their lifetime (Kearl, 2014). Rates of street harassment were higher for Latino and Black than White respondents, and they were higher for LGBT than heterosexual and cisgender respondents. The majority of respondents who experienced any street harassment experienced it more than once, and most (52%) reported that their first experience occurred by the age of 17. Many of those who experience street harassment fear that it will escalate, and this can prevent people from having equal and safe access to public spaces.

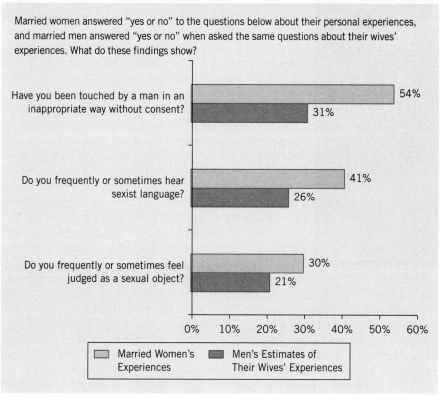

Figure 14.3 Men's Estimates of Women's Sex-Based Harassment Experiences.

Married women answered "yes or no" to the questions below about their personal experiences, and married men answered "yes or no" when asked the same questions about their wives' experiences. What do these findings show?

Have you been touched by a man in an inappropriate way without consent? 54% / 31%

Do you frequently or sometimes hear sexist language? 41% / 26%

Do you frequently or sometimes feel judged as a sexual object? 30% / 21%

0% 10% 20% 30% 40% 50% 60%

Married Women's Experiences

Men's Estimates of Their Wives' Experiences

Source: PerryUndem (2017).

Stop and Think

How do we determine which specific behaviors and comments constitute sex-based harassment? Some seem easy to identify as harassment (e.g., demanding sex from an employee), whereas others seem less clear-cut (e.g., commenting on how gorgeous a coworker looks). In defining harassment, how do we account for the fact that people differ in what they find offensive? What factors must be considered in developing a clear definition of sexual harassment?

Bari-Ellen Roberts, a financial analyst at Texaco, was subjected to racialized sex-based harassment at work. She became the lead plaintiff in a class action lawsuit against Texaco, and in 1996, Texaco was forced to pay out $176 million to 1,500 current and former Black employees for racial discrimination.

Source: Ted Thai/The LIFE Images Collection/ Getty Images

Race and ethnicity can interact with sex to produce unique harassment experiences, such as *racialized sex-based harassment*, which involves incidents where race-based and sex-based harassment are simultaneously present. Consider the case of Bari-Ellen Roberts, a Black female employee at Texaco who was called "a smart-mouthed little colored girl" by three White male Texaco senior executives during a board meeting (B.-E. Roberts & White, 1998). As other examples, some Black women report that White male coworkers use phrases in their presence such as "sexy black ass" or "big, sexy, Black women" (Buchanan & Ormerod, 2002, p. 115) while Latina women report coworkers' use of inappropriate pet names for them, such as "mamacita" (Cortina, 2001, pp. 167–168). This type of racialized sex-based harassment predicts higher job stress, lower job satisfaction, and increased depression and anxiety among Black women and Latinas (Buchanan & Fitzgerald, 2008; Cortina, Fitzgerald, & Drasgow, 2002).

Sexual orientation and gender identity interact with sex to impact the nature of sex-based harassment, as you may recall from Chapter 11 ("Work and Home"). In a study of workplace climate for LGBT employees in the United States, the majority (58%) reported overhearing derogatory comments or jokes about LGBT individuals (Human Rights Campaign, 2009). Moreover, of transgender individuals who are open about their identity at work, 47% experience adverse job consequences (e.g., being fired or denied a promotion), and 78% experience other forms of discrimination or mistreatment due to their transgender or gender-nonconforming identities. This mistreatment is more pronounced for transgender people of color (Grant et al., 2011).

Rates of sex-based harassment also vary by culture. In a survey of women in 16 of the world's largest cities, Bogota, Mexico City, Lima, and Delhi were rated as having the most dangerous public transportation systems for women (in terms of being able to travel safely without being verbally harassed or attacked), and New York, Tokyo, Beijing, and London were rated as having the safest public transportation systems for women (Thomson Reuters Foundation, 2014). Some research suggests that sex-based harassment is more common in cultures with greater **power distance** and higher levels of *collectivism*. Power distance is the extent to which a culture has and accepts unequal distributions of status and power among its members (Hofstede, 2001) while collectivism is a cultural orientation in which group needs are prioritized over individual needs. (You may recall reading about collectivistic cultures in Chapter 5, "The Contents and Origins of Gender Stereotypes.") For instance, China and India are high in power distance and collectivism, and men in these countries report being more likely to commit sex-based harassment than are men in the United States (Luthar & Luthar, 2008). Furthermore, people from Pakistan, Ecuador, the Philippines, Taiwan, and Turkey (collectivistic, high-power-distance cultures) assign more blame to victims of sex-based harassment and less blame to perpetrators than people from Canada, Germany, the Netherlands, and the United States (individualistic, low-power-distance cultures). This may reflect the greater tendency in individualistic cultures to protect individual rights in contrast to the greater tendency in collectivistic cultures to preserve social harmony (Sigal et al., 2005).

Jennifer Berdahl (2007) proposes that the primary motivation for sex-based harassment is the desire to protect one's own sex-based status and to punish people who deviate from traditional gender roles (recall our discussion of this topic in Chapter 11, "Work and Home"). For instance, women who have more agentic traits, are less feminine, or who identify as feminists have a heightened risk for sex-based harassment (Maass, Cadinu, Guarnieri, & Grasselli, 2003). Similarly, women in male-dominated organizations experience more harassment than women in female-dominated organizations. Why? Some researchers propose that women's presence in male-dominated organizations threatens men's gender identity or challenges the legitimacy of men's higher social status. In fact, men in one experiment committed more sex-based harassment toward a woman after they experienced a threat to their masculinity (Maass et al., 2003). And as noted, men who violate gender role norms more frequently experience sex-based harassment, typically at the hands of other men. For instance, fathers who are active caregivers report being harassed at work for not being "manly" enough (Berdahl & Moon, 2013).

Power distance: The extent to which a culture has and accepts unequally distributed levels of status and power among its members.

What Explains Gender-Based Aggression and Violence?

How can we make sense of various forms of gender-based aggression? To understand the causes of gender-based aggression, some researchers focus on person-level, individual factors. For example, individuals who experienced childhood abuse or witnessed domestic violence as children are more likely to perpetrate intimate partner violence as adults (Whitefield, Anda, Dube, & Felitti, 2003). Furthermore, individuals who have difficulty regulating their emotions tend to perpetrate more intimate partner violence (Shorey, Brasfield, Febres, & Stuart, 2011), as do men who abuse alcohol and who hold hostile, sexist attitudes about women (Renzetti, Lynch, & DeWall, 2015). Hostile attitudes toward women also play a role in men's sexual assault tendencies. According to the *confluence model of sexual aggression*, two primary factors that predict men's sexual aggression against women are hostile attitudes toward women and a preference for impersonal sex that lacks emotional closeness (Malamuth, Linz, Heavey, Barnes, & Acker, 1995). These two factors jointly predict male-to-female sexual assault among college students, community samples, and convicted sex offenders (Forbes, Adams-Curtis, & White, 2004; Widman, Olson, & Bolen, 2013). Other risk factors for sexual assault perpetration among college men include having more adverse childhood events, having more antisocial personality traits, engaging in more risky behavior, and approving of the use of alcohol to gain sexual compliance (G. H. Burgess, 2007; Zinzow & Thompson, 2015). Finally, the greater average physical size and strength of men relative to women likely plays a role in their greater tendencies toward gender-based aggression. In general, the larger the person, the more likely he or she is to behave aggressively, both between and within the sexes. This likely occurs because smaller individuals risk greater injury when they aggress (DeWall, Bushman, Giancola, & Webster, 2010).

Despite these individual risk factors, no single profile of a violent person can accurately describe all perpetrators of violence. With a phenomenon as complex as gender-based aggression, individual-level factors cannot provide a full explanation. Some researchers thus look beyond individual factors and take a more comprehensive view of interactive forces that underlie gender-based aggression. In this section, we consider factors ranging from the biological to the sociocultural.

Biological Factors

Testosterone. Men, compared with women, have higher average concentrations of testosterone, an androgen produced by both sexes (see Chapter 3, "The Nature and Nurture of Sex and Gender"). Boys and girls do not differ much in their testosterone levels until puberty, when the testosterone levels increase greatly in boys. By adulthood, men's testosterone levels are about 15 times higher, on average, than women's, although there is within-sex variation in testosterone levels (Severson & Barclay, 2015). It is tempting to conclude that testosterone and aggression are linked. After all, men tend to be more aggressive than women, they tend to have higher testosterone, and both aggression and testosterone levels peak in young adulthood. This pattern holds true for nonhuman animals as well. Nearly all male mammals show more physical aggression than females of the same species. One exception, however, is the spotted hyena. Female spotted hyenas are more physically aggressive, muscular, and dominant than their male counterparts, and they also have relatively high testosterone levels compared with females of other mammalian species (Goymann, East, & Hofer, 2001).

We should be careful, however, in drawing links between nonhuman animal behavior and human behavior. The links between testosterone and aggression in humans are fairly weak (Book, Starzyk, & Quinsey, 2001) and weaker than those found among non-human animals (Benton, 1983). Moreover, links between testosterone and aggression in humans are correlational, and correlation does not equal causation. Testosterone may influence aggressive behavior, but competitive social situations can cause changes in testosterone. For instance, testosterone levels rise and fall in response to winning or losing sports matches (Archer, 1991), and holding a gun briefly in a laboratory increases men's testosterone levels (Klinesmith, Kasser, & McAndrew, 2006). In short, testosterone is a complex hormone, and its role in human aggression requires further study.

Evolved jealousy. Evolutionary psychologists emphasize male jealousy as a primary motive for men's violence against women (M. I. Wilson & Daly, 1996). Recall from Chapter 10 ("Interpersonal Relationships") that male paternity was uncertain throughout most of humans' evolutionary history. Because conception occurs inside a woman's body, ancestral men—lacking the benefits of modern paternity-testing technology—could not be 100% certain that any given child belonged to them. Faced with this *paternity uncertainty*, men may have evolved heightened sensitivity to cues of a partner's infidelity or impending desertion because a female partner who mates with other men may become impregnated by them. Thus, a man who remains indifferent to his partner's infidelity risks two undesired outcomes: First, he may not pass on his own genes, and second, he may get duped into investing resources to raise someone else's offspring (a phenomenon referred to as *cuckoldry*). According to this perspective, men's jealousy is an adaptive strategy that facilitates reproductive success. Note also that jealousy may motivate men to control their partners with *mate retention tactics*, including violence (Buss & Shackelford, 1997). In support of this theory, jealousy is the most frequent reason offered for male-initiated intimate partner violence (M. I. Wilson & Daly, 1996).

Sociocultural Factors

Although biology plays a role in gender-based aggression, biological factors do not make aggression inevitable. Cultures vary widely in aggressive tendencies, with aggression, violence, and warfare occurring frequently in some societies (e.g., Afghanistan, Chad, and Sudan) and almost never in others. Consider the Che Wong of Malaysia, whose language lacks words for aggression, war, quarreling, and fighting (Bonta, 1993). In North America, contemporary nonaggressive cultures include the Amish, the Hutterites, and the Mennonites. This suggests that cultural norms can influence how people interpret and respond to conflict situations. In this section, we examine how honor, power, structural inequality, and other contextual factors impact gender-based aggression.

Honor cultures. **Honor cultures**—typically found in the Middle East, Southeast Asia, Latin America, and the southern United States—are reputation-based cultures in which norms dictate that men defend their own reputations and those of their family members, with violence if necessary (Nisbett & Cohen, 1996). Men in honor cultures also police the behavior of their family members, and women are expected to avoid any behavior (e.g., sexual promiscuity and infidelity) that could dishonor or shame the family. In these cultures, people perceive men as less honorable and manly if their wives commit infidelity (Vandello & Cohen, 2003). Rates of male-to-female violence tend to be relatively high in honor cultures, and community members generally accept male violence that is committed against wives in retaliation for infidelity (Vandello, Cohen, Grandon, & Franiuk, 2009). For example, **honor killings** typically involve the murder of a female relative who has shamed the family by, for example, committing infidelity, refusing an arranged marriage, seeking a divorce, or being raped (Abu-Rabia, 2011). Consider the case of Gul Meena, a 12-year-old Pakistani girl who was married off to a 60-year-old man and survived regular beatings by him before she fled to Afghanistan with a boyfriend at age 17. After tracking them down, Gul's brother attacked them with an axe, killing Gul's boyfriend and severely injuring her (A. J. Rubin, 2012). These attacks, which occur in the thousands every year around the world, stem from ingrained cultural beliefs that place personal and family honor at the center of all social life.

The same cultural emphasis on family honor can also motivate other forms of violence against intimate partners. In some South Asian countries, such as Pakistan, India, Nepal, and Bangladesh, it is not uncommon for women to experience dowry deaths or acid attacks. In *dowry deaths*, a bride's husband or in-laws murder her after her family fails to provide an adequate dowry (goods provided by the bride's family to the groom at marriage; Babu & Babu, 2011). In some cases of dowry deaths, brides commit suicide to escape the violent threats made by their husbands or in-laws. In *acid attacks*, rejected men throw sulfuric acid onto women or girls to punish them for refusing marriage proposals or denying sex (Patel, 2014). Despite being illegal in many countries, these violent practices are still frequently tolerated or excused in the name of family honor.

Honor culture:
A culture in which individual and family honor is at the center of all social life and men are expected to defend their own and their family's honor with violence if necessary.

Honor killing:
The murder of a—typically female—family member who is perceived to have brought shame or dishonor to the family.

Pakistani Sabira Sultana was burned as a teenager by her husband for not providing a dowry. She has since undergone 35 reconstructive surgeries, provided by a charitable medical foundation in Pakistan.

Source: Paul Bronstein/ Getty Images News/ Getty Images

Male discrepancy stress: Anxiety that boys and men feel about not living up to masculine expectations set by society.

Socioeconomic dependence perspective: The hypothesis that men use violence as a means of maintaining control over partners who are economically dependent on them and thus unlikely to leave.

Precarious manhood. Even outside honor cultures, men may use aggression to "save face" following challenges to their gender status. As discussed in Chapter 4 ("Gender Development"), people in many cultures view manhood as a more precarious social status than womanhood (Vandello & Bosson, 2013). That is, people see manhood as something that must be proven and that can be lost through unmanly behaviors, and this may encourage some men to prove their manhood to others with the use of aggression. To illustrate this idea, Bosson and colleagues had some men braid a mannequin's hair, a stereotypically feminine task that was intended to challenge men's gender status (Bosson, Vandello, Burnaford, Weaver, & Wasti, 2009). In a control group, men braided rope, which was a more gender-neutral version of the braiding task. All men were then given the option of either solving a "brainteaser" puzzle or punching a heavy bag. Just as predicted, more men in the hair-braiding group (50%) chose the punching activity, relative to the men in the control group (22%). In another experiment, all men punched a heavy bag after braiding either hair or rope, and the men who had braided hair punched harder than those who braided rope. Although these studies did not measure aggression toward another person, it is not difficult to imagine that men might use aggression against others to reestablish threatened manhood. In fact, men who are higher in **male discrepancy stress**—anxiety about not being masculine enough—commit more violence against intimate partners (Reidy, Berke, Gentile, & Zeichner, 2014). Of course, just because boys and men sometimes behave aggressively as a display of masculinity, it does not mean that others actually view them as masculine for doing so. One study found that women do not find men's aggression as attractive and desirable as men assume they will (Vandello, Ransom, Hettinger, & Askew, 2009).

Power and structural gender inequality. Some theoretical models focus on the role of patriarchal social structures in gender-based aggression and violence (Dobash & Dobash, 1979). On the one hand, according to the **socioeconomic dependence perspective**, when men have more power and financial resources than women, they might be more likely to use intimate partner violence as a means of exerting and maintaining control. On the other hand, according to the **status inconsistency perspective**, when men are in relationships with female partners who have greater status and financial power than they do, they may feel emasculated and thus use intimate partner violence to experience power (Atkinson, Greenstein, & Lang, 2005). While there is little evidence to support the socioeconomic dependence perspective in terms of intimate partner violence, you may recall from Chapter 6 that countries characterized by greater gender inequality also have higher national levels of male-to-female sexual violence in general (Yodanis, 2004). Thus, patriarchal power structures are associated with increases in some—but not all—types of gender-based aggression.

What about the status inconsistency perspective? A study of 42,000 randomly sampled women from the 28 European Union countries found that the three EU countries with the highest levels of male-to-female intimate partner violence were Denmark, Finland, and Sweden, and the three EU countries with the lowest levels were Poland, Austria, and Croatia (Agency for Fundamental Rights, 2014). This finding is called the *Nordic paradox* because Nordic countries simultaneously have the highest gender equality and the highest levels of male-to-female intimate partner violence in Europe. Consistent with the status inconsistency perspective, researchers explain the Nordic paradox in terms of backlash against Nordic women for occupying a relatively high status in society (Gracia & Merlo, 2016). Note, of course, that this pattern is correlational, which means that an unmeasured third variable might explain it. Can you think of any third variables that might explain the Nordic paradox?

Beyond intimate partner violence, several systematic forms of aggression against women and girls around the world reflect issues of power. In cultures that are higher in hostile sexism, men may express dominance and reinforce the structural inequality of women and girls though ritualized forms of aggression. For example, **female genital mutilation** (sometimes called female genital cutting or female circumcision) is the practice of removing or injuring the female external genitalia for nonmedical reasons. This practice, most common in parts of Africa, the Middle East, and Asia, reflects the beliefs that it encourages modesty, reduces sexual libido, and increases girls' and women's beauty and desirability as marriage partners. Worldwide, over 200 million girls, most under the age of 15, have been injured in this manner (WHO, 2017a). Despite leading to long-lasting negative health consequences and being condemned by the WHO, genital mutilation persists in many places because its proponents see it as a valued cultural ritual and an important part of cultural identity.

Status inconsistency perspective: The hypothesis that men engage in partner violence more often when they feel threatened by partners who have greater economic status and power than they do.

Female genital mutilation: Removing or injuring the external genitalia of girls or young women for nonmedical reasons. Also known as female genital cutting or female circumcision.

Stop and Think

Is female genital mutilation unconditionally wrong? What about other cultural practices that surgically alter the genitals, such as male circumcision or surgery to "correct" the genitals of infants who are born intersex? How do we decide whether or not a cultural practice constitutes harmful aggression, particularly if it has wide cultural acceptance?

In some cultures, families arrange the marriage of girls under the age of 18—and sometimes as young as 5—to much older men. **Child marriage** occurs around the world but predominates in South Asia, Africa, and Latin America (Nour, 2009). In most cases, child brides do not meet their future husbands before the wedding. Several organizations, including the United Nations Population Fund and the WHO, call child marriages a violation of human rights and work to stop this practice. Similarly, many countries define this practice as child rape.

Child marriage: Arranged marriages of girls to much older men.

Sex trafficking:
Forced,
nonconsensual
recruitment and
retention of persons
for sexual use and
exploitation.

I³ theory: The
theory that partner
violence depends
on the interplay
of three factors:
provocation
by a partner
(instigation), forces
that create a strong
urge to aggress
(impellance),
and forces
that decrease
the likelihood
of aggression
(inhibition).

Given that female genital mutilation and child marriage occur in cultural contexts that value these practices, they complicate the use of the term *aggression*. Remember that social psychologists define aggression as behavior "intended to harm" a person or animal. But if a culture believes that female genital mutilation enhances girls' beauty and value, then can we fairly label this practice *aggression*? There is disagreement about this question, but we cover these practices here because of their roots in structural gender inequalities. In cultural contexts in which girls and women systematically lack power, access to resources, and educational opportunities, they become especially vulnerable to exploitation and abuse. In these contexts, men (and sometimes women) use aggression against women and girls as a tool to reinforce power differences and maintain the gender hierarchy. And when the value of girls and women is tied largely to their childbearing abilities or to their abilities to provide sexual gratification, it becomes more socially acceptable to target them with physical aggression and violence.

Finally, the trafficking of young women and children into prostitution remains widespread in many parts of the world (Hodge & Lietz, 2007). **Sex trafficking** refers to the forced, nonconsensual recruitment and retention of persons for sexual use and exploitation. While difficult to know precisely how many people are victims of sex trafficking, the International Labour Organization (ILO, 2014) estimates that there are about 4.5 million victims worldwide, with most being girls and women. Sex trafficking occurs throughout the world, with particularly high rates in Burma, Turkmenistan, Algeria, Belarus, and Venezuela (U.S. Department of State, 2016). In the United States, the cities with the largest child sex industries are Atlanta, Miami, and San Diego (Dank et al., 2014), with an estimate of over 100,000 victims of child sex trafficking across the United States (Kotrla, 2010). Many experts describe the sex trafficking industry in economic terms of supply, demand, costs, and benefits. As long as societies routinely encourage the commodification of sex, consumers will demand it, and sex trafficking will rise to meet that demand. Furthermore, sex trafficking will remain a serious problem as long as its profits outweigh the physical and criminal risks of traffickers (Wheaton, Schauer, & Galli, 2010). The ILO (2014) estimates that profits from sex trafficking worldwide are about $99 billion annually.

An unnamed young female victim of human trafficking in India waits in a police station after being rescued on September 16, 2013.

Source: MANAN VATSYAYANA/AFP/Getty Images

I³ theory. Note that explanations for gender-based aggression rooted in jealousy, honor, and patriarchy better explain heterosexual male-to-female violence than female-to-male, male-to-male, and female-to-female violence. In contrast, the **I³** (pronounced *I-cubed*) **theory**, which examines intimate partner violence through the lens of self-regulation, can explain violence across relationship types. According to this theory, whether or not a conflict situation escalates into intimate partner violence depends on the interplay of three processes: instigation, impellance, and inhibition. *Instigation* refers to provocations by the partner in conflict situations. *Impellance* refers to dispositional or situational forces (e.g., an aggressive personality or intoxication) that increase the likelihood of aggression in response to instigation while *inhibition* refers to dispositional or situational factors (e.g., self-control or the presence of a police officer) that decrease the likelihood of aggression. Thus, I³ theory conceptualizes intimate partner violence as a product of competing urges to aggress and to inhibit aggression following partner provocation. In support of I³ theory, a combination of strong provocation and weak inhibitory control does, in fact, predict intimate partner violence (Finkel et al., 2012).

What Is the Relationship Between Pornography and Sexual Aggression?

Definitions and Prevalence

Now that we have considered some explanations for gender-based aggression, let's turn to a more applied area: the relationship between pornography and sexual aggression. Pornography is among the most frequently viewed material on the Internet, more popular than other commonly viewed material, including maps, weather forecasts, dictionaries, and games. From 2009 to 2010, about 4% of the top million visited websites were sex-related, and about 13% of all Web searches were for erotic content (Ogas & Gaddam, 2011). Perhaps not surprisingly, pornography is very profitable, typically generating more revenue annually than all mainstream Hollywood studios combined (Bridges, Wosnitzer, Scharrer, Sun, & Liberman, 2010). Given the popularity of pornography, sexuality researchers have long been interested in the connection between pornography use and sexual aggression.

To discuss this issue, we must first define pornography. Early legal definitions lacked specificity, focusing primarily on whether material was obscene, offensive, or lacking in social value; later legal definitions focused more on sexually explicit material that depicted the abuse of women (Sunstein, 1986). There are many types of pornography, but here we will focus primarily on **aggressive pornography**, or sexually explicit material that is meant to arouse and that contains acts of physical or verbal aggression, degradation, or humiliation. In contrast, **erotica** is sexually explicit material that is meant to arouse but that is nonaggressive.

Aggressive pornography: Sexually explicit material that is meant to arouse and that contains acts of physical or verbal aggression, degradation, or humiliation.

Erotica: Sexually explicit nonaggressive material that is meant to arouse.

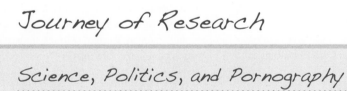

Journey of Research

Science, Politics, and Pornography

Pornography, or at least the graphic display of human sexuality, has existed for millennia around the world. Ancient Greek and Roman frescos depicted graphic sex acts. In the second century, India gave us the *Kama Sutra*, a love manual that included descriptions of creative sexual positions. For centuries, Japanese artists created erotic woodblock prints called *shunga*. And filmmakers began making sexually

(Continued)

explicit movies almost as soon motion pictures were invented.

Politicians, religious leaders, and feminist scholars have voiced concern about pornography for decades, but scientific research on pornography—and its effects on aggression and violence toward women—did not begin until the late 1960s and early 1970s. In 1969, President Lyndon Johnson set up the President's Commission on Obscenity and Pornography. Based on research showing that the availability of pornography did not lead to an increase in sexual crimes after Denmark legalized pornography in 1969 (Kutchinsky, 1970), the commission concluded that there was no evidence that pornography was a serious social problem.

Pornography briefly entered a period of mainstream acceptance in the early 1970s with the release of films such as *Deep Throat*, which was a box office hit. While some praised pornography as a sign of increased sexual freedom, religious leaders criticized it as an indication of moral decay, and feminists scholars argued that pornography exploits women and encourages sexual violence against them (Brownmiller, 1975). As pornography made its way into homes on videocassette tapes in the 1980s, President Ronald Reagan set up a commission in 1985 to investigate its effects. The commission, which consisted of a majority of antipornography activists, concluded that pornography had harmful effects on its users, although several psychologists immediately criticized the report as biased and inaccurate (Wilcox, 1987).

Scientific research on pornography grew during the 1980s. During this decade, researchers began to distinguish between nonviolent *erotica* and *aggressive pornography* (Malamuth, 1984), a distinction that proved important in predicting sexual aggression. However, in the early 1990s, the growth of the Internet made public access to pornography so easy that it became difficult for researchers to locate adequate numbers of "control" participants, or people who had no exposure to pornography (Liew, 2009).

Despite increasing research on pornography and aggression over the past four decades, the research community remains divided about whether exposure to pornography causes sexually violent attitudes and behavior. Some meta-analyses of experimental studies show that pornography exposure increases aggressive behavior (M. Allen, D'Alessio, & Brezgel, 1995), but research findings are inconsistent. This led Neil Malamuth and his colleagues to conclude that some individuals are both more likely to seek out pornography *and* more likely to be impacted by it negatively. That is, the individuals who show the greatest negative effects from watching aggressive pornography are men who are already predisposed toward sexual aggression and who watch pornography frequently (Malamuth, Hald, & Koss, 2012).

Researching pornography remains challenging. Pornography researchers face complex ethical considerations and a lack of federal research funds. In addition, pornography consumption is now so common that its meaning has changed from something private and stigmatized to something more mainstream and normative. Given the increasing acceptance and use of pornography in many Western cultures, understanding its effects is more important than ever.

Pornography and Sexual Aggression

What percentage of pornographic material contains images of violence, degradation, or humiliation of women? To answer this question, Ana Bridges and her colleagues randomly selected scenes from the 50 top-selling pornographic videos from December 2004 to June 2005 (Bridges et al., 2010). They found that 88% of scenes contained physical aggression (mostly spanking, gagging, and slapping), and about 49% of scenes contained verbal aggression, such as name-calling (see Table 14.3). The perpetrators of aggression in these videos were overwhelmingly men while the targets were women. Notably, targets of aggression in these videos usually reacted with pleasure or responded neutrally to their aggressive treatment. A more recent analysis of 400 videos from top pornography websites found lower rates of aggression, with 40% of scenes containing physical violence, most all of which portrayed women as the targets (Klaassen & Peter, 2015).

Given the frequent depictions of aggression and degradation in pornography, some scholars view pornography as dangerous because it represents women as objects who exist for the pleasure of others (Dines, 2010). In contrast, other scholars view pornography as a healthy form of sexual expression. One study of over 800 adult pornography users found that 75% of them were "recreational users" who watch pornography occasionally, have low levels of distress or guilt associated with pornography viewing, and report relatively high levels of sexual satisfaction and functioning (Vaillancourt-Morel et al., 2017).

So who is correct? As you may guess, not all pornography is the same, nor do all individuals engage with and react to it in the same way. Many factors predict whether pornography is healthy or harmful. The **sexual callousness model** attempts to account for the harmful effects of pornography (Zillmann & Weaver, 1989). This model argues

Sexual callousness model: A model proposing that repeated exposure to pornography desensitizes and habituates viewers, leading to callous sexual attitudes toward women.

Table 14.3	**Aggressive Acts Depicted in Pornography.** These values are the percentages of total pornographic scenes (in best-selling pornography videos) that contain each type of aggression. As you can see, men are most often portrayed as the aggressor in these scenes while women are most often portrayed as the targets of the aggression.
Any physical violence	88.2%
Spanking	75.3%
Gagging	53.9%
Open-handed slapping	41.1%
Hair pulling	37.2%
Choking	27.6%
Verbal aggression	48.7%
Sex of the aggressor	70.3% men
Sex of the target of aggression	94.4% women

Source: Based on a content analysis of best-selling pornographic videos from 2004–2005 (Bridges et al., 2010).

that repeated exposure to pornography can desensitize and habituate viewers, leading to callous attitudes toward sex. Ultimately, this desensitization can disinhibit viewers' sexually aggressive tendencies. In addition, pornography that portrays aggressors being rewarded for sexual aggression (e.g., female partners responding positively to victimization) may undermine men's inhibitions against acting on rape desires (Malamuth, 1984). Finally, aggressive pornography may skew viewers' perceptions of normal or typical sexual encounters, leading to the perception that sexual aggression is normative and expected (Häggström-Nordin, 2005).

The evidence supporting this theoretical model is mixed. Some (but not all) correlational research finds an association between pornography consumption and sexual aggression, but the effect sizes are small. A meta-analysis of correlational studies found that greater exposure to pornography predicted more real-life sexual aggression among both men ($r = 0.29$) and women ($r = 0.26$; P. J. Wright, Tokunga, & Kraus, 2016). In contrast, studies that examine associations on the cultural level find that as pornography becomes more widely available in cultures, rape rates do not tend to increase, and sometimes they decrease (Kutchinsky, 1991). For instance, sexual assault rates in the United States have been decreasing for at least 20 years, just as pornography has become more readily available via the Internet (C. J. Ferguson & Hartley, 2009).

Reviews of experimental studies similarly draw mixed conclusions. Some reviews find causal relationships between exposure to pornography and both aggressive behavior and acceptance of sexual violence (M. Allen et al., 1995; Malamuth, Addison, & Koss, 2000). In contrast, other reviews find slim evidence for a causal effect of pornography on aggression (C. J. Ferguson & Hartley, 2009). These inconsistencies may reflect differences in the types of pornography being viewed and the features of the people viewing it. Exposure to erotica is typically not associated with aggression, but aggressive pornography exposure can cause harmful outcomes (Malamuth et al., 2000). Also, regular exposure to pornography is most likely to activate and reinforce aggressive tendencies among men who are already at high risk for sexual aggression (Malamuth et al., 2012). For these men, aggressive pornography exposure may intensify already existing desires or lower inhibitions against acting on their aggressive impulses. Moreover, only a small subset (about 12%) of people who consume pornography use it compulsively, meaning that they view it quite frequently, go to great lengths to obtain it, and feel addicted to it. These viewers, who are mostly men, experience intrusive sexual thoughts that they cannot control and report less satisfaction in their sex lives (Vaillancourt-Morel et al., 2017).

Questions about the effects of aggressive pornography on sexual violence are especially important because children and young adolescents in the United States are increasingly exposed to Internet pornography. In one nationally representative sample of Internet users ages 10–17, 42% reported being exposed to online pornography at least once in the past year, and most of the exposure occurred unintentionally, by accidentally landing on a pornographic site (Wolak, Mitchell, & Finkelhour, 2007). In short, young people today have far greater exposure to pornographic images than in past generations. What consequences do you think this might have on the development of young people's sexual attitudes, beliefs, and experiences? This question merits further consideration.

CHAPTER SUMMARY

14.1 Analyze research on sex differences and similarities across different types of aggression.

Aggression refers to behavior intended to harm another person or animal. Unlike most other animals that rely primarily on physical aggression, humans have a wide repertoire of aggressive behaviors, some direct and physical and others more covert. Physical aggression includes behaviors such as hitting, kicking, shoving, or biting. Verbal aggression includes behaviors such as yelling or teasing. Indirect or relational aggression includes behaviors such as spreading rumors or excluding someone socially. While violence—defined as extreme physical aggression—is relatively rare—and especially among women—verbal and indirect aggression occur more frequently.

In comparison with women, men commit more physical violence, such as homicides and serious physical assaults, in most cultures. Men are also more often victims of violence, with the exception of sexual assault and intimate partner violence. Sexual, gender, and racial/ethnic minorities face disproportionate rates of aggression. Sex differences in physical aggression are larger in studies that include younger participants, occur in natural settings, and examine unprovoked aggression. Members of all sexes use verbal and indirect aggression with roughly the same frequency. Cyberbullying is becoming more common but shows only small sex differences. Children who both perpetrate and experience cyberbullying are more likely to attempt suicide.

14.2 Evaluate the gender dynamics of intimate partner violence, sexual assault, and sex-based harassment.

Rates of intimate partner violence vary across cultures, but nearly a third of women around the world experience this form of aggression in their lifetime. Intimate partner violence occurs with similar frequency in same-sex and heterosexual relationships, but transgender individuals experience higher rates of intimate partner violence than cisgender individuals. By some metrics, men and women report roughly equal amounts of partner violence, at least in cultures where women have more status and power, but women more often experience severe injury from intimate partner violence. Women perpetrate slightly higher rates of *situational couple violence* than men, whereas men perpetrate *intimate terrorism* more frequently than women.

Sexual assault refers to nonconsensual sexual contact. Consent means that all parties have an unambiguous agreement, expressed through words or actions, to engage in sexual activity. In one large survey of college students in the United States, 19.0% of women and 6.1% of men reported experiencing attempted or completed sexual assault since entering college. Rates of rape in the U.S. population vary by race and ethnicity, with higher rates for Native American and Black women than for Hispanic and White women. Higher rates of sexual assault occur among the disempowered, including young people, developmentally disabled individuals, sex workers, impoverished and homeless people, undocumented immigrants, refugees, and prisoners. Rape survivors experience elevated rates of PTSD, anxiety, and depression. Most rapes are committed by men (regardless of victim sex) and by familiar individuals (acquaintances, relationship partners, or relatives). Rape myths—false beliefs about rape, rape survivors, and rapists—contribute to a culture of blaming survivors for their assaults. False accusations of rape are rare, and most perpetrators of rape escape prosecution and punishment, though this varies by race and ethnicity.

Sex-based harassment is behavior that derogates or humiliates an individual based on the individual's sex, sexual orientation, or gender identity. Sex-based harassment occurs frequently in workplace, school, and military settings, as well as in public spaces. Approximately 40%–60% of women and 10%–20% of men report workplace sex-based harassment in the United States, and rates of harassment are higher for racial, ethnic, sexual, and gender minority individuals. Women of color may experience racialized sex-based harassment, in which race-based and sex-based harassment are both present. Individuals who deviate from traditional gender role expectations have a heightened risk of sex-based harassment likely because they threaten the status quo.

14.3 Discuss biological and sociocultural factors that explain sex differences in gender-based aggression.

Both biological and sociocultural factors contribute to gender-based aggression. Testosterone, which is linked to aggression and dominance across species, may partly explain greater male physical aggression because men have higher concentrations of testosterone than women, particularly in puberty and young adulthood. But because testosterone can both produce and result from aggression, it cannot necessarily explain greater male aggression. The I^3 theory argues that partner violence emerges from a combination of strong provocation and weak inhibitory control in the aggressor. Cultural concepts of honor and precarious manhood may also play roles. In honor cultures, men often use physical aggression to defend their honor (their personal and family reputation). Manhood is a relatively precarious social status, and men may restore their threatened gender status by using aggression. Systemic gender inequality in society can help explain specific forms of aggression such as sex trafficking, female genital mutilation, child marriage, and honor killing, which all victimize girls and women more than boys and men. The status inconsistency perspective states that men engage in partner violence more often when women challenge men's greater status and power.

14.4 Use research findings on gender-based violence to understand the relationship between pornography and sexual aggression.

While erotica is sexually explicit nonaggressive material, aggressive pornography is sexually explicit material that contains acts of physical or verbal aggression, degradation, or humiliation. Aggression occurs frequently in pornography, with women most often the targets of the aggression. Feminist scholars view pornography as dangerous because it objectifies women and desensitizes viewers to aggression against women. Inconsistent findings leave researchers divided about whether pornography exposure causes sexually violent attitudes and behavior. Pornography varies in type, and not all individuals react to it the same way. Men who are predisposed toward sexual aggression tend to show the greatest negative effects from watching pornography, and only about 12% of people who consume pornography use it compulsively. Though debate continues on the harm caused by pornography, the majority of pornography users do not seem to suffer from negative consequences.

Test Your Knowledge: True or False?

14.1 Around the world, young men commit the vast majority of violent crimes. (True: About 85% of all homicides and serious assaults are committed by men, and the median age for committing homicide is 20.) [p. 479]

14.2 Girls use indirect, relational forms of aggression, such as gossip and spreading rumors, much more often than boys do. (False: Although early research suggested that girls were more likely than boys to use indirect aggression, recent reviews suggest sex differences that are close to zero.) [p. 483]

14.3 Between one-third and two-thirds of sexual assault victims around the world are age 15 or younger. (True. Most sexual assault targets people who are younger and more vulnerable.) [p. 490]

14.4 False allegations of rape are common. (False: Scholars estimate that only 5.2% of rape allegations are false, which is comparable to the percentage of false allegations of other felony crimes.) [p. 494]

14.5 Attractive women who embody ideals of femininity are most likely to be targeted for workplace sex-based harassment. (False: Women who have more agentic traits, who are low in femininity, or who identify as feminists are most likely to be targeted for sex-based harassment.) [p. 499]

Glossary

Achievement motivation: An individual's need to meet goals and accomplish tasks.

Agency: A dimension, stereotypically associated with men, that reflects traits such as competence, intelligence, assertiveness, and competitiveness.

Agender: Describes people who feel internally ungendered.

Aggression: Behavior intended to cause psychological or physical harm to another person or animal.

Aggressive pornography: Sexually explicit material that is meant to arouse and that contains acts of physical or verbal aggression, degradation, or humiliation.

Allele: A variant form of a gene.

Alliance formation hypothesis: The hypothesis that same-sex sexual activity is adaptive because it promotes emotional bonds and facilitates survival and resource sharing between pairs of friends.

Allies: Individuals who publicly support and promote the rights of disadvantaged group members but who are not themselves part of the disadvantaged group.

Ambivalent sexism theory: Theory proposing that gender relations are characterized by both negative (hostile sexism) and seemingly positive (benevolent sexism) attitudes toward women.

Androcentrism: A cultural ideology that defines men and their experiences as universal and treats women and their experiences as deviations from the male norm.

Androgyny: High levels of both stereotypically male-typed and female-typed traits.

Arranged marriage: Marriage in which third parties, such as parents or relatives, select potential marriage partners, with both partners having the right to refuse.

Asexual: Signifies having a lack of desire for sex or sexual partners.

Attachment theory: A theory that describes the processes by which adults and infants become attached and develop strong emotional bonds.

Attributional ambiguity: Difficulty in attributing negative treatment to group-based discrimination when other possible explanations for the treatment are present.

Audience problem: The tendency for observers to assume that platonic friends are romantically involved; especially likely to occur in cross-sex friendships.

Autism spectrum disorders: Developmental disorders typically characterized by difficulties with communicating and interacting with others, limited interests or activities, and repetitive behaviors.

Autonomous (love) marriage: Marriage in which individuals select their own partners.

Benevolent sexism: Subjectively positive but patronizing attitudes toward women who conform to traditional gender role norms.

Between-group variance: The difference between the average values for each group in a study.

Big Five personality dimensions: Five dimensions that many researchers agree capture most of the important variance in personality (extraversion, neuroticism, agreeableness, conscientiousness, and openness to experience).

Bigender: Describes people who shift between gender identities as woman and man.

Binge drinking: Consuming four or more alcoholic drinks within 1–2 hours for women and five or more drinks within 1–2 hours for men.

Biobehavioral model: A model that proposes that the links between romantic love and sexual desire are bidirectional and that prolonged proximity and touch in sex-segregated environments can lead people to develop novel sexual attractions.

Biosocial constructionist theory: A theory that explains how biological differences between women and men lead to sex-based labor divisions in society, which then shape the development of role-relevant skills and gender stereotypes.

Bisexual: Signifies being attracted to women and men.

Body mass index (BMI): A person's weight in kilograms divided by the square of height in meters.

Callous-unemotional traits: A personality factor consisting of low levels of empathy, guilt, and warmth.

Cesarean section (C-section) procedure: The use of surgery to deliver a baby through the mother's lower abdomen.

Child marriage: Arranged marriages of girls to much older men

Child-free by choice: The status of an individual or couple who decides not to have children.

Chosen families: The friend circles of many LGBT individuals that offer many of the resources and benefits of biological families but that consist largely of individuals who understand the unique challenges of being LGBT.

Chromosomes: The organized units of genes inside the cells of all living organisms. Every somatic cell in the human body has 23 pairs of chromosomes, with the mother and father each contributing one set of chromosomes.

Cisgender: Describes people who experience a match between their sex assigned at birth and their psychological gender identity.

Code switching: The process by which bilinguals and multilinguals switch back and forth between languages and their different cultural meaning systems.

Cognitive abilities: Mental skills, such as paying attention, reasoning, remembering, solving problems, speaking, and interpreting speech.

Cognitive theories: Theories that propose that children learn gender by progressing through a series of increasingly sophisticated cognitive stages and that the emergence of sex-typed cognitions causes children to learn sex-typed behaviors and preferences.

Collective action: Behavior enacted on behalf of a group with the goal of improving conditions for the entire group.

Collectivistic cultures: Cultures (often found in East Asia, Africa, and the Middle East) that value fitting in and group solidarity and prioritize group goals and needs over individual goals and needs.

Communion: A dimension, stereotypically associated with women, that reflects traits such as warmth, connectedness, generosity, and kindness.

Companionate love: A later stage of love characterized by calm feelings of warmth and emotional closeness.

Consensual nonmonogamy (CNM): A relationship arrangement in which all partners agree that it is acceptable to pursue sexual and/or romantic relationships with others.

Correlational design: A design in which a researcher tests the strength and direction of the associations between participant (nonmanipulated) variables.

Cross-sex behavior: Behavior that is strongly associated with a sex group other than one's own.

Cross-sex friendships: Friendships with people who do not share one's sex.

Cultural ideologies: Overarching sets of beliefs and assumptions about groups that justify unequal social hierarchies.

Cyberbullying: Verbal or relational aggression committed via the Internet, mobile phones, or other types of electronic or digital technologies.

d statistic: An effect size statistic that expresses the magnitude and direction of a difference between group means, or of the strength of association between variables, in standardized units.

Dating scripts: Stereotyped, cognitive representations of the sequences of events that take place during dates.

Decoding accuracy: The ability to read the nonverbal communications of others correctly.

Degendering theory: The theory that gender becomes a less central aspect of the self as people age.

Demand–withdraw pattern: An interpersonal relationship pattern in which one couple member criticizes or demands, and the other partner responds by withdrawing emotionally or physically.

Dendrites: Branch-like structures of neurons that receive neural messages from other neurons.

Dependent variable: An outcome variable; in an experiment, the dependent variable is the one hypothesized to change as a result of manipulation of an independent variable.

Differences (or disorders) of sex development (DSDs): Conditions present at birth in which sex development is atypical in terms of chromosomes, gonads, or anatomy.

Different cultures approach: The belief that boys and girls are socialized to use language so differently that they may as well come from different "cultures," which leads to miscommunication.

Diminutive: A form of a word used to indicate a smaller, less powerful, or more familiar version (e.g., booklet, duckling, mommy, and daddy).

Direct aggression: Overt verbal or physical behaviors aimed directly at another person, with the intention to harm.

Direction accuracy: Accuracy regarding the direction of a sex difference.

Discrepancy accuracy: Accuracy regarding the specific size (and direction) of a sex difference.

Display rules: Culture-specific norms that regulate how, when, and whether individuals should express particular emotions.

Dopamine: A neurotransmitter that is associated with feelings of reward, positive arousal, and intentional control of voluntary movement.

Double jeopardy hypothesis: Hypothesis that individuals who belong to two or more subordinate groups face more discrimination than individuals who belong to only one subordinate group.

Double standard of aging: The idea that women's social value declines with age as their beauty and sexual appeal fade while men's value increases with age as their life experience and social status increase.

Down syndrome: A genetic disorder characterized by physical growth delays, mild to moderate intellectual impairment, and distinct facial features.

Dualism: The scientific and philosophical position that the physical body and the mind (consciousness) are two fundamentally different entities.

Dyadic power: The power to choose intimate partners and relationships and to control the interactions and decisions that occur within those relationships.

Dyslexia: A learning disability characterized by impairments in reading, including problems with word recognition and spelling.

Effect size: A quantitative measure of the magnitude and direction of a difference between groups or of the strength of a relationship between variables.

Effortful control: The capacity for persistence, focus, and inhibitory control.

Electroencephalogram (EEG): A brain imaging technique that reads electrical activity in the brain with the use of sensors on the scalp.

Emerging adulthood: In Western industrialized nations, the period of life between ages 18 and 25 when people transition to more adult roles and responsibilities.

Emotion: A complex, internal, subjective reaction to an event or stimulus that includes physiological, psychological, and behavioral components. Basic emotions, such as joy, anger, and fear, are thought to be innate and universally expressed and recognized.

Emotional contagion: The tendency for people to synchronize their emotions automatically with the emotions of others, without necessarily being aware of it happening.

Emotional infidelity: When a member of a couple falls in love with someone else.

Emotional intelligence: The ability to identify and manage one's own emotions and the emotions of others, and to use emotions to solve problems.

Empathy: The tendency to feel the emotional state of another person and to see the world from another person's vantage point. Empathy has both affective and cognitive components.

Encoding accuracy: The ability to communicate nonverbally in a clear manner that others can interpret correctly.

Epigenetics: The study of the biological mechanisms that guide whether or not certain genes get expressed.

Equality: A principle in which each individual is treated the same, regardless of background.

Equity: A principle in which each individual is treated fairly, by taking background into account.

Erectile dysfunction: A condition characterized by loss of erectile function and difficulty achieving or maintaining an erection.

Erotica: Sexually explicit nonaggressive material that is meant to arouse.

Essentialist beliefs: Assumptions that observed sex differences reflect inherent, natural, biological differences between women and men.

Ethnic identity: A psychological sense of connectedness to one's racial or ethnic group.

Ethnocentrism: A cultural ideology that defines the dominant ethnic group as universal and treats other ethnic groups as deviations from the norm.

Evolutionary psychology: A theoretical approach that explains much of human thought and behavior in terms of genetically heritable adaptations that evolved because they helped ancestral humans survive and reproduce.

Ex post facto design: A nonexperimental design in which participants are assigned to conditions on the basis of a preexisting participant variable (e.g., sex) and compared on some dependent variable.

Expansion hypothesis: The prediction that occupying multiple social roles is associated with psychological and physical health benefits.

Experiment: A type of research design in which a researcher systematically manipulates at least one independent variable to observe whether this causes changes in at least one dependent variable.

Externalizing disorders: Antisocial, conduct, substance use, and impulsivity-related disorders, in which symptoms are directed outward, toward others.

Factor analysis: A statistical procedure used to identify clusters of related scores or items.

Fakaleiti: Transgender individuals from Tonga, an archipelago nation in the South Pacific, who are assigned male at birth but assume a relatively feminine manner. Similar to the fa'afafine in Samoa.

False rape allegations: Accusations of rape that the accuser knows to be false.

Familism: A set of collectivistic social values that promote loyalty, support, and interdependence among family members.

Fecundity hypothesis: The hypothesis that genes for same-sex sexuality get passed on genetically because the female relatives of gay men produce many offspring.

Female genital mutilation: Removing or injuring the external genitalia of girls or young women for nonmedical reasons. Also known as female genital cutting or female circumcision.

Feme covert: The legal status of married women in British common law and American colonial law, whereby women transferred their identities and rights to their husband upon marriage.

Femininity: Possession of physical and psychological attributes typically associated with women.

Feminisms: Movements for the social, political, and economic equality of women and men or, according to bell hooks, movements "to end sexism, sexist exploitation, and oppression."

Feminization of poverty: The global tendency for women to experience disproportionate rates of poverty.

Flexible work arrangements: Arrangements in which employees control the location or timing of their work (e.g., flexible schedules and telecommuting).

Flynn effect: The increase of about three points per decade in average population performance on IQ tests over time (across generations).

Focus group: A type of interview conducted in a semistructured group format and guided by a moderator.

Food deserts: Neighborhoods in which the lack of nearby grocery stores and easy public transportation limits residents' regular access to fresh, healthy food.

Fraternal birth order effect: Positive correlation between the number of older brothers a man has and his likelihood of identifying as gay.

Friends-with-benefits relationships: Arrangements in which two friends have occasional, casual sexual interactions without the expectation of a romantic relationship.

Functional magnetic resonance imaging (fMRI): A brain imaging technique that uses magnetic fields and radio waves to map brain activity.

Gay: Typically refers to a man who is attracted only (or primarily) to men.

Gender: The meanings that people give to the different sex categories. Gender consists of broad sets of attributes and tendencies (e.g., identities, traits, interests, roles, attitudes, stereotypes, and socialization practices) commonly associated with maleness and femaleness.

Gender aschematic: Lacking the tendency to use gender as a salient schema for understanding the world.

Gender binary: The conceptualization of gender as consisting of two opposite and nonoverlapping categories, such as masculine or feminine.

Gender confirmation procedures: Procedures (including hormone treatments, surgeries, and psychotherapies) that transgender individuals sometimes seek to bring their physical bodies into greater alignment with their psychological identities.

Gender constancy: The recognition that sex is (largely) fixed and does not change as a result of external, superficial features.

Gender diagnosticity (GD) score: The estimated probability that an individual is male or female given the individual's gender-related interests. A GD score of .85 means that the individual has an 85% chance of being male and a 15% chance of being female.

Gender discrimination: Unjust treatment based solely on one's sex, sexual orientation, or gender identity.

Gender dysphoria: A disorder characterized by clinically significant distress arising from the mismatch between one's assigned sex and psychological sense of gender.

Gender fluid: Describes people whose gender identity shifts or changes flexibly rather remaining constant.

Gender identity: Individuals' psychological experience of their gender and how they identify internally as a man, woman, or something else. In cognitive-developmental theory, gender identity is the cognitive ability to identify the self as a boy or a girl and to label others according to sex.

Gender intensification hypothesis: The hypothesis that gender role socialization pressures increase during adolescence, resulting in increases in adolescents' gendered self-views.

Gender paradox of suicide: A pattern in which girls and women more frequently exhibit nonfatal suicide behavior (suicidal ideation, suicide attempts, and nonsuicidal self-injury) while boys and men more frequently die from suicide.

Gender prescriptions: Traits that people believe women and men should have.

Gender proscriptions: Traits that people believe women and men should not have.

Gender role ideology hypothesis: The hypothesis that a couple's beliefs about gender roles influence the manner in which they divide housework and childcare.

Gender schema: A mental model about gender, based on prior learning and experience, that guides how people interpret, process, and remember new gender-relevant information.

Gender schematic: Having a tendency to use gender as a salient schema for understanding the world.

Gender stability: The understanding that sex remains (largely) constant across time.

Gender stereotypes: Shared beliefs about the traits, qualities, and tendencies associated with different sex categories.

Gender wage gap: The difference in earnings between men and women, usually expressed as a ratio (or percentage) of women's to men's median yearly earnings for full-time, year-round work. A gender wage gap of 1.00 would reflect gender parity.

Genderqueer: Describes people who identify as neither, both, or a combination of man and woman.

Gene-by-environment interaction: When a genetic effect on a trait or behavior emerges only under certain environmental circumstances or when the environmental effect on a trait or behavior depends on a person's genetic makeup.

Generalizability: The extent to which the findings of a study would apply beyond the sample in the original study to the larger population.

Generalization: The tendency to assume that a new member of a category has the same qualities as other category members.

Generic beliefs: Beliefs about categories as wholes, without reference to numbers or proportions.

Generic masculine: The use of male-gendered terms to refer not only to men but to mixed-sex groups, to human beings in general, or to individuals whose sex is unknown or unspecified.

Genes: Basic units of heredity passed down from parents to offspring, consisting of specific sequences of DNA (deoxyribonucleic acid) that carry instructions for the offspring's characteristics.

Genetics: The study of genes (the basic units of heredity) and how physical traits are inherited. Behavioral genetics is the study of how psychological traits are inherited.

Genital ridge: The precursor to female or male gonads (ovaries or testes). It appears identical in genetic female and male embryos.

Genital reconstructive surgery: Surgery that alters the appearance, location, or function of genital tissue. People seek genital reconstructive surgery for a wide range of reasons; transgender individuals may seek such surgery to bring the appearance or function of their genitalia into greater alignment with their psychological gender identity.

Genital tubercle: The undifferentiated embryonic structure that becomes the clitoris or the penis.

Genitalia: Internal and external reproductive organs. For females, these include the cervix, uterus, fallopian tubes, and ovaries (internal) and the labia and clitoris (external). For males, these include the seminal vesicles, vas deferens, and testes (internal) and penis and scrotum (external).

Glass ceiling: Invisible barriers in the workplace that prevent women from rising to top corporate positions.

Glass cliff effect: The tendency to place women into leadership positions under risky, precarious circumstances in which the likelihood of failure is high.

Gonads: The sex organs (ovaries and testes) that produce sex cells (egg and sperm) and sex hormones (estrogen and testosterone).

Grammatical gender: A type of classification system in certain languages, such as French and Hindi, in which most nouns are assigned a gender (masculine, feminine, and sometimes neutral).

Greater male variability hypothesis: The prediction that men show more variability than women in their distributions of scores on cognitive performance measures, leading them to be overrepresented in the very bottom and very top of score distributions.

Hegemonic masculinity: A culturally idealized version of manhood that reinforces men's control over women.

Heritability estimate: A statistic that specifies the proportion of total population variance in a given trait, such as gender identity, that is due to genetic differences among the people in the population. Heritability estimates (signified by h^2) can range from 0% to 100%.

Heterocentrism: A cultural ideology that defines heterosexuality as universal and treats sexual minority groups as deviations from the norm.

Heteronormative: The assumption that "normal" sexuality is heterosexual.

Heterosexual: Signifies being attracted only (or primarily) to persons of the other sex.

Highly active antiretroviral therapies (HAARTs): Drug treatments, usually consisting of a combination of at least three drugs, that suppress HIV replication.

Homosocial perspective: An approach that proposes that men achieve friendship intimacy in the context of cohesive, hierarchical units that share goals and joint activities and contain opposing emotions (e.g., competition and affection).

Honor culture: A culture in which individual and family honor is at the center of all social life and men are expected to defend their own and their family's honor with violence if necessary.

Honor killing: The murder of a— typically female—family member who is perceived to have brought shame or dishonor to the family.

Hormones: Chemical substances in the body that regulate bodily functions such as digestion, growth, and reproduction.

Hostile sexism: Negative, antagonistic attitudes toward women who violate traditional gender role norms.

Human immunodeficiency virus (HIV): A virus that attacks the body's immune system and makes it difficult for the body to fight diseases.

Hypothesis: A testable prediction about the outcome of a study, stated in terms of the variables tested.

I^3 theory: The theory that partner violence depends on the interplay of three factors: provocation by a partner (instigation), forces that create a strong urge to aggress (impellance), and forces that decrease the likelihood of aggression (inhibition).

Implicit physician biases: Automatic, nonconscious judgments and behaviors, based on stereotypes, that influence how physicians evaluate or treat patients.

Impulsivity: A personality factor that consists of traits such as sensation seeking, novelty seeking, and risk taking.

Independent variable: A variable that is assumed to cause changes in a dependent variable; in an experiment, the independent variable is systematically manipulated by the researcher.

Indirect (relational) aggression: Behaviors intended to harm another person's social relationships or status, often performed when the target is not physically present.

Individualistic cultures: Cultures (often found in western Europe and North America) that value independence and self-reliance and prioritize individual goals and needs over group goals and needs.

In-group bias: A preference for one's own social group over other groups.

Intelligence (or general mental ability): The general capacity to understand ideas, think abstractly, reason, solve problems, and learn.

Intelligence quotient (IQ): A score representing an individual's level of intelligence, as measured by a standardized intelligence test. IQ is calculated such that the average for an individual's same-age peers is always set to 100.

Interaction effect: A pattern in which the strength or direction of the association between an independent (or participant) variable and a dependent variable differs as a function of another independent (or participant) variable.

Internalized homophobia/: Self-directed antigay attitudes held by sexual minority persons.

Internalized transphobia: Self-directed transphobic attitudes held by transgender persons.

Internalizing disorders: Mental illnesses of mood, anxiety, and disordered eating, in which symptoms are directed inward, toward the self.

Intersectional invisibility hypothesis: The prediction that people with multiple subordinate identities are noticed less than those with one subordinate identity.

Intersectionality: The ways in which different forms of discrimination and oppression (e.g., sexism, racism, classism, heterosexism, and transphobia) interact to shape people's experiences.

Intersex: Individuals for whom the biological components of sex (chromosomes, hormones, genitals, and internal and external sex organs) do not consistently fit either the typical male pattern or the typical female pattern.

Intersexual selection: The process by which heritable features get passed down because they give an animal an advantage by increasing its attractiveness to other-sex mates.

Intersexuality: A condition in which biological components of sex (chromosomes, hormones, genitals, and internal and external sex organs) do not consistently fit the typical male pattern or the typical female pattern.

Interview: A qualitative method in which researchers ask participants open-ended questions in an unstructured, semistructured, or structured format.

Intimate partner violence: Any behavior intended to cause physical harm to a romantic partner.

Intimate terrorism: Intimate partner violence in which one partner (usually a man) repeatedly uses violence and fear to dominate and control the other.

Intrasexual selection: The process by which heritable features get passed down because they give an animal a competitive advantage in contests against other same-sex animals for access to mates.

Kibbutzim: Collective agricultural communities in Israel in which work and social roles reflect socialist principles, and community members pursue gender-egalitarian lifestyles.

Kin selection: Helping behavior that is costly to the helper in the short term but beneficial in the long term because it increases the survival likelihood of the helper's genetic relatives.

Laissez-faire leadership style: A hands-off leadership style in which workers are allowed to complete responsibilities however they want, as long as the job gets done.

Latino paradox: A phenomenon in which Latino Americans in the United States have health outcomes as good as, if not better than, those of non-Latino White people in the United States, despite tending to have a lower average income and less education.

Lesbian: Refers to a woman who is attracted only (or primarily) to women.

LGBT: An acronym for "lesbian, gay, bisexual, and transgender."

Life expectancy: The average length of time a person is expected to live, based on year of birth.

Love (attachment): Strong feelings of affection and attachment that go beyond mere warmth.

Magnetic resonance imaging (MRI): An imaging procedure that uses magnetic fields and radio waves to create high-resolution images of brain structures.

Male discrepancy stress: Anxiety that boys and men feel about not living up to masculine expectations set by society.

Male gaze: A mode of viewing others that is voyeuristic and sexual and that reflects men's patriarchal power over women and other objectified individuals.

Manspreading: The tendency for some men to spread out and adopt an expansive posture while sitting, thus taking up more space.

Masculinity: Possession of physical and psychological attributes typically associated with men.

Mate preferences: Qualities that people claim to desire in a potential sexual or romantic mate.

Maternal gatekeeping: Behaviors and attitudes by women that discourage men's involvement in domestic labor and childcare.

Maternal wall: Gender bias in which working mothers—but not working fathers—are perceived as less competent at their jobs.

Matriarchal: Describes a societal structure in which women/mothers occupy the leadership positions in the society and control how it operates.

Matrilineal society: A society that traces descent through the mother's kinship line and passes inheritance down from mothers to their offspring.

Matrilocal society: A society in which husbands typically live near their wives' families.

Maximalist approach: A tendency to emphasize differences between members of different sex groups and view them as qualitatively different.

Medicalization: The process whereby normal, natural physical conditions and transitions are viewed as medical illnesses that require diagnoses and treatments.

Menopause: The cessation of menstruation and fertility, accompanied by stable declines in estrogen levels, that usually occurs between the ages of 45 and 55.

Mental rotation ability: The ability to rotate an object in one's mind.

Meta-analysis: A quantitative technique for analyzing a large collection of results from individual studies for the purpose of integrating the research findings.

Microaggressions: Common, everyday insults and indignities directed toward members of subordinate social groups. They can be verbal or behavioral and need not be intentional on the part of the perpetrator.

Milestone models of sexual identity development: Models that identify the timing, sequence, and tone of different milestones that many sexual minority individuals experience.

Minimalist approach: A tendency to emphasize similarities between members of different sex groups.

Minority stress theory: A theory that proposes that belonging to a stigmatized group can create stressors that are unique to the minority experience.

Mirror neurons: Neurons that fire both when performing an action and when observing another individual perform the action.

Mixed-methods approach: A research approach that combines both qualitative and quantitative methods within the same study or same program of research to develop a more complete understanding of a phenomenon.

Model: In social learning theories, a person who performs a behavior that is observed and later imitated by a learner.

Modern sexism: Socially acceptable form of sexism consisting of a denial that women still face gender discrimination, coupled with resentment toward women who seek social change.

Morbidity-mortality paradox: A phenomenon in which women have higher rates of morbidity (sickness and disability) than men while men have higher rates of mortality (death) than women.

Motherhood mandate: The societal expectation that women should have children and invest significant time and energy in raising them.

Motherhood penalty: The wage penalty that working women—but not working men—experience following the birth of a child.

Muscle dysmorphia: A body image disorder characterized by an obsessive preoccupation with increasing one's muscularity and maintaining low body fat.

Narrative approach to sexual identity development: An approach that broadly considers how multiple sources of oppression and pride interact to shape sexual identity within specific contexts.

Natural selection: The evolutionary process by which heritable features that increase the likelihood of an organism's survival get passed down through genes.

Need to belong: The fundamental need for a small number of close relationships that offer frequent, positive interactions.

Neurosexism: Interpreting the findings from neuroscience research in ways that reinforce gender stereotypes without valid supporting evidence.

Neuroticism: The tendency to experience high levels of negative emotions.

Norepinephrine: A neuropeptide that is associated with sympathetic arousal and the "fight-or-flight" response.

Obese: Having a body mass index over 30.

Objectification theory: The theory stating that experiencing socialization within a cultural context that objectifies the female body encourages girls and women to internalize an outsider's perspective on themselves and engage in self-objectification.

Occupational feminization: The entrance of women in large numbers into a previously male-dominated occupation.

Occupational masculinization: The (relatively rare) entrance of men in large numbers into a previously female-dominated occupation.

Occupational segregation: The segregation of occupations by sex, such that men primarily work in occupations dominated by men, and women primarily work in occupations dominated by women.

Old boys' networks: Informal, inner circles of men who exclude women from decision making and use their influence to help other men.

Optimal sex: The binary (male or female) sex perceived to be most advantageous to assign to a newborn whose genitalia appear atypical at birth.

Orgasm gap: The tendency for women to have lower rates of orgasm than men during heterosexual sexual encounters.

Outliers: Values at the extreme ends of a statistical distribution.

Overweight: Having a body mass index between 25 and 30.

Overwork: Working 50 or more hours per week in paid employment.

Oxytocin: A neurotransmitter that facilitates bonding, connectedness, and coordination.

Pair-bonding system: A system in which two adult members of a species remain bonded to one another for the purpose of producing and raising offspring.

Pansexual: Signifies being attracted to people of all sexes and gender identities.

Parent–child interaction: Phenomenon in which a parent and child mutually influence one another and therefore jointly contribute to the child's development.

Parental investment theory: Theory proposing that the sex that invests more in parenting (usually female) will be more selective in its choice of mates and will prefer mates who have social status and resources.

Participant variable: A naturally occurring feature of research participants (e.g., sex, personality, or nationality) that is measured in a study rather than manipulated.

Partner homogamy: The tendency for people to bond and mate with others who are similar to them on demographic, personality, background, and physical attributes.

Passionate friendships: Friendships characterized by intense longing for proximity, high levels of affection, and large amounts of physical touch (e.g., cuddling and hand holding). For some sexual minority women, these friendships provide the context for their first same-sex sexual experiences.

Passionate love: An early stage of love characterized by arousal, urgent longing, and exhilaration.

Paternalistic chivalry: The norm that dictates that men should be protective of women and treat them as if they are special and virtuous.

Patriarchal: Describes a societal structure in which men/fathers occupy the leadership positions in the society and control how it operates.

Patrilineal society: A society that traces descent through the father's kinship line and passes inheritance down from fathers to their offspring.

Patrilocal society: A society in which wives typically live near their husbands' families.

Phase models of sexual identity development: Models that posit distinct phases of emotional, psychological, social, and behavioral experiences that mark transitions in self-knowledge as people develop a sexual identity.

Phrenology: The discredited study of how the size and shape of the cranium (skull) relates to mental abilities and personal attributes.

Physical aggression: Physical acts intended to cause injury or harm to others.

Plasticity (or neuroplasticity): The ability of the brain to reorganize and adapt physically throughout life in response to environmental changes.

Point-light display: A minimal animated figure represented by points of light, which is created by a computer that reads sensors attached to the joints of a moving person.

Political correctness: The social norm—often viewed as taken to an extreme—that people should avoid language or acts that might offend, marginalize, or exclude members of socially disadvantaged groups.

Polyamory: A type of consensual nonmonogamy in which adults have more than one other adult intimate relationship partner, with the knowledge and consent of all parties.

Polyandry: Marriage between one wife and multiple husbands; polyandry is very rare historically.

Polygyny: Marriage between one husband and multiple wives; polygyny is more common than polyandry and is practiced today in some Muslim-majority countries in Africa, the Middle East, and South Asia.

Polysexual: Signifies being attracted to people of many different sexes and gender identities.

Polyvictimization: Experiencing more than one type of aggressive victimization.

Postpartum depression: Depression following (or associated with) childbirth.

Postpositivism: An orientation that views empirical investigation as a useful method for acquiring knowledge but recognizes its inherent biases and values.

Power: The capacity to determine one's own and other people's outcomes.

Power distance: The extent to which a culture has and accepts unequally distributed levels of status and power among its members.

Precarious manhood hypothesis: Hypothesis that manhood, relative to womanhood, is widely conceptualized as a social status that is hard to earn and easy to lose and

that requires continual validation in the form of public action.

Preferential looking: A method for determining preferences among preverbal infants that involves showing them two different objects or stimuli and examining how much time they spend looking at each one.

Prefrontal cortex: A brain region involved in impulse control, emotion regulation, and planning behaviors.

Premenstrual syndrome: A diagnosable illness that some women experience before the onset of menstruation and that consists of symptoms including aches and pains, bloating, anxiety, anger, and moodiness.

Privilege: Automatic, unearned advantages associated with belonging to a dominant group.

Prototype: The most typical cognitive representation of a category; with social groups, the prototype is the cultural default for representing the group.

Prove-it-again bias: Gender bias in which stereotypes about women's unsuitability for high-status positions result in women having to work harder than men to prove their competence.

Pseudoscience: Beliefs and practices that are presented as scientific despite lacking a factual basis and not being subjected to proper scientific scrutiny.

Psychological disorder (or mental illness): A persistent disruption or disturbance of thought, emotion, or behavior that causes significant distress or impairment in functioning.

Punishment: Any response following a behavior that decreases the likelihood of the behavior occurring again.

Qualitative methods: Methods in which researchers collect in-depth, non-numerical information in order to understand participants' subjective experiences within a specific context. Examples include case studies, interviews, and focus groups.

Quantitative methods: Methods in which researchers convert variables of interest into numbers and use statistical analyses to test hypotheses. Examples include experimental, ex post facto, quasi-experimental, and correlational designs.

Quasi-experiment (or person-by-treatment design): A design in which the researcher measures at least one participant variable and manipulates at least one independent variable.

Queen bee syndrome: A phenomenon in which women who hold authority positions in male-dominated professions dissociate themselves from other women and treat women employees more critically.

Random assignment: A process of assigning participants to experimental conditions randomly, so that each person has an equal chance of ending up in each condition.

Rank-order accuracy: Accuracy regarding the relative sizes of sex differences across different domains.

Rape: Nonconsensual penetration of the mouth, vagina, or anus by the penis, fingers, or objects.

Rape myths: Widely held false beliefs about rape, rape victims, and rapists.

Reinforcement: Any response following a behavior that increases the likelihood of the behavior occurring again.

Relative income hypothesis: The hypothesis that the partner who contributes proportionally less to the household income will do more housework.

Reproductive justice: The human right to personal bodily autonomy, parenthood choices, and safe communities in which to raise children.

Resource control: Controlling the creation or distribution of essential and desirable goods, such as money, land, food, and other valued commodities.

Reverse causation: In correlational research, the possibility that the true cause-and-effect relationship between two variables is the reverse of what is initially assumed (also known as the directionality problem). For instance, instead of X causing Y, it is always possible that Y causes X.

Risk networks: Extended networks of individuals with whom people have sexual contact or engage in other risky practices (e.g., intravenous drug use) that can transmit disease.

Rumination: Passively and persistently focusing attention on one's negative mood, its causes, and its possible consequences.

Scientific method: A process by which researchers conduct systematic studies in order to test hypotheses derived from theory.

Scientific positivism: An orientation that emphasizes the scientific method and proposes that objective and value-free knowledge is attainable through empirical investigation.

Self-concept: The entire set of an individual's beliefs, feelings, and knowledge about the self.

Self-fulfilling prophecy: The interpersonal process in which a perceiver's expectation about a target influences the target's behavior in such a manner that the target's behavior fulfills the perceiver's expectation.

Self-objectification: Defining the self in terms of how the body appears to others instead of what the body can do or how the body feels.

Sex: A term used to categorize people according to whether they are male, female, or intersex.

Sex-based harassment (sexual harassment): Behavior that derogates or humiliates an individual based on the individual's sex, sexual orientation, or gender identity.

Sex binary: The conceptualization of sex as consisting of two opposite and nonoverlapping categories, such as male or female.

Sex differentiation: The complex processes that unfold as sex-undifferentiated embryos transition into individuals with male, female, or intersex internal and external genitalia. Although much of sex differentiation occurs prenatally, further differentiation occurs during puberty.

Sex ratio: The number of men per woman in a given population or locale.

Sex trafficking: Forced, nonconsensual recruitment and retention of persons for sexual use and exploitation.

Sex typing: In social learning theories, the processes by which individuals acquire gendered behavior patterns.

Sexism: Negative attitudes toward individuals based solely on their sex, combined with institutional and cultural practices that support the unequal status of women and men.

Sexual assault: Unwanted sexual contact without the explicit consent of the victim.

Sexual callousness model: A model proposing that repeated exposure to pornography desensitizes and habituates viewers, leading to callous sexual attitudes toward women.

Sexual desire (lust): A wish or urge to engage in sexual activities.

Sexual fluidity: The tendency for people's sexual orientation or sexual identity to change across time.

Sexual identity: The label used to describe a person's sexual orientation and the emotional reactions that the person has to this label.

Sexual infidelity: When a member of a couple has sexual contact with someone else.

Sexual minority: Referring to lesbian, gay, bisexual, and other non-heterosexual sexual orientations.

Sexual orientation: A complex, enduring pattern of cognitive, motivational, and behavioral tendencies that shapes how people experience and express their sexuality. Often framed more simply as the sex or sexes toward whom an individual feels attracted.

Sexual peak: The height of a person's interest in, enjoyment of, or engagement in sexual activity over time.

Sexual selection: The evolutionary process by which heritable features that increase the likelihood of successful mating get passed down through genes.

Sexuality: The capacity for sexual responses and experiences.

Situational couple violence: Intimate partner violence that results when heated conflicts escalate; committed by men and women about equally.

Social comparisons: Comparisons between the self and another person on a specific domain.

Social dominance orientation (SDO): The belief that inequality among social groups is right and fair because some people and groups should have more status than others.

Social learning theories: Theories that propose that children learn gendered beliefs, behaviors, and preferences by observing and imitating models and by receiving reinforcement and punishment from others.

Social network: The extended circle of people with whom there are regular interactions.

Social role theory: The theory that gender stereotypes stem from people's observations of the social and occupational roles that women and men typically perform.

Socioeconomic dependence perspective: The the hypothesis that men use violence as a means of maintaining control over partners who are economically dependent on them and thus unlikely to leave.

Socioeconomic status (SES): A measure of an individual's (or household's) total income, educational background, and occupation.

Spatial location memory: The ability to remember the location of objects in physical space.

Spatial perception: The ability to perceive, understand, and remember relations between objects in three-dimensional space.

Spatial visualization: The ability to represent and manipulate two- and three-dimensional objects mentally.

Stalled gender revolution: A historical trend in the United States in which women made large gains in the workforce between the 1960s and 1980s, but this began to plateau in the early 1990s.

Standard deviation: A statistical measure of variability that indicates how far the scores in a distribution deviate, on average, from the mean value of the distribution.

Statistical beliefs: Beliefs about categories that involve numbers or proportions.

Statistically significant difference: An observed difference that is very unlikely to have resulted due to chance.

Status incongruity hypothesis: The assumption that gender role–violating women are viewed negatively because they are seen as too dominant while gender role–violating men are viewed negatively because they are seen as too low in status. These perceptions violate the gender status hierarchy and make people uncomfortable.

Status inconsistency perspective: The hypothesis that men engage in partner violence more often when they feel threatened by partners who have greater economic status and power than they do.

Stereotype content model: Theory proposing that stereotypes about social groups fall along communion and agency dimensions and that groups may be seen as high or low on both dimensions.

Stereotype threat: Anxiety individuals feel when concerned that their behavior or performance might confirm a negative group stereotype.

Sticky floor: Barriers that keep low-wage workers, who are disproportionately likely to be women and racial and ethnic minority individuals, from being promoted.

Street harassment: Uninvited sexual attention or harassment from a stranger in a public space.

Strong Black woman schema: A set of beliefs about Black women as being strong, resilient, and able to persevere despite oppression.

Structural power: The power to shape societies and social systems.

Subjective well-being: People's feelings of both short-term positive emotions and long-term sense of satisfaction, meaning, and purpose in life.

System justification theory: The theory proposing that people are motivated to justify the sociopolitical system that governs them (even if it treats them unfairly) because doing so reduces uncertainty.

Teddy bear effect: The tendency for baby-faced (physically nonthreatening) Black men to have an advantage in seeking high-status positions because they do not activate people's stereotypes about Black men as aggressive.

Telomeres: Disposable DNA sequences at the ends of chromosome strands that protect the remaining genes on the chromosomes during cell division.

Think manager–think male effect: An effect in which stereotypes of men and good leaders overlap more strongly than stereotypes of women and good managers.

Third variable problem: In correlational research, the possibility that an unmeasured third variable (z) is responsible for the relationship between two correlated variables (x and y).

Tightrope: Gender bias in which employed women are viewed as less likable if they are assertive and as less competent if they are warm.

Time availability theory: The theory that the partner who spends less time in paid work will do more housework.

Tipping point theory: The theory that genes for same-sex sexuality get passed on because the same-sex relatives of gay and lesbian people have personalities that increase their likelihood of engaging in reproductive sex.

Transdiagnostic approach: An approach that views most psychological disorders as different manifestations of a few core, heritable, underlying dimensions.

Transformational leadership style: A style of leading that involves active mentorship, inspiring trust in subordinates, and encouraging others to develop to their full potential.

Transgender: Describes people whose psychological gender identity does not align with their assigned sex at birth.

Trigender: Describes people who shift among woman, man, and third gender identities.

Tug of war: Gender bias in which women feel like they have to compete against one another for access to limited positions, promotions, and workplace rewards.

Unacknowledged rape: An experience that meets the legal definition of rape but is not labeled as rape by the victim.

Unmitigated agency: A tendency to focus on the self to the neglect of other people.

Unmitigated communion: A tendency to focus on others to the neglect of the self.

Verbal aggression: Communications intended to cause harm to others.

Verbal fluency: The ability to generate words.

Verbal reasoning: The ability to understand and analyze concepts, often tested with analogies or word problems.

Violence: Severe forms of physical aggression that have extreme harm as their goal.

Visual dominance: A pattern of eye contact in which a person looks at others when speaking and looks away when listening.

Visual-spatial abilities: Cognitive skills that help individuals understand relationships between objects and navigate three-dimensional space.

Whorfian (linguistic relativity) hypothesis: A hypothesis stating that the structure of language determines the nature of the speaker's thoughts and worldviews.

Within-group variance: A measure of how spread out the values are among people within the same group (or within the same condition of an experiment).

Women-are-wonderful effect: The tendency for people to view stereotypes about women more favorably than they view stereotypes about men and, accordingly, to view (traditional, gender-conforming) women very positively.

Work flexibility stigma: Negative evaluations that workers receive for pursuing flexible work arrangements.

Work–family conflict: Feelings of stressful conflict between work life and home life, in which time spent in each domain detracts from contributions to the other domain.

Work–life balance: The manner in which people prioritize work and home life.

Work–life enrichment: Feelings of positive enrichment between work life and home life, in which a fulfilling job produces positive spillover into the home, and a satisfying home life produces positive spillover into work.

References

Aassve, A., Fuochi, G., & Mencarini, L. (2014). Desperate housework: Relative resources, time availability, economic dependency, and gender ideology across Europe. *Journal of Family Issues, 35*, 1000–1022.

AAUW. (2017). *The simple truth about the gender pay gap, spring 2017 edition.* Washington, DC: Author.

Abbate, J. (2012). *Recoding gender: Women's changing participation in computing.* Cambridge, MA: MIT Press.

Abbey, A. D., Jacques-Tiura, A. J., & Parkhill, M. R. (2010). Sexual assault among diverse populations of women: Common ground, distinctive features, and unanswered questions. In H. R. N. F. Landrine (Ed.), *Handbook of diversity in feminist psychology* (pp. 391–425). New York, NY: Springer.

Abbey, A., Zawacki, T., Buck, P. O., Clinton, A. M., & McAuslan, P. (2004). Sexual assault and alcohol consumption: What do we know about their relationship and what types of research are still needed? *Aggression and Violent Behavior, 9*, 271–303.

ABC News. (2015, May 6). U.S. is only industrialized nation without paid maternity leave. Retrieved from http://abcnews.go.com/Business/us-industrialized-nation-paid-maternity-leave/story?id=30852419

Abele, A. E., & Wojciszke, B. (2013). The Big Two in social judgment and behavior. *Social Psychology, 44*, 61–62.

Abrams, D., Viki, G. T., Masser, B., & Bohner, G. (2003). Perceptions of stranger and acquaintance rape: The role of benevolent and hostile sexism in victim blame and rape proclivity. *Journal of Personality and Social Psychology, 84*(1), 111–125.

Abu-Rabia, A. (2011). Family honor killings: Between custom and state law. *Open Psychology Journal, 4*, 34–44.

Adams, R. B., & Ferreira, D. (2009). Women in the boardroom and their impact on governance and performance. *Journal of Financial Economics, 94*, 291–309.

Addis, M. E. (2008). Gender and depression in men. *Clinical Psychology Science and Practice, 15*, 153–168.

Addis, M., & Mahalik, J. (2003). Men, masculinity, and the contexts of help seeking. *American Psychologist, 58*, 5–14.

Afifi, W. A., & Faulkner, S. L. (2000). On being 'just friends': The frequency and impact of sexual activity in cross-sex friendships. *Journal of Social and Personal Relationships, 17*, 205–222.

Agency for Fundamental Rights. (2014, March). *Violence against women: An EU-wide survey.* Retrieved from http://fra.europa.eu/en/publication/2014/violence-against-women-eu-wide-survey-results-glance

Agha, S. (2009). Structural correlates of female homicide: A cross-national analysis. *Journal of Criminal Justice, 37*, 576–585.

Agrillo, C., & Nelini, C. (2008). Childfree by choice: A review. *Journal of Cultural Geography, 25*, 347–363.

Ahn, J. N., Haines, E. L., & Mason, M. F. (2017). Gender stereotypes and the coordination of mnemonic work within heterosexual couples: Romantic partners manage their daily to-dos. *Sex Roles, 77*(7–8), 435–452.

Alaerts, K., Nackaerts, E., Meyns, P., Swinnen, S. P., & Wenderoth, N. (2011). Action and emotion recognition from point light displays: An investigation of gender differences. *PLOS One, 6*(6), e0155885.

Albarracin, J., & Plambeck, C. R. (2010). Demographic factors and sexist beliefs as predictors of condom use among Lantinos in the USA. *AIDS Care, 22*(8), 1021–1028.

Albuquerque, G. A., de Lima Garcia, C., da Silva Quirino, G., Alves, M. J. H., Belém, J. M., dos Santos Figueiredo, F. W., . . . de Abreu, L. C. (2016). Access to health services by lesbian, gay, bisexual, and transgender persons: Systematic literature review. *BMC International Health and Human Rights, 16*(1), 2.

Alexander, G. M., Wilcox, R., & Woods, R. (2009). Sex differences in infants' visual interest in toys. *Archives of Sexual Behavior, 38*, 427–433.

Alexander, M. G., & Fisher, T. D. (2003). Truth and consequences: Using the bogus pipeline to examine sex differences in self-reported sexuality. *Journal of Sex Research, 40*, 27–35.

Allen, C. (2014, February 28). How lego earned the wrath of the 'gender-neutral toys' crowd. *Los Angeles Times.* Retrieved from http://articles.latimes.com/2014/feb/28/opinion/la-oe-allen-lego-gender-neutral-toys-20140228

Allen, M., D'Alessio, D., & Brezgel, K. (1995). A meta-analysis summarizing the effects of pornography II: Aggression after exposure. *Human Communication Research, 22,* 258–283.

Allen, S. M., & Hawkins, A. J. (1999). Maternal gatekeeping: Mothers' beliefs and behaviors that inhibit greater father involvement in family work. *Journal of Marriage and Family, 61,* 199–212.

Allen, T. A., Johnson, R. C., Kiburz, K. M., & Shockley, K. M. (2013). Work–family conflict and flexible work arrangements: Deconstructing flexibility. *Personnel Psychology, 66,* 345–376.

Allen, T. D. (2012). The work and family interface. In S. W. J. Kozlowski (Ed.), *The Oxford handbook of organizational psychology* (pp. 1163–1198). New York, NY: Oxford University Press.

Allen, T. D., Lapierre, L. M., Spector, P. E., Poelmans, S. A. Y., O'Driscoll, M., Sanchez, J. I., . . . Woo, J-M. (2014). The link between national paid leave policy and work–family conflict among married working parents. *Applied Psychology, 63,* 5–28.

Allport, G. W. (1954). *The nature of prejudice.* Reading, MA: Addison Wesley.

Ambady, N., Hallahan, M., & Conner, B. (1999). Accuracy of judgments of sexual orientation from thin slices of behavior. *Journal of Personality and Social Psychology, 77,* 538–547.

American Psychiatric Association. (1980). *Diagnostic and statistical manual of mental disorders* (3rd ed.). Washington, DC: Author.

American Psychiatric Association. (2013). Gender dysphoria: Fact sheet. Retrieved from http://www.psychiatry.org/dsm5

American Psychological Association. (1977). Guidelines for nonsexist language in APA journals: Publication manual change sheet 2. *American Psychologist, 32,* 487–494.

American Psychological Association. (1983). *Publication manual of the American Psychological Association* (3rd ed.). Washington DC: Author.

American Psychological Association. (2008). Transgender, gender identity, and gender expression non-discrimination. Retrieved from http://www.apa.org/about/policy/ transgender.aspx

American Psychological Association (2009a). *Report of the Task Force on Appropriate Therapeutic Responses to Sexual Orientation.* Washington, DC: APA.

American Psychological Association. (2009b). *Report of the Task Force on Gender Identity and Gender Variance.* Washington, DC: Author.

American Psychological Association. (2010). *Publication manual of the American Psychological Association* (6th ed.). Washington, DC: Author.

American Psychological Association. (2012). Guidelines for psychological practice with lesbian, gay, and bisexual clients. *American Psychologist, 67,* 10–42.

American Psychological Association. (2017). *Ethnic and racial minorities and socioeconomic status.* Retrieved from https://www.apa.org/pi/ses/resources/publications/minorities.aspx

Amy Poehler on the not-a-feminist trend: 'I don't get it.' (2014, January 31). *Huffington Post.* Retrieved from http://www.huffingtonpost.com/2014/01/31/amy-poehler-feminism-elle_n_4702359.html

Anderson, K. J., & Leaper, C. (1998). Meta-analyses of gender effects on conversational interruption: Who, what, when, where, and how. *Sex Roles, 39,* 225–252.

Anderson, R. N. (2001). *Deaths: Leading causes for 1999. National Vital Statistics Reports, 49, No. 11.* Hyattsville, MD: National Center for Health Statistics. Retrieved from http://www.cdc.gov/nchs/data/nvsr/nvsr49/nvsr49_11.pdf

Anderson, V. N. (2009). What's in a label: Judgments of feminist men and feminist women. *Psychology of Women Quarterly, 33,* 206–215.

Anson, O., Levenson, A., & Bonneh, D. Y. (1990). Gender and health on the kibbutz. *Sex Roles, 22,* 213–236.

APA Task Force. (2007). *Report of the APA Task Force on the Sexualization of Girls.* Washington, DC: American Psychological Association.

Applegate, J. (1997, October 19). *Nature vs. nurture in men and women.* Retrieved from https://highered.nbclearn.com/portal/site/HigherEd/browse/?cuecard=45950

Arain, M., Haque, M., Johal, L., Mathur, P., Nel, W., Rais, A., . . . Sharma, S. (2013). Maturation of the adolescent brain. *Neuropsychiatric Disease and Treatment, 9,* 449–461.

Arboleda, V. A., Sandberg, D. E., & Vilain, E. (2014). DSDs: Genetics, underlying pathologies and psychosexual differentiation. *Nature Reviews Endocrinology, 10*(10), 603–615.

Arcelus, J., Mitchell, A. J., Wales, J., & Nielsen, S. (2011). Mortality rates in patients with anorexia nervosa and other eating disorders. *Archives of General Psychiatry, 68,* 724–731.

Archer, J. (1991). The influence of testosterone on human aggression. *British Journal of Psychology, 82,* 1–28.

Archer, J. (2000). Sex differences in aggression between heterosexual partners: A meta-analytic review. *Psychological Bulletin, 126,* 651–680.

Archer, J. (2004). Sex differences in aggression in real-world setting: A meta-analytic review. *Review of General Psychology, 8,* 291–322.

Archer, J. (2006). Cross-cultural differences in physical aggression between partners: A social-role analysis. *Personality and Social Psychology Review, 10,* 133–153.

Arias, E. (2015). *United States life tables, 2011. National Vital Statistics Reports, 64, No. 11.* Hyattsville, MD: National Center for Health Statistics. Retrieved from https://www.cdc.gov/nchs/data/nvsr/nvsr64/nvsr64_11.pdf

Arias, I., & Corso, P. (2005). Average cost per person victimized by an intimate partner of the opposite gender: A comparison of men and women. *Violence and Victims, 20,* 379–391.

Armstrong, E. A., England, P., & Fogarty, A. C. K. (2009). Orgasm in college hookups and relationships. In B. J. Risman (Ed.), *Families as they really are* (pp. 362–377). New York, NY: Norton.

Arrighi, B. A., & Maume, D. J. (2001). Workplace subordination and men's avoidance of housework. *Journal of Family Issues, 21,* 464–487.

Artime, T. M., McCallum, E. B., & Peterson, Z. D. (2014). Men's acknowledgement of their sexual victimization experiences. *Psychology of Men & Masculinity, 15,* 313–323.

Artis, J., & Pavalko, E. (2003). Explaining the decline in women's household labour: Individual change and cohort differences. *Journal of Marriage and Family, 65,* 746–761.

Ashburn-Nardo, L. (2017). Parenthood as a moral imperative? Moral outrage and the stigmatization of voluntarily childfree women and men. *Sex Roles, 76,* 393–401.

Ashburn-Nardo, L., Morris, K. A., & Goodwin, S. A. (2008). The Confronting Prejudiced Responses (CPR) Model: Applying CPR in organizations. *Academy of Management Learning & Education, 7,* 332–342.

Association of American Universities. (2015). *Report on the AAU campus climate survey on sexual assault and sexual misconduct.* Rockville, MD: Westat. Retrieved from https://www.aau.edu/sites/default/files/%40%20Files/Climate%20Survey/AAU_Campus_Climate_Survey_12_14_15.pdf

Atkinson M. P., Greenstein T. N., & Lang, M. M. (2005). For women, breadwinning can be dangerous: Gendered resource theory and wife abuse. *Journal of Marriage and Family, 67,* 1137–1148.

AuBuchon, P. G., & Calhoun, K. S. (1985). Menstrual cycle symptomatology: The role of social expectancy and experimental demand characteristics. *Psychosomatic Medicine, 47,* 35–45.

Aughinbaugh, A., Robles, O., & Sun, H. (2013). Marriage and divorce: Patterns by gender, race and educational attainment. *Monthly Labor Review, 136.* Retrieved from: http://www.bls.gov/opub/mlr/2013/article/marriage-and-divorce-patterns-by-gender-race-and-educational-attainment.htm

Aumann, K., Galinsky, E., & Matos, K. (2011). *The new male mystique.* New York, NY: Families and Work Institute.

Austen, I. (2015, November 4). Justin Trudeau is sworn in as prime minister of Canada. *New York Times.* Retrieved from https://www.nytimes.com/2015/11/05/world/americas/canada-justin-trudeau-sworn-in-as-prime-minister.html?_r=0

Avert.org. (2016, August 10). *Global HIV and AIDS statistics.* Retrieved from http://www.avert.org/global-hiv-and-aids-statistics

Babcock, L., Gelfand, M., Small, D., & Stayn, H. (2006). Gender differences in the propensity to initiate negotiations. In D. De Cremer, M. Zeelenberg, & J. K. Murnighan (Eds.), *Social psychology and economics* (pp. 239–262). Mahwah, NJ: Lawrence Erlbaum.

Babcock, L., & Laschever, S. (2009, January 29). The costs of not negotiating. *Harvard Business Review.* Retrieved from https://hbr.org/2009/01/is-talent-going-to-waste-in-yo

Babu, G. R., & Babu, B. V. (2011). Dowry deaths: A neglected public health issue in India. *International Health, 3,* 35–43.

Bachner-Melman, R., Zohar, A. H., Ebstein, R. P., Elizur, Y., & Constantini, N. (2006). How anorexic-like are the symptom and personality profiles of aesthetic athletes? *Medicine & Science in Sports & Exercise, 38,* 628–636.

Badgett, M. V. L., Lau, H., Sears, B., & Ho, D. (2007). *Bias in the workplace: Consistent evidence of sexual orientation and gender identity discrimination.* Los Angeles, CA: Williams Institute. Retrieved from https://williamsinstitute.law.ucla.edu/wp-content/uploads/Badgett-Sears-Lau-Ho-Bias-in-the-Workplace-Jun-2007.pdf

Badgett, M. V. L., Nezhad, S., Waaldijk, K., & van der Meulen Rodgers, Y. (2014, November). *The relationship between LGBT inclusion* and economic development: An analysis of emerging economies. Retrieved from https://williamsinstitute.law.ucla.edu/wp-content/uploads/lgbt-inclusion-and-development-november-2014.pdf

Bagemihl, B. (1999). *Biological exuberance: Animal homosexuality and natural diversity.* New York, NY: St. Martin's Press.

Bailey, J. M., Dunne, M. P., & Martin, N. G. (2000). Genetic and environmental influences on sexual orientation and its correlates in an Australian twin sample. *Journal of Personality and Social Psychology, 78,* 524–536.

Bailey, M. J., & Zucker, K. J. (1995). Childhood sex-typed behavior and sexual orientation: A conceptual analysis and quantitative review. *Developmental Psychology, 31,* 43–55.

Baldiga, K. (2013). Gender differences in willingness to guess. *Management Science, 60,* 434–448.

Baldridge, D. C., Eddleston, K. A., & Veiga, J. F. (2006). Saying no to being uprooted: The impact of family and gender on willingness to relocate. *Journal of Occupational and Organizational Psychology, 79,* 131–149.

Baldwin, J. D., & Baldwin, J. I. (1997). Gender differences in sexual interest. *Archives of Sexual Behavior, 26,* 181–210.

Balog, P., Janszky, I., Leineweber, C., Blom, M., Wamala, S. P., & Orth-Gomer, K. (2003). Depressive symptoms in relation to marital and work stress in women with and without coronary heart disease: The Stockholm Female Coronary Risk Study. *Journal of Psychosomatic Research, 54,* 113–119.

Baltes, B. B., Briggs, T. E., Huff, J. W., Wright, J. A., & Neuman, G. A. (1999). Flexible and compressed workweek schedules: A meta-analysis of their effects on work-related criteria. *Journal of Applied Psychology, 84,* 496–513.

Bank, B. J., & Hansford, S. L. (2000). Gender and friendship: Why are men's best same-sex friendships less intimate and supportive. *Personal Relationships, 7,* 63–78.

Barber, N. (2003). Divorce and reduced economic and emotional interdependence: A cross national study. *Journal of Divorce & Remarriage, 39*(3/4), 113–124.

Barber, N. (2008). Explaining cross-national differences in polygyny intensity: Resource- defense, sex ratio, and infectious diseases. *Cross-Cultural Research, 42,* 103–117.

Barlett, C., & Coyne, S. M. (2014). A meta-analysis of sex differences in cyber-bullying behavior: The moderating role of age. *Aggressive Behavior, 40,* 474–488.

Barnett, R. C., & Hyde, J. S. (2001). Women, men, work, and family: An expansionist theory. *American Psychologist, 56,* 781–796.

Baron, D. (2016, February 24). On the birthday of the (legal) generic masculine, let's declare it legally dead [Web log post]. Retrieved from https://illinois.edu/blog/view/25/331699

Baron-Cohen, S., & Wheelwright, S. (2004). The empathy quotient: An investigation of adults with Asperger syndrome or high functioning autism, and normal sex differences. *Journal of Autism and Developmental Disorders, 34*(2), 163–175.

Barr, A., Bryan, A., & Kenrick, D. T. (2002). Sexual peak: Socially shared cognitions about desire, frequency, and satisfaction in men and women. *Personal Relationships, 9,* 287–299.

Barrett, E. L. B., & Richardson, D. S. (2011). Sex differences in telomeres and lifespan. *Aging Cell, 10,* 913–921.

Bartels, A., & Zeki, S. (2000). The neural basis of romantic love. *NeuroReport, 11,* 1–6.

Bartindale, B. (2005, February 14). New UCSC chancellor no stranger to challenges. *Mercury News.* Retrieved from http://lazowska.cs.washington.edu/denice.sjmercury

Bartkowski, J. P. (2003). *The Promise Keepers: Servants, soldiers, and godly men.* New Brunswick, NJ: Rutgers University Press.

Basow, S. A. (2010). Gender in the classroom. In J. C. Chrisler & D. R. McCreary (Eds.), *Handbook of gender research in psychology* (pp. 277–295). New York, NY: Springer.

Basow, S. A., & Rubenfeld, K. (2003). "Troubles talk": Effects of gender and gender-typing. *Sex Roles, 48,* 183–187.

Baumeister, R. F. (1988). Should we stop studying sex differences altogether? *American Psychologist, 43,* 1092–1095.

Baumeister, R. F. (2000). Gender differences in erotic plasticity: The female sex drive as socially flexible and responsive. *Psychological Bulletin, 126,* 347–374.

Baumeister, R. F. (2007). *In there anything good about men?* Invited address, American Psychological Association.

Baumeister, R. F. (2010). *Is there anything good about men: How cultures flourish by exploiting men.* New York, NY: Oxford University Press.

Baumeister, R. F., Catanese, K. R., & Vohs, K. D. (2001). Is there a gender difference in strength of sex drive? Theoretical views, conceptual distinctions, and a review of relevant evidence. *Personality and Social Psychology Review, 5,* 242–273.

Baumeister, R. F., & Leary, M. R. (1995). The need to belong: Desire for interpersonal attachments as a fundamental human motivation. *Psychological Bulletin, 117,* 497–529.

Baumgardner, J., & Richards, A. (2010). *Manifesta: Young women, feminism, and the future.* New York, NY: Farrar, Straus, and Giroux.

Bavelas, J. B., Black, A., Lemery, C. R., & Mullett, J. (1986). "I show how you feel": Motor mimicry as a communicative act. *Journal of Personality and Social Psychology, 50*(2), 322–329.

Bays, A. (2016). Perceptions, emotions, and behaviors toward women based on parental status. *Sex Roles, 76*(3–4), 138–155.

Beaulieu, C. (2004). Intercultural study of personal space: A case study. *Journal of Applied Social Psychology, 34,* 794–805.

Becker, A., Burwell, R. A., Herzog, D. B., Hamburg, P., & Gilman, S. E. (2002). Eating behaviors and attitudes following prolonged exposure to television among ethnic Fijian adolescent girls. *British Journal of Psychiatry, 180,* 509–514.

Becker, J. C., Glick, P., Ilic, M., & Bohner, G. (2011). Damned if she does, damned if she doesn't: Consequences of accepting versus confronting patronizing help for the female target and male actor. *European Journal of Social Psychology, 41,* 761–773.

Becker, J. C., & Swim, J. K. (2011). Seeing the unseen: Attention to daily encounters with sexism as way to reduce sexist beliefs. *Psychology of Women Quarterly, 35,* 227–242.

Becker, J. C., & Wright, S. C. (2011). Yet another dark side of chivalry: Benevolent sexism undermines and hostile sexism motivates collective action for social change. *Journal of Personality and Social Psychology, 101,* 62–77.

Beemyn, G., & Rankin, R. (2011). *The lives of transgender people.* New York, NY: Columbia University Press.

Beere, C. A., King, D. W., Beere, D. B., & King, L. A. (1984). The Sex Role Egalitarianism Scale: A measure of attitudes toward equality between the sexes. *Sex Roles, 10,* 563–576.

Bem, S. L. (1974). The measurement of psychological androgyny. *Journal of Consulting and Clinical Psychology, 43,* 155–162.

Bem, S. L. (1981). Gender schema theory: A cognitive account of sex typing. *Psychological Review, 88,* 354–364.

Bem, S. L. (1983). Gender schema theory and its implications for child development: Raising gender-aschematic children in a gender-schematic society. *Signs, 8,* 598–616.

Bem, S. L. (1993). *The lenses of gender: Transforming the debate on sexual inequality.* New Haven, CT: Yale University Press.

Benard, S., & Correll, S. J. (2010). Normative discrimination and the motherhood penalty. *Gender & Society, 24,* 616–646.

Benatar, D. (2012). *The second sexism: Discrimination against men and boys.* Malden, MA: Wiley-Blackwell.

Bennett, J. (2016, January 30). She? Ze? They? What's in a gender pronoun? *New York Times.* Retrieved from http://www.nytimes.com/2016/01/31/fashion/pronoun-confusion-sexual-fluidity.html?_r=0

Benton, D. (1983). Do animals tell us anything about the relationship between testosterone and human aggression? In C. C. L. Davey (Ed.), *Animal models of human behavior.* New York, NY: John Wiley.

Berdahl, J. L. (2007). Harassment based on sex: Protecting social status in the context of gender hierarchy. *Academy of Management Review, 32,* 641–658.

Berdahl, J. L., Magley, V. J., & Waldo, C. R. (1996). The sexual harassment of men? *Psychology of Women Quarterly, 20,* 527–547.

Berdahl, J. L., & Moon, S. H. (2013). Workplace mistreatment of middle class workers based on sex, parenthood, and caregiving. *Journal of Social Issues, 69,* 341–366.

Berdahl, J. L., & Moore, C. (2006). Workplace harassment: Double jeopardy for minority women. *Journal of Applied Psychology, 91,* 426–436.

Berdahl, J. L., & Raver, J. L. (2011). Sexual harassment. In S. Zedeck (Ed.), *APA handbook of industrial and organizational psychology, Vol 3: Maintaining, expanding, and contracting the organization* (pp. 641–669). Washington, DC: APA.

Berenbaum, S. A., & Bailey, J. M. (2003). Effects on gender identity of prenatal androgens and genital appearance: Evidence from girls with congenital adrenal hyperplasia. *Journal of Clinical Endocrinology Metabolism, 88*(3), 1102–1106.

Berenbaum, S. A., Bryk, K. L. K., & Beltz, A. M. (2012). Early androgen effects on spatial and mechanical abilities: Evidence from congenital adrenal hyperplasia. *Behavioral Neuroscience, 126*(1), 86–96.

Berger, J. M., Levant, R., McMillan, K. K., Kelleher, W., & Sellers, A. (2005). Impact of gender role conflict, traditional masculine ideology, alexithymia, and age on men's attitudes toward psychological help seeking. *Psychology of Men & Masculinity, 6*, 73–78.

Bergold, S., Wendt, H., Kasper, D., & Steinmayr, R. (2017). Academic competencies: Their interrelatedness and gender differences at their high end. *Journal of Educational Psychology, 109*, 439–449.

Berkel, J., & de Waard, F. (1983). Mortality pattern and life expectancy of Seventh-day Adventists in the Netherlands. *International Journal of Epidemiology, 12*, 455–459.

Berkman, L. F., & Syme, S. L. (1979). Social networks, host resistance, and mortality: A nine-year follow-up study of Alameda county residents. *American Journal of Epidemiology, 109*, 186–204.

Berkowitz, T., Schaeffer, M. W., Maloney, E. A., Peterson, L., Gregor, C., Levine, S. C., & Beilock, S. L. (2015). Math at home adds up to achievement at school. *Science, 350*, 196–198.

Besnier, N. (2003). Crossing gender, mixing languages: The linguistic construction of transgenderism in Tonga. In J. Holmes & M. Meyerhoff (Eds.), *The handbook of language and gender* (pp. 279–301). Oxford, UK: Blackwell.

Best, D. L., & Williams, J. E. (2001). Gender and culture. In D. Matsumoto & D. Matsumoto (Eds.), *The handbook of culture and psychology* (pp. 195–219). New York, NY: Oxford University Press.

Bettencourt, A. A., & Miller, N. (1996). Gender differences in aggression as a function of provocation: A meta-analysis. *Psychological Bulletin, 119*, 422–447.

Betzig, L. (1989). Causes of conjugal dissolution: A cross-cultural study. *Current Anthropology, 30*, 654–676.

Beyrer, C., Baral, S. D., Van Griensven, F., Goodreau, S. M., Chariyalertsak, S., Wirtz, A. L., & Brookmeyer, R. (2012). Global epidemiology of HIV infection in men who have sex with men. *The Lancet, 380*, 367–377.

Bian, L., & Cimpian, A. (2016, February 10). *Are stereotypes accurate? A viewpoint from the cognitive science of concepts*. Retrieved from http://www.spsp.org/blog/are-stereotypes-accurate

Bianchi, S. M., Robinson, J. O., & Milkie, M. A. (2006). *The changing rhythms of American family life*. New York, NY: Russell Sage Foundation.

Bianchi, S. M., Sayer, L. C., Milkie, M. A., & Robinson, J. P. (2012). Housework: Who did, does or will do it, and how much does it matter? *Social Forces, 91*, 55–63.

Bieber, I., Dain, H. J., Dince, P. R., Drellich, M. G., Grand, H. G., Gundlach, R. R., . . . Bieber, T. B. (1962). *Homosexuality: A psychoanalytic study of male homosexuals*. New York, NY: Basic Books.

Bielby, W. T., & Bielby, D. D. (1992). I will follow him: Family ties, gender-role beliefs, and reluctance to relocate for a better job. *American Journal of Sociology, 97*, 1241–1267.

Biernat, M., & Wortman, C. B. (1991). Sharing of home responsibilities between professionally employed women and their husbands. *Journal of Personality and Social Psychology, 60*, 844–860.

Bigler, R. S., & Liben, L. S. (2007). Developmental intergroup theory: Explaining and reducing children's social stereotyping and prejudice. *Current Directions in Psychological Science, 16*, 162–166.

Binet, A., & Simon, T. (1908). Le developpement de l'intelligence chez les enfants [The development of intelligence in children]. *L'Année Psychologique, 14*, 1–90.

Birdwhistell, R. (1970). *Kinesics and context*. Philadelphia: University of Pennsylvania Press.

Bittman, M., England, P., Sayer, L., Folbre, N., & Matheson, G. (2003). When does gender trump money? Bargaining and time in household work. *American Journal of Sociology, 109*, 186–214.

Björkqvist, K., Österman, K., & Lagerspetz, K. M. J. (1994). Sex differences in in covert aggression among adults. *Aggressive Behavior, 20*, 27–33.

Black, M. C., Basile, K. C., Breiding, M. J., Smith, S. G., Walters, M. L., Merrick, M. T., . . . Stevens, M. R. (2011). *The National Intimate Partner and Sexual Violence Survey (NISVS): 2010 summary report*. Atlanta, GA: National Center for Injury Prevention and Control, Centers for Disease Control and Prevention. Retrieved from https://www.cdc.gov/violencepreven tion/pdf/nisvs_report2010-a.pdf

Blackless, M., Charuvastra, A., Derryck, A., Fausto-Sterling, A., Lauzanne, K., & Lee, E. (2000). How sexually dimorphic are we? Review and synthesis. *American Journal of Human Biology, 12*, 151–166.

Blackwell, D. L., Lucas, J. W., & Clarke, T. C. (2014). Summary health statistics for US adults: National health interview survey, 2012. *Vital and Health Statistics. Series 10, Data from the National Health Survey, 260*, 1–161.

Blair, K. L., & Pukall, C. F. (2014). Can less be more? Comparing duration vs. frequency of sexual encounters in same-sex and mixed-sex relationships. *Canadian Journal of Human Sexuality, 23*, 123–136.

Blanchard, R. (2001). Fraternal birth order and the maternal immune hypothesis of male homosexuality. *Hormones and Behavior, 40*, 105–114.

Blashill, A. J., & Powlishta, K. K. (2009). Gay stereotypes: The use of sexual orientation as a cue for gender-related attributes. *Sex Roles, 61*, 783–793.

Blau, F. D., & Kahn, L. D. (2003). Understanding international differences in the gender pay gap. *Journal of Labor Economics, 21*, 106–144.

Bleske, A. L., & Buss, D. M. (2000). Can men and women be just friends? *Personal Relationships, 7*, 131–151.

Bleske-Rechek, A. L., & Buss, D. M. (2001). Opposite-sex friendship: Sex differences and similarities in initiation, selection, and dissolution. *Personality and Social Psychological Bulletin, 27*, 1310–1323.

Blow, A. J., & Hartnett, K. (2005). Infidelity in committed relationships II: A substantive review. *Journal of Marital and Family Therapy, 31*(2), 217–233.

Bluhm, R. (2013a). New research, old problems: Methodological and ethical issues in fMRI research examining sex/gender differences in emotion processing. *Neuroethics, 6*, 319–330.

Bluhm, R. (2013b). Self-fulfilling prophecies: The influence of gender stereotypes on functional neuroimaging research on emotion. *Hypatia, 28*(4), 870–886.

Blurton Jones, N. G., Marlowe, F., Hawkes, K., O'Connell, J., (2000). Hunter-gatherer divorce rates and the paternal investment theory of human pair bonding. In L. Cronk, N. Chagnon, & W. Irons (Eds.), *Human behavior and adaptation: An anthropological perspective* (pp. 65–86). New York, NY: Elsevier.

Bobrow, D., & Bailey, J. M. (2001). Is male homosexuality maintained via kin selection? *Evolution and Human Behavior, 22*, 361–368.

Boerma, T., Hosseinpoor, A. R., Verdes, E., & Chatterji, S. (2016). A global assessment of the gender gap in self-reported health with survey data from 59 countries. *BMC Public Health, 16*, 675.

Bogaert, A. F. (2004). Asexuality: Prevalence and associated factors in a national probability sample. *Journal of Sex Research, 41*, 279–287.

Bogle, K. A. (2008). *Hooking up: Sex, dating, and relationships on campus.* New York: New York University Press.

Bohner, G. (2001). Writing about rape: Use of the passive voice and other distancing text features as an expression of perceived responsibility of the victim. *British Journal of Social Psychology, 40*, 515–529.

Bonta, B. (1993). *Peaceful peoples: An annotated bibliography.* Metuchen, NJ: Scarecrow.

Book, A. S., Starzyk, K. B., & Quinsey, V. L. (2001). The relationship between testosterone and aggression: A meta-analysis. *Aggression and Violent Behavior, 6*, 579–599.

Booth, A. L., Francesconi, M., & Frank, J. (2003). A sticky floors model of promotion, pay, and gender. *European Economic Review, 47*, 295–322.

Borkhoff, C. M., Hawker, G. A., Kreder, H. J., Glazier, R. H., Mahomed, N. N., & Wright, J. G. (2008). The effect of patients' sex on physicians' recommendations for total knee arthroplasty. *Canadian Medical Association Journal, 178*, 681–687.

Bornstein, M. H., Hahn, C., & Haynes, O. M. (2004). Specific and general language performance across early childhood: Stability and gender considerations. *First Language, 24*(3), 267–304.

Boroditsky, L, Schmidt, L, & Phillips, W. (2003). Sex, syntax, and semantics. In D. Gentner & S. Goldin-Meadow (Eds.), *Language in mind: Advances in the study of language and cognition* (pp. 61–80). Cambridge, MA: MIT Press.

Bos, H. M. W., van Balen, F., & van den Boom, D. C. (2004). Experience of parenthood, couple relationship, social support, and child-rearing goals in planned lesbian mother families. *Journal of Child Psychology and Psychiatry, 45*, 755–764.

Bosson, J. K., Johnson, A. B., Niederhoffer, K., & Swann, W. B. (2006). Interpersonal chemistry through negativity: Bonding by sharing negative attitudes about others. *Personal Relationships, 13*, 135–150.

Bosson, J. K., Pinel, E. C., & Vandello, J. A. (2010). The emotional impact of ambivalent sexism: Forecasts versus real experiences. *Sex Roles, 62*, 520–531.

Bosson, J. K., Vandello, J. A., Burnaford, R., Weaver, J., & Wasti, A. (2009). Precarious manhood and displays of physical aggression. *Personality and Social Psychology Bulletin, 35*, 623–634.

Bosson, J. K., Vandello, J. A., & Caswell, T. A. (2013). Precarious manhood. In M. K. Ryan & N. R. Branscombe (Eds.), *The SAGE handbook of gender and psychology* (pp. 115–130). Thousand Oaks, CA: Sage.

Bosson, J. K., Vandello, J. A., Michniewicz, K. S., & Lenes, J. G. (2012). American men's and women's beliefs about gender discrimination: For men, it's not quite a zero-sum game. *Masculinities and Social Change, 1*, 210–239.

Botelho-Urbanski, J. (2016, July 1). Baby Storm five years later: Preschooler on top of the world. *The Star*. Retrieved from https://www.thestar.com/news/gta/2016/07/11/baby-storm-five-years-later-preschooler-on-top-of-the-world.html

Bouchard, Jr., T. J. (1998). Genetic and environmental influences on adult intelligence and special mental abilities. *Human Biology, 70*, 257–279.

Bouris, A., Guilamo-Ramos, V., Pickard, A., Shiu, C., Loosier, P. S., Dittus, P., . . . Waldmiller, J. M. (2010).

A systematic review of parental influences on the health and well-being of lesbian, gay, and bisexual youth: Time for a new public health research and practice agenda. *Journal of Primary Prevention, 31*, 273–309.

Bourne, J. (2014, March 6). Why educating girls makes economic sense [Web log post]. Retrieved from http://www.globalpartnership.org/blog/why-educating-girls-makes-economic-sense

Bowlby, J. (1980). *Attachment and loss*. New York, NY: Basic Books.

Bowles, H. R., Babcock, L., & Lai, L. (2007). Social incentives for gender differences in the propensity to initiate negotiations: Sometimes it does hurt to ask. *Organizational Behavior and Human Decision Making Processes, 103*, 84–103.

Boxer, C. F., Noonan, M. C., & Whelan, C. B. (2015). Measuring mate preferences: A replication and extension. *Journal of Family Issues, 36*, 163–187.

Boysen, G. A., Vogel, D. L., Madon, S., & Wester, S. R. (2006). Mental health stereotypes about gay men. *Sex Roles, 54*, 69–82.

Bradford, J., Reisner, S. L., Honnold, J. A., & Xavier, J. (2013). Experiences of transgender-related discrimination and implications for health: Results from the Virginia transgender health initiative. *American Journal of Public Health, 103*, 1820–1829.

Branch, J. (2015, July 27). Dutee Chand, female sprinter with high testosterone level, wins right to compete. *New York Times*. Retrieved from https://www.nytimes.com/2015/07/28/sports/international/dutee-chand-female-sprinter-with-high-male-hormone-level-wins-right-to-compete.html

Branco, J. C., Motta, J., Wiener, C., Oses, J. P., Moreira, F. P., Spessato, B., . . . da Silva, R. (2017). Association between obesity and suicide in woman, but not in man: A population-based study of young adults. *Psychology, Health & Medicine, 22*(3), 275–281.

Brandt, M. J. (2011). Sexism and gender inequality across 57 societies. *Psychological Science, 22*, 1413–1418.

Brebner, J. (2003). Gender and emotions. *Personality and Individual Differences, 34*, 387–394.

Breiding, M. J., Chen, J., & Black, M. C. (2014, February). *Intimate partner violence in the United States—2010*. Atlanta, GA: National Center for Injury Prevention and Control, Centers for Disease Control and Prevention. Retrieved from https://www.cdc.gov/violenceprevention/pdf/cdc_nisvs_ipv_report_2013_v17_single_a.pdf

Brenner, O. C., Tomkiewicz, J., & Schein, V. E. (1989). The relationship between sex role stereotypes and requisite management characteristics revisited. *Academy of Management Journal, 32*, 662–669.

Brescoll, V. L., & Uhlman, E. L. (2008). Can an angry woman get ahead? Status conferral, gender and expression of emotion in the workplace. *Psychological Science, 19*, 268–275.

Brescoll, V. L., Uhlmann, E. L., Moss-Racusin, C., & Sarnell, L. (2011). Masculinity, status, and subordination: Why working for a gender stereotype violator causes men to lose status. *Journal of Experimental Social Psychology, 48*, 354–357.

Breslow, A. S., Brewster, M. E., Velez, B. L., Wong, S., Geiger, E., &

Soderstrom, B. (2015). Resilience and collective action: Exploring buffers against minority stress for transgender individuals. *Psychology of Sexual Orientation and Gender Diversity, 2*, 253–265.

Brewster, M. E., Velez, B. L., Mennicke, A., & Tebbe, E. (2014). Voices from beyond: A thematic content analysis of transgender employees' workplace experiences. *Psychology of Sexual Orientation and Gender Diversity, 1*, 159–169.

Bridges, A. J., Wosnitzer, R., Scharrer, E., Sun, C., & Liberman, R. (2010). Aggression and sexual behavior in best-selling pornography videos: A content analysis update. *Violence Against Women, 16*, 1065–1085.

Brines, J. (1994). Economic dependency, gender and the division of labor at home. *American Journal of Sociology, 100*, 652–688.

Brinkman, B. G., Isacco, A., & Rosen, L. A. (2016). College men's experiences of gender prejudice. *Journal of Men's Studies, 24*, 312–325.

Briton, N. J., & Hall, J. A. (1995). Beliefs about female and male nonverbal communication. *Sex Roles, 32*, 79–90.

Brody, L. R. (1999). *Gender, emotion, and the family.* Cambridge, MA: Harvard University Press.

Brody, L. R. (2000). The socialization of gender differences in emotional expression: Display rules, infant temperament, and differentiation. In A. H. Fischer (Ed.), *Gender and emotion: Social psychological perspectives* (pp. 24–47). Cambridge, UK: Cambridge University Press.

Brody, L. R., & Hall, J. A. (2010). Gender, emotion, and socialization.

In J. C. Chrisler & D. R. McCreary (Eds.), *Handbook of gender research in psychology*, (Vol. 1, pp. 429–454). New York, NY: Springer.

Brody, N. (1992). *Intelligence* (2nd ed.). San Diego, CA: Academic Press.

Broude, G. J., & Greene, S. J. (1976). Cross-cultural codes on twenty sexual attitudes and practices. *Ethnology, 15*, 409–429.

Brown, D. E. (1991). *Human universals.* Philadelphia, PA: Temple University Press.

Brownmiller, S. (1975). *Against our will.* New York, NY: Simon & Schuster.

Brubaker, M. D., Garrett, M. T., & Dew, B. J. (2009). Examining the relationship between internalized heterosexism and substance abuse among lesbian, gay, and bisexual individuals: A critical review. *Journal of LGBT Issues in Counseling, 3*, 62–89.

Bruckmuller, S., Ryan, M. K., Floor, R., & Haslam, S. A. (2014). The glass cliff: Examining why women occupy leadership positions in precarious circumstances. In S. Kumra, R. Simpson, & R. J. Burke (Eds.), *Oxford handbook of gender in organizations* (pp. 314–331). New York, NY: Oxford University Press.

Brush, S. G. (1978). Nettie Stevens and the discovery of sex determination by chromosomes. *Isis, 69*, 162–172.

Buchanan, N. T., & Fitzgerald, L. F. (2008). Effects of racial and sexual harassment on work and the psychological well-being of African American women. *Journal of Occupational Health Psychology, 13*, 137–151.

Buchanan, N. T., & Ormerod, A. J. (2002). Racialized sexual harassment

in the lives of African American women. *Women & Therapy, 25*(3–4), 107–124.

Buckner, C. E. (2009). Attitudes toward women scale. In J. Levine & M. Hogg (Eds.), *Encyclopedia of group processes and intergroup relations* (pp. 39–42). Thousand Oaks, CA: Sage.

Budig, M. J., & England, P. (2001). The wage penalty for motherhood. *American Sociological Review, 66*, 204–225.

Bures, F. (2016, November 28). Is PMS real? *Slate.* Retrieved from http://www.slate.com/articles/health_and_science/medical_examiner/2016/11/pms_might_be_a_cultural_syndrome_not_a_biologic_one.html

Burgess, G. H. (2007). Assessment of rape-supportive attitudes and beliefs in college men: Development, reliability, and validity of the rape attitudes and beliefs scale. *Journal of Interpersonal Violence, 22*, 973–993.

Burgess, M. C. R., Stermer, S. P., & Burgess, S. R. (2007). Sex, lies, and video games: The portrayal of male and female characters on video game covers. *Sex Roles, 57*, 419–433.

Burke, S. E., & LaFrance, M. (2016). Lay conceptions of sexual minority groups. *Archives of Sexual Behavior, 45*, 635–650.

Burleson, B. R., & Kunkel, A. (2006). Revisiting the different cultures thesis: An assessment of sex differences and similarities in supportive communication. In K. Dindia & D. J. Canary (Eds.), *Sex differences and similarities in communication* (Vol. 2, pp. 137–159). Mahwah, NJ: Lawrence Erlbaum.

Burling, R. (1963). *Rengsanggri: Family and kinship in a Garo village.*

Philadelphia: University of Pennsylvania Press.

Burrelli, J. (2008). *Thirty-three years of women in S&E faculty positions*. Arlington, VA: National Science Foundation. Retrieved from http://www.nsf.gov/statistics/infbrief/nsf08308/nsf08308.pdf

Burri, A., Spector, T., & Rahman, Q. (2015). Common genetic factors among sexual orientation, gender nonconformity, and number of sex partners in female twins: Implications for the evolution of homosexuality. *Journal of Sexual Medicine, 12,* 1004–1011.

Burt, M. R. (1980). Cultural myths and supports for rape. *Journal of Personality and Social Psychology, 38,* 217–230.

Burt, S. A., & Mikolajewski, A. J. (2008). Preliminary evidence that specific candidate genes are associated with adolescent-onset antisocial behavior. *Aggressive Behavior, 34,* 437–445.

Burton, C. M., Marshal, M. P., Chisolm, D. J., Sucato, G. S., & Friedman, M. S. (2013). Sexual minority-related victimization as a mediator of mental health disparities in sexual minority youth: A longitudinal analysis. *Journal of Youth and Adolescence, 42,* 394–402.

Buss, D. M. (1989). Sex differences in human mate preferences: Evolutionary hypotheses tested in 37 cultures. *Behavioral and Brain Sciences, 12,* 1–14.

Buss, D. M., & Kenrick, D. T. (1998). Evolutionary social psychology. In D. T. Gilbert, S. T. Fiske, & G. Lindzey (Eds.), *The handbook of social psychology* (pp. 982–1026). New York, NY: McGraw-Hill.

Buss, D. M., Larsen, R. J., Westen, D., & Semmelroth, J. (1992). Sex differences in jealousy: Evolution, physiology and psychology. *Psychological Science, 3,* 251–255.

Buss, D. M., & Schmitt, D. P. (2011). Evolutionary psychology and feminism. *Sex Roles, 64,* 768–787.

Buss, D. M., & Shackelford, T. K. (1997). From vigilance to violence: Mate retention tactics in married couples. *Journal of Personality and Social Psychology, 72,* 346–361.

Buss, D. M., Shackelford, T. K., Kirkpatrick, L. A., & Larsen, R. J. (2001). A half century of mate preferences: The cultural evolution of values. *Journal of Marriage and Family, 63,* 491–503.

Byrne, J. (2014, May). License to be yourself: Laws and advocacy for legal recognition of trans people. Retrieved from https://www.opensocietyfoundations.org/reports/license-byourself

Byrnes, J. P. Miller, D. C., & Schafer, W. D. (1999). Gender differences in risk taking: A meta-analysis. *Psychological Bulletin, 125,* 367–383.

Byron, K. (2005). A meta-analytic review of work-family conflict and its antecedents. *Journal of Vocational Behavior, 67,* 169–198.

Cable, N., Bartley, M., Chandola, T., & Sacker, A. (2013). Friends are equally important to men and women, but family matters more for men's well-being. *Journal of Epidemiology & Community Health, 67,* 166–171.

Cachelin, F. M., Dohm, F.-A., & Brown, M. (2009). Eating disorders in ethnic minority women: A review of the emerging literature. *Current Psychiatry Reviews, 5,* 182–193.

Cahill, L. (2006). Why sex matters for neuroscience. *Nature Reviews Neuroscience, 7*(6), 477–484.

Cahill, L. (2014). Fundamental sex difference in human brain architecture. *Proceedings of the National Academy of Science, 111,* 577–578.

Caldwell, J. E., Swan, S. C., & Woodbrown, V. D. (2012). Gender differences in intimate partner violence outcomes. *Psychology of Violence, 2,* 42–57.

Campbell, A., Shirley, L., & Caygill, L. (2002). Sex-typed preferences in three domains: Do two-year-olds need cognitive variables? *British Journal of Psychology, 93,* 203–217.

Campbell, R., Greeson, M. R., Bybee, D., & Raja, S. (2008). The co-occurrence of childhood sexual abuse, adult sexual assault, intimate partner violence, and sexual harassment: A mediational model of posttraumatic stress disorder and physical health outcomes. *Journal of Consulting and Clinical Psychology, 76,* 194–207.

Card, N. A., Stucky, B. D., Sawalani, G. M., & Little, T. D. (2008). Direct and indirect aggression during childhood and adolescence: A meta-analytic review of gender differences, intercorrelations, and relations to maladjustment. *Child Development, 79,* 1185–1229.

Carli, L. L., & Eagly, A. H. (2011). Gender and leadership. In A. Bryman, D. Collinson, K. Grint, B. Jackson, & M. Uhl-Bien (Eds.), *The SAGE handbook of leadership* (pp. 103–117). Thousand Oaks, CA: Sage.

Carneiro, P., Loken, K. V., & Salvanes, K. G. (2015). A flying start? Maternity leave benefits and long-run outcomes of children. *Journal of Political Economy, 123,* 365–412.

Carnevale, A. P., & Cheah, B. (2013). *Hard times: College majors, unemployment, and earnings.* Washington, DC: Georgetown Public Policy Institute. Retrieved from https://repository.library.georgetown.edu/bitstream/handle/10822/559304/HardTimes.2013.2.pdf?sequence=1

Carnevale, A. P., Strohl, J., & Melton, M. (2014). *What's it worth? The economic value of college majors.* Washington, DC: Georgetown University Center on Education and the Workforce. Retrieved from https://cew.georgetown.edu/wp-content/uploads/2014/11/whatsitworth-complete.pdf

Carr, E. R., & Szymanski, D. M. (2011). Sexual objectification and substance abuse in young women. *Counseling Psychologist, 39,* 39–66.

Carrère, S., & Gottman, J. M. (1999). Predicting divorce among newlyweds from the first three minutes of a marital conflict discussion. *Family Process, 38,* 293–301.

Carrington, C. (1999). *No place like home: Relationships and family life among lesbians and gay men.* Chicago, IL: University of Chicago Press.

Carrol, L., & Gilroy, P. J. (2002). Role of appearance and nonverbal behaviors in the perception of sexual orientation among lesbians and gay men. *Psychological Reports, 91,* 115–122.

Carter, C. S., DeVries, A. C., & Getz, L. L. (1995). Physiological substrates of mammalian monogamy: The prairie vole model. *Neuroscience and Biobehavioral Reviews, 19,* 303–314.

Carver, K., Joyner, K., & Udry, J. R. (2003). National estimates of adolescent romantic relationships. In. P. Florsheim (Ed.), *Adolescent romantic relations and sexual behavior: Theory, research, and practical implications* (pp. 23–56). Mahwah, NJ: Lawrence Erlbaum.

Case, K. A., Hensley, R., & Anderson, A. (2014). Reflecting on heterosexual and male privilege: Interventions to raise awareness. *Journal of Social Issues, 70,* 722–740.

Caspi, A., Sugden, K., Moffitt, T. E., Taylor, A., Craig, I. W., Harrington, H., . . . Poulton, R. (2003). Influence of life stress on depression: moderation by a polymorphism in the 5-HTT gene. *Science, 301,* 386–389.

Ceci, S. J., Ginther, D. K., Kahn, S., & Williams, W. M. (2014). Women in academic science: A changing landscape. *Psychological Science in the Public Interest, 15,* 75–141.

Ceci, S. J., & Williams, W. M. (2009). *The mathematics of sex: How biology and society conspire to limit talented women and girls.* London, UK: Oxford University Press.

Ceci, S. J., Williams, W. M., & Barnett, S. M. (2009). Women's underrepresentation in science: Sociocultural and biological considerations. *Psychological Bulletin, 135,* 218–261.

Center for Behavioral Health Statistics and Quality. (2015). *Behavioral health trends in the United States: Results from the 2014 National Survey on Drug Use and Health* (HHS Publication No. SMA 15-4927, NSDUH Series H-50). Retrieved from http://www.samhsa.gov/data

Centers for Disease Control and Prevention. (2015a). Current cigarette smoking among adults aged 18 and over, by sex, race, and age: United States: Selected years 1965–2014. Retrieved from https://www.cdc.gov/nchs/data/hus/2015/047.pdf

Centers for Disease Control and Prevention. (2015b). *Fatal injury reports, national and regional, 1999–2015.* Retrieved from https://webappa.cdc.gov/sasweb/ncipc/mortrate10_us.html

Centers for Disease Control and Prevention. (2015c). *Suicide: Facts at a glance.* National Center for Injury Prevention and Control. Retrieved from http://www.cdc.gov/violenceprevention/pdf/suicide-datasheet-a.PDF

Centers for Disease Control and Prevention. (2017). HIV by group. Retrieved from https://www.cdc.gov/hiv/group/index.html

Cha, Y., & Wheedon, K. A. (2014). Overwork and the slow convergence in the gender gap in wages. *American Sociological Review, 79,* 457–484.

Chambers, C. G., Graham, S. A., & Turner, J. N. (2008). When hearsay trumps evidence: How generic language guides preschoolers' inferences about unfamiliar things. *Language and Cognitive Processes, 23,* 749–766.

Chandrasekharan, S., Minear, M. A., Hung, A., & Allyse, M. (2014). Noninvasive prenatal testing goes global. *Science Translational Medicine, 6,* 231fs15.

Chang, A., McDonald, P., & Burton, P. (2010). Methodological choices in work–life balance research 1987 to 2006: A critical review. *International Journal of Human Resource Management, 21*(13), 2381–2413.

Changing birth certificate sex designations: State-by-state guidelines.

(2015, Feburary 3). Retrieved from http://www.lambdalegal.org/know-your-rights/transgender/changing-birth-certificate-sex-designations

Chaplin, T. M., & Aldao, A. (2013). Gender differences in emotion expression in children: A meta-analytic review. *Psychological Bulletin, 139*, 735–765.

Chapman, E. N., Kaatz, A., & Carnes, M. (2013). Physicians and implicit bias: How doctors may unwittingly perpetuate health care disparities. *Journal of General Internal Medicine, 28*, 1504–1510.

Chapman, K. R., Tashkin, D. P., & Pye, D. J. (2001). Gender bias in the diagnosis of COPD. *Chest, 119*, 1691–1695.

Chartrand, T. L., & Bargh, J. A. (1999). The chameleon effect: The perception–behavior link and social interaction. *Journal of Personality and Social Psychology, 76*, 893–910.

Chen, J. A., Granato, H., Shipherd, J. C., Simpson, T., & Lehavot, K. (2017). A qualitative analysis of transgender veterans' lived experiences. *Psychology of Sexual Orientation and Gender Diversity, 4*, 63–74.

Chenoweth, E., & Pressman, J. (2017, February 7). This is what we learned by counting the women's marches. *Washington Post*. Retrieved from https://www.washingtonpost.com/news/monkey-cage/wp/2017/02/07/this-is-what-we-learned-by-counting-the-womens-marches

Chentsova-Dutton, Y. E., & Tsai, J. L. (2007). Gender differences in emotional response among European Americans and Hmong Americans. *Cognition & Emotion, 21*, 162–181.

Cherney, I. D., & London, K. (2006). Gender-linked differences in the toys, television shows, computer games, and outdoor activities of 5- to 13-year-old children. *Sex Roles, 54*(9–10), 717–726.

Chi, W., & Li, B. (2008). Glass ceiling or sticky floor? Examining the gender earnings differential across the earnings distribution in urban China, 1987–2004. *Journal of Comparative Economics, 36*, 243–263.

Chivers, M. L., Rieger, G., Latty, E., & Bailey, J. M. (2004). A sex difference in the specificity of sexual arousal. *Psychological Science, 15*, 736–744.

Choudhary, E., Smith, M., & Bossarte, R. M. (2012). Depression, anxiety, and symptom profiles among female and male victims of sexual violence. *American Journal of Men's Health, 6*, 28–36.

Chrisler, J. C., & Caplan, P. (2002). The strange case of Dr. Jekyll and Ms. Hyde: How PMS became a cultural phenomenon and a psychiatric disorder. *Annual Review of Sex Research, 13*, 274–306.

Christov-Moore, L., Simpson, E. A., Coude, G., Grigaityte, K., Iacoboni, M., & Ferrari, P. F. (2014). Empathy: Gender effects in brain and behavior. *Neuroscience & Biobehavioral Reviews, 46*, 604–627.

Chu, M., & Kita, S. (2011). The nature of gestures' beneficial role in spatial problem solving. *Journal of Experimental Psychology: General, 140*, 102–116.

CIA. (2016). *World factbook*. Retrieved from https://www.cia.gov/library/publications/download/index.html

Cimpian, A., Brandone, A. C., & Gelman, S. A. (2010). Generic statements require little evidence for acceptance but have powerful implications. *Cognitive Science, 34*, 1452–1482.

Clark, A. E., & Georgellis, Y. (2013). Back to baseline in Britain: Adaptation in the British household panel survey. *Economica, 80*(319), 496–512.

Clark, R. D., & Hatfield, E. (1989). Gender differences in receptivity to sexual offers. *Journal of Psychology & Human Sexuality, 2*, 39–55.

Clark-Flory, T. (2008, February 28). Tina Fey: "Bitch is the new black." *Salon*. Retrieved from http://www.salon.com/2008/02/25/fey

Clausell, E., & Fiske, S. T. (2005). When do subgroup parts add up to the stereotype whole? Mixed stereotype content for gay male subgroups explains overall ratings. *Social Cognition, 23*, 161–181.

Clausen, J., & Levy, N. (2015). What is neuroethics? In J. Clausen & N. Levy (Eds.), *Handbook of neuroethics* (pp. v–vii). Dordrecht, Netherlands: Springer.

Clarke, L. H., & Griffin, M. (2008). Visible and invisible ageing: Beauty work as a response to ageism. *Ageing & Society, 28*, 653–674.

Clement, S., Schauman, O., Graham, T., Maggioni, F., Evans-Lacko, S., Bezborodovs, N., . . . Thornicroft, G. (2015). *Psychological Medicine, 45*, 11–27.

Coates, J. (2016). *Women, men and language: A sociolinguistic account of gender differences in language* (3rd ed.). London, UK: Routledge. (Original work published 2004)

Coats, E. J., & Feldman, R. S. (1996). Gender differences in nonverbal correlates of social status. *Personality and Social Psychology Bulletin, 22,* 1014–1022.

Cochran, S. V. (2010). Emergence and development of the psychology of men and masculinity. In J. C. Chrisler & D. R. McCreary (Eds.), *Handbook of gender research in psychology: Gender research in general and experimental psychology* (Vol. 1, pp. 43–58). New York, NY: Springer.

Cohen, D. K. (2013). Explaining rape during civil war: Cross-national evidence (1980–2009). *American Political Science Review, 107,* 461–477.

Cohen, J. (1988). *Statistical power analysis for the behavioral sciences* (2nd ed.). Hillsdale, NJ: Lawrence Erlbaum.

Cohen, J. R., & Single, L. E. (2001). An examination of the perceived impact of flexible work arrangements on professional opportunities in public accounting. *Journal of Business Ethics, 32,* 317–328.

Colapinto, J. (2000). *As nature made him: The boy who was raised as a girl.* New York, NY: Harper Perennial.

Cole, E. R. (2009). Intersectionality and research in psychology. *American Psychologist, 64*(3), 170–180.

Cole, E. R., Jayaratne, T. E., Cecchi, L. A., Feldbaum, M., & Petty, E. M. (2007). Vive la différence? Genetic explanations for perceived gender differences in nurturance. *Sex Roles, 57,* 211–222.

Collins, P. H. (2000). *Black feminist thought: Knowledge, consciousness, and the politics of empowerment* (2nd ed.). London, UK: Routledge Taylor & Francis Group.

Colom, R., Contreras, M. J., Arend, I., Leal, O. G., & Santacreu, J. (2004). Sex differences in verbal reasoning are mediated by sex differences in spatial ability. *Psychological Record, 54,* 365–372.

Colom, R., Juan-Espinosa, M., Abad, F., & García, L. F. (2000). Negligible sex differences in general intelligence. *Intelligence, 28,* 57–68.

Coltrane, S. (2000). Research on household labor: Modeling and measuring the social embeddedness of routine family work. *Journal of Marriage and Family, 62,* 1208–1233.

Combahee River Collective. (1995). Combahee River Collective statement. In B. Guy-Sheftall (Ed.), *Words of fire: An anthology of African American feminist thought* (pp. 232–240). New York, NY: New Press. (Original work published 1977)

Condry, J., & Condry, S. (1976). Sex differences: A study of the eye of the beholder. *Child Development, 47,* 812–819.

Conger, J. J. (1975). Proceedings of the American Psychological Association, Incorporated, for the year 1974: Minutes of the annual meeting of the Council of Representatives. *American Psychologist, 30,* 620–651.

Conley, T. D. (2011). Perceived proposer personality characteristics and gender differences in acceptance of casual sex offers. *Journal of Personality and Social Psychology, 100,* 309–329.

Conley, T. D. (2013). Beautiful, self-absorbed, and shallow: People of color perceive White women as an ethnically marked category. *Journal of Applied Social Psychology, 43,* 45–56.

Conley, T. D., Moors, A. C., Matsick, J. L., & Ziegler, A. (2013). The fewer the merrier?: Assessing stigma surrounding consensually non-monogamous romantic relationships. *Analyses of Social Issues and Public Policy, 13,* 1–30.

Conley, T. D., Moors, A. C., Matsick, J. L., Ziegler, A., & Valentine, B. A. (2011). Women, men, and the bedroom: Methodological and conceptual insights that narrow, reframe, and eliminate gender differences in sexuality. *Current Directions in Psychological Science, 20,* 296–300.

Connell, R. W., & Messerschmidt, J. W. (2005). Hegemonic masculinity: Rethinking the concept. *Gender & Society, 19,* 829–859.

Connor, J., Psutka, R., Cousins, K., Gray, A., & Kypri, K. (2013). Risky drinking, risky sex: A national study of New Zealand university students. *Alcoholism: Clinical & Experimental Research, 37,* 1971–1978.

Conrad, M. (2006). Aptitude is not enough: How personality and behavior predict academic performance. *Journal of Research in Personality, 40,* 339–346.

Conron, K. J., Mimiaga, M. J., & Landers, S. J. (2010). A population-based study of sexual orientation identity and gender differences in adult health. *American Journal of Public Health, 100,* 1953–1960.

Constantinople, A. (1973). Masculinity-femininity: An exception to a famous dictum? *Psychological Bulletin, 80,* 389–407.

Contreras, J. M., Banaji, M. R., & Mitchell, J. P. (2013). Multivoxel patterns in fusiform face area differentiate faces by sex and race. *PLOS One, 8,* e69684, 1–6.

Cook, T. D., & Campbell, D. T. (1979). *Quasi-experimentation: Design and analysis issues for field settings*. Boston, MA: Houghton Mifflin Company.

Coolidge, F. L., Thede, L. L., & Young, S. E. (2002). The heritability of gender identity disorder in a child and adolescent twin sample. *Behavior Genetics, 32*, 251–257.

Coontz, S. (2006). *Marriage, a history: How love conquered marriage*. New York, NY: Penguin.

Cooper, A., & Smith, E. L. (2011, November). *Homicide trends in the U.S., 1980–2008* (NCJ Publication No. 236018). Retrieved from https://www.bjs.gov/content/pub/pdf/htus8008.pdf

Cooper, M. (2000). Being the "go-to guy": Fatherhood, masculinity, and the organization of work in Silicon Valley. *Qualitative Sociology, 23*, 379–405.

Corbett, C., & Hill, C. (2012). *Graduating to a pay gap: The earnings of women and men one year after college graduation*. Washington, DC: AAUW.

Cornwell, C., Mustard, D. B., & Van Parys, J. (2013). Noncognitive skills and the gender disparities in test scores and teacher assessments: Evidence from primary school. *Journal of Human Resources, 48*, 236–264.

Cortina, L. M. (2001). Assessing sexual harassment among Latinas: Development of an instrument. *Cultural Diversity and Ethnic Minority Psychology, 7*, 164–181.

Cortina, L. M., Fitzgerald, L. F., & Drasgow, F. (2002). Contextualizing Latina experiences of sexual harassment: Preliminary tests of a structural model. *Basic and Applied Social Psychology, 24*, 295–311.

Costa, P. T., Jr., Terracciano, A., & McCrae, R. R. (2001). Gender differences in personality traits across cultures: Robust and surprising findings. *Journal of Personality and Social Psychology, 81*, 322–331.

Cox, M. J., Paley, B., Burchinal, M., & Payne, C. C. (1999). Marital perceptions and interactions across transition to parenthood. *Journal of Marriage and the Family, 61*, 611–625.

Craig, S. L., & Smith, M. S. (2014). The impact of perceived discrimination and social support on the school performance of multiethnic sexual minority youth. *Youth & Society, 46*(1), 30–50.

Crawford, M. (2001). Gender and language. In R. K. Unger (Ed.), *Handbook of the psychology of women and gender* (pp. 228–244). Hoboken, NJ: John Wiley.

Crawford, M., & Kaufman, M. R. (2008). Sex trafficking in Nepal: Survivor characteristics and long-term outcomes. *Violence Against Women, 14*, 905–916.

Crawford, M., Lee, I.-C., Portnoy, G., Gurung, A., Khati, D., Jha, P., & Regmi, A. C. (2009). Objectified body consciousness in a developing country: A comparison of mothers and daughters in the U.S. and Nepal. *Sex Roles, 60*, 174–185.

Crawford, M., & Marecek, J. (1989). Psychology reconstructs the female: 1968–1988. *Psychology of Women Quarterly, 13*, 147–165.

Crenshaw, K. (1993). Mapping the margins: Intersectionality, identity politics, and violence against women of color. *Stanford Law Review, 43*(6), 1241–1299.

Creswell, J. W., & Clark, V. L. P. (2011). *Designing and conducting mixed methods research* (2nd ed.). Thousand Oaks, CA: Sage.

Crisp, R. J., Hewstone, M., & Rubin, M. (2001). Does multiple categorization reduce intergroup bias? *Personality and Social Psychology Bulletin, 27*, 76–89.

Crosby, F., Clayton, S., Alksnis, O., & Hemker, K. (1986). Cognitive biases in the perception of discrimination: The importance of format. *Sex Roles, 14*, 637–646.

Cross, C. P., Copping, L. T., & Campbell, A. (2011). Sex differences in impulsivity: A meta-analysis. *Psychological Bulletin, 137*, 97–130.

Cuddy, A. J. C., Fiske, S. T., & Glick, P. (2004). When professionals become mothers, warmth doesn't cut the ice. *Journal of Social Issues, 60*, 701–718.

Cuddy, A. J. C., Fiske, S. T., Kwan, V. Y., Glick, P., Demoulin, S., Leyens, J., . . . Ziegler, R. (2009). Stereotype content model across cultures: Toward universal similarities and some differences. *British Journal of Social Psychology, 48*, 1–33.

Cuddy, A. J. C., Wilmuth, C. A., Yap, A. J., & Carney, D. R. (2015). Preparatory power posing affects nonverbal presence and job interview performance. *Journal of Applied Psychology, 100*(4), 1286–1295.

Cuddy, A. J. C., Wolf, E. B., Glick, P., Crotty, S., Chong, J., & Norton, M. I. (2015). Men as cultural ideals: Cultural values moderate gender stereotype content. *Journal of Personality and Social Psychology, 109*, 622–635.

Cullen-DuPont, K. (2000). Femme covert (feme covert). In *Encyclopedia of women's history in America* (2nd ed., p. 87). New York, NY: Facts on File.

Culpepper, L. (2009). Generalized anxiety disorder and medical illness. *Journal of Clinical Psychiatry, 70,* 20–24.

Cunningham, B., Hoyer, K. M., & Sparks, D. (2015). *Gender differences in science, technology, engineering, and mathematics (STEM) interest, credits earned, and NAEP performance in the 12th grade* (NCES 2015-075). Washington, DC: National Center for Education Statistics.

Cunningham, G. F., Leveno, K. J., Bloom, S. L., Spong, C. Y., Dashe, J. S., Hoffman, B. L., . . . Sheffield, J. S. (2014). *Williams obstetrics* (24th ed.). New York, NY: McGraw-Hill Education.

Cutler, S. E., & Nolen-Hoeksema, S. (1991). Accounting for sex differences in depression through female victimization: Childhood sexual abuse. *Sex Roles, 24,* 425–438.

Czopp, A. M., Monteith, M. J., & Mark, A. Y. (2006). Standing up for a change: Reducing bias through interpersonal confrontation. *Journal of Personality snd Social Psychology, 90,* 784–803.

Dahlhamer, J. M., Galinsky, A. M., Joestl, S. S., & Ward, B. W. (2016). Barriers to health care among adults identifying as sexual minorities: A U.S. national study. *American Journal of Public Health, 16,* 1116–1122.

Daly, M., & Wilson, M. (1988). *Homicide.* New York, NY: Aldine de Gruyter.

Danaher, K., & Crandall, C. S. (2008). Stereotype threat in applied settings re-examined. *Journal of Applied Social Psychology, 38,* 1639–1655.

Dank, M., Khan, B., Downey, P. M., Kotonias, C., Mayer, D., Owens, C., . . . Yu, L. (2014, March). *Estimating the size and structure of the underground commercial sex economy in eight major U.S. cities.* Retrieved from http://www.urban.org/sites/default/files/publication/22376/413047-estimating-the-size-and-structure-of-the-underground-commercial-sex-economy-in-eight-major-us-cities.pdf

Dar-Nimrod, I., & Heine, S. J. (2006). Exposure to scientific theories affects women's math performance. *Science, 314,* 435.

Darwin, C. (1871). *The descent of man, and selection in relation to sex* (Vol. 2). London, UK: John Murray, Albemarle Street.

Darwin, C. (1872). *The expression of the emotions in man and animals.* London, UK: John Murray.

David-Barrett, T., Rotkirch, A., Carney, J., Behncke Izquierdo, I., Krems, J. A., Townley, D., . . . Dunbar, R. I. M. (2015). Women favour dyadic relationships, but men prefer clubs: Cross-cultural evidence from social networking. *PLOS One, 10,* e0118329.

Davis, L. E., Williams, J. H., Emerson, S., & Hourd-Bryant, M. (2000). Factors contributing to partner commitment among unmarried African Americans. *Social Research, 24,* 4–15.

Davis, M. H. (1983). Measuring individual differences in empathy: Evidence for a multidimensional approach. *Journal of Personality and Social Psychology, 44,* 113–126.

Dawood, K., Kirk, K. M., Bailey, J. M., Andrews, P. W., & Martin, N. G. (2005). Genetic and environmental influences on the frequency of orgasm in women. *Twin Research and Human Genetics, 8,* 27–33.

Deary, I. J. (Ed.). (2009). Intelligence, health, and death: The emerging field of cognitive epidemiology [Special issue]. *Intelligence, 37.*

Deary, I. J., Whalley, L. J., Lemmon, H., Crawford, J. R., & Starr, J. M. (2000). The stability of individual differences in mental ability from childhood to old age: Follow-up of the 1932 Scottish mental survey. *Intelligence, 28,* 49–55.

Deaux, K. (1984). From individual differences to social categories: Analysis of a decade's research on gender. *American Psychologist, 39*(2), 105–116.

Deaux, K., & Lewis, L. L. (1983). Assessment of gender stereotypes: Methodology and components. *Psychological Documents, 13,* 25.

Deaux, K., & Lewis, L. L. (1984). Structure of gender stereotypes: Interrelationships among components and gender label. *Journal of Personality and Social Psychology, 46,* 991–1004.

Deaux, K., & Major, B. (1987). Putting gender into context: An interactive model of gender related behavior. *Psychological Review, 94,* 369–389.

Deaux, K., & Stewart, A. J. (2001). Framing gendered identities. In R. K. Unger (Ed.), *Handbook of the psychology of women and gender* (pp. 84–97). Hoboken, NJ: John Wiley.

Deeb, A., Mason, C., Lee, Y. S., & Hughes, I. A. (2005). Correlation between genotype, phenotype and sex of rearing in 111 patients with partial androgen insensitivity syndrome. *Clinical Endocrinology, 63,* 56–62.

Deering, K. N., Amin, A., Shoveller, J., Nesbitt, A., Garcia-Moreno, C., Duff, P., . . . Shannon, K. (2014). A systematic review of the correlates of violence against sex workers. *American Journal of Public Health, 104,* e42–e54.

Denmark, F., Russo, N. F., Frieze, I. H., & Sechzer, J. A. (1988). Guidelines for avoiding sexism in psychological research: A report of the Ad Hoc Committee on Nonsexist Research. *American Psychologist, 43,* 582–585.

Derks, B., Van Laar, C., & Ellemers, N., & de Groot, K. (2011). Gender-bias primes elicit queen-bee responses among senior policewomen. *Psychological Science, 22,* 1243–1249.

Derlega, V. J., Catanzaro, D., & Lewis, R, J, (2001). Perceptions about tactile intimacy in same-sex and opposite-sex participants' sexual orientation. *Psychology of Men & Masculinity, 2,* 124–132.

Deutsch, F. M., Servis, L. J., & Payne, J. D. (2001). Paternal participation in child care and its effects on children's self-esteem and attitudes toward gendered roles. *Journal of Family Issues, 22,* 1000–1024.

Devaux, M., & Sassi, F. (2013). Social inequalities in obesity and overweight in 11 OECD countries. *European Journal of Public Health, 23,* 464–469.

deVries, G. J., & Södersten, P. (2009). Sex differences in the brain: The relations between structure and function. *Hormones and Behavior, 55,* 589–596.

DeWall, C. N., Bushman, B. J., Giancola, P. R., & Webster, G. D. (2010). The big, the bad, and the boozed-up: Weight moderates the effect of alcohol on aggression. *Journal of Experimental Social Psychology, 46,* 619–623.

Dewey, C. (2013, October 27). 7 ridiculous restrictions on women's rights around the world. *Washington Post.* Retrieved from https://www.washingtonpost.com/news/worldviews/wp/2013/10/27/7-ridiculous-restrictions-on-womens-rights-around-the-world

Dhariwal, A., & Connolly, J. (2013). Romantic experiences of homeland and diaspora South Asian youth: Westernizing processes of media and friends. *Research on Adolescence, 23,* 45–56.

di Pellegrino, G., Fadiga, L., Fogassi, L., Gallese, V., & Rizzolatti, G. (1992). Understanding motor events: A neurophysiological study. *Experimental Brain Research, 91,* 176–180.

Diamond, L. M. (2002). "Having a girlfriend without knowing it": Intimate friendships among adolescent sexual-minority women. *Journal of Lesbian Studies, 6,* 5–16.

Diamond, L. M. (2003). What does sexual orientation orient? A biobehavioral model distinguishing romantic love and sexual desire. *Psychological Review, 110,* 173–192.

Diamond, L. M. (2005). A new view of lesbian subtypes: Stable versus fluid identity trajectories over an 8-year period. *Psychology of Women Quarterly, 29,* 119–128.

Diamond, L. M. (2008). Female bisexuality from adolescence to adulthood: Results from a 10- year longitudinal study. *Developmental Psychology, 44,* 5–14.

Diamond, L. M., & Huebner, D. M. (2012). Is good sex good for you? Rethinking sexuality and health. *Social and Personality Psychology Compass, 6,* 54–69.

Diamond, M. (2006). Biased-interaction theory of psychosexual development: "How does one know if one is male or female?" *Sex Roles, 55,* 589–600.

Diamond, M. (2013). Transsexuality among twins: Identity concordance, transition, rearing, and orientation. *International Journal of Transgenderism, 14,* 24–38.

Diekman, A. B., Brown, E. R., Johnston, A. M., & Clark, E. K. (2010). Seeking congruity between goals and roles: A new look at why women opt out of science, technology, engineering and mathematics careers. *Psychological Science, 21,* 1051–1057.

Diener, E., Suh, E., M., Lucas, R. E., & Smith, H. L. (1999). Subjective well-being: Three decades of progress. *Psychological Bulletin, 125,* 276–302.

Dilley, J. A, Simmons, K. W., Boysun, M. J., Pizacani, B. A., & Stark, M. J. (2010). Demonstrating the importance and feasibility of including sexual orientation in public health surveys: Health disparities in the Pacific Northwest. *American Journal of Public Health, 100,* 460–467.

Dillon, L. M., Nowak, N., Weisfeld, G. E., Weisfeld, C. C., Shattuck, K. S., Imamoglu, O. E., . . . Shen, J. (2015). Sources of marital conflict in five cultures. *Evolutionary Psychology, 13,* 1–15.

Dillon, S. (2005, January 18). Harvard chief defends his talk on women. *New York Times.* Retrieved from http://www.nytimes.com/2005/01/18/us/harvard-chief-defends-his-talk-on-women.html

DiMatteo, M. R., Morton, S. C., Lepper, H. S., Damush, T. M., Carney, M. F., Pearson, M., & Kahn, K. L. (1996). Cesarean childbirth and psychosocial outcomes: A meta-analysis. *Health Psychology, 15,* 303–314.

Dindia, K. (2006). Men are from North Dakota, women are from South Dakota. In K. Dindia & D. J. Canary (Eds.), *Sex differences and similarities in communication* (Vol. 2, pp. 3–20). Mahwah, NJ: Lawrence Erlbaum.

Dindia, K., & Allen, M. (1992). Sex differences in self-disclosure: A meta-analysis. *Psychological Bulletin, 112*(1), 106–124.

Dines, G. (2010). *Pornland: How porn has hijacked our sexuality.* Boston, MA: Beacon Press.

Dobash, R. E., & Dobash, R. P. (1979). *Violence against wives: A case against the patriarchy.* New York, NY: Free Press.

Dobash, R. P., Dobash, R. E., Wilson, M., & Daly, M. (1992). The myth of sexual symmetry in marital violence. *Social Problems, 39,* 71–91.

Dockterman, E. (2015, May 7). Miley Cyrus: 'It has a lot to do with being a feminist, but I'm finally O.K. with being alone.' *Time.* Retrieved from http://time.com/3850794/miley-cyrus-feminism-gay-rights-happy-hippie

Dodd, D. K., Russell, B. L., & Jenkins, C. (1999). Smiling in yearbook photos: Gender differences from kindergarten to adulthood. *Psychological Record, 49,* 543–554.

Dodd, E. H., Giuliano, T. A., Boutell, J. M., & Moran, B. E. (2001). Respected or rejected: Perceptions of

women who confront sexist remarks. *Sex Roles, 45,* 567–577.

Dodge, K. A., Gilroy, F. D., & Fenzel, L. M. (1995). Requisite management characteristics revisited: Two decades later. *Journal of Social Behavior and Personality, 10,* 253–264.

Doherty, R. W., Orimoto, L., Singelis, T. M., Hatfield, E., & Hebb, J. (1995). Emotional contagion: Gender and occupational differences. *Psychology of Women Quarterly, 19,* 355–371.

Donnelly, K., Twenge, J. M., Clark, M. A., Shaikh, S. K., Beiler-May, A., & Carter, N. T. (2016). Attitudes toward women's work and family roles in the United States, 1976–2013. *Psychology of Women Quarterly, 40,* 41–54.

Donovan, R. A. (2007). To blame or not to blame: Influences of target race and observer sex on rape blame attribution. *Journal of Interpersonal Violence, 22,* 722–736.

Dovidio, J. F., Ellyson, S. L., Keating, C. F., Heltman, K., & Brown, C. E. (1988). The relationship of social power to visual displays of dominance between men and women. *Journal of Personality and Social Psychology, 54,* 233–242.

Drescher, J. (2010). Queer diagnoses: Parallels and contrasts in the history of homosexuality, gender variance, and the *Diagnostic and Statistical Manual. Archives of Sexual Behavior, 39,* 427–460.

Drevenstedt, G. L., Crimmins, E. M., Vasunilashorn, S., & Finch, C. E. (2008). The rise and fall of excess male infant mortality. *Proceedings of the National Academy of Sciences, 105,* 5016–5021.

Drimonis, T. (2017, March 30). Victim-blaming newspaper headline

highlights need for better media training. *Daily Hive.* Retrieved from http://dailyhive.com/montreal/victim-blaming-newspaper-headline-highlights-need-for-better-media-training

Driscoll, T. R., Mitchell, R. J., Hendrie, A. L., Healey, S. H., Mandryk, J. A., & Hull, B. P. (2003). Unintentional fatal injuries arising from unpaid work at home. *Injury Prevention, 9,* 15–19.

Duarte-Guterman, P., Yagi, S., Chow, C., & Galea, L. A. M. (2015). Hippocampal learning, memory, and neurogenesis: Effects of sex and estrogens across the lifespan in adults. *Hormones and Behavior, 74,* 37–52.

Duckworth, A. L. & Seligman M. E. P. (2005). Self-discipline outdoes IQ in predicting academic performance of adolescents. *Psychological Science, 16,* 939–944.

Duncan, D. T., & Hatzenbuehler, M. L. (2014). Lesbian, gay, bisexual, and transgender hate crimes and suicidality among a population-based sample of sexual-minority adolescents in Boston. *American Journal of Public Health, 104,* 272–278.

Duraisamy, M., & Duraisamy, P. (2016). Gender wage gap across the wage distribution in different segments of the Indian labour market, 1983–2012: Exploring the glass ceiling or sticky floor phenomenon. *Applied Economics, 48,* 4098–4111.

Dutton, L., Koenig, K., & Fennie, K. (2008). Gynecologic care of the female-to-male transgender man. *Journal of Midwifery & Women's Health, 53,* 331–337.

Eagly, A. H. (1987). *Sex differences in social behavior: A social-role interpretation.* Hillsdale, NJ: Lawrence Erlbaum.

Eagly, A. H. (1994). On comparing women and men. *Feminism & Psychology*, *4*, 513–522.

Eagly, A. H. (2007). Female leadership advantage and disadvantage: Resolving the contradictions. *Psychology of Women Quarterly*, *31*, 1–12.

Eagly, A. H. (2013). The science and politics of comparing women and men: A reconsideration. In M. K. Ryan & N. R. Branscombe (Eds.), *The SAGE handbook of gender and psychology* (pp. 11–28). Thousand Oaks, CA: Sage.

Eagly, A. H., & Crowley, M. (1986). Gender and helping behavior: A meta-analytic review of the social psychological literature. *Psychological Bulletin*, *100*, 283–308.

Eagly, A. H., Johannesen-Schmidt, M. C., & Van Engen, M. L. (2003). Transformational, transactional, and laissez-faire leadership styles: A meta-analysis comparing women and men. *Psychological Bulletin*, *129*, 569–591.

Eagly, A. H., Karau, S. J., & Makhijani, M. G. (1995). Gender and the effectiveness of leaders: A meta-analysis. *Psychological Bulletin*, *117*, 125–145.

Eagly, A. H., & Mladinic, A. (1994). Are people prejudiced against women? Some answers from research on attitudes, gender stereotypes, and judgments of competence. In W. Stroebe & M. Hewstone (Eds.), *European review of social psychology* (Vol. 5, pp. 1–35). New York, NY: John Wiley.

Eagly, A. H., & Riger, S. (2014). Feminism and psychology: Critiques of methods and epistemology. *American Psychologist*, *69*, 685–702.

Eagly, A. H., & Steffen, V. J. (1984). Gender stereotypes stem from the distribution of women and men into social roles. *Journal of Personality and Social Psychology*, *46*, 735–754.

Eagly, A. H., & Wood, W. (1999). The origins of sex differences in human behavior: Evolved dispositions versus social roles. *American Psychologist*, *54*(6), 408–423.

Eagly, A. H., & Wood, W. (2013). Feminism and evolutionary psychology: Moving forward. *Sex Roles*, *69*, 549–556.

Earp, B. D. (2012). The extinction of masculine generics. *Journal for Communication and Culture*, *2*, 4–19.

Easton, J. A., Confer, J. C., Goetz, C. D., & Buss, D. M. (2010). Reproduction expediting: Sexual motivations, fantasies, and the ticking biological clock. *Personality and Individual Differences*, *49*, 516–520.

Eastwick, P. W., Eagly, A. H., Glick, P., Johannesen-Schmidt, M. C., Fiske, S. T., Blum, A., . . . Volpato, C. (2006). Is traditional gender ideology associated with sex-type mate preferences? A test in nine nations. *Sex Roles*, *54*, 603–614.

Eastwick, P. W., & Finkel, E. J. (2008). Sex differences in mate preferences revisited: Do people know what they initially desire in a romantic partner? *Journal of Personality and Social Psychology*, *94*, 245–264.

Eaton, A. A., & Rios, D. (2017). Social challenges faced by queer Latino college men: Navigating negative responses to coming out in a double minority sample of emerging adults. *Cultural Diversity and Ethnic Minority Psychology*.

Eaton, A. A., & Rose, S. (2011). Has dating become more egalitarian? A 35 years review using *Sex Roles*, *64*, 843–862.

Eaton, N. R. (2014). Transdiagnostic psychopathology factors and sexual minority mental health: Evidence of disparities and associations with minority stressors. *Psychology of Sexual Orientation and Gender Diversity*, *1*, 244–254.

Eaton, N. R., Keyes, K. M., Krueger, R. F., Balsis, S., Skodol, A. E., Markon, K. E., . . . Hasin, D. S. (2012). An invariant dimensional liability model of gender differences in mental disorder prevalence: Evidence from a national sample. *Journal of Abnormal Psychology*, *121*, 282–288.

Eaton, W. O., & Enns, L. R. (1986). Sex differences in human motor activity level. *Psychological Bulletin*, *100*, 19–28.

Eccles, J. S. (1984). Sex differences in achievement patterns. In T. B. Sonderegger (Ed.), *Nebraska symposium on motivation* (Vol. 32, pp. 97–132). Lincoln: University of Nebraska Press.

Eccles, J. S. (2007). Where are all the women? Gender differences in participation in physical science and engineering. In S. J. Ceci & W. M. Williams (Eds.), *Why aren't more women in science?* (pp. 199–210). Washington, DC: American Psychological Association.

Eccles, J. S., Adler, T., & Meece, J. L. (1984). Sex differences in achievement: A test of alternate theories. *Journal of Personality and Social Psychology*, *46*, 26–43.

Eccles, J. S., Wigfield, A., Flanagan, C., Harold, R., & Blumenfeld, P. B. (1993). Age and gender differences in children's self- and task-perceptions during elementary school. *Child Development*, *64*, 830–847.

Eckes, T. (2002). Paternalistic and envious gender stereotypes: Testing predictions from the stereotype content model. *Sex Roles*, *47*, 99–114.

Eisenberg, M. E., & Resnick, M. D. (2006). Suicidality among gay, lesbian and bisexual youth: The role of protective factors. *Journal of Adolescent Health*, *39*, 662–668.

Eisenberg, N., Spinrad, T. L., & Sadovsky, A. (2005). Empathy-related responding in children. In M. Killen & J. G. Smetana (Eds.), *Handbook of moral development* (pp. 517–549). Mahwah, NJ: Lawrence Erlbaum.

Ekman, P. (1972). Universal and cultural differences in facial expressions of emotion. In J. R. Cole (Ed.), *Nebraska symposium on motivation* (Vol. 19, pp. 207–283). Lincoln: University of Nebraska Press.

Elfenbein, H. A., & Ambady, N. (2002). On the universality and cultural specificity of emotion recognition: A meta-analysis. *Psychological Bulletin*, *128*(2), 203–235.

Eliot, L. (2009). *Pink brain, blue brain*. New York, NY: Mariner Books.

Eller, C. (2011). *Gentlemen and Amazons: The myth of matriarchal prehistory, 1861–1900*. Berkeley: University of California Press.

Ellis, H. (1894). *Man and woman: A study of human sexual characters*. London, UK: Walter Scott.

Ellis, H. (1915). *Sexual inversion* (3rd ed). Philadelphia, PA: F. A. Davis.

Ellis, L., & Ames, M. A. (1987). Neurohormonal functioning and sexual orientation: A theory of homosexuality-heterosexuality. *Psychological Bulletin*, *101*, 233–258.

Ellison, G., & Swanson, A. (2010). The gender gap in secondary school mathematics at high achievement levels: Evidence from the American Mathematics Competitions. *Journal of Economic Perspectives*, *24*, 109–128.

Else-Quest, N. M., Hyde, J. S., Goldsmith, H. H., & Van Hulle, C. A. (2006). Gender differences in temperament: A meta-analysis. *Psychological Bulletin*, *132*, 33–72.

Else-Quest, N. M., Hyde, J. S., & Linn, M. C. (2010). Cross-national patterns of gender differences in mathematics: A meta-analysis. *Psychological Bulletin*, *136*, 103–127.

Else-Quest, N. M., & Hyde, J. S. (2016). Intersectionality in quantitative psychological research: II. Methods and techniques. *Psychology of Women Quarterly*, *40*, 319–336.

Else-Quest, N. M., Mineo, C. C., & Higgins, A. (2013). Math and science attitudes and achievement at the intersection of gender and ethnicity. *Psychology of Women Quarterly*, *37*, 293–309.

Emens, E. F. (2004). Monogamy's law: Compulsory monogamy and polyamorous existence. *N.Y.U. Review of Law & Social Change*, *29*, 277–376.

Engber, D. (2016, August 5). Should Caster Semenya be allowed to compete against women? *Slate*. Retrieved from http://www.slate.com/articles/sports/fivering_circus/2016/08/should_caster_semenya_be_allowed_to_compete_against_women.html

England, P. (2010). The gender revolution: Uneven and stalled. *Gender and Society*, *24*, 149–166.

England, P., Shafer, E. F., & Fogarty, A. C. (2008). Hooking up and forming romantic relationships on today's college campuses. *Gendered Society Reader*, *3*, 531–593.

Ensmenger, N. (2010). *The computer boys take over: Computers, programmers, and the politics of technical expertise*. Cambridge, MA: MIT Press.

Erich, S., Kanenberg, H., Case, K., Allen, T., & Bogdanos, T. (2009). An empirical analysis of factors affecting adolescent attachment in adoptive families with homosexual and straight parents. *Children and Youth Services Review*, *31*, 398–404.

Erosheva, E. A., Kim, H.-J., Emlet, C., & Fredriksen-Goldsen, K. I. (2016). Social networks of lesbian, gay, bisexual, and transgender older adults. *Research on Aging*, *38*, 98–123.

Escribà-Agüir, V., & Artazcoz, L. (2011). Gender differences in postpartum depression: A longitudinal cohort study. *Journal of Epidemiology and Community Health*, *65*, 320–326.

Eskes, T., & Haanen, C. (2007). Why do women live longer than men? *European Journal of Obstetrics & Gynecology & Reproductive Biology*, *133*, 126–133.

Esqueda, C. W., & Harrison, L. A. (2005). The influence of gender role stereotypes, the woman's race, and level of provocation and resistance on domestic violence culpability attributions. *Sex Roles*, *53*(11/12), 821–834.

Esser, M. B., Hedden, S. L., Kanny, D., Brewer, R. D., Gfroerer, J. C., & Naimi, T. S. (2014). Prevalence of alcohol dependence among U. S.

adult drinkers, 2009–2011. *Preventing Chronic Disease, 11*, 1545–1151.

Evans, D. L., & Charney, D. S. (2003). Mood disorders and medical illness: A major public health problem. *Biological Psychiatry, 54*, 177–180.

Evans, E. M., Schweingruber, H., & Stevenson, H. W. (2002). Gender differences in interest and knowledge acquisition: The United States, Taiwan, and Japan. *Sex Roles, 47(3/4)*, 153–167.

Evans, R., Scourfield, J., & Moore, G. (2016). Gender, relationship breakdown, and suicide risk: A review of research in Western countries. *Journal of Family Issues, 37(16)*, 2239–2264.

Everett, B. (2015). Sexual orientation identity change and depressive symptoms: A longitudinal analysis. *Journal of Health and Social Behavior, 56*, 37–58.

Evertsson, M. (2014). Gender ideology and the sharing of housework and child care in Sweden. *Journal of Family Issues, 25*, 927–949.

Eysenck, M. W. (2011). *Fundamentals of cognition* (2nd ed.). Hove, England: Psychology Press.

Fabes, R. A., Martin, C. L., & Hanish, L. D. (2003). Young children's play quality in same-, other-, and mixed-sex peer groups. *Child Development, 3*, 921–932.

Fagot, B. I., & Leinbach, M. D. (1989). The young child's gender schema: Environmental input, internal organization. *Child Development, 60*, 663–672.

Fagot, B. I., Rodgers, C. S., & Leinbach, M. D. (2000). Theories of gender socialization. In T. Eckes &

H. M. Trautner (Eds.), *The developmental social psychology of gender* (pp. 65–89). Mahwah, NJ: Lawrence Erlbaum.

Fairburn, C. G., & Harrison, P. J. (2003). Eating disorders. *The Lancet, 361*, 407–416.

Fallon, A. (2011, June 2). V. S. Naipaul finds no woman writer his literary match—not even Jane Austen. *The Guardian*. Retrieved from https://www.theguardian.com/books/2011/jun/02/vs-naipaul-jane-austen-women-writers

Family Equality Council. (2017). *Second-parent adoption laws*. Retrieved from http://www.familyequality.org/get_informed/resources/equality_maps/second-parent_adoption_laws

Farber, B. A., & Nitzburg, G. C. (2016). Young adult self-disclosures in psychotherapy and on Facebook. *Counselling Psychology Quarterly, 29*, 76–89.

Farr, R. H., & Patterson, C. J. (2013). Coparenting among lesbian, gay, and heterosexual couples: Associations with adopted children's outcomes. *Child Development, 84*, 1226–1240.

Farris, C., Jaycox, L. H., Schell, T. L., Street, A. E., Kilpatrick, D. G., & Tanielian, T. (2016). Sexual harassment and gender discrimination findings: Active component. In A. R. Morral, Gore, K. L., & Schell, T. L. (Eds.), *Sexual assault and sexual harassment in the U.S. military: Volume 2. Estimates for Department of Defense service members from the 2014 RAND military workplace study*. Santa Monica, CA: RAND Corporation. Retrieved from http://www.rand.org/content/dam/rand/pubs/research_reports/RR800/RR870z2-1/RAND_RR870z2-1.pdf

Fassinger, R. E., & Miller, B. A. (1997). Validation of an inclusive model of sexual minority identity formation on a sample of gay men. *Journal of Homosexuality, 32*, 53–78.

Fattah, H. M. (2005, May 1). The basics; why Arab men hold hands. *New York Times*. Retrieved from http://query.nytimes.com/gst/fullpage.html?res=9C07E4D71E31F932A35756C0A9639C8B63

Fausto-Sterling, A. (1993, March/April). The five sexes. *The Sciences*, 20–25.

Fausto-Sterling, A. (2000). The five sexes, revisited: The varieties of sex will test medical values and social norms. *The Sciences, 40*, 18–23.

Feder, L. (2014). *Natural pregnancy*. Toronto, Canada: Hatherleigh Press.

Federal Bureau of Investigation. (2015a). Expanded homicide data table 1: Murder victims by race, ethnicity, and sex, 2015. *Crime in the United States, 2015*. Retrieved from https://ucr.fbi.gov/crime-in-the-u.s/2015/crime-in-the-u.s.-2015/tables/expanded_homicide_data_table_1_murder_victims_by_race_ethnicity_and_sex_2015.xls

Federal Bureau of Investigation. (2015b). *Hate crime statistics*. Retrieved from https://ucr.fbi.gov/hate-crime/2015

Federal Bureau of Investigation. (2015c). Table 42: Arrests by sex, 2015. *Crime in the United States, 2015*. Retrieved from https://ucr.fbi.gov/crime-in-the-u.s/2015/crime-in-the-u.s.-2015/tables/table-42

Federal Bureau of Investigation. (2015d). Table 43: Arrests by race and ethnicity, 2015. *Crime in the*

United States, 2015. Retrieved from https://ucr.fbi.gov/crime-in-the-u.s/2015/crime-in-the-u.s.-2015/tables/table-43

Fehr, B. (2006). A prototype approach to studying love. In R. J. Sternberg & K. Weis (Eds.), *The new psychology of love* (pp. 225–246). New Haven, CT: Yale University Press.

Feinberg, M., Willer, R., Stellar, J., & Keltner, D. (2012). The virtues of gossip: Reputational information sharing as prosocial behavior. *Journal of Personality and Social Psychology, 102*(5), 1015–1030.

Feingold, A. (1988). Cognitive gender differences are disappearing. *American Psychologist, 43*, 95–103.

Feldblum, C. R., & Lipnic, V. A. (2016, June). *Report of the EEOC select task force on the study of harassment in the workplace*. Retrieved from https://www.eeoc.gov/eeoc/task_force/harassment/upload/report.pdf

Feldman, M. B., & Meyer, I. H. (2007). Eating disorders in diverse lesbian, gay, and bisexual populations. *International Journal of Eating Disorders, 40*, 218–226.

Feldman, M. P., MacCulloch, M. J., & Orford, J. E (1971). Conclusions and speculations. In M. P. Feldman & M. J. MacCulloch (Eds.), *Homosexual behaviour: Therapy and assessment* (pp. 156–188). New York, NY: Pergamon Press.

Feng, J., Spence, I., & Pratt, J. (2007). Playing an action video game reduces gender differences in spatial cognition. *Psychological Science, 18*(10), 850–855.

Ferguson, A. (2017, June 16). M, F, or X: Oregon becomes first state to offer 'not specified' gender option on ID cards. *Washington Post*. Retrieved from https://www.washingtonpost.com/news/morning-mix/wp/2017/06/16/m-f-or-x-oregon-becomes-first-state-to-offer-not-specified-gender-option-on-id-cards/?utm_term=.562d3e2490c8

Ferguson, C. E., & Malouff, J. M. (2016). Assessing police classifications of sexual assault reports: A meta-analysis of false reporting rates. *Archives of Sexual Behavior, 45*, 1185–1193.

Ferguson, C. J. (2013). In the eye of the beholder: Thin-ideal media affects some, but not most, viewers in a meta-analytic review of body dissatisfaction in women and men. *Psychology of Popular Media Culture, 2*, 20–37.

Ferguson, C. J., & Hartley, R. D. (2009). The pleasure is momentary . . . the expense damnable? The influence of pornography on rape and sexual assault. *Aggression and Violent Behavior, 14*, 323–329.

Field, A. E., Sonneville, K. R., Crosby, R. D., Swanson, S. A., Eddy, K. T., Camargo, C. A., . . . Micali, N. (2014). Prospective associations of concerns about physique and the development of obesity, binge drinking, and drug use among adolescent boys and young adult men. *JAMA Pediatrics, 168*, 34–39.

Figueredo, A. J., Wolf, P. S. A., Olderbak, S. G., Sefcek, J. A., Frías-Armenta, M., Vargas-Porras, C., & Egan, V. (2015). Positive assortative pairing in social and romantic partners: A cross-cultural observational field study of naturally occurring pairs. *Personality and Individual Differences, 84*, 30–35.

Fine, C. (2010). *Delusions of gender: How our minds, society, and neurosexism create difference*. New York, NY: W. W. Norton.

Fine, C. (2013). Neurosexism in functional neuroimaging: From scanner to pseudo-science to psyche. In M. K. Ryan & N. R. Branscombe (Eds.), *The SAGE handbook of gender and psychology* (pp. 45–60). Thousand Oaks, CA: Sage.

Finkel, E. J., DeWall, C. N., Slotter, E. B., McNulty, J. K., Pond, R. S., & Atkins, D. C. (2012). Using I³ to clarify when dispositional aggressiveness predicts intimate partner violence perpetration. *Journal of Personality and Social Psychology, 102*, 533–549.

Finkel, E. J., & Eastwick, P. W. (2009). Arbitrary social norms influence sex differences in romantic selectivity. *Psychological Science, 20*(10), 1290–1295.

Fischer, A., & Evers, C. (2013). The social basis of emotion in men and women. In M. K. Ryan & N. R. Branscombe (Eds.), *The SAGE handbook of gender and psychology* (pp. 183–198). Thousand Oaks, CA: Sage.

Fischer, A. H., Rodriquez Mosquera, P. M., van Vianen, A. E. M., & Manstead, A. S. R. (2004). Gender and culture differences in emotion. *Emotion, 4*(1), 87–94.

Fischtein, D. S., Herold, E. S., & Desmarais, S. (2007). How much does gender explain in sexual attitudes and behaviors? A survey of Canadian adults. *Archives of Sexual Behavior, 36*, 451–461.

Fisher, B. S., Daigle L. E., Cullen, F. T., & Turner, M. G. (2003). Reporting sexual victimization to the police and others: Results from a national-level study of college women. *Criminal Justice and Behavior, 30*, 6–38.

Fisher, C., Hauck, Y., & Fenwick, J. (2006). How social context impacts on women's fears of childbirth: A Western Australian example. *Social Science & Medicine, 63*, 64–75.

Fisher, H. E. (1998). Lust, attraction, and attachment in mammalian reproduction. *Human Nature, 9*, 23–52.

Fisher, T. D., Moore, Z. T., & Pittenger, M.-J. (2012). Sex on the brain? An examination of frequency of sexual cognitions as a function of gender, erotophilia, and social desirability. *Journal of Sex Research, 49*, 69–77.

Fiske, S. T. (1998). Stereotyping, prejudice, and discrimination. In D. T. Gilbert, S. T. Fiske, & G. Lindzey (Eds.), *The handbook of social psychology* (4th ed., Vol. 2, pp. 357–411). Boston, MA: McGraw-Hill.

Fiske, S. T., Cuddy, A. J. C., & Glick, P. (2007). Universal dimensions of social cognition: Warmth and competence. *Trends in Cognitive Sciences, 11*, 77–83.

Fiske, S. T., Cuddy, A. J. C., Glick, P., & Xu, J. (2002). A model of (often mixed) stereotype content: Competence and warmth respectively follow from perceived status and competition. *Journal of Personality and Social Psychology, 82*, 878–902.

Fitzpatrick, M. J., & McPherson, B. J. (2010). Coloring within the lines: Gender stereotypes in contemporary coloring books. *Sex Roles, 62*, 127–137.

Fitzsimmons, E. (2014, December 20). A scourge is spreading. M.T.A.'s cure? Close your legs. *New York Times*. Retrieved from http://www.nytimes.com/2014/12/21/nyregion/MTA-targets-manspreading-on-new-york-city-subways.html

Fivush, R., & Buckner, J. P. (2003). Creating gender and identity through autobiographical narratives. In R. Fivush & C. A. Haden (Eds.), *Autobiographical memory and the construction of a narrative self: Developmental and cultural perspectives* (pp. 149–167). Mahwah, NJ: Lawrence Erlbaum.

Flore, P. C., & Wicherts, J. M. (2015). Does stereotype threat influence performance of girls in stereotyped domains? A meta-analysis. *Journal of School Psychology, 53*, 25–44.

Flores, A. R., Herman, J. L., Gates, G. J., & Brown, T. N. T. (2016). *How many adults identify as transgender in the United States?* Los Angeles, CA: Williams Institute. Retrieved from https://williamsinstitute.law.ucla.edu/wp-content/uploads/How-Many-Adults-Identify-as-Transgender-in-the-United-States.pdf

Flynn, J. R. (1987). Massive IQ gains in 14 nations: What IQ tests really measure. *Psychological Bulletin, 101*, 171–191.

Flynn, K. E., Lin, L., Bruner, D. W., Cyranowski, J. M., Hahn, E. A., Jeffery, D. D., . . . Weinfurt, K. P. (2016). Sexual satisfaction and the importance of sexual health to quality of life throughout the life course of U.S. adults. *Journal of Sexual Medicine, 13*(11), 1642–1650.

Fone, B. (2000). *Homophobia*. New York, NY: Picador.

Forbes, G. B., Adams-Curtis, L. E., & White, K. B. (2004). First- and second-generation measures of sexism, rape myths, and related beliefs, and hostility toward women: Their interrelationships and association with college students' experiences with dating aggression and sexual coercion. *Violence Against Women, 10*, 236–261.

Ford, C. S., & Beach, F. A. (1951). *Patterns of sexual behavior*. New York, NY: Harper & Row.

Forssman, T. (2015). Reflections on a journey through the southern Omo Valley, Ethiopia. *Digging Stick, 32*, 17–20.

Foucault, M. (1978). *The history of sexuality*. New York, NY: Pantheon.

Fraser, G. E., & Shavlik, D. J. (2001). Ten years of life: Is it a matter of choice? *Journal of the American Medical Association, 161*, 1645–1652.

Frazer, A. K., & Miller, M. D. (2008). Double standards in sentence structure: Passive voice in narratives describing domestic violence. *Journal of Language and Social Psychology, 28*(1), 62–71.

Frederick, D. A., & Essayli, J. H. (2016). Male body image: The roles of sexual orientation and body mass index across five national U.S. studies. *Psychology of Men & Masculinity, 17*, 336–351.

Frederick, D. A., John, H. K. S., Garcia, J. R., & Lloyd, E. A. (2017). Differences in orgasm frequency among gay, lesbian, bisexual, and heterosexual men and women in a U.S. national sample. *Archives of Sexual Behavior*, 1–16.

Fredrickson, B. L., & Roberts, T.-A. (1997). Objectification theory: Toward understanding women's lived experiences and mental health risks. *Psychology of Women Quarterly, 21*, 173–206.

Fredrickson, B. L., Roberts, T.-A., Noll, S. M., Quinn, D. M., & Twenge, J. M. (1998). That swimsuit becomes you: sex differences in self-objectification, restrained eating, and math performance. *Journal of Personality and Social Psychology*, 75, 269–284.

Fredriksen-Goldsen, K. I., Cook-Daniels, L., Kim, H.-J., Erosheva, E. A., Emlet, C. A., Hoy-Ellis C., & Muraco, A. (2014). Physical and mental health of transgender older adults: An at-risk and underserved population. *The Gerontologist*, 54, 488–500.

Fredriksen-Goldsen, K. I., Kim, H.-J., Barkan, S. E., Muraco, A., & Hoy-Ellis, C. P. (2013). Health disparities among lesbian, gay, and bisexual older adults: Results from a population-based study. *American Journal of Public Health*, 103, 1802–1809.

Fredriksen-Goldsen, K. I., Kim, H.-J., Shiu, C., Goldsen, J., & Emlet, C. (2015). Successful aging among LGBT older adults: Physical and mental health-related quality of life by age group. *The Gerontologist*, 55, 154–168.

Freud, A. (1949). Some clinical remarks concerning the treatment of cases of male homosexuality. *International Journal of Psychoanalysis*, 30, 196.

Freud, A. (1951). Clinical observations on the treatment of manifest male homosexuality. *Psychoanalytic Quarterly*, 20, 337–338.

Freud, S. (1920). The psychogenesis of a case of female homosexuality. *International Journal of Psychoanalysis*, 1, 125–149.

Frith, K. T., Shaw, P., & Cheng, H. (2005). The construction of beauty: A cross-cultural analysis of women's magazine advertising. *Journal of Communication*, 55, 56–70.

Frost, D. M., Meyer, I. H., & Schwartz, S. (2016). Social support networks among diverse sexual minority populations. *American Journal of Orthopsychiatry*, 86, 91–102.

Frostenson, S. (2017, January 31). The women's marches may have been the largest demonstration in U.S. history. *Vox*. Retrieved from http://www.vox.com/2017/1/22/14350808/womens-marches-largest-demonstration-us-history-map

Fry, R. (2010, October 7). The reversal of the college marriage gap. Pew Research Center. Retrieved from http://www.pewsocialtrends.org/2010/10/07/the-reversal-of-the-college-marriage-gap

Fryer, R. G., & Levitt, S. D. (2010). An empirical analysis of the gender gap in mathematics. *American Economic Journal: Applied Economics*, 2, 210–240.

Fulcher, M., Sutfin, E. L., & Patterson, C. J. (2008). Individual differences in gender development: Associations with parental sexual orientation, attitudes, and division of labor. *Sex Roles*, 58, 330–341.

Furman, D., Hejblum, B. P., Simon, N., Jojic, V., Dekker, C. L., Thiebaut, R., . . . Davis, M. M. (2014). Systems analysis of sex differences reveals an immunosuppressive role for testosterone in the response to influenza vaccination. *Proceedings of the National Academy of Sciences*, 111, 869–874.

Gagne, F., & St. Pere, F. (2002). When IQ is controlled, does motivation still predict achievement? *Intelligence*, 30, 71–100.

Galea, L. A. M., Kavaliers, M., Ossenkopp, K.-P., & Hampson, E. (1995). Gonadal hormone levels and spatial learning performance in the Morris water maze in male and female meadow voles, *microtus pennsylvanicus. Hormones and Behavior*, 29, 106–125.

Galinsky, A. D., Wang, C. S., Whitson, J. A., Anicich, E. M., Hugenberg, K., & Bodenhausen, G. V. (2013). The reappropriation of stigmatizing labels: The reciprocal relationship between power and self-labeling. *Psychological Science*, 24(10), 2020–2029.

Galinsky, A. M., & Sonenstein, F. L. (2011). The association between developmental assets and sexual enjoyment among emerging adults. *Journal of Adolescent Health*, 48, 610–615.

Galperin, A., & Haselton, M. (2010). Predictors of how often and when people fall in love. *Evolutionary Psychology*, 8, 5–28.

Gamble, V. N. (1997). Under the shadow of Tuskegee: African Americans and health care. *American Journal of Public Health*, 87, 1773–1778.

Gangstead, S. W., Haselton, M. G., & Buss, D. M. (2006). Evolutionary foundations of cultural variation: Evoked culture and mate preferences. *Psychological Inquiry*, 17, 75–95.

Gannon, L. (2002). A critique of evolutionary psychology. *Psychology, Evolution, & Gender*, 4(2), 173–218.

Gannon, L., Luchetta, T., Rhodes, K., Pardie, L., & Segrist, D. (1992). Sex bias in psychological research: Progress or complacency? *American Psychologist*, 47, 389–396.

Gates, G. J. (2010). *Sexual minorities in the 2008 General Social Survey: Coming out and demographic characteristics*. Los Angeles, CA: Williams Institute. Retrieved from https://williamsinstitute.law.ucla.edu/wp-content/uploads/Gates-Sexual-Minorities-2008-GSS-Oct-2010.pdf

Gazzola, S. B., & Morrison, M. A. (2014). Cultural and personally endorsed stereotypes of transgender men and transgender women: Notable correspondence or disjunction? *International Journal of Transgenderism, 15*, 76–99.

Geiger, W., Harwood, J., & Hummert, M. L. (2006). College students' multiple stereotypes of lesbians. *Journal of Homosexuality, 51*, 165–182.

Gergen, M. M. (2010). Qualitative inquiry in gender studies. In J. C. Chrisler & D. R. McCreary (Eds.), *Handbook of gender research in psychology* (pp. 103–131). New York, NY: Springer Science + Business Media.

Gewertz, D. (1981). *Sepik River societies: A historical enthnography of the Chambri and their neighbors*. New Haven, CT: Yale University Press.

Ghavami, N., & Peplau, L. A. (2012). An intersectional analysis of gender and ethnic stereotypes: Testing three hypotheses. *Psychology of Women Quarterly, 37*, 113–127.

Gilbert, L. A. (1993). *Two careers/one family*. Newbury Park, CA: Sage.

Gilbert, L. A., & Rader, J. (2001). Current perspectives on women's adult roles: Work, family, and life. In R. K. Unger (Ed.), *Handbook of the psychology of women and gender* (pp. 156–169). Hoboken, NJ: John Wiley.

Gilmore, D. D. (1990). *Manhood in the making*. New Haven, CT: Yale University Press.

Gimlin, D. L. (2007). What is "Body Work"? A review of the literature. *Sociology Compass, 1*, 353–370.

Gingold, H. G., Hancock, K. A., & Cerbone, A. R. (2006). A word about words: Stigma, sexual orientation/identity, and the "heterosexist default." *NYS Psychologist, 8*(4), 20–24.

Ginsburg, H. J., Ogletree, S. M., & Silakowski, T. D. (2003). Vulgar language: Review of sex differences in usage, attributions, and pathologies. *North American Journal of Psychology, 5*, 105–115.

Glick, P., & Fiske, S. T. (1996). The Ambivalent Sexism Inventory: Differentiating hostile and benevolent sexism. *Journal of Personality and Social Psychology, 70*, 491–512.

Glick, P., & Fiske, S. T. (1999). The Ambivalence Toward Men Inventory: Differentiating hostile and benevolent beliefs about men. *Psychology of Women Quarterly, 23*, 519–536.

Glick, P., Fiske, S. T., Mladinic, A., Saiz, J. L., Abrams, D., Masser, B., . . . López, W. L. (2000). Beyond prejudice as simple antipathy: Hostile and benevolent sexism across cultures. *Journal of Personality and Social Psychology, 79*, 763–775.

Glick, P., Lameiras, M., Fiske, S. T., Eckes, T., Masser, B., Volpato, C., . . . Wells, R. (2004). Bad but bold: Ambivalent attitudes toward men predict gender inequality in 16 nations. *Journal of Personality and Social Psychology, 86*, 713–728.

Glover, J. A., Galliher, R. V., & Lamere, T. G. (2009). Identity development and exploration among sexual minority adolescents: Examination of a multidimensional model. *Journal of Homosexuality, 56*, 77–101.

Goh, V. H., Tain, C., Tong, Y., Mok, P., & Ng, S. (2004). Sex and aging in the city: Singapore. *Aging Male, 7*, 219–226.

Goldberg, A. E. (2013). "Doing" and "undoing" gender: The meaning and division of housework in same-sex couples. *Journal of Family Theory and Review, 5*, 85–104.

Goldberg, A. E., Smith, J. Z., & Kashy, D. A. (2010). Preadoptive factors predicting lesbian, gay, and heterosexual couples' relationship quality across the transition to adoptive parenthood. *Journal of Family Psychology, 24*, 221–232.

Golden, C. (2008). The intersexed and the transgendered: Rethinking sex/gender. In J. Chrisler, C. Golden, & P. Rozee (Eds.), *Lectures on the psychology of women* (4th ed., pp. 136–152). New York, NY: McGraw-Hill.

Goldenberg, T., Stephenson, R., Freeland, R., Finneran, C., & Hadley, C. (2016). "Struggling to be the alpha": Sources of tension and intimate partner violence in same-sex relationships between men. *Culture, Health, & Sexuality, 18*, 875–889.

Gonzalez, J. (2015, May 29). Hispanic paradox: Why immigrants have a high life expectancy. *BBC*. Retrieved from http://www.bbc.com/news/world-us-canada-32910129

Goode, W. J. (1960). A theory of role strain. *American Sociological Review, 25*, 483–496.

Gottfredson, L. S. (1997). Mainstream science on intelligence: An editorial with 52 signatories, history, and bibliography. *Intelligence, 24*(1), 13–23.

Gottman, J. M., & Levenson, R. W. (2000). The timing of divorce:

Predicting when a couple will divorce over a 14-year period. *Journal of Marriage and Family, 62,* 737–745.

Gottman, J. M., Levenson, R. W., Swanson, C., Swanson, K., Tyson, R., & Yoshimoto, D. (2003). Observing gay, lesbian, and heterosexual couples' relationships. *Journal of Homosexuality, 45,* 65–91.

Götz, M., Hofmann, O., Brosius, H.-B., Carter, C., Chan, K., Donald, St. H., . . . Zhang, H. (2008). Gender in children's television worldwide: Results from a media analysis in 24 countries. *Televizion, 21,* 4–9.

Gough, B., Weyman, N., Alderson, J., Butler, G., & Stoner, M. (2008). "They did not have a word": The parental quest to locate a "true sex" for their intersex children. *Psychology & Health, 23,* 493–507.

Goymann, W., East, M. L., & Hofer, H. (2001). Androgens and the role of female "hyperaggressiveness" in spotted hyenas (Crocuta crocuta). *Hormones and Behavior, 39,* 83–92.

Grabe, S., Ward, L. M., & Hyde, J. S. (2008). The role of the media in body image concerns among women: A meta-analysis of experimental and correlational studies. *Psychological Bulletin, 134,* 460–476.

Gracia, E., & Merlo, J. (2016). Intimate partner violence against women and the Nordic paradox. *Social Science & Medicine, 157,* 27–30.

Graefe, D. R., & Lichter, D. T. (2002). Marriage among unwed mothers: Whites, Blacks and Hispanics compared. *Perspectives on Sexual and Reproductive Health, 34,* 286–293.

Graham, C., & Chattopadhyay, S. (2013). Gender and well-being around the world. *International Journal of Happiness and Development, 1,* 212–232.

Grant, J. M., Mottet, L. A., Tanis, J., Harrison, J., Herman, J. L., & Keisling, M. (2011). *Injustice at every turn: A report of the National Transgender Discrimination Survey.* Retrieved from http://endtransdiscrimination. org/PDFs/NTDS_Report.pdf

Grant, J. M., Mottet, L. A., Tanis, J., Herman, J. L., Harrison, J., & Keisling, M. (2010). *National Transgender Discrimination Survey report on health and health care.* Washington, DC: National Center for Transgender Equality and the National Gay and Lesbian Task Force.

Gray, J. (1992). *Men are from Mars, women are from Venus: A practical guide for improving communication and getting what you want in your relationships.* New York, NY: HarperCollins.

Green, A. R., Carney, D. R., Pallin, D. J., Ngo, L. H., Raymond, K. L., Iezzoni, L. I., & Banaji, M. R. (2007). Implicit bias among physicians and its prediction of thrombolysis decisions for black and white patients. *Journal of General Internal Medicine, 22,* 1231–1238.

Green, E. (2016, May 31). America's profound gender anxiety. *The Atlantic.* Retrieved from https://www.theatlantic.com/politics/archive/2016/05/americas-profound-gender-anxiety/484856

Greenhaus, J. H., & Powell, G. N. (2006). When work and family are allies: A theory of work–family enrichment. *Academy of Management Review, 31,* 72–92.

Greenspoon, J., & Lamal, P. (1987). A behavioristic approach. In L. Diamant (Ed.), *Male and female homosexuality: Psychological approaches* (pp. 109–127). New York, NY: Hemisphere.

Griffin, G. D., & Flanagan-Cato, L. M. (2012). Sex differences in the dendritic arbors of neurons in the hypothalamic ventromedial nucleus. *Physiology and Behavior, 97,* 151–156.

Griffith, J. W., Zinbarg, R. E., Craske, M. G., Mineka, S., Rose, R. D., Waters, A. M., & Sutton, J. M. (2010). Neuroticism as a common dimension in the internalizing disorders. *Psychological Medicine: A Journal of Research in Psychiatry and the Allied Sciences, 40,* 1125–1136.

Griffiths, A. J. F., Wessley, S. R., Carroll, S. B., & Doebley, J. (2015). *Introduction to genetic analysis* (11th ed.). New York, NY: W. H. Freeman & Company.

Gross, S. R. (2008). Convicting the innocent. *Annual Review of Law and Social Science, 4,* 173–192.

Grunow, D., Schulz, F., & Blossfeld, H.-P. (2012). What determines change in the division of housework over the course of marriage? *International Sociology, 27,* 289–307.

Guerrero, L. K., & Chavez, A. M. (2005). Relational maintenance in cross-sex friendships characterized by different types of romantic intent: An exploratory study. *Western Journal of Communication, 69,* 339–358.

Guimond, S., Branscombe, N. R., Brunot, S., Buunk, A. P., Chatard, A., Desert, M., . . . Yzerbet, V. (2007). Culture, gender, and the self: Variations and impact of social comparison processes. *Journal of Personality and Social Psychology, 92,* 1118–1134.

Guindon, G. E., & Boisclair, D. (2003). Past, current and future trends in tobacco use: HNP discussion paper. Washington, DC: World Bank. Retrieved from http://escholarship.org/uc/item/4q57d5vp

Guiso, L., Monte, F., Sapienza, P., & Zingales, L. (2008). Culture, gender, and math. *Science, 320*, 1164–1165.

Gundersen, J. R., & Gampel, G. V. (1982). Married women's legal status in eighteenth-century New York and Virginia. *William and Mary Quarterly, 39*, 114–134.

Gunderson, E. A., Ramirez, G., Levine, S. C., & Beilock, S. L. (2012). The role of parents and teachers in the development of gender-related math attitudes. *Sex Roles, 66*, 153–166.

Gurnsey, R., Roddy, G., & Troje, N. F. (2010). Limits of peripheral direction discrimination of point-light walkers. *Journal of Vision, 10*(2): 15, 1–17.

Guttentag, M., & Secord, P. F. (1983). *Too many women?: The sex ratio question.* Beverly Hills, CA: Sage.

Häggström-Nordin, E. (2005). Associations between pornography consumption and sexual practices among adolescents in Sweden. *International Journal of STD & AIDS, 16*, 102–107.

Haider, A. H., Schneider, E. B., Kodadek, L. M., Adler, R. R., Ranjit, A., Torain, M., . . . German, D. (2017). Emergency department query for patient-centered approaches to sexual orientation and gender identity: The EQUALITY Study. *JAMA Internal Medicine, 177*(6), 819–828.

Haines, E. L., Deaux, K., & Lofaro, N. (2016). The times they are a-changing . . . or are they not? A comparison of gender stereotypes, 1983–2014. *Psychology of Women Quarterly, 40*(3), 353–363.

Hakim, C. (2015). The male sexual deficit: A social fact of the 21st century. *International Sociology, 30*, 314–335.

Haldeman, D. (1994). The practice and ethics of sexual orientation conversion therapy. *Journal of Consulting and Clinical Psychology, 62*, 221–227.

Halim, M. L., Ruble, D., Tamis-LeMonda, C., & Shrout, P. E. (2013). Rigidity in gender-typed behaviors in early childhood: A longitudinal study of ethnic minority children. *Child Development, 84*(4), 1269–1284.

Hall, E. V., Galinsky, A. D., & Phillips, K. W. (2015). Gender profiling: A gendered race perspective on person-position fit. *Personality and Social Psychology Bulletin, 41*, 853–868.

Hall, J. A. (1984). *Nonverbal gender differences: Communication accuracy and expressive style.* Baltimore, MD: John Hopkins University Press.

Hall, J. A. (2006). How big are nonverbal sex differences? The case of smiling and nonverbal sensitivity. In K. Dindia & D. J. Canary (Eds.), *Sex differences and similarities in communication* (Vol. 2, pp. 59–81). Mahwah, NJ: Lawrence Erlbaum.

Hall, J. A. (2011). Sex differences in friendship expectations: A meta-analysis. *Journal of Social and Personal Relationships, 28*, 723–747.

Hall, J. A., Andrzejewski, S. A., & Yopchick, J. E. (2009). Prosocial correlates of interpersonal sensitivity: A meta-analysis. *Journal of Nonverbal Behavior, 33*, 149–180.

Hall, J. A., Coats, E. J., & LeBeau, L. S. (2005). Nonverbal behavior and the vertical dimension of social relations: A meta-analysis. *Psychological Bulletin, 131*, 898–924.

Hall, J. A., LeBeau, L. S., Reinoso, J. G., & Thayer, F. (2001). Status, gender, and nonverbal behavior in candid and posed photographs: A study of conversations between university employees. *Sex Roles, 44*, 677–692.

Hall, J. A., & Matsumoto, D. (2004). Gender differences in judgments of multiple emotions from facial expressions. *Emotion, 4*, 201–206.

Hall, J. C., Everett, J. E., & Hamilton-Mason, J. (2012). Black women talk about workplace stress and how they cope. *Journal of Black Studies, 43*, 207–226.

Hallal, P. C., Andersen, L. B., Bull, F., Guthold, R., Haskell, W., & Ekelund, U. (2012). Global physical activity levels: Surveillance progress, pitfalls, and prospects. *The Lancet, 380*, 247–257.

Halliwell, E., & Dittmar, H. (2003). A qualitative investigation of women's and men's body image concerns and their attitudes toward aging. *Sex Roles, 49*(11–12), 675–684.

Halpern, D. F. (1994). Stereotypes, science, censorship, and the study of sex differences. *Feminism & Psychology, 4*, 523–530.

Halpern, D. F. (2004). A cognitive-process taxonomy for sex differences in cognitive abilities. *Current Directions in Psychological Science, 13*, 135–139.

Halpern, D. F. (2012). *Sex differences in cognitive abilities* (4th ed.). Mahwah, NJ: Lawrence Erlbaum.

Halpern, D. F., Benbow, C. P., Geary, D. C., Gur, R. C., Hyde, J. S., & Gernsbacher, M. A. (2007). The science of sex differences in science and mathematics. *Psychological Science in the Public Interest, 8*, 1–51.

Halpern, D. F., Eliot, L., Bigler, R. S., Fabes, R. A., Hanish, L. D., Hyde,

J., . . . Martin, C. L. (2012). The pseudoscience of single-sex schooling. *Science, 333*, 1706–1707.

Halpern, D. F., Straight, C. A., & Stephenson, C. L. (2011). Beliefs about cognitive gender differences: Accurate for direction, underestimated for size. *Sex Roles, 64*, 336–347.

Hammer, J. H., Vogel, D. L., & Heimerdinger-Edwards, S. R. (2013). Men's help seeking: Examination of differences across community size, education, and income. *Psychology of Men & Masculinity, 14*, 65–75.

Hammond, W. P., Matthews, D., Mohottige, D., Agyemang, A., & Corbie-Smith, G. (2010). Masculinity, medical mistrust, and preventive health services delays among community-dwelling African-American men. *Journal of General Internal Medicine, 25*, 1300–1308.

Hampson, E., & Moffatt, S. D. (2004). The psychobiology of gender: Cognitive effects of reproductive hormones in the adult nervous system. In R. J. Sternberg, A. Eagly, & A. Beal (Eds.), *The psychology of gender* (2nd ed., pp. 38–64). New York, NY: Guilford Press.

Haning, R. V., O'Keefe, S. L., Randall, E. J., Kommor, M. J., Baker, E., & Wilson, R. (2007). Intimacy, orgasm likelihood, and conflict predict sexual satisfaction in heterosexual male and female respondents. *Journal of Sex & Marital Therapy, 33*, 93–113.

Harden, B. (2008, July 13). Japan's killer work ethic. *Washington Post.* Retrieved from http://www.washingtonpost.com/wp-dyn/content/article/2008/07/12/AR2008071201630.html

Hare-Mustin, R. T., & Marecek, J. (1988). The meaning of difference:

Gender theory, postmodernism, and psychology. *American Psychologist, 43*, 455–464.

Hare-Mustin, R. T., & Marecek, J. (1994). Asking the right questions: Feminist psychology and sex differences. *Feminism & Psychology, 4*, 531–537.

Harrell, Z. A. T., & Karim, N. M. (2008). Is gender relevant only for problem alcohol behaviors? An examination of correlates of alcohol use among college students. *Addictive Behaviors, 33*, 359–365.

Harrendorf, S., Heiskanen, M., & Malby, S. (Eds.). (2010). *International statistics on crime and justice.* Vienna, Austria: United Nations Office on Drugs and Crime. Retrieved from https://www.unodc.org/documents/data-and-analysis/Crime-statistics/International_Statistics_on_Crime_and_Justice.pdf

Harris, C. R. (2003). A review of sex differences in sexual jealousy, including self-report data, psychophysiological responses, interpersonal violence, and morbid jealousy. *Personality and Social Psychology Review, 7*, 102–128.

Harris, E. C., & Barraclough, B. (1997). Suicide as an outcome for mental disorders: A meta-analysis. *British Journal of Psychiatry, 170*, 205–228.

Hartmann, I. (2011, October 19). Does single-sex education breed sexism? *Salon.* Retrieved from http://www.salon.com/2011/10/19/sexism_education_alternet

Hassett, J. M., Siebert, E. R., & Wallen, K. (2008). Sex differences in rhesus monkey toy preferences parallel those of children. *Hormones and Behavior, 54*, 359–364.

Hatfield, E., Cacioppo, J. T., & Rapson, R. L. (1993). Emotional contagion. *Current Directions in Psychological Science, 2*, 96–99.

Hatfield, E., & Sprecher, S. (1995). Men's and women's preferences in marital partners in the United States, Russia, and Japan. *Journal of Cross-Cultural Psychology, 26*(6), 728–750.

Hatzenbuehler, M. L. (2014). Structural stigma and the health of lesbian, gay, and bisexual populations. *Current Directions in Psychological Science, 23*, 127–132.

Hatzenbuehler M. L., Bellatorre, A., Lee, Y., Finch, B., Muennig, P., & Fiscella, K. (2014). Structural stigma and all-cause mortality in sexual minority populations. *Social Science & Medicine, 103*, 33–41.

Hatzenbuehler, M. L., Keyes, K. M., & Hasin, D. S. (2009). State-level policies and psychiatric morbidity in lesbian, gay, and bisexual populations. *American Journal of Public Health, 99*, 2275–2281.

Hatzenbuehler, M. L., Slopen, N., & McLaughlin, K. A. (2014). Stressful life events, sexual orientation and cardiometabolic risk among young adults in the United States. *Health Psychology, 33*, 1185–1194.

Hawes, D. J., Dadds, M. R., Frost, A. J., & Hasking, P. A. (2011). Do childhood callous-unemotional traits drive change in parenting practices? *Journal of Clinical Child and Adolescent Psychology, 40*, 507–518.

Hazan, C., & Shaver, P. R. (1994). Attachment as an organizational framework for research on close relationships. *Psychological Inquiry, 5*, 1–22.

Hazan, C., & Zeifman, D. (1994). Sex and the psychological tether.

In D. Perlman & K. Bartholomew (Eds.), *Advances in personal relationships: A research annual* (Vol. 5, pp. 151–177). London, UK: Jessica Kingsley.

Hazen, A. L., & Soriano, F. I. (2007). Experiences with intimate partner violence among Latina women. *Violence Against Women, 13,* 562–582.

Heard, E., & Martienssen, R. (2014). Transgenerational epigenetic inheritance: Myths and mechanisms. *Cell, 157*(1), 95–109.

Heck, J. E., Sell, R. L., & Gorin, S. S. (2006). Health care access among individuals involved in same-sex relationships. *American Journal of Public Health, 96,* 1111–1118.

Hedges, L. V., & Nowell, A. (1995). Sex differences in mental test scores, variability, and numbers of high-scoring individuals. *Science, 269,* 41–45.

Hegarty, P., & Buechel, C. (2006). Androcentric reporting of gender differences in APA journals: 1965–2004. *Review of General Psychology, 10,* 377–389.

Hegewisch, A., & Ellis, E. (2015). *The gender wage gap by occupation 2014 and by race and ethnicity.* Washington, DC: Institute for Women's Policy Research. Retrieved from http://www.iwpr.org/publications/pubs/the-gender-wage-gap-by-occupation-2014-and-by-race-and-ethnicity

Hegewisch, A., & Hartmann, H. (2014). *Occupational segregation and the gender wage gap: A job half done.* Washington, DC: Institute of Women's Policy Research. Retrieved from http://www.iwpr.org/publications/pubs/occupational-segregation-and-the-gender-wage-gap-a-job-half-done

Heilman, M. E., & Okimoto, T. G. (2007). Why are women penalized for success at male tasks? The implied communality deficit. *Journal of Applied Psychology, 92,* 81–92.

Heilman, M. E., & Wallen, A. S. (2010). Wimpy and undeserving of respect: Penalties for men's gender-inconsistent success. *Journal of Experimental Social Psychology, 46,* 664–667.

Heilman, M. E., Wallen, A. S., Fuchs, D., & Tamkins, M. M. (2004). Penalties for success: Reactions to women who succeed in male gender-typed tasks. *Journal of Applied Psychology, 89,* 416–427.

Heimer, K. (2000). *Changes in the gender gap in crime and women's economic marginalization.* Retrieved from https://www.ncjrs.gov/criminal_justice2000/vol_1/02i.pdf

Heise, L., Ellsberg, M., & Gottmoeller, M. (2002). A global overview of gender-based violence. *International Journal of Gynecology and Obstetrics, 78,* 5–14.

Helgeson, V. S. (2003). Gender-related traits and health. In J. Suls & K. A. Wallston (Eds.), *Social psychological foundations of health and illness* (pp. 367–394). Malden, MA: Blackwell.

Helgeson, V. S., & Fritz, H. L. (1996). Implications of unmitigated communion and communion for adolescent adjustment to Type I diabetes. *Women's Health: Research on Gender, Behavior, and Policy, 2,* 163–188.

Helgeson, V. S., & Lepore, S. J. (2004). Quality of life following prostate cancer: The role of agency and unmitigated agency. *Journal of Applied Social Psychology, 34,* 2559–2585.

Helmreich, R. L., Spence, J. T., & Wilhelm, J. A. (1981). A psychometric analysis of the Personal Attributes Questionnaire. *Sex Roles, 7,* 1097–1108.

Helweg-Larsen, M., Cunningham, S. J., Carrico, A., & Pergram, A. M. (2004). To nod or not to nod: An observational study of nonverbal communication and status in female and male college students. *Psychology of Women Quarterly, 28,* 358–361.

Henley, N. M. (1995a). Body politics revisited: What do we know today? In P. J. Kalbfleisch & M. J. Cody (Eds.), *Gender, power, and communication in human relationships* (pp. 105–138). Hillsdale, NJ: Lawrence Erlbaum.

Henley, N. M. (1995b). Ethnicity and gender issues in language. In H. Landrine (Ed.), *Bringing cultural diversity to feminist psychology: Theory, research, and practice* (pp. 361–395). Washington, DC: American Psychological Association.

Henley, N. M., Miller, M., & Beazley, J. A. (1995). Syntax, semantics, and sexual violence: Agency and passive voice. *Journal of Language and Social Psychology, 14*(1–2), 60–84.

Hennenlotter, A., Dresel, C., Castrop, F., Ceballos Baumann, A. O., Wohlschlager, A. M., & Haslinger, B. (2008). The link between facial feedback and neural activity within central circuitries of emotion: New insights from botulinum toxin-induced denervation of frown muscles. *Cerebral Cortex, 19,* 537–542.

Herbenick, D., Reece, M., Schick, V., Sanders, S. A., Dodge, B., & Fortenberry, J. D. (2015). Sexual behavior in the United States: Results from a national probability sample of men and women ages 14–94. *Journal of Sexual Medicine, 7*(suppl 5), 255–265.

Herbst, K. L., Amory, J. K., Brunzell, J. D., Chansky, H. A., & Bremner, W. J. (2003). Testosterone administration to men increases hepatic lipase activity and decreases HDL and LDL size in 3 wk. *American Journal of Physiology, Endocrinology and Metabolism, 284*, E1112–E1118.

Herdt, G. H. (1982). Fetish and fantasy in Sambia initiation. In G. H. Herdt (Ed.), *Rituals of manhood* (pp. 44–98). Berkeley: University of California Press.

Herdt, G., & Polen-Petit, N. C. (2014). *Human sexuality: Self, society, and culture.* New York, NY: McGraw-Hill.

Herek, G. M. (2000). Homosexuality. In A. E. Kazdin (Ed.), *Encyclopedia of psychology* (Vol. 4, pp. 149–153). Washington, DC: American Psychological Association.

Herek, G. M., & Capitanio, J. P. (1996). "Some of my best friends": Intergroup contact, concealable stigma, and heterosexuals' attitudes toward gay men and lesbians. *Personality and Social Psychology Bulletin, 22*, 412–424.

Hettinger, V. E., Hutchinson, D., & Bosson, J. K. (2013). Influence of professional status on perceptions of romantic relationship dynamics. *Psychology of Men & Masculinity, 15,* 470–480.

Hewett, B., Western, M., & Baxter, J. (2006). Who decides? The social characteristics of who initiates marital separation. *Journal of Marriage and Family, 68,* 1165–1177.

Hewitt, J., & Alqahtani, M. (2003). Differences between Saudi and U.S. students in reaction to same- and mixed-sex intimacy shown by others. *Journal of Social Psychology, 143*(2), 233–242.

Heyes, C. (2015). Animal mind-reading: What's the problem? *Psychonomic Bulletin & Review, 22*, 313–327.

Heylens G., De Cuypere, G., Zucker, K. J., Schelfaut, C., Elaut, E., Van den Bossche, H., . . . T'Sjoen, G. (2012). Gender identity disorder in twins: A review of the case report literature. *Journal of Sexual Medicine, 9*, 751–757.

Hibbard, J. H., & Pope, C. R. (1993). The quality of social roles as predictors of morbidity and mortality. *Social Science & Medicine, 36*, 217–225.

Hill, C., & Kearl, H. (2011). *Crossing the line: Sexual harassment at school.* Washington, DC: AAUW. Retrieved from http://www.aauw .org/files/2013/02/Crossing-the-Line-Sexual-Harassment-at-School.pdf

Hill, D. B., & Willoughby, B. B. (2005). The development and validation of the Genderism and Transphobia Scale. *Sex Roles, 53,* 531–544.

Hill, J. P., & Lynch, M. E. (1983). The intensification of gender-related role expectations during early adolescence. In J. Brooks-Gunn & A. Petersen (Eds.), *Girls at puberty: Biological and psychosocial perspectives* (pp. 201–228). New York, NY: Plenum.

Hilliard, L. J., & Liben, L. S. (2010). Differing levels of gender salience in preschool classrooms: Effects on children's gender attitudes and intergroup bias. *Child Development, 81,* 1787–1798.

Hilmers, A., Hilmers, D. C., & Dave, J. (2012). Neighborhood disparities in access to healthy foods and their effects on environmental justice. *American Journal of Public Health, 102*, 1644–1654.

Himmelstein, M. S., & Sanchez, D. T. (2016). Masculinity impediments: Internalized masculinity contributes to healthcare avoidance in men and women. *Journal of Health Psychology, 21*, 1283–1292.

Hinduja, S., & Patchin, J. W. (2010). Bullying, cyberbullying, and suicide. *Archives of Suicide Research, 14,* 206–221.

Hines, M. (2004). Androgen, estrogen, and gender: Contributions of the early hormone environment to gender-related behavior. In A. H. Eagly, A. E. Beall, & R. J. Sternberg (Eds.), *The psychology of gender* (2nd ed., pp. 9–37). New York, NY: Guilford Press.

Hines, M. (2013). Sex and sex differences. In P. D. Zelazo (Ed.), *The Oxford handbook of developmental psychology (Vol 1): Body and mind* (pp. 164–201). New York, NY: Oxford University Press.

Hines, M., Ahmed, S. F., & Hughes, I. A. (2003). Psychological outcomes and gender-related development in complete androgen insensitivity syndrome. *Archives of Sexual Behavior, 32*(2), 93–101.

Hines, M., Brook, C., & Conway, G. S. (2004). Androgen and psychosexual development: Core gender identity, sexual orientation, and recalled childhood gender role behavior in women and men with congenital adrenal hyperplasia (CAH). *Journal of Sex Research, 41*(1), 75–81.

Hirsch, B. J., Mickus, M., & Boerger, R. (2002). Ties to influential adults among Black and White adolescents: Culture, social class, and family networks. *American Journal of Community Psychology, 30,* 289–303.

Hochschild, A. (1989). *The second shift: Working parents and the revolution at home.* New York, NY: Penguin.

Hodge, D. R., & Lietz, C. A., (2007). The international sexual trafficking of women and children: A review of the literature. *Affilia, 22,* 163–174.

Hoff Sommers, C. (2013, February 2). The boys at the back. *New York Times.* Retrieved from http://opinionator.blogs.nytimes.com/2013/02/02/the-boys-at-the-back

Hoff Sommers, C. (2014, February 1). No, women don't make less money than men. *Daily Beast.* Retrieved from http://www.thedailybeast.com/articles/2014/02/01/no-women-don-t-make-less-money-than-men.html

Hofstede, G. (2001). *Culture's consequences: Comparing values, behaviors, institutions, and organizations across nations* (2nd ed.). Thousand Oaks, CA: Sage.

Hogue, C. L. (1987). Cultural entomology. *Annual Review of Entomology, 32,* 181–199.

Holleran, S. E., Mehl, M. R., & Levitt, S. (2009). Eavesdropping on social life: The accuracy of stranger ratings of daily behavior from thin slices of natural conversations. *Journal of Research in Personality, 43,* 660–672.

Holmes, M. (Ed.). (2016). *Critical intersex.* London, UK: Routledge.

Holmstrom, A. J. (2004). The effects of the media on body image: A meta-analysis. *Journal of Broadcasting & Electronic Media, 48,* 196–217.

Hook, J. L. (2006). Care in context: Men's unpaid work in 20 countries, 1965–2003. *American Sociological Review, 71,* 639–660.

Hooker, E. (1957). The adjustment of the male overt homosexual. *Journal of Projective Techniques, 21,* 18–31.

Hooker, E. (1969). Parental relations and male homosexuality in patient and nonpatient samples. *Journal of Consulting and Clinical Psychology, 33,* 140–142.

hooks, b. (1981). *Ain't I a woman? Black women and feminism.* Cambridge, MA: South End Press.

hooks, b. (2000). *Feminist theory: From margin to center* (2nd ed.). Cambridge, MA: South End Press.

hooks, b. (2014). *Feminism is for everybody: Passionate politics* (2nd ed.). New York, NY: Routledge.

Houston, M., & Scott, K. D. (2006). Negotiating boundaries, crossing borders: The language of Black women's intercultural encounters. In B. J. Dow & J. T. Wood (Eds.), *The SAGE handbook of gender and communication* (pp. 397–414). Thousand Oaks, CA: Sage.

Howell, N. (1979). *Demography of the Dobe !Kung.* New York, NY: Academic Press.

Hudson, J. I., Hiripi, E., Pope, H. G., & Kessler, R. C. (2007). The prevalence and correlates of eating disorders in the National Comorbidity Survey Replication. *Biological Psychiatry, 61,* 348–358.

Hughto, J. M. W., Reisner, J. E., & Pachankis, J. E. (2015). Transgender stigma and health: A critical review of stigma determinants, mechanisms, and interventions. *Social Science & Medicine, 147,* 222–231.

Human Rights Campaign. (2009). *Degrees of equality: A national study examining workplace climate for LGBT individuals.* Retrieved from http://hrc-assets.s3-website-us-east-1.amazonaws.com//files/assets/resources/DegreesOfEquality_2009.pdf

Human Rights Campaign. (2017). The lies and dangers of efforts to change sexual orientation or gender identity. Retrieved from http://www.hrc.org/resources/the-lies-and-dangers-of-reparative-therapy

Hurtado, A. (1996). *The color of privilege: Three blasphemies on race and feminism.* Ann Arbor: University of Michigan Press.

Hurtado, A., & Sinha M. (2008). More than men: Latino feminist masculinities and intersectionality. *Sex Roles, 59,* 337–349.

Hutter, J. (1993). The social construction of homosexuals in the nineteenth century: The shift from the sin to the influence of medicine on criminalizing sodomy in Germany. In J. P. DeCecco & J. P. Elia (Eds.), *If you seduce a straight person, can you make them gay? Issues in biological essentialism versus social constructionism in gay and lesbian identities* (pp. 73–93). Binghamton, NY: Harrington Park Press.

Hutter Epstein, R. (2010). *Get me out: A history of childbirth from the garden of Eden to the sperm bank.* New York, NY: Norton.

Hwang, H., & Matsumoto, D. (2015). Evidence for the universality of facial expressions of emotion. In M. K. Mandal & A. Awasthi (Eds.), *Understanding facial expressions in* communication (pp. 41–56). New Delhi, India: Springer.

Hyde, J. S. (1984a). Children's understanding of sexist language. *Developmental Psychology, 20,* 697–706.

Hyde, J. S. (1984b). How large are gender differences in aggression? A developmental meta-analysis. *Developmental Psychology, 20,* 722–736.

Hyde, J. S. (1994). Should psychologists study gender differences? Yes, with some guidelines. *Feminism & Psychology, 4,* 507–512.

Hyde, J. S. (2005). The gender similarities hypothesis. *American Psychologist, 60,* 581–592.

Hyde, J. S. (2014). Gender similarities and differences. *Annual Review of Psychology, 65,* 373–398.

Hyde, J. S., Fennema, E., & Lamon, S. J. (1990). Gender differences in mathematics performance: A meta-analysis. *Psychological Bulletin, 107*(2), 139–155.

Hyde, J. S., Lindberg, S. M., Linn, M. C., Ellis, A., & Williams, C. (2008). Gender similarities characterize math performance. *Science, 321,* 494–495.

Hyde, J. S., & Linn, M. C. (1988). Gender differences in verbal ability: A meta-analysis. *Psychological Bulletin, 104,* 53–69.

Hyde, J. S., & Mertz, J. E. (2009). Gender, culture, and mathematics performance. *Proceedings of the National Academy of Sciences, 106,* 8801–8807.

Hyde, J. S., & Oliver, M. B. (2000). Gender differences in sexuality: Results from meta-analysis. In C. B. Travis & J. W. White (Eds.), *Sexuality, society, and feminism* (pp. 57–77).

Washington, DC: American Psychological Association.

Hymowitz, C., & Schellhardt, T. D. (1986, March 24). The glass ceiling: Why women can't seem to break the invisible barrier that blocks them from the top jobs. *Wall Street Journal,* 1D–32D.

Hynes, M., & Lopes Cardozo, B. (2000). Observations from the CDC: Sexual violence against refugee women. *Journal of Women's Health & Gender-Based Medicine, 9,* 819–823.

Ickes, W., Gesn, P. R., & Graham, T. (2000). Gender differences in empathic accuracy: Differential ability or differential motivation? *Personal Relationships, 7,* 95–109.

Iemmola, F., & Ciani, A. C. (2009). New evidence of genetic factors influencing sexual orientation in men: Female fecundity increase in the maternal line. *Archives of Sexual Behavior, 38,* 393–399.

Iervolino, A. C., Hines, M., Golombok, S. E., Rust, J., & Plomin, R. (2005). Genetic and environmental influences on sex-typed behavior during the preschool years. *Child Development, 76*(4), 826–840.

Ikizler, A. S., & Szymanski, D. M. (2014). A qualitative study of Middle Eastern/Arab American sexual minority identity development. *Journal of LGBT Issues in Counseling, 8,* 206–241.

Imbornoni, A. (n.d.). *Women's rights movement in the U.S.* Retrieved from http://www. infoplease.com/spot/womenstimeline1.html

Ingalhalikar, M., Smith, A. Parker, D., Satterthwaite, T. D., Elliott, M. A., Ruparel, K., . . . Verma, R. (2014). Sex differences in the structural

connectome of the human brain. *Proceedings of the National Academy of Science, 111*(2), 823–828.

Institute for Women's Policy Research. (2016, September). *The gender wage gap: 2015: Annual earnings difference by gender, race, and ethnicity.* Washington, DC: Author. Retrieved from http://www.iwpr.org/publications

Insurance Institute for Highway Safety. (2016). *Motor vehicle crash deaths by type and gender, 1975–2014.* Highway Loss Data Institute. Retrieved from http://www.iihs.org/iihs/topics/t/general-statistics/fatalityfacts/gender

International Labour Organization. (2007). *Equality at work: Tackling the challenges.* Report of the Director General, International Labour Conference. Geneva, Switzerland: Author. Retrieved from http://www.ilo.org/wcmsp5/groups/public/---dgreports/---dcomm/---webdev/documents/publication/wcms_082607.pdf

International Labour Organization. (2014, May). *Profits and poverty: The economics of forced labour.* Retrieved from http://www.ilo.org/wcmsp5/groups/public/---ed_norm/---declaration/documents/publication/wcms_243391.pdf

Ioannidis, J. P. A. (2012). Why science is not necessarily self-correcting. *Perspectives on Psychological Science, 7*(6), 645–654.

Itakura, H., & Tsui, A. B. M. (2004). Gender and conversational dominance in Japanese conversation. *Language in Society, 33,* 223–248.

Jackson, D. N., & Rushton, J. P. (2006). Males have greater g: Sex differences in general mental ability from 100,000 17- to 18-year-olds on the Scholastic Assessment Test. *Intelligence, 34,* 479–486.

Jackson, P. B., & Williams, D. (2006). The intersection of race, gender, and SES: Health paradoxes. In A. Schulz & L. Mullings (Eds.), *Gender, race, class, and health: Intersectional approaches* (pp. 131–162). San Francisco, CA: Jossey-Bass.

Jacobi, T., & Schweers, D. (2017). Justice, interrupted: The effect of gender, ideology and seniority at Supreme Court oral arguments. *Virginia Law Review.* Forthcoming. Northwestern Law & Econ Research Paper No. 17-03. Retrieved from https://ssrn.com/abstract=2933016

Jamal, A., Homa, D. M., O'Connor, E., Babb, S. D., Caraballo, R. S., Singh, T., . . . King, B. A. (2015). Current cigarette smoking among adults—United States, 2005–2014. *Morbidity and Mortality Weekly Report, 64,* 1233–1240.

Jameis Winston apologizes after saying girls should be 'silent and polite.' (2017, February 23). *The Guardian.* Retrieved from https://www.theguardian.com/sport/2017/feb/23/jameis-winston-girls-silent-polite-gentle

James, D., & Clarke, S. (1993). Women, men, and interruptions: A critical review. In D. Tannen (Ed.), *Gender and conversational interaction* (pp. 231–280). New York, NY: Oxford University Press.

James, D., & Drakich, J. (1993). Understanding gender differences in amount of talk: A critical review of the research. In D. Tannen (Ed.), *Gender and conversational interaction* (pp. 281–312). New York, NY: Oxford University Press.

James, W. (1884). What is an emotion? *Mind, 9*(34), 188–205.

Jankowiak, W. R., & Fischer, E. F. (1992). A cross-cultural perspective on romantic love. *Ethnology, 31,* 149–155.

Jaslow, R. (2012, February 15). Man suffers heart attack at Heart Attack Grill in Las Vegas: Report. *CBS News.* Retrieved from http://www.cbsnews.com/news/man-suffers-heart-attack-at-heart-attack-grill-in-las-vegas-report

Jay, T. (2009). The utility and ubiquity of taboo words. *Perspectives on Psychological Science, 4,* 153–161.

Jenkins, J. (2014). *Sickness absence in the labour market: February 2014.* London, UK: Office for National Statistics. Retrieved from http://www.ons.gov.uk/employmentandlabourmarket/peopleinwork/labourproductivity/articles/sicknessabsenceinthelabourmarket/2014-02-25

Ji, Y. (2015). Between tradition and modernity: "Leftover" women in Shanghai. *Journal of Marriage and Family, 77*(5), 1057–1073.

Joel, D., Berman, Z., Tavor, I., Wexler, N., Gaber, O., Stein, Y., . . . Assaf, Y. (2015). Sex beyond the genitalia: The human brain mosaic. *Proceedings of the National Academy of Sciences, 112,* 15468–15473.

Johnson, F. L. (2006). Transgressing gender in discourses across cultures. In B. J. Dow & J. T. Wood (Eds.), *The SAGE handbook of gender and communication* (pp. 415–431). Thousand Oaks, CA: Sage.

Johnson, K. J., & Tassinary, L. G. (2005). Perceiving sex directly and indirectly: Meaning in motion and morphology. *Psychological Science, 16,* 890–897.

Johnson, K. L., Gill, S., Reichman, V., & Tassinary, L. G. (2007). Swagger, sway, and sexuality: Judging sexual orientation from body motion and morphology. *Journal of Personality and Social Psychology, 93,* 321–334.

Johnson, M. P. (2008). *A typology of domestic violence: Intimate terrorism, violent resistance, and situational couple violence.* Boston, MA: Northeastern University Press.

Johnson, R. B., Onwuegbuzie, A. J., & Turner, L. A. (2007). Toward a definition of mixed methods research. *Journal of Mixed Methods Research, 1,* 112–133.

Jones, B. A., & Griffiths, K. M. (2015). Self-objectification and depression: An integrative systematic review. *Journal of Affective Disorders, 171,* 22–32.

Jones, B. A., Haycraft, E., Murjan, S., & Arcelus, J. (2016). Body dissatisfaction and disordered eating in trans people: A systematic review of the literature. *International Review of Psychiatry, 28,* 81–94.

Jones, C. M., & Healy, S. D. (2006). Differences in cue use and spatial memory in men and women. *Proceedings of the Royal Society B: Biological Sciences, 273,* 2241–2247.

Jones, D. S., Podolsky, S. H., & Greene, J. A. (2012). The burden of disease and the changing task of medicine. *New England Journal of Medicine, 366,* 2333–2338.

Jones, J. C., & Barlow, D. H. (1990). Self-reported frequency of sexual urges, fantasies, and masturbatory fantasies in heterosexual males and females. *Archives of Sexual Behavior, 19,* 269–279.

Jones, T.-V. (2016). Predictors of perceptions of mental illness and averseness to help: A survey of elite football players. *Journal of Mental Health, 25*, 422–427.

Jones, W. R. (2010). Eating disorders in men: A review of the literature. *Journal of Public Mental Health, 9*, 23–31.

Jorm, A. F., Anstey, K. J., Christensen, H., & Rodgers, B. (2004). Gender differences in cognitive abilities: The mediating role of health state and health habits. *Intelligence, 32*, 7–23.

Joseph, D. L., & Newman, D. A. (2010). Emotional intelligence: An integrative meta-analysis and cascading model. *Journal of Applied Psychology, 95*, 54–78.

Jost, A., Vigier, B., Prepin, J., & Perchellet, J. P. (1973). Studies on sex differentiation in mammals. *Recent Progress in Hormone Research, 29*, 1–41.

Jost, J. T., Chaikalis-Petritsis, V., Abrams, D., Sidanius, J., van der Toorn, J., & Bratt, C. (2012). Why men (and women) do and don't rebel: Effects of system justification on willingness to protest. *Personality and Social Psychology Bulletin, 38*, 197–208.

Jost, J. T., & Kay, A. C. (2005). Exposure to benevolent sexism and complementary gender stereotypes: Consequences for specific and diffuse forms of system justification. *Journal of Personality and Social Psychology, 88*, 498–509.

Jost, J. T., Kivetz, Y., Rubini, M., Guermandi, G., & Mosso, C. (2005). System justifying functions of complementary regional and ethnic stereotypes: Cross-national evidence. *Social Justice Research, 18*, 305–333.

Judd, L. L., Schettler, P. J., Coryell, W., Akiskal, H. S., & Fiedorowicz, J. G. (2013). Overt irritability/anger in unipolar major depressive episodes: Past and current characteristics and implications for long-term course. *JAMA Psychiatry, 70*, 1171–1180.

Judge, T. A., & Piccolo, R. F. (2004). Transformational and transactional leadership: A meta-analytic test of their relative validity. *Journal of Applied Psychology, 89*, 755–768.

Jussim, L., Crawford, J. T., Anglin, S. M., Chambers, J. R., Stevens, S. T., & Cohen, F. (2016). Stereotype accuracy: One of the largest and most replicable effects in all of social psychology. In T. D. Nelson (Ed.), *Handbook of prejudice, stereotyping, and discrimination* (2nd ed.) (pp. 31–63). New York, NY: Psychology Press.

Jussim, L., & Eccles, J. S. (1992). Teacher expectations: II. Construction and reflection of student achievement. *Journal of Personality and Social Psychology, 63*(6), 947–961.

Kahlenberg, S. G., & Hein, M. M. (2010). Progression on Nickelodeon? Gender-role stereotypes in toy commercials. *Sex Roles, 62*, 830–847.

Kahn, J. R., García-Manglano, J., & Bianchi, S. M. (2014). The motherhood penalty at midlife: Long-term effects of children on women's careers. *Journal of Marriage and Family, 76*, 56–72.

Kaighobadi, F., Shackelford, T. K., & Goetz, A. T. (2009). From mate retention to murder: Evolutionary psychological perspectives on men's partner-directed violence. *Review of General Psychology, 13*, 327–334.

Kalish, R., & Kimmel, M. (2011). Hooking up. *Australian Feminist Studies, 26*, 137–151.

Kalmijn, M., & Flap, H. (2001). Assortative meeting and mating: Unintended consequences of organized settings for partner choices. *Social Forces, 79*, 1289–1312.

Kann, L., Kinchen, S., Shanklin, S. L., Flint, K. H., Hawkins, J., Harris, W. A., . . . Zaza, S. (2014). Youth risk behavior surveillance, United States, 2013. *Morbidity and Mortality Weekly Report, 63*, 1–168. Retrieved from http://www.cdc.gov/mmwr/pdf/ss/ss6304.pdf

Kanny, D., Liu, Y., Brewer, R. D., & Lu, H. (2013). Binge drinking—United States, 2011. *Morbidity and Mortality Weekly Report, 62*, 77–80.

Kanter, R., & Caballero, B. (2012). Global gender disparities in obesity: A review. *Advances in Nutrition: An International Review Journal, 3*, 491–498.

Kaplan, D., & Rosenmann, A. (2014). Toward an empirical model of male homosocial relatedness: An investigation of friendship in uniform and beyond. *Psychology of Men & Masculinity, 15*, 12–21.

Kaplan, R. M., & Kronick, R. G. (2006). Marital status and longevity in the United States population. *Journal of Epidemiology & Community Health, 60*, 760–765.

Karraker, K. H., Vogel, D. A., & Lake, M. A. (1995). Parents' gender-stereotyped perceptions of newborns: The eye of the beholder revisited. *Sex Roles, 33*, 687–701.

Kasen, S., Chen, H., Sneed, J., Crawford, T., & Cohen, P. (2006). Social role and birth cohort influences on gender-linked personality traits in women: A 20-year longitudinal analysis. *Journal of Personality and Social Psychology, 91*, 944–958.

Katz, I., & Hass, R. G. (1988). Racial ambivalence and American value conflict: Correlational and priming studies of dual cognitive structures. *Journal of Personality and Social Psychology, 55,* 893–905.

Katz-Wise, S. L., & Hyde, J. S. (2012). Victimization experiences of lesbian, gay, and bisexual individuals: A meta-analysis. *Journal of Sex Research, 49,* 142–167.

Katz-Wise, S. L., Reisner, S. L., Hughto, J. W., & Keo-Meier, C. L. (2016). Differences in sexual orientation diversity and sexual fluidity in attractions among gender minority adults in Massachusetts. *Journal of Sex Research, 53,* 74–84.

Kaura, S. A., & Allen, C. M. (2004). Dissatisfaction with relationship power and dating violence perpetration by men and women. *Journal of Interpersonal Violence, 19,* 576–588.

Kearl, H. (2014). *Unsafe and harassed in public spaces: A national street harassment report.* Retrieved from http://www.stopstreetharassment .org/wp-content/uploads/2012/08/ National-Street-Harassment-Report-November-29-20151.pdf

Keller, C. (2001). Effect of teachers' stereotyping on students' stereotyping of mathematics as a male domain. *Journal of Social Psychology, 141*(2), 165–173.

Kelly, E. L., Moen, P., & Tranby, E. (2011). Changing workplaces to reduce work–family conflict: Schedule control in a white-collar organization. *American Sociological Review, 76,* 265–290.

Kennedy, P. (2007). *The first man-made man.* New York, NY: Bloomsbury.

Kenney-Benson, G. A., Pomerantz, E. M., Ryan, A. M., & Patrick, H. (2006). Sex differences in math performance: The role of children's approach to schoolwork. *Child Development, 42*(1), 11–26.

Kenrick, D. T., Keefe, R. C., Bryan, A., Barr, A., & Brown, S. (1995). Age preferences and mate choice among homosexuals and heterosexuals: A case for modular psychological mechanisms. *Journal of Personality and Social Psychology, 69,* 1166–1172.

Kenrick, D. T., Trost, M. R., & Sundie, J. M. (2004). Sex roles as adaptations: An evolutionary perspective on gender differences and similarities. In A. H. Eagly, A. E. Beall, & R. J. Sternberg (Eds.), *The psychology of gender* (2nd ed.) (pp. 65–91). New York, NY: Guilford Press.

Kessels, U., & Hannover, B. (2008). When being a girl matters less: Accessibility of gender- related self-knowledge in single-sex and coeducational classes and its impact on students' physics related self-concept of ability. *British Journal of Educational Psychology, 78,* 273–289.

Kessler, R. C., Aguilar-Gaxiola, S., Alonso, J., Chatterji, S., Lee, S., Ormel, J., . . . Wang, P. S. (2009). The global burden of mental disorders: An update from the WHO World Mental Health (WMH) surveys. *Epidemiologia e Psichiatria Sociale, 18,* 23–33.

Kessler-Harris, A. (2003). *Out to work: A history of wage earning women in the United States.* New York, NY: Oxford University Press.

Ketterer, S. (2015, September 30). The 'wage gap' myth that won't die. *Wall Street Journal.* Retrieved

from http://www.wsj.com/articles/ the-wage-gap-myth-that-wont-die-1443654408

Keyes, C. L. M., Shmotkin, D., & Ryff, C. D. (2002). Optimizing well-being: The empirical encounter of two traditions. *Journal of Personality and Social Psychology, 82,* 1007–1022.

Khaleeli, H. (2014, April 16). Hijra: India's third gender claims its place in law. *The Guardian.* Retrieved from https://www.theguardian.com/soci ety/2014/apr/16/india-third-gender-claims-place-in-law

Khazan, O. (2014, May 23). 'Pushy' is used to describe women twice as often as men. *The Atlantic.* Retrieved from http://www.theatlantic.com/busi ness/archive/2014/05/pushy-is-used-to-describe-women-twice-as-often-as-men/371291

Kidd, S. A. (2002). The role of qualitative research in psychological journals. *Psychological Methods, 7,* 126–138.

Killermann, S. (2013). *The social justice advocate's handbook: A guide to gender.* Austin, TX: Impetus Books.

Killewald, A. (2012). A reconsideration of the fatherhood premium: Marriage, co-residence, biology, and fathers' wages. *American Sociological Review, 78,* 96–116.

Kimball, M. M. (2001). Gender similarities and differences as feminist contradictions. In R. K. Unger (Ed.), *Handbook of the psychology of women and gender* (pp. 66–83). Hoboken, NJ: John Wiley.

Kimmel, M. S. (2006). *Manhood in America: A cultural history* (2nd ed.). New York, NY: Oxford University Press.

Kimmel, M. S., & Messner, M. (1989). *Men's lives*. New York, NY: Macmillan.

King, M., & Ussher, J. M. (2012). It's not all bad: Women's construction and lived experience of positive premenstrual change. *Feminism & Psychology, 23*, 399–417.

Kinsey, A. C., Pomeroy, W. B., & Martin, C. B. (1948). *Sexual behavior in the human male*. Philadelphia, PA: W. B. Saunders.

Kinsey, A., Pomeroy, W., Martin, C., & Gebhard, P. (1953). *Sexual behavior in the human female*. Philadelphia, PA: W. B. Saunders.

Kirkpatrick, R. C. (2000). The evolution of human homosexual behavior. *Current Anthropology, 41*, 385–413.

Kirkwood, T. (2010). Why women live longer. *Scientific American, 303*, 34–35.

Kite, M. E., & Deaux, K. (1987). Gender belief systems: Homosexuality and the implicit inversion theory. *Psychology of Women Quarterly, 11*, 83–96.

Kite, M. E., Deaux, K., & Haines, E. L. (2008). Gender stereotypes. In F. L. Denmark & M. A. Paludi (Eds.), *Psychology of women: A handbook of issues and theories* (2nd ed., pp. 205–236). Westport, CT: Greenwood Press.

Kite, M. E., Stockdale, G. D., Whitley, B. J., & Johnson, B. T. (2005). Attitudes toward younger and older adults: An updated meta-analytic review. *Journal of Social Issues, 61*, 241–266.

Kitzinger, C. (Ed.). (1994). Should psychologists study sex differences? *Feminism & Psychology, 4*, 501–546.

Klaassen, M. J. E., & Peter, J. (2015). Gender (in)equality in internet pornography: A content analysis of popular pornographic Internet videos. *Journal of Sex Research, 52*, 721–735.

Klawitter, M. (2014). Meta-analysis of the effects of sexual orientation on earnings. *Industrial Relations, 54*, 4–32.

Klebs, T. A. E. (1876). *Handbook of pathological anatomy*. Berlin, Germany: A. Hirschwald.

Klein, A., & Golub, S. A. (2016). Family rejection as a predictor of suicide attempts and substance misuse among transgender and gender nonconforming adults. *LGBT Health, 3*, 193–199.

Klein, C., & Gorzalka, B. B. (2009). Continuing medical education: Sexual functioning in transsexuals following hormone therapy and genital surgery: A review. *Journal of Sexual Medicine, 6*(11), 2922–2939.

Klein, M. C., Sakala, C., Simkin, P., Davis-Floyd, R., Rooks, J. P., & Pincus, J. (2006). Roundtable discussion: Part 2. Why do women go along with this stuff? *Birth, 33*, 245–250.

Klesse, C. (2006). Polyamory and its "others": Contesting the terms of non-monogamy. *Sexualities, 9*, 565–583.

Klinesmith, J., Kasser, T., & McAndrew, F. (2006). Guns, testosterone, and aggression: An experimental test of a mediational hypothesis. *Psychological Science, 17*, 568–571.

Knapton, S. (2015, September 20). The astonishing village where little girls turn into boys at aged 12. *The Telegraph*. Retrieved from http://www.telegraph.co.uk/science/2016/03/12/the-astonishing-village-where-little-girls-turn-into-boys-aged-1

Kneidinger, L. M., Maple, T. L., & Tross, S. A., (2001). Touching behavior in sport: Functional components, analysis of sex differences, and ethological considerations. *Journal of Nonverbal Behavior, 25*, 43–62.

Knight, G. P., Fabes, R. A., & Higgins, D. A. (1996). Concerns about drawing causal inferences from meta-analyses: An example in the study of gender differences in aggression. *Psychological Bulletin, 119*(3), 410–421.

Knight, G. P., Guthrie, I. K., Page, M. C., & Fabes, R. A. (2002). Emotional arousal and gender differences in aggression: A meta-analysis. *Aggressive Behavior, 28*, 366–393.

Know your rights: Transgender people and the law. (2016). Retrieved from http://www.aclu.org/know-your-rights/transgender-people-and-law

Kochanek, K. D., Arias, E., & Anderson, R. N. (2015). Leading causes of death contributing to decrease in life expectancy gap between Black and White populations: United States 1999–2013. NCHS Data Brief: No. 218. Hyattsville, MD: National Center for Health Statistics. Retrieved from http://www.cdc.gov/nchs/data/databriefs/db218.pdf

Kochanska, G., & Kim, S. (2012). Early attachment organization with both parents and future behavior problems: From infancy to middle childhood. *Child Development, 84*, 283–296.

Koenig, A. M., & Eagly, A. H. (2014). Evidence for the social role theory of stereotype content: Observations of groups' roles shape stereotypes. *Journal of Personality and Social Psychology, 107*, 371.

Koenig, A. M., Eagly, A. H., Mitchell, A. A., & Ristikari, T. (2011). Are leader stereotypes masculine? A meta-analysis of three research paradigms. *Psychological Bulletin, 137*, 616–642.

Kohlberg, L. A. (1966). A cognitive-developmental analysis of children's sex role concepts and attitudes. In E. E. Maccoby (Ed.), *The development of sex differences* (pp. 82–173). Stanford, CA: Stanford University Press.

Kolb, D. M., & Porter, J. L. (2015, April 16). "Office housework" gets in women's way. *Harvard Business Review.* Retrieved from https://hbr .org/2015/04/office-housework-gets-in-womens-way

Koopman, C., Vaartjes, I., Heintjes, E. M., Spiering, W., van Dis, I., Herings, R. M. C., & Bots, M. L. (2013). Persisting gender differences and attenuating age differences in cardiovascular drug use for prevention and treatment of coronary heart disease, 1998–2010. *European Heart Journal, 34*, 3198–3205.

Koppel, M., Argamon, S., & Shimoni, A. R. (2002). Automatically categorizing written texts by author gender. *Literary & Linguistic Computing, 17*, 401–412.

Koratayev, A. (2003). Division of labor by gender and postmarital residence in cross-cultural perspective: A reconsideration. *Cross-Cultural Research, 37*, 335–372.

Koropeckyj-Cox, T., Romano, V., & Moras, A. (2007). Through the lenses of gender, race, and class: Students' perceptions of childless/childfree individuals and couples. *Sex Roles, 56*(7–8), 415–428.

Kosciw, J. G., Diaz, E. M., & Greytak, E. A. (2008). *National School Climate Survey 2007: The experiences of lesbian, gay, bisexual and transgender youth in our nation's schools.* New York, NY: GLSEN.

Koss, M. P., & Kilpatrick, D. G. (2001). Rape and sexual assault (pp. 177–187). In E. Gerrity, T. M. Keane, & F. Tuma (Eds.), *The mental health consequences of torture.* New York, NY: Springer.

Kotrla, K. (2010). Domestic minor sex trafficking in the United States. *Social Work, 55*, 181–187.

Kovacs, D. M., Parker, J. G., & Hoffman, L. W. (1996). Behavioral, affective, and social correlates of involvement in cross-sex friendship in elementary school. *Child Development, 67*(5), 2269–2286.

Kovess-Masfety, V., Boyd, A., van de Velde, S., de Graaf, R., Vilagut, G., Haro, J. M., . . . Alonso, J. (2014). Are there gender differences in service use for mental disorders across countries in the European Union? Results from the EU-World Mental Health survey. *Journal of Epidemiology and Community Health, 68*, 649–656.

Krafft-Ebing, R. (1965). *Psychopathia sexualis* (H. Wedeck, Trans.). New York, NY: Putnam. (Original work published 1886)

Krafft-Ebing, R. (1998). *Psychopathia sexualis.* New York, NY: Arcade. (Original work published 1886)

Kramer, M. D., Krueger, R. F., & Hicks, B. M. (2008). The role of internalizing and externalizing liability factors in accounting for gender differences in the prevalence of common psychopathological syndromes. *Psychological Medicine, 38*, 51–61.

Kramer, M. S., Chalmers B., Hodnett, E. D., Sevkovskaya, Z., Dzikovich, I., Shapiro, S., . . . Helsing, E. (2001). Promotion of Breastfeeding Intervention Trial (PROBIT): A randomized trial in the Republic of Belarus. *Journal of the American Medical Association, 285*, 413–420.

Kraus, M. W., Huang, C., & Keltner, D. (2010). Tactile communication, cooperation, and performance: An ethological study of the NBA. *Emotion, 10*, 745–749

Krebs, C. P., Lindquist, C. H., Warner, T. D., Fisher, B. S., & Martin, S. L. (2007). *The campus sexual assault (CSA) survey.* Washington, DC: National Institutes of Justice. Retrieved from https://www.ncjrs. gov/pdffiles1/nij/grants/221153.pdf

Kring, A. M., & Gordon, A. H. (1998). Sex differences in emotion: Expression, experience, and physiology. *Journal of Personality and Social Psychology, 74*, 686–703.

Krueger, R. F. (1999). Personality traits in late adolescence predict mental disorders in early adulthood: A prospective–epidemiological study. *Journal of Personality, 67*, 39–65.

Krueger, R. F., & Eaton, N. R. (2015). Transdiagnostic factors of mental disorders. *World Psychiatry, 14*, 27–29.

Kruger, D. J., Fisher, M. L., & Wright, P. (2013). A framework for integrating evolutionary and feminist perspectives in psychological research. *Journal of Social, Evolutionary, and Cultural Psychology, 7*(4), 299–303.

Kruger, D. J., & Nesse, R. M. (2006). An evolutionary life-history framework for understanding sex differences in human mortality rates. *Human Nature, 17*, 74–97.

Krysinska, K., Batterham, P. J., & Christensen, H. (2017). Differences in the effectiveness of psychosocial interventions for suicidal ideation and behaviour in women and men: A systematic review of randomised controlled trials. *Archives of Suicide Research, 21*(1), 12–32.

Kuchynka, S. L., Salomon, K., Bosson, J. K., El-Hout, M., Kiebel, E., Cooperman, C., & Toomey, R. (2017). Hostile and benevolent sexism and college women's STEM outcomes. *Psychology of Women Quarterly.*

Kulik, L. (2011). Developments in spousal power relations: Are we moving toward equality? *Marriage & Family Review, 47,* 419–435.

Kuntzman, G. (2004, February 23). An unusual love story. *Newsweek.* Retrieved from http://gersh kuntzman.homestead.com/files/Gay_Penguins.htm

Kurdek, L. A. (2004). Are gay and lesbian cohabiting couples *really* different from heterosexual married couples? *Journal of Marriage and Family, 66,* 880–900.

Kurdek, L. A. (2006). Differences between partners from heterosexual, gay, and lesbian cohabiting couples. *Journal of Marriage and Family, 68,* 509–528.

Kutchinsky, B. (1970). *Studies on pornography and sex crimes in Denmark.* Copenhagen, Denmark: New Social Science Monographs.

Kutchinsky, B. (1991). Pornography and rape: Theory and practice? Evidence from crime data in four countries where pornography is easily available. *International Journal of Law and Psychiatry, 14,* 47–64.

Kutlu, H. A., & Akbiyik, F. (2011). Clitoral length in female newborns: A new approach to the assessment of clitoromegaly. *Turkish Journal of Medical Sciences, 41*(3), 495–499.

Lachance-Grzela, M., & Bouchard, G. (2010). Why do women do the lion's share of housework? A decade of research. *Sex Roles, 63,* 767–780.

LaFrance, M., & Banaji, M. (1992). Toward a reconsideration of the gender–emotion relationship. In M. S. Clark (Ed.), *Emotion and social behavior* (pp. 178–201). Newbury Park, CA: Sage.

LaFrance, M., Hecht, M. A., & Paluck, E. L. (2003). The contingent smile: A meta-analysis of sex differences in smiling. *Psychological Bulletin, 129,* 305–334.

LaFrance, M., & Vial, A. C. (2016). Gender and nonverbal behavior. In D. Matsumoto, H. C. Hwang, & M. G. Frank, (Eds.), *APA handbook of nonverbal communication* (pp. 139–161). Washington, DC: American Psychological Association.

Lamb, M. E. (1987). Introduction: The emergent American father. In M. E. Lamb (Ed.), *The father's role: Cross-cultural perspectives* (pp. 3–26). Hillsdale, NJ: Lawrence Erlbaum.

Lamb, M. E. (1997). The development of father–infant relationships. In M. E. Lamb (Ed.), *The role of the father in child development* (3rd ed., pp. 104–120). Hoboken, NJ: John Wiley.

Lamm, C., Decety, J., & Singer, T. (2011). Meta-analytic evidence for common and distinct neural networks associated with directly experienced pain and empathy for pain. *Neuroimage, 54,* 2492–2502.

Landivar, K. (2013). *Disparities in STEM employment by sex, race, and Hispanic origin.* American Community Surveys Report. Washington, DC: U.S. Census Bureau. Retrieved from https://www.census.gov/prod/2013pubs/acs-24.pdf

Landrine, H. (1985). Race × class stereotypes of women. *Sex Roles, 13,* 65–75.

Lang, C., & Kuhnle, U. (2008). Intersexuality and alternative gender categories in non-Western cultures. *Hormone Research, 69,* 240–250.

Langhinrichsen-Rohling, J. (2010). Controversies involving gender and intimate partner violence in the United States. *Sex Roles, 62,* 179–193.

Langhinrichsen-Rohling, J., McCullars, A., & Misra, T. A. (2012). Motivations for men and women's intimate partner violence perpetration: A comprehensive review. *Partner Abuse, 3,* 429–468.

Langlois, J. H., & Downs, A. C. (1980). Mothers, fathers, and peers as socialization agents of sex-typed play behaviors in young children. *Child Development, 51*(4), 1237–1247.

Lansford, J. E., Skinner, A. T., Sorbring, E., Di Glunta, L., Deater-Deckard, K., Dodge, K. A., . . . Chang, L. (2012). Boys' and girls' relational and physical aggression in nine countries. *Aggressive Behavior, 38,* 298–308.

LaResche, L. (1999). Gender considerations in the epidemiology of chronic pain. In I. K. Crombie, P. R. Croft, S. T. Linton, L. LaResche, & M. Von Korff (Eds.), *Epidemiology of pain* (pp. 43–52). Seattle, WA: IASP Press.

Larsen, K. S., & Long, E. (1988). Attitudes toward sex roles: Traditional or egalitarian? *Sex Roles, 19,* l–12.

Larson, R., & Pleck, J. (1999). Hidden feelings: Emotionality in boys and men. In R. A. Dienstbier & D. Bernstein (Eds.), Nebraska symposium on motivation: Gender and motivation (Vol. 45, pp. 25-74). Lincoln, NE: University of Nebraska Press.

Larson, R. W., & Richards, M. H. (1994). Family emotions: Do young adolescents and their parents experience the same states? *Journal of Research on Adolescence, 4*(4), 567–583.

Larson, R. W., & Verma, S. (1999). How children and adolescents spend time across the world: Work, play, and developmental opportunities. *Psychological Bulletin, 125,* 701–736.

LaSala, M. C. (2005). Extradyadic sex and gay male couples: Comparing monogamous and nonmonogamous relationships. *Families in Society, 85,* 405–412.

Laska, M. N., VanKim, N. A., Erickson, D. J., Lust, K., Eisenberg, M. E., & Rosser, B. R. S. (2015). Disparities in weight and weight behaviors by sexual orientation in college students. *American Journal of Public Health, 105,* 111–121.

Lau, C. Q. (2012). The stability of same-sex cohabitation, different-sex cohabitation, and marriage. *Journal of Marriage and Family, 74,* 973–988.

Laughlin, K. A., Gallagher, J., Cobble, D. S., Boris, E., Nadasen, P., Gilmore, S., & Zarnow, L. (2010). Is it time to jump ship? Historians rethink the waves metaphor. *Feminist Formations, 22*(1), 76–135.

Laumann, E. O., Gagnon, J. H., Michael, R. T., & Michaels, S. (1994). *The social organization of sexuality: Sexual practices in the United States.* Chicago, IL: University of Chicago Press.

Lauritsen, J. L., & Heimer, K. (2009, December). *Gender and violent victimization, 1973–2005* (Document No.: 229133). Retrieved from https://www.ncjrs.gov/pdffiles1/nij/grants/229133.pdf

Law, D. J., Pellegrino, J. W., & Hunt, E. B. (1993). Comparing the tortoise and the hare: Gender differences and experience in dynamic spatial reasoning tasks. *Psychological Science, 4*(1), 35–40.

Lawson, J. F., James, C., Jannson, A.-U. C., Koyama, N. F., & Hill, R. A. (2014). A comparison of heterosexual and homosexual mating preferences in personal advertisements. *Evolution and Human Behavior, 35,* 408–414.

Leaper, C., Anderson, K. J., & Sanders, P. (1998). Moderators of gender effects on parents' talk to their children: A meta-analysis. *Developmental Psychology, 34,* 3–27.

Leaper, C., & Ayres, M. M. (2007). A meta-analytic review of gender variations in adults' language use: Talkativeness, affiliative speech, and assertive speech. *Personality and Social Psychology Review, 11,* 328–363.

Leaper, C., & Holliday, H. (1995). Gossip in same-gender and cross-gender friends' conversations. *Personal Relationships, 2,* 237–246.

Leaper, C., & Robnett, R. D. (2011). Women are more likely than men to use tentative language, aren't they? A meta-analysis testing for gender differences and moderators. *Psychology of Women Quarterly, 35*(1), 129–142.

Leaper, C., & Smith, T. E. (2004). A meta-analytic review of gender variations in children's language use: Talkativeness, affiliative speech, and assertive speech. *Developmental Psychology, 40,* 993–1027.

Lee, G. R., DeMaris, A., Bavis, S., & Sullivan, R. (2001). Gender differences in the depressive effect of widowhood in later life. *Journal of Gerontology B, 56,* 56–61.

Leman, P. J., Ahmed, S., & Ozarow, L. (2005). Gender, gender relations, and the social dynamics of children's conversations. *Developmental Psychology, 41*(1), 64–74.

Lemaster, P., Delaney, R., & Strough, J. (2017). Crossover, degendering, or . . . ? A multidimensional approach to life-span gender development. *Sex Roles, 76*(11–12), 669–681.

Lennon, M. C., & Rosenfield, S. (1994). Relative fairness and the division of housework: The importance of options. *American Journal of Sociology, 100,* 506–531.

Lev, A. I. (2013). Gender dysphoria: Two steps forward, one step back. *Clinical Social Work Journal, 41,* 288–296.

Levanon, A., England, P., & Allison, P. (2009). Occupational feminization and pay: Assessing causal dynamics using 1950–2000 Census data. *Social Forces, 88,* 865–891.

Leve, L. D., & Fagot, B. I. (1997). Gender-role socialization and discipline processes in one- and two-parent families. *Sex Roles, 36,* 1–21.

Leviatan, U., & Cohen, J. (1985). Gender differences in life expectancy among Kibbutz members. *Social Science & Medicine, 21,* 545–551.

Lewinsohn, P. M., Rohde, P., Seeley, J. R., & Baldwin, C. L. (2001). Gender differences in suicide attempts from adolescence to young adulthood.

Journal of the American Academy of Child & Adolescent Psychiatry, 40, 427–434.

Li, G., Kung, K. F., & Hines, M. (2017). Childhood gender-typed behavior and adolescent sexual orientation: A longitudinal population-based study. *Developmental Psychology, 53*(4), 764–777.

Li, N. P., & Kenrick, D. T. (2006). Sex similarities and differences in preferences for short-term mates: What, whether, and why. *Journal of Personality and Social Psychology, 90*, 468–489.

Li, N. P., Valentine, K. A., & Patel, L. (2011). Mate preferences in the U.S. and Singapore: A cross-cultural test of the mate preference priority model. *Personality and Individual Differences, 50*, 291–294.

Li, Z. H., Connolly, J., Jiang, D., Pepler, D., & Craig, W. (2010). Adolescent romantic relationships in China and Canada: A cross-national comparison. *International Journal of Behavioral Development, 32*, 113–120.

Liew, J. (2009, December 2). All men watch porn, scientists find. *The Telegraph*. Retrieved from http://www.telegraph.co.uk/women/sex/6709646/All-men-watch-porn-scientists-find.html

Lightdale, J. R., & Prentice, D. A. (1994). Rethinking sex differences in aggression: Aggressive behavior in the absence of social roles. *Personality and Social Psychology Bulletin, 20*, 34–44.

Lilienfeld, S. O. (2017). Microaggressions: Strong claims, inadequate evidence. *Perspectives on Psychological Science, 12*, 138–169.

Lindberg, S. M., Hyde, J. S., Petersen, J. L., & Linn, M. C. (2010). New trends in gender and mathematics performance: A meta-analysis. *Psychological Bulletin, 136*, 1123–1135.

Lindner, D., & Tantleff-Dunn, S. (2017). The development and psychometric evaluation of the self-objectification beliefs and behaviors scale. *Psychology of Women Quarterly*. Retrieved from http://journals.sagepub.com/doi/pdf/10.1177/0361684317692109

Lindsey, E. W. (2016). Same-gender peer interaction and preschoolers' gender-typed emotional expressiveness. *Sex Roles, 75*(5–6), 231–242.

Linn, M. C., & Petersen, A. C. (1985). Emergence and characterization of sex differences in spatial ability: A meta-analysis. *Child Development, 56*, 1479–1498.

Lipman, J. (2015, August 13). Let's expose the gender pay gap. *New York Times*. Retrieved from https://www.nytimes.com/2015/08/13/opinion/lets-expose-the-gender-pay-gap.html

Lippa, R. A. (1991). Some psychometric characteristics of gender diagnosticity measures: Reliability, validity, consistency across domains, and relationship to the Big Five. *Journal of Personality and Social Psychology, 61*, 1000–1011.

Lippa, R. A. (2001). On deconstructing and re-constructing masculinity-femininity. *Journal of Research in Personality, 35*, 168–207

Lippa, R. A. (2005a). *Gender, nature, and nurture*. Mahwah, NJ: Lawrence Erlbaum.

Lippa, R. A. (2005b). Subdomains of gender-related occupational interests: Do they form a cohesive bipolar M-F dimension? *Journal of Personality, 73*, 693–729.

Lippa, R. A. (2006). Is high sex drive associated with increased sexual attraction to both sexes? It depends on whether you are male or female. *Psychological Science, 17*, 46–52.

Lippa, R. A. (2007). The preferred traits of mates in a cross-national study of heterosexual and homosexual men and women: An examination of biological and cultural influences. *Archives of Sexual Behavior, 36*, 193–208.

Lippa, R. A. (2009). Sex differences in sex drive, sociosexuality, and height across 53 nations: Testing evolutionary and social structural theories. *Archives of Sexual Behavior, 38*, 631–651.

Lippa, R. A., Collaer, M. L., & Peters, M. (2010). Sex differences in mental rotation and line angle judgments are positively associated with gender equality and economic development across 53 nations. *Archives of Sexual Behavior, 39*, 990–997.

Lippa, R. A., Martin, L. R., & Friedman, H. S. (2000). Gender-related individual differences and mortality in the Terman longitudinal study: Is masculinity hazardous to your health? *Personality and Social Psychology Bulletin, 26*, 1560–1570.

Lippa, R. A., Preston, K., & Penner, J. (2014). Women's representation in 60 occupations from 1972 to 2010: More women in high-status jobs, few women in things-oriented jobs. *PLOS One, 9*, e95960.

Liss, M., Crawford, M., & Popp, D. (2004). Predictors and correlates of collective action. *Sex Roles, 50*(11/12), 771–779.

Liss, M., Schiffrin, H. H., Mackintosh, V. H., Miles-McLean, H., & Erchull, M. J. (2013). Development and validation of a quantitative measure of intensive parenting attitudes. *Journal of Child and Family Studies, 22*, 621–636.

Littleton, H. L., Rhatigan, D. L., & Axsom, D. (2007). Unacknowledged rape: How much do we know about the hidden rape victim? *Journal of Aggression, Maltreatment & Trauma, 14*, 57–74.

Liu, F. (2017). Chinese young men's construction of exemplary masculinity: The hegemony of chenggong. *Men and Masculinities*, 1–23.

Livingston, R. W., & Pearce, N. A. (2009). The teddy-bear effect: Does having a baby face benefit Black chief executive officers? *Psychological Science, 20*, 1229–1236.

Livingston, R. W., Rosette, A. S., & Washington, E. F. (2012). Can an agentic Black woman get ahead? The impact of race and interpersonal dominance on perceptions of female leaders. *Psychological Science, 23*, 354–358.

Löckenhoff, C. E., Chan, W., McCrae, R. R., De Fruyt, F., Jussim, L., De Bolle, M., . . . Terracciano, A. (2014). Gender stereotypes of personality: Universal and accurate? *Journal of Cross-Cultural Psychology, 45*, 675–694.

Lockshin, M. D. (2005). Sex differences in autoimmune disease. *Handbook of Systemic Autoimmune Diseases, 4*, 3–10.

Lombardo, M. V., Ashwin, E., Auyeung, B., Chakrabarti, B., Taylor, K., Hackett, G., . . . Baron-Cohen, S. (2012). Fetal testosterone influences sexually dimorphic gray matter in the human brain. *Journal of Neuroscience, 32*, 674–680.

Longman, J. (2016, August 18). Understanding the controversy over Caster Semenya. *New York Times.* Retrieved from http://www.nytimes.com/2016/08/20/sports/caster-semenya-800-meters.html

Lorber, J. (1994). *Paradoxes of gender.* New Haven, CT: Yale University Press.

Lorde, A. (1984). *Sister outsider: Essay and speeches.* Trumansburg, NY: Crossing Press.

Loughnan, S., Fernandez-Campos, S., Vaes, J., Anjum, G., Aziz, M., Harada, C., . . . Tsuchiya, K. (2015). Exploring the role of culture in sexual objectification: A seven nations study. *Revue internationale de psychologie sociale, 28*, 125–152.

Lu, L. (2005). Sex differences and conjugal interdependence on parenthood stress and adjustment: A dyadic longitudinal Chinese study. *Marriage & Family Review, 36*, 75–93.

Lucas, R. E. (2005). Time does not heal all wounds: A longitudinal study of reaction and adaptation to divorce. *Psychological Science, 16*(12), 945–950.

Lucas, R. E., & Gohm, C. L. (2000). Age and sex differences in subjective well-being across cultures. In E. Diener & E. M. Suh (Eds.), *Subjective well-being across cultures.* Cambridge, MA: MIT Press.

Lucas-Thompson, R. G., Goldberg, W. A., & Prasue, J. (2010). Maternal work early in the lives of children and its distal associations with achievement and behavior problems: A meta-analysis. *Psychological Bulletin, 136*, 915–942.

Lumley, J. & Astbury, J. (1982). Advice in pregnancy: Perfect remedies, imperfect science. In M Enkin & I. Chalmers (Eds.), *Effectiveness and satisfaction in antenatal care* (Vol. 81). New York, NY: Cambridge University Press.

Lun, V. M.-C., & Bond, M. H. (2016). Achieving subjective well-being around the world: The moderating influence of gender, age, and national goals for socializing children. *Journal of Happiness Studies, 17*, 587–608.

Luna-Firebaugh, E. M. (2006). Violence against American Indian women and the Services-Training-Officers-Prosecutors Violence Against Indian Women (STOP VAIW) program. *Violence Against Women, 12*, 125–136.

Luthar, H. K., & Luthar, V. K. (2008). Likelihood to sexually harass: A comparison among American, Indian, and Chinese students. *International Journal of Cross Cultural Management, 8*, 59–77.

Luy, M. (2003). Causes of male excess mortality: Insights from cloistered populations. *Population and Development Review, 29*, 647–676.

Lytton, H., & Romney, D. M. (1991). Parents' differential socialization of boys and girls: A meta-analysis. *Psychological Bulletin, 109*, 267–296.

Lyubomirsky, S. (2008). *The how of happiness: A scientific approach to getting the life you want.* New York, NY: Penguin.

Maass, A., Cadinu, M., & Galdi, S. (2013). Sexual harassment: Motivations and consequences. In M. K. Ryan & N. R. Branscombe (Eds.), *The SAGE handbook of gender and psychology* (pp. 341–358). Thousand Oaks, CA: Sage.

Maass, A., Cadinu, M., Guarnieri, G., & Grasselli, A. (2003). Sexual harassment under social identity threat: The computer harassment paradigm. *Journal of Personality and Social Psychology, 85*, 853–870.

Macarow, A. (2015, February 9). These eleven countries are way ahead of the U.S. on trans issues. Retrieved from http://www.attn.com/stories/868/transgender-passport-status

Maccoby, E. E., & Jacklin, C. N. (1974). *The psychology of sex differences* (Vol. 1). Stanford, CA: Stanford University Press.

MacGeorge, E. L., Graves, A. R., Feng, B., Gillihan, S. J., & Burleson, B. R. (2004). The myth of gender cultures: Similarities outweigh differences in men's and women's provision of and responses to supportive communication. *Sex Roles, 50*, 143–175.

Machin, S., & Pekkarinen, T. (2008). Global sex differences in test score variability. *Science, 322*, 1331–1332.

Machizawa, S., & Hayashi, K. (2012). Birthing across cultures: Toward the humanization of childbirth. In J. Chrisler (Ed.), *Reproductive justice: A global concern* (pp. 231–248). Santa Barbara, CA: ABC-CLIO.

Mackenzie, C. S., Reynolds, K., Cairney, J., Streiner, D. L., & Sareen, J. (2012). Disorder- specific mental health service use for mood and anxiety disorders: Associations with age, sex, and psychiatric comorbidity. *Depression and Anxiety, 29*, 234–242.

MacNell, L., Driscoll, A., & Hunt, A. N. (2015). What's in a name: Exposing gender bias in student ratings of teaching. *Innovative Higher Education, 40*, 291–303.

MacPhee, D., Fritz, J., & Miller-Heyl, J. (1996). Ethnic variations in personal social networks and parenting. *Child Development, 67*(6), 3278–3295.

Macur, J., & Schweber, N. (2012, December 16). Rape case unfolds on web and splits city. *New York Times*. Retrieved from http://www.nytimes.com/2012/12/17/sports/high-school-football-rape-case-unfolds-online-and-divides-steubenville-ohio.html?pagewanted=all&_r=1&

Madan, A. K., Cooper, L., Gratzer, A., & Beech, D. J. (2006). Ageism in breast cancer surgical options by medical students. *Tennessee Medicine, 99*, 37–38.

Madon, S. (1997). What do people believe about gay males? A study of stereotype content and strength. *Sex Roles, 37*, 663–685.

Magnuson, M. J., & Dundes, L. (2008). Gender differences in "social portraits" reflected in MySpace profiles. *Cyberpsychology & Behavior, 11*(2), 239–241.

Major, B. (2012). Gender patterns in touching behavior. In C. Mayo & N. M. Henley (Eds.), *Gender and nonverbal behavior* (pp. 15–38). New York, NY: Springer-Verlag.

Malacrida, C., & Boulton, T. (2014). The best laid plans? Women's choices, expectations, and experiences in childbirth. *Health, 18*, 41–59.

Malamuth, N. M. (1984). Aggression against women: Cultural and individual causes. In N. M. Malamuth & E. Donnerstein (Eds.), *Pornography and sexual aggression* (pp. 19–52). New York, NY: Academic Press.

Malamuth, N. M., Addison, T., & Koss, M. (2000). Pornography and sexual aggression: Are there reliable effects and can we understand them? *Annual Review of Sex Research, 11*, 26–91.

Malamuth, N. M., Hald, G. M., & Koss, M. (2012). Pornography, individual differences in risk and men's acceptance of violence against women. *Sex Roles, 66*, 427–439.

Malamuth, N. M., Linz, D., Heavey, C. L., Barnes, G., & Acker, M. (1995). Using the confluence model of sexual aggression to predict men's conflict with women: A 10-year follow-up study. *Journal of Personality and Social Psychology, 69*, 353–369.

Mallett, R. K., Ford, T. E., & Woodzicka, J. A. (2016). What did he mean by that? Humor decreases attributions of sexism and confrontation of sexist jokes. *Sex Roles, 75*, 272–284.

Mallett, R. K., & Wagner, D. E. (2011). The unexpectedly positive consequences of confronting sexism. *Journal of Experimental Social Psychology, 47*, 215–220.

Malmusi, D., Artazcoz, L., Benach, J., & Borrell, C. (2012). Perception or real illness? How chronic conditions contribute to gender inequalities in self-rated health. *European Journal of Public Health, 22*, 781–786.

Malone, C. N. (2000). Near confinement: Pregnant women in the nineteenth-century British novel. *Dickens Studies Annual, 29*, 367–385.

Maloney, E. A., Ramirez, G., Gunderson, E. A., Levine, S. C., & Beilock, S. L. (2015). Intergenerational effects of parents' math anxiety on children's math achievement and anxiety. *Psychological Science, 26*(9), 1480–1488.

Maltz, D. N., & Borker, R. A. (1982). A cultural approach to male–female miscommunication. In J. J. Gumperz (Ed.), *Language and social identity* (pp. 196–216). Cambridge, UK: Cambridge University Press.

Mandel, H. (2013). Up the down staircase: Women's upward mobility and the wage penalty for occupational feminization, 1970–2007. *Social Forces, 91*, 1183–1207.

Maragh-Bass, A. C., Torain, M., Adler, R., Ranjit, A., Schneider, E., Shields R. Y., . . . Haider, A. H. (2017). Is it okay to ask: Transgender patient perspectives on sexual orientation and gender identity collection in healthcare. *Academic Emergency Medicine, 24*, 655–667.

Marecek, J., Crawford, M., & Popp, D. (2004). On the construction of gender, sex, and sexualities. In A. H. Eagly, A. E. Beall, & R. J. Sternberg (Eds.), *The psychology of gender* (2nd ed., pp. 192–216). New York, NY: Guilford.

Margolis, H. S. (2016, June 28). *To live really long, be female and Japanese.* Retrieved from http://www.margolis.com/our-blog/to-live-really-long-be-female-and-japanese

Marlowe, F. (2000). Paternal investment and the human mating system. *Behavioral Processes, 51*, 45–61.

Marshall, J. (2014). Mirror neurons. *Proceedings of the National Academy of Science, 111*, 6531.

Martel, M. M. (2013). Sexual selection and sex differences in the prevalence of childhood externalizing and adolescent internalizing disorders. *Psychological Bulletin, 139*, 1221–1259.

Martin, C. L., Eisenbud, L., & Rose, H. A. (1995). Children's gender-based reasoning about toys. *Child Development, 66*, 1453–1471.

Martin, C. L., & Ruble, D. (2004). Children's search for gender cues: Cognitive perspectives on gender development. *Current Directions in Psychological Science, 13*, 67–70.

Martin, C. L., Ruble, D. N., & Szkrybalo, J. (2002). Cognitive theories of early gender development. *Psychological Bulletin, 128*(6), 903–933.

Martin, L. A., Neighbors, H. W., & Griffith, D. M. (2013). The experience of symptoms of depression in men vs women: Analysis of the National Comorbidity Survey Replication. *JAMA Psychiatry, 70*, 1100–1106.

Martin-Storey, A., Cheadle, J. E., Skalamera, J., & Crosnoe, R. (2015). Exploring the social integration of sexual minority youth across high school contexts. *Child Development, 86*, 965–975.

Martins, Y., Tiggemann, M., & Kirkebride, A. (2007). Those Speedos become them: The role of self-objectification in gay and heterosexual men's body image. *Personality and Social Psychology Bulletin, 33*, 634–647.

Martinez, G., Daniels, K., & Chandra, A. (2012). Fertility of men and women aged 15–44 years in the United States: National Survey of Family Growth, 2006–2010. *National Health Statistics Reports, 51*, 1–29.

Mason, T. B., Lewis, R. J., Gargurevich, M., & Kelley, M. L. (2016). Minority stress and intimate partner violence perpetration among lesbians: Negative affect, hazardous drinking, and intrusiveness as mediators. *Psychology of Sexual Orientation and Gender Diversity, 3*, 236–246.

Mast, M. S., & Sczesny, S. (2010). Gender, power, and nonverbal behavior. In J. C. Chrisler & D. R. McCreary (Eds.), *Handbook of gender research in psychology* (Vol. 1, pp. 411–425). New York, NY: Springer.

Master, A., Cheryan, S., Moscatelli, A., & Meltzoff, A. N. (2017). Programming experience promotes higher STEM motivation among first-grade girls. *Journal of Experimental Child Psychology, 160*, 92–106.

Mathews, C. E., Chen, K. Y., Freedson, P. S., Buchowski, M. S., Beech, B. M., Pate, R. R., & Troiano, R. P. (2008). Amount of time spent in sedentary behaviors in the United States, 2003–2004. *American Journal of Epidemiology, 167*, 875–881.

Mathews, T. J., & Hamilton, B. E. (2005). *Trend analysis of the sex ratio at birth in the United States.* National Vital Statistics Reports, 53, No. 20. Hyattsville, MD: National Center for Health Statistics. Retrieved from https://www.cdc.gov/nchs/data/nvsr/nvsr53/nvsr53_20.pdf

Mathews, T. J., & Hamilton, B. E. (2016). *Mean age of mothers is on the rise: United States, 2000–2014* (NCHS Data Brief, No. 232). Hyattsville, MD: National Center for Health Statistics.

Matos, K. (2015). *Modern families: Same- and different-sex couples negotiating at home.* New York, NY: Families and Work Institute. Retrieved from http://www.familiesandwork.org/downloads/modern-families.pdf

Matsick, J. L., & Conley, T. D. (2016). Cultural stereotypes and personal beliefs: Perceptions of heterosexual men, women, and people. *Psychology of Sexual Orientation and Gender Diversity, 3*, 113–128.

Matsumoto, D. (2006). Culture and nonverbal behavior. In V. Manusov & M. L. Patterson (Eds.), *The SAGE handbook of nonverbal communication* (pp. 219–235). Thousand Oaks, CA: Sage.

Matsumoto, D., Yoo, S. H., Fontaine, J., Anguas-Wong, A. M., Arriola, M., Ataca, B., . . . Gross, E. (2008). Mapping expressive differences around the world: The relationship between emotional display rules and individualism versus collectivism. *Journal of Cross-Cultural Psychology*, *39*(1), 55–74.

Matthes, J., Prieler, M., & Adam, K. (2016). Gender-role portrayals in television advertising across the globe. *Sex Roles*, *75*, 314–327.

Mazur, E., & Kozarian, L. (2010). Self-presentation and interaction in blogs of adolescents and young emerging adults. *Journal of Adolescent Research*, *25*(1), 124–144.

Mayer, J. D., Roberts, R. D., & Barsade, S. G. (2008). Human abilities: Emotional intelligence. *Annual Review of Psychology*, *59*, 507–536.

Maylor, E. A., Reimers, S., Choi, J., Collaer, M. L., Peters, M., & Silverman, I. (2007). Gender and sexual orientation differences in cognition across adulthood: Age is kinder to women than to men regardless of sexual orientation. *Archives of Sexual Behavior*, *36*(2), 235–249.

McAndrew, F. T. (2008). Can gossip be good? *Scientific American Mind*, *19*, 26–33.

McAndrew, F. T. (2014). The "sword of a woman": Gossip and female aggression. *Aggression and Violent Behavior*, *19*(3), 196–199.

McCabe, J., Fairchild, E., Grauerholz, L., Pescosolido, B. A., & Tope, D. (2011). Gender in twentieth-century children's books: Patterns of disparity in titles and central characters. *Gender & Society*, *25*, 197–226.

McCall, L. (2005). The complexity of intersectionality. *Signs: Journal of Women in Culture and Society*, *30*(3), 1771–1800.

McCarthy, A., Lee, K., Itakura, S., & Muir, D. W. (2008). Gaze display when thinking depends on culture and context. *Journal of Cross-Cultural Psychology*, *39*(6), 716–729.

McCarthy, M. M., Auger, A. P., Bale, T. L., DeVries, G. J., Dunn, G. A., Forger, N. G., . . . Wilson, M. E. (2009). The epigenetics of sex differences in the brain. *Journal of Neuroscience*, *29*(41), 12815–12823.

McClure, E. B. (2000). A meta-analytic review of sex differences in facial expression processing and their development in infants, children, and adolescents. *Psychological Bulletin*, *126*(3), 424–453.

McCrae, R. R., Martin, T. A., Hrebícková, M., Urbánek, T., Willemsen, G., & Costa, P. J. (2008). Personality trait similarity between spouses in four cultures. *Journal of Personality*, *76*, 1137–1163.

McDonnell, A., & Mehta, C. M. (2016). We could never be friends: Representing cross-sex friendship on celebrity gossip web sites. *Psychology of Popular Media Culture*, *5*, 74–84.

McFarlane, D. R., & Nikora, R. D. (2014). Women's issues and American health care policy (1960s–present). In T. R. Oliver (Ed.), *Guide to U.S. health and health care policy* (pp. 277–292). Washington, DC: CQ Press.

McGinn, K. L., Ruiz Castro, M., & Long Lingo, E. (2015). *Mums the word! Cross-national effects of maternal employment on gender inequalities at work and at home*. Harvard Business School Working Paper, No. 15-094.

McHale, S. M., Crouter, A. C., & Whiteman, S. (2003). The family contexts of gender development in childhood and adolescence. *Social Development*, *12*, 125–148.

McHale, S. M., Updegraff, K. A., Shanahan, L., Crouter, A. C., & Killoren, S. E. (2005). Siblings' differential treatment in Mexican American families. *Journal of Marriage and Family*, *67*(5), 1259–1274.

McHugh, M. C., & Frieze, I. H. (1997). The measurement of gender-role attitudes: A review and commentary. *Psychology of Women Quarterly*, *21*, 1–16.

McHugh, M. C., Koeske, R. D., & Frieze, I. H. (1986). Issues to consider in conducting nonsexist psychological research: A guide for researchers. *American Psychologist*, *41*, 879–890.

McIntosh, P. (1989, July/August). *White privilege: Unpacking the invisible knapsack*. Retrieved from http://nationalseedproject.org/white-privilege-unpacking-the-invisible-knapsack

McIntosh, P. (2012). Reflections and future directions for privilege studies. *Journal of Social Issues*, *68*, 194–206.

McKinlay, J. B. (1996). Some contributions from the social system to gender inequalities in heart disease. *Journal of Health and Social Behavior*, *37*, 1–26.

McLain, L., & Brown, S. L. (2017). The roles of fathers' involvement and coparenting in relationship quality among cohabitating and married parents. *Sex Roles*, 76, 334–345.

McLanahan, S. S., & Kelly, E. L. (2006). The feminization of poverty. In *Handbook of the sociology of gender* (pp. 127–145). New York, NY: Springer.

McNall, L. A., Nicklin, J. M., & Masuda, A. D. (2010). A meta-analytic review of the consequences associated with work–family enrichment. *Journal of Business Psychology*, 25, 381–396.

Mead, M. (1935). *Sex and temperament in three primitive societies*. New York, NY: William Morrow and Company.

Mehl, M. R., Vazire, S., Ramirez-Esparza, N., Slatcher, R. B., & Pennebaker, J. W. (2007). Are women really more talkative than men? *Science*, 317, 82.

Meier, M. H., Slutske, W. S., Heath, A. C., & Martin, N. G. (2009). The role of harsh discipline in explaining sex differences in conduct disorder: A study of opposite-sex twin pairs. *Journal of Abnormal Child Psychology*, 37, 653–664.

Melhuish, E. C., Sylva, K., Sammons, P., Siraj-Blatchford, I., Taggart, B., Phan, M., & Malin, A. (2008). Preschool influences on mathematics achievement. *Science*, 321, 1161–1162.

Mendle, J., & Ferrero, J. (2012). Detrimental psychological outcomes associated with pubertal timing in adolescent boys. *Developmental Review*, 32, 49–66.

Mendle, J., Turkheimer, E., & Emery, R. E. (2007). Detrimental psychological outcomes associated with early pubertal timing in adolescent girls. *Developmental Review*, 27, 151–171.

Menz, F., & Al-Roubaie, A. (2008). Interruptions, status and gender in medical interviews: The harder you brake, the longer it takes. *Discourse & Society*, 19(5), 645–666.

Mercer, C. H., Tanton, C., Prah, P., Erens, B., Sonnenberg, P., Clifton, S., . . . Copas, A. J. (2013). Changes in sexual attitudes and lifestyles in Britain through the life course and over time: Findings from the National Surveys of Sexual Attitudes and Lifestyles (Natsal). *The Lancet*, 382, 1781–1794.

Merten, J. (2005). Culture, gender and the recognition of basic emotions. *Psychologia*, 48, 306–316.

Mesch, D. J., Brown, M. S., Moore, Z. I., & Hayat, A. D. (2011). Gender differences in charitable giving. *International Journal of Nonprofit and Voluntary Sector Marketing*, 16, 342–355.

Meyer, I. H. (2003). Prejudice, social stress, and mental health in lesbian, gay, and bisexual populations: Conceptual issues and research evidence. *Psychological Bulletin*, 129, 674–697.

Meyer, V. (2003). Medicalized menopause, U.S. style. *Health Care for Women International*, 24, 822–830.

Meyer-Bahlburg, H. F. L. (2005). Gender identity outcome in female-raised 46, XY persons with penile agenesis, cloacal exstrophy of the bladder, or penile ablation. *Archives of Sexual Behavior*, 34, 423–438.

Michniewicz, K. S., Vandello, J. A., & Bosson, J. K. (2014). Men's (mis) perceptions of the gender threatening consequences of unemployment. *Sex Roles*, 70(3–4), 88–97.

Milestones in the American gay rights movement. (n.d.). Retrieved from http://www.pbs.org/wgbh/americanexperience/features/timeline/stonewall

Miller, C. C., & Willis, D. (2015, June 27). Maiden names, on the rise again. *New York Times*. Retrieved from http://www.nytimes.com/2015/06/28/upshot/maiden-names-on-the-rise-again.html

Miller, D. I., & Halpern, D. F. (2014). The new science of cognitive sex differences. *Trends in Cognitive Sciences*, 18, 37–45.

Miller, E. M. (2000). Homosexuality, birth order, and evolution: Toward an equilibrium reproductive economics of homosexuality. *Archives of Sexual Behavior*, 29, 1–34.

Million Women Study Collaborators. (2003). Breast cancer and hormone-replacement therapy in the Million Women Study. *The Lancet*, 362, 419–427.

Minino, A. M., Heron M. P., Murphy, S. L., & Kochanek, K. D. (2007). *Deaths: Final data for 2004*. National Vital Statistics Reports, 55, No. 19. Hyattsville, MD: National Center for Health Statistics. Retrieved from https://www.cdc.gov/nchs/data/nvsr/nvsr59/nvsr59_04.pdf

Mirgain, S. A., & Cordova, J. V. (2007). Emotion skills and marital health: The association between observed and self-reported emotion skills, intimacy, and marital satisfaction. *Journal of Social and Clinical Psychology*, 26, 983–1009.

Mischel, W. (1966). A social learning view of sex differences in behavior. In E. E. Maccoby (Ed.), *The development of sex differences* (pp. 57–81). Stanford, CA: Stanford University Press.

Mitchell, J. E., Baker, L. A., & Jacklin, C. N. (1989). Masculinity and femininity in twin children: Genetic and environmental factors. *Child Development, 60*, 1475–1485.

Miyake, A., Kost-Smith, L. E., Finkelstein, N. D., Pollock, S. J., Cohen, G. L., & Ito, T. A. (2010). Reducing the gender achievement gap in college science: A classroom study of values affirmation. *Science, 330*, 1234–1237.

Mizock, L., & Hopwood, R. (2016). Conflation and interdependence in the intersection of gender and sexuality among transgender individuals. *Psychology of Sexual Orientation and Gender Diversity, 3*, 93–103.

Moen, P., Kelly, E., & Hill, R. (2011). Does enhancing work-time control and flexibility reduce turnover? A naturally occurring experiment. *Social Problems, 58*, 69–98.

Moffitt, T. E., Caspi, A., Belsky, J., & Silva, P. A. (1992). Childhood experience and the onset of menarche: A test of a sociobiological model. *Child Development, 63*(1), 47–58.

Moghadam, V. M. (2010). Transnational feminisms. In J. Lee & S. M. Shaw (Eds.), *Women worldwide: Transnational feminist perspectives on women* (pp. 15–46). New York, NY: McGraw-Hill.

Molin, A. (2012, November 28). In Sweden, playtime goes gender neutral for the holidays. *Wall Street Journal.* Retrieved from http://www.wsj.com/articles/SB100014241278873242054045781473734222297406

Molloy, L. E., Gest, S. D., Feinberg, M. E., & Osgood, D. W. (2014). Emergence of mixed-sex friendship groups during adolescence: Developmental associations with substance use and delinquency. *Developmental Psychology, 50*, 2449–2461.

Mondschein, E. R., Adolph, K. E., & Tamis-LeMonda, C. S. (2000). Gender bias in mothers' expectations about infant crawling. *Journal of Experimental Child Psychology, 77*, 304–316.

Money, J., Hampson, J. G., & Hampson, J. (1955). An examination of some basic sexual concepts: The evidence of human hermaphroditism. *Bulletin of the Johns Hopkins Hospital, 97*(4), 301–319.

Mongeau, P. A., Knight, K., Williams, J., Eden, J., & Shaw, C. (2013). Identifying and explicating variation among friends with benefits relationships. *Journal of Sex Research, 50*, 37–47.

Monin, J. K., & Clark, M. S. (2011). Why do men *benefit* more from marriage than do women? Thinking more broadly about interpersonal processes that occur within *and* outside of marriage. *Sex Roles, 65*, 320–326.

Monroe, K., Ozyurt, S., Wrigley, T., & Alexander, A. (2008). Gender equality in academia: Bad news from the trenches, and some possible solutions. *Perspectives on Politics, 6*, 215–233.

Monteith, M. (2014, May). *The self-regulation of prejudice: When we see it, when we don't.* MPA Presidential Address presented at the Midwestern Psychological Association, Chicago, IL.

Moore, F. R., Cassidy, C., Law Smith, M. J., & Perrett, D. I. (2006). The effects of female control of resources on sex-differentiated mate preferences. *Evolution and Human Behavior, 27*, 193–205.

Moradi, B., & Huang, Y.-P. (2008). Objectification theory and psychology of women: A decade of advances and future directions. *Psychology of Women Quarterly, 32*, 377–398.

Moraga, C., & Anzaldúa, G. (Eds.). (1981). *This bridge called my back: Writings by radical women of color.* Watertown, MA: Persephone Press.

Morman, M. T., Schrodt, P., & Tornes, M. J. (2012). Self-disclosure mediates the effects of gender orientation and homophobia on the relationship quality of male same-sex friendships. *Journal of Social and Personal Relationships, 30*, 582–605.

Morris, N. (2013, January 10). 100,000 assaults. 1,000 rapists sentenced. Shockingly low conviction rates revealed. *Independent.* Retrieved from http://www.independent.co.uk/news/uk/crime/100000-assaults-1000-rapists-sentenced-shockingly-low-conviction-rates-revealed-8446058.html

Moss-Racusin, C. A., Dovidio, J. F., Brescoll, V. L., Graham, M. J., & Handelsman, J. (2012). Science faculty's subtle gender biases favor male students. *Proceedings of the National Academy of Sciences, 109*, 16474–16479.

Moss-Racusin, C. A., Phelan, J. E., & Rudman, L. A. (2010). When men break the gender rules: Status incongruity and backlash against modest men. *Psychology of Men & Masculinity, 11*, 140–151.

Mudege, N. N., & Ezeh, A. C. (2009). Gender, aging, poverty and health: Survival strategies of older men and women in Nairobi slums. *Journal of Aging Studies, 23*(4), 245–257.

Mukherjee, S. (2016). *The gene: An intimate history*. New York, NY: Scribner.

Mulac, A. (2006). The gender-linked language effect: Do language differences really make a difference? In K. Dindia & D. J. Canary (Eds.), *Sex differences and similarities in communication* (Vol. 2, pp. 219–239). Mahwah, NJ: Lawrence Erlbaum.

Muller, K. (1970). Land diving with the Pentecost Islanders. *National Geographic, 138*(6), 796–817.

Munro, D. (2017). A trans timeline. Retrieved from http://www.transmediawatch.org/timeline.html

Munthali, A. C., & Zulu, E. M. (2007). The timing and role of initiation rites in preparing young people for adolescence and responsible sexual and reproductive behaviour in Malawi. *African Journal of Reproductive Health, 11*, 150–167.

Murnen, S. K., & Karazsia, B. T. (2017). A review of research on men's body image and drive for muscularity. In R. F. Levant & Y. J. Wong (Eds), *The psychology of men and masculinities* (pp. 229–257). Washington, DC: American Psychological Association.

Murphy, E., & Oesch, D. (2015). *The feminization of occupations and change in wages: A panel analysis of Britain, Germany, and Switzerland*. SOEP—The German Socio-Economic Panel Study at DIW Berlin, 731-2015.

Murray-Close, D., Nelson, D. A., Ostrov, J. M., Casas, J. F., & Crick, N. R. (2016). Relational aggression: A developmental psychopathology perspective. In D. Cohen & D. Cicchetti (Eds.), *Developmental psychopathology, genes and environment*

(pp. 660–723). Hoboken, NJ: John Wiley.

Musick, K. (2002). Planned and unplanned childbearing among unmarried women. *Journal of Marriage and Family, 64*(4), 915–929.

Mustanski, B., Birkett, M., Kuhns, L. M., Latkin, C. A., & Muth, S. Q. (2015). The role of geographic and network factors in racial disparities in HIV among young men who have sex with men: An egocentric network study. *AIDS and Behavior, 19*, 1037–1047.

Myers, J. E., Madathil, J., & Tingle, L. R. (2005). Marriage satisfaction and wellness in India and the United States: A preliminary comparison of arranged marriages and marriages of choice. *Journal of Counseling & Development, 83*, 183–190.

Nadal K. L. (2013). That's so gay! Microaggressions and the lesbian, gay, bisexual, and transgender community. Washington, DC: American Psychological Association.

Nakazawa, J., & Shwalb, D. W. (2013). Fathering in Japan: Entering an era of involvement with children. In D. W. Shwalb, B. J. Shwalb, & M. E. Lamb (Eds.), *Fathers in cultural context*. New York, NY: Routledge.

Nardi, P., & Sherrod, D. (1994). Friendship in the lives of gay men and lesbians. *Journal of Social and Personal Relationships, 11*, 185–199.

National Center for Education Statistics. (2012). *Digest of education statistics. Table 318.30: Bacehlor's master's, and doctor's degrees conferred by postsecondary institutions, by sex of student and discipline division: 2011–2012*. Retrieved from https://nces.

ed.gov/programs/digest/d13/tables/dt13_318.30.asp

National Center for Education Statistics. (2016). Fast facts. Retrieved from https://nces.ed.gov/fastfacts/display.asp?id=372

National Center for Health Statistics. (2015). *Health, United States, 2014: With special feature on adults aged 55–64*. Hyattsville, MD: Centers for Disease Control. Retrieved http://www.cdc.gov/nchs/data/hus/hus14.pdf

National Center for Health Statistics. (2016). *Health, United States, 2015: With special feature on racial and ethnic health disparities*. Hyattsville, MD: Centers for Disease Control. Retrieved from https://www.cdc.gov/nchs/data/hus/hus15.pdf#015

National Institute on Drug Abuse. (2010). *Diagnosis of HIV infection among adults and adolescents, by sex and transmission category*. Retrieved from https://www.drugabuse.gov/longdesc/diagnosis-hiv-infection-among-adults-adolescents-by-sex-transmission-category-2010

Neal, J. W. (2010). Hanging out: Features of urban children's peer social networks. *Journal of Social and Personal Relationships, 27*, 982–1000.

Needham, B., & Hill, T. D. (2010). Do gender differences in mental health contribute to gender differences in physical health? *Social Science & Medicine, 71*, 1472–1479.

Neisser, U., Boodoo, G., Bouchard, Jr., T, J., Boykin, A. W., Brody, N., Ceci, S. J., . . . Urbina, S. (1996). Intelligence: Knowns and unknowns. *American Psychologist, 51*(2), 77–101.

Nelson, L. J., Padilla-Walker, L. M., Carroll, J. S., Madsen, S. D., Barry,

C. M., & Badger, S. (2007). 'If you want me to treat you like an adult, start acting like one!' Comparing the criteria that emerging adults and their parents have for adulthood. *Journal Of Family Psychology, 21*(4), 665–674.

Nelson, M. R., & Paek, H.-J. (2005). Cross-cultural differences in sexual advertising content in a transnational women's magazine. *Sex Roles, 53,* 371–383.

Nelson, S. K., Kushlev, K., English, T., Dunn, E. W., & Lyubomirsky, S. (2013). In defense of parenthood: Children are associated with more joy than misery. *Psychological Science, 24,* 3–10.

Neumann, S. A., & Waldstein, S. R. (2001). Similar patterns of cardiovascular response during emotional activation as a function of affective valence and arousal and gender. *Journal of Psychosomatic Research, 50,* 245–253.

New, J., Krasnow, M. M., Truxaw, D., & Gaulin, S. J. C. (2007). Spatial adaptations for plant foraging: Women excel and calories count. *Proceedings of the Royal Society B: Biological Sciences, 274,* 2679–2684.

Newcomb, M. E., & Mustanski, B. (2010). Internalized homophobia and internalizing mental health problems: A meta-analytic review. *Clinical Psychology Review, 30,* 1019–1029.

Nguyen, H.-H. D., & Ryan, A. M. (2008). Does stereotype threat affect test performance of minorities and women? A meta-analysis of experimental evidence. *Journal of Applied Psychology, 93,* 1314–1334.

Nicholas, C. L. (2004). Gaydar: Eyegaze as identity recognition among gay men and lesbians. *Sexuality and Culture, 8*(1), 60–86.

Nicholson, L. (2010). Feminism in "waves": Useful metaphor or not? *New Politics, 12*(4). Retrieved from http://newpol.org/content/feminism-waves-useful-metaphor-or-not

Nisbett, R. E., Aronson, J., Blair, C., Dickens, W., Flynn, J., Halpern, D. T., & Turkheimer, E. (2012). Intelligence: New findings and theoretical developments. *American Psychologist, 67,* 130–159.

Nisbett, R. E., & Cohen, D. (1996). *Culture of honor.* Boulder, CO: Westview Press.

Nissan, T., Shapira, O., & Liberman, N. (2015). Effects of power on mental rotation and emotion recognition in women. *Personality and Social Psychology Bulletin, 41,* 1425–1437.

Nolan, J., & Scott, J. (2009). Experiences of age and gender: Narratives or progress and decline. *International Journal of Aging & Human Development, 69*(2), 133–158.

Noland, M., Moran, T., & Kotschwar, B. (2016). *Is gender diversity profitable? Evidence from a global survey.* Washington, DC: Peterson Institute for International Economics.

Nolen-Hoeksema, S. (1991). Responses to depression and their effects on the duration of depressive episodes. *Journal of Abnormal Psychology, 100,* 569–582.

Nolen-Hoeksema, S. (2001). Gender differences in depression. *Current Directions in Psychological Science, 10,* 173–176.

Nolen-Hoeksema, S. (2012). Emotion regulation and psychopathology: The role of gender. *Annual Review of Clinical Psychology, 8,* 161–187.

Norona, J. C., Preddy, T. M., & Welsh, D. P. (2016). How gender shapes emerging adulthood. In J. J. Arnett (Ed.), *The Oxford handbook of emerging adulthood* (pp. 62–86). New York, NY: Oxford University Press.

Norris, A. L., Marcus, D. K., & Green, B. A. (2015). Homosexuality as a discrete class. *Psychological Science, 26*(12), 1843–1853.

Nour, N. M. (2009). Child marriage: A silent health and human rights issue. *Obstetrics & Gynecology, 2,* 51–56.

Nowak, K. L. (2003). Sex categorization in computer-mediated communication (CMC): Exploring the utopian promise. *Media Psychology, 5,* 83–103.

Nugent, B. M., & McCarthy, M. M. (2011). Epigenetic underpinnings of developmental sex differences in the brain. *Neuroendocrinology, 93,* 150–158.

Nyborg, H. (2005). Sex-related differences in general intelligence g, brain size, and social status. *Personality and Individual Differences, 39,* 497–509.

Nyostrom, K., & Ohrling, K. (2004). Parenthood experiences during the child's first year: Literature review. *Journal of Advanced Nursing, 46,* 319–330.

Oakes, M. E., & Slotterback, C. S. (2004). Prejudgments of those who eat a "healthy" versus an "unhealthy" food for breakfast. *Current Psychology, 23,* 267–278.

O'Brien, M., & Nagle, K. J. (1987). Parents' speech to toddlers: The effect of play context. *Journal of Child Language, 14,* 269–279.

O'Doherty, J. K., & Holm, L. (1999). Preferences, quantities and concerns: Socio-cultural perspectives on the gendered consumption of foods. *European Journal of Clinical Nutrition, 53*, 351–359.

OECD. (2016). *Gender wage gap.* OECD Employment Database. Retrieved from https://data.oecd.org/earnwage/gender-wage-gap.htm

Ofreneo, M. A. P., & Montiel, C. J. (2010). Positioning theory as a discursive approach to understanding same-sex intimate violence. *Asian Journal of Social Psychology, 13*, 247–259.

Ogas, O., & Gaddam, S. (2011). *A billion wicked thoughts: What the Internet tells us about sexual relationships.* New York, NY: Plume.

O'Leary, A., Fisher, H. H., Purcell, D. W., Spikes, P. S., & Gomez, C. A. (2007). Correlates of risk patterns and race/ethnicity among HIV-positive men who have sex with men. *AIDS and Behavior, 11*, 706-715.

Olivardia, R., Pope, Jr., H. G., Borowiecki, J. J., & Cohane, G. H. (2004). Biceps and body image: The relationship between muscularity and self-esteem, depression, and eating disorder symptoms. *Psychology of Men & Masculinity, 5*, 112–120.

Olson, K. R., Key, A. C, & Eaton, N. R. (2015). Gender cognition in transgender children. *Psychological Science, 26*, 467–474.

Onnela, J.-P., Waber, B. N., Pentland, A., Schnorf, S., & Lazer, D. (2014). Using sociometers to quantify social interaction patterns. *Scientific Reports, 4*, 1–8.

Orenstein, P. (2011, December 29). Should the world of toys be gender-free? *New York Times.* Retrieved from http://www.nytimes.com/2011/12/30/opinion/does-stripping-gender-from-toys-really-make-sense.html?_r=0

Ortner, T. M., & Sieverding, M. (2008). Where are the gender differences? Male priming boosts spatial skills in women. *Sex Roles, 59*, 274–281.

Osborne, D., & Davies, P. G. (2012). When benevolence backfires: Benevolent sexists opposition to elective and traumatic abortion. *Journal of Applied Social Psychology, 42*(2), 291–307.

Otter, M., Schrander-Stumpel, C., & Curfs, L. (2010). Triple X syndrome: A review of the literature. *European Journal of Human Genetics, 18*, 265–271.

Oudekerk, B. A., Allen, J. P., Hessel, E. T., & Molloy, L. E. (2015). The cascading development of autonomy and relatedness from adolescence to adulthood. *Child Development, 86*(2), 472–485.

Owen, J., & Fincham, F. D. (2011). Effects of gender and psychosocial factors on "friends with benefits" relationships among young adults. *Archives of Sexual Behavior, 40*, 311–320.

Owen J., Tao, K., & Rodolfa, E. (2010). Microaggressions and women in short-term psychotherapy: Initial evidence. *Counseling Psychologist, 38*, 923–946.

Owens, G. M. (2008). Gender differences in health care expenditures, resource utilization, and quality of care. *Journal of Managed Care Pharmacy, 14*(suppl S), S2–S6.

Ozdemir, A. (2008). Shopping malls: Measuring interpersonal distance under changing conditions across cultures. *Field Methods, 20*, 226–248.

Ozturk, M. B., & Tatli, A. (2016). Gender identity inclusion in the workplace: Broadening diversity management research and practice through the case of transgender employees in the U.K. *International Journal of Human Resource Management, 27*, 781–802.

Padgett, D. K., Patrick, C., Burns, B. J., & Schlesinger, H. J. (1994). Ethnic differences in use of inpatient mental health services by blacks, whites, and Hispanics in a national insured population. *Health Services Research, 29*, 135–153.

Pahlke, E., Hyde, J. S., & Allison, C. M. (2014). The effects of single-sex compared with coeducational schooling on students' performance and attitudes: A meta-analysis. *Psychological Bulletin, 140*, 1042–1072.

Paine, T. (1999). *Rights of man.* Mineola, NY: Dover. (Original work published 1791)

Paoletti, J. B. (2012). *Pink and blue: Telling the boys from the girls in America.* Bloomington: Indiana University Press.

Parent, M. C., DeBlaere, C., & Moradi, B. (2013). Approaches to research on intersectionality: Perspectives on gender, LGBT, and racial/ethnic identities. *Sex Roles, 68*(11), 639–645.

Paris, B. J. (1994). *Karen Horney: A psychoanalyst's search for self-understanding.* New Haven, CT: Yale University Press.

Parish, A. R., & De Waal, F. M. (2000). The other "closest living relative": How bonobos (Pan paniscus) challenge traditional assumptions about females, dominance, intra- and intersexual interactions, and hominid evolution. In D. LeCroy & P. Moller (Eds.), *Evolutionary perspectives on human reproductive behavior* (pp. 97–113). New York, NY: New York Academy of Sciences.

Park, B., Banchefsky, S., & Reynolds, E. B. (2015). Psychological essentialism, gender, and parenthood: Physical transformation leads to heightened essentialist conceptions. *Journal of Personality and Social Psychology, 109,* 949–967.

Park, G., Yaden, D. B., Schwartz, H. A., Kern, M. L., Eichstaedt, J. C., Kosinski, M., . . . Seligman, M. E. P. (2016). Women are warmer but no less assertive than men: Gender and language on Facebook. *PLOS One, 11*(5), e0155885.

Parker, K. (2015, June 18). 5 facts about today's fathers. Pew Research Center. Retrieved from http://www.pewresearch.org/fact-tank/2015/06/18/5-facts-about-todays-fathers

Parra, A., Oliva, A., & del Carmen Reina, M. (2015). Family relationships from adolescence to emerging adulthood: A longitudinal study. *Journal of Family Issues, 36*(14), 2002–2020.

Parra-Cardona, J. R., Córdova, D., Holtrop, K., Villarruel, F. A., & Wieling, E. (2008). Shared ancestry, evolving stories: Similar and contrasting life experiences described by foreign born and U.S. born Latino parents. *Family Process, 47,* 157–172.

Pash, C. (2016, October 5). A third gender option is now recognized by an Australian health insurer. *Business Insider Australia.* Retrieved from http://www.businessinsider.com .au/a-third-gender-option-is-now-recognised-by-an-australian-health-insurer-2016-10

Pasterski, V. L., Geffner, M. E., Brain, C., Hindmarsh, P., Brook, C., & Hines, M. (2005). Prenatal hormones and postnatal socialization by parents as determinants of male-typical toy play in girls with congenital adrenal hyperplasia. *Child Development, 76*(1), 264–278.

Patel, M. (2014). A desire to disfigure: Acid attack in India. *International Journal of Criminology and Sociological Theory, 7*(2), e39702–e39702.

Paterson, K. K. (2016, July 13). When rape became a war crime (Hint: It's not when you think) [Web log post]. Retrieved from http://www .womenundersiegeproject.org/blog/ entry/when-rape-became-a-war-crime-hint-its-not-when-you-think1

Patterson, C. J. (2004). Lesbian and gay parents and their children: Summary of research findings. In *Lesbian and gay parenting: A resource for psychologists.* Washington, DC: American Psychological Association.

Patterson, C. J. (2006). Children of lesbian and gay parents. *Current Directions in Psychological Science, 15,* 241–244.

Pauletti, R. E., Cooper, P. J., & Perry, D. G. (2014). Influences of gender identity on children's maltreatment of gender-nonconforming peers: A person × target analysis of aggression. *Journal of Personality and Social Psychology, 106,* 843–866.

Paulus, R. (2016, October 20). A brief history of the ways men have tried to cure impotence. *Mel Magazine.* Retrieved from https:// melmagazine.com/a-brief-history-of-the-ways-men-have-tried-to-cure-impotence-dbe4d16203fe

Paustian-Underdahl, S. C., Walker, L. S., & Woehr, D. J. (2014). Gender and perceptions of leadership effectiveness: A meta-analysis of contextual moderators. *Journal of Applied Psychology, 99,* 1129–1145.

Payne, D. L., Lonsway, K. A., & Fitzgerald, L. F. (1999). Rape myth acceptance: Exploration of its structure and its measurement using the Illinois rape myth acceptance scale. *Journal of Research in Personality, 33,* 27–68.

Paynter, A., & Leaper, C. (2016). Heterosexual dating double standards in undergraduate women and men. *Sex Roles, 75,* 393–406.

Peck, E. (2016, October 26). When a company is failing, female CEOs get blamed more frequently than men. *Huffington Post.* Retrieved from http://www.huffingtonpost.com/ entry/female-ceoblame_us_581 00af0e4b001e247df34c5?utm_ hp_ref=gender-equality

Pedersen, W. C., Miller, L. C., Putcha-Bhagavatula, A. D., & Yang, Y. (2002). Evolved sex differences in the number of partners desired? The long and the short of it. *Psychological Science, 13*(2), 157–161.

Pelham, B. W., & Blanton, H. (2013). *Conducting research in psychology: Measuring the weight of smoke* (4th ed.). Belmont, CA: Thomson Wadsworth.

Peplau, L. A., & Fingerhut, A. W. (2007). The close relationships of lesbians and gay men. *Annual Review of Psychology, 58,* 405–424.

Pérez-Peña, R. (2015, September 21). 1 in 4 women experience sexual assault on campus. *New York Times.* Retrieved from https://www.nytimes.com/2015/09/22/us/a-third-of-college-women-experience-unwanted-sexual-contact-study-finds.html?_r=0

Perlow, L. A. (2012). Sleeping with your smart phone: How to break the 24/7 habit and change the way you work. Cambridge, MA: Harvard Business Review Press.

Perls, T., & Fretts, R. (1998). Why women live longer than men. *Scientific American, 9,* 100–107.

Pernice-Duca, F. M. (2010). An examination of family and social support networks as a function of ethnicity and gender: A descriptive study of youths from three ethnic reference groups. *Journal of Youth Studies, 13*(3), 391–402.

Perrin, P. B., Heesacker, M., Tiegs, T. J., Swan, L. K., Lawrence, A. W., Smith, M. B., . . . Mejia-Millan, C. M. (2011). Aligning Mars and Venus: The social construction and instability of gender differences in romantic relationships. *Sex Roles, 64,* 613–628.

PerryUndem. (2017, January 17). *The state of the Union on gender equality, sexism, and women's rights.* PerryUndem Research/Communication. Retrieved from https://www.scribd.com/document/336804316/PerryUndem-Gender-Equality-Report

Petersen, J. L., & Hyde, J. S. (2010). A meta-analytic review of research on gender differences in sexuality, 1993–2007. *Psychological Bulletin, 136,* 21–38.

Petrides, K. V., & Furnham, A. (2006). The role of trait emotional intelligence in a gender specific

model of organizational variables. *Journal of Applied Social Psychology, 36,* 552–569.

Pettit, B., & Western, B. (2004). Mass imprisonment and the life course: Race and class inequality in U.S. incarceration. *American Sociological Review, 69*(2), 151–169.

Pew Research Center. (2013a, March 12). Gun ownership trends and demographics. Retrieved from http://www.people-press.org/2013/03/12/section-3-gun-ownership-trends-and-demographics

Pew Research Center (2013b, December 11). On pay gap, millennial women near parity—for now. Retrieved from http://www.pewsocialtrends.org/2013/12/11/on-pay-gap-millennial-women-near-parity-for-now

Pew Research Center. (2015, December 17). The American family today. Retrieved from http://www.pewsocialtrends.org/2015/12/17/1-the-american-family-today

Phillips, A. (2016, April 15). Mississippi's new law allowing refusal of service to LGBT people is the most sweeping yet. *Washington Post.* Retrieved from https://www.washingtonpost.com/news/the-fix/wp/2016/04/05/mississippis-new-religious-freedom-law-is-the-most-sweeping-weve-seen-yet-heres-what-it-does

Piccinelli, M., & Wilkinson, G. (2000). Gender differences in depression. Critical review. *British Journal of Psychiatry, 177,* 486–492.

Picho, K., Rodriguez, A., & Finnie, L. (2013). Exploring the moderating role of context on the mathematics performance of females under

stereotype threat: A meta-analysis. *Journal of Social Psychology, 153,* 299–333.

Pietschnig, J., & Voracek, M. (2015). One century of global IQ gains: A formal meta-analysis of the Flynn effect (1909–2013). *Perspectives on Psychological Science, 10,* 282–306.

Pihet, S., Etter, S., Schmid, M., & Kimonis, E. R. (2015). Assessing callous-unemotional traits in adolescents: Validity of the Inventory of Callous-Unemotional Traits across gender, age, and community/institutionalized status. *Journal of Psychopathology and Behavioral Assessment, 37,* 407–421.

Pillsworth, E. G., & Haselton, M. G. (2005). The evolution of coupling. *Psychological Inquiry, 16,* 98–104.

Pilver, C. E., Kasl, D., Desai, R., & Levy, B. R. (2011). Exposure to American culture is associated with premenstrual dysphoric disorder among ethnic minority women. *Journal of Affective Disorders, 130,* 334–341.

Pines, A. M., & Zaidman, N. (2003). Gender, culture, and social support: A male-female, Israeli Jewish-Arab comparison. *Sex Roles, 49*(11–12), 571–586.

Pinker, S. (2011). *The better angels of our nature.* New York, NY: Viking.

Pinquart, M., & Sörensen, S. (2001). Gender differences in self-concept and psychological well-being in old age: A meta-analysis. *Journal of Gerontology: Psychological Sciences, 56B,* P195–P213.

Plant, E. A., Kling, K. C., & Smith, G. L. (2004). The influence of gender and social role on the interpretation of facial expressions. *Sex Roles, 51,* 187–196.

Planty, M., Langton, L., Krebs, C., Berzofsy, M., & Smiley-McDonald, H. (2013). *Female victims of sexual violence, 1994–2010.* Washington, DC: Bureau of Justice Statistics. Retrieved from http://www.bjs.gov/content/pub/pdf/fvsv9410.pdf

Poisson, J. (2013, November 15). Remember Storm? We check in on the baby being raised gender-neutral. *Toronto Star.* Retrieved from http://www.thestar.com/life/parent/2013/11/15/remember_storm_we_check_in_on_the_baby_being_raised_genderneutral.html

Pollick, F. E., Kay, J. W., Heim, K., & Stringer, R. (2005). Gender recognition from point-light walkers. *Journal of Experimental Psychology: Human Perception and Performance, 31*(6), 1247–1265.

Pomerantz, E. M., Ng, F. F., & Wang, Q. (2004). Gender socialization: A parent × child model. In A. H. Eagly, A. E. Beall, & R. J. Sternberg (Eds.), *The psychology of gender* (pp. 120–142). New York, NY: Guilford Press.

Pomerleau, C. S., & Snedecor, S. M. (2008). Validity and reliability of the weight control smoking scale. *Eating Behaviors, 9,* 376–380.

Post, C., & Byron, K. (2015). Women on boards and firm financial performance: A meta-analysis. *Academy of Management Journal, 58,* 1546–1571.

Poulin-Dubois, D., & Serbin, L. A. (2006). Infants' knowledge about gender stereotypes and categories. *Enfance, 58,* 283–292.

Powell, M. P., & Schulte, T. (2011). *Turner syndrome.* In S. Goldstein &

C. R. Reynolds (Eds.), *Handbook of neurodevelopmental and genetic disorders in children* (2nd ed., pp. 261–275). New York, NY: Guilford Press.

Prattala, R., Paalanen, L., Grinberga, D., Helasoja, V., Kasmel, A., & Petkeviciene, J. (2007). Gender differences in the consumption of meat, fruit and vegetables are similar in Finland and the Baltic countries. *European Journal of Public Health, 17,* 520–525.

Pratto, F., & Pitpitan, E. V. (2008). Ethnocentrism and sexism: How stereotypes legitimize six types of power. *Social and Personality Psychology Compass, 2,* 2159–2176.

Pratto, F., Sidanius, J., & Levin, S. (2006). Social dominance theory and the dynamics of intergroup relations: Taking stock and looking forward. *European Review of Social Psychology, 17,* 271–320.

Pratto, F., Sidanius, J., Stallworth, L. M., & Malle, B. F. (1994). Social dominance orientation: A personality variable predicting social and political attitudes. *Journal of Personality and Social Psychology, 67,* 741–763.

Pratto, F., & Walker, A. (2004). The bases of gendered power. In A. E. Beall, A. H. Eagly, & R. J. Sternberg (Eds.), *The psychology of gender* (pp. 242–268). New York, NY: Guilford Press.

Prewitt-Freilino, J. L., Caswell, T. A., & Laakso, E. K. (2012). The gendering of language: A comparison of gender equality in countries with gendered, natural gender, and genderless languages. *Sex Roles, 66,* 268–281.

Priess, H. A., Lindberg, S. M., & Hyde, J. S. (2009). Adolescent

gender-role identity and mental health: Gender intensification revisited. *Child Development, 80,* 1531–1544.

Purdie-Vaughns, V., & Eibach, R. P. (2008). Intersectional invisibility: The distinctive advantages and disadvantages of multiple subordinate-group identities. *Sex Roles, 59,* 377–391.

Quinn, J. M., & Wagner, R. K. (2015). Gender differences in reading impairment and in the identification of impaired readers: Results from a large-scale study of at-risk readers. *Journal of Learning Disabilities, 48*(4), 433–445.

Quinn, P. C., & Liben, L. S. (2014). A sex difference in mental rotation in infants: Convergent evidence. *Infancy, 19,* 103–116.

Quinn, P. C., Yahr, J., Kuhn, A., Slater, A. M., & Pascalis, O. (2002). Representation of the gender of human faces by infants: A preference for female. *Perception, 31,* 1109–1121.

Quintana, N., Rosenthal, J., & Krehely, J. (2010). *On the streets: The federal response to gay and transgender homeless youth.* Retrieved from https://www.americanprogress.org/issues/lgbt/report/2010/06/21/7983/on-the-streets

Radmacher, K., & Azmitia, M. (2006). Are there gendered pathways to intimacy in early adolescents' and emerging adults' friendships? *Journal of Adolescent Research, 21,* 415–448.

Rafferty, Y. (2013). International dimensions of discrimination and violence against girls: A human rights perspective. *Journal of International Women's Studies, 14,* 1–23.

Rahman, Q., & Hull, M. S. (2005). An empirical test of the kin selection hypothesis for male homosexuality. *Archives of Sexual Behavior, 34*, 461–467.

Rakhkovskaya, L. M., & Warren, C. S. (2014). Ethnic identity, thin-ideal internalization, and eating pathology in ethnically diverse college women. *Body Image, 11*, 438–445.

Randle, A. A., & Graham, C. A. (2011). A review of the evidence on the effects of intimate partner violence on men. *Psychology of Men & Masculinity, 12*(2), 97–111.

Rangecroft, A. (2016, January 6). Where new dads are encouraged to take months off work. *BBC News Magazine*. Retrieved from http://www.bbc.com/news/magazine-35225982

Rani, M., & Lule, E. (2004). Exploring the socioeconomic dimension of adolescent reproductive health: A multicountry analysis. *International Family Planning Perspectives, 30*, 110–117.

Ranson, K. E., & Urichuk, L. J. (2008). The effect of parent–child attachment relationships on child biopsychological outcomes: A review. *Early Child Development and Care, 178*, 129–152.

Rape Abuse and Incest National Network. (2016). What consent looks like. Retrieved from https://www.rainn.org/articles/what-is-consent

Ratliff, K. A., Redford, L., Conway, J. G., & Smith, C. T. (2016). Engendering support: Hostile sexism predicts voting for Donald Trump over Hillary Clinton in the 2016 U.S. presidential election. Manuscript submitted for publication.

Rawlins, W. K. (2009). *The compass of friendship: Narratives, identities,* *and dialogues*. Thousand Oaks, CA: Sage.

Rawstron, K. (2014, December). *NSW Registrar of Births, Deaths and Marriages v. Norrie*: Implications for sex segregation studies. Retrieved from https://www.tasa.org.au/wp-content/uploads/2014/12/Rawston-K.pdf

Reddy, S. (2012, January 6). 'Good guy' goes for girls. *Wall Street Journal*. Retrieved from http://www.wsj.com/articles/SB10001424052970203513604577143034143271506

Regner, I., Smeding, A., Gimmig, D., Thinus-Blanc, C., Monteil, J.-M., & Huguet, P. (2010). Individual differences in working memory moderate stereotype-threat effects. *Psychological Science, 21*, 1646–1648.

Reidy, D. E., Berke, D. S., Gentile, B., & Zeichner, A. (2014). Man enough? Masculine discrepancy stress and intimate partner violence. *Personality and Individual Differences, 68*, 160–164.

Reilly, D. (2012). Gender, culture, and sex-typed cognitive abilities. *PLOS One, 7*, e39904.

Reiter, S., Bryen, D. N., & Shachar, I. (2007). Adolescents with intellectual disabilities as victims of abuse. *Journal of Intellectual Disabilities, 11*, 371–387.

Renzetti, C. M., Lynch, K. R., & DeWall, C. N. (2015). Ambivalent sexism, alcohol use, and intimate partner violence perpetration. *Journal of Interpersonal Violence*. Advance online publication.

Rescorla, L. A., Bochicchio, L., Achenbach, T. M., Ivanova, M. Y., Almqvist, F., Begovac, I., . . . Verhulst, F. C. (2014). Parent–teacher agreement on children's problems in 21 societies. *Journal of Clinical Child and Adolescent Psychology, 43*, 627–642.

Reuben, E., Sapienza, P., & Zingales, L. (2014). How stereotypes impair women's careers in science. *Proceedings of the National Academy of Sciences, 111*, 4403–4408.

Richards, Z., & Hewstone, M. (2001). Subtyping and subgrouping: Processes for the prevention and promotion of stereotype change. *Personality and Social Psychology Review, 5*, 52–73.

Richeson, J. A., Todd, A. R., Trawalter, S., & Baird, A. A. (2008). Eye-gaze direction modulates race-related amygdala activity. *Group Processes & Intergroup Relations, 11*(2), 233–246.

Riddoch, C. J., Andersen L. B., Wedderkopp, N., Harro, M., Klasson-Heggebo, L., Sardinha, L. B., . . . Ekelund, U. (2004). Physical activity levels and patterns of 9- and 15-yr-old European children. *Medicine & Science in Sports & Exercise, 36*, 86–92.

Ridgeway, C. L. (2001). Gender, status, and leadership. *Journal of Social Issues, 57*, 637–655.

Riela, S., Rodriguez, G., Aron, A., Xu, X., & Acevedo, B. P. (2010). Experiences of falling in love: Investigating culture, ethnicity, gender, and speed. *Journal of Social and Personal Relationships, 27*, 43–493.

Riessman, C. K. (1990). *Divorce talk: Women and men make sense of personal relationships*. Piscataway, NJ: Rutgers University Press.

Riley, E. A., Clemson, L., Sitharthan, G., & Diamond, M. (2013).

Surviving a gender-variant childhood: The views of transgender adults on the needs of gender-variant children and their parents. *Journal of Sex & Marital Therapy, 39,* 241–263.

Rizzolatti, G., & Craighero, L. (2004). The mirror neuron system. *Annual Review of Neuroscience, 27,* 169–192.

Robbins, N. K., Low, K. G., & Query, A. N. (2016). A qualitative exploration of the "coming out" process for asexual individuals. *Archives of Sexual Behavior, 45*(3), 751–760.

Roberts, B. E., & White, J. E. (1998). *Roberts vs. Texaco: A true story of race and corporate America.* New York, NY: Avon Books.

Roberts, J., Griffiths, F. E., Verran, A., & Ayre, C. (2015). Why do women seek ultrasound scans from commercial providers during pregnancy? *Sociology of Health & Illness, 37,* 594–609.

Roberts, T.-A. (1991). Gender and the influence of evaluations on self-assessments in achievement settings. *Psychological Bulletin, 109,* 297–308.

Roberts, T. A., & Pennebaker, J. W. (1995). Gender differences in perceiving internal state: Toward a his-and-hers model of perceptual cue use. *Advances in Experimental Social Psychology, 27,* 143–175.

Robertson, K. F., Smeets, S., Lubinski, D., & Benbow, C. P. (2010). Beyond the threshold hypothesis: Even among gifted and top math-science graduate students, cognitive abilities, vocational interests, and lifestyle preference matter for career choice, performance, and persistence. *Current Directions in Psychological Science, 19,* 346–351.

Robinson, K. (2015, August 10). Target ditches gender labels on toys, home and entertainment. *NBC News.* Retrieved from http://www.nbcnews.com/news/us-news/target-ditches-gendered-labels-toys-home-entertainment-n406741

Robles, R., Fresán, A., Vega-Ramírez, H., Cruz-Islas, J., Rodríguez-Pérez, V., Domínguez- Martínez, T., & Reed, G. M. (2016). Removing transgender identity from the classification of mental disorders: A Mexican field study for ICD-11. *Lancet Psychiatry, 3,* 850–859.

Roe-Sepowitz, D. E., Gallagher, J., Risinger, M., & Hickle, K. (2014). The sexual exploitation of girls in the United States: The role of female pimps. *Journal of Interpersonal Violence, 30,* 2814–2830.

Rogier, S. A., & Padgett, M. Y. (2004). The impact of utilizing a flexible work schedule on the perceived career advancement potential of women. *Human Resource Development Quarterly, 15,* 89–106.

Rosario, M., Schrimshaw, E. W., & Hunter, J. (2011). Homelessness among lesbian, gay, and bisexual youth: Implications for subsequent internalizing and externalizing symptoms. *Journal of Youth and Adolescence, 41,* 544–560.

Rosenfeld, M. J. (2014). Couple longevity in the era of same-sex marriage in the United States. *Journal of Marriage and Family, 76,* 905–918.

Rosin, H. (2013, August 30). The wage gap lie. *Slate.* Retrieved from http://www.slate.com/articles/double_x/doublex/2013/08/gender_pay_gap_the_familiar_line_that_women_make_77_cents_to_every_man_s.html

Ross, J. L., Roeltgen, D. P., Kushner, H., Zinn, A. R., Reiss, A., Bardsley, M. Z., . . . Tartaglia, N. (2012). Behavioral and social phenotypes in boys with 47,XYY syndrome or 47,XXY Klinefelter syndrome. *Pediatrics, 129,* 769–778.

Ross, L. (2011, March). Understanding reproductive justice. Retrieved from https://www.trustblackwomen.org/our-work/what-is-reproductive-justice/9-what-is-reproductive-justice

Rostosky, S. S., Black, W. W., Riggle, E. B., & Rosenkrantz, D. (2015). Positive aspects of being a heterosexual ally to lesbian, gay, bisexual and transgender (LGBT) people. *American Journal of Orthopsychiatry, 85,* 331–338.

Roter, D. L., Hall, J. A., & Aoki, Y. (2002). Physician gender effects in medical communication: A meta-analytic review. *Journal of the American Medical Association, 288,* 756–764.

Rowe, M. (1981). The minutiae of discrimination: The need for support. In B. L. Forisha, & B. H. Goldman (Eds.), *Outsiders on the inside: Women and organizations* (pp. 155–171). Englewood Cliffs, NJ: Prentice-Hall.

Rozin, P., Hormes, J. M., Faith, M. S., & Wansink, B. (2012). Is meat male? A quantitative multimethod framework to establish metaphoric relationships. *Journal of Consumer Research, 39,* 629–643.

Rubel, A. N., & Bogaert, A. F. (2015). Consensual nonmonogamy: Psychological well-being and relationship quality correlates. *Journal of Sex Research*, *52*, 961–982.

Rubin, A. J. (2012, December 1). With help, Afghan survivor or "honor killing" inches back. *New York Times*. Retrieved from http://www.nytimes.com/2012/12/02/world/asia/doctors-and-others-buck-tradition-in-afghan-honor-attack.html

Rubin, J. Z., Provenzano, F. J., & Luria, Z. (1974). The eye of the beholder: Parents' views on sex of newborns. *American Journal of Orthopsychiatry*, *44*, 512–519.

Rudd, M. D., Berman, A. L., Joiner, T. J., Nock, M. K., Silverman, M. M., Mandrusiak, M., . . . Witte, T. (2006). Warning signs for suicide: Theory, research, and clinical applications. *Suicide and Life-Threatening Behavior*, *36*(3), 255–262.

Ruderman, M. N., Ohlott, P. J., Panzer, K., & King, S. N. (2002). Benefits of multiple roles for managerial women. *Academy of Management Journal*, *45*, 369–386.

Rudman, L. A., & Mescher, K. (2013). Penalizing men who request a family leave: Is flexibility stigma a femininity stigma? *Journal of Social Issues*, *69*, 322–340.

Rudman, L. A., Mescher, K., & Moss-Racusin, C. A. (2012). Reactions to gender egalitarian men: Perceived feminization due to stigma-by-association. *Group Processes & Intergroup Relations*, *16*, 572–599.

Rudman, L. A., Moss-Racusin, C. A., Phelan, J. E., & Nauts, S. (2012). Status incongruity and backlash effects: Defending the gender hierarchy motivates prejudice against female leaders. *Journal of Experimental Social Psychology*, *48*, 165–179.

Ruhm, C. J. (2000). Parental leave and child health. *Journal of Health Economics*, *19*, 931–960.

Ruigrok, A. N. V., Salimi-Khorshidi, G., Lai, M.-C., Baron-Cohen, S., Lombardo, M. V., Tait, R. J., & Suckling, J. (2014). A meta-analysis of sex differences in human brain structure. *Neuroscience and Biobehavioral Reviews*, *39*, 34–50.

Russell, E. M., DelPriore, D. J., Butterfield, M. E., & Hill, S. R. (2013). Friends with benefits, but without the sex: Straight women and gay men exchange trustworthy mating advice. *Evolutionary Psychology*, *11*, 132–147.

Russell, S. T., & Consolacion, T. B. (2003). Adolescent romance and emotional health in the United States: Beyond binaries. *Journal of Clinical and Adolescent Psychology*, *32*, 499–508.

Russell, S. T., & Fish, J. N. (2016). Mental health in lesbian, gay, bisexual, and transgender (LGBT) youth. *Annual Review of Clinical Psychology*, *12*, 465–487.

Russo, N. F. (1976). The motherhood mandate. *Journal of Social Issues*, *32*, 143–153.

Rust, J., Golombok, S., Hines, M., & Johnston, K. (2000). The role of brothers and sisters in the gender development of preschool children. *Journal of Experimental Child Psychology*, *77*, 292–303.

Rutherford, A., & Granek, L. (2010). Emergence and development of the psychology of women. In J. C. Chrisler & D. R. McCreary (Eds.), *Handbook of gender research in psychology: Gender research in general and experimental psychology* (Vol. 1, pp. 19–41). New York, NY: Springer.

Ryan, C., Huebner, D., Diaz, R. M., & Sanchez, J. (2009). Family rejection as a predictor of negative health outcomes in White and Latino lesbian, gay, and bisexual young adults. *Pediatrics*, *123*, 346–352.

Ryan, C., Russell, S. T., Huebner, D., Diaz, R., & Sanchez, J. (2010). Family acceptance in adolescence and the health of LGBT young adults. *Journal of Child and Adolescent Psychiatric Nursing*, *23*, 205–213.

Ryan, M. K., & Haslam, S. A. (2005). The glass cliff: Evidence that women are overrepresented in precarious leadership positions. *British Journal of Management*, *16*, 81–90.

Rydell, R. J., McConnell, A. R., & Beilock, S. L. (2009). Multiple social identities and stereotype threat: Imbalance, accessibility, and working memory. *Journal of Personality and Social Psychology*, *96*, 949–966.

Sadiqi, F. (2003). Women and linguistic space in Morocco. *Woman and Language*, *26*(1), 35–43.

Saewyc, E., Skay, C., Richens, K., Reis, E., Poon, C., & Murphy, A. (2006). Sexual orientation, sexual abuse, and HIV-risk behaviors among adolescents in the Pacific Northwest. *American Journal of Public Health*, *96*, 1104–1110.

Sagan, C. (1980). *Broca's brain: Reflections on the romance of science*. New York, NY: Presidio Press.

Saginak, K. A., & Saginak, M. A. (2005). Balancing work and family: Equity, gender, and marital satisfaction. *Family Journal*, *13*, 162–166.

Salisbury, C. M., & Fisher, W. A. (2014). "Did you come?" A qualitative exploration of gender differences in beliefs, experiences, and concerns regarding female orgasm occurrence during heterosexual sexual interactions. *Journal of Sex Research, 51*(6), 616–631.

Salomon, K., Burgess, K. D., & Bosson, J. K. (2015). Flash fire and slow burn: Women's cardiovascular reactivity and recovery following hostile and benevolent sexism. *Journal of Experimental Psychology: General, 144,* 469–479.

Samal, J. (2016). The unabated female feticide is leading to bride crises and bride trade in India. *Journal of Family Medicine and Primary Care, 5*(2), 503–505.

Samar, R. G., & Alibakhshi, G. (2007). The gender linked differences in the use of linguistic strategies in face-to-face communication. *Linguistics Journal, 3*(3), 59–71.

Sandserson, C. A., Rahm, K. B., & Beigbeder, S. A. (2005). The link between the pursuit of intimacy goals and satisfaction in close same-sex friendships: An examination of the underlying processes. *Journal of Social and Personal Relationships, 22,* 75–98.

Sasson, S., & Paul, L. A. (2014). Labeling acts of sexual violence: What roles do assault characteristics, attitudes, and life experiences play? *Behavior and Social Issues, 23,* 35–49.

Saunders, D. G. (2002). Are physical assaults by wives and girlfriends a major social problem? A review of the literature. *Violence Against Women, 8*(12), 1424–1448.

Savage-McGlynn, E. (2012). Sex differences in intelligence in younger and older participants of the Raven's Standard Progressive Matrices Plus. *Personality and Individual Differences, 53,* 137–141.

Savin-Williams, R. C., & Diamond, L. M. (2000). Sexual identity trajectories among sexual- minority youths: Gender comparisons. *Archives of Sexual Behavior, 29*(6), 607–627.

Sawyer, K., Salter, N., & Thoroughgood, C. (2013). Studying individual identities is good, but examining intersectionality is better. *Industrial and Organizational Psychology, 6,* 80–84.

Scarr, S., & McCartney, K. (1983). How people make their own environments: A theory of genotype -> environment effects. *Child Development, 54,* 424–435.

Schein, V. E. (1973). The relationship between sex role stereotypes and requisite management characteristics. *Journal of Applied Psychology, 57,* 95–100.

Schein, V. E. (1975). Relationships between sex role stereotypes and requisite management characteristics among female managers. *Journal of Applied Psychology, 60,* 340–344.

Schein, V. E., Mueller, R., & Jacobson, C. (1989). The relationship between sex role stereotypes and requisite management characteristics among college students. *Sex Roles, 20,* 103–110.

Scheithauser, H., Haag, N., Mahlke, J., & Ittel, A. (2008). Gender and age differences in the development of relational/indirect aggression: First results of a meta-analysis. *European Journal of Developmental Science, 2,* 176–189.

Schieman, S., & Van Gundy, K. (2000). The personal and social links between age and self-reported empathy. *Social Psychology Quarterly, 63,* 152–174.

Schiff, W., & Oldak, R. (1990). Accuracy of judging time to arrival: Effects of modality, trajectory, and gender. *Journal of Experimental Psychology: Human Perception and Performance, 16,* 303–316.

Schmader, T., & Johns, M. (2003). Converging evidence that stereotype threat reduces working memory capacity. *Journal of Personality and Social Psychology, 85,* 440–452.

Schmidt, F. L., & Hunter, J. (2004). General mental ability in the world of work: Occupational attainment and job performance. *Journal of Personality and Social Psychology, 86,* 162–173.

Schmitt, D. P. (2005). Sociosexuality from Argentina to Zimbabwe: A 48-nation study of sex, culture, and strategies of human mating. *Behavioral and Brain Sciences, 28,* 247–275.

Schmitt, D. P., Shackleford, T. K., Duntley, J., & Tooke, W. (2002). Is there an early-30s peak in female sexual desire? Cross-sectional evidence from the United States and Canada. *Canadian Journal of Human Sexuality, 11,* 1–18.

Schmitt, D. P., Youn, G., Bond, B., Brooks, S., Frye, H., Johnson, S., . . . Stoka, C. (2009). When will I feel love? The effects of culture, personality, and gender on the psychological tendency to love. *Journal of Research in Personality, 43,* 830–846.

Schnittker, J., & Bacak, V. (2014). The increasing predictive validity of self-rated health. *PLOS One, 9,* e84933.

Schoenfeld, E. A., Bredow, C. A., & Huston, T. L. (2012). Do men and women show love differently in marriage? *Personality and Social Psychology Bulletin, 38,* 1396–1409.

Schoonover, K., & McEwan, B. (2014). Are you really just friends? Predicting the audience challenge in cross-sex friendships. *Personal Relationships, 21*, 387–403.

Schrader, M. P., & Wann, D. L. (1999). High-risk recreation: The relationship between participant characteristics and degree of involvement. *Journal of Sport Behavior, 22*, 426–441.

Schützwohl, A. (2005). Sex differences in jealousy: The processing of cues to infidelity. *Evolution & Human Behavior, 26*, 288–299.

Schwartz, C. R., & Graf, N. L. (2009). Assortative matching among same-sex and different-sex couples in the United States, 1990–2000. *Demographic Research, 21*, 843–878.

Schwartz, H. A., Eichstaedt, J. C., Kern, M. L., Dziurzynski, L., Ramones, S. M., Agrawal, M., . . . Ungar L. H. (2013). Personality, gender, and age in the language of social media: The open-vocabulary approach. *PLOS One, 8*(9), e73791.

Scott, K. D. (2000). Crossing cultural borders: 'Girl' and 'look' as markers of identity in Black women's language use. *Discourse & Society, 11*(2), 237–248.

Scott, S. M., Wallander, J. L., Depaoli, S., Elliott, M. N., Grunbaum, J. A., Tortolero, S. R., . . . Schuster, M. A. (2015). Gender role orientation is associated with health-related quality of life differently among African-American, Hispanic, and White youth. *Quality of Life Research: An International Journal of Quality of Life Aspects of Treatment, Care & Rehabilitation, 24*(9), 2139–2149.

Scutti, S. (2017, January 2). "The protocol of the day was to lie": NYC issues first US "intersex" birth certificate. *CNN.* Retrieved from http://www.cnn.com/2016/12/30/health/intersex-birth-certificate/index.html

Seedat, S., Scott, K. M., Angermeyer, M. C., Berglund, P., Bromet, E. J., Brugha, T. S., . . . Kessler, R. C. (2009). Cross-national associations between gender and mental disorders in the World Health Organization World Mental Health Surveys. *Archives of General Psychiatry, 66*, 785–795.

Sen, A. (1990, December 20). More than 100 million women are missing. *New York Review of Books, 37*, 20.

Sendén, M. G., Bäck, E. A., & Lindqvist, A. (2015). Introducing a gender-neutral pronoun in a natural gender language: The influence of time on attitudes and behavior. *Frontiers in Psychology, 6.*

Sentencing Project. (2007). *Women in the criminal justice system: Briefing sheets.* Retrieved from http://www.sentencingproject.org/wp-content/uploads/2016/01/Women-in-the-Criminal-Justice-System-Briefing-Sheets.pdf

Sentencing Project. (2015). *Fact sheet: Incarcerated women and girls.* Retrieved from http://www.sentencingproject.org/wp-content/uploads/2016/02/Incarcerated-Women-and-Girls.pdf

Serbin, L. A., Zelkowitz, P., Doyle, A., Gold, D., & Wheaton, B. (1990). The socialization of sex-differentiated skills and academic performance: A mediational model. *Sex Roles, 23*, 613–628.

Sesko, A. K., & Biernat, M. (2010). Prototypes of race and gender: The invisibility of Black women. *Journal of Experimental Social Psychology, 46*, 356–360.

Settles, I. H., Pratt-Hyatt, J. S., & Buchanan, N. T. (2008). Through the lens of race: Black and White women's perceptions of womanhood. *Psychology of Women Quarterly, 32*, 454–468.

Severson, A., & Barclay, R. S. (2015). Testosterone levels by age. Retrieved from http://www.healthline.com/health/low-testosterone/testosterone-levels-by-age#Overview1

Shackelford, T. K., Schmitt, D. P., & Buss, D. M. (2005). Universal dimensions of human mate preferences. *Personality and Individual Differences, 39*, 447–458.

Shapiro, A. F., Gottman, J. M., & Carrère, S. (2000). The baby and the marriage: Identifying factors that buffer against decline in marital satisfaction after the baby arrives. *Journal of Family Psychology, 14*, 59–70.

Shapiro, D. N., Rios, D., & Stewart, A. J. (2010). Conceptualizing lesbian sexual identity development: Narrative accounts of socializing structures and individual decisions and actions. *Feminism & Psychology, 20*, 491–510.

Shapka, J. D., & Keating, D. P. (2003). Effects of a girls-only curriculum during adolescence: Performance, persistence, and engagement in mathematics and science. *American Educational Research Journal, 40*, 929–960.

Sheets, V. L., & Wolfe, M. D. (2001). Sexual jealousy in heterosexuals, lesbians, and gays. *Sex Roles, 44*, 255–276.

Sheff, E. (2013). *The polyamorists next door.* New York, NY: Rowman & Littlefield.

Sheltzer, J., & Smith, J. C. (2014). Elite male faculty in the life sciences employ fewer women. *Proceedings of the National Academy of Sciences, 111,* 10107–10112.

Shepard, L. D. (2012). The impact of polygamy on women's mental health: A systematic review. *Epidemiology and Psychiatric Sciences, 22,* 47–62.

Shepard, R. N., & Metzler, J. (1971). Mental rotation of three-dimensional objects, 171, 701–703.

Shi, Y., & Kennedy, J. (2016). Delayed registration and identifying the "Missing Girls" in China. *China Quarterly, 228,* 1018–1038.

Shields, S. (1975). Functionalism, Darwinism, and the psychology of women. *American Psychologist, 30,* 739–754.

Shields, S. A. (1982). The variability hypothesis: The history of a biological model of sex differences in intelligence. *Signs: Journal of Women in Culture and Society, 7,* 769–797.

Shields, S. A. (2002). *Speaking from the heart: Gender and the social meaning of emotion.* Cambridge, UK: Cambridge University Press.

Shields, S. A. (2007). Passionate men, emotional women: Psychology constructs gender difference in the late 19th century. *History of Psychology, 10*(2), 92–110.

Shields, S. A. (2008). Gender: An intersectionality perspective. *Sex Roles, 59,* 301–311.

Shor, E., Roelfs, D. J., Bugyi, P., & Schwartz, J. E. (2012). Meta-analysis of marital dissolution and mortality: Reevaluating the intersection of gender and age. *Social Science & Medicine, 75,* 46–59.

Shorey, R. C., Brasfield, H., Febres, J., & Stuart, G. L. (2011). An examination of the association between difficulties with emotion regulation and dating violence perpetration. *Journal of Aggression, Maltreatment & Trauma, 20,* 870–885.

Sidanius, J., & Pratto, F. (1999). *Social dominance: An intergroup theory of social hierarchy and oppression.* Cambridge, UK: Cambridge University Press.

Siever, M. D. (1994). Sexual orientation and gender as factors in socioculturally acquired vulnerability to body dissatisfaction and eating disorders. *Journal of Consulting and Clinical Psychology, 62,* 252–260.

Sigal, J., Gibbs, M. S., Goodrich, C., Rashid, T., Anjum, A., Hsu, D, . . . Wei-Kang, P. (2005). Cross-cultural reactions to academic sexual harassment: Effects of individualist vs. collectivist culture and gender of participants. *Sex Roles, 52,* 201–215.

Signorella, M. L., Bigler, R. S., & Liben, L. S. (1997). A meta-analysis of children's memories for own-sex and other-sex information. *Journal of Applied Developmental Psychology, 18,* 429–445.

Silverstein, L. B., & Auerbach, C. F. (1999). Deconstructing the essential father. *American Psychologist, 54,* 397–407.

Simons, L., Schrager, S. M., Clark, L. F., Belzer, M., & Olson, J. (2013). Parental support and mental health among transgender adolescents. *Journal of Adolescent Health, 53,* 791–793.

Simpson, J. A., Farrell, A. K., Orina, M., & Rothman, A. J. (2015). Power and social influence in relationships. In M. Mikulincer & P. R. Shaver (Eds.), *APA handbook of personality and social psychology* (Vol. 3, pp. 393–420). Washington, DC: American Psychological Association.

Simpson, P. A., & Stroh, L. K. (2004). Gender differences: Emotional expression and feelings of personal inauthenticity. *Journal of Applied Psychology, 89*(4), 715–721.

Sims, C. M., Noel, N. E., & Maisto, S. A. (2007). Rape blame as a function of alcohol presence and resistance type. *Addictive Behaviors, 32,* 2766–2775.

Sin, N. L., & Lyubomirsky, S. (2009). Enhancing well-being and alleviating depressive symptoms with positive psychology interventions: A practice-friendly meta-analysis. *Journal of Clinical Psychology, 65,* 467–487.

Sinozich, S., & Langton, L. (2014). *Rape and sexual assault victimization among college-age females, 1995–2013.* Washington, DC: Bureau of Justice Statistics. Retrieved from http://www.bjs.gov/content/pub/pdf/fvsv9410.pdf

Sirois, M. (2016, August 8). A word of caution on gender reveal parties. *Huffington Post.* Retrieved from http://www.huffingtonpost.com/entry/a-word-of-caution-on-gender-reveal-parties_us_57a8f834e4b08f5371f1d001

Slater, A., & Tiggemann, M. (2015). Media exposure, extracurricular activities, and appearance-related comments as predictors of female adolescents' self-objectification. *Psychology of Women Quarterly, 39,* 375–389.

Small, D. A., Gelfand, M., Babcock, L., & Gettman, H. (2007). Who goes to the bargaining table? The influence of gender and framing on the initiation of negotiation. *Journal of Personality and Social Psychology, 93,* 600–613.

Smirnova, J., & Cai, W. (2015, August 19). See where women outnumber men around the world (and why). *Washington Post*. Retrieved from https://www.washingtonpost.com/news/worldviews/wp/2015/08/19/see-where-women-outnumber-men-around-the-world-and-why

Smith, A. (2010). *The theory of moral sentiments*. London, UK: Alex Murray. Retrieved from http://www.earlymoderntexts.com/assets/pdfs/smith1759.pdf (Original work published 1759)

Smith, B. (2015, May 20). Caster Semenya: "What I dream of is to become Olympic champion." *BBC*. Retrieved from http://www.bbc.com/sport/athletics/32805695

Smith, C. A., Johnston-Robeldo, I., McHugh, M. C., & Chrisler, J. C. (2010). Words matter: The language of gender. In J. C. Chrisler & D. R. McCreary (Eds.), *Handbook of gender research in psychology* (Vol. 1, pp. 361–377). New York, NY: Springer.

Smith, C. A., & Konik, J. (2011). Feminism and evolutionary psychology: Allies, adversaries, or both? An introduction to a special issue. *Sex Roles, 64*, 595–602.

Smith, C. A., Konik, J. A., & Tuve, M. V. (2011). In search of looks, status, or something else? Partner preferences among butch and femme lesbians and heterosexual men and women. *Sex Roles, 64*, 658–668.

Smith, D. (2004, February 7). Love that dare not squeak its name. *New York Times*. Retrieved from http://www.nytimes.com/2004/02/07/arts/love-that-dare-not-squeak-its-name.html

Smith, J. C. S., Vogel, D. L., Madon, S., & Edwards, S. R. (2011). The power of touch: Nonverbal communication within married dyads. *Counseling Psychologist, 39*, 764–787.

Smith, P. H., Kasza, K. A., Hyland, A., Fong, G. T., Borland, R., Brady, K., . . . McKee, S. A. (2015). Gender differences in medication use and cigarette smoking cessation: Results from the International Tobacco Control Four Country Survey. *Nicotine & Tobacco Research, 17*, 463–472.

Snipp, C. M., & Cheung, S. Y. (2016). Changes in racial and gender inequality since 1970. *Annals of the American Academy of Political and Social Science, 663*, 80–98.

Snyder, J. A., Fisher, B. S., Scherer, H. L., & Daigle, L. E. (2012). Unsafe in the camouflage tower: Sexual victimization and perceptions of military academy leadership. *Journal of Interpersonal Violence, 27*, 3171–3194.

Sobal, J. (2005). Men, meat, and marriage: Models of masculinity. *Food and Foodways, 13*, 135–138.

Solnick, S. J. (2001). Gender differences in the Ultimatum Game. *Economic Inquiry, 39*, 189–200.

Sontag, S. (1978). The double standard of ageing. In V. Carver & P. Liddiard (Eds.), *An ageing population* (pp. 72–80). Milton Keynes, UK: Open University Press.

South, S. J. (1991). Sociodemographic differentials in mate selection preferences. *Journal of Marriage and the Family, 53*, 928–940.

South, S. J., & Trent, K. (1988). Sex ratios and women's roles: A cross-national analysis. *American Journal of Sociology, 93*, 1096–1115.

Spearman, C. E. (1904). 'General intelligence' objectively determined and measured. *American Journal of Psychology, 15*, 201–293.

Spelke, E. S. (2005). Sex differences in intrinsic aptitude for mathematics and science? A critical review. *American Psychologist, 60*, 950–958.

Spence, J. T. (1993). Gender-related traits and gender ideology: Evidence for a multifactorial theory. *Journal of Personality and Social Psychology, 64*, 624–635.

Spence, J. T., & Buckner. C. (1995). Masculinity and femininity: Defining the undefinable. In P. J. Kalbfleisch & M. J. Cody (Eds.), *Gender, power, and communication in human relationships* (pp. 105–138). Hillsdale, NJ: Lawrence Erlbaum.

Spence, J. T., & Buckner, C. E. (2000). Instrumental and expressive traits, trait stereotypes, and sexist attitudes: What do they signify? *Psychology of Women Quarterly, 24*, 44–62.

Spence, J., & Helmreich, R. (1972). The Attitudes Toward Women Scale: An objective instrument to measure attitudes toward the rights and roles of women in contemporary society. *JSAS Catalog of Selected Documents in Psychology, 2*, 66.

Spence, J. T., Helmreich, R. L., & Stapp, J. (1974). The Personal Attributes Questionnaire: A measure of sex-role stereotypes and masculinity-femininity. *JSAS Catalog of Selected Documents in Psychology, 4*, 43–44.

Spencer, S. J., Steele, C. M., & Quinn, D. M. (1999). Stereotype threat and women's math performance. *Journal of Experimental Social Psychology, 35*, 4–28.

Spinath, B., Eckert, C., & Steinmayr, R. (2014). Gender differences in school success: What are the roles of students' intelligence, personality and motivation? *Education Research, 56,* 230–243.

Sprecher, S., & Felmlee, D. (1997). The balance of power in romantic heterosexual couples over time from "his" and "her" perspectives. *Sex Roles, 37,* 361–379.

Sprecher, S., & Regan, P. C. (2002). Liking some things (in some people) more than others: Partner preferences in romantic relationships and friendships. *Journal of Social and Personal Relationship, 19,* 463–481.

Sprecher, S., Sullivan, Q., & Hatfield, E. (1994). Mate selection preferences: Gender differences examined in a national sample. *Journal of Personality and Social Psychology, 66,* 1074–1080.

Sprecher, S., & Toro-Morn, M. (2002). A study of men and women from different sides of Earth to determine if men are from Mars and women are from Venus In their beliefs about love and romantic relationships. *Sex Roles, 46,* 131–147.

Stanford sexual assault: Read the full text of the judge's controversial decision. (2016, June 14). *The Guardian.* Retrieved from https://www.theguardian.com/us-news/2016/jun/14/stanford-sexual-assault-read-sentence-judge-aaron-persky

Statistic Brain. (2012). Arranged/forced marriage statistics. Retrieved from http://www.statisticbrain.com/arranged-marriage-statistics

Statistics Canada. (2016). Victims and persons accused of homicide, by age and sex (accused), CANSIM, table 253-0003. *Homicide Survey, Canadian Centre for Justice Statistics.* Retrieved from http://www.statcan.gc.ca/tables-tableaux/sum-som/l01/cst01/legal10b-eng.htm

Stavans, I. (Ed.). (2010). *Quinceañera.* Santa Barbara, CA: Greenwood.

Steinem, G. (1983). *Outrageous acts and everyday rebellions.* New York, NY: Hold, Rinehart, & Winston.

Steiner, M., & Born, L. (2000). Advances in the diagnosis and treatment of premenstrual dysphoria. *CNS Drugs, 13,* 287–304.

Stevenson, M. R., & Black, K. N. (1988). Paternal absence and sex-role development: A meta-analysis. *Child Development, 59,* 793–814.

Stolte, I. G., Dukers, N. H. T. M., Geskus, R. B., Coutinho, R. A., & Wit, J. B. F. (2004). Homosexual men change to risky sex when perceiving less threat of HIV/AIDS since availability of highly active antiretroviral therapy: A longitudinal study. *AIDS, 18,* 303–309.

Stoltenborgh, M., van Ijzendoorn, M. H., Euser, E. M., & Bakermans-Kranenburg, M. J. (2011). A global perspective on child sexual abuse: Meta-analysis of prevalence around the world. *Child Maltreatment, 16,* 79–101.

Stone, E. A., Shackelford, T. K., & Buss, D. M. (2007). Sex ratio and mate preferences: A cross-cultural investigation. *European Journal of Social Psychology, 37,* 288–296.

Stoppard, J. M., & Gunn Gruchy, C. (1993). Gender, context, and expression of positive emotion. *Personality and Social Psychology Bulletin, 19,* 143–150.

Stout, J. G., & Dasgupta, N. (2011). When *he* doesn't mean *you*: Gender-exclusive language as ostracism. *Personality and Social Psychology Bulletin, 36,* 757–769.

Strack, F., Martin, L. L., & Stepper, S. (1988). Inhibiting and facilitating conditions of the human smile: A nonobtrusive test of the facial feedback hypothesis. *Journal of Personality and Social Psychology, 54,* 768–777.

Strand, S., Deary, I. J., & Smith, P. (2006). Sex differences in Cognitive Ability Test scores: A UK national picture. *British Journal of Educational Psychology, 76,* 463–480.

Straus, M. A. (2005). Women's violence toward men is a serious social problem. In D. R. Loseke, R. J. Gelles, & M. M. Cavanaugh (Eds.), *Current controversies on family violence* (pp. 55–78). Thousand Oaks, CA: Sage.

Straus, M. A. (2009). Why the overwhelming evidence on partner physical violence by women has not been perceived and is often denied. *Journal of Aggression, Maltreatment & Trauma, 18,* 552–571.

Stricker, L. J., & Ward, W. C. (2004). Stereotype threat, inquiring about test takers' ethnicity and gender, and standardized test performance. *Journal of Applied Social Psychology, 34,* 665–693.

Strolovitch, D. Z. (2006). Do interest groups represent the disadvantaged? Advocacy at the intersections of race, class, and gender. *Journal of Politics, 68,* 894–910.

Strousma, D. (2014). The state of transgender health care: Policy, law, and medical frameworks. *American Journal of Public Health, 104*(3), e31–e38.

Su, R., Rounds, J., & Armstrong, P. I. (2009). Men and things, women and people: A meta-analysis of sex differences in interests. *Psychological Bulletin, 135,* 859–884.

Suarez, E., & Gadalla, T. M. (2010). Stop blaming the victim: A meta-analysis on rape myths. *Journal of Interpersonal Violence*, 25(11), 2010–2035.

Sue, D. W. (2010). *Microaggressions in everyday life: Race, gender, and sexual orientation*. Hoboken, NJ: John Wiley.

Sue, D. W., Capodilupo, C. M., Torino, G. C., Bucceri, J. M., Holder, A. M. B., Nadal, K. L., & Esquilin, M. (2007). Racial microaggressions in everyday life: Implications for clinical practice. *American Psychologist*, 62, 271–286.

Sullivan, O. (2006). *Changing gender relations, changing families: Tracing the pace of change over time*. Lanham, MD: Rowman and Littlefield.

Summers, L. H. (2005, January 14). *Remarks at NBER Conference on Diversifying the Science & Engineering Workforce*. Retrieved from http://www.harvard.edu/presi dent/speeches/summers_2005/ nber.php

Sunstein, C. (1986). Pornography and the first amendment. *Duke Law Journal*, 4, 589–627.

Susukida, R., Mojtabai, R., & Mendelson, T. (2015). Sex differences in help seeking for mood and anxiety disorders in the National Comorbidity Survey–Replication. *Depression and Anxiety*, 32, 853–860.

Suvilehto, J. T., Glerean, E., Dunbar, R. I. M., Hari, R., & Nummenmaa, L. (2015). Topography of social touching depends on emotional bonds between humans. *Proceedings of the National Academy of Sciences*, 112, 13811–13816.

Swartout, K. M. (2013). The company they keep: How peer networks influence male sexual aggression. *Psychology of Violence*, 3, 157–171.

Swim, J. K. (1994). Perceived versus meta-analytic effect sizes: An assessment of the accuracy of gender stereotypes. *Journal of Personality and Social Psychology*, 66, 21–36.

Swim, J. K., Aikin, K. J., Hall, W. S., & Hunter, B. A. (1995). Sexism and racism: Old-fashioned and modern prejudices. *Journal of Personality and Social Psychology*, 68, 199–214.

Swim, J. K., Eyssell, K. M., Murdoch, E. Q., & Ferguson, M. J. (2010). Self-silencing to sexism. *Journal of Social Issues*, 66, 493–507.

Swim, J. K., & Hyers, L. L. (2009). Sexism. In T D. Nelson (Ed.), *Handbook of prejudice, stereotyping, and discrimination* (pp. 407–430). New York, NY: Psychology Press.

Szymanski, D. M., & Gupta, A. (2009). Examining the relationship between multiple internalized oppressions and African American lesbian, gay, bisexual, and questioning persons' self-esteem and psychological distress. *Journal of Counseling Psychology*, 56, 110–118.

Szymanski, D. M., Kashubeck-West, S., & Meyer, J. (2008). Internalized heterosexism: Measurement, psychosocial correlates, and research directions. *Counseling Psychologist*, 36, 525–574.

Tach, L. M., & Eads, A. (2015). Trends in the economic consequences of marital and cohabitation dissolution in the United States. *Demography*, 52, 401–432.

Taki, Y., Thyreau, B., Kinomura, S., Sato, K., Goto, R., Kawashima, R., & Fukuda, H. (2011). Correlations among brain gray matter volumes, age, gender, and hemisphere in healthy individuals. *PLOS One*, 6(7), e22734.

Talbot, M. (2012, January 2). Stumptown girl: An indie-rock star satirizes hipster culture, on "Portlandia." *New Yorker*. Retrieved from http://www.newy orker.com/magazine/2012/01/02/ stumptown-girl

Tamm, A., Kasearu, K., Tulviste, T., & Trommsdorff, G. (2016). Maternal values and parenting and Estonian, German, and Russian adolescents' friendship satisfaction. *Personal Relationships*, 23, 249–264.

Tamres, L. K., Janicki, D., & Helgeson, V. S. (2002). Sex differences in coping behavior: A meta-analytic review and an examination of relative coping. *Personality and Social Psychology Review*, 6, 2–30.

Taylor, J. K. (2007). Transgender identities and public policy in the United States: The relevance for public administration. *Administration & Society*, 39(7), 833–856.

Tebbe, E., & Moradi, B. (2016). Suicide risk in trans populations: An application of minority stress theory. *Journal of Counseling Psychology*, 63, 520–533.

Techasrivichien, T., Darawuttimaprakorn, N., Punpuing, S., Musumari, P. M., Lukhele, B. W., El-saaidi, C., . . . Kihara, M. (2016). Changes in sexual behavior and attitudes across generations and gender among a population-based probability sample from an urbanizing province in Thailand. *Archives of Sexual Behavior*, 45, 367–382.

Ten years of "X" passports, and no protection from discrimination. (2013, January 12). Retrieved from https://oii.org.au/21597/ten-years-of-x-passports-and-no-protection-fromdiscrimination

Teng, F., You, J., Poon, K.-T., Yang, Y., You, J., & Jiang, Y. (2017). Material-ism predicts young Chinese women's self-objectification and body surveil-lance. *Sex Roles, 76,* 448–459.

Terlecki, M. S., & Newcombe, N. S. (2005). How important is the digital divide? The relation of computer and videogame usage to gender differ-ences in mental rotation ability. *Sex Roles, 53,* 433–441.

Terman, L. M. (1916). *The measure-ment of intelligence: An explanation of and a complete guide for the use of the Stanford revision and extension of the Binet-Simon intelligence scale.* Boston, MA: Houghton Mifflin.

Terman, L. M., & Miles, C. C. (1936). *Sex and personality: Studies in masculinity and femininity.* New York, NY: McGraw-Hill.

Thebaud, S. (2010). Masculin-ity, bargaining, and breadwinning: Understanding men's housework in the cultural context of paid work. *Gender & Society, 24,* 330–354.

Thoits, P. A. (1986). Multiple identi-ties: Examining gender and marital status differences in distress. *Ameri-can Sociological Review, 51,* 259–272.

Thomas, J. R., & French, K. E. (1985). Gender differences across age in motor performance: A meta-analysis. *Psychological Bulletin, 98,* 260–282.

Thomas, K. (2008, July 30). A lab is set to test the gender of some female athletes. *New York Times.* Retrieved from http://www.nytimes.com/2008/07/30/sports/olympics/30gender.html

Thompson-Woolley, H. (1903). *The mental traits of sex: An empirical inves-tigation of the normal mind in men and women.* Chicago, IL: University of Chicago Press.

Thomson Reuters Foundation. (2014, October 31). *Most danger-ous transport systems for women.* Retrieved from http://news.trust.org/spotlight/most-dangerous-transport-systems-for-women/?tab=results

Throckmorton, W. (1998). Efforts to modify sexual orientation: A review of outcome literature and ethical issues. *Journal of Mental Health Coun-seling, 20,* 283–304.

Thurstone, L. L., & Thurstone, T. G. (1941). Factorial studies of intel-ligence. Chicago, IL: University of Chicago Press.

Tiedens, L. Z. (2001). Anger and advancement versus sadness and subjugation: The effect of negative emotion expressions on social status conferral. *Journal of Personality and Social Psychology, 80*(1), 86–94.

Tiefer, L. (1994). The medicalization of impotence: Normalizing phal-locentrism. *Gender and Society, 8,* 363–377.

Tiefer, L. (2006). The Viagra phe-nomenon. *Sexualities, 9,* 273–294.

Tobin, D. D., Menon, M., Menon, M., Spatta, B. C., Hodges, E. E., & Perry, D. G. (2010). The intrapsychics of gender: A model of self-socialization. *Psychological Review, 117,* 601–622.

Tone, A. (2012). Medicalizing repro-duction: The Pill and home preg-nancy tests. *Journal of Sex Research, 49,* 319–327.

Topping, A. (2017, January 15). Half of fathers want less stressful job to help more with child rearing. *The Guardian.* Retrieved from https://www.theguardian.com/lifeandstyle/2017/jan/16/half-of-fathers-want-less-stressful-job-to-help-more-with-child-rearing

Toro-Morn, M., & Sprecher, S. (2003). A cross-cultural compari-son of mate preferences among uni-versity students; the United States vs. the People's Republic of China (PRC). *Journal of Comparative Family Studies, 34,* 151–170.

Travis, C. B., & White, J. W. (Eds.). (2000). *Sexuality, society, and femi-nism: Psychology of women, 4.* Wash-ington, DC: American Psychological Association.

Treas, J., & Drobnic, S. (2010). *Dividing the domestic: Men, women, & household work in cross-national perspective.* Palo Alto, CA: Stanford University Press.

Trent, K., & South, S. J. (2011). Too many men? Sex ratios and women's partnering behavior in China. *Social Forces, 90*(1), 247–267.

Trivers, R. L. (1972). Parental invest-ment and sexual selection. In B. G. Campbell (Ed.), *Sexual selection and the descent of man: 1871–1971* (pp. 136–179). Chicago, IL: Aldine de Gruyter.

Troiano, R. P., Berrigan, D., Dodd, K. W., Masse, L. C., Tilert, T., & McDowell, M. (2007). Physical activ-ity in the United States measured by accelerometer. *Medicine & Science in Sports & Exercise, 40,* 181–188.

Trommsdorff, G., & John, H. (1992). Decoding affective communica-tion in intimate relationships. *Euro-pean Journal of Social Psychology, 22,* 41–54.

Truman, J. L., & Langton, L. (2015, August). *Criminal victimization, 2014* (NCJ Publication No. 248973). Retrieved from https://www.bjs.gov/content/pub/pdf/cv15.pdf

Tsai, J. L., Ang, J. Y. Z., Blevins, E., Goernandt, J., Fung, H. H., Jiang, D., . . . Haddouk, L. (2016). Leaders' smiles reflect cultural differences in ideal affect. *Emotion, 16*(2), 183–195.

Turchik, J. A., & Wilson, S. M. (2010). Sexual assault in the U.S. military: A review of the literature and recommendations for the future. *Aggression and Violent Behavior, 15*, 267–277.

Turkheimer, E., & Halpern, D. F. (2009). Sex differences in variability for cognitive measures: Do the ends justify the genes? *Perspectives on Psychological Science, 4*, 612–614.

Turner, H. A., Finkelhor, D., & Ormrod, R. (2010). Poly-victimization in a national sample of children and youth. *American Journal of Preventative Medicine, 38*, 323–330.

Turner, J. C., Hogg, M. A., Oakes, P. J., Reicher, S. D., & Wetherell, M. S. (1987). *Rediscovering the social group: A self-categorization theory*. Oxford, England: Basil Blackwell.

Turner, N. (2013, May 28). 10 things that American women could not do before the 1970s. *Ms. Magazine Blog*. Retrieved from http://msmagazine.com/blog/2013/05/28/10-things-that-american-women-could-not-do-before-the-1970s

Twenge, J. M. (1997). Changes in masculine and feminine traits over time: A meta-analysis. *Sex Roles, 36*, 305–325.

Twenge, J. M., Campbell, W. K., & Foster, C. A. (2003). Parenthood and marital satisfaction: A meta-analytic review. *Journal of Marriage and Family, 65*, 574–583.

Twenge, J. M., Sherman, R. A., & Wells, B. E. (2015). Changes in American adults' sexual behavior and attitudes, 1972–2012. *Archives of Sexual Behavior, 44*, 2273–2285.

Tylka, T. L., & Sabik, N. J. (2010). Integrating social comparison theory and self-esteem within objectification theory to predict women's disordered eating. *Sex Roles, 63*, 18–31. doi:10.1007/s11199-010-9785-3

Uchino, B. N. (2006). Social support and health: A review of physiological processes potentially underlying links to disease outcomes. *Journal of Behavioral Medicine, 29*, 377–387.

Uecker, J. E., & Regnerus, M. D. (2010). Bare market: Campus sex ratios, romantic relationships, and sexual behavior. *Sociological Quarterly, 51*, 408–435.

Umberson, D., Chen, M. D., House, J. S., & Hopkins, K. (1996). The effect of social relationships on psychological well-being: Are men and women really so different? *American Sociological Review, 61*, 837–857.

UN Women. (2016a). Facts and figures: HIV and AIDS, prevalence and new infections. Retrieved from http://www.unwomen.org/en/what-we-do/hiv-and-aids/facts-and-figures#notes

UN Women. (2016b). Facts and figures: Leadership and political participation. Retrieved from http://www.unwomen.org/en/what-we-do/leadership-and-political-participation/facts-and-figures#sthash.xmalh8Pd.dpuf

UNESCO. (2013). Girls' education — the facts. Retrieved from http:// en.unesco.org/gem-report/sites/gem-report/files/girls-factsheet-en.pdf

UNESCO. (2016, July). *Leaving no one behind: How far on the way to universal primary and secondary education?* (Policy Paper No. 37). Retrieved from http://unesdoc.unesco.org/images/0024/002452/245238E.pdf

Unger, C. A. (2014). Care of the transgender patient: The role of the gynecologist. *American Journal of Obstetrics and Gynecology, 210*, 16–26.

Unger, R. K. (1979). Toward a redefinition of sex and gender. *American Psychologist, 34*(11), 1085–1094.

Unger, R. K. (Ed.). (2001). *Handbook of the psychology of women and gender*. Hoboken, NJ: John Wiley.

Unger, R., & Crawford, M. (1996). *Women and gender: A feminist psychology*. New York, NY: McGraw-Hill.

Upadyaya, K., & Eccles, J. S. (2014). How do teachers' beliefs predict children's interest in math from kindergarten to sixth grade? *Merrill-Palmer Quarterly, 60*(4), 403–430.

U.S. Bureau of Labor Statistics. (2005, January). Labor force statistics from the current population survey: 2004 annual averages—Household data—Tables from employment and earnings. Retrieved from http://www.bls.gov/cps/cps_aa2004.htm

U.S. Bureau of Labor Statistics. (2009, July). *Highlights of women's earnings in 2008*. Washington, DC: U.S. Department of Labor. Retrieved from https://www.bls.gov/opub/reports/womens-earnings/archive/womensearnings_2008.pdf

U.S. Bureau of Labor Statistics. (2015a). *Annual social and economic supplements to the Current Population Survey (CPS): Wives who earn more than their husbands, 1987–2013.* Washington, DC: Author. Retrieved from https://blsmon1.bls.gov/cps/wives-earn-more.htm

U.S. Bureau of Labor Statistics. (2015b). Fatal occupational injuries by worker characteristics and event or exposure, 2015. *Census of fatal occupational injuries.* Washington, DC: U.S. Department of Labor. Retrieved from https://www.bls.gov/iif/oshcfoi1.htm

U.S. Bureau of Labor Statistics. (2015c). *Women in the labor force: A databook, 2015.* Retrieved from https://www.bls.gov/opub/reports/womens-databook/archive/women-in-the-labor-force-a-databook-2015.pdf

U.S. Census Bureau. (2010). *Centenarians: 2010. 2010 Census Special Reports.* Retrieved from https://www.census.gov/prod/cen2010/reports/c2010sr-03.pdf

U.S. Census Bureau. (2012). *Households and families: 2010.* Retrieved from http://www.census.gov/prod/cen2010/briefs/c2010br-14.pdf

U.S. Census Bureau. (2015a). *Estimated median age at first marriage, by sex: 1890 to the present; current population survey.* Washington, DC: Author. Retrieved from http://www.census.gov/hhes/families/data/marital.html

U.S. Census Bureau. (2015b). *Living arrangements of children, Table CH-1.* Retrieved from http://www.census.gov/hhes/families/data/children.html

U.S. Department of Education. (2011). *Writing 2011: National assessment of educational progress at grades 8 and 12.* National Center for Education Statistics. Washington, DC: Government Printing Office. Retrieved from http://www.nationsreportcard.gov/writing_2011/writing_2011_report

U.S. Department of Health and Human Services. (2000). A historical review of efforts to reduce smoking in the United States. In *Reducing tobacco use: A report of the surgeon general* (pp. 29–52). Atlanta, GA: Centers for Disease Control and Prevention.

U.S. Department of Housing and Urban Development. (2015). *The 2015 annual homeless assessment report (AHAR) to Congress.* Retrieved from https://www.hudexchange.info/resources/documents/2015-AHAR-Part-1.pdf

U.S. Department of State. (2016, June). *Trafficking in persons (TIP) report.* Retrieved from https://www.state.gov/documents/organization/258876.pdf

Usdansky, M. L. (2011). The gender-equality paradox: Class and incongruity between work–family attitudes and behaviors. *Journal of Family Theory and Review, 3,* 163–178.

Ussher, J. M., & Perz, J. (2013). PMS as a gendered illness linked to the construction and relational experience of hetero-femininity. *Sex Roles, 68,* 132–150.

Uzzell, D., & Horne, N. (2006). The influence of biological sex, sexuality and gender role on interpersonal distance. *British Journal of Social Psychology, 45,* 579–597.

Vacharkulksemsuk, T., Reit, E., Khambatta, P., Eastwick, P. W., Finkel, E. J., & Carney, D. R. (2016). Dominant, open nonverbal displays are attractive at zero-acquaintance. *Proceedings of the National Academy of Sciences, 113,* 4009–4014.

Vaillancourt-Morel, M.-P., Blais-Lecours, S., Labadie, C., Bergeron, S., Sabourin, S., & Godbout, N. (2017). Profiles of cyberpornography use and sexual well-being in adults. *Journal of Sexual Medicine, 14,* 78–85.

Vainapel, S., Shamir, O. Y., Tenenbaum, Y., & Gilam, G. (2015). The dark side of gendered language: The masculine-generic form as a cause for self-report bias. *Psychological Assessment, 27*(4), 1513–1519.

Valla, J. M., & Ceci, S. J. (2011). Can sex differences in science be tied to the long reach of prenatal hormones? Brain organization theory, digit ratio (2D/4D), and sex differences in preferences and cognition. *Perspectives on Psychological Science, 6,* 134–146.

van Anders, S. M., Steiger, J., & Goldey, K. L. (2015). Effects of gendered behavior on testosterone in women and men. *Proceedings of the National Academy of Sciences, 112*(45), 13805–13810.

van Anders, S. M., Tolman, R. M., & Jainagaraj, G. (2014). Examining how infant interactions influence men's hormones, affect, and aggression using the Michigan Infant Nurturance Simulation Paradigm. *Fathering, 12,* 143–160.

van Engen, M. L., & Willemsen, T. M. (2004). Sex and leadership styles: A meta-analysis of research published in the 1990s. *Psychological Reports, 94,* 3–18.

van Hooff, J. H. (2011). Rationalising inequality: Heterosexual couples' explanations and justifications for the division of housework along traditionally gendered lines. *Journal of Gender Studies, 20,* 19–30.

Van Loo, K. J., & Rydell, R. J. (2014). Negative exposure: Watching another woman subjected to dominant male behavior during a math interaction can induce stereotype threat. *Social Psychological and Personality Science, 5*(5), 601–607.

van Steenbergen, E. F., Ellemers, N., & Mooijaart, A. (2007). How work and family can facilitate each other: Distinct types of work–family facilitation and outcomes for women and men. *Journal of Occupational Health Psychology, 12,* 279–300.

Vandello, J. A., & Bosson, J. K. (2013). Hard won and easily lost: A review and synthesis of theory and research on precarious manhood. *Psychology of Men and Masculinity, 14,* 101–113.

Vandello, J. A., Bosson, J. K., Cohen, D., Burnaford, R. M., & Weaver, J. R. (2008). Precarious manhood. *Journal of Personality and Social Psychology, 95,* 1325–1339.

Vandello, J. A., & Cohen, D. (2003). Male honor and female fidelity: Implicit cultural scripts that perpetuate domestic violence. *Journal of Personality and Social Psychology, 84,* 997–1010.

Vandello, J. A., Cohen, D., Grandon, R., & Franiuk, R. (2009). Stand by your man: Indirect cultural prescriptions for honorable violence and feminine loyalty. *Journal of Cross-Cultural Psychology, 40,* 81–104.

Vandello, J. A., Hettinger, V. E., Bosson, J. K., & Siddiqi, J. (2013). When equal isn't really equal: The masculine dilemma of seeking work flexibility. *Journal of Social Issues, 69,* 303–321.

Vandello, J. A., Ransom, S., Hettinger, V., & Askew, K. (2009). Men's misperceptions about the acceptability and attractiveness of aggression. *Journal of Experimental Social Psychology, 45,* 1209–1219.

VanderLaan, D. P., Ren, Z., & Vasey, P. L. (2013). Male androphilia in the ancestral environment: An ethnological analysis. *Human Nature, 24,* 375–401.

Vasey, P. L. (1993). Homosexual behavior in primates: A review of evidence and theory. *International Journal of Primatology, 16,* 173–204.

Vasey, P. L., & VanderLaan, D. P. (2009). Maternal and avuncular tendencies in Samoa: A comparative study of women, men and fa'afafine. *Human Nature, 20,* 269–281.

Velez, B. L., Campos, I. D., & Moradi, B. (2015). Relations of sexual objectification and racist discrimination with Latina women's body image and mental health. *Counseling Psychologist, 43,* 906–935.

Verma, R. S., & Huq, A. (1987). Sex ratio of children with trisomy 21 or Down syndrome. *Cytobios, 51,* 145–148.

Verna, B. A., Nichols, L. P., Plegue, M. A., Moniz, M. H., Rai, M., & Chang, T. (2016). Advice given by community members to pregnant women: A mixed methods study. *BMC Pregnancy and Childbirth, 16,* 349.

Verweij, K. J. H., Mosing, M. A., Ullén, F., & Madison, G. (2016). Individual difference in personality masculinity-femininity: Examining the effects of genes, environment, and prenatal hormone transfer. *Twin Research and Human Genetics, 19,* 87–96.

Vescio, T. K., Schlenker, K. A., & Lenes, J. G. (2010). Power and sexism. In A. Guinote & T. Vescio (Eds.), *The social psychology of power* (pp. 363–382). New York, NY: Guilford Press.

Viki, G. T., Abrams, D., & Hutchison, P. (2003). The "true" romantic: Benevolent sexism and paternalistic chivalry. *Sex Roles, 49,* 533–537.

Viki, G. T., Abrams, D., & Masser, B. (2004). Evaluating stranger and acquaintance rape: The role of benevolent sexism in perpetrator blame and recommended sentence length. *Law and Human Behavior, 28*(3), 295–303.

Viña, J., Borrás, C., Gambini, J., Sastre, J., & Pallardó, F. V. (2005). Why females live longer than males: Control of longevity by sex hormones. *Science's SAGE KE, 23,* pe17.

Vingerhoets, A., & Scheirs, J. (2000). Sex differences in crying: Empirical findings and possible explanations. In A. H. Fischer (Ed.), *Gender and emotion: Social psychological perspectives* (pp. 143–165). Cambridge, UK: Cambridge University Press.

Violence Against Women Act of 1994/2013, Pub. L. 103-322, 42 U.S.C. §§ 13707–14040.

Voeller, B. (1990). Some uses and abuses of the Kinsey scale. In D. P. McWhirter, S. A. Saunders, & J. Machover Reinisch (Eds.), *Homosexuality-heterosexuality: Concepts of sexual orientation* (pp. 32–38). New York, NY: Oxford University Press.

Vogel, D. L., Wester, S. R., Heesacker, M., & Madon, S. (2003). Confirming gender stereotypes: A social role perspective. *Sex Roles, 48,* 519–528.

Volkmar, F. E., Szatmari, P., & Sparrow, S. S. (1993). Sex differences in pervasive developmental disorders. *Journal of Autism and Developmental Disorders, 23*, 579–591.

Vonk, R., & Ashmore, R. D. (2003). Thinking about gender types: Cognitive organization of female and male types. *British Journal of Social Psychology, 42*, 257–280.

Voyer, D., Postma, A., Brake, B., & Imperato-McGinley, J. (2007). Gender differences in object location memory: A meta-analysis. *Psychonomic Bulletin & Review, 14*, 23–28.

Voyer, D., Voyer, S., & Bryden, M. P. (1995). Magnitude of sex differences in spatial abilities: A meta-analysis and consideration of critical variables. *Psychological Bulletin, 117*, 250–270.

Vrugt, A., & Luyerink, M. (2000). The contribution of bodily posture to gender stereotypic impressions. *Social Behavior and Personality: An International Journal, 28*, 91–103.

Vukasović, T., & Bratko, D. (2015). Heritability of personality: A meta-analysis of behavior genetic studies. *Psychological Bulletin, 141*(4), 769–785.

Wade, C. (2008). Critical thinking: Needed now more than ever. In D. S. Dunn, J. S. Halonen, & R. A. Smith (Eds.), *Teaching critical thinking in psychology: A handbook of best practices* (pp. 11–21). Chichester, West Sussex, UK: Wiley-Blackwell.

Wade, L. D., Kremer, E. C., & Brown, J. (2005). The incidental orgasm: The presence of clitoral knowledge and the absence of orgasm for women. *Women & health, 42*, 117–138.

Wade, T. D., Keski-Rahkonen, A., & Hudson, J. (2011). Epidemiology of eating disorders. In M. Tsuang & M. Tohen (Eds.), *Textbook in psychiatric epidemiology* (3rd ed., pp. 343–360). New York, NY: John Wiley.

Wade, T. J., Auer, G., & Roth, T. M. (2009). What is love: Further investigation of love acts. *Journal of Social, Evolutionary, and Cultural Psychology, 3*, 290–304.

Wadsworth, T. (2016). Marriage and subjective well-being: How and why context matters. *Social Indicators Research, 126*, 1025–1048.

Walby, S., & Allen, J. (2004). *Domestic violence, sexual assault and stalking: Findings from the British Crime Survey*. London, UK: Home Office Research, Development and Statistics Directorate. Retrieved from http://eprints.lancs.ac.uk/3515/1/Domesticviolencefindings_2004_5BritishCrimeSurvey276.pdf

Walker, R. (1992, January/February). Becoming the third wave. *Ms.*, 39–41.

Wallen, K., & Lloyd, E. A. (2011). Female sexual arousal: Genital anatomy and orgasm in intercourse. *Hormones and Behavior, 59*, 780–792.

Wallentin, M. (2009). Putative sex differences in verbal abilities and language cortex: A critical review. *Brain and Language, 108*, 175–183.

Walton, G. M., & Spencer, S. J. (2009). Latent ability: Grades and test scores systematically underestimate the intellectual ability of negatively stereotyped students. *Psychological Science, 20*, 1132–1139.

Wang, M.-H., & Baskin, L. S. (2008). Endocrine disruption, genital development, and hypospadias. *Journal of Andrology, 29*(5), 499–505.

Wang, W., & Parker, K. (2014, September 24). Record share of Americans have never married as values, economics, and gender patterns change. Pew Research Center. Retrieved from http://www.pewsocialtrends.org/2014/09/24/record-share-of-americans-have-never-married

Wang, Y. N. (2016). Balanced authenticity predicts optimal well-being: Theoretical conceptualization and empirical development of the authenticity in relationships scale. *Personality and Individual Differences, 94*, 316–323.

Wardle, J., Haase, A. M., Steptoe, A., Nillapun, M., Jonwutiwes, K., & Bellisle, F. (2004). Gender differences in food choice: The contribution of health beliefs and dieting. *Annals of Behavioral Medicine, 27*, 107–116.

Wasserman, B. D., & Weseley, A. J. (2009). ¿Qué? Quoi? Do languages with grammatical gender promote sexist attitudes? *Sex Roles, 61*, 634–643.

Watson, N. N., & Hunter, C. D. (2015). Anxiety and depression among African American women: The costs of strength and negative attitudes toward psychological help-seeking. *Cultural Diversity and Ethnic Minority Psychology, 21*, 604–612.

Weeden, K. (2005). Is there a flexiglass ceiling? Flexible work arrangements and wages in the United States. *Social Science Research, 34*, 454–482.

Weich, S., Sloggett, A., & Lewis, G. (2001). Social roles and the gender difference in rates of the common mental disorders in Britian: A 7-year, population-based cohort study. *Psychological Medicine, 31*, 1055–1064. doi:10.1017/S0033291701004263

Weichold, K., Silbereisen, R. K., & Schmitt-Rodermund, E. (2003). Short-and long-term consequences of early versus late physical maturation in adolescents. In C. Hayward (Ed.), *Puberty and psychopathology* (pp. 241–276). Cambridge, UK: Cambridge University Press.

Weinrich, J. D., & Klein, F. (2002). Bi-gay, bi-straight, and bi-bi: Three bisexual subgroups identified using cluster analysis of the Klein Sexual Orientation Grid. *Journal of Bisexuality, 2,* 109–139.

Weiss, E. M., Kemmler, G., Deisenhammer, E. A., Fleischhacker, W. W., & Delazer, M. (2003). Sex differences in cognitive functions. *Personality and Individual Differences, 35,* 863–875.

Wellman, J. D., Liu, X., & Wilkins, C. L. (2016). Priming status-legitimizing beliefs: Examining the impact on perceived anti-White bias, zero-sum beliefs, and support for affirmative action among White people. *British Journal of Social Psychology, 55,* 426–437.

Wert, S. R., & Salovey, P. (2004). A social comparison account of gossip. *Review of General Psychology, 8,* 122–137.

Wertz, F. J. (2014). Qualitative inquiry in the history of psychology. *Qualitative Psychology, 1,* 4–16.

West, C., & Zimmerman, D. H. (1987). Doing gender. *Gender & Society, 1,* 125–151.

Weston, K. (2005). *Families we choose: Lesbians, gays, kinship.* New York, NY: Columbia University Press.

What's next for the women's movement? (2017, March 4). *The Guardian.* Retrieved from https://www.theguardian.com/world/2017/mar/05/whats-next-for-the-womens-movement-march-equality

Wheaton, E. M., Schauer, E. J., & Galli, T. V. (2010). Economics of human trafficking. *International Migration, 48,* 114–141.

Whitaker, D. J., Haileyesus, T., Swahn, M., & Saltzman, L. S. (2007). Differences in frequency of violence and reported injury between relationships with reciprocal and nonreciprocal intimate partner violence. *American Journal of Public Health, 97,* 941–947.

Whitam, F. L., & Zent, M. (1984). A cross-cultural assessment of early cross-gender behavior and familial factors in male homosexuality. *Archives of Sexual Behavior, 13,* 427–439.

White, A., de Sousa, B. C., de Visser, R. O., Hogston, R., Madsen, S. A., Makara, P., . . . Zatonski, W. (2011). *The state of men's health in Europe.* Brussels, Belgium: European Commission.

White, S., & Yamawaki, N. (2009). The moderating influence of homophobia and gender-role traditionality on perceptions of male rape victims. *Journal of Applied Social Psychology, 39,* 1116–1136.

White Hughto, J. M., & Reisner, S. L. (2016). A systematic review of the effects of hormone therapy on psychological functioning and quality of life in transgender individuals. *Transgender Health, 1*(1), 21–31.

Whitefield, C. L., Anda, R. F., Dube, S. R., & Felitti, V. J. (2003). Violent childhood experiences and the risk of intimate partner violence in adults: Assessment in a large health maintenance organization. *Journal of Interpersonal Violence, 18,* 166–185.

Whiting, B. B., & Edwards, C. P. (1988). *Children of different worlds: The formation of social behavior.* Cambridge, MA: Harvard University Press.

Whitley, B. E., Nelson, A. B., & Jones, C. J. (1999). Gender differences in cheating attitudes and classroom cheating behavior: A meta-analysis. *Sex Roles, 41,* 657–680.

Whorf, B. L. (1956). The relation of habitual thought and behavior to language. In J. B. Carroll (Ed.), *Language, thought, and reality: Selected writings of Benjamin Lee Whorf* (pp. 134–159). Cambridge, MA: MIT Press.

Widman, L., Olson, M. A., & Bolen, R. M. (2013). Self-reported sexual assault in convicted sex offenders and community men. *Journal of Interpersonal Violence, 28,* 1519–1536.

Wiesemann, C., Ude-Koeller, S., Sinnecker, G. H. G., & Thyen, U. (2010). Ethical principles and recommendations for the medical management of differences of sex development (DSD)/intersex in children and adolescents. *European Journal of Pediatrics, 169*(6), 671–679.

Wilcox, B. L. (1987). Pornography, social science, and politics: When research and ideology collide. *American Psychologist, 42,* 941–943.

Wilkie, J. E. B., & Bodenhausen, G. V. (2012). Are numbers gendered? *Journal of Experimental Psychology: General, 141,* 206–210.

Wilkie, J. R., Ferree, M. M., & Ratcliff, K. S. (1998). Gender and fairness: Marital satisfaction in two-earner couples. *Journal of Marriage and Family, 60,* 577–594.

Williams, D. R., & Jackson, P. B. (2015). Social sources of racial disparities in health. *Health Affairs, 24,* 325–334.

Williams, D. R., Mohammed, S. A., Leavell, J., & Collins, C. (2010). Race, socioeconomic status and health: Complexities, ongoing challenges and research opportunities. *Annals of the New York Academy of Science, 1186,* 69–101.

Williams, D. R., Priest, N., & Anderson, N. B. (2016). Understanding associations among race, socioeconomic status, and health: Patterns and prospects. *Health Psychology, 35,* 407–411.

Williams, J. C. (2010). *Reshaping the work–family debate: Why men and class matter.* Cambridge, MA: Harvard University Press.

Williams, J. C., Berdahl, J. L., & Vandello, J. A. (2016). Beyond work–life integration. *Annual Review of Psychology, 67,* 515–539.

Williams, J. C., & Dempsey, R. (2014). *What works for women at work: Four patterns working women need to know.* New York, NY: New York University Press.

Williams, J. C., Phillips, K., & Hall, E. (2014). *Double jeopardy? Gender bias against women of color in science.* San Francisco, CA: UC Hastings Center for WorkLife Law.

Williams, J. C., Phillips, K., & Hall, E. R. (2015). *Double jeopardy: Gender bias against women in STEM.* University of California Hastings College of Law, Center for WorkLife Law. Retrieved from http://www

.toolsforchangeinstem.org/tools/double-jeopardy-report

Williams, J. E., & Best, D. L. (1990). *Sex and psyche: Gender and self viewed cross-culturally.* Thousand Oaks, CA: Sage.

Williams, M. E., & Fredriksen-Goldsen, K. I. (2014). Same-sex partnerships and the health of older adults. *Journal of Community Psychology, 42,* 558–570.

Williams, P. B. (2015, June 24). Mysterious Islamic tribe where women have sex with different men, don't wear a veil and own property. Retrieved from http://peacebenwilliams.com/mysterious-islamic-tribe-where-women-have-sex-with-different-men-dont-wear-a-veil-and-own-property

Williams, W., & Ceci, S. J. (2015). National hiring experiments reveal 2:1 faculty preference for women on STEM tenure track. *Proceedings of the National Academy of Sciences, 112,* 5360–5365.

Willoughby, B. J., Farero, A. M., & Busby, D. M. (2014). Exploring the effects of sexual desire discrepancy among married couples. *Archives of Sexual Behavior, 43,* 551–562.

Willoughby, B. J., & Vitas, J. (2012). Sexual desire discrepancy: The effect of individual differences in desired and actual sexual frequency on dating couples. *Archives of Sexual Behavior, 41,* 477–486.

Wilson, C. A., & Davies, D. C. (2007). The control of sexual differentiation of the reproductive system and brain. *Reproduction, 133,* 331–359.

Wilson, J. P., Remedios, J. D., & Rule, N. O. (2017). Interactive effects of

obvious and ambiguous social categories on perceptions of leadership: When double-minority status may be beneficial. *Personality and Social Psychology Bulletin, 43,* 888–900.

Wilson, M., & Daly, M. (1985). Competitiveness, risk taking, and violence: The young male syndrome. *Ethology and Sociobiology, 6,* 59–73.

Wilson, M., & Daly, M. (1992). The man who mistook his wife for a chattel. In J. Barkow, L. Cosmides, & J. Tooby (Eds.), *The adapted mind* (pp. 289–322). New York, NY: Oxford University Press.

Wilson, M. I., & Daly, M. (1996). Male sexual proprietariness and violence against wives. *Current Directions in Psychological Science, 5,* 2–7.

Wingood, G. M., & DiClemente, R. J. (2000). Application of the theory of gender and power to examine HIV-related exposures, risk factors, and effective interventions for women. *Health and Education Behavior, 27*(5), 539–565.

Winkler, D., Pjrek, E., & Kasper, S. (2005). Anger attacks in depression: Evidence for a male depressive syndrome. *Psychotherapy and Psychosomatics, 74,* 303–307.

Woelfle, J., Hoepffner, W., Sippell, W. G., Brämswig, J. H., Heidemann, P., Deiß, D., . . . Albers, N. (2002). Complete virilization in congenital adrenal hyperplasia: Clinical course, disease management and disease-related complications. *Clinical Endocrinology, 56,* 231–238.

Wolak, J., Mitchell, K., & Finkelhour, D. (2007). Unwanted and wanted exposure to online pornography in a national sample of youth internet users. *Pediatrics, 119,* 247–257.

Wolff, J. R., Allen, K. D., Himes, H. L., Fish, A. E., & Losardo, J. R. (2014). A retrospective examination of completed sexual and gender minority youth suicides in the United States: What can be learned from written online media? *Journal of Gay & Lesbian Mental Health*, *18*(1), 3–30. doi:10.1080/19359705.2013.827607

Wollstonecraft, M. (1992). *A vindication of the rights of woman*. London, UK: Penguin Books. (Original work published 1792)

Wood, J. T. (2015). *Gendered lives: Communication, gender, and culture* (11th ed.). Stamford, CT: Cengage.

Wood, R. G., Corcoran, M. E., & Courant, P. N. (1993). Pay differences among the highly paid: The male–female earnings gap in lawyers' salaries. *Journal of Labor Economics*, *11*, 417–441.

Wood, W., & Eagly, A. H. (2012). Biosocial construction of sex differences and similarities in behavior. *Advances in Experimental Social Psychology*, *46*, 55–123.

Wood, W., & Eagly, A. H. (2013). Biology or culture alone cannot account for human sex differences and similarities. *Psychological Inquiry*, *24*, 241–247.

Woodin, E. M. (2011). A two-dimensional approach to relationship conflict: Meta-analytic findings. *Journal of Family Psychology*, *25*, 325–335.

Woodley, M. A. (2011). Heterosis doesn't cause the Flynn effect: A critical examination of Mingroni (2007). *Psychological Review*, *118*(4), 689–693.

Woodzicka, J. A., & LaFrance, M. (2001). Real versus imagined gender harassment. *Journal of Social Issues*, *57*, 15–30.

Woolley, H. T. (1910). Psychological literature: A review of the recent literature on the psychology of sex. *Psychological Bulletin*, *7*, 335–342.

World Bank. (2015). Labor force, female (% of total labor force). Retrieved from http://data.worldbank.org/indicator/SL.TLF.TOTL.FE.ZS

World Economic Forum. (2015). *The global gender gap index 2015*. Retrieved from http://reports.weforum.org/global-gender-gap-report-2015/rankings

World Economic Forum. (2016). *The global gender gap report 2016 rankings*. Retrieved from http://reports.weforum.org/global-gender-gap-report-2016/rankings

World Health Organization. (2013). *Global and regional estimates of violence against women: Prevalence and health effects of intimate partner violence and non-partner sexual violence*. Retrieved from http://apps.who.int/iris/bitstream/10665/85239/1/9789241564625_eng.pdf?ua=1

World Health Organization. (2016, November). *Intimate partner and sexual violence against women fact sheet*. Retrieved from: http://www.who.int/mediacentre/factsheets/fs239/en

World Health Organization. (2017a, February). *Female genital mutilation fact sheet*. Retrieved from: http://www.who.int/mediacentre/factsheets/fs241/en

World Health Organization. (2017b). *Global Health Observatory (GHO) data: Life expectancy data by country*. Retrieved from http://apps.who.int/gho/data/view.main.SDG2016LEXv?lang=en

World Health Organization. (2017c). *Global Health Observatory (GHO) data: Obesity*. Retrieved from http://www.who.int/gho/ncd/risk_factors/obesity_text/en

World Heart Federation. (2014). *Global dietary changes threaten health*. Retrieved from: http://www.world-heart-federation.org/what-we-do/awareness/children-youth/fact-sheets/

Worley, T. R., & Samp, J. (2016). Complaint avoidance and complaint-related appraisals in close relationships: A dyadic power theory perspective. *Communication Research*, *43*, 391–413.

Worthington, R. L., Navarro, R. L., Savoy, H. B., & Hampton, D. (2008). Development, reliability, and validity of the Measure of Sexual Identity Exploration and Commitment (MOSIEC). *Developmental Psychology*, *44*, 22–33.

Worthington, R. L., & Reynolds, A. L. (2009). Within-group differences in sexual orientation and identity. *Journal of Counseling Psychology*, *56*, 44–55.

Worthington, R. L., Savoy, H. B., Dillon, F. R., & Vernaglia, E. R. (2002). Heterosexual identity development: A multidimensional model of individual and social identity. *Counseling Psychologist*, *30*, 496–531.

Wright, P. J., Tokunga, R. S., & Kraus, A. (2016). A meta-analysis of pornography consumption and actual acts of sexual aggression in general population studies. *Journal of Communication, 66,* 183–205.

Wright, S. C. (2010). Collective action and social change. In J. F. Dovidio, M. Hewstone, P. Glick, & V. M. Esses (Eds.), *Handbook of prejudice, stereotyping, and discrimination* (pp. 577–595). Thousand Oaks, CA: Sage.

Wyatt, G. E., Davhana-Maselesele, M., Zhang, M., Wong, L. H., Nicholson, F., Der Sarkissian, A., . . . Myers, H. F. (2017). A longitudinal study of the aftermath of rape among rural South African women. *Psychological Trauma: Theory, Research, Practice, and Policy, 9,* 309–316.

Xue, B., Johnson, A. K., & Hay, M. (2013). Sex differences in angiotensin II- and aldosterone-induced hypertension: The central protective effects of estrogen. *American Journal of Physiology, 305,* 459–463.

Yamawaki, N., Ostenson, J., & Brown, C. R. (2009). The functions of gender role traditionality, ambivalent sexism, injury, and frequency of assault on domestic violence perception. *Violence Against Women, 15*(9), 1126–1142.

Yan, X., Wang, M., & Zhang, Q. (2012). Effects of gender stereotypes on spontaneous trait inferences and the moderating role of gender schematicity: Evidence from Chinese undergraduates. *Social Cognition, 30,* 220–231.

Yang, C. Y., Decety, J., Lee, S., Chen, C., & Cheng, Y. (2009). Gender differences in the mu rhythm during empathy for pain: An electroencephalographic study. *Brain Research, 1251,* 176–184.

Yang, G. S., Huesmann, L. R., & Bushman, B. J. (2014). Effects of playing a violent video game as male versus female avatar on subsequent aggression in male and female players. *Aggressive Behavior, 40,* 537–541.

Yap, M., & Konrad, A. M. (2009). Gender and racial differentials in promotions: Is there a sticky floor, a mid-level bottleneck, or a glass ceiling? *Industrial Relations, 64,* 593–619.

Yodanis, C. L. (2004). Gender inequality, violence against women, and fear: A cross-national test of the feminist theory of violence against women. *Journal of Interpersonal Violence, 19,* 655–675.

Yoffe, E. (2015, September 24). The problem with campus sexual assault surveys. *Slate.* Retrieved from http://www.slate.com/articles/double_x/doublex/2015/09/aau_campus_sexual_assault_survey_why_such_surveys_don_t_paint_an_accurate.html

York, E. A. (2008). Gender differences in the college and career aspirations of high school valedictorians. *Journal of Advanced Academics, 19,* 578–600.

Yousaf, O., Popat, A., & Hunter, M. S. (2015). An investigation of masculinity attitudes, gender, and attitudes toward psychological help-seeking. *Psychology of Men & Masculinity, 16,* 234–237.

Zahn-Waxler, C., Shirtcliff, E. A., & Marceau, K. (2008). Disorders of childhood and adolescence: Gender and psychopathology. *Annual Review of Clinical Psychology, 4,* 275–303.

Zaidi, A. U., & Shuraydi, M. (2002). Perceptions of arranged marriages by young Pakistani Muslim women living in a Western society. *Journal of Comparative Family Studies, 33,* 495–514.

Zell, E., Krizan, Z., & Teeter, S. R. (2015). Evaluating gender similarities and differences using metasynthesis. *American Psychologist, 70,* 10–20.

Zentner, M., & Eagly, A. H. (2015). A sociocultural framework for understanding partner preferences of women and men: Integration of concepts and evidence. *European Review of Social Psychology, 26,* 328–373.

Zietsch, B. P., Morley, K. I., Shekar, S. N., Verweij, K. H., Keller, M. C., Macgregor, S., . . . Martin, N. G. (2008). Genetic factors predisposing to homosexuality may increase mating success in heterosexuals. *Evolution and Human Behavior, 29,* 424–433.

Zillmann, D., & Weaver, J. B. (1989). Pornography and men's sexual callousness toward women. In D. Zillmann & J. Bryant (Eds.), *Pornography: Research advances and policy considerations* (pp. 95–125). Hillsdale, NJ: Lawrence Erlbaum.

Zimmer-Gembeck, M. J., & Collins, W. A. (2003). Autonomy development during adolescence. In G. R. Adams & M. D. Berzonsky (Eds.), *Blackwell handbook of adolescence* (pp. 175–204). Malden, MA: Blackwell.

Zimmerman, D., & West, C. (1975). Sex roles, interruptions and silences in conversations. In B. Thorne & N. Henley (Eds.), *Language and sex: Difference and dominance* (pp. 105–129). Rowley; MA: Newbury House.

Zinzow, H. M., & Thompson, M. (2015). A longitudinal study of risk factors for repeated sexual coercion and assault in U.S. college men. *Archives of Sexual Behavior, 44,* 213–222.

Zivony, A., & Lobel, T. (2014). The invisible stereotypes of bisexual men. *Archives of Sexual Behavior, 43,* 1165–1176.

Zucker, A. N. (2004). Disavowing social identities: What it means when women say, "I'm not a feminist, but . . ." *Psychology of Women Quarterly, 28,* 423–435.

Zuk, M. (2009). The sicker sex. *PLOS Pathogens, 5,* e1000267.

Zuk, M., & McKean, K. A. (1996). Sex differences in parasite infections: Patterns and processes. *International Journal of Parasitology, 26,* 1009–1024.

Index

AAU (Association of American Universities) report on sexual assault, 478
achievement motivation, 242
acid attacks, 501
acronyms, 29
activism
  feminisms, 21–25
  gay rights movements, 27
  intersectionality, 30
  men's movements, 26–27
  transgender movement, 27–29
  women's movements, 17–21
adolescence
  puberty, 131–133
  relationships, 133–136
  self-concepts, 136–137
adulthood
  cultural ideals of, 137–139
  emerging adulthood, 133
affirmative action, 209
agency, 152–153, 472
  See also gender stereotypes
agender, defined, 9
aggression
  confluence model of sexual aggression, 499
  defined, 478
  explanation for, 499–505
  forms of, 485–499
  microaggressions, 206
  and pornography, 505–508
  relational aggression, 265, 479, 483
  sex differences in, 479–485
  and testosterone, 6, 500
aggressive pornography, 505–506

aging, double standard of aging, 141–142
AIS (androgen insensitivity syndrome), 88–89
alcohol abuse, 420–421
alleles, 237
alliance formation hypothesis, *309*, 312
allies, 214
Ambivalence Toward Men Inventory (AMI), 199–200, 202
Ambivalent Sexism Inventory (ASI), 198, 202
ambivalent sexism theory, 184
American Psychological Association, 259
Anaxagoras, 84–85
androcentrism, 63
androgyny
  defined, 8
  and health, 11
antigen, 312
Armstrong, Lance, 91
aromantic individuals, 298
arranged marriage, 349–350
As Nature Made Him: The Boy Who Was Raised as a Girl (Colapinto), 94
asexual
  defined, 11
  label of, 10
  sexual identitification of, 298
ASI (Ambivalent Sexism Inventory), 198, 202
Association of American Universities (AAU) report on sexual assault, 478
athletes, 14, 75–77, 91–92
attachment, 299
attachment theory, 363

Attitudes Toward Women Scale (AWS), 201
attraction, role of sex and gender in, 339–346
attributional ambiguity, 210
audience problem, 337
autism spectrum disorders autism spectrum disorders, 237
autonomous marriages, 350

babies, 113
balanced authenticity, 473
battered wives, 485–488
Baumeister, Roy, 322
Becker, Anne, 462
"Becoming the Third Wave" article (Walker), 21
bedarche, *90*
behavioral genetics, *309*
Bem, Sandra, 292, 298
Bem Sex-Role Inventory (BSRI), 46
Benatar, David, 190
benevolent sexism, 196–199
Berdahl, Jennifer, 386, 499
between-group variance, 60
biases
  implicit physician biases, 427
  against men, 385–386
  prove-it-again bias, 382
  publication bias, 42
  in sex difference research, 63–65
  tightrope bias, 383
  against women, 382–383
  See also gender discrimination
Bieber, Irving, 296
Biernat, Monica, 193
Big Five personality dimensions, 173–174
bigender, defined, 9–10
Binet, Alfred, 226

binge drinking, 421
biobehavioral model,
    310, 314
biological factors of gender, 6
biological sex, idea of, 6–7
biosocial constructionist theory,
    100, 103–107, 170–171
biparental care, 300–301
Birkenhead drill, 184
birth, 436–439
    See also parenting
bisexual
    defined, 10
    stereotypes, 164
Bodenhausen, Galen, 13
body image disorders,
    psychological health,
    458–465
body mass index
    (BMI), 423
body posture,
    273–274
Bogaert, Anthony, 298
Bonds, Barry, 91
Bonobo chimpanzees, 185–186
Boy Scouts of America, 4
boys
    body image, 458
    See also men
brain structure, 98–100, 224–226
Bridges, Ana, 506
Broca's Brain: Reflections on the
    Romance of
    Science (Sagan), 44
Brownstein, Carrie, 299
BSRI (Bem Sex-Role
    Inventory), 46
bullying, 483
Burns, Ursula, 157

CAH (congenital adrenal
    hyperplasia), 88
CAIS (complete androgen
    insensitivity syndrome), 6, 88
calabi, 90
Calkins, Mary Whiton, 21
callous-unemotional
    (CU) traits, 454

Calment, Jeanne, 408
Caspi, Avshalom, 78
Cesarean section (C-section)
    procedures, 436–437
Chand, Dutee, 76
child marriage, 503–504
childbirth, 436–439
    See also parenting
childcare, 375
child-free by choice, 361
children, gender-nonconforming,
    127–131
chosen families, 338
chromosomes, 81–82, 87–88
cisgender
    defined, 9
    privilege, 15
Clinton, Hillary Rodham, 4, 262
CNM (consensual
    nonmonogamy), 350–351
code switching, 268–269
cognitive abilities
    overview, 222–224
    biopsychosocial model of, 238
    brain structure, 224–226
    dualism, 224, 226
    Flynn effect, 226–227
    influences on, 237–242
    intelligence quotient (IQ),
        226–227
    phrenology, 225–226
    quantitative performance,
        231–232
    relevance of, 242–250
    stereotypes, 173
    variability of, 235–237
    verbal performance, 228–231
    visual-spatial performance,
        232–235
Colapinto, John, 94
collective action, 212
collectivistic cultures, 177–178
Collins, Patricia, 10
Combahee River Collective,
    159–160
communication
    intersectionality in, 268–269
    stereotypes, 174

communion, 152, 472
companionate love, 300
complete androgen insensitivity
    syndrome (CAIS), 6, 88
comradeships, 335
conflict, 355–358
    See also divorce
confluence model of sexual
    aggression, 499
Confronting Prejudiced Responses
    Model, 210–211
congenital adrenal hyperplasia
    (CAH), 88
Conley, Terri, 156, 164, 315–317
consensual nonmonogamy
    (CNM), 350–351
consent, 489
Constantinople, Anne,
    11, 46
conversion therapies, 295–296
Coontz, Stephanie, 332
Cooper, Marianne, 397
correlational designs, 52
Cover the Athlete campaign, 14
Cox, Laverne, 4
cranioscopy,
    225–226
Crawford, Mary, 56
critical thinking, 31–32
Crosby, Faye, 210
cross-sex friendships, 134,
    336–337
    See also friendships
crying, 278
    See also emotions
C-section (Cesarean section)
    procedures, 436–437
CU (callous-unemotional)
    traits, 454
Cuddy, Amy, 177
cultural ideologies, 190–191
cultural/difference feminism, 23
    See also feminisms
cultures
    cognitive abilities context,
        177–178
    different cultures approach, 262
    gender stereotypes across, 154

honor cultures, 501
individualistic vs. collectivistic, 177–178
Curie, Marie, 250
cyberbullying, 483
Cyrus, Miley, 299

d statistics, 58
DA (dopamine), 299–300, 455
Darwin, Charles, 223, 283–284
dating, 134–136, 344–346
dating scripts, 344
death, 410–413
Deaux, Kay, 9–10
Defense of Marriage Act (DOMA), 332
degendering theory, 140
demand-withdraw pattern, 358
dendrites, 225
Denton, Denice, 222
dependent variables, 47–49
depression, 456–457
Diagnostic and Statistical Manual of Mental Disorders (DSM), 446–448
Diamond, Lisa, 301, 314–315, 322
Diekman, Amanda, 247
diet, 421, 429
differences,sex, research on, 38–43
differences/or disorders/of sex development (DSDs), 86
different cultures approach, 262
diminutives, 260
direct aggression, 479
direction accuracy, 172
discrepancy accuracy, 172
discrimination
    gender discrimination, 205–214
    and health care, 429–434
    institutional, 467
    LGBT individuals, 466

display rules, 277
divorce, 190, 358–359
documentation, gender options on, 12
DOMA (Defense of Marriage Act), 332
domestic labor, 376–378
dominance. *See* power
dominant groups, 16–17
dopamine (DA), 299–300, 455
double jeopardy hypothesis, 192–195
double standard of aging, 141–142
double standards, 344–345
dowry deaths, 501
DSDs (differences/or disorders/of sex development), 86
DSM (Diagnostic and Statistical Manual of Mental Disorders), 446–448
dualism, 224, 226
dyadic power, 186–188
dyslexia, 237

Eagly, Alice, 6
eating and body image disorders, role of sex and gender in, 458–465
effect sizes, 57–63
effort-based learning, 243
effortful control, 454
electroencephalogram (EEG) technology, 286
Eliot, George, 256
Eliot, Lise, 99
Ellis, Havelock, 310
emerging adulthood, 133
emotional contagions, 284
emotional infidelity, 355
emotional intelligence, 286
emotional investment, 345–346
emotional restraint, 335
emotions
    expression of, 280

role of sex and gender in, 277–286
empathy, 283–286
encoding accuracy, 282
epigenetics, 79
Equal Pay Day, 388
equality, 17, 18, 208
equity, 17, 18, 352–354
erectile dysfunction, 325
erotica, 505–506
essentialism, 67
essentialist beliefs, 362
estradiol, 311
ethnic identity, 463
Evans, Mary Ann, 256
evolutionary psychology, 100–103, 168–169
ex post facto designs, 50
expansion hypothesis, 399, 451
experiments, 47–48
externalizing disorders, 439, 446, 453–458
eye contact, 271–272

fa'afafine, 77, *90*, 298
Facebook, 265–266
factor analysis, 227
fakaleiti, 268–269
false rape allegations, 494
familism, 134, 298
family leave policies, 400–402
family relationships, role of sex and gender in, 359–364
family roles, and work, 398–402
Fausto-Sterling, Anne, 6, 76
fecundity hypothesis, *310*, 313
feedback, sensitivity to, 242
female deficit model, 63
female genital mutilation, 503–504
female-to-male (FtM) individuals, 97
feme covert, 346
The Feminine Mystique (Friedan), 21

femininity
    conceptualizations of, 46–47
    defined, 11–12
feminisms
    and evolutionary
        psychology, 103
    types of, 21–25
    See also women's movements
feminization of poverty, 431, 481
file drawer problem, 42
Fischer, Agneta, 282
Fiske, Susan, 184
flexible work arrangements,
    399–402
Flynn effect, 226–227
food deserts, 429
force, 188–189
fraternal birth order effect, *309,*
    311–312
Freud, Sigmund, 295,
    311, 315
Friedan, Betty, 21
friends with benefits relationships
    (FWBs), 337–338, 345
    See also friendships
friendships, role of sex and gender
    in, 134–136, 334–339
FtM (female-to-male)
    individuals, 97
functional magnetic resonance
    imaging (fMRI), 98, 225, 286

gait, 274–275
Gall, Franz Joseph,
    224–225
gay
    defined, 10
    stereotypes, 163–164
gay rights movements, 27
GD (gender diagnosticity)
    score, 47
gender
    complexity of, 11–16
    defined, 6
    influence of, 14
    and leadership,
        379–380
    use of term, 5

gender asymmetry perspective,
    487–488
gender binary, defined, 6
gender confirmation procedures,
    96–97
gender development, theories of,
    113–127
gender diagnosticity (GD)
    score, 47
gender discrimination, 205–214
gender dysphoria, 29, 94–95,
    447–448
gender equality, 208
gender expression, use of term, 5
gender fluid
    defined, 9–10
    sexual identitification
        of, 299
gender harassment, 496
gender identity
    overview, 9–10
    defined, 9
    nature vs.
        nurture debate, 86–92
    theory of, 9
    use of term, 5
gender intensification hypothesis,
    133, 450
gender minorities, psychological
    health, 465–468
gender norms, flipping, 14
gender paradox of suicide,
    457–458
gender prescriptions, 165
gender proscriptions, 165
gender role attitudes,
    use of term, 5
gender role ideology
    hypothesis, 377
gender roles, use of term, 5
gender socialization practices,
    140–141
gender stereotypes
    accuracy of, 172–177
    across cultures, 154
    across multiple domains,
        174–175
    agency, 152–153

biosocial constructionist
    theory, 170–171
cognitive
    stereotypes, 173
communion, 152–153
components of,
    150–151
consequences of,
    165–168
defined, 148
evolutionary psychology,
    168–169
intersectionality,
    159–163
nonverbal and verbal
    communication
    stereotypes, 174
origins, 168–171
personality stereotypes,
    173–174
prototypes, 162
sexual orientation stereotypes,
    163–164
social role theory,
    169–170
status incongruity hypothesis,
    165–166
stereotype content model,
    152–153
subgroups, 158–159
think manager-think male
    effect, 156–157
transgender
    stereotypes, 163
universality of, 177–178
use of term, 5
women-are-wonderful effect,
    155–156
gender symmetry perspective,
    487–488
gender traits, use of term, 5
gender wage gap, 386–398
gender-fair research designs,
    67–68
gender-inclusive depression
    scale, 456
gender-nonconforming children,
    127–131

genderqueer, defined, 9
gene-by-environment interactions, 78–79
generalizability, 55
generalizations, 149–150
    See also gender stereotypes
generic beliefs, vs. statistical beliefs, 176–177
generic masculine, 257–258
genes, 78, 87
genetics, 79, 413
genital reconstructive surgery (GRS), 12, 96, 321
genital ridge, 82
genital tubercle, 83
genitalia, 82–83
Gerber, Henry, 27
glass ceiling, 381
glass cliff effect, 381–382
Glick, Peter, 184
Global Gender Gap Index, 207
gonads, 82
Goode, William, 399
Gottman, John, 355–357
grammatical gender, 260
Gray, John, 262
greater male variability hypothesis, 236–237
guevedoces, 89
Guimond, Serge, 137

HAARTs (highly active antiretroviral therapies), 418–419
Haley, Charles, 444, 469
Halpern, Diane, 66
Hannah, Lucy, 408
happiness, 470–473
Harris, Christine, 357
health
    and androgyny, 11
    biological factors affecting, 413–416
    and longevity, 415–416
    social factors affecting, 416–428

health care
    accessing, 425–427
    and discrimination, 429–434
hegemonic masculinity, 17, 139
Helgeson, Vicki, 423–424
heritability estimates, 95
Herman, Tom, 4
Hermaphroditus, 87
heteronormative assumptions, 164
heterosexual
    defined, 11
    label of, 10
    privilege, *15*
heterosexuality
    etymology of, 293
    use of term, 294
hierarchical social structures, 16–17, 184–186
    See also matriarchal societies; patriarchal societies
highly active antiretroviral therapies (HAARTs), 418–419
hijras, 8, 77, *90*
HIV (human immunodeficiency virus), 418–419
Hochschild, Arlie, 373
homelessness, 466–467
homophobia, 298–299, 335, 467–468
Homosexualität, use of term, 293
homosexuality
    etymology of, 293
    as a psychological disorder, 27
    use of term, 294
homosocial perspective, 335
honor cultures, 501
honor killings, 501
hookups, 320, 345
Hopkins, Nancy, 222
hormones
    estradiol, 311
    human growth hormones, 91
    influences of, 415
    and sex differentiation, 82–83
    and sexual orientation, 311
    testosterone, 6, 311, 500

hostile sexism, 196–199
human growth hormones, 91
human immunodeficiency virus (HIV), 418–419
human trafficking, 504–505
Hunter, Tyra, 27, 434
Hyde, Janet, 228, 231
hyperandrogenism, 88
hypotheses, 44

I3 theory, 504–505
IAAF (International Association of Athletics Federations), 76
ICE (Intersex Campaign for Equality), 29
ikumen project, 376
implicit physician biases, 427
impulsivity, 454
independent variables, 47–48
indirect aggression, 479
individualistic cultures, 177–178
inequality
    representation between women and men, 208
    structures of, 16–17
infants, 113
intelligence, 173, 223, 226–227
    See also cognitive abilities
interaction effects, 51
interdisciplinary psychological approach, 30–31
interest-based learning, 243
internalized homophobia, 298–299, 467–468
internalized transphobia, 467–468
internalizing disorders, 439, 446, 448–452
International Association of Athletics Federations (IAAF), 76
International Classification of Diseases and Related Health Problems (ICD), 446, 448

interpersonal attraction, role of sex and gender in, 339–346
intersectional invisibility hypothesis, 193–195
intersectionality
    overview, 10
    in communication, 268–269
    defined, 11
    and eating disorders among women, 463–464
    and gender stereotypes, 159–163
    and help-seeking, 469–470
    and power, 192–195
Intersex Campaign for Equality (ICE), 29
intersexual selection, 101
intersexuality
    overview, 6
    defined, 7, 76
    optimal sex or optimal gender, 92–93
    and sex differentiation, 86–92
intimate partner violence, 485–488
intimate terrorism, 486
intrasexual selection, 101
invisibility, 193–195
It Gets Better Project, 131

Jacklin, Carol Nagy, 39
jealousy, 355–357, 500–501
jobs, gendered division of, 104–105, 141
Jones, Susannah Mushatt, 408
Jorgenson, Christine (born George), 447
Jorm, Anthony, 228
Jussim, Lee, 176
justice, and privilege, 494–495

karojisatsu, 397
kathoey, 77, 90
Kaufman, Michelle, 56
kawe-kawe, 90

Keenan, Sara Kelly, 12
Kellogg, John Harvey, 438
Kertbeny, Karl-Maria, 293
kibbutzim, 428
Kiernan, James, 293, 297
Kimmel, Michael, 139
kin selection theory, 310, 312
Kinsey, Alfred, 297, 323
Klinefelter syndrome, 12, 87
Knauss, Sarah, 408
Koenig, Anne, 157
Koppel, Moshe, 256
Krafft-Ebing, Richard von, 310
Kuntzman, Gersh, 292
kwolu-aatmwol, 90

labor divisions, 371–372
labor market, gendered division of, 104–105, 141
ladyboys, 77
laissez-faire leadership style, 380
language
    outdated, 294
    pronouns, 9, 65, 257–258
    and social perception, 257–262
Latino paradox, 410
leadership, and gender, 379–380
Ledbetter, Lilly, 390
leftover women, 187
lesbians
    defined, 10
    stereotypes, 163–164
LGBT individuals
    defined, 26
    discrimination of, 466
    friendships, 338
    homelessness, 466–467
    physical health of, 431–434
    teens, 131
    victimization of, 466
liberal feminism, 23
    See also feminisms

life expectancy, changes in, 409–410
linguistic relativity hypothesis. See Whorfian hypothesis
Lippa, Richard, 47
Livingston, Robert, 281
longevity, and health, 415–416
Lorber, Judith, 14
love, 299
love marriages, 350
lust, 299

Maccoby, Eleanor, 39
MacFarlane, Alex, 12
MacNell, Lillian, 148
magnetic resonance imaging (MRI), 98
mahuwahine, 298
male discrepancy stress, 502
male gaze, 465–466
male privilege, 15, 494–495
male-to-female (MtF) individuals, 97
Maloney, Erin, 243
manhood, cultural ideals of, 137–139
mansplaining, 207
manspreading, 273–274
marriage
    contemporary relationships, 347–351
    Defense of Marriage Act (DOMA), 332
    history of, 346–347
    and power, 190
Marshall, Brandon, 444, 469
masculine generic, 65
masculinity
    conceptualizations of, 46–47
    defined, 11–12
    hegemonic masculinity, 139
mastectomy, 96
Master, Allison, 248
masturbation, 321
mate preferences, 339–342
mate selection, 342–343
maternal gatekeeping, 378
maternal wall, 382

matriarchal societies, 16, 184–186
matrilineal societies, 185
matrilocal society, 186
Matsick, Jes, 164
maximalist approach, 40–41
May-Welby, Norrie, 12
McGwire, Mark, 91
McIntosh, Peggy, 14
Mead, Margaret, 185
media, role in objectification
    theory, 461–462
medicalization, of reproductive
    health, 434–439
medicalization of sexuality,
    325–326
members of the LGB community,
    use of term, 294
men
    Ambivalence Toward Men
        Inventory (AMI),
        199–200, 202
    biases against, 385–386
    and emotions, 278–280
    erectile dysfunction, 325
    greater male variability
        hypothesis, 236–237
    health care, 426
    and intimate partner violence,
        487–488
    men's movements, 26–27
    physical health of, 412–413
    psychological health of,
        456–457
    risk networks, 418–419
    sex drive of, 318–319
    sexism against, 204–205
    and women's movements,
        24–25
    See also boys
Men Are From Mars, Women Are
    From Venus (Gray 1992), 262
menopause, 325
mental illness. See psychological
    health
mental rotation ability, 234
meritocracy, 209
meta-analyses, 57–63
metoidioplasty, 96

M-F Test, 46
microaggressions, 206
    See also gender discrimination
Miles, Catharine Cox, 46
milestone models of sexual
    identity development,
    306–308
minimalist approach, 40–41
minority stress theory, 431, 466
mirror neurons, 284–285
mixed methods approach, 56–57
modern sexism, 201–202
Money, John, 93
Monteith, Margo, 16
morbidity, 410–413
morbidity-mortality paradox, 411
mortality, 410–413
motherhood mandate, 138
motherhood penalty, 396
MRI (magnetic resonance
    imaging), 98
MS (Modern Sexism) scale, 201
MtF (male-to-female)
    individuals, 97
Mulac, Anthony, 256
muscle dysmorphia, 464–465
mustergil, 8, 90
myth of matriarchy, 185

nadleehe, 90
Naipaul, V. S., 256
National Organization for Men
    Against Sexism (NOMAS), 26
natural selection, 101
nature
    and the brain, 99–100
    vs. nurture, 78–79
need to belong, 333
neurohormonal theory, 309
neuroplasticity, 99
neurosexism, 100
neuroticism, 452
newborn babies, 113
Nicholson, Linda, 18
Nolen-Hoeksema, Susan, 450
NOMAS (National
    Organization for Men
    Against Sexism), 26

nonbinary identification,
    examples, 8, 77, 90
nonverbal communication
    role of sex and gender in,
        270–276
    stereotypes, 174
Nordic paradox, 503
norepinephrine, 300
Normalsexualit't, use of term, 293
nurture, vs. nature, 78–79
Nyborg, Helmuth, 222, 227

Obama, Barack, 281
obesity, 423
objectification theory, 460–462
occupational feminization,
    393–394
occupational masculinization, 394
occupational segregation, 391
office housework, 390
old boys' networks, 381
O'Neal, Shaquille, 91
optimal sex or optimal gender,
    92–93
orgasm frequency, 319–322
orgasm gap, 320
outliers, 235
overweight, 423
overwork, 397
oxytocin, 273

Paine, Thomas, 259
pair-bonding system, 300–301
PAIS (partial androgen
    insensitivity syndrome), 88
pansexual
    defined, 11
    label of, 10
pansexual individuals, 298
PAQ (Personal Attributes
    Questionnaire), 46
parental investment theory,
    101–102, 315, 341
parental rejection, 466
parenting, role of sex and gender
    in, 359–364
parents, relationships with,
    133–134

partial androgen insensitivity syndrome (PAIS), 88
participant variables, 50
partner homogamy, 342–343
passionate friendships, 314, 338–339
passionate love, 299
paternalistic chivalry, 344
paternity uncertainty, 355
patriarchal societies, 16, 184–186
patrilineal societies, 185
patrilocal society, 185
Personal Attributes Questionnaire (PAQ), 46
personal space, 272
personality stereotypes, 173–174
person-by-treatment designs, 50–51
PFC (prefrontal cortex), 454–455
phalloplasty, 96
phase models of sexual identity development, 304–307
Phelps, Michael, 91
phrenology, 225–226
physical aggression, defined, 478–479
Pinker, Steven, 226
Planet 50-50 by 2030: Step It Up for Gender Equality initiative, 4
plasticity, 99
PMS (premenstrual syndrome), 436–439
Poehler, Amy, 23
point-light display, 275
political correctness, 257
polyamory, 351–352
polyandry, 350
polygyny, 350
polysexual
    defined, 11
    label of, 10
polyvictimization, 490
positivism, 66–67
postpartum depression, 360
postpositivism, 66–67
poverty, 141, 431, 481

power
    and cultural ideologies, 190–191
    double jeopardy hypothesis, 192–195
    exertion of, 188–191
    and force, 188–189
    intersectional invisibility hypothesis, 193–195
    and privilege, 192
    and resource control, 190
    structural vs. dyadic, 186–188
    structures of, 16–17
    See also sexism
power distance, 498–499
power poses, 273–274
precarious manhood hypothesis, 139
prefrontal cortex (PFC), 454–455
pregnancy, 436–439
    See also parenting
premenstrual syndrome (PMS), 436–439
privilege, 14–16, 192, 494–495
Project 375, 444
Promise Keepers, 26
pronouns
    gender-neutral, 9
    generic masculine, 257–258
    masculine generic, 65
    See also language
Protestant work ethic, 203
prototypes, 162
prove-it-again bias, 382
pseudoscience, 225–226
psychological disorder (or mental illness) definition, defined, 446
psychological health
    overview, 445–448
    eating and body image disorders, 458–465
    externalizing disorders, 453–458
    happiness and well-being, 470–473
    help-seeking, 468–470

internalizing disorders, 448–452
    psychological disorder (or mental illness) definition, 446
    sexual and gender minorities, 465–468
    stigma surrounding, 444
The Psychology of Sex Differences (Maccoby and Jacklin), 39
puberty
    development in, 131–133
    relationships, 133–136
    self-concepts, 136–137
    sex differentiation, 84
    transition to young adulthood, 131–133
publication bias, 42

qualitative research methods, 54–55
quantitative performance, 231–232
quantitative research methods, 47–54
quasi-experiments, 50–51
queen bee syndrome, 383

radical feminism, 23
    See also feminisms
random assignments, 48–49
rank-order accuracy, 174
rape, 488–495
rape myths, 491–492
Reimer, David, 94
rejection, 466
relational aggression, 265, 479, 483
relationships, with parents, 133–134
relative income hypothesis, 377
reproductive health, medicalization of, 434–439
reproductive justice, 24
research, See sex difference research
resource control, 190
response styles theory, 450

Ressler, Cali, 402
reverse causation, 52
risk networks, 418–419
Roberts, Bari-Ellen, 498
Roberts, Tomi-Ann, 242
Roosevelt, Franklin D., 13
rumination, 450–451
RuPaul, 269
Rydell, Robert, 274

Sagan, Carl, 44
Salomon, Kristen, 196
same-sex couples, 27
same-sex sexuality,
    use of term, 294
SAT (Scholastic Aptitude Test),
    240–241
Savage, Dan, 131, 351
SBW (strong Black woman)
    schema, 470
scarcity hypothesis, 399, 451
Schein, Victoria, 156
Schoenfeld, Elizabeth, 354
Scholastic Aptitude Test (SAT),
    240–241
science, 43–45
scientific method, 44–45
scientific positivism, 66–67
SDO (social dominance
    orientation), 202–203
self-concepts, 136–137
self-fulfilling prophecies, 167
self-objectification, 460–462
Semenya, Caster, 75–77, 88
separation, 358–359
    See also divorce
SES (socioeconomic status),
    430–431
Sesko, Amanda, 193
sex
    complexity of, 11–16
    defined, 6
    use of term, 5
*Sex and Temperament in Three
    Primitive Societies* (Mead
    1935), 185
sex binary, defined, 6
sex difference research

Bem Sex-Role
    Inventory (BSRI), 46
biases, 63–65
challenges, 66–69
effect sizes, 57–63
gender diagnosticity (GD)
    score, 47
history of, 39
meta-analyses, 57–63
M-F Test, 46
mixed methods approach,
    56–57
Personal Attributes
    Questionnaire (PAQ), 46
qualitative research methods,
    54–55
quantitative research methods,
    47–54
sex differentiation
    defined, 80
    intersexuality, 86–92
    types of, 80–84
sex ratio theory, 186–188
sex trafficking, 504–505
sex verification testing, 76
sex-based harassment, 495–499
sex-gender correspondence,
    use of term, 5
sexism
    overview, 184
    ambivalent sexism theory, 196
    attitudes of, 203–204
    benevolent sexism, 196–199
    hostile sexism, 196–199
    social dominance orientation
        (SDO), 202–203
    system justification theory, 203
    use of term, 195
    See also power
sexual aggression. *See* aggression
sexual assault, 478, 488–495
sexual behavior, 302
sexual callousness model, 507
sexual coercion, 496
sexual desire, 299
sexual fluidity, 322
sexual harassment. *See* sex-based
    harassment

sexual identity
    overview, 297–299
    milestone models of
        development, 306–308
    phase models of development,
        304–307
    See also sexual orientation
sexual infidelity, 355
sexual inversion theory, 163
sexual minority individuals
    issues, 27
    psychological health, 465–468
    use of term, 294
sexual orientation
    overview, 10, 292–295
    complexity of, 303
    development of, 304–308
    differences in, 309–315
    motivation components of,
        299–301
    sexual behavior, 302
    sexual identity, 297–299
    stereotypes, 163–164
    use of term, 5
    See also sexual identity
sexual orientation change efforts
    (SOCEs), 295–296
sexual peak, 323–325
sexual satisfaction, 319–322
sexual selection, 101
sexuality
    changes in, 323–326
    defined, 292
    medicalization of, 325–326
    role of sex and gender in,
        315–322
Sheldon, Alice B., 256
sickness, 410–413
Simon, Theodore, 226
single-sex classrooms, 244–246
SisterSong Women of Color
    Reproductive Justice
    Collective, 24
situational couple violence, 486
smiling, 271
    See also emotions
Smith, Adam, 283
smoking, 419–420

SOCEs (sexual orientation change efforts), 295–296
social comparisons, 461
social constructivism, 66–67
social dominance orientation (SDO), 202–203
social factors of gender, 6
social networking, 134–136
social networks, role of sex and gender in, 333–334
social role theory, 169–170
socialist feminism, 23
See also feminisms
socialization practices, 140–141
socioeconomic dependence perspective, 502
socioeconomic status (SES), 430–431
Sontag, Susan, 141
Soranus, 438
spansexual, 12
spatial location memory, 234
spatial perception, 234
spatial visualization, 234
Spearman, Charles, 227
speed-dating, 315–316
Spence, Janet, 9, 47
stalled gender revolution, 373
standard deviation, 58
statistical beliefs, vs. generic beliefs, 176–177
status incongruity hypothesis, 165–166
status inconsistency perspective, 502–503
Steinem, Gloria, 261
STEM fields, 246–250
stereotype content model, 152–153
See also gender stereotypes
stereotype threats, 166, 239–241
steroids, 91
Stevens, Nettie, 85
Stewart, Abigail, 9–10
sticky floor, 382
Stocker-Witterick, Storm, 110–112
stonewalling, 358

street harassment, 496
strong Black woman (SBW) schema, 470
structural power, 186–188
subjective well-being (SWB), 470–471
subordinate groups, 16–17
suicide, gender paradox of, 457–458
Sultana, Sabira, 502
Summers, Lawrence, 222
surgical procedures, 96
Swartout, Kevin, 52
sworn virgins, 8, *90*
system justification theory, 203

teddy bear effect, 281–282, 384
Teena, Brandon, 27
telomeres, 414
Terman, Lewis, 46, 226
terminology, changing, 97
testosterone
    and aggression, 6, 500
    and sexual orientation, 311
thin ideal internalization, 463
think manager-think male effect, 156–157
third sex status, *90*
third variable problem, 52
Thompson, Jody, 402
Thompson-Woolley, Helen, 39
Tiedens, Larissa, 281
tightrope bias, 383
time availability theory, 376–377
tipping point theory, *310,* 313–314
Tiptree, James, Jr., 256
Toom, Nong, 77
touch, 272
transdiagnostic approach, 446–447
transformational leadership style, 380
transgender individuals
    defined, 9
    gender confirmation procedures, 96
    stereotypes, 163

transgender movement, 27–29
transmen, 97
transnational feminism, 23
    See also feminisms
transphobia, 467–468
transwomen, 97
trigender, defined, 9–10
Trump, Donald J., 4, 18
Tsai, Jeanne, 271
tug of war, 383
Turner, Brock, 494–495
Twenge, Jean, 136
two-spirit people, 8, 298

unacknowledged rape, 491
Unger, Rhoda, 6, 11
unmitigated agency, 423–425, 472
unmitigated communion, 423–425, 472
unprotected receptive anal intercourse (URAI), 418–419
unwanted sexual attention, 496

Vacharkulksemsuk, Tanya, 274
vaginoplasty, 96
Vallum, Joshua, 27
van Anders, Sari, 99
Van Loo, Katie, 274
verbal aggression, 479, 482
verbal communication
    role of sex and gender in, 262–270
    stereotypes, 174
verbal fluency, defined, 230
verbal performance, 228–231
verbal reasoning, defined, 231
victim blaming, 493
victimization, 466
video games, 481
violence
    defined, 479
    explanation for, 499–505
    factors, 452
    forms of, 485–499
    and power, 188–189
visual dominance, 272

visual-spatial abilities, defined, 232–233
visual-spatial performance, 232–235

Wade, Carole, 31
Walker, Rebecca, 21
well-being, psychological health, 470–473
Whorfian hypothesis, 257, 260
wife beating, 485–488
Wilkie, James, 13
Williams, J. E., 177
Williams, Serena, 91
Williamson, Mercedes, 27
within-group variance, 60
Wollstonecraft, Mary, 259
womanhood, cultural ideals of, 137–139
womanism, 23
    See also feminisms

women
    bias against, 382–383
    double standard of aging, 141–142
    eating and body image disorders, 463–464
    and emotions, 278–280
    and intimate partner violence, 487–488
    leftover women, 187
    menopause, 325
    physical health of, 412–413
    pregnancy, 436–439
    psychological health of, 456–457
    sex drive of, 318–319
women-are-wonderful effect, 155–156
women's movements, 17–21
    See also feminisms
work
    domestic, 372–378

    and family roles, 398–402
    labor divisions, 371–372
work flexibility stigma, 401
work-family conflict, 399
work-family enrichment, 399
work-family interface, 398
workforce
    cultural ideals of, 138, 141
    gendered division of, 104–105
    role of sex and gender in, 379–386
work-life balance, 399
work-life enrichment, 400

young adulthood, transition to, 131–133
Yousafzai, Malala, 4, 208

ze (pronoun), 9
zir (pronoun), 9